PSYC 103

INTRODUCTION TO PSYCHOLOGY

DEPARTMENT OF PSYCHOLOGY
UNIVERSITY OF CINCINNATI
CINCINNATI, OH

WILEY
Custom Services

ISBN 0-471-27225-6

Psychology

Brain, Behavior, & Culture

Third Edition

Drew Westen

Boston University

John Wiley & Sons, Inc.

New York   Chichester   Weinheim   Brisbane   Singapore   Toronto

DEDICATION

To Laura and Mackenzie

ACQUISITIONS EDITOR	Ellen Schatz
SENIOR DEVELOPMENT EDITOR	Nancy Perry
SENIOR PRODUCTION EDITOR	Elizabeth Swain
MARKETING MANAGER	Kevin Molloy
INTERIOR DESIGN	Laura C. Ierardi
COVER DESIGN	Harold Nolan
ILLUSTRATION EDITOR	Sandra Rigby
ILLUSTRATIONS	Third edition updated by Fine Line Illustration, Inc.
PHOTO RESEARCHER	Mary Ann Price
PHOTO EDITOR	Sara Wight
COVER AND CHAPTER OPENERS, FINE ART RESEARCH	Steven Diamond
COVER PHOTO	"Ideal Woman" by Robert Silvers

This book was set in 10/12 Palatino Light by LCI Design, color separation was done by Banta Digital Group, it was printed and bound by Von Hoffmann Press. The cover was printed by Von Hoffmann Press.

This book is printed on acid-free paper.

To order books or for customer service, call 1(800)-CALL-WILEY (225-5945).

Library of Congress Cataloging in Publication Data:
Westen, Drew, 1959–
    Psychology : brain, behavior & culture / Drew Westen. — 3rd ed.
       p.   cm.
    Includes bibliographical references and index.
    ISBN 0-471-38754-1 (alk. paper)
    1. Psychology. I. Title.

BF121.W44 2001
150—dc21   2001033245

Printed in the United States of America

10 9 8 7 6 5 4 3 2 1

Preface

Psychology: Brain, Behavior, & Culture emerged from several years of teaching introductory psychology at the University of Michigan. My goal was to try to translate a style of teaching into the written word, a style that is at once personal and informal—engaging students by presenting material relevant to their own concerns and interests—yet highly conceptual and scientifically rigorous.

My aim from the start has also been to try to give students a sense of the "big picture" of how we think, feel, and behave, and how our evolving science continually addresses and readdresses the central questions that brought most of us into the field—questions about the relation between psychological events and their neural underpinnings, between cognition and emotion, between cultural processes and human evolution, between nature and nurture, and so forth. Introductory psychology is probably the last time most students—and psychologists—get a broad purview of the depth and breadth of our field. In fact, I suspect one of the greatest personal benefits for those of us who teach introductory psychology is that we are continually exposed to new information, often in domains far from our own areas of expertise, that stretch and challenge our imaginations.

◆ What's New in the Third Edition

Writing a textbook is always a balancing act, with each edition adjusting scales that tipped too far in one direction in the last. Probably the most difficult balance to achieve in writing an introductory text is how to cover what we know (at least for now) and what's on the cutting edge without writing an encyclopedia, particularly when the field is moving forward rapidly. Another balancing act involves helping students who need more structure to learn the material, without placing roadblocks in the path of students who would find most pedagogical devices contrived and distracting. The new features in this edition reflect these competing demands.

Saying More with Less

This edition of *Psychology: Brain, Behavior, & Culture* is leaner than the last. Cutting back while adding new material is a Sisyphean task. With the help of several reviewers, I have cut the book by about 15%, which will undoubtedly lead to statistically significant decreases in back pain by students and professors alike. The material now more easily fits into both semester and quarter courses, although professors will still need to pick and choose what they want to cover. I have also moved one or two sections of each chapter that some professors found too detailed but others appreciated onto the Web, where professors can assign it or students who are interested can find it. The kind of material now on the Wiley website (www.wiley.com/college/westen) includes discussions of nearsightedness and farsightedness (Chapter 4), sleep disorders (Chapter 9), methodological issues in studying cognitive changes with aging (Chapter 13), the impact of daycare on children's welfare and attachment patterns (Chapter 14), and self-attribution (Chapter 17).

The book is *scaled* down but not *dumbed* down. In tightening the book's belt, I was careful not to eliminate central concepts or reduce the overall complexity of the material, except in specific places where multiple reviewers let me know that I had aimed too high in the last edition. I was also vigilant not to cut material that gives students an understanding of the *process of scientific discovery*—descriptions of studies that allow students to get into the mind of the researchers in order to understand not just the *conclusions* they reached but the *process* by which they arrived at those conclusions and generated the next hypothesis.

Key Pedagogical Changes: An Integrated Package

The most important changes in this edition are pedagogical. We surveyed professors and students to find out how this text could better help them meet their teaching and learning challenges. Using their feedback, we have worked to create an integrated study package for students built into the structure of the text, without cluttering the margins or adding infantilizing pedagogical gimmicks that distract from the narrative.

- **Central Questions.** The chapters now all have an integrated structure, beginning with the **Central Questions** that guide research in that area of the field and returning to those questions at the end. In between, students are challenged to think about those questions as

Central Questions

- To what extent is coping related to intelligence? Does general problem-solving ability make people better able to cope with social and emotional sources of stress?

they apply to new material. For example, we begin Chapter 3 with questions about the relation between psychological processes and their underlying neuroanatomy, and conclude with a discussion of how and why we would want to track down brain–behavior relationships. In Chapter 11, we begin with a central question about the role of cognition in generating and regulating emotion and stress. Later, students are challenged to consider an offshoot of that broader question, regarding the relation between intelligence and coping (and in particular, whether intellect buffers people in the face of stressful experiences).

In this edition, we have also done something we believe is completely novel with the art program in a textbook, integrating photos with the text in a way that fosters critical thinking and helps students see the connections between concepts presented in different chapters. Instead of using photos primarily to brighten the color of the book or provide interesting diversions (both lofty aims, of course), we have used the photos to *link concepts and visual images*, through two new pedagogical features, called **Making Connections** and **Apply & Discuss**.

- **Making Connections** illustrates and links material from different chapters, so that students can see the threads that tie the discipline together. For example, as they consider the prevalence of airplane phobias in Chapter 15, students are reminded of data on prepared learning from Chapter 5 on learning.

Making Connections

Although plane crashes kill far fewer people than cigarettes, phobias of flying are far more common than cigarette phobias. Learning theorists have proposed that we are biologically *prepared* to fear certain stimuli, such as extreme heights, darkness, and snakes, which posed dangers to our ancestors (Chapter 5).

- **Apply and Discuss** combines visual imagery with critical thinking to challenge students to apply what they have just learned. For example, in discussing principles of learning (Chapter 5), students see a photograph of former Indiana basketball coach Bobby Knight, who was fired after repeatedly behaving aggressively toward athletes and other students. They are asked to think about the conditions under which aggression is punished and reinforced, and why people sometimes repeatedly produce responses that produce aversive consequences. The visual example pulls students in, while the questions require them to apply what they have just learned about reinforcement and punishment to a case that requires them to grapple with the concepts.

We made two additional changes in this edition to help students study and focus on key concepts.

- Where previously we **boldfaced** key words in the text, now we have also *italicized the definitions of those words* in the text where they appear and tightened the definitions, so that students can readily understand every term introduced.
- Each chapter now ends with a list of **Key Terms** with page numbers, so that students can be certain that they understand all the major terms introduced in the chapter.

Keeping Pace with Emerging Knowledge

Every chapter has been updated to keep apace with a rapidly moving body of knowledge. Some of the highlights in this edition are as follows.

- Chapter 3, Biological Bases of Mental Life and Behavior, includes new research on the role of the basal ganglia in automatic information processing and responding to subtle social cues.
- Chapter 4, Sensation and Perception, includes new research on "referred pain" that can occur when limbs are removed or damage has occurred to a nerve.
- Chapter 5, Learning, presents new research on the neural systems involved in classical conditioning and avoidance learning.
- Chapter 6, Memory, includes a discussion of Schacter's "seven sins of memory" and recent research on the accuracy of people's "flashbulb" memories of the O. J. Simpson verdict.
- Chapter 7, Thought and Language, includes new material on cultural differences in thinking between East and West.
- Chapter 8, Intelligence, reports recent neuroimaging research on the "g" factor, or general intelligence.
- Chapter 9, Consciousness, includes new neuroimaging research on conscious control, as occurs in experimental procedures such as the Stroop task.
- Chapter 10, Motivation, includes substantially updated sections on the mechanisms of hunger and satiety.
- Chapter 11, Emotion, Stress, and Coping, presents new research on emotional forecasting (people's predictions, and mispredictions, of the way they will feel if certain events happen) and longitudinal research on childhood predictors of health-promoting and high-risk behaviors.
- Chapter 12, Personality, describes the latest research on the behavior genetics of personality traits.
- Chapter 13, Physical and Cognitive Development, presents cutting-edge research on the development of categorization in infants, and the latest research on cognitive functioning that does and does not decline with aging.

Apply & Discuss

Coach Bobby Knight at Indiana University lost his coaching job despite one of the most successful careers in the history of college basketball after repeatedly attacking students.
- How do people learn when aggression is likely to be reinforced or punished?
- Why do people sometimes produce responses destined to lead to aversive consequences?

- Chapter 14, Social Development, includes the most recent research on stability and change in attachment, based on longitudinal studies that have now completed their second decade, and provides a detailed discussion of the recent controversy over whether parents really make a difference in their children's development.
- Chapter 15, Psychological Disorders, includes a state-of-the art discussion of genetic and environmental contributions to schizophrenia.
- Chapter 16, Treatment of Psychological Disorders, presents the latest thinking and research on what works for whom, including the strengths and limitations of efficacy trials and effectiveness studies.
- Chapter 17, Attitudes and Social Cognition, includes a discussion of recent neuroimaging research on cognitive dissonance, which finds that amnesics show dissonance reduction even though they cannot explicitly remember what they have said or done that would lead to it.
- Chapter 18, Interpersonal Processes, presents new research on the variables involved in maintenance of long-term relationships.

Balanced Coverage of Multiple Perspectives

A theme over these three editions has been the attempt to acquaint students not just with seminal research but with the conceptual frameworks that guide that research across subdisciplines. Thus, the first chapter introduces the concept of *perspectives* in psychology. With this edition, I have once again tried to describe the strengths and limitations of the major perspectives, with increased emphasis on cognitive and evolutionary perspectives and on potential integrations across perspectives. Based on feedback from reviewers, I have also increased emphasis on the role of scientific method in evaluating explanations from each perspective, and use the perspectives to raise challenging questions. For example, in discussing psychodynamic explanations, I have focused on hypotheses that have received empirical support and deleted more speculative discussions.

◆ A Proven Pedagogical Framework

Those are some of the new features that distinguish this edition from the last. Several key features, however, remain from the first two editions, which give this book its distinctive "signature." They arose from five objectives I had as I set out to write this book:

- To focus on both the biological basis of psychology and the role of culture in shaping basic psychological processes;
- To provide a conceptual orientation that would capture the excitement and tensions in the field;
- To help students understand the logic of scientific discovery and hypothesis-testing as applied to psychological questions;
- To suggest ways of integrating psychological theories and knowledge across subfields; and
- To employ language that would be sophisticated but engaging.

Biology and Culture: A Micro to Macro Approach

A consistent theme of the book, introduced in the first chapter, is that biology and culture form the boundaries of psychology. Understanding people means attending simultaneously to biological processes, psychological experience, and cultural and historical context. The focus on biological and neural underpinnings echoes one of the major trends in contemporary psychological science, as technological developments allow progressively more sophisticated understanding of the neural substrates of psychological experience. The focus on culture has been a central feature of this book since I began work on it in 1986. *Cross-cultural material is not tacked onto this book; it is integral to it.* My first book, *Self and Society* (1985), was on culture and personality, and a background in anthropology and sociology informs my understanding of the way people think, feel, learn, behave, and develop.

Each chapter of this book contains two extended discussions that show the way psychological experience is situated between the nervous system and cultural experience.

- **From Brain to Behavior** focuses on concepts and findings from biopsychology and the neurosciences, providing a detailed discussion of a specific issue, such as the way damage to the brain can alter personality (Chapter 3), the role of the dorsolateral prefrontal cortex in thinking (Chapter 7), or the neuroanatomy of emotion (Chapter 11), or long-term memory (Chapter 6; see below). One of the key features of this text, however, is the integration of neuroscientific research into the fabric of the narrative.

The Neuropsychology of Long-Term Memory

From Brain to Behavior

How distinct are these varieties of LTM? Are researchers simply splitting hairs, or are they really "carving nature at its joints," making distinctions where distinctions truly exist?

Some of the most definitive data supporting distinctions among different types of memory are neuroanatomical studies, including case studies of patients with neurological damage, brain imaging with normal and brain-damaged patients, and experimental studies with animals (Gabrieli, 1998; Gluck & Myers, 1997; Squire, 1992, 1995).

- **A Global Vista** uses ethnographic material and cross-cultural studies to explore psychological phenomena in other cultures, with an eye to addressing the universality or culture-specificity of psychological theories and observations. For example, menopause has a very different meaning, and hence different symptoms, in a Mayan village than it does in North America (Chapter 13), and parenting styles fostering autonomy that are adaptive in Western, technologically developed societies are not necessarily optimal everywhere (Chapter 14; see below). Like research in the neurosciences, cross-cultural research is integrated into the structure of each chapter, so that students do not balkanize cross-cultural issues as distinct from the "psychology of white people" but instead ask cross-cultural questions from the start.

Parental Acceptance and Rejection in Cross-Cultural Perspective

A Global Vista

One of the most important ways parents vary across and within cultures is the extent to which they are accepting or rejecting of their children (Rohner, 1975a, 1986; Veneziano & Rohner, 1998). Parents can express acceptance verbally through praise, compliments, and support, or nonverbally through hugging, approving glances, and smiling. Like acceptance, parents can express rejection verbally (bullying or harsh criticism) or nonverbally (hitting, beating, shaking, or simply neglecting).

These special features flow integrally from the text and are not presented as isolated "boxes." Thus, students will get the message that biological and cultural material is integral to understanding psychology, not somehow superfluous or added on.

Conceptual Orientation

The book is conceptually oriented. It attempts, within the limits of my objectivity and expertise (considerable limits, no doubt), to give a fair and compelling account of the different perspectives psychologists take in understanding psychological phenomena. I have a healthy respect for each approach and assume that if thousands of my colleagues find an approach compelling, it probably contains something that students should know.

- **Perspectives.** From the start, students are challenged to think about psychological phenomena from multiple perspectives. Chapter 1 is not perfunctory; it introduces four perspectives—*cognitive, evolutionary, behavioral, and psychodynamic*—in enough depth to allow students to begin conceptualizing psychological data rather than simply memorizing a list of facts, names, or studies. At the same time, I have avoided slavishly introducing paragraphs on each perspective in every chapter, since some perspectives obviously apply better to certain phenomena than to others.
- **Commentary.** Although I have made every effort to present controversies in a balanced way, the danger in doing so is that one loses one's voice, and the last thing I wanted to write was a book with intellectual laryngitis. Thus, in **Commentary** sections, I periodically comment on issues of method that bear on the conclusions being reached; or after presenting both sides of a debate, I let the reader know where I stand on controversial issues, such as the existence of repressed memories of sexual abuse. I have presented versions of some of these commentaries on National Public Radio's *All Things Considered*.

Research Focus

This book is about psychological science. A student should come out of an introductory psychology class not only with a sense of the basic questions and frameworks for answering them but also with an appreciation for how to obtain psychological knowledge. Thus, Chapter 2 is devoted to research methods, and the style reflects an effort to engage, not intimidate, so that students can see how methods actually make a difference. The statistical supplement that immediately follows it, which even the most seriously math-phobic can understand, is included in the body of the text rather than cast off at the end as an impenetrable appendix. From start to finish, students read about specific studies so that they can learn about the logic of scientific investigation.

Integrative Approach

Solo-authoring an introductory text is probably presumptive evidence of mental instability (and is clearly a cause of it as well), but I could not have produced this book any other way, because my aim was to engage students in the enterprise of thinking about the whole person, not just the parts. As one psychologist put it (Holt, 1976), the human psyche is not the handiwork of an obsessive-compulsive god who created cognition on one day, affect on another, motivation on another, and so forth, and made sure they all stayed neatly in their own territories. Too often our efforts to classify and label lead us to try to separate the inseparable. The integrative bent of the book stems primarily from my own work as a researcher, which has focused on integrating clinical and experimental perspectives as well as concepts and methods from different psychological traditions.

Wherever possible, this book tries to delineate some of the links that our best intellectual efforts often obscure. For example, Chapter 7 presents connectionist models in some detail, linking them to concepts of association described in Chapter 1, Chapter 5 on associative learning, and Chapter 6 on associative memory. Multiple chapters revisit connectionist models, such as research on psychomotor slowing in Chapter 13 and research on stereotype activation and prejudice in Chapter 17. Similarly, in various places throughout the book, I present avenues of integration across theoretical perspectives. Chapter 6 on memory concludes by linking the expanded understanding of memory characteristic of the last decade to research from multiple traditions that can now be incorporated under the larger tent of cognitive neuroscience. Students are challenged to consider the link between classical and operant conditioning and implicit and procedural memory and to consider the evolutionary challenge to the concept of an all-purpose, general processing brain.

Language

Above all, I wanted to avoid writing in "textese," a language that presents dry summaries of data for students to memorize instead of engaging them in *thinking* about psychology. *Psychology: Brain, Behavior, & Culture* offers a solid and comprehensive account of the principles of psychology in what I hope is an accessible, lively, and thought-provoking style.

- Throughout the book, I aim at clarity and introduce terminology only when it enlightens, not obscures. I am not shy about using metaphor or weaving a narrative, but not a single term in this book is defined by context alone. If students need to understand a concept, they will see the definition in the same sentence in which the word is boldfaced and will see the definition "jump out at them" in italics. I have also tried to keep the language at a level appropriate to college students, but if they have to look up an occasional word, I will not lose sleep over it. (I had to look up a few in writing it!)

- As a teacher and writer, I try to make use of one of the most robust findings in psychology: that memory and understanding are enhanced when target information is associated with vivid and personally relevant material. Each chapter begins with an experiment, a case, or an event that lets students know why the topic is important and why anyone might be excited about it. None of the cases is invented, this is real material, and the questions raised in the opening study or vignette reemerge throughout each chapter. Chapter 2, for example, begins with the case of a young woman who lost her entire family in a car accident and found herself suddenly contracting one minor ailment after another until finally starting to talk about the event with a psychologist. I then juxtapose this with an experiment by James Pennebaker on the influence of emotional expression on physical health to show how a researcher can take a striking phenomenon or philosophical question (the relation between mind and body) and turn it into a researchable question.

Learning Aids

I have tried to avoid pedagogy that is condescending or unnecessary. One student complained to me in an e-mail message that her biggest problem with the book was that her roommate kept stealing it from the bookshelf and reading it! In my experience students never follow up on annotated recommendations for future reading, so I have not cluttered the ends of chapters with them. On the other hand, most students need guidance in studying the material. Therefore, in addition to the new pedagogy added in this edition—*Central Questions, Making Connections, Apply & Discuss*, italicized definitions, and key terms—I have retained the learning aids from the last edition that have proven effective in helping students learn: *Interim Summaries*, a feature called *One Step Further*, and *Chapter Summaries*.

■ **Interim Summaries.** At the end of major sections, **Interim Summaries** recap the "gist" of what has been presented, not only to help students consolidate their knowledge of what they have read but also to alert them if they failed to "get" something important (see below). The inclusion of these summaries reflects both feedback from professors and the results of research suggesting that distributing conceptual summaries throughout a chapter and presenting them shortly after students have read the material is likely to optimize learning.

◆ **INTERIM SUMMARY**

Learning refers to any enduring change in the way an organism responds based on its experience. Learning theories assume that experience shapes behavior, that learning is adaptive, and that only systematic experimentation can uncover laws of learning. Principles of association are fundamental to most accounts of learning.

■ **One Step Further.** This edition, like the last, includes a feature called **One Step Further**. Like the other recurring features in the book, these discussions flow naturally from the text but are highlighted in color. Generally, these are advanced discussions of some aspect of the topic, usually with a strong methodological or conceptual focus. These sections are intended to be assigned by professors who prefer a high-level text, or to be read by students who find the topic intriguing and want to learn more about it even if it isn't assigned. Highlighting these sections gives professors—and students—some choice about what to read or not to read.

For example, in Chapter 4, the **One Step Further** section addresses signal detection theory, which some professors consider central to introductory coverage of sensation and perception and others consider too advanced. In Chapter 6, this feature describes research tracking down the neuropsychology of working memory, linking primate studies, basic laboratory research with humans, and the latest neuroimaging research (see below).

One Step Further

The Neuropsychology of Working Memory

Recently researchers have begun tracking down the neuropsychology of working memory. The emerging consensus is that working memory is "orchestrated," or directed, by the *prefrontal cortex*, a region of the brain long known to be involved in the most high-level cognitive functions. When information is temporarily stored and manipulated, the prefrontal cortex is activated along with whichever posterior regions (that is, regions toward the back of the brain) normally process the kind of

■ **Chapter Summaries.** Each chapter concludes with a summary of the major points, organized under the headings in which they were presented. These summaries provide an outline of the chapter.

Summary

1. **Psychopathology** refers to patterns of thought, feeling, or behavior that disrupt a person's sense of well-being or social or occupational functioning.

The Cultural Context of Psychopathology

2. The concept of mental illness varies historically and cross-culturally. Cultures differ in the ways they describe and pattern psychopathol-

with most psychological disorders, the roots of alcoholism lie in genetics, environment, and their interaction.

12. **Schizophrenia** is a disorder or set of disorders in which people lose touch with reality, experiencing both **positive symptoms** (such as **hallucinations, delusions**, and **loosening of associations**) and **negative symptoms** (such as flat affect and poor social skills). Schizophrenia is a highly heritable disease of the brain, although environmental circumstances such as a critical

Organization

I tried to organize *Psychology: Brain, Behavior, & Culture* in a way that would be convenient for most instructors and yet follow a coherent design. Of course, different instructors organize things differently, but I do not think many will find the organization idiosyncratic.

Teaching the material in the order presented is probably optimal, for chapters do build on each other. For example, Chapter 9 on consciousness presupposes knowledge of the distinction posed in Chapter 6 between implicit and explicit memory. However, if instructors want to rearrange the order of chapters, they can certainly do so, as material mentioned from a previous chapter is cross-referenced so that students can easily find any information they need.

Illustration and Design

When I began this enterprise, I had no idea what it meant to put together a whole textbook. As a person with minimal use of his right hemisphere, I assumed that some editorial type would come up with figures and tables. This assumption was an example of a well-known psychological phenomenon, wishful thinking. After fifteen years of working on this project, and tutelage from a number of reviewers as well as some of those "editorial types" at Wiley, I think I finally figured out how to educate the right hemisphere, even if mine does not work so well. I took tremendous care to select and design only figures and tables that actually add something and that do not just make the pages look less ominous.

◆ Supplementary Materials

Psychology: Brain, Behavior, and Culture, Third Edition features a full line of teaching and learning resources developed to help professors create a more dynamic and innovative learning environment.

These resources—including print, software, and Web-based materials—are integrated with the text and take an active learning approach to help build students' ability to think clearly and critically.

For Instructors

Instructor's Manual. Prepared by Paul J. Wellman of Texas A&M University, this comprehensive resource includes for each text chapter an outline, student learning objectives, outline/lecture organizer (referenced to text pages), lecture topic extensions, in-class demonstrations and discussion questions, out-of-class student exercises, Web site resources, suggested Web links, software, videos, PowerPoint presentations, and numerous student handouts.

Instructor's Resource CD-ROM. This multiplatform CD-ROM is an invaluable resource for in-class lectures and out-of-class preparation. It includes

- The entire **Instructor's Manual**
- The student **Study Guide**
- The **Computerized Test Bank**
- *NEW!* **Interactive Animations,** prepared by Marvin Lee of Shenandoah University and Margaret Olimpieri of Westchester Community College. The interactive modules help students understand concepts featured in the text. Each interactive animation includes a preface, a summary and questions to reinforce students' understanding of the module.
- **PowerPoint Presentation Slides and Lecture Notes**, created and developed by Paul J. Wellman of Texas A&M University, which are comprised of 450 original lecture slides and 215 art slides that can be sequenced and customized by instructors to fit any lecture. The PowerPoint slides contain a combination of key concepts, images, and problems from the textbook for use in the classroom. Designed according to the organization of the material in the textbook, this series of electronic transparencies can be used to illustrate concepts visually and graphically.
- Over 50 **video clips** to help reinforce complex concepts during class presentations. Among these video clips are segments entitled
  - Neurotransmitter Action
  - Stanley Milgram's Original Research
  - Narcolepsy in Action
  - Confirmation of Zimbardo's Prison Study
  - Schizophrenia
  - Piaget's Conservation and Object Permanence
  - Kohler's Study with Chimps and Insight
  - Sample Therapy Sessions from Ellis

Web CT and Blackboard Courses. Web CT and Blackboard courses, prepared by John S. Conklin of Camosun College, are available with this edition of the textbook. This powerful Web program allows professors to set up their own on-line course with chat rooms, bulletin boards, quizzing, and student tracking. These course-management systems are tools that facilitate the organization and delivery of course materials on the Web. Easy to use, these tools help broaden communication, and provide in-depth content for easy and flexible course administration and sophisticated online testing and diagnostic systems.

Computerized Test Bank. Prepared by Dennis C. Cogan and Ravi Prasad of Texas Tech University-Lubbock, this multiplatform CD-ROM has nearly 2,000 test items, which have been meticulously proofread and reviewed. Each multiple-choice question has been linked to the text's learning objectives, coded "Factual" or "Applied," and referenced to its source in the text. The easy-to-use test-generation program fully supports graphics, print tests, student answer sheets, and answer keys quickly and easily. The software's advanced features allow you to create an exam to your exact specifications, with an easy-to-use interface.

Transparencies. Full-color traditional acetate transparencies of illustrations from the text are available for professors who cannot or do not wish to use the slides available on the *Instructor's Resource CD-ROM*.

Video Library. A number of the videotapes available to adopters of the text are new to this edition. Please contact your local Wiley representative for details of this rich resource.

Westen *Psychology 3e* **Web Site at www.wiley.com/college/westen.** Our on-line resources add a rich, interactive learning experience designed to give professors the tools they need to teach and students the tools and foundations needed to grasp concepts and expand their critical thinking skills. The Westen *Psychology 3e* Web Site provides instructors with the following.

- Instructor's Manual
- Test Bank
- Student Study Guide
- Web CT Guide Answers to Central Questions
- Apply & Discuss
- Chapter Summaries
- Interactive Animations
- Vocabulary Flashcards
- In the News
- Web Links
- PowerPoint Slides and Lecture Notes
- On-line Guide
- Additional Reading Suggestions
- Supplementary Content

For Students

Study Guide. Written by Alastair Younger of the University of Ottawa, the *Study Guide* offers students a comprehensive way to review materials from the text and test their knowledge. Each chapter in the text has a corresponding chapter in the *Study Guide*. Six tools help students master the material:

- Chapter Outlines
- Learning Objectives
- Key Terms
- Fill-In Exercises
- Critical Thinking Exercises
- Sample Test Questions with Answers

Take Note! This notebook contains the art illustrations in Westen *Psychology, 3e* that students will see in lectures from the transparencies. The notebook is designed for students to take notes directly on the illustrations during classroom lectures. *Take Note!* is also a valuable resource for students to help prepare for exams.

Westen *Psychology 3e* **Web Site at** <u>www.wiley.com/college/westen</u>. Students have access to the following supplements to help them succeed in the course.

- *NEW!* **Vocabulary Flash Cards** Prepared by Marvin Lee of Shenandoah University, this interactive module gives students the opportunity to test their knowledge of vocabulary terms. In addition, students can take self-tests and monitor their progress throughout the semester.

- *NEW!* **Interactive Animations.** Prepared by Marvin Lee of Shenandoah University and Margaret Olimpieri of Westchester Community College, the interactive modules help students understand concepts featured in the text. Each interactive animation includes a preface and a summary to reinforce students' understanding of the module.

- **PowerPoint Presentation Slides and Lecture Notes.** The *PowerPoint slides*, prepared by Paul Wellman, contain a combination of key concepts, images, and problems from the textbook. Designed according to the organization of the material in the textbook, this series of electronic transparencies can be used to reinforce introductory psychology concepts visually and graphically when students are studying the subject matter, writing term papers, or preparing for exams.

- **Supplementary Content** on topics from each chapter. Look for the Web icon in each chapter.

- **On-Line Guide.** This Web guide covers the basics of the Internet and how to use search engines efficiently. This helpful guide covers some of the following topics:
  - Basic Computer Configuration, Software, Service Providers
  - Internet Structure, Netscape Commands
  - Search Engines
  - Anatomy of a Web Site
  - Psychology Links
  - Understanding HTML, Creating Your Own Web Pages
  - Additional Reading
  - Self-Tests
  - Discussion Questions
  - Homework Assignments
  - Web Activities, which provide active Web links, explanatory text, and questions

Acknowledgments

This project began many years ago—in 1987—and several people have played important roles at different points in the endeavor. For the present edition, a very special thanks go to Dr. Matthew Lieberman, a rising star at the University of California at Los Angeles, who helped update multiple chapters. Dr. Lieberman had just received his doctorate in social psychology from Harvard when he signed on to help update this edition, but in the year or two since has emerged as a leader of the new field of cognitive social neuroscience. His insight into a range of topics, from the basal ganglia to classic research in social psychology, was invaluable. Thanks, Matt.

Other people played important roles in prior editions. The initial plan for the book in the mid-1980s was to co-write it with a talented writer, Jean Stein, who helped write the first draft of the first half of the first edition. Several other people also contributed in earlier stages, notably Judy Block, Colleen Coffey, Dr. Alfred Kellam, Dr. Carol Holden, Dr. Lauren Korfine, Dr. Barbara Misle, Dr. Patricia Harney, and Karen Schenkenfeldter. Like Jean, they helped lay the foundations, and their efforts, too, are greatly appreciated. I have also gained from the work of multiple talented research assistants, including (but not limited to) Michelle Levine and, most importantly, Samantha Glass, who has seen me through two editions. To all of them I am very grateful.

Finally, perhaps the most important reviewer and critic who read (and taught from) this book, and who had to feign excitement as I repeatedly told her about the latest developments in functional neuroimaging of the earlobe, is my wife, Dr. Laura Westen.

◆ Reviewers

Over the past fifteen years, this book has been shaped by the insightful comments of dozens of colleagues and would look nothing like it does now without their tireless efforts. In particular, for this edition I would like to thank Sandra Frankmann of the University of Southern Colorado for her meticulous reviews of every word and every figure of every chapter. From the prior edition, I would like to thank Walt Lonner of Western Washington University, who advised me on cross-cultural coverage for many chapters and gave feedback on others, and Paul Watson of the University of Tennessee for his uncanny ability throughout the years to notice where my prose was getting sloppy, my thoughts confused, or my coverage idiosyncratic. Several other professors have provided invaluable feedback on multiple chapters of the new and prior editions.

Reviewers for the Third Edition

Millicent H. Abel, *Western Carolina University*
George Adler, *University College of the Cariboo*
John D. Bonvillian, *University of Virginia*
John P. Broida, *University of Southern Maine*
Robert B. Branstrom, *United Behavioral Health*
Adam Butler, *University of Northern Iowa*
Kelly B. Cartwright, *Christopher Newport University*
Dennis Cogan, *Texas Tech University*
Ken Cramer, *University of Windsor*
Hank Davis, *University of Guelph*
Daniel L. C. DeNeui, *Elon College*
Joseph R. Ferrari, *DePaul University*
Oney D. Fitzpatrick, Jr., *Lamar University*
Sandra P. Frankmann, *University of Southern Colorado*
Jennifer J. Freyd, *University of Oregon*
Larry Hawk, *University at Buffalo*
Thomas Herrman, *University of Guelph*
Julia C. Hoigaard, *University of California, Irvine*

Norman E. Kinney, *Southeast Missouri State University*

Karsten Look, *Columbus State Community College*

Stephen Madigan, *University of Southern California*

J. L. Mottin, *University of Guelph*

William H. Overman, *University of North Carolina at Wilmington*

Donald J. Polzella, *University of Dayton*

Hillary R. Rodman, *Emory University*

Michael K. Russell, *Bucknell University*

Robert DeBrae Russell, *University of Michigan-Flint*

Sheldon Solomon, *Brooklyn College*

Paul Stager, *York University*

Angela D. Tigner, *Nassau Community College*

Paul J. Wellman, *Texas A&M University*

Robert W. Weisberg, *Temple University*

Reviewers for Prior Editions

Eugene Aidman, *University of Ballarat*

Gary Allen, *University of South Carolina*

Gordon Allen, *Miami University*

Harvard L. Armus, *University of Toledo*

Elaine Baker, *Marshall University*

Robert Batsell, *Southern Methodist University*

Carol M. Batt, *Sacred Heart University*

Col. Johnson Beach, *United States Military Academy-West Point*

Richard Belter, *University of West Florida*

John B. Best, *Eastern Illinois University*

Kathleen Bey, *Palm Beach Community College*

Paul Bloom, *University of Arizona*

Toni L. Blum, *Stetson University*

Joanna Boehnert, *University of Guelph*

John D. Bonvillian, *University of Virginia*

Douglas A. Bors, *University of Toronto-Scarborough*

Bruce Bridgeman, *University of California, Santa Cruz*

Nathan Brody, *Wesleyan University*

Robert Brown, *Georgia State University*

James Butler, *James Madison University*

Simone Buzwell, *Swinburne University of Technology*

Mark Byrd, *University of Canterbury (New Zealand)*

Susan Calkins, *University of North Carolina-Greensboro*

Barbara K. Canaday, *Southwestern College*

George A. Cicala, *University of Delaware*

Toon Cillessen, *University of Connecticut*

John M. Clark, *Macomb Community College*

Margaret Cleek, *University of Wisconsin-Madison*

Patricia Colby, *Skidmore College*

James Dalziel, *University of Sidney*

Hank Davis, *University of Guelph*

Peter Ditto, *Kent State University*

Allen Dobbs, *University of Alberta*

Mark Dombeck, *Idaho State University*

William Domhoff, *University of California, Santa Cruz*

Eugene B. Doughtie, *University of Houston*

Wendi Gardner, *Northwestern University*

Richard Eglsaer, *Sam Houston State University*

J. Gregor Fetterman, *Arizona State University*

Nelson Freedman, *Queens University*

Herbert Friedman, *College of William and Mary*

Mauricio Gaborit, S. J., *St. Louis University*

Adrienne Ganz, *New York University*

Mark Garrison, *Kentucky State University*

Nellie Georgiou, *Monash University*

Marian Gibney, *Phoenix College*

William E. Gibson, *Northern Arizona University*

Marvin Goldfried, *State University of New York-Stony Brook*

Mary Alice Gordon, *Southern Methodist University*

Charles R. Grah, *Austin Peay State University*

Leonard Green, *Washington University*

Mary Banks Gregerson, *George Washington University*

Joseph Guido, *Providence College*

Robert Guttentag, *University of North Carolina-Greensboro*

Richard Halgin, *University of Massachusetts-Amherst*

Douglas Herrmann, *Indiana State University*

Linda Hort, *Griffith University*

Julia Jacks, *University of North Carolina-Greensboro*

Timothy Jay, *North Adams State College*

James Johnson, *Illinois State University*

Lance K. Johnson, *Pasadena City College*

Robert Johnston, *College of William and Mary*

Kevin Kennelly, *University of North Texas*

Lynne Kiorpes, *New York University*

Stephen B. Klein, *Mississippi State University*

Keith Kluender, *University of Wisconsin-Madison*

James M. Knight, *Humboldt State University*

James Kopp, *University of Texas-Arlington*

Emma Kraidman, *Franciscan Children's Hospital, Boston*

Philip Langer, *University of Colorado-Boulder*

Randy J. Larsen, *Washington University*

Len Lecci, *University of North Carolina-Wilmington*

Peter Leppmann, *University of Guelph*

Alice Locicero, *Lesley College*

Matthew Margres, *Saginaw Valley State University*

Richard M. Martin, *Gustavus Adolphus College*
Donald McBurney, *University of Pittsburgh*
Ann Meriwether, *University of Michigan*
Eleanor Midkiff, *Eastern Illinois University*
David Mitchell, *Southern Methodist University*
Robert F. Mosher, *Northern Arizona University*
David I. Mostofsky, *Boston University*
John Mullennix, *Wayne State University*
Andrew Neher, *Cabrillo College*
John B. Nezlek, *College of William and Mary*
Constance Pilkington, *College of William and Mary*
Dorothy C. Pointkowski, *San Francisco State University*
Felicia Pratto, *University of Connecticut*
J. Faye Pritchard, *La Salle University*
David Rabiner, *University of North Carolina-Greensboro*
Freda Rebelsky, *Boston University*
Bradley C. Redburn, *Johnson County Community College*
Laura Reichel, *Metropolitan State College of Denver*
Paul Roberts, *Murdoch University*
Hillary R. Rodman, *Emory University*
Daniel Roenkert, *Western Kentucky University*
Lawrence Rosenblum, *University of California-Riverside*
Alexander Rothman, *University of Minnesota*
Kenneth W. Rusiniak, *Eastern Michigan University*
Ina Samuels, *University of Massachusetts-Boston*

Karl E. Scheibe, *Wesleyan University*
Richard Schiffman, *Rutgers University*
David A. Schroeder, *University of Arkansas*
Alan Searlman, *St. Lawrence University*
Robert Sekuler, *Brandeis University*
Norm Simonson, *University of Massachusetts*
Steven Sloman, *Brown University*
J. Diedrick Snoek, *Smith College*
Sheldon Solomon, *Skidmore College*
Paul Stager, *York University*
Margo A. Storm, *Temple University*
Chehalis Strapp, *Western Oregon University*
Perry Timmermans, *San Diego City College*
David Uttal, *Northwestern University*
D. Rene Verry, *Millikin University*
Malcolm Watson, *Brandeis University*
Paul J. Watson, *University of Tennessee-Chattanooga*
Paul Waxer, *York University*
Russell H. Weigel, *Amherst College*
Joel Weinberger, *Adelphi University*
Cheryl Weinstein, *Harvard Medical School*
Cara Wellman, *Indiana University*
Paul J. Wellman, *Texas A&M University*
Macon Williams, *Illinois State University*
Jeremy M. Wolfe, *Massachusetts Institute of Technology*
Billy Wooten, *Brown University*
David M. Wulff, *Wheaton College*
Todd Zakrajsek, *Southern Oregon State College*
Thomas Zentall, *University of Kentucky*

◆ Student Reviews

We also benefited considerably from students' comments in reviews and in focus groups. Thanks to the students who provided their feedback as they used the text and/or evaluated the new pedagogy, as well as to the following faculty members and graduate students who coordinated focus groups and reviews.

For the Third Edition

DePaul University: Joseph Ferrari
University of Northern Iowa: Adam Butler
University of Southern Colorado: Sandra P. Frankmann
University of Texas-Austin: Wendy Domjan

For Prior Editions

Canisius College: Harvey Pines
Johnson County Community College: Tody Klinger
Ohio State University Faculty: Alexis Collier
Southern Illinois University-Carbondale: Gordon Pitz
University of Minnesota-Minneapolis: Gail Peterson
University of New Mexico-Albuquerque: Robert J. Sutherland

University of Oklahoma-Norman: Richard Reardon
University of Tennessee-Knoxville: William H. Calhoun

Finally, I'd like to offer my deep appreciation to the extraordinary team at Wiley. As Psychology editor, Ellen Schatz used her extraordinary talent, insight, and intellect to guide the development of the project, filling the enormous shoes of Chris Rogers, who shepherded the project for several years and helped elaborate its vision. Harriett Prentiss has worked on every edition of the textbook, teaching me how to eliminate useless phrases and wordy sentences, and has probably taught me more about writing than anyone since my twelfth-grade English teacher. Most importantly, this edition I would like to thank Nancy Perry, the developmental editor for the book, who guided every stage of this revision, as she had done for the First Edition. She has an extraordinary ability to catch ambiguous clauses and inhospitable figures and captions, and an inimitable way of kindly asking questions like, "Are you sure you want to keep that phrase?" Her appreciation of the writing process, as well as of where it can go astray, has made her a tremendous contributor to what is best described as a team effort in creating and revising a textbook of this size and scope. To her, a special thanks this edition. Hilary Newman and Sandra Rigby have done a superb job developing the photography and artwork programs, respectively. They performed an impressive balancing act in giving me autonomy while sharing their expertise whenever my defective right hemisphere led me astray. My thanks also go to Art Ciccone, who helped render accurate technical illustrations in the first edition; the artists at Fine Line Illustrations, who did an extraordinary job of turning my sketches into illustrations that are both aesthetically appealing and edifying; Harry Nolan, who supervised the design with great creativity; Laura Ierardi at LCI Design, who gave this edition its exciting new look; Elizabeth Swain, a master at overseeing and managing production; Lili DeGrasse and Lili Kalish, who helped pull the final project together; and Ilse Wolfe, Associate Director of Marketing, and Charity Robey, Senior Marketing Manager. More generally, I couldn't ask for a better publisher, from the extraordinary efforts of a gifted editorial and production staff, to the marketing and sales force who put this book in your hands, and to a CEO, Will Pesce, and a Chairman of the Board, Brad Wiley, II, who are committed to publishing textbooks that edify and excite rather than just sell.

Drew Westen
Boston

About the Author

Drew Westen is Research Associate Professor in the Department of Psychology and Director of the Adolescent and Adult Personality Programs at the Center for Anxiety and Related Disorders at Boston University. He received his B.A. at Harvard University, an M.A. in Social and Political Thought at the University of Sussex (England), and his Ph.D. in Clinical Psychology at the University of Michigan, where he subsequently taught for six years. While at the University of Michigan, he was honored two years in a row by the *Michigan Daily* as the best teaching professor at the university, and was the recipient of the first Golden Apple Award for outstanding undergraduate teaching. More recently, he was selected as a G. Stanley Hall Lecturer by the American Psychological Association. Professor Westen is an active researcher who is on the editorial boards of multiple journals, including *Clinical Psychology:*  *Science and Practice, Psychological Assessment,* and the *Journal of Personality Disorders.* His major areas of research are personality disorders, eating disorders, emotion regulation, implicit processes, psychotherapy effectiveness, and adolescent psychopathology. His series of videotaped lectures on abnormal psychology, called *Is Anyone Really Normal?,* was published by the Teaching Company, in collaboration with the Smithsonian Institution. He also provides psychological commentaries on political issues for *All Things Considered* on National Public Radio. His main loves outside of psychology are his wife, Laura, and his baby daughter, Mackenzie. He also writes comedy music, has performed as a stand-up comic in Boston, and has performed and directed improvisational comedy for the President of the United States.

Contents in Brief

Contents

Chapter 12 ◆ Personality 402

Chapter 13 ◆ Physical and Cognitive Development 439

Chapter 14 ◆ Social Development 473

Chapter 15 ◆ Psychological Disorders   515

Chapter 16 ◆ Treatment of Psychological Disorders   558

Chapter 9
Consciousness

Matias Morales, *Ecological Sleep*. Kactus Foto, Santiago, Chile/Superstock.

lmost a century ago, a Swiss physician named Claparede shook hands with a patient suffering from Korsakoff's disorder, which produces amnesia for recent events (Chapter 6). Claparede had concealed a pin between his fingers, which pricked the patient as their hands clasped. At their next meeting, the patient had no memory of having met Claparede, but she found herself inexplicably unwilling to shake his hand (Cowey, 1991). What the patient knew (that the good doctor was not so good) and what she *consciously* knew (that she was meeting a doctor, whom she need not fear) were two very different things.

Amnesics are not the only people who can respond to a stimulus at different levels of consciousness. As we shall see, we all do, but the signs are often more subtle.

We begin this chapter by discussing the nature and functions of consciousness, examining the way attention focuses consciousness at any given time on a narrow subset of the thoughts and feelings of which a person could be aware. We then examine multiple perspectives on consciousness and explore the neural basis of consciousness. The remainder of the chapter is devoted to **states of consciousness**—*qualitatively different patterns of subjective experience*, including ways of experiencing both internal and external events. We start with the most basic distinction, between waking and sleeping, exploring the stages of sleep and the nature of dreaming. We conclude by examining several altered states of consciousness—deviations from the normal waking state—including meditation, religious experiences, hypnosis, and drug-induced states.

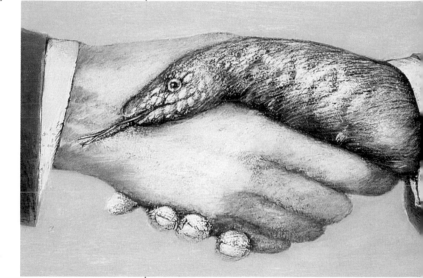

Throughout, we focus on a central question: How does each of the major perspectives in psychology contribute to our understanding of consciousness? As we will see, these seemingly incompatible vantage points may be starting to find some common ground.

◆ The Nature of Consciousness

Consciousness, *the subjective awareness of mental events*, is easier to describe than to define. William James (1890) viewed consciousness as a constantly moving stream of thoughts, feelings, and perceptions. Following in the footsteps of the French philosopher René Descartes, who offered the famous proposition *cogito ergo sum* ("I think, therefore I am"), James also emphasized a second aspect of consciousness, the consciousness of self. James argued that part of being conscious of any particular thought is a simultaneous awareness of oneself as the author or owner of it.

Functions of Consciousness

Why do we have consciousness at all? Two of the functions of consciousness are readily apparent: Consciousness monitors the self and the environment, and it regulates

Central Questions

■ What light does each of the major perspectives—psychodynamic, behavioral, cognitive, and evolutionary—shed on consciousness?

Apply & Discuss

■ What is the role of consciousness in typing?
■ To what extent is consciousness involved in knowing which keys to press while typing?

Red	Yellow	Green
Blue	Red	**Yellow**
Green	Blue	Red

Figure 9.1   The Stroop color-naming task. The task is to name the color of the ink in which each word is printed as quickly as possible while ignoring the words themselves. Try it yourself—the task is very difficult because the word interferes with color naming when the word is printed in a different color (e.g., when "green" is written in red).

thought and behavior (Kihlstrom, 1987). Consciousness as a *monitor* is analogous to a continuously moving video camera, surveying potentially significant perceptions, thoughts, emotions, goals, and problem-solving strategies. The regulatory or *control function* of consciousness allows people to initiate and terminate thought and behavior in order to attain goals. People often rehearse scenarios in their minds, such as asking for a raise or confronting a disloyal friend. Consciousness is often engaged when people choose between competing strategies for solving a problem (Mandler & Nakamura, 1987; Wegner & Bargh, 1998).

These two functions of consciousness—monitor and control—are intertwined, because consciousness monitors inner and outer experience to prevent and solve problems. For example, consciousness often "steps in" when automatized processes (procedural knowledge) are not successful. In this sense, consciousness is like the inspector in a garment factory: It does not make the product, but it checks to make sure the product is made correctly. If it finds an imperfection, it institutes a remedy (Gilbert, 1989, p. 206).

Recent neuroimaging evidence suggests that the dorsolateral prefrontal cortex, which is involved in working memory and conscious decision making (Chapters 6 and 7), is activated when people exercise conscious control. Researchers in one study (MacDonald et al., 2000) demonstrated this using the *Stroop test*, in which subjects are presented a word printed in color and then have to name the color quickly while ignoring the word. This task can be very difficult, particularly if the word itself is the name of a *color*, because the subject has to name the color of the ink and ignore the competing color name—a task that requires considerable conscious attention (Figure 9.1).

The researchers found that the Stroop task leads to activation of the dorsolateral prefrontal cortex, as subjects "put their mind to" the job of ignoring the words while naming the color (Figure 9.2). Interestingly, a different part of the cortex, the anterior cingulate, becomes active only when the color of the ink and the word conflict but not when the color of the ink is congruent with the word (e.g., "red" printed in red ink). This suggests that the anterior cingulate is involved in consciously regulating conflicting cues and perhaps in inhibiting responses that are incorrect.

From an evolutionary standpoint, consciousness probably evolved as a mechanism for directing behavior in adaptive ways that was superimposed on more primitive psychological processes such as conditioning (Reber, 1992). Indeed, William James, who was heavily influenced by Darwin, explained consciousness in terms of its function: fostering adaptation. Consciousness is often "grabbed" by things that are unexpected, unusual, contradictory (as in the Stroop task), or contrary to expecta-

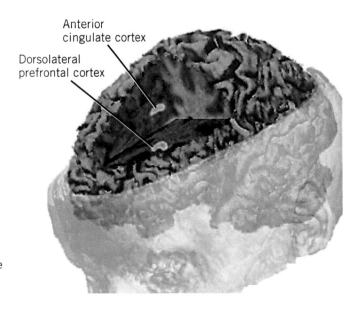

Anterior cingulate cortex

Dorsolateral prefrontal cortex

Figure 9.2   Neural pathways in controlling and monitoring tasks. Participants showed more activation in the dorsolateral prefrontal cortex when preparing to exert conscious control but showed more activation in the anterior cingulate when monitoring for conflicts. *Source*: MacDonald et al., 2000.

tions—precisely the things that could affect well-being or survival. Much of the time people respond automatically to the environment, learning and processing information without much attention. Important choices, however, require more careful conscious consideration.

◆ INTERIM SUMMARY

> **Consciousness** refers to the subjective awareness of mental events. **States of consciousness** are qualitatively different patterns of subjective experience, including ways of experiencing both internal and external events. Consciousness plays at least two functions: monitoring the self and the environment and controlling thought and behavior. Consciousness probably evolved as a mechanism for directing behavior in adaptive ways that was superimposed on more primitive psychological processes that continue to function without conscious awareness.

Consciousness and Attention

At any given time, people are dimly aware of much more than what is conscious. For example, while reading the newspaper a person may have some vague awareness of the radiator clanking, voices in the next room, and the smell of breakfast cooking, but none of these is at the center of awareness or consciousness.

Attention

Attention refers to *the process of focusing conscious awareness*, providing heightened sensitivity to a limited range of experience requiring more extensive information processing. *Selection*—of a particular object, a train of thought, or a location in space where something important might be happening—is the essence of attention (Posner & DiGirolamo, 2000). Attention is generally guided by some combination of external stimulation, which naturally leads us to focus on relevant sensory information, and activated goals, which lead us to attend to thoughts, feelings, or stimuli relevant to obtaining these goals.

Filtering in and Filtering Out   Some psychologists have likened attention to a filtering process through which only more important information passes (Broadbent, 1958). For example, people frequently become so engrossed in conversation with one person that they tune out all the other conversations in the room— an important skill at a loud party. However, if they hear someone mention their name across the room, they may suddenly look up and focus attention on the person who has just spoken the magic word. This phenomenon, called the *cocktail party phenomenon* (Cherry, 1953), suggests that we implicitly process much more information than reaches consciousness.

On the other hand, *people also sometimes divert attention from information that may be relevant but emotionally upsetting*, a process called **selective inattention**. This can be highly adaptive, as when students divert their attention from the anxiety of taking a test to the task itself. It can also be maladaptive, as when people ignore a darkening birthmark on their arm that could be malignant.

Components of Attention   Attention actually consists of at least three functions: orienting to sensory stimuli, controlling behavior and the contents of consciousness, and maintaining alertness (see Posner, 1995). Different neural networks, relying on different neurotransmitter systems, appear to be involved in these three functions (Robbins, 1997).

Orienting, which has been studied most extensively in the visual system (Robertson & Rafal, 2000), involves turning sensory organs such as the eyes and ears toward a stimulus. It also involves spreading extra activation to the parts of the cortex that are

Apply & Discuss

■ What parts of the brain are involved as a person notices that her baby is playing with something, categorizes the object as dangerous, and moves the object away from the baby?

processing information about the stimulus and probably inhibiting activation of others. When we attend to a stimulus, such as a mosquito buzzing around the room, the brain uses the same circuits it normally uses to process information that is not the focus of attention. For example, watching the mosquito activates the "what" and "where" visual pathways in the occipital, temporal, and parietal lobes. What attention does is to enhance processing at those cortical locations (Rees et al., 1997). Orienting to stimuli activates neural circuits in the midbrain (such as the superior colliculi, which help control eye movements), thalamus (which directs attention to particular sensory systems), and parietal lobes (which, among other functions, direct attention to particular locations).

A second function of attention is to control the contents of consciousness, such as deciding how much to listen as someone is talking. Despite our subjective experience of consciously controlling what we attend to, the situation is more the other way around: To notice something consciously, unconscious attentional mechanisms have to alert us to its potential significance. Thus, paradoxically, consciousness is, to a large degree, regulated *outside* of consciousness, by unconscious attentional mechanisms that focus conscious awareness. Controlling the contents of consciousness and controlling voluntary behavior involve areas of the frontal lobes and basal ganglia known to be involved in thought, movement, and self-control.

The third function of attention, maintaining alertness, is crucial in tasks ranging from focusing on test items in the face of anxiety, to staying alert for hours while watching a radar screen to detect seemingly small but potentially meaningful changes. A whole network of neurons from the reticular formation (involved in regulating states of alertness) through the frontal lobes appear to be involved in alertness (Posner, 1995).

Divided Attention

Everyone has had the experience of being on the telephone and having someone in the room begin talking at the same time. Trying to follow two such conversations is an example of **divided attention**, *splitting attention between two complex tasks* (see Craik et al., 1996).

One way researchers study divided attention is through **dichotic listening** tasks, in which *subjects are fitted with earphones, and different information is simultaneously presented to the left and right ears* (Figure 9.3). Subjects can be instructed to attend only to the information from one ear by repeating aloud what they hear in that ear, a procedure called shadowing.

Subjects can become so adept at shadowing that they are completely unable to recognize information in the unattended channel. Nevertheless, the information does appear to be processed to some degree, as demonstrated in research on priming, in which exposure to a stimulus (such as a word) affects performance on tasks involving related stimuli (Chapter 6). For example, subjects who hear "England" (the prime) in the unattended channel in a dichotic listening study may have no recollection of having heard the name of any country. When compared to control subjects who have not been similarly primed, however, they are more likely to say "London" if asked to name a capital city and will more quickly fill in the missing letters when asked for the name of a city when presented with LO—.

Divided attention can be seen in such everyday but remarkably complex events as listening to a lecture while simultaneously taking notes. Psychologists have even trained subjects to take dictation while reading (Spelke et al., 1976). Sometimes people accomplish such feats by rapidly shifting attention back and forth between the two tasks. Much of the time, however, they solve attentional dilemmas by automatizing one task or the other (Chapter 6). Automatization develops through practice, as actions previously performed with deliberate conscious effort are eventually processed automatically. While students listen to a lecture, their primary focus of consciousness is on the lecturer's current words, while a largely automatic process, perhaps drawing on some subset of attentional processes, allows note taking.

Figure 9.3 A dichotic listening task. Subjects are fitted with earphones, and different information is transmitted into each ear simultaneously. Subjects often show effects of information presented in the unattended channel, even when they have no conscious recognition of it.

◆ **INTERIM SUMMARY**

> **Attention** refers to the process of focusing conscious awareness, providing heightened sensitivity to a limited range of experience requiring more extensive information processing. Attention consists of at least three functions: orienting to sensory stimuli, controlling behavior and the contents of consciousness, and maintaining alertness. **Divided attention**, which often involves automatizing one or more tasks or rapidly shifting attention between them, refers to the capacity to split attention or cognitive resources between two or more tasks.

The Normal Flow of Consciousness

A major component of the normal flow of consciousness is **daydreaming**—*turning attention away from external stimuli to internal thoughts and imagined scenarios*. Some daydreams are pleasurable fantasies, whereas others involve planning for future actions or conversations with significant others. In one large-scale study of daydreaming, all subjects reported daydreaming daily (Singer, 1975). Another research team found that college students daydream about half the time they are conscious, if daydreaming includes thoughts about something other than what is currently happening in the person's environment, such as thinking about an upcoming date while sitting in the library (Klinger, 1992).

Psychologists study the normal flow of consciousness using **experience-sampling** techniques, in which *participants report on the contents of consciousness at specified times* (Larson, 1997; Singer & Kolligian, 1987). For example, after being instructed simply to report the contents of their consciousness, they may come into the laboratory and talk aloud, often while performing a task. Psychologists then code their verbal responses into categories, such as emotional tone, relevance to the task at hand, ways of solving the task, and so forth.

Beeper studies are *an experience-sampling technique that has provided a more natural window to the flow of consciousness in everyday life*. In these studies, participants carry pagers or palm-top computers and report their experience when "beeped" at various points during the day (Affleck et al., 2000; Larsen, 1996). In one study, researchers randomly selected 75 high school students within several categories, such as sex, grade, and social class (a stratified random sample; Chapter 2) (Csikszentmihalyi & Larson, 1984). For an entire week, they beeped the students at some point during every two-hour period (except, of course, at night). Participants then immediately filled out a brief form reporting what they were doing and with whom, what they were thinking and feeling, and how intensely they were feeling it. Some of the results were quite unexpected. For example, when subjects were with their families, their negative thoughts outnumbered their positive thoughts by about 10 to 1.

◆ **INTERIM SUMMARY**

> Prominent in the normal flow of conscious experience are **daydreams**, in which the person turns attention away from external stimuli to internal thoughts and imagined scenarios, often for pleasure or for problem solving. Psychologists learn about the normal flow of consciousness through **experience-sampling** techniques, such as **beeper studies**, in which participants carry pagers or palm-top computers and report on aspects of consciousness when they are paged at random intervals.

◆ Perspectives on Consciousness

Consciousness occupied a central role in the first textbook on psychology, written by William James in 1890, and figured prominently in Freud's work. When behaviorism came into ascendance, however, consciousness as a focus of investigation receded from the consciousness of the scientific community and remained that way until the 1980s. Behaviorists rejected the idea of a conscious mind as an agent that chooses, intends, or makes decisions (Skinner, 1974, p. 169). Organisms as primitive as snails respond to environmental contingencies, but one would not propose that snails therefore have consciousness.

Until about a decade ago, cognitive psychologists paid little attention to consciousness, either. As we saw in Chapters 6 and 7, however, that all changed with the surge of research on implicit memory and cognition. Spurred by developments in neuroscience and neuroimaging that provide a new window on consciousness, cognitive scientists—as well as philosophers, neurologists, biologists, and even physicists—have begun rethinking consciousness (e.g., Cohen & Schooler, 1997; Edelman, 1989). In this section we examine psychodynamic and cognitive perspectives on consciousness and explore some emerging common ground.

The Psychodynamic Unconscious

Freud (1900) defined consciousness as one of three mental systems called the conscious, preconscious, and unconscious (Figure 9.4). **Conscious mental processes** *involve subjective awareness of stimuli, feelings, or ideas* (e.g., consciousness of the sentence you just read—if you were paying attention). **Preconscious mental processes** *are not presently conscious but could be readily brought to consciousness* if the need arose, such as the smell of bacon cooking in the background or the name of a city that is not currently in mind but could easily be retrieved. **Unconscious mental processes** *are inaccessible to consciousness because they would be too anxiety provoking to acknowledge and thus have been repressed* (Chapter 12).

Freud likened repression to a censor: Just as a repressive government censors ideas or wishes it considers threatening, so, too, does the mind censor threatening thoughts from consciousness. Thus, a person may remember an abusive father with love and admiration and have little access to unhappy memories because admitting the truth would be painful. Unconscious processes of this sort are *dynamically unconscious*—that is, kept unconscious for a reason. According to Freud, keeping mental contents out of awareness requires continuing psychological effort or energy, a postulate that has received empirical support in recent years (Wegner & Wheatley, 1999). Freud (1915) recognized that many other psychological processes are *descriptively unconscious*, that is, not conscious even though they are not threatening, such as the processes by which readers are converting symbols on this page into words with psychological meaning.

Subliminal Perception

In the 1940s and 1950s, as part of the New Look in perception (Chapter 4), researchers tested hypotheses derived from Freud's theory of consciousness. Studies of **subliminal perception**—*perception of stimuli below the threshold of consciousness*—used a device called a *tachistoscope*, which can flash images too quickly for conscious recognition but slowly enough to be registered outside awareness (Dixon, 1971, 1981; Erdelyi, 1985; Weinberger, in press). Figure 9.5 describes one such study.

Although experiments in subliminal perception went out of favor for almost 30 years, more recently both cognitive and psychodynamic researchers have breathed new life into subliminal research, demonstrating that subliminal presentation of stimuli can indeed influence thought and emotion (Morris et al., 1998; Shevrin et al., 1996; Weinberger & Hardaway, 1990; Whalen et al., 1998). For instance, subliminal presentation of a happy or sad face directly prior to exposure to a novel visual stimulus (such as a Chinese letter) affects the extent to which subjects like it (Murphy & Zajonc, 1993). Subliminal presentation of the face seems to "tag" the stimulus with an emotional connotation. Other studies have shown that participants subliminally primed with a word (e.g., "beach") will more quickly recognize words semantically related to it (e.g., "sand"), even though they never consciously registered the prime (Marcel, 1983).

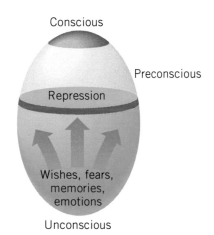

Figure 9.4 Freud's model of consciousness. Conscious mental processes are those of which a person is subjectively aware. Preconscious mental processes are not presently conscious but could readily be brought to consciousness. Unconscious mental processes are inaccessible to consciousness because they have been repressed.

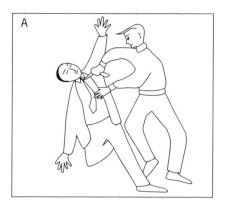 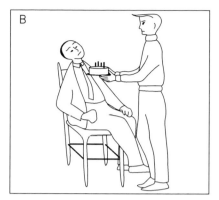 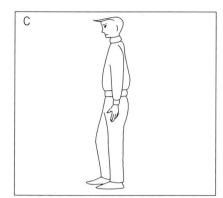

Figure 9.5 Subliminal perception. Participants were presented subliminally with either slide A, a boy behaving aggressively, or slide B, a boy behaving altruistically. Participants were then shown a neutral picture of the boy and asked to judge his personality. Participants who had seen slide A described the boy as aggressive, whereas those who had seen slide B described him as altruistic. *Source.* Eagle, 1959.

Psychologists have not been the only people interested in subliminal processing. In the 1950s, rumors flew that movie theaters were manipulating consumers by subliminally presenting messages like "eat popcorn" and "buy Coke." In the 1980s, parents expressed fears about subliminal messages in rock music, such as backward messages encouraging violence. More recently, a storm of controversy emerged when U.S. presidential candidate George W. Bush ran an attack ad against his rival, Al Gore, which subliminally paired the word "rats" with Gore. Media pundits and advertising executives were quick to deny that subliminal messages of this sort could have any effect—surprisingly, without ever talking to psychologists who had studied the issue scientifically.

Although the impact of subliminal messages on consumers is not likely to be particularly large, research on subliminal priming clearly demonstrates that presenting people with subliminal stimuli that are positive or negative can influence their emotional reactions and behaviors (Glassman & Andersen, 1997; Weinberger, in press). For consumers who already have a strong preference or clearly thought-out rationale for or against a product or candidate, however, subliminal effects are likely to be relatively weak motivators of consumer behavior. A person who is already thirsty may become somewhat more likely to buy a soft drink after a subliminal message, but a person whose stomach is full is unlikely to make a run for the popcorn. Backward messages have no effect whatsoever because they cannot be perceived (Kirk & Rogers, 1994; Trappey, 1996).

Critics cried foul play when George W. Bush's campaign ran an advertisement in which the word "rats" appeared, at one-third of a second, superimposed on a message about his opponent, then Vice President Al Gore. Bush responded that the idea of subliminal perception was "weird and bizarre" and that the subliminal message had appeared by accident. (Apparently rats had eaten their way into a $2 million advertisement!)

Unconscious Emotion and Motivation

The proposition that unconscious cognitive and perceptual processes can influence behavior is no longer controversial. Historically, however, the most distinctively psychodynamic hypothesis is that motivational and emotional processes can be unconscious as well. This proposition has now also gained experimental support (see Bargh & Barndollar, 1996; Epstein, 1994; Westen, 1998).

With respect to motivation, research suggests a distinction between conscious and unconscious motivational systems similar to the distinction between implicit and explicit memory in cognitive science. Numerous studies have shown that when people are not attending to their conscious goals and values, they tend to act on implicit motives (McClelland et al., 1989). As described below, other studies show that priming people with words associated with their motives (e.g., priming people with *success*, which is associated to the need for achievement) makes them more likely to act on these motives, even though they may be completely unaware that they have been primed (Bargh & Barndollar, 1996).

Making Connections

When people are consciously focusing on their motives or goals, these goals tend to direct their behavior. When they are not, however, their unconscious or implicit motives control their behavior. That is probably why New Years' resolutions are usually short-lived (Chapter 10).

Emotional processes can also influence thought and behavior without being conscious. This can be seen in research with patients with Korsakoff's disorder, like the woman whose case began this chapter, who have severe amnesia. In one study, Korsakoff's patients preferred a person described a week earlier as having positive traits over someone described more negatively, even though they had no recollection of having seen either one before (Johnson et al., 1985). Similar findings emerge in subliminal priming studies of patients without neurological damage (see Lazarus & McCleary, 1951), using measures ranging from facial muscle movements indicating distress to brain wave activity assessed by EEG (see Ohman, 1994; Wong et al., 1994). These findings are of particular relevance to the psychodynamic hypothesis that individuals can respond emotionally to people or situations without knowing why.

Other researchers have found that people can regulate their emotions outside of awareness by keeping distressing thoughts, feelings, and memories out of consciousness (Paulhus et al., 1997; Vaillant, 1992). This can sometimes be adaptive, particularly if nothing can be done to change an uncomfortable situation. However, people who chronically keep themselves unaware of their emotions may pay a physical toll: They are more likely to suffer from asthma, heart disease, and other illnesses than people who are more aware of their unpleasant feelings and can therefore take steps to try to deal with the things that are distressing them (Asendorph & Sherer, 1983; Pennebaker, 1997a; Shedler et al., 1993; D. Weinberger, 1990).

The Cognitive Unconscious

The **cognitive unconscious** of cognitive research refers to *information-processing mechanisms that operate outside of awareness* (such as implicit memory) rather than information the person is *motivated* to keep from awareness. In other words, the cognitive unconscious includes what Freud called *descriptively* but not *dynamically* unconscious processes.

Information-processing models often use the terms *consciousness* and *working memory* interchangeably, viewing consciousness as an "on-line" workspace for focusing attention on perceptions, memories, and skills relevant for solving current problems. As we saw in Chapters 6 and 7, most models now distinguish explicit (conscious) and implicit (unconscious) memory and cognition, such as conscious problem-solving strategies versus automatic, unconscious heuristics. Connectionist models further propose that information processing occurs simultaneously in multiple, relatively separate neural networks, most of which are unconscious (Chapter 7). The brain synthesizes a unitary conscious experience from the various activated unconscious networks, "highlighting" those that best fit the data (Baars, 1988, 1997; Mandler, 1997; Searle, 2000).

Distinguishing Unconscious Cognitive Processes

From a cognitive perspective, John Kihlstrom (1987, 1996) distinguishes unconscious from preconscious cognitive processes, both of which occur outside of awareness. *Unconscious cognitive processes* are skills or procedures that operate without awareness and are not accessible to consciousness under any circumstance. *Preconscious cognitive processes* refer to associations and schemas (declarative knowledge) activated below the threshold of consciousness that influence conscious thought and behavior. The activity of preconscious processes can be seen experimentally in subliminal priming procedures as well as in everyday life, as when a person cannot get a song "out of his head" that keeps returning because it continues to be preconsciously activated.

Kihlstrom adds a third aspect of consciousness—consciousness of self—to account for two unusual phenomena. The first is that people given hypnotic suggestions to perform certain actions may do them without any sense of having chosen to do so. The second involves *dissociative disorders*, in which memories or feelings are literally disassociated from consciousness, such as cases of multiple personality (Chapter 15).

According to Kihlstrom, these phenomena suggest, as William James asserted, that part of normal consciousness involves consciousness of self. In other words, consciousness includes an activated representation of self linked with the thought or action, so that the person sees her thoughts or actions as *hers*.

The Functions of Conscious and Unconscious Processes

Some cognitive theorists have examined the complementary functions, strengths, and weaknesses of conscious and unconscious processes in everyday behavior. Unconscious processes, notably skills and associative processes such as priming and classical conditioning, are extremely fast and efficient (Baars & McGovern, 1996; Mandler, 1997). Since they are usually based on considerable learning, they tend to lead to adaptive responses that make sense in light of observed regularities in the environment (such as avoiding stimuli that would lead to pain or danger).

Another strength of unconscious processes is that they can operate simultaneously. When solving a problem, for example, multiple networks can "collect data" at the same time and come up with independent and "well-researched" potential solutions. Consciousness, in contrast, has limited capacity: We can only form one "scene" at a time in our conscious minds; we cannot, for example, see the classic ambiguous Gestalt figure as both two faces and a vase simultaneously (Chapter 1). We can switch rapidly back and forth between two views of a scene or among tasks that require attention, but ultimately, each will draw conscious cognitive resources from the other. On the other hand, conscious processes are more flexible than unconscious processes, and because consciousness is not limited to quasi-independent networks operating in parallel in their own small domains, consciousness can survey the landscape and consider the "big picture."

One theory suggests that unconscious processes operating in parallel are like independent teams of "experts," each offering its own advice on how to solve a problem or make a decision (Baars, 1988, 1997). Consciousness is thus like a blackboard on which each team of experts fights to present its solution or several teams brainstorm "at the board" to develop novel answers that none alone could produce. If a "team" manages to get its message on the blackboard, its "solution" is advertised throughout the system and leads other experts to begin trying to find solutions along those lines.

In more technical terms, a central role of consciousness is to redistribute activation among the tens, hundreds, or thousands of networks ("team of experts") active at any given time (Mandler, 1997). When conscious goals are active, they spread extra activation to networks associated with goal attainment. If a person is trying to make a decision or solve a problem, the networks activated below consciousness all vie for conscious access. Those that seem to provide the best potential solutions become represented in consciousness. Becoming conscious in turn spreads further activation to them and inhibits activation of less compelling alternatives.

Central Questions

- In what ways do cognitive and psychodynamic views of consciousness diverge or disagree?
- In what ways do these two views converge or agree?

◆ INTERIM SUMMARY

Freud distinguished types of mental activities: **conscious** processes, of which the person is currently subjectively aware; **preconscious** processes, which are not presently conscious but could be readily brought to consciousness; and **unconscious** processes, which are dynamically kept from consciousness because they are threatening. Studies of **subliminal perception** have shown that perception of stimuli below the threshold of consciousness can indeed have an impact on conscious thought and behavior. Recent research also supports the psychodynamic hypothesis that emotional and motivational processes can occur outside of awareness. Researchers from a cognitive perspective have been studying the **cognitive unconscious**, which focuses on information-processing mechanisms that operate outside of awareness, such as procedural knowledge and implicit memory. Implicit processes tend to be rapid and to operate simultaneously. Conscious processes are slower and less efficient for tasks that require instant responses but are useful for "shining a spotlight" on problems that require more careful consideration.

Commentary

An Integrated View of Consciousness

Fifteen years ago, summarizing psychologists' views of conscious and unconscious processes was easy: Psychoanalysts believed in them, behaviorists did not, cognitive scientists were not particularly interested, and evolutionary psychology was just getting off the ground and had not yet weighed in on the subject. Today, we are beginning to see a rare convergence of views. The state of the art might be summarized as follows.

In humans, as in other animals, most behavior is controlled through implicit processes. Conscious processing is too limited in capacity to regulate and monitor the range of stimuli and goals confronting a person at any given time. Associative learning mechanisms, such as those studied by behaviorists, are generally rapid and efficient, and they served our pre-human ancestors well, long before consciousness arrived on the scene (Reber, 1992). The vast majority of perceptual, cognitive, emotional, and motivational processes are implicit and are thus not available to introspection. We can see the *impact* of our own implicit processes and form conscious representations of them (e.g., recognizing the kinds of people or situations that "push our buttons"), but our brains are not constructed to give us direct access to them.

Some processes to which we *could* have access, such as thoughts, fantasies, or motives of which we are ashamed, can also become inaccessible to consciousness if we learn that keeping them from consciousness reduces our discomfort. The mechanisms for keeping uncomfortable material outside of awareness or transforming it into conscious representations that are not threatening (e.g., "I'm not a competitive person; I'm only competitive with *myself*") are themselves a form of procedural knowledge or skill. These procedures are learned like any other: Those that reduce uncomfortable feelings are reinforced (Chapter 5).

Consciousness is a specialized function that monitors our current state in relation to the environment for the purpose of maximizing adaptation. Consciousness is particularly "grabbed" by news; that is, it is most likely to shine its spotlight on information that is novel or unexpected or on procedures that are not working optimally (Baars & McGovern, 1996). Its control function involves overriding procedures that are ineffective or bringing together quasi-independent "experts" to help provide flexible solutions that cannot be obtained while running on automatic pilot.

While multiple processes operate in parallel to solve problems outside of awareness, attentional mechanisms also operate outside awareness to "prioritize" cognitive resources, spreading extra activation to those resources that might be adaptively significant or help solve current goals. Once a perception, thought, goal, or motive enters consciousness, it further spreads activation to those neural networks that are relevant to it. Much of the time this increases the likelihood that aspects of those neural networks will become conscious. However, activated networks can influence behavior outside of awareness, and threatening information can be inhibited from consciousness even while it is maximally active.

From Brain to Behavior

The Neuropsychology of Consciousness

Subjectively, consciousness is the seat of who we are; to lose consciousness permanently is to lose existence as a psychological being. So what neural structures produce conscious awareness and regulate states of consciousness?

Insights from Neurological Disorders

One way to learn about the neural pathways involved in consciousness is to examine neurological conditions that disrupt it. People with split brains, whose two hemispheres function independently following severing of the corpus callosum, provide one window to the neuropsychology of consciousness. An instructive case, described in Chapter 3, concerned a ten-year-old boy who could only answer written questions orally when inquiries were made to the left hemisphere, suggesting that information presented to his right hemisphere lacked access to conciousness—although he could spell answers using his left hand when questions were addressed to his right hemisphere (LeDoux et al., 1977). The feelings spelled by his nonverbal right hemisphere were consistently more negative than those of his left hemisphere, raising questions about the unity of consciousness across the hemispheres.

Blindsight   Another phenomenon that bears on the neural underpinnings of consciousness is blindsight (Chapter 4). Pursuing observations made by neurologists in the early part of the twentieth century, researchers have examined patients who are, in one sense, totally blind: If shown an object, they deny having seen it. They typically have lesions to the primary visual cortex in the occipital lobes, a region central to visual sensation, so their inability to see makes neurological sense. Yet if asked to describe the object's geometric form (e.g., triangle or square) or give its location in space (to the right or left, up or down), they do so with accuracy far better than chance, frequently protesting all the while that they cannot do the task because they cannot see (Weiskrantz, 1997; Weiskrantz et al., 1974)!

The neural basis for blindsight is not entirely clear, but one hypothesis, derived in part from animal research, points to the role of two neural pathways involved in vision (Figure 9.6). In the evolutionarily more recent pathway, neurons of the optic nerve carrying sensory information project to the thalamus via the optic tract; the information is subsequently transmitted to the primary visual cortex in the occipital lobes. This pathway is responsible for conscious visual perception and for determining the precise nature of stimuli.

The other pathway is evolutionarily older. Neurons carrying information from the retina project to a midbrain structure responsible for vision in animals such as frogs and birds that lack the highly specialized visual cortex of humans. From there the information passes through the thalamus and eventually on to the cortex. In blindsight, this second pathway appears to allow some visual processing at the midbrain level, even though the first pathway is rendered inoperative by damage to the visual cortex. Thalamic processing may also permit some recognition of what an object is even though this thalamic knowledge cannot be consciously accessed—and may lead to emotional reactions to it even though the person has no idea what he has seen (Chapter 11).

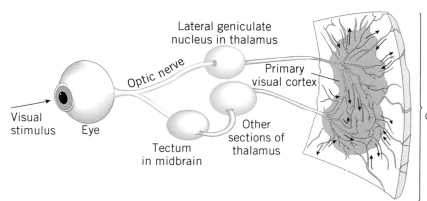

Visual stimulus   Eye
Optic nerve
Lateral geniculate nucleus in thalamus
Primary visual cortex
Tectum in midbrain
Other sections of thalamus
Section of occipital lobe

Figure 9.6   Blindsight. In blindsight, the neural pathway from the lateral geniculate nucleus in the thalamus to the primary visual cortex, which allows consciousness of visual images, is inoperative. However, a second, evolutionarily older pathway through the midbrain remains intact, permitting the implicit ability to locate visual stimuli.

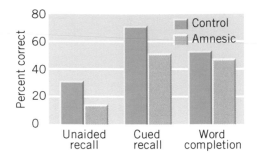

Figure 9.7 Priming effects in amnesia. Participants were shown word lists including words like *absent*, *income*, and *motel* and asked to recall the words. Amnesic patients were impaired on both unaided recall and cued recall. However, amnesic patients exhibited normal priming effects when they completed three-letter fragments (e.g., *ABS*) with the first word that came to mind. *Source:* Squire, 1986.

Amnesia Studies with amnesics have shown that people can remember things implicitly even while lacking any consciousness of having seen them. In one series of studies (Squire, 1986), researchers showed amnesic and normal subjects a word list and asked them to recall the words with and without cues. When later tested for explicit memory, amnesic subjects were considerably impaired on both free-recall (recall without cues) and cued-recall tasks (in which participants were given the first three letters of the word) (Figure 9.7). However, amnesics were as likely as neurologically intact subjects to use words from the list when shown the first three letters of the word and simply asked to complete them with the first words that came to mind.

Implicit memory can show up in some unusual ways in amnesic patients. In one study, researchers had amnesic and normal subjects play the computer game *Tetris* for several hours over 3 days (Stickgold et al., 2000). Amnesics were just as likely to report *Tetris*-related imagery while nodding off to sleep those nights, even though they had no explicit recollection of having played! Similarly, a psychologist told a joke to a Korsakoff's patient whose ability to remember new experiences was virtually nonexistent (Jacoby & Kelley, 1987). Predictably, the man laughed, but the next time he heard the joke, he thought the joke was "dumb." The patient had apparently anticipated the punch line unconsciously, even though he had no conscious recollection of it.

Where Is Consciousness Located?

So where is consciousness located in the brain? Research over the past two decades has made increasingly clear that this is probably not the right question to ask about any psychological phenomenon. Consciousness, like most psychological functions, involves a distributed network of neurons rather than a single "center." The better question, then, is, "What neural structures are involved in the experience of consciousness?"

The answer to this question, too, has a twist: It depends on which meaning of consciousness one has in mind. If one simply means the state of being conscious (as opposed to being unconscious or asleep), then hindbrain and midbrain structures, especially the reticular formation, are particularly important (Bogen, 1995; Franklin et al., 1988; Szymusiak et al., 1989). For example, neuroimaging of surgical patients undergoing anesthesia finds reduced activity in the midbrain (as well as the thalamus, which plays an important role in conscious awareness) (Fiset et al., 1999). Similarly, damage to the reticular formation through head injury in humans or lesioning in animals can lead to loss of consciousness or coma. The pons and medulla are also involved in regulating states of conscious arousal (Figure 9.8); in contrast, we can lose an entire cerebral hemisphere and remain conscious.

But consciousness has another meaning, which has been our focus thus far in this chapter: consciousness as the center of subjective awareness. In this sense, consciousness is distributed across a number of neural pathways, most of them found in the cortex as well as the reticular formation and the thalamus (Newman, 1995). The reticular formation extends throughout much of the hindbrain and sends axons through the midbrain (in the tegmentum). These fibers then synapse with nuclei in the thalamus, which in turn synapse with parts of the cortex. A region of particular importance is the prefrontal cortex (Goldman-Rakic, 1995), which is involved in momentarily storing, manipulating, or calling up information from various senses into working memory and hence making them conscious (Chapter 6).

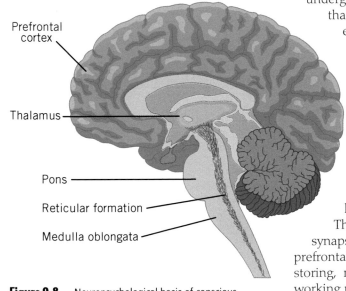

Figure 9.8 Neuropsychological basis of consciousness. The hindbrain and midbrain structures involved in conscious arousal and in shifts from waking to sleep include the reticular formation, pons, and medulla. Midbrain reticular regions, the thalamus, and the prefrontal cortex play a particular role in shining a conscious "spotlight" on thoughts, feelings, or perceptions.

Recent positron emission tomography (PET) data have in fact confirmed that when subjects are consciously attending to stimuli, a pathway from the midbrain sections of the reticular formation through the region of the thalamus to which it projects becomes activated (Kinomura et al., 1996). Once the cortex is activated and the person attends to a stimulus, it sends messages back down to another region of the thalamus that signals the first region to limit its activation to the most relevant details of the stimulus, "shining a spotlight" on information that needs to be highlighted and inhibiting attention to irrelevant details (see Crick & Koch, 1998). Thus, the thalamus and cortex appear to have a feedback loop, in which the thalamus and reticular formation "illuminate" a large terrain, the cortex sends messages back to narrow the focus, and the thalamus in turn helps the cortex focus its conscious spotlight on a more specific target (Newman, 1995).

Not all areas of the cortex have direct access to consciousness. Some researchers have suggested that early sensory processing areas like area V1 in the visual cortex (one of the first sensory "stops" along the road to visual perception; Chapter 4) do not have connections to the prefrontal cortex and hence cannot directly influence conscious experience (Crick & Koch, 1998). A series of creative neuroimaging studies support this theory. The Necker cube (Figure 9.9), the outline of a see-through cube, produces two distinct conscious percepts that subjectively seem to alternate every few seconds. Because the Necker cube casts a constant image on the retina, and hence a constant "image" on the primary visual cortex, this means that the subjective experience of alternating percepts or images is independent of sensory activation V1. However, changes in conscious attention—even without moving the eyes—can alter activation levels in V1 This suggests that consciousness can focus the spotlight on the sensory building blocks of perception and hence alter perception of what is ultimately seen (Lumer & Rees, 1999; Smith et al., 2000; Watanabe et al., 1998).

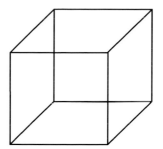

Figure 9.9   The Necker cube.

◆ INTERIM SUMMARY

An integrated view suggests that consciousness is a specialized processing function that monitors and controls current states for the purpose of maximizing adaptation. Consciousness thus highlights or inhibits information based on its relevance to adaptation and its emotional consequences. Consciousness involves a network of neurons distributed throughout the brain. Damage to hindbrain structures, particularly the reticular formation, can lead to a complete loss of consciousness. The neural networks that "shine a spotlight" on perceptions, thoughts, emotions, or goals at any moment appear to involve the prefrontal cortex, the thalamus, and midbrain regions of the reticular formation.

◆ Sleep and Dreaming

We have focused thus far on waking consciousness. We now turn to the major series of changes that occur in consciousness every 24 hours: the sleep–wake cycle. Those who lament that life is too short would be horrified to realize that they will sleep away roughly a third of their time on the earth, about 25 years. Infants sleep two-thirds of each day, and elderly people, about one-fourth.

The Nature and Evolution of Sleep

Sleep evolved over 3 billion years ago in some organisms, and the mechanisms that govern the biological clock in humans are apparently over 500 million years old (Lavie, 1996). Although not all animals show the characteristic EEG signs of sleep (described below), nearly all animals show behavioral signs of sleeping: minimal movement, a stereotyped posture, and a high degree of stimulation needed to arouse them. They differ, however, in how much they sleep (Figure 9.10)

Individuals differ widely in the amount of sleep they both need and get, with most people sleeping between 6.5 and 8.5 hours a night (Lavie, 1996). As people get older, they tend to require less sleep. The number of hours people sleep is related to mortal-

Central Questions

■ Why might sleep have evolved?

■ Why might it make adaptive sense for our consciousness to wax and wane with the cycles of the sun?

Figure 9.10 Average hours of sleep per night. Animals vary according to the amount of sleep they need; humans lie somewhere in the middle.

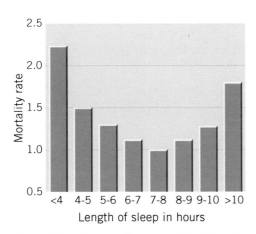

Figure 9.11 Sleep duration and mortality. Mortality rates are highest among those at the extremes, who report sleeping less than five or more than ten hours per night. (Mortality rate is scaled against the group with the lowest mortality rate, those who sleep eight hours.) *Source:* Adapted from Kripke et al., 1979.

ity rates, although the reasons for this are unclear. People who report sleeping for unusually long *or* unusually short durations are prone to die earlier than people whose reported sleep is closer to average (Figure 9.11).

Researchers have documented rare cases of people who require minimal sleep with no adverse consequences, such as a 70-year-old English nurse who was observed to sleep only one hour every night (Borbély, 1986). Legend has it that Leonardo DaVinci had the unusual habit of sleeping 15 minutes every four hours. Interestingly, from the late 1960s to the early 1990s, college students reported sleeping about an hour less on the average per night (Hicks & Pelligrini, 1991).

Circadian Rhythms

The cycle of sleep and waking in humans and other animals, like the ebb and flow of body temperature, hormones, and other life support processes, is a circadian rhythm. A **circadian rhythm** (from the Latin, *circa*, meaning "about," and *diem*, meaning "day") is *a cyclical biological process that evolved around the daily cycles of light and dark*. Expectant mothers can attest to the fact that circadian rhythms begin before birth: Fetuses begin showing rhythms of sleep and activity by the sixth month in utero.

Rhythms akin to sleep–wake cycles may exist in daytime as well as in sleep. Research supports the distinction between "day people" and "night people," finding that people peak in their alertness and arousal at different times of the day (Wallace, 1993). Researchers studying mice have tracked down the genes responsible for controlling their internal "clock" by examining mutant mice whose clocks do not tick correctly (Antoch et al., 1997; Shearman et al., 2000).

Human circadian rhythms are controlled largely by the hypothalamus but are influenced by light and dark. A special neural tract that projects from the retina to the hypothalamus responds only to relatively intense light, such as sunlight. During periods of darkness, the pineal gland in the middle of the brain produces a hormone called *melatonin*; melatonin levels gradually diminish during daylight hours. Melatonin influences not only sleep but also sexual arousal. Thus, during the winter months, when the number of daylight hours diminishes, so, too, does sexual arousal. The old saying that "a young man's fancy turns to thoughts of love" in the springtime thus has more than a grain (or gram) of hormonal truth (see Lavie, 1996).

Circadian rhythms account for the difficulties people experience when they cross time zones (jet lag) or have frequently changing work shifts. Nurses, medical residents on call, police, pilots, and flight attendants, whose shifts change from day to day or week to week, suffer greater incidence of health problems, in part because of disrupted circadian rhythms (Monk, 1997; Tan, 1991). Although some people seem to function well despite these frequent disruptions in their sleep cycle, others become irritable and inefficient—not particularly comforting traits to see in pilots or doctors in training. Prescription melatonin has proven effective for some people in reducing jet lag, presumably by "recalibrating" the body to the light–dark cycle of the new time zone (Arendt et al., 1997; Claustrat et al., 1992).

Sleep Deprivation

No one knows precisely what functions sleep serves. Some researchers emphasize its role in conserving energy, since sleep turns down the body's "thermostat" at night (Berger & Phillips, 1995). Others emphasize a restorative function, in which sleep "freshens" both body and mind; as we will see, still others point to a potential role in consolidating memories learned during the day (see Stickgold, 1998; Walsh & Lindblom, 1997).

People have known of the ill effects of extreme sleep deprivation for at least 2000 years. In Roman times and during the Middle Ages, sleep deprivation was used as a form of torture. Long-term sleep deprivation reduces the functioning of the immune system and makes the body more vulnerable to diseases ranging from common colds to cancer (Everson, 1997). Rats deprived of sleep die after two or three weeks (Rechtscaffen et al., 1989).

As anyone knows who has ever had a bad night's sleep, the time required to fall asleep drops substantially after even a single sleepless night (Carskadon & Dement, 1982). Researchers have recently discovered that a neurotransmitter substance (actually, a modulatory neurotransmitter, which regulates the activity of other neurotransmitters) in the thalamus and in structures deep within the cerebrum increases with each additional hour an animal is awake (Porkka-Heiskanen et al., 1997). This neurotransmitter, called *adenosine*, plays an inhibitory role in the brain, shutting down the systems that normally lead to arousal and hence fostering sleep when an animal has been awake too long.

Insomnia, or *inability to sleep*, affects virtually everyone at some point, but for some people it is a chronic problem. Although "sleeping pills" are sometimes appropriate and may offer temporary relief, they should always be taken with caution. Sleeping pills can lead to more, rather than less, trouble sleeping, as the person becomes dependent on them or the brain develops a tolerance, requiring higher doses to achieve the same effect (Lavie, 1996). Table 9.1 lists some suggestions by a major sleep researcher for reducing or avoiding insomnia.

In 1959, a New York disk jockey, Peter Tripp, stayed awake for 200 hours, or about eight days, as part of a "wakeathon" for charity (Luce, 1966). As time went on, Tripp deteriorated considerably, developing hallucinations (such as the belief that his bureau drawer was on fire), delusions, and paranoid thinking, all of which disappeared after a good night's sleep. Although such extreme reactions have been noted for over a century in cases of long-term sleep deprivation, other people show much less dramatic symptoms.

Sleep disorders range from insomnia to chronic nightmares. To learn more about them, go to www.wiley.com/college/westen and click on **Chapter 9: Sleep Disorders.**

Table 9.1 ◆ Suggestions for Avoiding or Reducing Insomnia

1. Avoid spending too much time in bed. If you are awake, get out. Do not let the bed become a conditioned stimulus associated with insomnia and anxiety.

2. Do not try to force sleep. Go to bed when you are ready, and get out if you are not.

3. Do not keep a brightly lit, ticking clock near the bed.

4. Avoid physical activity late at night. It activates the autonomic nervous system, which is incompatible with sleep.

5. Avoid coffee, chocolate, or alcohol before bedtime. Caffeine will keep you up, even if you do not think it affects you, and alcohol often causes people to wake up in the middle of the night.

6. Keep a regular sleep schedule. If you have insomnia, you need more of a routine than most people.

7. Do not eat a large meal before bedtime. If you wake up, do not visit the refrigerator.

8. Avoid sleeping during the day if you have insomnia.

Source: Adapted from P. Lavie, *The Enchanted World of Sleep* (A. Berris, Trans.), Yale University Press, New Haven, CT, 1996, pp. 176–177.

◆ **INTERIM SUMMARY**

People spend roughly one-third of their lives asleep. The sleep cycle is governed by **circadian rhythms**, cyclical biological "clocks" that evolved around the daily cycles of light and dark. The functions of sleep are not yet known, although sleep appears to be involved in restoration and maintenance of bodily processes such as homeostasis, immune functioning, and consolidation of memory.

Stages of Sleep

Sleep proceeds through a series of stages (Figure 9.12). To study these stages, researchers use EEG (Chapter 2), attaching electrodes to subjects' heads to assess electrical activity in the brain. (They also attach electrodes at the corners of the eyes to track eye movements.) In general, as people move from a waking state through deeper stages of sleep, their brain waves become slower and more rhythmic, decreasing from over 14 cycles per second (cps) in the waking state to as little as $^1/_2$ cps in deep sleep (Dement & Kleitman, 1957). (The number of cycles per second is a gross measure of rate of neural firing and hence of mental activity.)

Early Stages of Sleep

As Figure 9.12 shows, normal waking brain activity has an irregular pattern with a high mental activity level, evidenced in a large number of cycles per second (known as *beta waves*). As people close their eyes and relax, *alpha waves* (8 to 12 cps) emerge, signaling a slowing of mental activity and a transition into sleep.

Stage 1 sleep is brief (only a few minutes), marked by the appearance of slower *theta waves* (3 to 7 cps). Physiological changes accompany this shift from drowsiness into sleep as eye movements slow, muscles relax, and blood pressure drops, bringing the body into a calm, quiet state.

Stage 2 sleep is marked by an EEG pattern of slightly larger waves interrupted by bursts of low-amplitude activity (called *sleep spindles*) and slow, high-amplitude waves called *K complexes* (Halasz, 1993). During Stage 2, sleep deepens, as alpha activity disappears.

Stage 3 sleep is marked by large, slow, rhythmic *delta waves* (less than 1 cps). When delta waves comprise more than 50 percent of recorded brain activity, the person has entered Stage 4 sleep. Together, Stages 3 and 4 constitute what is called *delta sleep*, a deep sleep characterized by relaxed muscles, decreased rate of respiration, and slightly lower body temperature. People aroused from delta sleep are groggy and disoriented. During delta sleep, muscles apparently rest and rejuvenate, since people deprived of it frequently complain of muscle aches and tension.

Rapid Eye Movement Sleep

Delta sleep is followed by a kind of sleep that is qualitatively different from the preceding stages. Stage 4 sleep is interrupted, and the sleep stages occur in reverse order, through Stages 3 and 2. But instead of entering Stage 1, suddenly the eyes begin to dart around as if the sleeper were watching a play. At this point, the person enters **rapid eye movement (REM) sleep**, *a qualitatively different stage of sleep that is named for the darting eye movements that characterize it*. Because REM sleep is so different, *Stages 1 to 4 are often collectively called simply* **non-REM (**or **NREM) sleep**.

In REM sleep, autonomic activity increases: Pulse and blood pressure quicken, respiration becomes faster and irregular, and both males and females evidence signs of sexual arousal that may last for several minutes. At the same time, muscle movement is largely "turned off" (which is a good thing, or we would act out our dreams). The EEG during REM sleep resembles the irregular, faster pattern of waking life, suggesting that, although the body is not moving, the brain is quite active. The function

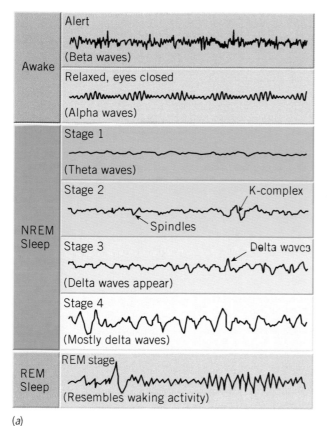

(a)

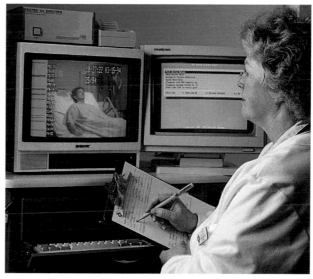

(b)

Figure 9.12 Stages of sleep. (a) As people move from a waking state through deeper stages of sleep, their brain waves become slower and more rhythmic, decreasing from over 14 cycles per second in the waking state to as little as one-half cycle per second in deep sleep. (b) A subject in a sleep laboratory is outfitted with electrodes on the forehead and scalp to measure brain waves using EEG. Electrodes are applied next to the eyes for a similar instrument, an electro-oculogram, to measure eye movements.

of REM sleep is not clear, but if a person is repeatedly awakened from it, the brain will return to it with increasing persistence.

The mental activity that occurs during REM sleep is dreaming. Roughly 80 percent of the time when people are awakened from REM sleep, they report dream activity. Although many people believe they do not dream, the evidence suggests that everyone dreams several times a night, even though they may not remember dreaming. Dreaming also occurs during NREM sleep, but less frequently, and the dreams often consist of a simple experience, such as "I dreamed I smelled fish" (Antrobus, 1991; Foulkes, 1995).

Recent PET studies find that a network of neurons, beginning at the pons and extending through the thalamus and amygdala, are active during REM sleep (Maquet et al., 1996). Visual association areas in the occipital and temporal lobes, which are active when people form mental images and identify objects, are also activated during REM sleep, but the primary visual cortex is not (Braun et al., 1998). At the same time, areas of the prefrontal cortex involved in consciousness and attention are inactive or inhibited.

These findings are particularly interesting in light of the fact that watching an event in normal waking consciousness (as opposed to "watching" a dream) involves both primary visual cortex and prefrontal attentional mechanisms. Together, these findings suggest that dreaming involves a neurologically distinct kind of consciousness that does not rely on normal waking attentional mechanisms. These findings may also explain why dreams are often highly emotional—because the amygdala is very active—and why dreamers can uncritically accept bizarre story lines—because the frontal circuits involved in critical thinking and social judgment are shut off during dreaming.

After a period of REM sleep, the person descends again through Stage 2 and on to delta sleep. A complete cycle of REM and NREM sleep occurs about every 90 minutes

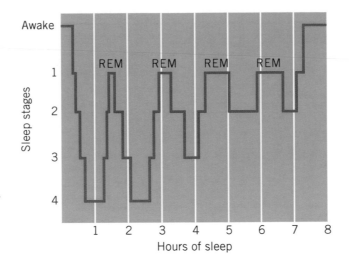

Figure 9.13 REM sleep. The stages of sleep follow a cyclical pattern that repeats about every 90 minutes, from Stage 1 through delta sleep and back again. As the night progresses, the person spends less time in deeper sleep and more time in REM sleep. *Source:* Cartwright, 1978.

(Figure 9.13). However, as the night progresses, the person spends less of the 90 minutes in delta sleep and more in REM sleep. Rapid eye movement sleep recurs four or five times a night and accounts for about 25 percent of all time asleep (on the average, two hours per night). Thus, over the course of a lifetime, the average person spends an estimated 50,000 hours—2000 days, or six full years—dreaming (Hobson, 1988).

◆ **INTERIM SUMMARY**

Sleep proceeds through a series of stages that can be assessed by EEG. The major distinction is between **rapid eye movement (REM)** and **non-REM (NREM) sleep**. Most dreaming occurs in REM sleep, in which the eyes dart around and the EEG takes on an active pattern resembling waking consciousness.

Three Views of Dreaming

For thousands of years, humans have speculated about the nature and significance of dreams. Some cultures view dreams as indices of the dreamer's deepest desires, revelations from the spiritual world, or sources of supernatural power (Bourguignon, 1979). Here we address three contemporary psychological views of dreaming: psychodynamic, cognitive, and biological.

A Psychodynamic View

Freud (1900) believed that dreams, like all mental events, have meaning but must be deciphered by someone skilled in dream interpretation. As communications spoken in the language of the unconscious, which is irrational and wishful, dreams are often vague, illogical, or bizarre and thus require translation into the language of rational waking consciousness. For example, in dreams two people are often condensed into one, or thoughts about one person are displaced onto someone else (that is, attributed to the wrong person).

According to Freud, unconscious processes are associative processes. Thus, ideas are connected by their relationship to one another along networks of association, not by logic. During sleep, a person is not using conscious, rational processes to create or monitor the story, so one thought or image can easily be activated in place of another. Because associative thinking replaces logical thought, Freud saw dreams as "the insanity of the night." For example, a man who was angry at his father had a dream of murdering his father's best friend, presumably because anger and murder were associatively linked, as were his father and his father's friend.

Freud distinguished between the **manifest content**, *the story line of the dream*, and the **latent content**, *the dream's underlying meaning*. To uncover the latent content of a dream, the dreamer free-associates to each part of the dream (that is, simply says aloud whatever thoughts come to mind about it), while the dream analyst tries to trace the networks of association.

Freud proposed that the underlying meaning of every dream is an unconscious wish, typically a forbidden sexual or aggressive desire. He suggested that people often rapidly forget their dreams upon awakening because dreams contain anxiety-provoking thoughts that are repressed during normal waking consciousness. The empirical data do not support the hypothesis that dream content is generally associated with sexual and aggressive wishes (see Fisher & Greenberg, 1997). Most contemporary psychodynamic psychologists believe, instead, that the latent content of a dream can be a wish, a fear, or anything else that is emotionally pressing. Probably the most central aspect of the psychodynamic approach today is its view of dreaming as *associative thought* laden with *emotional concerns*. This form of thought requires interpretation because the story line has not been constructed using the rational thought processes characteristic of conscious mental activity.

A Cognitive View

A cognitive perspective suggests that dreams are cognitive constructions that reflect the concerns and metaphors people express in their waking thought (Antrobus, 1991; Domhoff, 1996; Hall, 1951; Kerr et al., 1978). In other words, dreams are simply a form of thought. At times, they may even serve a problem-solving function, presenting dreamers with potential solutions to problems they are facing during the day (e.g., Cartwright, 1996).

Dreams rely on the same metaphors people use in everyday thinking. However, conscious monitoring is deactivated during dreaming, so metaphoric thinking is relatively unconstrained, leading to images or events that may seem bizarre to the conscious mind (Lakoff, 1997). Dreams also show cognitive development: Children's dreams lack the sophistication of adult dreams (Foulkes, 1982).

A Grammar of Dreams   One cognitive view that shares many points with Freud's theory was proposed by dream researcher David Foulkes (1995; and in Kerr et al., 1978). Like many contemporary psychodynamic psychologists, Foulkes disagrees that the latent meaning of every dream is an unconscious wish. He proposes instead that dreams simply express current concerns of one sort or another, in a language with its own peculiar grammar. The manifest content is constructed from the latent content through rules of transformation, that is, rules for putting a thought or concern into the "language" of dreaming.

Decoding dream language thus requires a knowledge of those rules of transformation, just as a transformational grammar allows linguists to transform the surface structure of a sentence into its deep structure, or meaning (Chapter 7). In everyday language, the sentence "The boy threw the ball" can be transformed into "The ball was thrown by the boy." In dream language, the thought "I am worried about my upcoming exam" can be translated into a dream about falling off a cliff.

Dreams and Current Concerns   Empirical research supports the view that dreams are related to current concerns, whether wishes, fears, or preoccupations of other sorts (Domhoff, 1996). A study of dreams of Israeli medical students five weeks into the Gulf War, when Israel was under threat of missile attacks, found that over half the dream reports dealt with themes of war or attack (Lavie, 1996). Other research finds that the extent to which people's dreams express wishes for intimacy correlates with their desires for intimacy by day (Evans & Singer, 1994). Similarly, people who report high well-being during waking hours also report fewer nightmares (Zadra & Donderi, 2000).

Making Connections

If dreaming is a kind of thought, theories of thinking ought to be useful in understanding even an unusual form of cognition (Chapter 7).

■ How might events of the day before prime implicit "thinking" at night? What could lead the content of a dream to bear a relation to the content of thoughts shortly before going to bed—or what Freud called the "day residue" of the dream?

■ How might activation of networks during the day result in "problem solving" in dreams? Could dream activity be "productive" even if the person is not consciously trying to solve the problem at night? If so, how might this occur?

Gender and cross-cultural differences also support the view that dreams express concerns similar to those that people experience in their waking consciousness (Domhoff, 1996). Just as males tend to be more aggressive than females by day, their dreams show a greater ratio of aggressive to friendly interactions than women's dreams. Similarly, the Netherlands and Switzerland are two of the least violent technologically developed societies, whereas the United States is the most violent. Incidents involving physical aggression are about 20 percent more prevalent in the dreams of U.S. males and females than among their Dutch and Swiss counterparts.

A Biological View

Some dream researchers argue that dreams are biological phenomena with no meaning at all (e.g., Crick & Mitchison, 1983). According to one such theory (Hobson, 1988; Hobson & McCarley, 1977), dreams reflect cortical interpretations of random neural signals initiated in the midbrain during REM sleep. These signals are relayed through the thalamus to the visual and association cortexes, which try to understand this information in their usual way, namely, by using existing knowledge structures (schemas) to process the information. Because the initial signals are essentially random, however, the interpretations proposed by the cortex rarely make logical sense.

Many dream researchers, however, criticize this view, arguing that the presence of dreams during NREM sleep challenges this explanation of dreaming. Further, the lack of evidence linking specific patterns of midbrain activation with specific patterns of dream content suggests that a biological interpretation is at least incomplete (Foulkes, 1995; Squier & Domhoff, 1998).

More recently, biologically oriented researchers have offered another view that emphasizes the role of sleep and dreaming in learning and memory. If they are right, the next time you are tempted to stay up all night to prepare for a big exam, think again: Sleep appears to be involved in the consolidation of memory. Memories for newly learned material are stronger after eight hours of sleep than after eight hours of wakefulness (Smith, 1985). Researchers are just beginning to track down the mechanisms, but the data suggest that during sleep the cortex and hippocampus work together to consolidate newly learned material, that is, to solidify it so it "sticks" (Chapter 6). According to this view, during NREM sleep, the hippocampus "replays" what it has "learned" during the day and activates relevant parts of the cortex to consolidate the memory (Chrobak & Buzsaki, 1994; Wilson & McNaughton, 1994). During REM sleep, activity appears to flow in the other direction—from the cortex to the hippocampus—erasing old memories from the hippocampus that are now fully consolidated in the cortex (Holscher et al., 1997; Stickgold, 1998).

Integrating the Alternative Models

Are these three models of dreaming really incompatible? The psychodynamic and cognitive views converge on the notion that dreams express current ideas and concerns in a highly symbolic language that requires decoding. They differ over the extent to which those concerns involve motives and emotions, although dreams probably express motives (wishes and fears) as well as ideas. Many motives have cognitive components, such as representations of wished-for or feared states (Chapter 10). Thus, a fear of failing an examination includes a representation of the feared scenario and its possible consequences. What applies to cognition, then, probably applies to many aspects of motivation as well, so dreams are as likely to express motives as beliefs.

Even the biological view of dreams as cortical interpretations of random midbrain events is not necessarily incompatible with either the psychodynamic or the cognitive view. The interpretive processes that occur at the cortical level involve the same structures of meaning—schemas, associational networks, and emotional processes—posited by Freud and Foulkes. Hence, even random activation of these structures would produce dreams that reveal something about the organization of thoughts and

You would wish to be responsible for everything except your dreams! What miserable weakness, what lack of logical courage! Nothing contains more of your own work than your dreams! Nothing belongs to you so much! Substance, form, duration, actor, spectator—in these comedies you act as your complete selves!

NIETZSCHE,
Thus Spake Zarathustra

feelings in the person's mind, particularly those that have received chronic or recent activation. Further, neurons activated during the day should be more readily triggered at night, leading to likely similarities of content in daytime and nighttime thoughts. The memory consolidation theory is even more congruent with psychodynamic and cognitive theories, because what matters during the day is what is likely to be replayed and consolidated by night.

◆ **INTERIM SUMMARY**

Freud viewed dreams as a window to the language of unconscious associative thoughts, feelings, and wishes. He distinguished the **latent content**, or underlying meaning, from the **manifest content**, or story line. Although Freud believed that the latent content of every dream is an unconscious sexual or aggressive wish that has been repressed, empirical data do not support this view. Most psychodynamic theorists instead believe that the latent content can be a wish, a fear, or anything else that is emotionally pressing. The cognitive perspective suggests that dreams are the outcome of cognitive processes and that their content reflects the concerns and metaphors people express in their waking cognition. One biological view of dreaming proposes that dreams reflect cortical interpretations of random neural signals arising from the midbrain during REM sleep. Another points to the role of sleep and dreaming in memory consolidation, as the hippocampus and cortex work together to consolidate memories and then "wipe the slate clean" in the hippocampus. These three perspectives are probably not incompatible.

◆ Altered States of Consciousness

Sleep is the most common example of a psychological state in which normal waking consciousness is suspended, but it is not the only one. In **altered states of consciousness**, *the usual conscious ways of perceiving, thinking, and feeling are modified or disrupted*. Altered states are often culturally patterned and occur through meditation, hypnosis, ingestion of drugs, and religious experiences.

Meditation

In **meditation**, *the meditator develops a deep state of tranquility by altering the normal flow of conscious thoughts*. Many religions, such as Buddhism, believe that meditation leads to a deepened understanding of reality (Ornstein, 1986). By focusing attention on a simple stimulus or by concentrating on stimuli that are usually in the background of awareness (such as one's breathing), meditation shuts down the normal flow of self-conscious inner dialogue (J. Weinberger, personal communication, 1992). With the usual goal-directed flow of consciousness disrupted, the procedures that normally direct conscious attention are "de-automatized" or disrupted.

Meditation can produce a state of serenity that is reflected in altered brain wave activity. Some forms of meditation facilitate the alpha waves characteristic of the relaxed state of falling into sleep. Others produce beta activity, and still others even produce theta waves, which are rarely observed except in subjects who are fully asleep (Jangid et al., 1988; Matsuoka, 1990). As a result, some experienced meditators in the East can perform remarkable feats, such as meditating for hours in the bitter cold.

Hypnosis

Another type of altered state, hypnosis, was named after Hypnos, the Greek god of sleep, because of the superficial resemblance between the hypnotic state and sleep. **Hypnosis** is *characterized by deep relaxation and suggestibility* (proneness to follow

Making Connections

Some approaches to psychotherapy use altered states such as meditation to reduce stress and approach irrational fears in a more relaxed state, allowing the person to overcome them (Chapter 16).

A hypnotist places a subject in a hypnotic trance.

the suggestions of the hypnotist). The subject is likely to experience a number of changes in consciousness, including an altered sense of time, self, volition (voluntary control over actions), and perception of the external world. For instance, a subject directed to raise her arm may have no sense of initiating the action but feel instead as if the arm has a mind of its own (Bowers, 1976).

As a skeptic taking a weekend workshop on clinical hypnosis a few years ago, I was personally shocked when, after two unsuccessful attempts at being hypnotized, I found my arm suddenly rising when instructed that I would feel like my wrist was tied to a helium balloon. Two weeks later, having learned to control mild pain under hypnosis, I decided to try the same technique on myself on an airplane, playing the roles of both hypnotist and hypnotic subject, when I could not shake a nasty headache (a procedure called *self-hypnosis*). The procedure worked—a throbbing sinus headache transformed itself into a vague, dull pain—but I still wonder what the person sitting next to me thought when my arm began to head for the ceiling as I sat motionless with my eyes closed at 30,000 feet!

Not everyone can be hypnotized. People differ in **hypnotic susceptibility**, *the capacity to enter into deep hypnotic states* (Hilgard, 1965, 1986). People who are highly hypnotizable tend to be able to form vivid visual images and to become readily absorbed in fantasy, daydreams, movies, and the like (see Kunzendorf et al., 1996).

Hypnotic Effects

Hypnosis can produce an array of unusual effects, although, as we will see, researchers disagree on the extent to which many of these effects are either genuine or unique to hypnosis. For example, if told they are about to smell a beautiful flower, subjects will smile peacefully rather than reflexively turn their heads when ammonia is placed under their noses. Under hypnosis, people can experience amnesia (for example, for events that occurred while under hypnosis) or its opposite, *hypermnesia*, the recall of forgotten memories. A hypnotist can induce *age regression*, in which hypnotic subjects feel as if they are reliving an earlier experience. Under hypnosis, one subject spoke a language he did not consciously remember but was spoken in his home when he was a very young child (Nash, 1988).

Hypnosis has clear and well-documented therapeutic effects (Kirsch et al., 1995). Hypnotized subjects often demonstrate *hypnotic analgesia*, an apparent lack of pain despite pain-inducing stimulation. Some hypnotic subjects have undergone surgery without anesthesia and shown no signs of conscious pain. Hypnosis can, in fact, be useful in minimizing the experience of pain in many situations, ranging from the dentist's chair to the treatment of burn injuries (Mulligan, 1996; Patterson & Ptacek, 1997). Controlled scientific studies have even shown that hypnotized subjects can rid themselves of warts (Noll, 1994; Sinclair-Gieben & Chalmers, 1959) and stop blood from flowing profusely from lacerated skin (Bowers, 1976; Ornstein, 1986).

The Hidden Observer

Ernest Hilgard (1986) experimented extensively with hypnotic phenomena and told the story of a striking event that led him down a productive path of scientific research. In a class demonstration of hypnosis, he hypnotized a student to become deaf, telling him he could hear nothing until Hilgard touched his right shoulder. Hilgard then banged together large wooden blocks near the subject's ears and even fired off a starter pistol, to which the subject did not respond.

A student in the room wondered whether "some part" of the subject could still hear him, so Hilgard, confident this was not the case, told the subject, "Perhaps there is some part of you that is hearing my voice.... If there is, I should like the index finger of your right hand to rise." To the surprise of both instructor and students, the finger rose. The hypnotized student then asked Hilgard to restore his hearing and tell him what had just happened, explaining, "I felt my finger rise in a way that was not a spontaneous twitch, so you must have done something to make it rise, and I want to know what you did" (Hilgard, 1986, p. 186).

Hilgard then instructed the subject, "When I place my hand on your arm.... I can be in touch with that part of you that listened to me before and made your finger rise.... But this hypnotized part of you, to whom I am now talking, will not know what you are saying." The *hidden observer*—the part of the subject's consciousness that raised the finger—then fully described what had happened, including hearing the slamming wooden blocks. When Hilgard lifted his hand and again asked what had happened in the last few minutes, the subject had no idea (pp. 187–188).

Hilgard's discovery of the hidden observer led him to conduct some fascinating experiments on hypnotic analgesia. In the basic design, the subject places her hand and forearm in ice water and reports the degree of pain produced, from 0 (no pain) to 10 (pain so severe that she wants to pull out her hand). In a normal waking state, the person usually hits 10 in less than a minute. When given a suggestion for hypnotic analgesia, subjects often report no pain and would keep their arm in the water indefinitely if allowed. However, when given the suggestion for the hidden observer to rate the pain using the same 0 to 10 scale, subjects report steadily increasing pain (Figure 9.14).

Hypnosis and Memory

Some advocates of hypnosis have claimed that hypnosis can restore forgotten memories. In the late 1970s, a busload of children and their driver were kidnapped at gunpoint. Later, under hypnosis, the driver relived the experience from beginning to end and was able to recall the kidnappers' license plate number with enough clarity to lead to their apprehension.

One researcher found that subjects under hypnosis could even recall events that occurred under anesthesia (Levinson, 1965). While a surgeon was removing a small lump from the lower lip of a patient, the doctor made the comment, "Good gracious...it may be a cancer!" For the next three weeks, the patient was inexplicably depressed. The investigator then hypnotized the woman and induced hypnotic regression to the day of the operation. She remembered the exclamation "Good gracious" and then, crying profusely, recalled, "He is saying this may be malignant" (p. 201). The researcher subsequently demonstrated the capacity for recall of similar events experimentally with a sample of dental patients. Since then, a number of memory researchers have demonstrated both implicit and explicit memory for events occurring during anesthesia, such as later recognition of word lists presented while surgery patients were completely unconscious (Bonebakker et al., 1996; Cork, 1996).

Despite such examples, many psychologists have expressed concern about the use of hypnosis to retrieve memories of crime scenes or experiences from childhood such as sexual abuse. Others have questioned the scientific validity of hypnosis as an aid to memory enhancement for legal purposes (Lynn et al., 1997). In fact, the limits of hypnosis are substantial enough that many states outlaw the use of hypnotically induced memories in court testimony. One of the major problems is that people under hypnosis are highly suggestible, and a subtle inflection or leading question can lead hypnotized eyewitnesses to report more than they actually know (Wagstaff, 1984). Hypnosis may also lower the threshold for feeling confident enough to report a memory. This can increase the capacity to recall actual memories, such as the license plate of the school bus kidnappers described above, but it can also increase the tendency to mistake beliefs, hypotheses, fantasies, or suggestions for true memories (Malpass & Devine, 1980). Controversy continues over the conditions under which hypnosis leads to genuine or distorted memories and is likely to do so for some time (Appelbaum et al., 1997; McConkey, 1995).

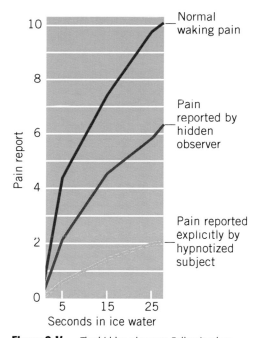

Figure 9.14 The hidden observer. Following hypnotic suggestion for analgesia, hypnotized subjects reported minimal pain (bottom line) when their hand was immersed in ice water. However, the "hidden observer" (middle line) reported pain midway between normal consciousness of pain during immersion (top line) and conscious reports under hypnosis. *Source:* Hilgard, 1986, p. 190.

One Step Further

Is Hypnosis Real?

Hypnosis has drawn considerable skepticism since it first received scientific attention in the nineteenth century, in part because of a history of charlatans using stage hypnosis mixed with liberal doses of deception (such as planting subjects). As we will see in Chapter 17, research over many decades has demonstrated that social pressure can lead people to perform peculiar, deviant, or destructive behavior, even in a normal state of consciousness (see Kirsch & Lynn, 1998). Several researchers have produced evidence to suggest that hypnotic subjects are simply playing the role they believe they are expected to play (Murrey et al., 1992; Spanos et al., 1996).

Other critics contend that aspects of hypnotic suggestion that are not *unique* to hypnosis, such as heavy reliance on imagery, actually account for hypnotic effects. For example, people instructed to use vivid visual images can often accomplish the same feats as hypnotized subjects, such as eliminating warts (Spanos et al., 1988).

Data supporting the validity of hypnosis, however, come from studies in which subjects are given *posthypnotic suggestions*—commands to perform a behavior on demand once they are out of the hypnotic trance. In a study designed to test the hypothesis that hypnotized subjects are simply playing roles (and that they are not really in an altered state), the investigators compared the behavior of subjects instructed to act *as if* they were hypnotized with the behavior of true hypnotized subjects (Orne et al., 1968). When both groups of subjects were distracted from assigned tasks and thus diverted from thinking about what they were supposed to do, hypnotized subjects were three times as likely to carry out the posthypnotic suggestion as simulators.

Neuroscientific data also provide evidence for the validity of hypnosis as an altered state. Not only do studies find distinct EEG patterns in hypnotized subjects (De-Pascalis & Perrone, 1996), but recent neuroimaging studies support the distinctness of hypnotic states as well. In one study, researchers suggested to hypnotized subjects that they should see color images in black and white (Kosslyn et al., 2000). Remarkably, their brain scans showed decreased activation in a part of the cortex that processes color (at the borders of the occipital and temporal lobes; Chapter 3), compared with activation while viewing color images without the suggestion. When the researchers made the same suggestion to the same individuals *without* hypnosis, they showed no reduction in the color area of the cortex. These findings suggest that hypnosis can, in fact, dramatically influence basic components of perceptual experience that psychologists have generally assumed to be independent of people's intentions.

Other strong evidence comes from studies in which hypnotic subjects have endured painful medical procedures, including surgery, without anesthesia. Although some skeptics argue that these patients may be "faking it," it is difficult to imagine undergoing an operation without anesthesia simply to please an experimenter (Bowers, 1976). (I wish the participants in my own studies were so compliant!)

At this juncture, the most appropriate conclusion is probably that hypnosis is, in fact, an altered state of consciousness, at least in highly hypnotizable subjects. However, some or many of its effects can be produced under other conditions, such as use of imagery, relaxation, or social pressure.

◆ INTERIM SUMMARY

Altered states of consciousness, in which the usual conscious ways of perceiving, thinking, and feeling are modified or disrupted, are often brought about through meditation, hypnosis, ingestion of drugs, and religious experiences. **Meditation** creates a deep state of tranquility by altering the normal flow of conscious thoughts. **Hypnosis** is an altered state characterized by deep relaxation and suggestibility.

Drug-Induced States of Consciousness

The most common way people alter their state of consciousness (other than by going to sleep, of course) is by ingesting **psychoactive substances**—*drugs that operate on the nervous system to alter mental activity*. In the West, people use many psychoactive substances, ranging from caffeine in coffee and nicotine in tobacco, to medications that relieve depression or anxiety (Chapter 16), to drugs that seriously impair functioning, such as cocaine and heroin. Some psychoactive drugs resemble the molecular structure of naturally occurring neurotransmitters and thus have similar effects at synapses. Others alter the normal processes of synthesis, release, reuptake, or breakdown of neurotransmitters (Chapter 3) and consequently affect the rate of neural firing in various regions of the brain.

The action of psychoactive substances cannot, however, be reduced entirely to their chemical properties. Their impact also depends on cultural beliefs and expectations. Native Americans who use peyote (a potent consciousness-altering drug) in religious rituals typically experience visions congruent with their religious beliefs, as well as feelings of reverence or religious awe and relief from physical ailments. In contrast, Anglo-Americans using the same drug often experience frightening visions, extreme mood states, and a breakdown in normal social inhibitions (Wallace, 1959).

The major types of psychoactive substances in widespread use include alcohol and other depressants, stimulants, hallucinogens, and marijuana. We briefly examine each in turn.

Alcohol and Other Depressants

Depressants are *substances that depress, or slow down, the nervous system*. Common depressants are barbiturates and benzodiazepines. *Barbiturates* ("downers") provide a sedative or calming effect and in higher doses can be used as sleeping pills. *Benzodiazepines*, or anti-anxiety agents, serve as tranquilizers; common examples are Valium and Xanax (Chapter 16). Depressants can produce both psychological and physical dependence.

Contrary to what many people who rely on alcohol to elevate their mood believe, alcohol is a depressant. Researchers are still tracking down the precise neural mechanisms by which alcohol slows down central nervous system activity, but like other sedatives, alcohol appears to enhance the activity of the neurotransmitter GABA (gamma-aminobutyric acid) (Buck, 1996). Because GABA inhibits norepinephrine, which is involved in anxiety reactions, alcohol can reduce anxiety. Alcohol also enhances the activity of dopamine and endorphins, which provide pleasurable feelings that reinforce behavior (De Witte, 1996; Di Chiara et al., 1996). Thus, alcohol derives its powerful effects from its capacity both to diminish unpleasant feelings and heighten pleasurable ones.

Cross-culturally, alcohol is the most widely used psychoactive substance. In moderate doses—wine with dinner or a drink after work—alcohol can enhance experience and even have positive health consequences, but the social costs of abuse of alcohol and other substances are staggering. In the United States, approximately one in seven people abuse alcohol, and another one in 20 misuse other psychoactive substances. The number of people killed in alcohol-related accidents in the United States every year surpasses the total number killed in the entire Vietnam War [Group for the Advancement of Psychiatry (GAP), 1991]. A Swedish study found that reported alcohol consumption in 1973 predicted mortality rates in a large sample followed up over the next 20 years (Andreasson & Brandt, 1997).

Alcohol and Expectations As with psychoactive substances in general, expectations about alcohol's effects, shaped by culture and personal experience, can sometimes have as much impact on behavior as the drug's direct effects on the nervous system (see Collins et al., 1990; Hittner, 1997). This appears to be true cross-culturally (Velez-Blasini, 1997).

O God, that men should put an enemy in their mouths to steal away their brains; that we should, with joy, pleasance, revel and applause, transform ourselves into beasts!

SHAKESPEARE,
Othello (II, iii)

Central Questions

■ From a cognitive perspective, how do expectations and beliefs about alcohol affect the way people behave when they are under the influence (or *believe* they are under the influence) of alcohol? How do these expectations develop, and at what point(s) in the drinking process (e.g., before, during, or after ingestion or intoxication) do they get activated?

■ From a psychodynamic perspective, why might people be more likely to behave in deviant ways when they are under the influence (or believe they are under the influence) of alcohol?

Several studies have sought to distinguish the causal roles of two independent variables: whether subjects are drinking alcohol and whether they *think* they are drinking alcohol. The researchers place participants in one of four groups. In one, participants drink an alcoholic beverage and are told they are drinking alcohol; in another, they drink alcohol but are told they are not. (The flavor of the drink makes alcohol detection impossible.) In the other two groups, participants drink a nonalcoholic beverage and are either informed or misinformed about what they are drinking.

The results of these investigations can help "distill" the relative contributions of biology and beliefs to the effects of alcoholic consumption. For example, male subjects who think they are drinking alcohol report greater sexual arousal and less guilt when exposed to sexually arousing stimuli, whether or not they have actually been drinking alcohol. This is even more likely to occur if they have strong beliefs about the impact of alcohol on arousal (see Abrams & Wilson, 1983; Hull & Bond, 1986). More generally, people are more likely to behave in ways that are deviant, dangerous, or antisocial if they can attribute their behavior to alcohol.

Consequences of Alcohol Use and Abuse Alcohol abuse is involved in many violent crimes, including assault, rape, spouse abuse, and murder, but precisely how alcohol contributes to aggression is not entirely clear (see Bushman, 1997; Bushman & Cooper, 1990). One theory suggests that it disengages normal inhibitions; that is, alcohol contributes to aggression "not by stepping on the gas but rather by paralyzing the brakes" (Muehlberger, 1956, cited in Bushman & Cooper, 1990, p. 342). A related theory suggests that alcohol facilitates aggression by derailing other psychological processes that normally decrease the likelihood of aggression, such as the ability to assess risks accurately. A third theory suggests that violence-prone individuals drink so that they can have an excuse for aggression, particularly since they tend to believe that alcohol makes them aggressive. All three processes can operate together: An angry, violent person may drink in part to dull his conscience and to provide himself an excuse for his actions.

Long-term ingestion of alcohol produces physical changes in the brain that can seriously affect cognitive functioning, sometimes to the point of dementia (confusion and disorientation) or Korsakoff's syndrome (as in the vignette that opened this chapter). Imaging techniques such as CT scans reveal that roughly half of alcoholics show cerebral atrophy, and many show subcortical damage as well. Some of the behavioral changes associated with these physiological changes appear to be reversible, however, if the person stops drinking (Bowden, 1990).

Stimulants

Stimulants are *drugs that increase alertness, energy, and autonomic reactivity* (such as heart rate and blood pressure). These drugs range from commonly used substances like nicotine and caffeine to more potent ones such as amphetamines and cocaine.

Nicotine increases heart rate and blood pressure while often decreasing emotional reactivity. Thus, cigarette smokers often report that smoking increases their arousal and alertness while also providing a soothing effect. The reason is that nicotine has receptors in both branches of the autonomic nervous system—sympathetic (which increases arousal) and parasympathetic (which reduces it). When one of these branches is active, nicotine tends to produce stronger effects in the other—thus both arousing the slothful and soothing the stressed. Over the long term, however, smoking can cause cancer, heart disease, and other life-threatening conditions.

Caffeine is found in coffee, tea, chocolate, soft drinks, and some nonprescription drugs (such as aspirin products, decongestants, and sleep suppressants). Whereas moderate amounts of caffeine can help a person stay awake, high doses can produce symptoms indistinguishable from anxiety disorders, such as "the jitters" or even panic.

Amphetamines lead to hyperarousal and a feeling of "speeding," where everything seems to move quickly. The molecular structure of amphetamines is similar to that of the neurotransmitters dopamine and norepinephrine. Stimulation of norepinephrine receptors appears to produce alertness, while stimulation of dopamine receptors produces euphoria and increased motor activity. Amphetamines can induce psychosis in vulnerable individuals, death by overdose, or ill health in chronic users, who essentially circumvent the normal signals sent by the brain to protect the body from fatigue and overuse.

Cocaine has held an attraction for people since about A.D. 500, when the Inca in Peru learned about the powers of the coca leaf, from which cocaine is derived. The Inca used the coca leaf in religious ceremonies and even treated it as money to compensate laborers (not a strategy recommended for future industrialists, since it also leads to absenteeism and ill health). In the late 1800s, physicians discovered cocaine's anesthetic properties; soon many medicines and elixirs were laced with cocaine.

In the nineteenth century, cocaine was an ingredient of many elixirs, including Coca-Cola.

Cocaine causes hyperarousal, leading to a "rush" that can last a few minutes to several hours. Cocaine is one of the most potent pleasure-inducing substances, as well as one of the most addictive, ever discovered. Experimental animals will press a lever thousands of times to receive a single dose (Siegel, 1990). Like other stimulants, it appears to increase the activity of norepinephrine and dopamine. Chronic use depletes these neurotransmitters and can cause chronic depression similar to the crash that occurs when the initial high is over (GAP, 1991).

Cocaine produces diminished judgment and an inflated sense of one's own abilities. Regular use can also produce paranoia. One study found that 68 percent of cocaine-dependent men in a rehabilitation program reported paranoid experiences on cocaine that lasted several hours, long after the cocaine high was over (Satel et al., 1991). Moreover, 38 percent of the patients who reported paranoia actually responded by arming themselves with guns or knives. A recent study found that two-thirds of the assailants in domestic violence cases had consumed both cocaine and alcohol on the day they beat their spouse or children (Brookoff et al., 1997).

Hallucinogens

Hallucinogens derive their name from **hallucinations**—*sensations and perceptions that occur in the absence of external stimulation.* **Hallucinogens** *alter sensory data to produce bizarre or unusual perceptions.* While under the influence of hallucinogens, people may experience time as speeding up or slowing down or sense colors bursting from the sky, walls moving, or ants crawling under their skin.

Humans have used hallucinogens for thousands of years, but their impact and cultural meaning differ dramatically. In many cultures, people use hallucinogens largely during cultural rituals, as when Australian aboriginal boys ingest hallucinogenic plants during ceremonies initiating them into manhood (Grob & Dobkin de Rios, 1992). In these settings, the meaning of hallucinations is established by the elders, who consider the drugs essential for bringing the young into the community of adults. In the contemporary West, individuals ingest these substances for recreation and with minimal social control, so the effects are more variable, and vulnerability to addiction is high.

Hallucinogenic drug use in Europe and North America dramatically increased in the 1960s with the discovery of the synthetic hallucinogen *lysergic acid diethylamide (LSD)*. By the late 1970s, concern over the abuse of LSD and other drugs, such as PCP ("angel dust") and hallucinogenic mushrooms ("shrooms"), intensified, and with good scientific reason: Chronic use of LSD is associated with psychotic symptoms, depression, paranoia, lack of motivation, and changes in brain physiology (Kaminer & Hrecznyj, 1991; Smith and Seymour, 1994). Some chronic users repeatedly experience strange visual phenomena, such as seeing trails of light or images as they move their hands. Even when they are not experiencing these symptoms, their EEGs show a pattern of abnormal firing of neurons in visual pathways of the brain (Abraham & Duffy, 1996). The long-term effects of even occasional use of LSD are not entirely clear, although tragic events have occurred with LSD use, such as people walking out of windows and falling to their death.

Marijuana

The use of *marijuana* has been a subject of controversy for decades. Marijuana use among young people peaked in 1979 in the United States, with 60.4 percent of high school seniors reporting having tried the drug at least once. That number dropped to 35.3 percent in 1993, with the percentages fluctuating slightly throughout the 1990s and into the current century (see Hansen & O'Malley, 1996).

Marijuana produces a state of being high, or "stoned," during which the individual may feel euphoric, giddy, unself-conscious, or contemplative. During a marijuana high, judgment is moderately impaired, problem solving becomes less focused and efficient, and attention is more difficult to direct; some people report paranoia or panic symptoms.

For decades, people have speculated about the detrimental effects of marijuana, but few credible scientific studies have documented negative effects from occasional recreational use (Castle & Ames, 1996). In fact, the most definitive study in this area, a longitudinal follow-up of young adults observed since early childhood, actually found occasional marijuana users and experimenters to be healthier psychologically than either abusers *or* abstainers (Shedler & Block, 1990). Other research finds that marijuana abuse, but not occasional use, is a risk factor for use of harder drugs (Kouri et al., 1995).

Nevertheless, marijuana, like harder drugs, artificially manipulates dopamine reward circuits in the brain (Wickelgren, 1997) and can produce unwanted consequences. For example, residual effects on attention, working memory, and motor abilities can make users unaware of subtle impairment at work, at school, or at the wheel (Pope et al., 1995). Chronic or heavy use, particularly beyond adolescence, is a symptom of psychological disturbance (Chapter 15) and can contribute to deficits in social and occupational functioning. As with other drugs, smoking during pregnancy may have risks for the developing fetus (see Chandler et al., 1996; Fried, 1995).

In sum, like alcohol, the extent to which marijuana has negative psychological consequences probably depends on whether or not it is abused.

◆ INTERIM SUMMARY

The most common way people alter their state of consciousness is by ingesting **psychoactive substances**, drugs that operate on the nervous system to alter mental activity. Drugs have their effects not only physiologically but also through cultural beliefs and expectations. **Depressants** such as alcohol slow down, or depress, the nervous system. **Stimulants**, such as amphetamines and cocaine, increase alertness, energy, and autonomic reactivity. **Hallucinogens** such as LSD produce **hallucinations**, sensations and perceptions that occur without external sensory stimulation. Marijuana is a controversial drug that produces a "high" that may include a mixture of pleasurable feelings and a sense of calm or panic and paranoia.

A Global Vista — Religious Experiences in Cross-Cultural Perspective

Religious experiences are *subjective experiences of being in contact with the divine or spiritual.* They range from relatively ordinary experiences, such as listening passively to a sermon, to altered states of consciousness in which a person feels at one with nature or the supernatural. In his classic work, *The Varieties of Religious Experience*, William James (1902) describes the more dramatic forms of religious experience. In this state, the person experiences a sense of peace and inner harmony, perceives the world and self as having changed dramatically in some way, and has "the sense of perceiving truths not known before" (p. 199). James quotes the manuscript of a clergyman (1902, p. 67):

I remember the night, and almost the very spot on the hilltop where my soul opened out, as it were, into the Infinite, and there was a rushing together of the two worlds, the inner and the outer.... The ordinary sense of things around me faded.... It was like the effect of some great orchestra when all the separate notes have melted into one swelling harmony.

Experiences people consider spiritual occur in a wide variety of settings and may or may not involve organized religion (Wolman, 2001). In most societies, however, dramatic religious experiences occur in the context of ritualized religious practices. For example, in a *possession trance*, the person who is "possessed" believes another person or a supernatural being enters his soul. The altered state typically occurs through drumming, singing, dancing, and crowd participation (Bourguignon, 1979). Many born-again Christian churches include possession trances as part of their regular religious practices (see, e.g., Griffith et al., 1984).

The use of ritualized altered states dates back at least to the time of the Neanderthals. Graves of prehistoric human remains in northern Iraq contained medicinal substances that are still used today to induce trancelike states. The "vision quest" of some Native American tribes frequently included religious trance states. During these states, a young person being initiated into adulthood would come in contact with ancestors or a personal guardian and emerge as a full member of adult society (Bourguignon, 1979). John Lame Deer, a Sioux medicine man, describes an experience that in certain respects resembles that of the Western clergyman quoted by James (Lame Deer & Erdoes, 1972, pp. 14–15):

> I was still lightheaded and dizzy from my first sweatbath in which I had purified myself before going up the hill. Even now, an hour later, my skin still tingled. But it seemed to have made my brain empty.... Blackness was wrapped around me like a velvet cloth. It seemed to cut me off from the outside world, even from my own body. It made me listen to voices within me. I thought of my forefathers, who had crouched on this hill before me.... I thought I could sense their presence.... I trembled and my bones turned to ice.

Like James's clergyman, Lame Deer describes a breakdown in the normal boundaries of the inner and outer worlds. Both men also describe a sense of being touched by a presence beyond themselves and an altered experience of reality, perception, and consciousness.

Ritualized religious experiences are simultaneously cultural and psychological phenomena. For individuals, they offer a sense of security, enlightenment, and oneness with something greater than themselves. For the group, they provide a sense of solidarity, cohesiveness, and certainty in shared values and beliefs. The individual is typically swept away in the experience, losing the self-reflective component of consciousness and experiencing a dissolution of the boundaries between self and nonself.

The French sociologist Emile Durkheim (1915) described this phenomenon as "collective effervescence," in which the individual's consciousness seems dominated by the "collective consciousness." Most readers have probably experienced collective effervescence, either during religious ceremonies or in less profound circumstances, such as rock concerts and sporting events. Collective events of this sort, many of which involve chanting or rhythmic movement and speech, seem to tap into a basic human capacity for this kind of altered state.

Humans seem predisposed to be moved by collective experiences. Top, a Balinese ritual; bottom, a spontaneous "ritual" at a rock festival in North America.

◆ Central Questions: Perspectives on Consciousness

Like the attentional mechanisms that direct the consciousness of individuals, scientific communities have mechanisms that bring phenomena in and out of focus at various times. In the heyday of behaviorism, consciousness was relegated to the periphery of psychological awareness. As we have seen, recent developments in cognitive science have generated renewed interest in the roles of conscious and unconscious processes.

This renewed interest may actually contribute to integration across the theoretical perspectives in psychology. Interest in unconscious processes brings the field squarely back to one of the central tenets of psychoanalytic theory, that much of mental life is unconscious, including thoughts, feelings, and motivations—but this time on a much firmer scientific foundation. Paradoxically, the growing literature on unconscious processes has also produced new interest in learning that occurs without awareness, a central focus of behavioral research. We may discover that the conditioned emotional responses of the behaviorist and the unconsciously triggered emotional reactions of the psychoanalyst are not as far apart as they once seemed—and they may have much in common with associations between emotions and memories studied by cognitive psychologists.

Researchers studying consciousness have also increasingly relied on a functionalist approach common to both William James and current evolutionary psychologists. In this view, consciousness serves the functions of monitoring and controlling the self and the environment. It allows us to examine and sometimes override automatic procedures, unconscious motives, dysfunctional conditioned emotional responses, and operant responses normally triggered outside awareness.

Issues of consciousness and unconsciousness have become a central focus of psychological attention at the turn of the twenty-first century just as they were a century ago. This time, however, we may have the tools to test and refine our hypotheses in previously unimagined ways—and perhaps to synthesize a unitary experience from the parallel lines of investigation that previously divided the consciousness of the psychological community.

Summary

The Nature of Consciousness

1. **Consciousness** refers to the subjective awareness of percepts, thoughts, feelings, and behavior. It performs two functions: monitoring the self and environment and controlling thought and behavior. **Attention** is the process of focusing awareness, providing heightened sensitivity to a limited range of experience requiring more extensive information processing. **Divided attention** means splitting attention between two or more stimuli or tasks.

2. Psychologists study the flow of consciousness through **experience-sampling** techniques, such as **beeper studies**. Even such a private experience as consciousness is in part shaped by cultural practices and beliefs, which influence aspects of subjective awareness, such as the experience of time and the focus on internal psychological states.

Perspectives on Consciousness

3. Freud distinguished among conscious, preconscious, and unconscious processes. **Conscious mental processes** are at the center of subjective awareness. **Preconscious mental processes** are not presently conscious but could be readily brought to consciousness. Dynamically unconscious processes—or the system of mental processes Freud called the **unconscious**—are thoughts, feelings, and memories that are inaccessible to consciousness because they have been kept from awareness because they are threatening. Research over several decades has demonstrated that subliminal presentation of stimuli can influence conscious thought and behavior. Emotional and motivational processes can also be unconscious or implicit.

4. The **cognitive unconscious** refers to information-processing mechanisms that occur outside of awareness, notably unconscious procedures or skills and preconscious associational processes such as those that occur in priming experiments. Cognitive theorists have argued that consciousness is a mechanism for flexibly bringing together quasi-independent processing modules that normally operate in relative isolation and for solving problems that automatic processes cannot optimally solve.

5. Hindbrain and midbrain structures, notably the reticular formation, play a key role in regulating states of wakefulness and arousal. Like most psychological functions, consciousness appears to be distributed across a number of neural pathways, in-

volving a circuit running from the reticular formation through the thalamus, from the thalamus to the cortex (particularly the prefrontal cortex), and back down to the thalamus and midbrain regions of the reticular formation.

Sleep and Dreaming

6. The sleep–wake cycle is a **circadian rhythm**, a cyclical biological process that evolved around the daily cycles of light and dark. Sleep proceeds through a series of stages that cycle throughout the night. Most dreaming occurs during REM sleep, named for the bursts of darting eye movements.

7. Freud distinguished between the **manifest content**, or story line, and the **latent content**, or underlying meaning, of dreams. Freud believed the latent content is always an unconscious wish, although most contemporary psychodynamic psychologists believe that wishes, fears, and current concerns can underlie dreams. Cognitive theorists suggest that dreams express thoughts and current concerns in a distinct language with its own rules of transformation. Some biological theorists contend that dreams have no meaning; in this view, dreams are cortical interpretations of random neural impulses generated in the midbrain. Others focus on the role of sleep and dreaming in memory consolidation. These three approaches to dreaming are not necessarily incompatible.

Altered States of Consciousness

8. In **altered states of consciousness**, the usual conscious ways of perceiving, thinking, and feeling are changed. **Meditation** is an altered state in which the person narrows consciousness to a single thought or expands consciousness to focus on stimuli that are usually at the periphery of awareness. **Hypnosis**, characterized by deep relaxation and suggestibility, appears to be an altered state, but many hypnotic phenomena can be produced under other conditions. In altered states that occur during **religious experiences**, the person feels a sense of oneness with nature, others, or the supernatural and experiences a breakdown in the normal boundaries between self and nonself.

9. **Psychoactive substances** are drugs that operate on the nervous system to alter patterns of perception, thought, feeling, and behavior. **Depressants**, the most widely used of which is alcohol, slow down the nervous system. **Stimulants** (such as nicotine, caffeine, amphetamines, and cocaine) increase alertness, energy, and autonomic reactivity. **Hallucinogens** create **hallucinations**, in which sensations and perceptions occur in the absence of any external stimulation. Marijuana leads to a state of being high—euphoric, giddy, unself-conscious, or contemplative. **Psychoactive substances** alter consciousness biologically, by facilitating or inhibiting neural transmission at the synapse, and psychologically, through expectations shaped by cultural beliefs.

Key Terms

altered states of consciousness 323
attention 305
beeper studies 307
circadian rhythms 316
cognitive unconscious 310
conscious mental processes 308
consciousness 303
daydreaming 307

depressants 327
dichotic listening 306
divided attention 306
experience sampling 307
hallucinations 329
hallucinogens 329
hypnosis 323
hypnotic susceptibility 324
insomnia 317

latent content 321
manifest content 321
meditation 323
non-REM (NREM) sleep 318
preconscious mental processes 308
psychoactive substances 327
rapid eye movement (REM) sleep 318

religious experiences 330
selective inattention 305
states of consciousness 303
stimulants 328
subliminal perception 308
unconscious mental processes 308

Chapter 10
Motivation

Peter Malone, *Dreams.*

Since 1981, when an article in the *New York Times* informed the world of a new "gay cancer," knowledge about AIDS in the general population has increased tremendously. Researchers eventually discovered that heterosexuals were at risk as well. In fact, 75 percent of HIV-positive people around the world have been infected through heterosexual transmission (Miller et al., 1993).

Although AIDS is a deadly, contagious disease, the risk of contracting the HIV virus is substantially diminished in people who use condoms. Thus, one would expect condom use to be nearly universal among sexually active people who are not in exclusive relationships. Surprisingly, however, this is not the case. Among sexually active college students, for example, only half report consistently using condoms (Civic, 2000). Physicians in San Francisco, a city whose gay population has been decimated by the virus, report that condom use among young gay males had returned to pre-AIDS levels less than 15 years after the appearance of the disease (Hamilton, 1994).

In light of all the knowledge about AIDS transmission and prevention, why do people continue to engage in unsafe sexual practices? One explanation is cognitive: People simply do not understand the risks. However, research has shown little relation between people's knowledge of how to prevent AIDS and their tendency to engage in high-risk behavior (Moatti et al., 1997; Winslow et al., 1992).

An alternative hypothesis is that the problem lies less in cognition than in motivation (see Cooper et al., 1998). A person might cope with fear of contracting the HIV virus by downplaying the probability that he could contract it and hence behave in ways that *maximize* his danger. For someone else, the motivation to please a partner who dislikes condoms—and thereby to avoid rejection—may supersede the goal of avoiding AIDS (Miller et al., 1993). Alternatively, a person high in sensation seeking, who is motivated to experience new and exciting activities, may be less likely to practice safe sex (Stein et al., 1994).

This chapter focuses on **motivation**—*the driving force behind behavior, that leads us to pursue some things and avoid others*. The word *motivation* comes from the Latin *movere* (meaning *to move*), reflecting the fact that motives "move" us. We first examine the major perspectives on motivation and then consider some of the most important motives that guide

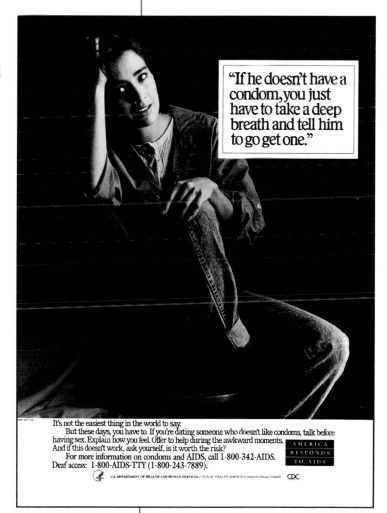

"If he doesn't have a condom, you just have to take a deep breath and tell him to go get one."

It's not the easiest thing in the world to say.
But these days, you have to. If you're dating someone who doesn't like condoms, talk before having sex. Explain how you feel. Offer to help during the awkward moments. And if this doesn't work, ask yourself, is it worth the risk?
For more information on condoms and AIDS, call 1-800-342-AIDS.
Deaf access: 1-800-AIDS-TTY (1-800-243-7889).

AMERICA RESPONDS TO AIDS

U.S. DEPARTMENT OF HEALTH AND HUMAN SERVICES / PUBLIC HEALTH SERVICE / Centers for Disease Control   CDC

human behavior across cultures. Developing an adequate classification of motives is no easy task. Here we follow one of the first efforts, proposed by Henry Murray (1938). Murray distinguished between biological needs (e.g., for food and sex) and nonbiological, or "psychogenic" (literally, *psychologically generated*) needs. Psychogenic needs, more commonly called *psychosocial motives*, include needs for order, dominance, achievement, autonomy, aggression, nurturance, and so forth. As we will see, this classification is useful, but we should not assume that any motive is "purely" biological or psychosocial. As Sir Francis Bacon wisely observed, the subtlety of nature is far greater than the subtlety of any mind trying to comprehend and categorize it.

Throughout the chapter, several basic issues repeatedly emerge. The first is the extent to which people are driven by internal needs or pulled by external goals or stimuli. Does the presence of a condom in a nearby drawer increase the likelihood of its use, or must the goal be internal to matter in a moment of passion?

A second and related issue is the extent to which human motivation is rooted in biology or influenced by culture and environment. Do the motives of a Western corporate executive and a tribal chief in the Sudan differ dramatically, or do both individuals rise to their position out of similar needs for power or achievement?

A third issue is the relative importance of thoughts, feelings, and arousal in motivation. Can a person simply be motivated by a thought or goal, or must goals be connected with feeling or arousal to be motivating? In other words, what transforms a thought or daydream into an intention that directs behavior?

◆ INTERIM SUMMARY

Motivation refers to the driving force behind behavior that leads us to pursue some things and avoid others. Motives can be divided into biological needs and psychosocial needs (such as needs for dominance, power, achievement, and relatedness to others), although few motives are strictly biological or learned.

◆ Perspectives on Motivation

Motivation has two components: *what* people want to do (the goals they pursue), and *how strongly* they want to do it. A number of perspectives offer insight into both of these components.

Evolutionary Perspective

In the early part of this century, psychologists assumed that humans, like other animals, had **instincts**—*relatively fixed patterns of behavior produced without learning* (Tinbergen, 1951). An example is the mating ritual of the ring dove, which must perform an elaborate, stereotyped sequence of behaviors in exactly the right manner to attract a mate. If the male does not bow and coo at the proper point in the ritual, the female will not be receptive (Lehrman, 1956). (Male humans whose dancing is less than elegant may feel some kinship with this poor creature.)

Most psychologists eventually abandoned instinct theory, for a number of reasons. For one, human behavior varies so substantially across cultures that the motives that seemed "instinctive" in one culture (such as motives for wealth in the West) did not seem so powerful in others. Perhaps more importantly, one of the most distinctive features of human behavior is its *flexibility*—seen in our ability to find novel ways to solve problems or to bow and coo when it suits us. Thus, many psychologists came to argue that learning, not instinct, directs human behavior.

Central Questions

- To what extent are we driven by internal needs or pulled by external stimuli?
- To what extent does human motivation reflect biological, environmental, and cultural influences?
- What are the roles of thoughts, feelings, and arousal in motivation?

Apply & Discuss

Many animals have elaborate courting rituals that precede mating.

■ To what extent do human "rituals" and those of other animals reflect common evolutionary roots? Are the similarities just accidental (and amusing) or do they reflect similar evolutionary histories?

Maximizing Inclusive Fitness

Contemporary evolutionary psychologists contend that motivational systems, like other psychological attributes, have been selected by nature for their ability to maximize reproductive success—that is, survival and reproduction (see Buss, 1999). For some motives, this is an unremarkable claim. Organisms that do not replenish their energy by eating do not survive and reproduce. Nature has thus designed humans and other animals with intricate systems for maintaining basic life-support processes.

Some evolutionary explanations, however, are much more controversial. As we saw in Chapter 1, evolutionary theorists have argued that evolution selects animals that maximize their inclusive fitness, which refers to their own reproductive success plus their influence on the reproductive success of genetically related individuals (Hamilton, 1964). This theory makes mathematical sense. The probability that any given gene of an individual who protects his child will be available in the gene pool in the next generation is 50 percent because his child shares half his genes. The probability jumps to 75 percent for someone who protects his child *plus* his niece (one-half from his child and one-fourth from his niece). Over many generations, this difference becomes substantial. Applied to other species, such as honeybees, the theory of inclusive fitness has produced some stunningly accurate predictions about the way organisms behave toward kin of varying degrees of relatedness (e.g., Anderson & Ricklefs, 1995; Sundstrom et al., 1996).

Evolutionary psychologists are generally careful to distinguish the theory that evolution *favors* organisms that maximize their inclusive fitness from the assumption that organisms deliberately *seek* to maximize their inclusive fitness, as if they carry inclusive fitness calculators in their pockets. Nevertheless, some basic motivational mechanisms presumably evolved to help organisms select courses of action that foster survival, reproduction, and the care and protection of kin. These mechanisms should guide their behavior so that their degree of investment is roughly proportional to their degree of relatedness.

So how do organisms—whether bees or humans—know who their sons, brothers, or cousins are? Recent research suggests that some species are actually endowed with chemical mechanisms (pheromones) for kin recognition. Pheromones are similar to hormones, except that they allow cell-to-cell communication *between* rather than *within* organisms (Figure 10.1). They are typically detected by specialized neural circuits in the olfactory system (Chapter 4) and may have the same or similar effects as hormones (Sorenson, 1996).

Whether pheromonal communication leads to increased investment in close relatives is unknown, but it does help members of some species avoid mating with members of other species (which wastes precious mating time) and avoid incest, which can produce genetically defective offspring and hence reduce reproductive success (Blaustein & Waldman, 1992; Wilson & Bossert, 1996). In one study, the experimenter allowed female crickets to choose where they would spend their time in an area divided into four territories

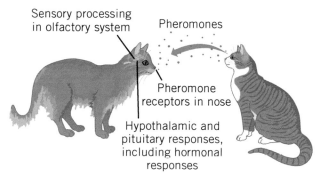

Sensory processing in olfactory system

Pheromones

Pheromone receptors in nose

Hypothalamic and pituitary responses, including hormonal responses

Figure 10.1 Pheromonal communication. Pheromones activate sexual and other responses much as hormones do, except that they are secreted by other animals instead of by the animal's own endocrine system.

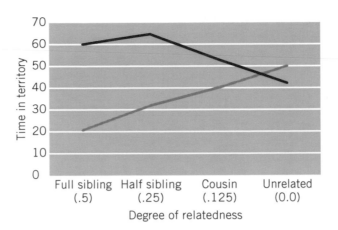

Figure 10.2 Pheromonal mechanisms for kin recognition in crickets. In normal females (blue line), the smaller the degree of relatedness, the more time spent in the territory of a male cricket. Females whose pheromone receptors were covered with wax (red line) did not show the same inverse relationship between degree of relatedness and amount of time in the territory. *Source:* Adapted from Simmons, 1990, p. 194.

Apply & Discuss

■ To what degree does familiarity influence caretaking behavior in humans? In other words, do we tend to care about (and for) people with whom we interact regularly?

■ Has the fact that people in technologically developed societies may live hundreds or thousand of miles from their families derailed the evolutionary mechanisms that lead people to care for blood relatives?

Nearly all men can stand adversity, but if you want to test a man's character, give him power.

ABRAHAM LINCOLN

(Simmons, 1990). Potential male mates were not present, but the experimenter marked each territory with the scent (from droppings) of a male who was a full sibling, a half sibling, a cousin, or an unrelated cricket. Thus, the females could spend time in the territory of male crickets related to them by .5, .25, .125, or 0, respectively.

The results were striking: The amount of time females spent in each territory was inversely proportional to degree of relatedness; that is, the more distant the relation, the more time spent "in the neighborhood" (Figure 10.2). The mechanism for kin recognition proved to be chemical, since female crickets whose pheromone receptors were covered with wax showed no preference for unrelated males.

Humans probably do not rely on pheromones for kin recognition; however, as suggested in Chapter 1, they probably make use of other mechanisms, such as degree of familiarity, particularly from childhood. Throughout the course of much of human evolution, people who grew up together were more than likely family members, so longtime familiarity, particularly from childhood, would be a rough index of degree of kinship, if an imperfect one. In fact, just as crickets avoid sexual contact with other crickets with the scent of family, marriage among children who grow up together in Israeli communal living arrangements, or *kibbutzim*, is almost nonexistent (Shepher, 1978).

Multiple Motivational Systems

From an evolutionary point of view, humans and other animals are likely to have multiple motivational systems—innate response tendencies, many with their own distinct neural circuitry—that evolved to solve particular problems of adaptation. From an evolutionary point of view, the motives we pursue, like the ways we think and behave, evolved over the millions of years of evolution in response to evolutionary pressures.

Central to evolutionary accounts is the notion that organisms evolve through natural selection in directions that maximize survival and reproduction, and this should be no less true of motives than any other psychological functions. The primary motives that emerge in cross-cultural research are power and love, which is not surprising from an evolutionary perspective (Buss, 1991). Power allows animals to dominate potential rivals, establish status (which females tend to find attractive in males), and protect their "turf." Indeed, competition for status is nearly universal among animals, and certainly among primates, where baboon males can be seen to jockey for power in the bush much as human executives jockey in the boardroom. That "love" is a basic motive across cultures also makes evolutionary sense. Love is involved in caring for offspring, mates, kin, and friends who can be counted on "like a brother" or "like a sister." The fact that we use phrases like these to describe close friends may not be accidental.

Not all motives for intimacy, of course, are brotherly or sisterly. The amount of time we spend on activities related to mating or making ourselves attractive to potential mates—and the number of poems, novels, and movies with a central theme of "boy meets girl," "meeting Mr. Right," unfaithful lovers, and so forth—is a testimony to the power of natural selection. Motives related to mating include sexual motivation, competition for desirable partners, making sure our mates are faithful (Chapter 18), and a host of others. Other motives related to reproduction involve motives for parental care, which exist in nearly every animal species. That parents awakened in the middle of the night by a crying baby generally respond with affection rather than aggression is a true testimony to the power of natural selection!

A key evolutionary assumption is that psychological systems—whether motivational, cognitive, or otherwise—serve functions that may have evolved independently in response to particular evolutionary pressures (Buss, 1991, 2000; Cosmides & Tooby, 1995). Just as specialized neural circuits in the cortex and amygdala allow us to recognize the meaning of facial expressions (warning us, for example, that someone is angry and potentially threatening), specific circuits also regulate sexual desire or probably our attunement (and response) to the auditory frequency of a baby's cry.

◆ INTERIM SUMMARY

According to evolutionary theory, evolution selects animals that maximize their inclusive fitness (their own reproductive success plus their influence on the reproductive success of genetically related individuals). Maximizing inclusive fitness entails a range of motives, such as selecting and competing for mates, taking care of offspring, caring about other genetically related individuals, forming useful alliances, and maintaining one's own survival through eating, drinking, keeping the body warm, and so forth.

Psychodynamic Perspective

The psychodynamic perspective also emphasizes the biological basis of motivation. Humans are animals, and their motives reflect their animal heritage. According to Freud, humans, like other animals, are motivated by **drives**, *internal tension states that build up until they are satisfied*. He proposed two basic drives: sex and aggression. The sexual drive includes desires for love, lust, and intimacy, whereas the aggressive drive includes not only blatantly aggressive or sadistic impulses but desires to control or master other people and the environment. These drives may express themselves in subtle ways. Aggression, for example, can underlie sarcastic comments or enjoyment of violent movies.

Changing Views of Motivation: What Are Our Basic Motives?

Initially Freud had proposed self-preservation and sex as the two basic drives, much like the contemporary concept of reproductive success, which includes survival and reproduction. His decision to change from self-preservation to aggression stemmed in part from living through one world war and witnessing the beginning of another. If aggression on such a massive scale kept breaking through in the most "civilized" societies, he reasoned, it must be a basic motivational force.

Psychodynamic views of motivation have advanced considerably in the half century since Freud's death. Today, many psychoanalysts, like evolutionary psychologists, think in terms of multiple motivational systems, each of which evolved under the influence of natural selection (e.g., Bowlby, 1969; Lichtenberg, 1983). In addition to sexual and aggressive desires, psychodynamic theorists now emphasize two other motives in particular: the need for relatedness to others (independent of sexual desire) and the need for self-esteem (feeling good about oneself) (Aron, 1996; Bowlby, 1969, 1973; Fairbairn, 1954; Kohut, 1977; Mitchell, 1988).

Just as psychodynamic theorists have moved away from Freud's dual-instinct theory (sex and aggression), many have also moved away from his abstract notion of "drives" to two concepts that seem closer to the data of clinical observation: wishes and

Making Connections

Few psychologists (or even psychoanalysts) now accept Freud's theory of aggression as an instinct that builds up until discharged. However, the ethnic warfare in Eastern Europe, the Middle East, and Africa in our own times may lead us to think carefully before discarding the idea that a readiness for aggression is an innate human characteristic (Chapter 18).

fears (Brenner, 1982; Holt, 1976). A *wish* is a representation of a desired state that is associated with emotion or arousal. Wishes range from the obvious and commonplace, such as desires to be promoted at work, to the less obvious and unconscious, such as competitive desires that the individual would feel guilty to acknowledge. Once a wish is achieved, it may become temporarily deactivated or less intense. A *fear* is a representation of an undesired state that is associated with unpleasant feelings. Fears, too, range from the obvious (e.g., a child's fear of being punished) to the less obvious (the child's fear that if she misbehaves her mother will not love her anymore).

Unconscious Motivation

Perhaps the most distinctive aspect of the psychodynamic theory of motivation is the view that motives can be unconscious. An individual may be tremendously competitive in school or sports but vehemently assert that "I'm only competitive with myself." The child of an abusive alcoholic parent may desperately want to avoid an alcoholic mate but just keeps "finding" herself in relationships with abusive alcoholic men.

Until recently, the evidence for unconscious motivation was largely clinical and anecdotal. However, laboratory evidence now supports the distinction between unconscious motives and the conscious motives people can self-report (Bargh & Chartrand, 1999; McClelland et al., 1989; Westen, 1998).

To study unconscious motives, researchers often use the Thematic Apperception Test (Morgan & Murray, 1935). The **Thematic Apperception Test (TAT)** consists of *a series of ambiguous pictures about which subjects make up a story*. Researchers then code the stories for motivational themes: Do the stories describe people seeking success or achievement? Power? Affiliation with other people? Intimacy in a close relationship?

A person taking the Thematic Apperception Test (TAT).

The motives researchers code from people's TAT stories are in fact highly predictive of their behavior over time. For example, in samples from both the United States and India, the number of times an individual's stories express themes of achievement predicts success in business over many years (McClelland et al., 1989). Similarly, the number of intimacy themes expressed in stories at age 30 predicts the quality of marital adjustment almost 20 years later (McAdams & Vaillant, 1982).

Another way to measure motives is simply to ask people: "Is achievement important to you? Is power? Is intimacy?" Interestingly, the correlation between conscious, self-reported motives and the inferred motives expressed in TAT stories is typically zero. People who demonstrate high achievement motivation in their stories, for example, do not necessarily report high motivation to achieve.

Although the discrepancy could simply mean that one of the two assessment methods is invalid, in fact, each type of measure predicts different kinds of behavior. For instance, achievement motivation assessed by the TAT is far more predictive of long-term entrepreneurial success than the same motive assessed by self-report. However, if subjects in the laboratory are told they must do well on a task they are about to undertake, self-reported achievement motivation is far more predictive of effort and success than TAT-expressed motivation. How can both types of measure predict achievement behavior but not predict each other?

David McClelland and his colleagues (1989) found a solution to this paradox, making a distinction similar to that between implicit and explicit memory (Chapter 6). The TAT taps implicit (unconscious) motives, whereas self-reports reflect explicit (conscious) motives. Implicit or unconscious motivation is expressed over time without conscious effort or awareness, whereas explicit or self-reported motivation becomes activated when people focus conscious attention on tasks and goals. Conscious motives, which are more flexible and controllable, can override unconscious motives but often only temporarily, as anyone knows who has ever made—and broken—a New Year's resolution.

Further research suggests that the two kinds of motives, implicit and explicit, reflect different kinds of child-rearing experiences. For example, parental demands for control, mastery, and autonomy in early life (e.g., early and rigid feeding schedules or toilet training) predict implicit need for achievement decades later. In contrast, parents' *explicit* teaching about values (such as the importance of doing well) predicts later explicit motives (Koestner et al., 1991b; McClelland & Pilon, 1983).

◆ **INTERIM SUMMARY**

Freud argued that humans are motivated by two **drives**—internal tension states that build up until they are satisfied—sex and aggression. Contemporary psychodynamic theorists emphasize other needs as well, notably self-esteem and relatedness, and conceptualize motives in terms of wishes and fears. The most distinctive aspect of the psychodynamic approach is its distinction between conscious (explicit) and unconscious (implicit) motives, which is receiving increasing empirical support.

Behaviorist Perspective

Although behaviorists usually prefer to avoid terms such as *motivation* that suggest a causal role for internal states, the theory of operant conditioning offers (if only "implicitly") one of the clearest and most empirically supported views of motivation: Humans, like other animals, are motivated to produce behaviors rewarded by the environment and to avoid behaviors that are punished.

Learning theorists recognized many years ago, however, that the internal state of the organism influences reinforcement. A pellet of food will reinforce a hungry rat but not a sated one. Clark Hull (1943, 1952) and other behaviorists addressed this issue through their own concept of *drive*. All biological organisms have needs, such as those for food, drink, and sex. Unfulfilled needs lead to drives, defined by these theorists as states of arousal that motivate behavior. **Drive-reduction theories** *propose that motivation stems from a combination of drive and reinforcement.*

According to this view, deprivation of basic needs creates an unpleasant state of tension; as a result, the animal begins emitting behaviors. If the animal in this state happens to perform an action that reduces the tension (as when a hungry dog finds food on the dinner table), it will associate this behavior with drive reduction. Hence, the behavior will be reinforced (and the family may have to set another plate). In this example, the drive is a **primary drive**, that is, *an innate drive such as hunger, thirst, and sex.*

"I can't explain it. I see that guy coming up the walkway and I go postal."

Most human behaviors, however, are not directed toward fulfilling primary drives. Especially in wealthier societies, people spend much of their waking time in activities such as earning a living, playing, or studying. The motives for these behaviors are secondary, or acquired, drives. A **secondary drive** is *a drive learned through conditioning and other learning mechanisms such as modeling*. An originally neutral stimulus comes to be associated with drive reduction and thus itself becomes a motivator. For example, in many cultures, the desire for money is a secondary drive that ultimately permits the satisfaction of many other primary and secondary drives.

Although drive-reduction theories explain a wide range of behaviors, they leave others unexplained. Why, for instance, do people sometimes stay up until 3:00 A.M. to finish a riveting novel, even though they are exhausted? And why are some people unable to refuse dessert, even after a filling meal? Such behaviors seem motivated more by the presence of *an external stimulus or reward*—called an **incentive**—than by an internal need state.

Incentives control much of human behavior, as when a person not previously hungry is enticed by the smells of a bakery or an individual not previously sexually aroused becomes excited by an attractive, scantily clad body on a beach. In these cases, stimuli *activate* drive states rather than eliminate them. Drive-reduction theories also have difficulty explaining motives to create stimulation, encounter novelty, or avoid boredom, which are present to varying degrees in different individuals (Zuckerman, 1994) and even in other animal species (Premack, 1962).

◆ INTERIM SUMMARY

> Implicit in the theory of operant conditioning is that humans and other animals are motivated to repeat behaviors that lead to reinforcement and avoid behaviors associated with punishment. Some behavioral theorists have proposed **drive-reduction theories**, which assert that deprivation of basic needs creates an unpleasant state of tension; if the animal produces a behavior that reduces that tension, the behavior is reinforced. Some drives, called **primary drives**, are innate, whereas others, called **secondary drives**, are learned through their association with primary drives.

Making Connections

Expectancies—expectations about the things we value and the behaviors necessary to produce them—are central to cognitive accounts of learning, motivation, and personality. For children in ethnic minority groups with a history of discrimination, role models shape expectancies about what is possible or impossible and about what they imagine they can and cannot accomplish (Chapters 5 and 12).

Cognitive Perspective

Cognitive theories provide an alternative approach to motivation. One such theory we have encountered before is *expectancy–value theory* (Chapter 7). Expectancy–value theories view motivation as a joint function of the value people place on an outcome and the extent to which they believe they can attain it. That is, we are driven to attain goals that matter a lot to us but that we also believe we can accomplish. Becoming a rock star may be my wildest dream, but if I know I am tone-deaf and unable to play any instrument, I am unlikely to be motivated to grow my hair and abandon a tenured faculty position (unless I hear of an opening in Hole or Stone Temple Pilots, for which such skills may not be a prerequisite).

A considerable body of research has demonstrated the extent to which children's beliefs about their abilities influence their motivation (and subsequent achievement) in school (Wigfield & Eccles, 2000). Students of similar *actual* ability levels often differ tremendously in their success depending on their *perceived* ability. Similarly, research finds that unemployed workers' expectancies about their likelihood of success in job seeking, together with the value they place on work, predict the probability that they will hold a job a year later (Lynd-Stevenson, 1999).

Goal-Setting Theories

Cognitive approaches to motivation often focus on **goals**—*desired outcomes established through social learning*—such as getting good grades or making a good impression at a party (Bandura, 1999; Cantor, 1990). A cognitive theory widely used by organizational psychologists interested in worker motivation is goal-setting theory (Locke, 1996; Locke & Latham, 1990). The core proposition of **goal-setting theory** is that *conscious goals regulate much of human behavior*, especially performance on work tasks (Locke, 1991, p. 18). Goals represent desired outcomes that differ in some way from a person's current situation. A salesperson may set a goal of selling 100 computers next month, which is 15 more than she sold last month. Goals activate old solutions that have worked before and encourage efforts to create new solutions if the old ones fail.

Research using this theory suggests that maximum job performance occurs only under certain conditions (Locke, 1991; Smith et al., 1996). The person must (a) experience a discrepancy between what she has and wants; (b) define specific goals (e.g., "I've got to improve my serve") rather than general ones (e.g., "I have to play better"); (c) receive continuing feedback that allows her to gauge her progress toward the goal; (d) believe she has the ability to attain the goal; (e) set a high enough goal to remain motivated (so that the goal is not met too early or too easily); and (f) have a high degree of commitment to the goal.

Students can readily apply this theory to improve their classroom performance. Suppose, for example, they want to learn the material in this textbook. If so, they should set specific goals, such as finishing a section of a chapter before a certain time. To give themselves feedback, they should then glance at the words in bold in the interim summary and see if they can define them all before reading the definitions. If they do not understand a term, they should go back to that section of the text and re-read it. If they have momentary failures along the way, they should remind themselves of prior successes rather than jumping to global conclusions about their incompetence. If they find their motivation flagging, they might set themselves more challenging goals, such as responding to the features in the margins that require them to apply the material.

Self-Determination Theory and Intrinsic Motivation

Thirty years ago, Edward Deci began exploring a paradox that has captured psychologists' attention ever since. Thousands of studies from a behaviorist point of view had shown that rewarding people for performing behaviors increases their likelihood to perform them in the future. But does reward increase people's **intrinsic motivation**—their *enjoyment of and interest in an activity for its own sake*—or does it simply make them more likely to perform the behavior when they can expect an external (or "extrinsic") reward (Deci et al., 1999; Leeper, 1981; Ryan & Deci, 2000)? This question has profound implications for school, work, and parenting. Do we increase a child's interest in mathematics by rewarding her for good grades or does rewarding her inadvertently extinguish her intrinsic interest in the subject?

Deci offered a controversial and counterintuitive prediction—that reward can actually stifle intrinsic pleasure in learning—a prediction largely supported by available data (Deci et al., 1999; Rawsthorne & Elliot, 1999). The most recent version of the theory, called **self-determination theory**, suggests that *people have three innate needs—competence, autonomy, and relatedness to others*—and that intrinsic motivation flourishes when these needs are fulfilled rather than compromised (Ryan & Deci, 2000).

Rewards (as well as threats, such as strict deadlines accompanied with stiff consequences) tend to compromise people's sense of autonomy. As a result, even though they may develop competence in a domain (such as math or science), they are likely to see the motivation as forced on them and hence to lose intrinsic interest. Thus, the effects of a reward on motivation depend on how the individual perceives the situation. If the person views the reward as compromising her self-determination, intrinsic motivation will decline. If she perceives a reward (such as praise) as an indicator of her competence and not as a bribe or threat, the reward is likely to *increase* intrinsic motivation.

In many respects, this theory places motives in a social context. A supportive social environment that encourages autonomy and independence is likely to be fertile ground for the development of intrinsic motivation. Thus, when possible, parents who want to foster intrinsic motivation in school would do well to praise and support their children's interests and successes. If they do reward success (for example, with cash for a good report card), they should emphasize the child's *competence* rather than her *compliance*.

Implicit Motives: A Cognitive Perspective on Unconscious Motivation

Although self-determination theory is a cognitive theory, it has drawn heavily from other perspectives. For example, Deci derived his theory that children have innate needs for challenge and mastery from the psychoanalyst Robert White (1959), and the theory is certainly compatible with many humanistic approaches to personality that focus on innate needs for growth or self-development (Chapter 12).

Another cognitive approach to motivation that "crosses theoretical lines" is the work of Jonathan Bargh on **implicit motives**, *motives that can be activated and expressed outside of awareness*. According to Bargh, just as well-learned cognitive procedures can become automatic and occur without conscious awareness (see Chapter 7), so, too, can well-learned goals. Drawing upon principles of association, they argue that if an individual frequently chooses the same goal in a certain situation (e.g., trying to look smart in school), that goal will become associated with the situation. As a result, whenever that situation arises (as when a teacher or professor asks a question in class), the goal state will be activated and guide behavior, whether or not the person has any conscious awareness of the intention (Bargh & Barndollar, 1996, p. 8).

In a series of studies, Bargh and his colleagues tested this hypothesis using priming techniques usually used to assess implicit memory (see Bargh, 1997). They primed subjects by having them make words out of scrambled letters, under one of two conditions. In one condition, the words were related to achievement (e.g., "strive"); in the other, the words were related to affiliation (e.g., "friend"). Next, they informed participants that the study was over but asked if they could help an experimenter down the hall who was allegedly conducting an entirely separate experiment.

In this "second experiment," subjects found themselves in a situation of motivational conflict: Each was assigned an incompetent partner (a confederate of the experimenters) and given a puzzle task on which they would receive a joint score reflecting their work as a team. Thus, subjects could succeed—by essentially ignoring what the partner had to say and likely making their partner feel humiliated and stupid—or they could be more interpersonally sensitive but receive a lower score.

As predicted, subjects who had been primed with achievement words outperformed subjects primed with affiliation words (as well as control subjects who had been exposed to neutral primes). When debriefed at the end of the study, none of the subjects had any idea of the connection between the two "experiments." Thus, similar to the conclusions reached by David McClelland and his colleagues (1989), Bargh suggests that motives, like other psychological processes, can be activated either implicitly or explicitly and can guide our behavior even when we have no idea how (or whether) they became active.

◆ INTERIM SUMMARY

According to expectancy–value theories, people are motivated to perform a behavior to the extent that they value the potential outcome and believe they can attain it. **Goal-setting theory** argues that conscious goals regulate much of human action. **Intrinsic motivation** refers to enjoyment of and interest in an activity for its own sake. According to **self-determination theory**, people have innate needs for competence, autonomy, and relatedness, and intrinsic motivation flourishes when these needs are fulfilled. **Implicit motives** are motives that can be activated and expressed outside of conscious awareness.

A Hierarchy of Needs

An alternative approach to motivation was advanced by Abraham Maslow (1962, 1970). According to Maslow's **hierarchy of needs**, *lower level needs, beginning with basic survival, must be fulfilled before higher level needs guide a person's behavior*

(Figure 10.3). At the most basic level are *physiological needs*, such as those for water and food. Next are safety needs, for security and protection. Having satisfied physiological and safety needs to some extent, people are motivated to pursue closeness and affiliation with other people, or what Maslow calls *belongingness needs*. Next in the hierarchy are *esteem needs*, including both self-esteem and the esteem of others.

At the highest level are **self-actualization needs**, *motives to express one-self and grow*, or to actualize one's potential. Self-actualization needs differ from all the previous levels in that they are not *deficiency needs*; that is, they are not generated by a *lack* of something (food, shelter, closeness, the esteem of others). Rather, they are *growth needs*—motives to expand and develop one's skills and abilities.

Many behaviors reflect multiple needs. Going to work, for example, can "bring home the bacon" as well as satisfy needs for esteem, affiliation, and self-actualization. According to Maslow, however, people can spend their lives focused on motives primarily at one level and not develop beyond it. People who are starving are unlikely to think much about art, and motives for self-expression may take a back seat in people who desperately need the esteem of others. In contrast, self-actualized individuals are no longer preoccupied with where they will get their dinner or who will hold them in esteem and are thus free to pursue moral, cultural, or aesthetic concerns. Maslow offered prominent examples of self-actualizers—Gandhi, Martin Luther King, Jr., and Eleanor Roosevelt—but believed that few people reach this level.

Maslow's theory of self-actualization has proven difficult to test (Neher, 1991). However, one organizational psychologist, Clayton Alderfer, refined and applied aspects of Maslow's model to motivation in the workplace (Alderfer, 1972, 1989). Alderfer was a consultant to a small manufacturing company that was having trouble motivating its workers. In interviewing the employees, he noticed that their concerns seemed to fall into three categories: material concerns such as pay, fringe benefits, and physical conditions in the plant; relationships with peers and supervisors; and opportunities to learn and use their skills on the job. His observations led to **ERG theory**, which essentially *condenses Maslow's hierarchy to three levels of need: existence, relatedness, and growth (hence ERG)*.

According to ERG theory, worker satisfaction and motivation vary with the extent to which a job matches a given worker's needs. Workers whose primary concern is pay are unlikely to appreciate attempts to give them more training to expand their skills. In general, however, the best job provides good pay and working conditions, a chance to interact with other people, and opportunities to develop one's skills, thus satisfying the major needs. This theory offers testable hypotheses, although the empirical evidence for it remains sketchy.

◆ INTERIM SUMMARY

Maslow proposed a **hierarchy of needs**—from needs that are basic to survival to needs that guide behavior only once the person has fulfilled needs lower down the hierarchy. The hierarchy includes physiological needs, safety needs, belongingness needs, esteem needs, and **self-actualization needs** (needs to express oneself and grow). **ERG theory**, which applied Maslow's model to the workplace, proposes that workers are motivated by three kinds of needs: existence, relatedness, and growth.

Applying the Perspectives on Motivation

How might the different theoretical approaches to motivation explain the puzzling scenario with which this chapter began—the apparent lack of motivation for protection against HIV infection many people demonstrate in sexual situations?

From an evolutionary perspective, one answer lies in the discrepancy between the current environment and the circumstances in which our ancestors evolved.

Self–actualization
(e.g., creative art,
service to others)

Esteem (e.g., respect from peers)

Love or belongingness (e.g., intimacy)

Safety (e.g., housing, money)

Physiological (e.g., hunger, thirst)

Figure 10.3 Maslow's hierarchy of needs. Except for self-actualization, all of Maslow's needs are generated by a lack of something, such as food or shelter.

Apply & Discuss

■ To what extent does factory work on this production line satisfy the motives described by Maslow and ERG theory?

■ What could employers do to increase employee satisfaction in jobs such as this?

Central Questions

■ How might the basic perspectives on motivation—evolutionary, psychodynamic, behaviorist, cognitive, as well as Maslow's hierarchy of needs—explain why people often fail to protect themselves from exposure to HIV?

■ How might the different theoretical approaches explain the self-inflicted pain people endure in order to sport a tattoo or pierced body parts?

■ How would Maslow account for such behavior?

Humans have neural programs for sexual arousal that were engineered over millennia; AIDS, like other deadly venereal diseases (notably syphilis), is a new disease (in evolutionary time). Thus, these neural programs do not include momentary breaks for condoms. Distaste for condoms should be particularly high among males, who can lose erections while searching for or wearing condoms, whose reproductive success may be compromised by their application, who face less risk of AIDS transmission than females from heterosexual intercourse, and who in many cultures attract females through apparent bravery ("Nothing scares me, babe").

From a psychodynamic perspective, sex is a basic human motivation, and people are prone to self-deception and wishful thinking; the fact that people frequently deny the risk to themselves of unprotected sex should thus come as no surprise. Furthermore, any sexual encounter reflects multiple motives, and the balance of these motives can sometimes override good judgment. For example, people have casual sex for many reasons beyond biological drive. These include self-esteem motives (to feel desirable), wishes to feel physically or emotionally close to someone, and motives for dominance (the feeling of conquest). Casual, unprotected sex may also reflect blatantly self-destructive motives, as was the case with a suicidal young gay man who regularly attended bath houses at the height of media attention to the epidemic.

From a behaviorist perspective, sexual behavior, like all behavior, is under environmental control. If condom use is punishing (because it "breaks the mood," decreases genital sensations, or leads to whining by male partners), it will diminish over time. Partners who consent to unsafe sex may also be negatively reinforced for doing so by the cessation of complaining or cajoling and positively reinforced by praise or enjoyable sex.

From a cognitive perspective, people's expectancies about the probable outcomes of high-risk behavior can simply be wrong because of misinformation or inattention to media messages. Moreover, because HIV may not lead to symptoms of AIDS for many years, unprotected sexual contact produces no immediate feedback to deter its continued practice. In fact, the absence of immediate consequences probably bolsters erroneously optimistic expectancies.

From Maslow's perspective, sexual behavior can satisfy both physiological and belongingness needs, so it is likely a powerful source of motivation. When the behavior is life threatening, safety needs should be activated; however, the absence of any obvious negative impact of high-risk behavior for several years could provide a false sense of safety and allow other motives to be expressed in behavior.

A Global Vista　　Cultural Influences on Motivation

Although the major approaches to motivation take the individual as their starting point, cross-cultural work suggests that culture plays a substantial role in shaping motivation (Benedict, 1934). For example, some societies, such as the United States, view the personal accumulation of material wealth as a worthy end of individual endeavor and even celebrate wealthy people (achievers of the American Dream). In contrast, other cultures disapprove of accumulating material goods for oneself or one's family, considering it a crime against the community or a mark of poor character. The Kapauka Papuans of New Guinea strictly punish individual wealth (Pospisil, 1963). Disapproval or sanctions against individual consumption are common in agricultural or peasant societies, where resources tend to be limited and people tend to be oriented more to the good of the community (Foster, 1965).

Psychologist Erich Fromm (1955) argued that a culture's socioeconomic system shapes people's motivations so that they *want* to act in ways that the system *needs* them to act. In other words, for an economic system to work, it must create individuals whose personal needs match the needs of the system. A capitalist economy such as our own depends on workers and consumers to be materialistic. If advertisements for digital cameras or rewriteable CD drives did not motivate people, entrepreneurs would not create them, and ultimately the economy would stagnate.

The impact of culture can be seen in the conditions that foster intrinsic motivation in children. Contemporary Western cultures are highly individualistic and hence place a high premium on autonomy and self-direction. In contrast, most non-Western cultures are much more group centered. In these cultures, getting along with others, honoring one's family and parents, and participating in the life of the community tend to be more highly valued (Chapter 18).

Recent research suggests that these differences may translate into differences in the kinds of experiences that produce intrinsic motivation (Iyengar & Lepper, 1999). In one study, Anglo-American and Asian-American children (who spoke their parents' native language in the home and hence were not fully assimilated into U.S. culture) were asked to solve a set of anagrams (scrambled words). In one condition, the children were given choices to maximize their sense of self-determination. For example, the anagrams were taken from one of several categories (e.g., words related to animals, food, or San Francisco), and children in this condition were allowed to pick the category. They were also allowed to choose the color of the marker they would use to record their answers. In another condition, children were given no choices. In fact, they were told that their mother had chosen the category of words and the color of the marker for them.

Afterward the children were allowed to play in the room for a few minutes and were told that they could do some more word puzzles if they wanted or that they could play some other games, such as solving crossword puzzles. The investigators then recorded how much time the children continued to solve the anagrams, as a measure of their intrinsic motivation (that is, whether they found the task intrinsically interesting enough to continue with it even though the experiment was presumably over).

As predicted, Anglo-American children were more likely to show intrinsic motivation for solving anagrams in the first condition, in which they chose the categories and colors themselves (Figure 10.4). In contrast, the Asian-American children demonstrated the *opposite* pattern: They showed more intrinsic motivation to solve anagrams when they believed that the relevant choices had been made by their mothers. These results suggest that principles of motivation may not be culturally invariant and that the extent to which a culture emphasizes autonomy and individualism may influence the extent to which threats to autonomy influence what people find interesting and worth pursuing.

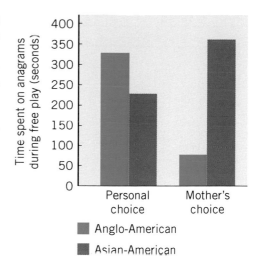

Figure 10.4 Culture and intrinsic motivation. Anglo-American children who were given choices spent more time continuing to solve anagrams after they were no longer required to do so. Asian-American children, in contrast, showed more intrinsic motivation to solve anagrams when their mothers made the choices for them. *Source:* Adapted from Iyengar & Lepper, 1999, p. 354.

◆ **INTERIM SUMMARY**

Social and cultural practices play a substantial role in shaping motives. Influences on what children come to find intrinsically motivating may be very different depending on whether they come from a culture that emphasizes individualism and personal control over choices.

◆ Eating

Having explored the major perspectives in motivation, we now turn to specific motives, beginning with eating. The motivation to eat is biologically based, but the story is not that simple. Even as I write these words, I am struggling, as many readers undoubtedly do while writing term papers, to keep my mind from drifting into the refrigerator where it does not belong. In general, however, the function of eating is not to relieve anxiety, frustration, or boredom but to convert what were once the cells of other living organisms into energy.

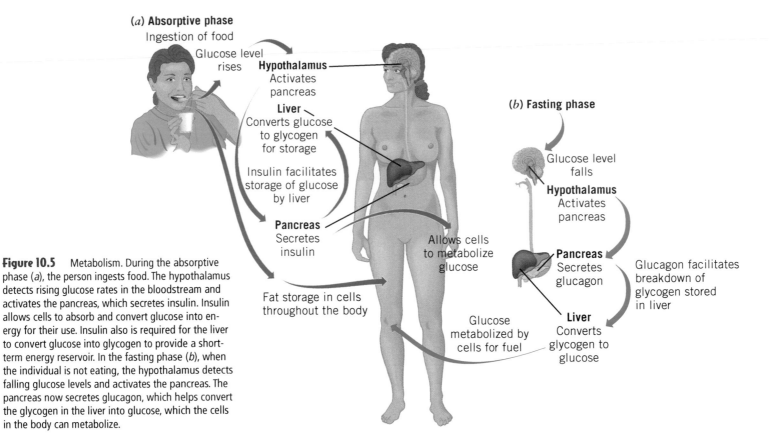

Figure 10.5 Metabolism. During the absorptive phase (*a*), the person ingests food. The hypothalamus detects rising glucose rates in the bloodstream and activates the pancreas, which secretes insulin. Insulin allows cells to absorb and convert glucose into energy for their use. Insulin also is required for the liver to convert glucose into glycogen to provide a short-term energy reservoir. In the fasting phase (*b*), when the individual is not eating, the hypothalamus detects falling glucose levels and activates the pancreas. The pancreas now secretes glucagon, which helps convert the glycogen in the liver into glucose, which the cells in the body can metabolize.

Metabolism refers to *the processes by which the body transforms food into energy* for moving muscles, maintaining body heat, operating the nervous system, and building and maintaining organ tissue. Much of that energy comes from *glucose*, a simple sugar. What makes metabolism a complex process is that the body has to maintain energy at all times, even though we cannot be eating at all times.

Metabolism thus has two phases (Figure 10.5): absorptive and fasting. In the **absorptive phase**, *the person is ingesting food*. During this phase, the body "runs" on some of the food it is absorbing but puts additional reserves into short- and long-term stores. The short-term "fuel tanks" store carbohydrates, by converting glucose to a more complex sugar (*glycogen*), which is stored throughout the body but particularly in the liver. The long-term energy tanks, located under the skin and in the abdomen, contain primarily fats (lipids). Fat cells are capable of expanding enormously when reserves are high. From an evolutionary perspective, the ability to store fat served our ancestors well. When winter came and food was scarce, they had both extra reserves of body fuel and an extra layer of warmth.

The second phase of metabolism, the **fasting phase**, *occurs when a person is not eating*, as the body converts its short- and long-term reserves into energy. In starvation, both these sources of fuel become depleted, and the body starts converting proteins into fuel, often breaking down muscle.

Homeostasis

Biological functions such as eating, drinking, and sleeping are regulated by a process called **homeostasis**, which refers to *the body's tendency to maintain a relatively constant state that permits cells to live and function*. Homeostasis literally means "standing still" (or, more accurately, "standing similarly"). Homeostasis requires mechanisms for both *detecting* the state of the system (e.g., whether the body has enough nutrients) and *correcting* the situation to restore the system to the desired state (e.g., searching for food).

Cells in the body can only live within a fairly narrow range of conditions (e.g., at the right temperature and bathed in the right amount of water). Thus, humans, like other animals, evolved systems for regulating these conditions. These systems work much like a thermostat in a house. If the thermostat ("the detector") is set at 70 degrees, the furnace remains off if the temperature inside meets or exceeds 70 degrees. When the temperature drops below that point, a circuit running from the system's thermometer switches on the furnace long enough to restore the temperature to 70 degrees (the correcting mechanism). Once feedback from the thermostat signals that the goal is attained, the furnace is again deactivated.

Eating is part of a complex homeostatic process: Energy reserves become depleted, and the person becomes hungry and eats. As the fuel tanks become full, ingestion stops, until reserves again become depleted. Like other homeostatic systems, the system that regulates food intake includes several features. First, the system has a **set point** (or set points), a *biologically optimal level the system strives to maintain* (in this case, nutrients that provide fuel for cells to do their work). Second, the system must have **feedback mechanisms** that *provide information regarding the state of the system with respect to the variables being regulated*. Thus, the body contains receptors that monitor, for example, how much sugar is in the bloodstream and provide feedback to the brain. Finally, the system must have **corrective mechanisms** that *restore the system to its set point when needed* (in this case, finding and ingesting food).

Two features of this description of homeostatic process are worth noting. First, although homeostatic processes most obviously apply to biological needs (e.g., for food, water, and air), similar mechanisms are involved in regulating many motives, such as maintaining closeness to people to whom we are deeply attached (Bowlby, 1969). Similar processes occur with regulation of emotional states as well (Chapter 11). For example, an unemployed person who feels stressed after two unsuccessful months on the job market may work even harder to find a job or may start drinking to kill the emotional pain. Both are mechanisms aimed at turning off a painful "feedback" signal (distress), although one is more likely to restore his financial security and self-esteem.

Second, in many motivational systems, particularly biological ones such as hunger and thirst, there may be a substantial lag between the time corrective mechanisms have kicked in to restore the system to homeostasis and the time the system registers their effects. For example, by the time a hungry person has eaten enough to restore his energy reserves, only a small part of the food he may have scarfed down has actually been digested—which means that the receptors designed to detect nutrient levels do not yet have all the "data" necessary to turn off eating. Thus, the body has evolved two separate systems, one for "turning on" eating and the other for turning it off. *Mechanisms for turning off ingestive behavior* are known as **satiety mechanisms**—that is, mechanisms designed to make us feel *sated* so we will close our mouths long enough to let the food "sink in."

◆ INTERIM SUMMARY

Metabolism, the processes by which the body transforms food into energy, has two phases: the **absorptive phase**, in which the person is ingesting food, and the **fasting phase**, during which the body converts its short- and long-term stores into energy. **Homeostasis** refers to the body's tendency to maintain a relatively constant state that permits cells to live and function. Homeostatic processes, including those involved in eating, have several common features. These include a **set point**, or optimal level the system strives to maintain; **feedback mechanisms** that provide the system with information regarding the state of the system with respect to the set point; and **corrective mechanisms** that restore the system to its set point when needed. **Satiety mechanisms** turn off ingestive behavior.

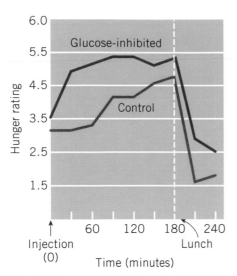

Figure 10.6 Hunger and glucose levels. The blue line depicts data from the experimental group, who received injections of a drug that suppresses blood-sugar levels. The red line illustrates data from the control group, who received a saline-solution injection. As the figure illustrates, subjects whose blood-sugar level had been artificially lowered (the glucose-inhibited group) felt considerably more hungry than the control group, even after a meal. *Source:* Thompson & Campbell, 1977.

What Turns Hunger On?

Feelings of hunger caused by physiological need ultimately derive from dropping levels of glucose and lipids in the bloodstream as the body draws increasingly on its long-term stores. Because the nervous system can use glucose (and cannot, like the rest of the body, metabolize fats), it has its own glucose detectors (located on the "brain" side of the blood–brain barrier) that detect falling blood-sugar levels (Carlson, 1999). The body has additional detectors that monitor both glucose and fats, located in the liver, which send specific signals to the brain (Woods et al., 2000). Signals from both liver and brain receptors appear to converge in the brain stem and together play a significant role in feelings of hunger.

Although most people think they become hungry because their stomachs feel empty, glucose levels probably play the most important role in producing feelings of hunger. Even people whose stomachs have been removed because of cancer nonetheless report feeling hunger (Janowitz & Grossman, 1949).

Although we cannot ask rats how hungry they are, injecting small amounts of glucose into their bloodstream when glucose levels begin to drop delays feeding behavior (Campfield et al., 1985). In humans, subjective sensations of hunger increase as glucose levels decrease. Figure 10.6 compares the reported sensations of hunger in two groups of well-fed subjects, one of whom received an injection of a drug that suppresses blood glucose levels. The experimental group felt hungrier, even after a meal (Thompson & Campbell, 1977). In another study, the investigators continuously recorded participants' glucose levels, subjective ratings of hunger, and requests for food (Campfield et al., 1996). Just after momentary decreases in glucose levels, subjects tended to feel hungry and ask for food.

The Role of the Hypothalamus Above the brain stem, the hypothalamus (Figure 10.7) plays a key role in hunger and eating, as it does in virtually all homeostatic processes (Lawrence et al., 1999). Researchers once believed that one section of the hypothalamus—the lateral hypothalamus—was the "on" switch for eating, whereas another region—the ventromedial hypothalamus—was the "off" switch (Anand & Brobeck, 1951; Teitelbaum, 1961). They based this theory in part on the fact that lesions to the lateral hypothalamus led rats to stop eating, and lesions to the ventromedial hypothalamus led them to eat ravenously.

The theory turned out to have several problems. For example, rats with damage to the lateral hypothalamus show deficits in other motivated behaviors, such as thirst and sex. More recent research suggests that eating, like virtually all psychological functions, reflects the action of neural circuits that run throughout the brain, and that, although the hypothalamus plays a central role, it is not the brain's "eating center" (Sakurai et al., 1998; Winn, 1995).

The lateral hypothalamus does, in fact, play a central role in initiating eating. A neurotransmitter found in this region, called *neuropeptide Y*, is particularly important in turning on eating, and the ventromedial hypothalamus is particularly important in producing off signals. What complicates things, however, is that both regions of the hypothalamus contain chemicals that can turn eating off *and* on, and both require substantial input from brain stem circuits that integrate information about blood glucose levels, taste, and smell. The hypothalamus also feeds information to the cortex, particularly the frontal cortex, which regulates the motor behaviors involved in finding and ingesting food.

The Role of External Cues in Eating Hunger is the prime motivator for eating, but external factors also influence the inclination to eat. In fact, desire for a food can be motivated either by hunger or simply by its palatability, or taste. Moreover, these two sources of eating motivation are mediated by different neural pathways and neurotransmitters (Berridge, 1996). Palatability plays an important role even in animals not

Lateral hypothalamus

Ventromedial hypothalamus

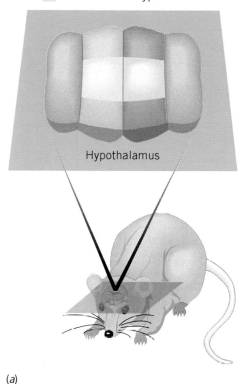

Hypothalamus

(a)

(b)

Figure 10.7   The hypothalamus and eating. (a) Decades ago, researchers began studying the roles of the ventromedial hypothalamus (*ventral* meaning toward the bottom of the brain, and *medial* meaning toward the middle) and lateral hypothalamus (*lateral* meaning on the sides) in eating. (b) Destruction of the ventromedial hypothalamus can lead to obesity in rats.

known for their gourmet tastes (Capaldi & VandenBos, 1991; Warwick et al., 1993). Rats, like humans, like variety in their diets, and as pet owners can attest, dogs and cats may grow tired of a brand of food and walk away from a delightful and nutritious bowl of horse meat or tuna innards even if they are hungry. Some taste preferences are in-born, such as the preference of human infants and baby rats for sweet tastes, while others depend on exposure and learning.

Some researchers argue that learned factors of this sort play a larger role in arousal of hunger than homeostatic processes (Woods et al., 2000). For example, rats fed consistently at particular times of day will develop classically conditioned hormonal and other chemical responses that prepare the body for food and "turn on" eating behavior. Much of eating is also regulated by learning and habit, as people learn to eat at particular times of day or in particular situations.

Another external factor that influences the motive to eat is the presence of other people. One study gave subjects pocket-sized cards on which they were to record both their food intake and dining companions for seven consecutive days (de Castro & Brewer, 1992). The more people present, the more subjects ate. Meals eaten with a large group of people were 75 percent larger than meals eaten alone.

What Turns Hunger Off?

Although hunger and satiety signals certainly interact, the mechanisms that stop eating are not the same ones that start it. The signals that stop eating begin with tastes and smells, some learned and some innate, that signal that certain food is better left alone. And noticing that our plate is empty or that other people are no longer eating can certainly signal that dinnertime is over.

Central Questions

■ Do people differ in the extent to which their eating behavior reflects feelings (e.g., taste and mood), cognitions (e.g., knowledge about calories and body image), and arousal (hunger)?

■ How might these differences develop?

Feelings of satiety (fullness, or satiation), however, usually begin in the stomach and intestines. Not only does the stomach wall have stretch receptors that send messages to the brain signaling that enough is enough, but even more important are receptors in the stomach and intestines that detect levels of nutrients. For example, rats will eat more when their stomachs are full of saline solution than of a high-calorie liquid, suggesting that glucose receptors are involved in feelings of satiety as well as hunger (Angel et al., 1992; Deutsch & Gonzalez, 1980). Over the long run, knowing when to stop is also regulated by a protein, called leptin, which is secreted by well-stocked fat cells.

◆ **INTERIM SUMMARY**

Feelings of hunger derive from dropping levels of glucose and lipids in the bloodstream, which are detected by receptors in the liver and brain stem. This information is transmitted to regions of the hypothalamus involved in both hunger and satiety. Eating is also influenced by external cues, such as palatability, time of day, and presence of other people. Satiety occurs through a number of mechanisms, beginning with tastes and smells but primarily through detection of nutrients in the stomach and intestines.

Obesity

Obesity is one of the easiest to recognize, and most difficult to treat, physical or medical conditions (Devlin et al., 2000). **Obesity** is defined as *body weight 15 percent or more above the ideal for one's height and age*. By this criterion, about one-third of the adult population of the United States is obese, and the percentage is growing (as is the author, whose body weight has steadily increased over three editions).

In industrialized countries, fatness tends to be inversely correlated with socioeconomic status; that is, people in lower social classes tend to be more obese. In developing nations, the direction of this correlation is reversed: the richer, the fatter (at least for women) (Sobal & Stunkard, 1989). The situation in the developing world probably approximates the state of affairs through most of human evolution. Particularly for women, whose pregnancies could extend into times of scarcity, larger *internal* food reserves were adaptive in the face of variable *external* reserves. In fact, societies in which food is scarce tend to associate beauty with bulk, since women who are healthy and have more resources tend to be heavier (Triandis, 1994). From an evolutionary point of view, human eating behavior evolved in conditions of scarcity and unpredictability, leading to evolved mechanisms that likely influence us to eat at our physiological limits when food is available (Pinel et al., 2000). These mechanisms may not be so adaptive when people have to hunt for food on menus instead of in forests.

Obesity places people at increased risk for a number of medical problems, such as heart disease, high blood pressure, and diabetes (Brownell & Rodin, 1994; Pinel et al., 2000). The mortality rates of overweight people are up to four times higher than in people of normal weight (Foreyt, 1987; Woo et al., 1998). On the other hand, the ways people try to lose weight—such as overreliance on "diet pills," semistarvation diets, and self-induced vomiting—can also lead to health risks (Berg, 1999).

Culture, Gender, and Conceptions of Weight and Obesity

Although obesity can be defined objectively, the subjective experience of being overweight varies considerably by individual, gender, and culture. North American culture is preoccupied with thinness, particularly for women. At any given moment, two-thirds of high school girls report that they are trying to lose weight (Rosen & Gross, 1987). From age 9 to 14, girls (unlike boys) show steady increases in concerns about their weight as well as tendencies to binge at least once a month, probably reflecting their efforts to keep their weight down by overly restricting food intake (Field et al., 1999). In Western culture, stereotypes about the obese are extremely negative (Crandall, 1994) and begin as early as kindergarten (Hsu, 1989; Rothblum, 1992). Children who are overweight are teased and often develop both lowered self-esteem and negative expectations about the way others will treat them (Miller & Downey, 1999).

Whereas most white women complain about their weight even when their weight is biologically in the "ideal" range, African-American culture has different norms (Rand and Kuldau, 1990). In one study, African-American women were heavier than their white counterparts, but they were more satisfied with their weight and less likely to find weight on other people (particularly women) unattractive (Harris et al., 1991). Overall, men were more concerned about the weight of their dates than women were, but African-American men were less likely than white men to refuse to date a woman because of her weight. Other research finds that white women rate heavier women (especially other white women) negatively on multiple dimensions (such as attractiveness, intelligence, and popularity), whereas African-American women do not (Hebl and Hetherton, 1998).

Views of beauty and obesity vary not only across and within cultures but also historically. Compared to the "Rubenesque" view of beauty of just a few centuries ago (expressed in the art and culture of the period, in which the artist Rubens was painting nudes that might today be used in advertisements for weight-loss programs!), the prototypes of feminine beauty portrayed in the mass media today look emaciated. The standards have even changed considerably since the 1950s, when the ideal was the voluptuous beauty of Marilyn Monroe, replete with large breasts and slightly protruding abdomen.

The way others behave toward obese people in our culture may actually lead them to *behave* less attractively. In one study, obese and nonobese women conversed on the phone with other subjects who did not know them and could not see them (Miller et al., 1991). College student raters, unaware of the subjects' weights (or even of what the study was about), then listened to the recorded conversations and rated the women on their social skills, likeability, and probable physical attractiveness. Not only did the raters view the obese women more negatively on all dimensions, but correlations between pounds overweight and every other variable suggested that coders could judge physical appearance from purely auditory cues: The heavier the subject, the less socially skilled, likable, and physically attractive she was perceived to be.

Cultures set standards for body types that are considered attractive and unattractive. In Renoir's time, beautiful meant bountiful. Even in the 1950s and 1960s, the standard of beauty was considerably plumper than it is now. Marilyn Monroe, for example, would probably be considered chubby today—and might well have difficulty making it on television. A study of Playboy's *centerfolds and Miss America Pageant contestants found a 10 percent decrease in the ratio of weight to height in both groups from the late 1950s to the late 1970s. This was paralleled by a dramatic increase in the number of articles on dieting in popular women's magazines (Garner et al., 1980, cited in Hsu, 1989).*

CLOSE TO HOME JOHN McPHERSON

NO SMOKING

McPHERSON 12-26

"I wish you'd renew your membership at the health club."

Causes of Obesity

Obesity likely has many causes, with both nature and nurture playing starring roles. As with IQ, however, biology appears to be the more substantial contributor.

Biology and Obesity   Twin studies reveal that both body weight and the amount of fat in a person's body are highly heritable. Body weight of adoptees correlates with the weight of their biological parents but not with their adoptive parents (Allison et al., 1994; Bouchard, 1989). Heritability for obesity is estimated to range from 30 to 70%, which is extremely high (Devlin et al., 2000). Even the amount a person eats is highly heritable, although family environment during childhood also influences food intake years later (de Castro, 1993; Faith et al., 1999).

Tracking down the genes that contribute to obesity is difficult because so many processes influenced by genetics can contribute—such as those regulating hunger, satiety, metabolic rate, fat storage or activity levels. In fact, researchers have already isolated at least 200 genes likely to contribute to normal and abnormal weight (Yager, 2000). Two physiological factors have received attention for many years, both of which show substantial heritability. The first is the number and size of fat cells in the body. Obese people have many more fat cells than average-weight individuals, and the cells they do have tend to be larger (Hirsch & Knittle, 1970). Unfortunately, fat cells that develop early in life do not disappear when a person later attempts to lose weight; they only shrink.

The second physiological factor is the body's tendency to maintain a relatively constant weight, or set point. **Set-point theory** suggests that *each person has a natural weight to which his or her body gravitates*. If a person starts to gain weight above the set point, his metabolism will increase. Thus, even though the person consumes more calories, the body burns these more efficiently than before, making further weight gain difficult. Conversely, if the person starts to lose weight, the body compensates by slowing down metabolism, requiring fewer calories to maintain the same weight (Keesey & Corbett, 1984; Williams & Thompson, 1993).

The implication of this homeostatic process is probably painfully clear to dieters: The more you lose, the harder losing becomes. As weight drops, so, too, does metabolic level, so that even maintaining the loss becomes difficult. Set-point theory may explain why the long-term success rate of virtually every diet devised over the last 40 years is dismal, no matter how impressive its advertised short-term gains. In the long run, the vast majority of dieters gain back every ounce of weight they took off (Garner & Wooley, 1991; Miller, 1999; Katahn & McMinn, 1990).

Despite many discouraging statistics, studies suggest that weight control through diet and exercise seems to be possible for a subset of people who want to lose weight. However, researchers do not yet know what defines that subset and hence who these people are (Brownell & Rodin, 1994).

Environmental and Psychological Factors in Obesity   Biological factors alone do not control weight. The fact that obesity rates in the United States have doubled since 1900 points to the significance of environmental influences and the possibility of reversing them (Brownell & Rodin, 1994). A case in point is the Pima Indians (see Devlin et al., 2000). In Mexico, where they have to search for food actively every day to survive, individuals weigh on average almost 60 pounds less than their more sedentary Arizona relatives, who share their genetics. Whereas starvation was once a major cause of mortality, in technologically developed societies the opposite of obesity may be the greater threat.

Similarly, as noted above, women of higher socioeconomic status in technologically developed countries are substantially less obese than women of lower socioeconomic status. The difference between the two groups appears to reflect environmental factors: diet, efforts to restrain eating, and trips to the gym (Garner & Wooley, 1991). Thus, as with IQ, genetics plays a central role in accounting for individual differences in body mass, but group differences may be under greater environmental control.

Other environmental factors substantially affect body weight and obesity. For example, Europeans are often astonished by the size of food portions in U.S. restaurants, and with good reason: One of the best ways to cut obesity is simply to limit portions and to change expectations about how much food should be on the plate (Hill & Peters, 1998). A recent experimental study of children's eating patterns found that cutting back on time watching television and playing video games resulted in decreased fatness (Robinson, 1999). Thus, although DNA plays a key role in obesity, so, too, do Nintendo and McNuggets.

The psychological factors involved in obesity are not entirely clear, in part because different people become obese for different reasons (Friedman & Brownell, 1995; Rodin et al., 1989). One frequent psychological correlate of obesity is low self-esteem (Bruch, 1970; Miller & Downey, 1999). Whether self-esteem problems cause or reflect obesity, however, is unclear; the relationship probably runs in both directions, with people sometimes eating to assuage their pain and others feeling bad about themselves *because of* their weight. Anxiety appears to be another psychological variable relevant to obesity (Greeno & Wing, 1994; Palme & Palme, 1999). Both clinical and experimental data suggest that some people overeat to control anxiety (Ganley, 1989; Slochower, 1987). Further, people who are morbidly obese (at least 100 pounds or 100 percent over ideal body weight) are more likely to suffer from depressive, anxiety, and personality disorders (Black et al., 1992).

Another important variable is the motivation to diet or exercise. Exercising is strongly predictive of weight control, but only 15 percent of dieters continue their exercise regimens after reaching their weight goal (Katahn & McMinn, 1990). Health psychologists are attempting to understand the reasons people smoke, eat too much, fail to see the doctor when they are becoming sick, and fail to exercise and are beginning to zero in on some of the reasons for this seemingly "irrational" behavior (Chapter 11).

Making Connections

■ Given that virtually all women in the West are exposed to the same skinny models, why do some women develop eating disorders while others do not?

■ How firm is the line between eating disorders and the preoccupation with issues of food and weight shown by many girls and women in the West (Chapter 15)?

◆ INTERIM SUMMARY

Obesity—having a body weight more than 15 percent above the ideal for one's height and age—is highly prevalent in some countries, particularly the United States. Attitudes about weight vary considerably by culture, class, ethnic group, and level of affluence of a society. The causes of obesity lie in both nature and nurture: Differences among individuals in body fat are highly heritable, although dietary factors and exercise can also strongly influence weight. **Set-point theory** suggests that lost weight is difficult to maintain because of homeostatic processes that keep body fat in some relatively narrowly specified range.

◆ Sexual Motivation

Like hunger, sex is a universal drive based in biology, but its expression varies considerably from culture to culture and from person to person. In fact, sexual motivation is even more variable than hunger. Most people eat two or three meals a day, whereas sexual appetites defy generalizations. Sexual behavior is driven as much by fantasies as by hormones; indeed, the primary sexual organ in humans is arguably not the genitals but the brain.

Apply & Discuss

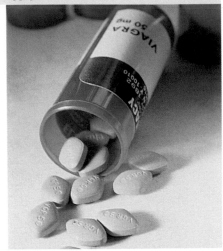

Many people have problems with sexual functioning at some point in their lives. These include trouble getting and keeping an erection, premature ejaculation, inhibited desire, and sexual inhibitions of other sorts that lead to reduced sexual satisfaction or to marital distress.

■ How freely should doctors dispense Viagra without thoroughly examining a patient and his partner psychologically as well as physically?

Although psychoanalysis broke down many of the Victorian taboos against discussing sexuality, sex did not become a respectable area of scientific research until Alfred Kinsey and his colleagues published two massive volumes on the sexual behavior of the human male and female (Kinsey et al., 1948, 1953). Many of Kinsey's findings, based on interviews with thousands of adults, provoked shock and outrage. For instance, some 37 percent of males and 13 percent of women reported having engaged in homosexual activity at some time in their lives. More recent research finds slightly lower rates of male homosexual activity but otherwise paints a similar picture (Seidman & Reider, 1994). The average sexually active person reports having intercourse between one and three times a week and becomes sexually active between ages 17 and 19 (although many start earlier or later).

Since the time of the Kinsey report, and especially since the sexual revolution of the 1960s and 1970s, sexual attitudes and practices have become much more liberal. For example, in a study that used the original Kinsey data for comparison, both white and black women reported earlier age at first intercourse, a wider range of sexual practices, a larger number of sexual partners, and reduced likelihood of marrying their first lover (Wyatt et al., 1988a,b).

The Sexual Response Cycle

A major step forward in the scientific study of sex was William Masters and Virginia Johnson's (1966) pathbreaking book, *Human Sexual Response*. By observing several hundred women and men in the laboratory, Masters and Johnson discovered that *similar physiological changes take place during sex in both women and men*, a pattern they termed the **sexual response cycle** (Figure 10.8).

The sexual response cycle begins with a phase of *excitement*, characterized by increased muscle tension, engorgement of blood vessels in the genitals causing erection of the penis and lubrication of the vagina, and often a skin flush. Maximum arousal occurs during the second, or *plateau*, phase. During this stage, heart rate, respiration, muscle tension, and blood pressure reach their peak. The third phase, *orgasm*, is characterized by vaginal contractions in females and expulsion of semen in males. During the fourth phase, *resolution*, physiological and psychological functioning gradually return to normal.

The subjective experience of orgasm is very similar in men and women. When given written descriptions of orgasms, psychologists, medical students, and gynecolo-

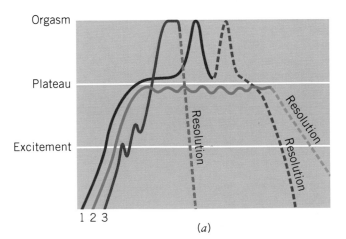

(*a*)

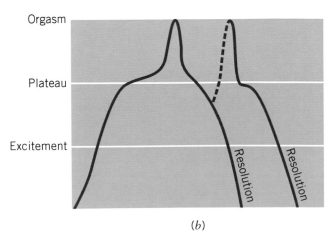

(*b*)

Figure 10.8   Sexual response cycles. Part (*a*) depicts the variations of sensation in women's sexual response. Part (*b*) illustrates the typical male sexual response cycle. The two are practically indistinguishable, except for the greater variability in women's experience. *Source:* Masters & Johnson, 1966, p. 5.

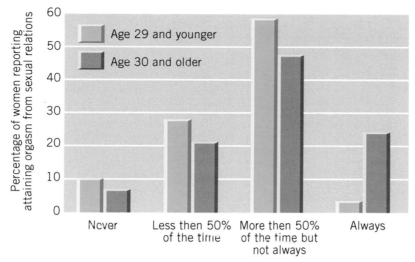

Figure 10.9 Female orgasm. Most women achieve orgasm most of the time during sex with male partners, but women over 30 have learned to do so more often. *Source:* Butler, 1976.

gists are unable to distinguish men's from women's if not told the writer's gender (Vance & Wagner, 1976). This makes some sense, given that women and men experience similar rhythmic muscular contractions during orgasm.

However, the female sexual response cycle does seem to be more variable. Women describe a few different types of orgasm, from mild pulsations to a sharp climax to repeated sensations of orgasm (Bardwick, 1971). In addition, many women do not reach orgasm with every sexual encounter (Figure 10.9), but they do report a sense of sexual release even without experiencing orgasm (Butler, 1976).

In many animal species, females and males are genetically programmed to follow very specific, stereotyped mating rituals, with attraction and mating behavior often controlled by pheromones. In the American cockroach, pheromone detection leads the male to touch its antennae to the female's antennae, spread its wings, and turn 180 degrees in a courtship dance (Seelinger & Schuderer, 1985). Even in species less reliant on pheromonal communication, mating behavior is often rigidly instinctive.

Humans do not have the same kinds of genetically based mating rituals or mating seasons as other animals. However, biological influences on human dating and mating are obvious, from the "plumage" displayed by both sexes at a fraternity mixer, to scents with names like "Passion" and "Musk," to the simple fact that most humans choose to mate only with members of their own species.

Biology and Sexual Motivation

Many key aspects of sexual behavior in humans and other animals is under hormonal control. Hormones have two effects on the nervous system and behavior: organizational and activational.

Organizational Effects Hormones exert **organizational effects** *on the circuitry, or "organization," of the brain* and thereby influence sexual behavior. In humans, these effects occur prenatally. Fetuses will develop into females unless something very particular happens. This "something particular" is the presence of two kinds of hormones secreted in the third month of pregnancy. One hormone "turns off" female development. The other set of hormones, called *androgens* (of which the most important is *testosterone*), "turns on" male development. Doctors can often tell the sex of a fetus by the fourth month using ultrasound (provided the fetus is not so modest that it keeps its legs together during the whole procedure). Other hormones, such as estrogen, appear to have organizational effects that lead to nonreproductive differ-

Human sexuality differs substantially from sexuality in other animal species—or does it?

What can go wrong in bed
(other than insomnia)?
Go to www.wiley.com/college/westen
and click on **Chapter 10: Sexual Dysfunction.**

ences between males and females, such as cognitive differences (McEwen, 1998; Chapter 3).

The fact that some hormones turn male development on while others turn female development off explains some otherwise perplexing syndromes (Money, 1987; Money & Ehrhardt, 1972). In **androgen insensitivity syndrome**, *a genetic male develops female genitalia.* The testes secrete androgens, but a genetic defect leads to an absence of androgen receptors. Thus, the body responds as if no androgen were present. The child is reared as a girl, usually leading a perfectly normal life, except that she does not develop internal female organs (and hence is sterile) because the hormone secreted by the testes that *turns off* female development continues to function. Interestingly, people with this disorder, who are by all outward appearances female, are rarely attracted to other females, even though they have testes instead of ovaries. (Their testicles are not externally visible.)

A very different course of development occurs in **congenital adrenal hyperplasia**, *a condition in which the adrenal glands secrete too much androgen, leading to masculinization of the genitals in females.* The result is an enlarged clitoris and labia that may resemble a penis and scrotum. (In utero, the tissue that becomes the scrotum in males will become labia if the testes do not secrete androgens.) Among a sample of women with this very rare disorder who would discuss their sexual orientation, roughly half reported that they were homosexual or bisexual (Money et al., 1984).

In rodents, the organizational effects of hormones continue postnatally. As a result, psychologists can study these effects experimentally (rather than by studying "experiments of nature," such as androgen insensitivity syndrome) by surgically removing the testes in males (castration) or the ovaries in females (ovariectomy). Male rats castrated at birth become sexually receptive to males if given female hormones in adulthood, manifesting the characteristic female mating behavior of hunching over and exposing the hindquarters (Edwards & Einhorn, 1986; Olster & Blaustein, 1989).

Activational Effects   Once the brain circuitry is in place, hormones exert **activational effects**, *activating brain circuits that produce psychobiological changes,* such as the development of secondary sex characteristics (e.g., breasts in adolescent females and facial hair in males). When puberty begins, for example, the hypothalamus sends signals to the pituitary to secrete hormones that in turn activate the testes and ovaries.

In males, hormones produce fluctuations in sexual arousal. Studies show a direct association between levels of testosterone in the bloodstream and sexual activity, desire, and arousal in men (Schiavi et al., 1991; Udry et al., 1985). One study demonstrated the relationship experimentally by administering doses of testosterone to adult males (Alexander et al., 1997). During the time in which their testosterone levels were chemically inflated, the men reported more sexual desire and enjoyment when presented with erotic auditory stimulation. They also showed increased attention to sexual words presented in the unattended channel in a dichotic listening task. The data are less clear for women (see Hedricks, 1994; Regan, 1996).

Culture and Sexual Behavior

Although biology plays an important role in sexual motivation, anthropological studies show enormous cultural diversity in both the ways people carry out sexual acts and the types of behaviors they consider acceptable (Davis & Whitten, 1987). Among the Basongye people of the Congo, for instance, the conventional position for intercourse is for partners to lie facing each other with the woman on her left side and the man on his right; the woman lifts her right leg to allow the man to enter (Merriam, 1971). In many parts of Australia, Melanesia, and India, the woman typically lies on her back as the man squats between her legs (Gebhard, 1971), whereas in Western culture the male lying prone on top of the female is more typical.

Apply & Discuss

■ Are most males innately wired to find the female form appealing, or is this attraction primarily learned behavior?

Cultures also differ in their conceptions of male and female sexuality. Some, such as our own, view men as having greater sexual needs. Other cultures believe just the opposite (Gordon & Shankweiler, 1971; Griffitt, 1987).

◆ **INTERIM SUMMARY**

Sexual motivation and behavior are highly variable across cultures and individuals. Masters and Johnson discovered a common pattern of physiological changes that takes place in both women and men during sex called the **sexual response cycle**. Hormones influence sexual behavior through both **organizational effects**, which influence the developing circuitry of the brain, and **activational effects**, in which hormones activate those circuits.

Sexual Orientation

Sexual orientation refers to *the direction of a person's enduring sexual attraction: to members of the same sex, the opposite sex, or both.* Determining a person's sexual orientation is not as easy as it may seem. Many people report having occasional homosexual fantasies or encounters even though they are not homosexual. Stigma, discrimination, religious values, and violence directed against homosexuals lead some people whose sexual motives and fantasies are primarily homosexual to behave heterosexually or to abstain from sex, to deny their homosexuality, or to take on the trappings of a heterosexual life-style, such as marriage to a member of the opposite sex.

Prevalence of Homosexuality   An exclusive homosexual orientation is rare among animals, but homosexual behaviors occur frequently among many species, from lizards to chimpanzees (Money, 1987; Srivastava et al., 1991). The incidence of homosexuality has varied substantially historically and cross-culturally (Adams, 1985; Herdt, 1997). In a large part of the world, stretching from Sumatra throughout Melanesia, males almost universally participate in homosexual activities several years before they reach marriageable age (Herdt, 1984, 1997; Money & Ehrhardt, 1972). Yet even in some of these cultures, in which homosexual activity is normative during a particular time in life, the concept of homosexuality as a permanent state does not exist (Herdt, 1997).

In contemporary Western societies, approximately 2 to 7 percent of men and 1 percent of women consider themselves homosexual, although the numbers vary depending on how researchers phrase the questions (see Ellis & Ames, 1987; Pillard et al., 1981). Until relatively recently, both laypeople and the psychiatric community considered homosexuality a disorder; in fact, the official diagnostic manual of the American Psychiatric Association classified it as a disorder until 1973.

People harbor many misperceptions about homosexuality, but one of the most pervasive is that homosexuality is a sexual *preference*. Psychologist John Money (1987), who has conducted some of the best-known research on homosexuality (and on sexuality in general), argues that people no more choose their sexual orientation than they select their native language or decide to be right handed.

Early Markers of Homosexual Orientation   An accumulating body of research demonstrates that children who prefer to dress or act in ways typically associated with the opposite sex are more likely to become homosexual than other children; this is especially true in males (Bailey & Zucker, 1995). In fact, the best predictor of male homosexuality in adulthood is the presence in childhood of marked behavioral characteristics of the opposite sex, sometimes called "sissy" behavior (Bell et al., 1981; Green, 1987). Although this pattern applies only to a subset of homosexual men, and cross-gender behavior is present in some boys who do not become homosexual, it is a strong predictor nonetheless.

Consider an example described in an interview with the mother of an eight-year-old boy (Green, 1987, pp. 2–3):

Mother: He acts like a sissy. He has expressed the wish to be a girl. He doesn't play with boys. He's afraid of boys, because he's afraid to play boys' games. He used to like to dress in girls' clothing. He would still like to, only we have absolutely put our foot down. And he talks like a girl, sometimes walks like a girl, acts like a girl.

Interviewer: What was the very earliest thing that you noticed?

Mother: Wanting to put on a blouse of mine, a pink and white blouse which if he'd put it on it would fit him like a dress. And he was very excited about the whole thing, and leaped around and danced around the room. I didn't like it and I just told him to take it off and I put it away. He kept asking for it.

Interviewer: You mentioned that he's expressed the wish to be a girl. Has he ever said, "I am a girl"?

Mother: Playing in front of the mirror, he'll undress for bed, and he's standing in front of the mirror and he took his penis and he folded it under, and he said, "Look, Mommy, I'm a girl."

A cross-cultural study reported the same finding in females: A major characteristic distinguishing homosexual and heterosexual females in Brazil, Peru, the Philippines, and the United States was cross-gendered childhood behavior (Whitam & Mathy, 1991). Lesbians in all four cultures were more interested in boys' toys and clothes and less interested in "girl things" as defined by their cultures than were their heterosexual peers.

From Brain to Behavior

The Biology of Homosexuality

If sexual orientation is not a matter of conscious choice, what are its causes? Homosexuality is probably the end result of many causes, some environmental and some biological. However, most environmental hypotheses (such as absent or weak fathers and dominant mothers) have received little empirical support.

Researchers who emphasize the nature side of the nature–nurture question have had more success, particularly in explaining male homosexuality (Figure 10.10). One study found differences in the neuroanatomy of homosexual and heterosexual men (LeVay, 1991). The investigator compared the brains of homosexual men (who died of AIDS complications) with men and women presumed to be heterosexual. He found that one specific set of nuclei in the hypothalamus was twice as large in heterosexual men as in women and homosexual men.

A more recent study compared the EEG patterns of heterosexual and homosexual men and women while performing a mental rotation task (at which men usually excel) and a verbal task (at which women usually outperform men). Heterosexual and lesbian women did not differ substantially from each other on either task. However, gay men's EEG patterns looked more like those of heterosexual women than heterosexual men on the mental rotation task (Wegesin, 1998). Across a number of studies, a clear finding has also emerged that homosexual men and women are more likely than heterosexuals to be left handed. This suggests early differences between heterosexuals and homosexuals (or, more likely, a subset of homosexual men and women) in the organization of the brain (Lalumiere et al., 2000).

The Behavioral Genetics of Homosexuality

What causes these differences? An increasing body of evidence from behavioral genetics suggests that homosexuality in both men and women is highly heritable (Bailey et al., 1999). Several studies have found a higher incidence of homosexuality among male relatives of male homosexuals than in the general population (Buhrich

Apply & Discuss

■ If homosexuality is substantially influenced by genetics, is there any difference between intolerance toward homosexuality and persecution of people with blue eyes or diabetes (both of which also show considerable heritability)?

et al., 1991). Whereas rates of homosexuality in the general population are estimated at 2 to 7 percent, nearly 25 percent of brothers of male homosexuals in one study were reportedly homosexual (Pillard et al., 1981, 1982).

The most definitive study to date found concordance rates for homosexuality much higher among identical than fraternal twins and adoptive brothers (Bailey & Pillard, 1991). Concordance for homosexuality was 52 percent for monozygotic twins, 22 percent for dizygotic twins, and 11 percent for adoptive brothers, with heritability estimated somewhere between .31 and .74.

The same research group conducted one of the only studies of heritability of homosexuality in women and found a similar pattern: 48 percent concordance for monozygotic twins, 16 percent for dizygotic, and 6 percent for adoptive sisters, with heritability estimates ranging from .27 to .76 (Bailey et al., 1993). Other research similarly finds increased rates of lesbianism among the biological relatives of homosexual women (Pattatucci and Hamer, 1995).

Recently, researchers have begun to investigate the genetics of homosexuality experimentally. One team of investigators *created* male homosexuality in fruit flies by inserting genetic material to produce mutations (Yamamoto et al., 1996). These "gay" fruit flies all showed mutations at precisely the same chromosomal locus that has been shown to distinguish heterosexual fruit flies from a bisexual breed. Although generalizations from fruit flies to humans obviously require caution, the fact that genetic alteration in any organism can predictably alter sexual orientation is clearly of importance.

The data thus suggest that homosexuality is substantially, but certainly not entirely (and probably not in all cases), influenced by genetics. If, as appears to be the case, sexual orientation is in part a preference exercised by our genes instead of our souls, this has substantial implications for public policy and attitudes.

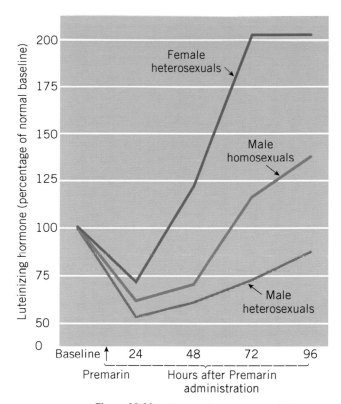

Figure 10.10 Hormonal response in male homosexuals. This figure depicts the changes in the amount of a hormone called luteinizing hormone (LH) as a response to injections of a drug called Premarin. Premarin increases LH in women and increases testosterone in men. Heterosexual men and women showed the expected hormonal responses to Premarin injection. The response of homosexual males, however, was intermediate between heterosexual men and women. *Source:* Gladue et al., 1984, p. 1496.

◆ **INTERIM SUMMARY**

Sexual orientation refers to the direction of a person's enduring sexual attraction, to members of the same or opposite sex. Attitudes toward homosexuality differ substantially across cultures. The causes of homosexuality are likely numerous, but particularly for males, mounting evidence suggests that homosexuality is highly heritable and does not likely reflect a "choice."

◆ Psychosocial Motives

Unlike sex, **psychosocial needs** (*personal and interpersonal motives for achievement, power, self-esteem, affiliation, intimacy, and the like*) are less obviously biological; however, many of these needs are strongly influenced by evolved tendencies rooted in our biology. Human infants, like the young of other species, have an inborn tendency to form intense social bonds with their primary caretakers, and toddlers spontaneously exhibit joy at their achievements and frustration at their failures. Once again, nature and nurture jointly weave even the most socially constructed fabrics.

Two major clusters of goals people pursue everywhere are **relatedness** (sometimes called "communion," referring to *motives for connectedness with others*), and **agency** (*motives for achievement, autonomy, mastery, power, and other self-oriented goals*) (Bakan, 1966; McAdams, 1999; Woike et al., 1999).

Needs for Relatedness

People have a number of interpersonal needs (Baumeister & Leary, 1995; Weiss, 1986). The earliest to arise in children are related to attachment (Chapter 14). **Attachment motivation** refers to *the desire for physical and psychological proximity (closeness) to another person*, so that the individual experiences comfort and pleasure in the other person's presence. Attachment motives form the basis for many aspects of adult love (Cassidy & Shaver, 1999; Main et al., 1985).

A related need common among adults and older children in some cultures is **intimacy**, *a special kind of closeness characterized by self-disclosure, warmth, and mutual caring* (McAdams et al., 1996; Reis & Shaver, 1988). Intimacy needs are often satisfied in adult attachment relationships and deep friendships.

Another social motive is the need for **affiliation**, or *interaction with friends or acquaintances*. Most people need to be with and communicate with other people, whether that means obtaining support after an upsetting experience, sharing good news, or playing sports together. Individuals differ in the extent to which they seek intimate versus affiliative relationships. Some people have many friends and acquaintances but have little need for intimacy. Others desire one or two intimate friends and have little need for a broad social network (Reis & Shaver, 1988; Weiss, 1986).

Social relationships, particularly with people in whom one can confide, are important for both physical and mental health (Chapter 11). For example, women who report having at least one confidante are 10 times less likely to suffer depression following a stressful event than women who do not have someone in whom they can confide (Brown et al., 1975). Lack of supportive relationships is a risk factor for mortality as well (Farmer et al., 1996; House et al., 1988a).

◆ INTERIM SUMMARY

Two clusters of **psychosocial needs** pursued cross-culturally are **relatedness** and **agency** (achievement, autonomy, mastery, power, and other self-oriented goals). Needs for relatedness include attachment, intimacy, and affiliation. Although relatedness needs are psychosocial, the failure to fulfill them can have powerful biological effects, such as sickness or mortality.

Achievement and Other Agency Motives

Pride at mastery appears to emerge spontaneously in the second year of life.

Motives for power, competence, achievement, autonomy, and self-esteem form a second cluster of motives common to humans throughout the world. As early as the second year of life, infants seem to desire to be competent and effective, even when they are not rewarded by their parents (Kagan et al., 1978). This can be clearly seen in the persistence and pride shown by young children as they learn to walk.

According to some theorists (e.g., Epstein, 1998; White, 1959), humans have an innate need to know and understand the world around them and to feel competent in the exercise of their knowledge. Pleasure in knowing and displeasure in feeling uncertain may have evolved as mechanisms that foster exploration of the environment.

Another self-oriented motive is self-esteem. Theorists of many theoretical persuasions—psychodynamic (Kohut, 1971), humanistic (Rogers, 1959), and cognitive–social (Moretti & Higgins, 1999), among others—view self-esteem motivation—the need to view oneself in a positive light—as a fundamental motivator of behavior (Chapter 17).

Need for Achievement

The **need for achievement**—*to do well, to succeed, and to avoid failure*—is the best researched psychosocial motive. This is not surprising in view of our culture's emphasis on personal achievement in school, sports, careers, and practically every domain in which our actions can be described in terms of success and failure.

People high in achievement motivation tend to choose moderately difficult tasks (those with about a 50/50 chance of success) over very easy or very difficult tasks (Atkinson, 1977; Slade & Rush, 1991). They enjoy being challenged and take pleasure in accomplishing a difficult task but are often motivated to avoid failure. In one classic study, subjects played a ring-toss game and were free to choose their own distance from the target (Atkinson & Litwin, 1960). Those who scored high in achievement motivation selected distances that were challenging but not impossible. In contrast, subjects who scored low in achievement motivation and had a high fear of failure stood either very close to the target or impossibly far, which guaranteed either success or a good excuse for failing.

How do experimental findings such as these translate into everyday behaviors? People with a high need for achievement tend to work more persistently than others to achieve a goal, and they take more pride in their accomplishments when they succeed (Atkinson, 1977). Not surprisingly, they are consequently more likely to succeed. They also tend to attribute their past successes to their abilities and their past failures to forces beyond their control, which increases confidence and persistence in the face of adverse feedback (Dweck, 1975; Weiner, 1974). Students with high achievement motivation are likely to select a major that suits their abilities, commit to a study schedule that is rigorous but not impossible, and work hard to succeed within those limits.

The consequences of achievement motivation extend far beyond the classroom. In an economically depressed area of India, where government programs had been ineffective in raising the standard of living, psychologist David McClelland undertook an experiment with far-reaching consequences. He taught local businessmen to fantasize about high achievement and to problem-solve ways to succeed (McClelland, 1978; McClelland & Winter, 1969). Over time, they began new businesses and employed new workers at a much higher rate than businessmen in a comparable town in the same region. In Western cultures, achievement motivation predicts not only occupational success but even people's earnings as much as 25 years later (Dunifon & Duncan, 1998).

Components of Achievement Motivation

As with other motives, people do not express achievement motivation in every domain. For example, an achievement-oriented premedical student may place little value in succeeding in literature courses and may be undisturbed by her failure to bake a fluffy soufflé. From a cognitive perspective, motives may be expressed selectively because they are hierarchically organized, with some sections of the hierarchy carrying more motivational weight than others (Figure 10.11).

Achievement goals themselves appear to reflect a blend of at least three motives: performance-approach, performance-avoidance, and mastery goals (Elliot & Harackiewicz, 1996; Rawsthorne & Elliott, 1999). **Performance goals** are *motives to achieve at a particular level, usually a socially defined standard*, such as getting an A in a class (Dweck, 1986). The emphasis of performance goals is on the *outcome*—on success or failure in meeting a standard.

Some people are more *motivated to attain a goal* (**performance-approach goals**), whereas others are more *motivated by the fear of not attaining it* (**performance-avoidance goals**). Thus, if I am skiing, I may be motivated by the desire to know (and tell people) I skied a black-diamond slope—a slope of considerable difficulty. Skiing a tough slope is a performance-approach goal. Alternatively, I may stay on the baby slopes to avoid skiing down the hill on my buttocks, a performance-avoidance goal.

Performance goals, whether for approach or avoidance, are about achieving a concrete outcome—obtaining success or avoiding failure. In contrast, **mastery goals** are *motives to increase one's competence, mastery, or skill*. If I am motivated by mastery goals, my interest is in developing my skill or technique—enjoying the sheer pleasure of skiing more quickly or competently—not in being able

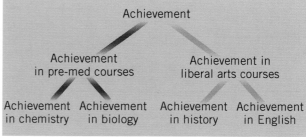

Figure 10.11 Cognitive structure of achievement motivation. A premedical student attaches different motivational weights to different sections of the hierarchy. Red lines indicate strong motivation; blue lines indicate weaker motivation

Making Connections

■ Performance-approach goals and performance-avoidance goals are related to both operant conditioning (Chapter 5) and emotion (Chapter 11). Performance-approach goals are linked to positive reinforcement and positive (pleasurable) emotions, such as pride and excitement. Performance-avoidance goals are linked to punishment, negative reinforcement (avoidance of aversive consequences), and negative (unpleasant) emotions such as anxiety, guilt, shame, and sadness.

to brag about my exploits or to avoid the snickers of even little children passing by. (My own goals in skiing are probably now apparent.)

The three types of goals underlying achievement actually predict different outcomes. For example, children with high performance-approach goals tend to get good grades, but they may or may not develop intrinsic interest in the material (Elliott & Church, 1997). Students with high performance-avoidance goals tend to get both low grades and less intrinsic pleasure from what they are doing, presumably because of their preoccupation with fears of failure. Children motivated by mastery goals often get good grades as well as develop intrinsic interest in the material.

In the future, researchers are likely to tease apart fine-grained distinctions such as these in most motivational systems. In fact, multiple motives probably underlie most behavior. Asking someone out for dinner may reflect needs for affiliation, attachment, food, sex, altruism, and self-esteem—and a central task of the person being asked out may involve figuring out which motives are primary.

Parenting, Culture, and Achievement

The need for achievement is primarily a learned motive, which numerous studies have linked to patterns of child rearing. Children with high achievement motivation tend to have parents who encourage them to attempt new tasks slightly beyond their reach, praise success when it occurs, encourage independent thinking, discourage complaining, and prompt their children to try new solutions when they fail (McClelland, 1985; Weiss & Schwarz, 1996; Winterbottom, 1953).

Parenting always occurs within a cultural context, and motivation for achievement varies considerably across cultures and historical periods. David McClelland and his colleagues spent years exploring the links among culture, child rearing, and achievement. One hypothesis, based on the theory that cultures teach motives through the stories they tell, is that a culture's myths, folk tales, and children's stories should be related to its child-rearing practices and level of economic development. A prominent children's story in our own achievement-oriented society is *The Little Engine That Could*. From a psychological standpoint, the moral of this story is simple: Those who expect success and strive for it despite adversity will succeed ("I think I can, I think I can....").

In one study, McClelland and his colleagues (1953) rated the folktales of eight Native American cultures for the extent to which they expressed achievement themes. Another set of coders independently rated the cultures for independence training, noting the age at which training began and the strength and frequency of punishment for failure to behave autonomously. The results were striking: The more achievement themes in folk tales, the more focus on autonomy and independence in child rearing (Table 10.1).

Table 10.1 ◆ Ranking of Cultures on Need for Achievement and Independence Training

Culture	Rank	
	Need for Achievement Measured from Folktales	Independence Training (Age and Severity)
Navajo	1	1
Central Apache	2	2
Hopi	3	4
Comanche	4	3
Sanpoil	5	5.5
Western Apache	6	5.5
Paiute	7	7
Flatheads	8	8

Source: Adapted from McClelland et al., 1953, p. 294.

◆ INTERIM SUMMARY

Agency needs include motives such as power, competence, achievement, autonomy, and self-esteem. The **need for achievement**—to succeed and to avoid failure—affects the goals people pursue in everyday life, the tasks they choose to tackle, and the extent to which they persist in the face of difficulty. Achievement goals themselves reflect a blend of at least three motives: **performance-approach goals** (the desire to meet a socially defined standard), **performance-avoidance goals** (the desire to avoid failure, particularly when it is publicly observable), and **mastery goals** (the desire to master the skill). Parenting practices, which themselves reflect cultural values, substantially affect achievement motivation.

◆ Central Questions:
The Nature and Causes of Human Motives

Having explored a variety of motives from multiple perspectives, we return to the basic questions with which we began. First, to what extent are people pulled by internal needs or pushed by external stimuli? Examination of the most biological of needs—hunger and sex—makes clear that even where a motive is undeniably rooted in biology, its strength depends in part on whether an appropriate stimulus presents itself, whether the stimulus is a hot fudge sundae or a hot date. A stimulus by itself, however, never motivates behavior unless the person has acquired some motivational tendency toward it. A hot fudge sundae that calls one person's name will have no effect on another who is indifferent to ice cream or chocolate.

A second and related question concerns the extent to which human motivation is rooted in biology or in culture and experience. As in nearly every other discussion of nature and nurture in this book, the answer is an intellectually unsatisfying "yes." Much as doing so might make us more comfortable, we cannot neatly parse motives into biological and psychosocial, because the most biological needs are shaped by culture and experience, and the most psychosocial motives draw on innate tendencies.

The third question pertains to the roles of thought, feeling, and arousal in motivation: Do people act on the basis of cognition? Emotion? Generalized arousal? The most likely answer is that motivation typically requires both cognition and some form of emotional energy or arousal. To put it another way, cognitive representations or thoughts provide the direction or goals of a motive, and feelings provide the strength or force behind it, but neither alone is likely to move anyone anywhere. In neuropsychological terms, the cortex provides the map for life's journeys, but the hypothalamus and limbic system largely provide the fuel. In the next chapter, we continue to examine the fuel as we explore emotion—and consider what happens if the vehicle begins to sputter under stress.

Summary

Perspectives on Motivation

1. **Motivation** refers to the moving force that energizes behavior. It includes two components: what people want to do (the direction in which activity is motivated) and how strongly they want to do it (the strength of the motivation). Although some motives (e.g., eating and sex) are more clearly biologically based and others (e.g., relatedness to others and achievement) are more psychogenic or psychosocial, both types of motives have roots in biology and are shaped by culture and experience.

2. Evolutionary psychologists argue that basic human motives derive from the tasks of survival and reproduction. They have expanded the concept of reproductive success to include inclusive fitness, which means that natural selection favors organisms that survive, reproduce, and foster the survival and reproduction of their kin. Natural selection has endowed humans and other animals with motivational mechanisms that lead them to maximize their inclusive fitness.

3. Freud believed that humans, like other animals, are motivated by internal tension states, or **drives**, for sex and aggression. Contemporary psychodynamic theorists focus less on drives than on wishes and fears. They emphasize motives for relatedness and self-esteem, as well as sex and aggression, and contend that many human motives are unconscious.

4. Behavioral theorists use the term *drive* to refer to motivation activated by a need state (such as hunger). According to **drive-reduction theories**, deprivation of basic needs creates an unpleasant state of tension that leads the animal to act. If an action happens to reduce the tension, the behavior is reinforced. Innate drives such as hunger, thirst, and sex are **primary drives**; with **secondary drives**, an originally neutral stimulus comes to be associated with drive reduction and hence itself becomes a motivator.

5. Cognitive theorists often speak of **goals**, valued outcomes established through social learning. **Expectancy–value theories** assert that motivation is a joint function of the value people place on an outcome and the extent to which they believe they can attain it. **Goal-setting theory** proposes that conscious goals regulate much of human action, particularly in work tasks. **Self-determination theory** suggests that people are most likely to develop **intrinsic motivation** in a task or domain (that is, a genuine interest in the activity for its own sake) when learning is accompanied by feelings of competence, autonomy (that is, control over their own actions, rather than control by others), and relatedness to others (a supportive, noncontrolling interpersonal environment). Recently, cognitive researchers have begun to apply experimental methods to study **implicit motives**, which occur outside awareness.

6. According to Maslow's **hierarchy of needs**, basic needs must be met before higher level needs become active. Maslow's hierarchy includes physiological, safety, belongingness, esteem, and self-actualization needs.

Eating

7. Many motives, particularly biological motives related to survival, involve **homeostasis**, the body's tendency to maintain a relatively constant state, or internal equilibrium, that permits cells to live and function. Homeostatic systems such as hunger and thirst share a number of common features, including a **set point** (a biologically optimal level the system strives to maintain); **feedback mechanisms** (which provide the system with information regarding the state of the system with respect to the variables being regulated) and **corrective mechanisms** (mechanisms that restore the system to its set point when needed).

8. **Metabolism** refers to the processes by which the body transforms food into energy. It includes an **absorptive phase**, in which the body is absorbing nutrients; and a **fasting phase**, in which the body is converting short- and long-term fuel stores into energy useful for the brain and body.

9. Eating is regulated both by hunger and by **satiety mechanisms** (mechanisms for turning off eating). Hunger increases as glucose (and, to some extent, lipid) levels fall in the bloodstream. These falling levels signal the brain that short- and long-term fuels stores are diminishing. Hunger also reflects external cues, such as the palatability of food, learned meal times, and the presence of other people. The body relies on multiple mechanisms to signal satiety (fullness), although the most important are receptors in the intestines that let the body know that the "fuel tanks" will soon be full.

10. **Obesity** is a condition characterized by a body weight over 15 percent above the ideal for one's height and age. Genetic factors and dietary fat intake are strong predictors of body fat.

Sexual Motivation

11. Sexual motivation is driven by both fantasies and hormones and is shaped by culture. Hormones control sexual behavior in humans and other animals through **organizational effects** (influencing the structure of neural circuitry) and **activational effects** (activating physiological changes that depend on this circuitry).

12. **Sexual orientation** refers to the direction of a person's enduring sexual attraction—to members of the same sex, the opposite sex, or both. Accumulating evidence on homosexuality suggests a substantial biological influence in both men and women.

Psychosocial Motives

13. **Psychosocial needs** are personal and interpersonal motives for such ends as mastery, achievement, power, self-esteem, affiliation, and intimacy. Across cultures, the two major clusters of motives are **agency** (self-oriented goals, such as mastery or power) and **relatedness** (interpersonal motives for connection, or communion, with others).

14. The **need for achievement** refers to a motive to succeed and to avoid failure, which is heavily influenced by cultural and economic conditions. Underlying achievement motivation are **performance goals** (to approach or achieve a socially visible standard) or **mastery goals** (to master the skill).

15. Even for needs undeniably rooted in biology, such as hunger and sex, the strength of a motive depends in part on whether appropriate stimuli impinge on the organism. Motives also often reflect a subtle blend of innate factors (nature) and learning and culture (nurture). Motivation usually requires both cognition (representations that provide the direction of motivation) and emotional energy or arousal (providing the "fuel," or strength, of motivation).

Key Terms

Chapter 11
Emotion, Stress, and Coping

Pablo Picasso, *Weeping Woman*, 1937. © ARS, Tate Gallery, London/Art Resource.

Forecasting the weather is an imprecise art, as anyone knows who has ever planned a weekend at the beach based on a weather report. But meteorology seems like an exact science compared with **emotional forecasting**—*predicting our own emotional reactions to future events* (Gilbert et al., 1998; Wilson et al., 2000b). People are usually good forecasters in the short run, but in the long run, they have trouble distinguishing sunshine from an emotional hail storm.

Researchers in one set of studies documented just how inexact emotional forecasting can be (Gilbert et al., 1998). They asked professors early in their careers at the University of Texas to predict how they would feel at several points in the future if they did or did not get tenure (Gilbert et al., 1998). (Tenure is a major event in the life of a professor because it means job security and freedom to write what they believe without the risk of being fired.) Most professors believed that the tenure decision would have a major impact on their well-being years down the road.

To test these forecasts, the researchers contacted everyone who had actually been up for tenure at the same university over the *prior* 10 years and asked them to rate how they felt about their lives. Those who had recently lost a tenure decision did, in fact, feel worse than those who made it, but the effect only lasted about *three months*. By a year, those who had achieved the goal that had seemed so important all those years were no happier than those who had not! Similar findings emerge when people are asked to predict how they would feel if their university's football team lost a crucial game, or if their favorite candidate were defeated in an election. What we feel and what we imagine we will feel are often very different things.

In this chapter we explore the nature of emotion, the related concept of stress, and the strategies people use to regulate their emotions and cope with stress. Throughout, we wrestle with two central questions. First, what is the function of emotion? Second, what is the relation between emotion and cognition? How does emotion affect cognition, and how do cognitive processes in turn affect the way people feel?

Central Questions

- To what extent does emotion guide behavior in adaptive ways?
- What is the role of cognition in generating and regulating emotional and stressful reactions?

◆ Emotion

Everyone has an intuitive sense of what an emotion is, but emotion can be exceedingly difficult to define. Imagine explaining the concept of emotion to someone who has never experienced one (such as a tax collector). **Emotion**, or **affect** (a synonym for emotion, pronounced with the accent on the first syllable, like *apple*), is an *evaluative response (a positive or negative feeling) that typically includes some combination* *of physiological arousal, subjective experience, and behavioral or emotional expression.* We examine each component of emotion in turn.

Physiological Components

Over a century ago, William James (1884) argued that emotion is rooted in bodily experience. According to James, an emotion-inducing stimulus elicits visceral, or gut, reactions and voluntary behaviors such as running or gesturing. The physical experience in turn leads the person to feel aroused, and the arousal stimulates the subjective experience of, for example, fear. In this view, confronting a bear on a camping trip causes a person to run, and running produces fear.

James thus offered a counterintuitive proposition: We do not run because we are afraid; rather, we become afraid because we run (Figure 11.1*a*). James's theory is sometimes called the *peripheral theory of emotion* because it sees the origins of emotion in the peripheral nervous system. Recall that the peripheral nervous system controls both muscle movements and autonomic responses such as racing heart and shortness of breath in the face of fear-eliciting stimuli. At about the same time that James developed his theory, the Danish physiologist Carl Lange (1885) proposed a similar view (which no doubt made both of their hearts pound and fists clench, leading them to feel angry). Thus, the **James–Lange theory** states that *emotions originate in peripheral nervous system responses that the central nervous system then interprets* (see Lang, 1994).

Personally, I never found the James–Lange theory all that compelling until recently, when I had my own "James–Lange moment." My wife awakened me to tell me that she was pregnant. Although we were trying to have a baby, most of what I felt as I opened my eyes that morning was terror! Later that day, alone on the elevator at work, I experienced a strange sensation in my face. I reached up, touched my face, and felt a grin from ear to ear. I then thought, "Hmmm. I must be excited," and suddenly felt the emotion that goes with a big grin—which has grown even bigger now that our baby is four months old.

On a more empirical note, as the James–Lange theory would predict, some emotional experiences—particularly sexual arousal, fear, and anger—do appear to be blunted in individuals with spinal cord lesions that prevent them from moving or experiencing gut feelings (Hohmann, 1966; Jasmos & Hakmiller, 1975). One man with a cervical spinal cord lesion (a lesion near the neck, which cuts off almost all autonomic

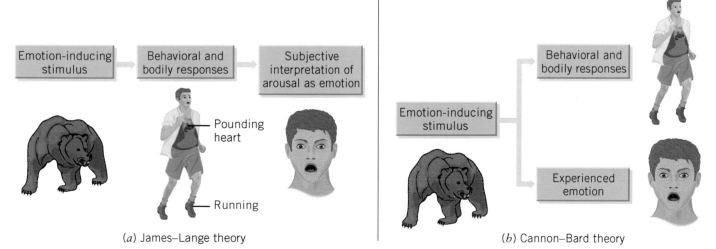

(a) James–Lange theory   (b) Cannon–Bard theory

Figure 11.1 The James–Lange and Cannon–Bard theories of emotion. In the James–Lange theory (a), a stimulus leads to a peripheral nervous system response, which in turn is interpreted as an emotion. In the Cannon–Bard theory (b), the stimulus produces simultaneous peripheral responses and subjective experience.

signals) compared his feelings of sexual arousal before and after the accident (Hohmann, 1966, p. 148):

> Before I got hurt...I would get a hot, tense feeling all over my body. I've got out and necked a few times since I was hurt, but it doesn't do anything for me. I day-dream once in a while about it, and when I'm around a bunch of guys I talk big, but I just don't get worked up anymore.

Other cases of spinal cord injury do not, however, support the James–Lange theory (Bermond et al., 1991), and the theory was challenged on other grounds over a half century ago by Walter Cannon (1927) and Philip Bard (1934). Cannon and Bard noted that autonomic responses are typically slow, occurring about one to two seconds after presentation of a stimulus. In contrast, emotional responses are immediate and often precede both autonomic reactions and behaviors such as running. Further, many different emotional states are linked to the same visceral responses, so that arousal is too generalized to translate directly into discrete emotional experiences. For instance, muscle tension and quickened heart rate accompany sexual arousal, fear, and rage, which people experience as very different emotional states. Thus, the alternative view, known as the **Cannon–Bard theory**, states that *emotion-inducing stimuli simultaneously elicit both an emotional experience, such as fear, and bodily responses, such as sweaty palms* (Figure 11.1b).

Cannon and Bard's first criticism (about the relative speed of autonomic and emotional responses) continues to be valid. However, their second criticism, that visceral arousal is general, has been challenged by more recent research. In fact, although some forms of arousal are probably general, different emotions are in fact associated with distinct patterns of autonomic activity, such as heart rate acceleration, finger temperature, and skin conductance (a measure of sweat on the palms related to arousal or anxiety, also known as *galvanic skin response*, or *GSR*) (Ekman, 1992; Levenson, 1992; Levenson et al., 1990). Anger and fear, for example, produce greater heart rate acceleration than happiness. This makes evolutionary sense, because anger and fear are related to fight-or-flight responses, which require the heart to pump more blood to the muscles.

Anger and fear are also distinguishable from each other autonomically. The language we use to describe anger ("hot under the collar") appears to be physiologically accurate: People who are angry get "heated" in their surface skin temperatures. Data from non-Western cultures such as Indonesia suggest that these links between emotional experience and physiology are similar cross-culturally and appear to be wired into the brain (Levenson et al., 1992).

◆ INTERIM SUMMARY

Emotion, or **affect**, is an evaluative response that typically includes physiological arousal, subjective experience, and behavioral or emotional expression. The **James–Lange theory** asserts that emotions originate in peripheral nervous system responses, which the central nervous system then interprets. The **Cannon–Bard theory** argues that emotion-inducing stimuli simultaneously elicit both an emotional experience and bodily responses. Although people likely experience some forms of general arousal that require interpretation, different emotions are associated with distinct patterns of emotional activation.

Subjective Experience

The most familiar component of emotion is *subjective experience*, or what it feels like to be happy, sad, angry, or elated. Individuals differ tremendously in the intensity of their emotional states (Bryant et al., 1996; Larsen et al., 1996), and these differences already begin to be apparent in preschool children (Cole et al., 1997). At the extreme high end of the bell curve of emotional intensity in adults are people with severe personality disorders (Chapter 15), whose emotions spiral out of control (M. Linehan, 1987; Wagner & Linehan, 1999).

At the other end of the bell curve are people with a psychological disorder called *alexithymia*, the inability to recognize one's own feelings (Sifneos, 1973; Taylor & Taylor, 1997). (*A-lexi-thymia* literally means *without language for emotion*.) People with alexithymia often report what seem to be meaningful, painful, or traumatic experiences with bland indifference. One alexithymic patient told his doctor about a "strange event" that had occurred the previous day. He had found himself shaking and felt his eyes tearing and wondered if he had been crying. The patient showed no recognition that his tears could have been related to frightening news he had received that morning about the results of a biopsy (D. Hulihan, personal communication, 1992). People with alexithymia appear to pay a toll for their inability to feel: They are more likely to suffer from stress-related illnesses such as chronic pain and ulcers (Fukunishi et al., 1997).

Making Connections

In *Girl Interrupted*, Angelina Jolie plays a young woman with borderline personality disorder, a psychological disorder characterized by intense emotions, particularly anger and depression, that spiral out of control (Chapter 15).

Emotional Disclosure

Just as being unaware of one's feelings can lead to illness, knowing and attending to them can have a positive impact on health (Chapter 2). In one study, Holocaust survivors spoke for one to two hours about their experiences during World War II. The investigators then measured the extent to which they had talked emotionally about traumatic events (Pennebaker et al., 1989). The more emotion they expressed as they recounted the events, the better their health for over a year later. In another study, patients with painful arthritis spoke into a tape recorder for 15 minutes a day about either stressful or trivial events (Kelley et al., 1997). Those who spoke about stressful events were in better emotional and physical shape three months later, and the more unpleasant emotion they experienced while discussing stressful events, the less painful their joints were three months later. The moral of the story? No pain, no gain.

Researchers have been tracking down some of the precise mechanisms through which emotional disclosure affects health (Pennebaker, 1997; Pennebaker & Seagal, 1999). Writing about stressful or unpleasant events has been shown to increase the functioning of specific cells in the immune system (the system of cells in the body that fight off disease). Disclosure also decreases autonomic reactivity that keeps the body on red alert (or chronically yellow alert) and takes its toll over time.

Perhaps most importantly, disclosure permits a change in cognitive functioning that allows the person to rework the traumatic experience in thought and memory. People who benefit from disclosure tend to begin with disorganized, disjointed narratives about the event, suggesting emotional disruption of their thinking. After writing, their narratives become more coherent. The more complex and coherent people's narratives after disclosing traumatic events, the more their health improves (Suedfeld & Pennebaker, 1997).

Feeling Happy

Although psychologists tend to focus on unpleasant emotions such as anxiety and depression, increasingly researchers have begun studying the subjective experience of happiness (Diener, 2000; Myers, 2000). Men and women tend to be equally happy, as do older and younger people (contrary to many people's emotional forecasts about their own sense of well-being as they age; see Chapter 14). Rates of reported happiness do, however, differ across cultures. The percentage of people who describe themselves as "very happy" ranges from a low of 10 percent in Portugal to a high of 40 percent in the Netherlands.

One predictor of happiness is the extent to which a culture is more individualistic or collectivistic: People in individualistic cultures, which focus on the needs and desires of individuals, tend to be happier than people in collectivist cultures, which emphasize the needs of the group. Another predictor is political: The correlation between life satisfaction and the number of uninterrupted years of democracy in a country is .85, which is one of the largest observed correlations ever produced in psychology between two seemingly dissimilar variables (Inglehart, 1990).

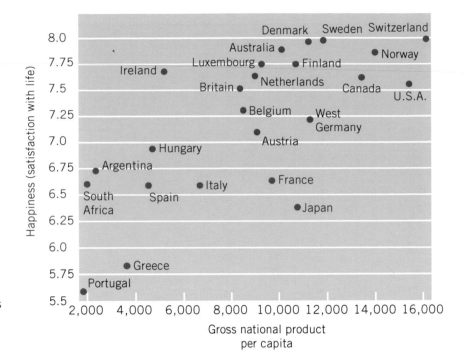

Figure 11.2 Happiness in 24 nations. Happiness is strongly correlated with gross national product (GNP), a measure of economic prosperity. *Source:* Adapted from Myers and Diener, 1995, p. 13.

Does money buy happiness? Yes and no. Across cultures, the correlation between self-reported happiness and economic prosperity is substantial (Figure 11.2). Interestingly, however, within cultures, happiness and income are not highly correlated. Apparently, a decent income is necessary but not sufficient for happiness. Other variables that predict happiness are a large network of close friends and strong religious faith (Myers, 2000).

◆ INTERIM SUMMARY

> The subjective experience of emotion refers to what the emotion feels like to the individual. People differ tremendously in emotional intensity. Acknowledging, talking about, and thinking about feelings can have a positive impact on health. The extent to which people experience happiness is relatively stable across age and gender but differs substantially across cultures.

Emotional Expression

A third component of emotion is **emotional expression**, *the overt behavioral signs of emotion*. People express feelings in various ways, including facial expressions, posture, gestures, and tone of voice.

Facial Expression and Emotion

In a twist on William James's peripheral hypothesis of emotion, some theorists argue that the face is the primary center of emotion (Tomkins, 1962, 1980). Whereas James asserted that we feel afraid because we run, these theorists argue that we feel afraid because our face shows fear. In this view, emotion consists of muscular responses located primarily in the face (and, secondarily, muscular and glandular responses throughout the body).

Different facial expressions are, in fact, associated with different emotions (Ekman, 1992; Izard, 1971, 1997). The relationship between emotion and facial muscle movements is uniform enough across individuals and cultures that electrodes attached to the face to detect muscle movements allow psychologists to assess directly both the *valence* (positive or negative tone) and intensity of emotion (Tassinary & Cacioppo, 1992). Inter-

Then imitate the action of the tiger:
Stiffen the sinews, summon up the blood,
Disguise fair nature with hard-favored rage;
Then lend the eye a terrible aspect;
Let it pry through the portage of the head
Like the brass cannon...
Now set the teeth and stretch the nostril wide,
Hold hard the breath and bend up every spirit
To his full height!

SHAKESPEARE,
Henry V, III i

(a)   (b)   (c)

Figure 11.3   Creating fear in the face. Participants instructed to (a) raise their eyebrows and pull them together, (b) then raise their upper eyelids, and (c) stretch their lips back toward their ears showed physiological changes consistent with fear.

estingly, across cultures some similarity even exists in the colors people use to describe emotions, such as the association of anger with seeing red—perhaps because anger is associated with facial flushing and an increase in temperature (see Hupka et al., 1997).

Facial expressions not only *indicate* a person's emotional state, they also *influence* the physiological and subjective components of the emotion. In a classic study, researchers gave participants specific directions to contract their facial muscles in particular ways, for instance, as in Figure 11.3 (Ekman et al., 1983). Though the participants (actors) had not been instructed to show a particular emotion, they created expressions characteristic of fear, anger, sadness, happiness, surprise, and disgust. Participants held each expression for ten seconds, while the experimenters measured their heart rate and finger temperature.

The researchers found a striking causal relation between the simple act of changing facial expression and patterns of autonomic response (Figure 11.4). More recent research has found that when people imitate positive and negative expressions in

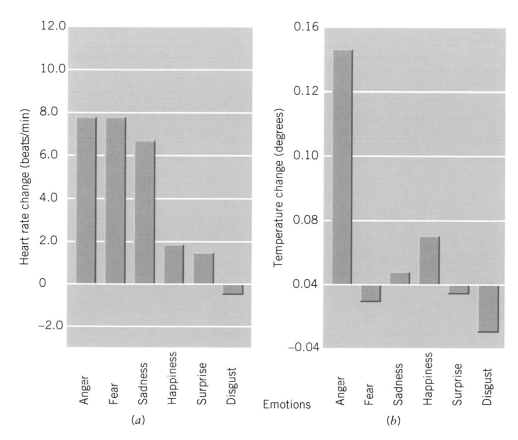

Figure 11.4   Facial expression and physiological response. The figure shows changes in heart rate and finger temperature associated with certain emotional expressions. Anger, fear, and sadness elevate heart rate, but of these three emotions, only anger also increases temperature. People presumably learn to distinguish these affects based on subtle physiological cues such as these. *Source:* Ekman et al., 1983, p. 1209.

Apply & Discuss

Research suggests that moving muscles in the face can lead to changes in emotion. Whoever wrote the lyric about letting a smile be your umbrella on a rainy day may have been a savvy psychologist.

- When is "putting on a happy face" adaptive?
- When is it maladaptive?
- In what ways can keeping a stiff upper lip influence the way *other* people respond, which, in turn, may affect health and happiness?

photographs, their own emotions tend to change accordingly (Kleinke et al., 1998). Still other studies document distinct EEG activity associated with the different posed emotions and changes in subjective experience that accompany them (Ekman & Davidson, 1993; Izard, 1990; Lanzetta et al., 1976). Similar effects appear to occur with other nonverbal expressions of emotion: People who receive positive feedback about their appearance experience more pride when they receive the feedback while standing upright rather than hunching over (Stepper & Strack, 1993)!

Not only do emotions differ from one another physiologically, but so do genuine and false emotional displays. True and fake smiles appear to be physiologically different and rely on different sets of muscles (Ekman, 1992; Ekman & Keltner, 1997). True smiles use eye muscles not used in fake smiles. Interestingly, children have some capacity to detect these differences as early as the preschool years (Banerjee, 1997).

Culture and Emotional Display Rules

Before research documented the physiological and anatomical differences among emotions, psychologists and sociologists hotly debated whether people across cultures ascribe the same meaning to a smile or a frown. In fact, some facial expressions are universally recognized (see Ekman & Oster, 1979; Scherer & Wallbott, 1994). Participants in one classic study viewed photographs showing the faces of North American actors expressing fear, anger, happiness, and other emotions. Participants from diverse cultural groups, ranging from Swedes and Kenyans to members of a preliterate tribe in New Guinea with minimal Western contact, all recognized certain emotions (Ekman, 1971).

Cross-cultural studies have identified six facial expressions recognized by people of every culture examined (Figure 11.5): surprise, fear, anger, disgust, happiness, and sadness (Ekman & Oster, 1979). Shame and interest also may have universal facial expressions (Izard, 1977). These findings suggest that some emotions are biologically linked not only to distinct autonomic states but also to certain facial movements, which people in all cultures can decode.

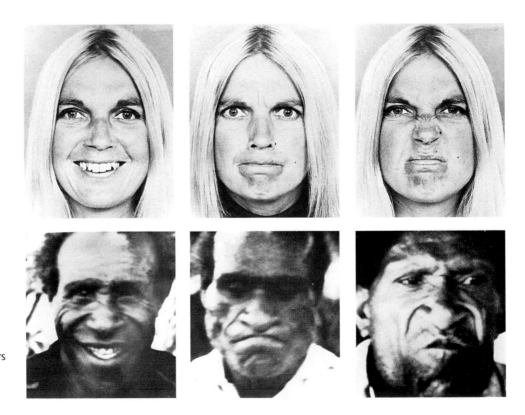

Figure 11.5 Universal facial expressions. Members of the remote Fore tribe of New Guinea recognize Western facial expressions, just as Western college students recognize the expressions on Fore faces.

Not all facial expressions, however, are the same from culture to culture. People learn to control the way they express many emotions, using *patterns of emotional expression considered appropriate within their culture or subculture*, called **display rules** (Ekman & Friesen, 1975; Ekman et al., 1982). Some of these differences appear to reflect such simple variables as geography: A study of a large sample of participants from 26 countries found, as many observers and travelers had long believed, that both within and across countries, southerners tend to be more emotionally expressive than northerners (Pennebaker et al., 1997).

In another study, Japanese and North American participants viewed a film depicting a painful adolescent initiation ceremony involving ritual circumcision. When they were unaware that they were being observed, participants from the two cultures showed the same facial responses. When participants believed they might be observed, however, their reactions were quite different. The North Americans still showed revulsion, but the Japanese, socialized to show far less emotion, masked their expressions (Ekman, 1977). Interestingly, when looking at facial displays of emotion, the Japanese tend to rate facial displays as less intense than Westerners but view the internal experience as *more* intense, suggesting that when they see a facial display, they expect it to be somewhat masked (Matsumoto et al., 1999).

Gender and Emotional Expression

Do display rules differ by gender as well as culture? The best evidence available suggests that women probably experience emotion more intensely, are better able to read emotions from other people's faces and nonverbal cues, and express emotion more intensely and openly than men (Brody, 1999; Brody & Hall, 2000). For example, a recent study found that women and men differed in both emotional expression and autonomic arousal while watching emotional films, suggesting that men and women differ in their experience of emotion (Kring & Gordon, 1998).

These distinctions apply to children as well. While watching videotapes of emotional interactions, girls show facial expressions that more closely match those of the people on the videos, suggesting greater emotional empathy; they are also better at verbally describing the emotions of the people they view (Strayer and Roberts, 1997). Interestingly, even children as young as three years old recognize that females are more likely to express fear, sadness, and happiness and that males are more likely to express anger (Birnbaum, 1983).

The reasons for gender differences in emotion are a matter of debate (Brody, 1999). On the one hand, they likely reflect adaptation to the roles that men and women have historically tended to occupy. Women are generally more comfortable with emotions such as love, happiness, warmth, shame, guilt, and sympathy, which foster affiliation and caretaking. Men, on the other hand, are socialized to compete and to fight; hence, they avoid "soft" emotions that display their vulnerabilities to competitors and enemies or discourage them from asserting their dominance when the need arises (Brody & Hall, 2000).

Parents talk to their children differently about emotion from at least the time they are toddlers. They talk more about feelings with girls, implicitly teaching them how—and how much—to think about and express their emotions (Cervantes & Callahan, 1998; Dunn et al., 1987). Little boys, in contrast, learn that only "sissies" cry and that feeling scared and showing signs of emotional vulnerability are unmanly.

Gender differences also make sense from an evolutionary perspective. Nurturing children, for example, requires attention to feelings—which can be dysfunctional for males when they are fighting, defending territory, or competing with other males for mates. This is not, of course, absolute: Men who understand others well, which means being able to read their emotions, are likely to be more socially successful and to compete more successfully for females. Thus, males may have pressures both to feel and not to feel.

◆ **INTERIM SUMMARY**

Emotional expression refers to the overt behavioral signs of emotion. Different facial muscles are associated with different emotions. Facial expressions not only indicate but can influence the subjective experience of emotion. **Display rules** are patterns of emotional expression considered appropriate within a culture or subculture. Display rules differ not only by culture but also by gender. Women appear to experience emotions more intensely and to read people's emotions more accurately.

A Taxonomy of Emotions

Some aspects of emotion, then, are universal, whereas others vary by culture and gender. How many emotions do humans experience, and how many of these are innate?

Basic Emotions

Psychologists have attempted to produce a list of **basic emotions**, *emotions common to the human species, with characteristic physiological, subjective, and expressive components* (Ekman, 1999; Izard & Buechler, 1980). Basic emotions are similar to primary colors in perception: All other emotions and emotional blends are derived from them.

Although theorists generate slightly different lists, and some even argue against the existence of basic emotions (Ortony & Turner, 1990), most classifications include five to nine emotions (J. Russell, 1991). All theorists list anger, fear, happiness, sadness, and disgust. Surprise, contempt, interest, shame, guilt, joy, trust, and anticipation sometimes make the roster (Plutchik, 1980; Shaver et al., 1987; Tomkins, 1980). Similar lists of basic emotions were compiled years ago in India (Lynch, 1990) and in China, where an encyclopedia from the first century B.C. included the following entry (*The Li Chi*, cited in Russell, 1991, p. 426):

> What are the feelings of men? They are joy, anger, sadness, fear, love, disliking, and liking. These seven feelings belong to men without their learning them.

Beyond the basic emotions, cultures vary in the extent to which they elaborate and distinguish emotional states (Kitayama & Markus, 1994; Mesquita, 1997; J. Russell, 1991). The Tahitian language has 46 different words for anger (much as English has several terms, such as annoyance, frustration, and rage) but no word for sadness. The Tahitians do not even have a word for *emotion*. In some African languages, the same word denotes both anger and sadness; members of these cultures seldom seem to distinguish between the two.

Positive and Negative Affect

A distinction that is perhaps even more basic than the basic emotions is between **positive affect** (*pleasant emotions*) and **negative affect** (*unpleasant emotions*). Researchers discovered the distinction between positive and negative affect through factor analysis, a statistical procedure that combines variables that are highly correlated with each other into superordinate variables, called factors (Chapter 8). Factor analyses of people's ratings of their tendency to experience a variety of emotions suggest that these two factors, positive and negative affect, underlie people's self-reported emotions across cultures (see Watson, 2000; Watson & Clark, 1992; Watson & Tellegen, 1985). Within these two factors, emotions are substantially intercorrelated. In other words, people who frequently experience one negative emotion, such as guilt, also tend to experience others, such as anxiety and sadness.

Brain imaging studies suggest that positive and negative affect are largely neurologically distinct, although they share *some* neural pathways. In other words, some emotional pathways lead to a general sense of emotional arousal, whereas others add a specific valence (positive or negative) (Lane et al., 1997).

Apply & Discuss

■ Can complex emotions be read from the face?
■ What other cues may be necessary to "read" emotional blends?

Approach and Avoidance   Positive and negative affect appear to motivate different kinds of behavior and to involve different regions of the cerebral cortex. Positive affect drives pleasure-seeking, approach-oriented behavior, whereas negative affect leads to avoidance (Chapter 5; see also Davidson, 1992; Gray, 1994; Lang, 1995). Approach-oriented feelings and motives are processed to a greater extent in the left frontal lobe, whereas avoidance-oriented feelings and motives are associated with right frontal activation. These circuits appear to be in place by early childhood. For example, four-year-olds who show greater left than right activation by EEG tend to be more socially competent and less interpersonally isolated than four-year-olds who show little difference between the hemispheres or greater right frontal activation (Fox et al., 1995).

A growing body of research suggests not only that people differ substantially in the extent to which they experience positive and negative affect but also that these differences play a central role in the way they live their lives (Chapters 10, 12, and 15). People who are particularly prone to negative affect may organize their lives around preventing potentially aversive events from occurring. In contrast, people who are more driven by positive affect tend to seek novel and exciting events.

For most people, positive and negative affect provide an internal set of checks and balances, leading them to pursue things they enjoy but putting on the brakes when they are about to get themselves into trouble. People who are high on one and low on the other, in contrast, are at risk for psychological problems: They may be vulnerable to depression and anxiety on the one hand or excessive risk taking and antisocial behavior on the other.

Positive and negative affect are regulated by different neurotransmitter systems, leading some researchers to suggest that an individual's tendency to experience one more than the other is related to differences in neurotransmitter functioning (Cloninger, 1998). According to one hypothesis, people who are fear driven have an abundance of or greater reaction to norepinephrine. People who are reward or pleasure driven, in contrast, are slaves to dopamine.

Part of the tendency to experience positive and negative emotions is heritable. For positive affect, estimated heritability (based on studies of twins reared together and apart) is .40. For negative affect, heritability is even higher, at .55 (Gabbay, 1992; Watson & Tellegen, 1985).

Anger

An emotion that does not neatly fit into this distinction between positive and negative affect is anger. Subjectively, anger can feel unpleasant, but anger and aggression can also have pleasurable components, as anyone knows who has ever fantasized about revenge. Anger can sometimes lead to withdrawal, as when people "swallow it" and say nothing. More often, however, anger is an approach-oriented emotion, because it leads people to approach and attack the object of their anger.

Interestingly, EEG research finds that people who tend to be angry show greater relative activity in the left versus the right frontal lobe, the standard pattern for positive affect (Harmon-Jones & Allen, 1998). This suggests either that anger is more akin to positive affect or that the asymmetry between left and right frontal functioning has less to do with the emotion itself than with the tendency to approach or avoid.

An Emotion Hierarchy

How can the various theories of emotion be reconciled, with their competing claims about the number of emotions and the relative importance of biology and culture? One solution (Figure 11.6) is to organize emotions hierarchically (Fischer et al., 1990). The most universal categories are positive and negative affect. All cultures make this distinction, and it is the first drawn by young children, who use words such as *nice*, *mean*, *good*, *bad*, *like*, and *don't like*. Physiological data (such as EEG responses) suggest that these factors are already distinct in infancy (Belsky et al., 1996).

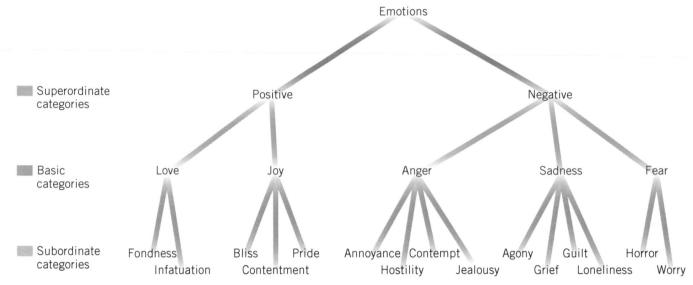

Figure 11.6 An emotion hierarchy. Emotions may be arranged hierarchically, with universal categories at the superordinate and basic levels and categories that vary by culture at the subordinate level. *Source:* Fischer et al., 1990, p. 90.

The basic emotions at the next level of the hierarchy also apply across cultures. Below this level, however, most emotion concepts are culturally constructed. Western culture, for example, distinguishes different forms of love, such as infatuation, fondness, sexual love, nonsexual love, and puppy love. Indian culture, in contrast, distinguishes only two forms of love: *vatsalya bhava*, a mother's love for her child, and *madhurya bhava*, erotic love (Lynch, 1990). Children recognize these culture-specific distinctions much later than the basic emotions.

◆ INTERIM SUMMARY

Basic emotions—such as anger, fear, happiness, sadness, and disgust—are common to the human species and include characteristic physiological, subjective, and expressive components. Beyond the basic emotions, different cultures distinguish different emotional states. Probably the most fundamental distinction is between **positive affect** (pleasant emotions) and **negative affect** (unpleasant emotions), with positive affect associated with approach-oriented motives and negative affect associated with avoidance-oriented emotions. These emotional systems are to a substantial degree neurologically distinct. Emotions appear to be organized hierarchically, with positive and negative affect at the superordinate level, followed by basic emotions and then more culture-specific emotions.

From Brain to Behavior

The Neuropsychology of Emotion

Poets often locate emotion in the heart, whereas theorists with a less romantic bent of mind locate it in the face or the peripheral nervous system. Still other researchers have searched for the neural circuits underlying emotion in the central nervous system. They have found that affect, like cognition, is distributed throughout the nervous system and not located in any particular region. Three areas of the brain, however, are particularly important: the hypothalamus, limbic system, and cortex.

The Hypothalamus

Psychologists have known about the role of the hypothalamus in emotion since the 1930s (Papez, 1937). The hypothalamus is a central link in a neural circuit that converts emotional signals generated at higher levels of the brain into autonomic and endocrine responses. (Recall from Chapter 3 that the hypothalamus links the brain to the pituitary gland, which in turn activates other glands in the endocrine system.) In some species, motivation is largely controlled by the hypothalamus and hence by instinctive responses and the emotions linked to them. Thus, electrical stimulation of regions of the hypothalamus can produce attack, defense, or flight reactions, with corresponding emotions of rage or terror.

The Limbic System

In other animals, such as humans, behavior is controlled less by instinct than by learning, which is guided by emotional responses to stimuli. Central to emotional reactions are structures in the limbic system, particularly the amygdala (LeDoux, 1989, 1995). Decades ago, researchers discovered that lesioning a large temporal region (which later turned out primarily to involve the amygdala) produced a peculiar syndrome in monkeys (Kluver & Bucy, 1939). The monkeys no longer seemed to understand the emotional significance of objects in their environment, even though they had no trouble recognizing or identifying them. The animals showed no fear of previously feared stimuli and were generally unable to use their emotions to guide behavior. They would, for example, eat feces or other inedible objects that normally elicited disgust or indifference.

Researchers have subsequently found that lesioning the neurons connecting the amygdala with a specific sense, such as vision or hearing, makes monkeys unable to register the emotional significance of objects perceived by that sense (LeDoux, 1989). The amygdala, with its dense connections to hippocampus (which is involved in memory), plays a crucial role in associating sensory and other information with pleasant and unpleasant feelings. This allows humans and other animals to adjust their behavior based on positive and negative emotional reactions to objects or situations they encounter. For example, in rats, neurons in a region of the amygdala that receives auditory information respond differently to a tone following classical conditioning of an emotional response (fear) to that tone (Rogan et al., 1997). In humans, neuroimaging data suggest that the amygdala plays a crucial role in detecting *other* people's emotions as well, particularly from observing their facial expressions (Scott et al., 1997).

Two Systems for Processing Emotion

Recent data from a variety of species point to two distinct circuits involving the amygdala that produce emotional responses, particularly fear (Armony & LeDoux, 2000; LeDoux, 1995). The first circuit is evolutionarily primitive and requires no cortical involvement. The thalamus, which processes and routes sensory information to various parts of the brain, sends some relatively simple sensory information directly to the amygdala. This information can elicit an immediate emotional response (such as fear in response to a snake approaching).

Conditioning can occur through this thalamo-limbic circuit, even when links between the amygdala and the cortex have been severed, as long as the neural connections between the amygdala and the hippocampus are intact. (The hippocampus is involved in forming associations between stimuli and emotional reactions.) Thus, an animal can have a rapid response to a stimulus previously associated with fear or pain even before the cortex "knows" anything about what is happening. For primitive vertebrates, this simple circuit was probably the sole basis of emotional reaction.

In humans and many other animals, however, the amygdala is also connected to higher processing centers in the cortex. Thus, when the thalamus sends sensory information to the amygdala, it simultaneously routes information to the cortex for more thorough examination. The cortex then transmits signals down to the amygdala. A second emotional response may then occur, based on this more complex information processing.

Thus, the emotional reaction to a stimulus may occur in two stages, reflecting the semi-independent action of these two pathways (Figure 11.7). One is a quick re-

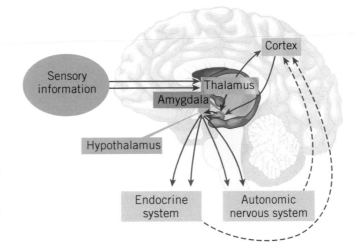

Figure 11.7 Two circuits for emotion processing. Emotionally relevant information is relayed from the thalamus simultaneously to the amygdala and the cortex. The first (blue arrows) leads to immediate responses. The second pathway (red solid arrows) allows the person to evaluate the stimulus on the basis of stored knowledge and goals. Both pathways activate the hypothalamus, which produces autonomic and endocrine changes that the cortex must interpret (dotted red arrows, indicating feedback to the cortex). *Source:* Adapted from LeDoux, 1995.

sponse based on a cursory reaction to gross stimulus features, involving a circuit running from the thalamus to the amygdala. (A dark shadow in the water frightens a swimmer.) The second process is slower, based on a more thorough cognitive appraisal, involving a thalamus-to-cortex-to-amygdala circuit. (The bather realizes that the dark shadow is a buoy.) The initial thalamus-to-amygdala response typically occurs faster because it involves fewer synaptic connections; that is, the circuit is shorter and hence faster.

The existence of two circuits for emotional processing raises fascinating questions about what happens when the affective reactions generated by these two circuits are in conflict. For example, a cancer patient may have an immediate aversive conditioned response to the room in which she receives chemotherapy (Chapter 5). At the same time, she recognizes that what happens in this room may be key to her survival. As a result of this second reaction, involving higher level cortical processing, she overrides the avoidance behavior that would ordinarily be elicited by the conditioned emotional response and keeps appearing for her treatments.

The Cortex

The cortex plays several roles with respect to emotion. As noted above, it allows people to consider whether a stimulus is safe or harmful. People with damage to the regions of the frontal cortex that receive input from the amygdala have difficulty making choices guided by their emotions (Chapter 7) (Damasio, 1994).

The cortex has a number of other emotional functions as well. One is its role in interpreting the meaning of peripheral responses, as when a person's shaky knees and dry throat while speaking in front of a group clue her in that she is anxious (Pribram, 1980). The frontal cortex plays a central role, as well, in regulating facial displays of emotion for social purposes, such as amplifying, minimizing, or feigning an emotion (Borod, 1992; Rinn, 1984).

The right and left hemispheres of the cortex appear to be specialized, with the right hemisphere dominant in processing emotional cues from others and producing facial displays of emotion (Borod, 1992). In addition, as discussed earlier, approach-related emotions are associated with activation of the left frontal cortex, whereas avoidance-related emotions are linked to activation of the right frontal lobe (Davidson, 1992; Sutton & Davidson, 1997). People who tend toward more left- than right-hemisphere activation generally experience more positive then negative affect, whereas people who show the opposite pattern of hemispheric activation tend to have more negative mood states (Figure 11.8).

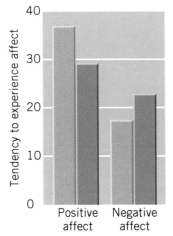

Figure 11.8 Emotional experience and hemisphere activation. The figure shows mean positive and negative affect scores for participants with a strong tendency toward left- versus right-midfrontal activation. As can be seen, participants with a bias toward left-relative to right-hemisphere activation reported more positive and less negative affect. *Source:* Adapted from Tomarken et al., 1992, p. 681.

Emotion Regulation

Because emotions feel good or bad and can draw positive or negative responses from other people, from early in life people learn to regulate their emotions. **Emotion regulation** (or **affect regulation**) refers to *efforts to control emotional states* (Westen et al., 1997; Gross, 2000; Kopp, 1989).

People can regulate emotions before or after they occur. Whether they try to regulate an emotion before or after the fact, however, has important psychological and physiological consequences. For example, people often *reframe* the meaning of an event before it occurs, trying to put it in a perspective that will make them less upset. In contrast, they may try to *suppress* the emotion after the fact, that is, try not to feel it or show it to others. Although reframing events before they occur often leads to diminished negative feelings, suppression does not. In fact, suppression leads to more sympathetic nervous system activity—that is, arousal—including increased heart rate (Gross, 1998). Suppression also interferes with the ability to engage in other tasks, because it essentially keeps the person "working overtime" to keep the feeling at bay (Richards & Gross, in press).

Just as people regulate emotions, they similarly regulate **moods**, which are *relatively extended emotional states*. Whereas emotions often grab attention and disrupt ongoing activities, moods provide a background sense of positive or negative well-being (Oatley & Jenkins, 1992). Because moods, like emotions, include subjective feelings of pleasure and pain, they also become targets for emotion regulation strategies.

Emotion regulation strategies can be viewed as a form of procedural knowledge (Chapter 6); that is, they are procedures people use to try to alter their emotional states (Westen, 1994). Many of these strategies are conscious, as when people exercise to "blow off steam" or take their mind off whatever is bothering them. Much of the time, however, people learn what regulates their emotions in everyday life, as they learn many procedures, implicitly. Some people, for example, regularly handle distress by avoiding awareness of unpleasant emotions (Weinberger, 1990). Stable styles of emotion regulation are already observable by the time children enter preschool (Cole et al., 1996; Eisenberg et al., 2000).

Men and women tend to regulate different emotions. Men more often inhibit expressions of fear and sadness, whereas women are more likely to inhibit anger (Brody & Hall, 2000; Brody et al., 1995). This makes sense in light of gender differences in motivation for power versus motivation to maintain relationships (Fischer, 2000). How much gender differences in regulation of anger are really differences in *display* of anger is not entirely clear, however. Recent research finds, for example, that women express as much anger as men—but only if the target of the anger is not present.

Making Connections

Infants and young children learn to regulate their emotions in the context of their primary relationships. Children who feel secure in their relationships with their parents learn that they can find comfort through closeness. Others, particularly those whose parents are themselves uncomfortable with intimacy and physical affection, may learn to "go it alone" and try to shut off feelings of dependence (Chapter 14).

◆ INTERIM SUMMARY

Emotional processes are distributed throughout the nervous system. The amygdala is involved in evaluating the emotional significance of a stimulus. It is also involved in detecting other people's emotions from their facial expression and vocal tone. The emotional reaction to a stimulus appears to occur through two distinct neural pathways: a quick response based on a circuit running from the thalamus to the amygdala, and a slower response based on a more thorough cognitive appraisal, based on a thalamus-to-cortex-to-amygdala circuit. In both cases, the amygdala then passes information on to the hypothalamus, which is involved in regulating autonomic responses. The cortex plays multiple roles with respect to emotion, such as interpreting the meaning of events and translating emotional reactions into socially desirable behaviors. **Emotion regulation** (or **affect regulation**) refers to efforts to control emotional states.

Perspectives on Emotion

Having examined the components of emotion and its basis in the nervous system, we now turn to *perspectives* on emotion. We already explored the behavioral perspective on emotion in some detail in Chapter 5, which emphasizes conditioned emotional responses, such as fear upon seeing a doctor approaching with a hypodermic needle. Each of the other perspectives offers insight into emotion as well.

Psychodynamic Perspective

A growing body of evidence supports a central, and somewhat counterintuitive, contention of psychodynamic theory: that people can be unconscious of their own emotional experience, and that unconscious emotional processes can influence thought, behavior, and even health (Singer, 1990). Researchers from multiple perspectives are increasingly converging on the same view (Westen, 1985, 1998). For example, in one study (see Moray, 1969), the experimenter repeatedly paired neutral words with electric shock, which eventually led to a classically conditioned emotional response to the words (anxiety or fear). Next, the experimenter presented the fear-inducing words in the unattended channel of a pair of headphones as participants attended to the other channel (a dichotic listening procedure; see Chapter 9). The researcher then measured anxious arousal by assessing skin conductance (Chapter 5). The words elicited a physiological response (a GSR), even though participants had no conscious awareness that they had heard them. Thus, participants reacted emotionally to stimuli perceived but never consciously heard.

Psychodynamic theory also suggests that we regularly delude ourselves about our own abilities and attributes to avoid the unpleasant emotional consequences of seeing ourselves more objectively. A growing body of research supports this hypothesis as well (e.g., Pratkanis, et al., 1994; G. Vaillant, 1992). One set of studies tested the hypothesis that people who disavow negative thoughts and feelings about themselves will pay a price physiologically (Shedler et al., 1993). In the first part of the experiment, participants filled out a questionnaire about their mental health and then described in detail their earliest memories. Participants who self-reported themselves as happy and healthy on the questionnaire but whose early memories were filled with unpleasant emotion (which is empirically associated with psychological disturbance) were categorized as having "illusory mental health."

Next, the experimenters presented subjects with a potentially anxiety-provoking task, such as making up TAT stories (Chapter 10) or answering items from an IQ test. Subjects with illusory mental health exhibited numerous signs of psychological distress, including elevated heart rate and blood pressure, which are related to heart disease. These subjects also consistently scored highest on indirect measures of anxiety, such as sighing and stammering. All the while, however, they consciously reported the *least* anxiety, suggesting the presence of unacknowledged anxiety (Figure 11.9). Several other researchers have presented similar data on people who tend to keep themselves unaware of their emotions (e.g., Asendorpf & Scherer, 1983; Bell & Cook, 1998; Brosschot & Janssen, 1998; D. Weinberger, 1990).

Cognitive Perspectives

As far back as the fifth century B.C., Western thinkers have viewed emotion as a disruptive force in human affairs. Plato, for example, believed that reason must rein in the passions, which otherwise distort rational thinking. Psychologists now study the impact of feelings on cognitive processes such as memory and judgment empirically, as well as studying the reverse—the influence of cognition on emotion (Dalgleish and Power, 1999; Power & Dalgleish, 1997). (Research on emotional forecasting, such as the study with which this chapter began, represents another example of a cognitive approach to emotion.)

Interpretation and Emotion You have just climbed four flights of stairs to your apartment on a hot, humid day to be confronted by a roommate complaining about dirty dishes in the sink. Your heart is racing, and your face feels flushed. Are you angry? Or is your body simply registering the impact of four flights of stairs in the

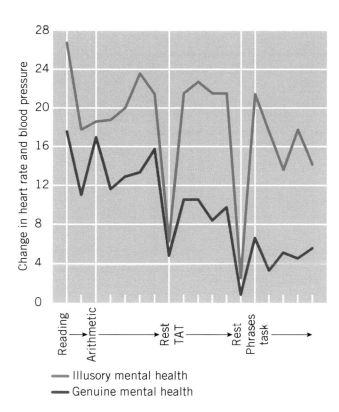

Figure 11.9   Illusory mental health. Participants who were judged high but who self-reported themselves to be low in distress showed substantially larger heart rate and blood pressure increases while performing such mildly stressful tasks as solving arithmetic questions and making up stories in response to TAT cards. Note, however, that during resting periods participants who deluded themselves showed as little reactivity as genuinely healthy participants, suggesting that their unconscious anxiety is activated only when performing a potentially threatening task. *Source:* Shedler et al., 1993.

heat? The way you react may well depend on the **attributions** (*inferences about causes*) you make about these bodily sensations.

In a classic paper, Stanley Schachter and Jerome Singer (1962) argued that a cognitive judgment or attribution is crucial to emotional experience. That is, when people experience a state of nonspecific physiological arousal, which could be anger, happiness, or any other feeling, they try to figure out what the arousal means. If situational cues suggest that they should be afraid, they interpret the arousal as fear; if the cues suggest excitement, they interpret their arousal as excitement. Thus, according to the **Schachter–Singer theory**, *emotion involves two factors: physiological arousal and cognitive interpretation* (Figure 11.10).

To test their hypothesis, Schachter and Singer injected subjects with either adrenalin (a hormone involved in emotional arousal) or an inert placebo and then correctly informed, misinformed, or told them nothing about the possible effects of the injection. Participants then went to a waiting room, where they were joined by a confederate of the experimenter posing as another participant. The confederate either behaved

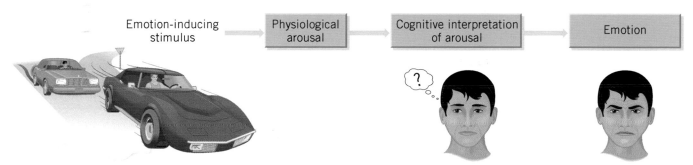

Figure 11.10   The Schachter–Singer theory of emotion. According to Schachter and Singer, people must interpret their arousal (e.g., when cut off by a speeding car) in order to experience a specific emotion.

angrily and stormed out of the room (designed to elicit anger) or playfully threw paper wads into the wastebasket, flew paper airplanes, and generally enjoyed himself (designed to elicit euphoria).

Schachter and Singer predicted that participants who knew they had been injected with an arousing drug would attribute their arousal to the drug, whereas those who became aroused but did not know why would think they were either angry or euphoric, depending on the condition. The results were as predicted, suggesting that emotional experience is not simply the subjective awareness of arousal. Rather, it is a complex cognitive–affective state that includes inferences about the meaning of the arousal.

Schachter and Singer's conclusions have drawn criticism on a number of grounds (see Leventhal & Tomarken, 1986). First, the findings have not been easy to replicate (Maslach, 1979; Mezzacappa et al., 1999). Second, research shows that people can feel anxious or angry even after taking medication that blocks physiological arousal (Cleghorn et al., 1970; Erdmann & van Lindern, 1980). These data suggest that arousal may intensify emotional experience but may not be necessary for an emotion to occur (Reisenzein, 1983). Perhaps most importantly, as the research reviewed earlier suggests, different emotions have distinct physiological correlates; thus, emotion is not simply the interpretation of general arousal.

Nevertheless, numerous studies support the view that *some* degree of interpretation is involved in the experience of many emotional states. For instance, distinguishing between being tired (or fatigued) and being depressed requires interpretation, because the two physiological states share many common features. Excessive caffeine intake can also lead to arousal, which can be misattributed as anxiety and even contribute to the development of panic attacks (Chapter 15).

Cognition and Appraisal   In Schachter and Singer's study, participants initially became aroused by a shot of adrenalin. In normal life, however, people typically become aroused by their experiences rather than by injection. According to many cognitive theorists, people's emotions reflect their judgments and appraisals of the situations or stimuli that confront them (Lazarus, 1999b; Scherer, 1999; Smith & Ellsworth, 1985). For example, an event that affects a person's well-being in the present can lead to joy or distress, whereas an event that influences the person's potential well-being in the future can generate hope or fear (Ortony et al., 1988).

Many of these cognitive principles operate cross-culturally (Mauro et al., 1992; Scherer, 1997). Others, however, depend on cultural conceptions of causality. For example, some preliterate societies believe that prolonged illness is the result of sorcery (Whiting & Child, 1958). Hence, the ill person or his loved ones may direct anger about the illness toward an accused sorcerer. The increased incidence in the United States of malpractice suits against physicians may reflect a similar process, as people look for someone to blame for tragedies.

Cognitive processes also play a central role in interpreting *other* people's emotions. For example, although facial expressions are a major source of information about people's emotions, knowledge about the situation can influence or sometimes override information from the face. In one study, the researchers showed participants the face of a woman that had been unambiguously interpreted in prior studies as expressing fear (Carroll & Russell, 1996). Along with the photograph, however, they told participants that the woman had made a reservation at a fancy restaurant and was kept waiting for over an hour as celebrities and others walked in and were seated immediately. When she reminded the maitre d' of her reservation, he told her that the tables were now full and the wait would likely be over an hour. With this information about the circumstances, the vast majority of participants interpreted the expression as anger, not fear.

These findings suggest that not only emotions but also interpretations of emotion reflect cognitive appraisals. From a connectionist point of view (Chapter 7), facial expressions provide a powerful, "hard-wired" set of constraints that influence the interpretation of another person's emotion. However, they are not the only constraints. In everyday life, knowledge about the situation also constrains inferences and may color the way a person interprets another's facial expression.

Cognitive appraisals often underlie emotions, but they do not always do so. Indeed, emotional responses can sometimes precede complex cognitive evaluations of a stimulus—or as psychologist Robert Zajonc (1980) put it, "preferences need no inferences." Zajonc demonstrated this using a phenomenon called the *mere exposure effect*, whereby people become more positive about stimuli the more times they are exposed to them. The experimenters briefly exposed participants several times to Japanese ideographs (written characters). When later asked about their preferences for particular characters, as expected from the mere exposure effect, participants preferred characters they had previously seen, even when they did not consciously recognize having seen them (Zajonc, 1980). Zajonc thus concluded that the subjective sense of liking or disliking a stimulus may occur independently of cognitions about that stimulus. At the very least, affect may precede the *conscious* cognitive appraisals proposed by many theorists.

Influence of Emotion and Mood on Cognition   Just as cognition can influence emotion, so, too, can emotion and mood influence ongoing thought and memory. For example, anxiety can reduce working memory capacity and explicit problem solving by distracting the person from the task at hand (Eysenck, 1982; Richardson, 1996a). Mood can also influence the way people make judgments, inferences, and predictions (Forgas, 1995; Mayer et al., 1992; Ochsner & Schacter, 2000). People who are depressed, for example, tend to underestimate the probability of their own success and overestimate the probability of bad events occurring in the future (Beck, 1976, 1991). Once again, anger does not appear to be a classically negative affect: Whereas fear generally leads to pessimistic judgments of the future, anger can actually lead to optimistic judgments (Lerner & Keltner, 2000).

Emotional states influence both the encoding and retrieval of information in long-term memory (Bower, 1989; Kenealy, 1997; Mathews & Macleod, 1994). Individuals in a positive mood tend both to store and to retrieve more positive information (Isen, 1984, 1993). Positive mood also tends to facilitate memory more generally, independent of its emotional quality (Levine & Burgess, 1997). Negative moods also affect encoding and retrieval, but the mechanisms are more complex. Negative mood at retrieval facilitates recall of negative words, because they are associatively linked in memory by the feeling common to both of them (Ochsner, 2000). However, people actively fight negative moods because they are aversive, so they try to retrieve more positive information (Josephson et al., 1996; Boden and Baumeister, 1997). Thus, a motivational process (regulating a negative mood) may counteract an automatic cognitive process (recall of information congruent with current thought and mood).

Emotional processes can also have a direct physiological effect on memory: Stressful emotional experiences can alter the structure of the brain (Gould et al., 1998). In one study, monkeys in one condition were exposed to an emotionally threatening encounter—being placed in another monkey's cage, who attacked until the "intruder" cowered in the corner. Compared to monkeys in a control condition, the traumatized monkeys showed a reduction in neural cells in the hippocampus, a neural structure that plays a crucial role in memory (Chapter 6).

Evolutionary Perspectives

The evolutionary perspective on emotion derives from Charles Darwin's (1872) view that emotions serve an adaptive purpose. Darwin stressed their communicative function: Animals, including humans, signal their readiness to fight, run, or attend to each other's needs through a variety of postural, facial, and other nonverbal communications (see Buck, 1986). A baby's cry sends a signal to its parents, just as bared teeth display anger. These communications regulate social behavior and increase the individual's chances of survival.

The similarities of facial expressions of emotions such as anger show their common evolutionary roots.

Darwin's theory explains why basic emotional expressions are wired into the organism and recognized cross-culturally. In fact, brain-imaging studies demonstrate the existence of hard-wired neural circuits that function to recognize emotion in other people. As we have seen, the amygdala includes specific regions that allow people to recognize emotions such as fear and anger from other people's faces.

Emotion and Motivation Evolutionary theorists also view emotion as a powerful source of motivation—an *internal* communication that something must be done (Izard, 1977; Lang, 1995; Plutchik, 1980, 1997; Tomkins, 1962). In fact, the words "motivation" and "emotion" share the same Latin root, *movere*, which means to move. For example, when people are threatened, they feel fear, which in turn leads them to deal with the threatening situation through either fight or flight. Emotions and drives may also operate in tandem to motivate action, as when excitement accompanies sexual arousal (Tomkins, 1986). Table 11.1 shows how emotional reactions motivate behaviors that promote survival and reproduction (Plutchik, 1980).

Jealousy: An Evolutionary View An emotion that is less well understood is jealousy. Why do people become jealous in intimate sexual relationships?

One series of studies tested evolutionary hypotheses about men's and women's concerns about their partners' fidelity (Buss et al., 1992). From an evolutionary perspective, females can have only a limited number of children during their lifetimes. Thus, to maximize their reproductive success, they should seek relationships with males who have resources to contribute to the care of their offspring. In fact, crosscultural evidence demonstrates that one of the main mate selection criteria used by females is male resources, whether cattle or Corvettes (Chapter 18). From a female's point of view, then, infidelity by a mate accompanied by emotional commitment to the other woman is a major threat to resources because the male is likely to divert resources or even switch mates.

For males, the situation is different. If a male commits himself to an exclusive relationship with a female, he must be certain that the offspring in whom he is investing are his own. Because a man can never be entirely certain of paternity, the best he can do is prevent his mate from copulating with any other males. In males, then, jealousy should focus less on the female's emotional commitment or resources than on her tendency to give other males sexual access. (Evolutionary psychologists are not particularly romantic in their descriptions of relationships, although I have it on good authority that they often marry, fall in love, and devote resources to children they believe are their offspring.)

Table 11.1 ◆ Evolutionary Links between Emotion and Behavior in Humans and Other Animals

Stimulus Event	Emotion	Behavior
Threat	Fear, terror, anxiety	Fight, flight
Obstacle	Anger, rage	Biting, hitting
Potential mate	Joy, ecstasy, excitement	Courtship, mating
Loss of valued person	Sadness, grief	Crying for help
Group member	Acceptance, trust	Grooming, sharing
New territory	Anticipation	Examining, mapping
Sudden novel object	Surprise	Stopping, attending

Source: Adapted from Plutchik, 1980, p. 16.

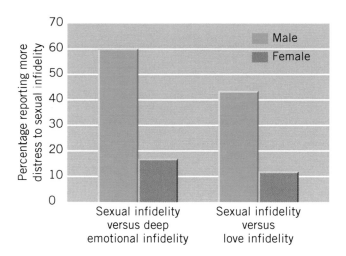

Figure 11.11 Jealousy in males and females. The figure shows the percentage of participants reporting more distress to the sexual infidelity scenario than to imagining their lover either becoming deeply attached to someone else (left) or falling in love with someone else (right). Men are more concerned than women with sexual infidelity, and this is particularly true of those who have actually been in a committed sexual relationship. *Source:* Buss et al., 1992.

Indeed, in species ranging from insects to humans, males take extreme measures to prevent other males from inseminating their mates (Hasselquist & Bensch, 1991). Male birds in some species refuse to let a female out of their sight for days after insemination. In humans, male sexual jealousy is the leading cause of homicides and of spouse battering cross-culturally (Daly & Wilson, 1988).

To test the evolutionary hypothesis that males and females differ in their reasons for jealousy, college students were asked to "imagine that you discover that the person with whom you've been seriously involved became interested in someone else" (Buss et al., 1992). Participants were to choose which of two scenarios would upset them more: "imagining your partner forming a deep emotional attachment to that person" or "imagining your partner enjoying passionate sexual intercourse with that person." They were then asked a second question involving similar scenarios contrasting love and sex: "imagining your partner falling in love with that other person" or "imagining your partner trying different sexual positions with that other person."

As Figure 11.11 shows, 60 percent of males reported greater distress at the thought of sexual infidelity in response to the first question, compared to only 17 percent of the females, who were more concerned about emotional attachment. The second question yielded similar results, as did a third study in which the investigators measured distress *physiologically* rather than by self-report, using indicators such as pulse and subtle facial movements (such as a furrowed brow, which is associated with negative affect).

The evolutionary interpretation of these findings has not gone unchallenged (DeSteno and Salovey, 1996; Harris and Christenfeld, 1996). For example, the findings could be equally attributed to culture, because these studies were conducted in a single culture. More recently, however, cross-cultural researchers have found similar sex differences in countries as diverse as Germany and China, although these differences were slightly less pronounced than in the United States, suggesting both cultural and evolutionary influences on feelings of jealousy (Buunk et al., 1996; Geary et al., 1995).

◆ INTERIM SUMMARY

According to psychodynamic theory, people can be unconscious of their emotional experience and can act on affects even when they lack subjective awareness of them. According to the **Schachter–Singer theory**, a cognitive approach to emotion, emotion occurs as people interpret their physiological arousal. Subsequent research suggests that cognitive appraisals influence emotion and that mood and emotion can affect thought and memory. From an evolutionary perspective, emotion serves an important role in communication between members of a species. It is also a powerful source of motivation.

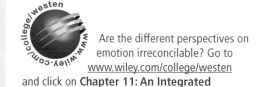

Are the different perspectives on emotion irreconcilable? Go to www.wiley.com/college/westen and click on **Chapter 11: An Integrated Perspective on Emotion.**

Eight years of stress can take a remarkable toll on the body. President Bill Clinton appeared to age tremendously during his years in the White House, as have other presidents before him.

◆ Stress

Emotion and stress are closely related concepts. **Stress** refers to *a challenge to a person's capacity to adapt to inner and outer demands*. Stressful experiences typically produce physiological and emotional arousal and elicit cognitive and behavioral efforts to cope with the stress.

Stress as a Psychobiological Process

Stress is a psychobiological process, with both physiological and psychological components and consequences. An early contribution to the understanding of stress was Walter Cannon's (1932) description of the fight-or-flight response (Chapter 3), in which an organism prepares for danger with endocrine and sympathetic nervous system activation. If the danger does not abate, however, the organism remains perpetually aroused. This can lead to deteriorating health as the body continues to divert its resources away from everyday maintenance and toward emergency readiness.

Another major contribution occurred when a young Canadian scientist, Hans Selye, accidentally uncovered some of the physiological mechanisms of stress. Selye (1936, 1976) was experimenting with what he thought was a new sex hormone, which he injected into rats to test its effects. What he ultimately discovered was that a wide range of stressful events, from injections of various substances (including his "sex hormone") to fatigue to extreme cold, led the body to respond with a **general adaptation syndrome** *consisting of three stages: alarm, resistance, and exhaustion.*

The first stage, *alarm*, involves release of adrenalin and other hormones such as cortisol as well as activation of the sympathetic nervous system. This is what occurs biologically in fight-or-flight responses: Blood pressure, heart rate, respiration, and blood sugar rise as blood is diverted from the gastrointestinal tract to muscles and other parts of the body that may be called upon for an emergency response.

The alarm stage cannot last indefinitely, however, and the body may eventually enter the second stage, *resistance*. The parasympathetic nervous system returns respiration and heart rates to normal. However, blood glucose levels remain high (for energy), and some stress-related hormones (including adrenalin and cortisol) continue to circulate at elevated levels. Essentially, the organism remains on red alert, with heightened energy and arousal, but it has begun to adapt to a higher level of stress.

Remaining on red alert takes its toll, making the organism especially vulnerable to illness. Overworked college students in the resistance stage, for example, are susceptible to influenza, mononucleosis, and whatever garden-variety colds happen to be making the rounds. The situation is analogous to a country that deploys all its military troops to one border to protect against an invasion, leaving its other borders unprotected.

If the resistance phase lasts long enough, the body eventually wears down, and the organism enters a third stage, *exhaustion*. Physiological defenses break down, resulting in greatly increased vulnerability to serious or even life-threatening disease. Organs such as the heart that are vulnerable genetically or environmentally (from smoking, too much lifelong cholesterol intake, etc.) are the first to go during this stage.

Stress as a Transactional Process

A major step forward in the study of stress came when Richard Lazarus developed his *transactional model* of stress. According to this view, stress is typically a *transaction* between the individual and the environment, rather than a property of either the person or the environment alone (Lazarus, 1981, 1993). Just as the amount of stress on a rope is jointly determined by the quality of the rope and the amount of weight pulling on it, so, too, is the amount of stress people experience a joint function of their internal resources and the external situations "tugging" at them.

Stress entails an individual's perception that demands of the environment tax or exceed her available psychosocial resources. That is, stress depends on the *meaning* of an event to the individual. An event that fills one person with excitement, such as a new business opportunity, can make another feel overwhelmed and anxious. The extent to which an event is experienced as stressful therefore depends on the person's appraisal of both the situation and her ability to cope with it.

Lazarus's model identifies two stages in the process of stress and coping (neither of which is necessarily conscious). In a **primary appraisal** of the situation, *the person decides whether the situation is benign, stressful or irrelevant*. If she appraises the situation as stressful (e.g., the professor who fails to make tenure), she must determine what to do about it. In the second stage, **secondary appraisal**, *the person evaluates the options and decides how to respond* (e.g., deciding that she is better off leaving the university to work for an Internet firm and make a better living). Both stages involve emotional forecasting, predicting what feelings the situation will produce (primary appraisal) and predicting the likely emotional impact of each potential response (secondary appraisal).

Lazarus distinguishes three types of stress. The first is *harm* or *loss*, as when a person loses a loved one or something greatly valued, such as a job. The second is *threat*, which refers to anticipation of harm or loss. The third form of stress is *challenge*, which refers to opportunities for growth that may nonetheless be fraught with disruption and uncertainty. Examples of challenges include getting married or entering college. These events can be exceedingly stressful—that is, psychologically and physiologically taxing—because of all the changes and adjustments they entail, even though they are also accompanied by positive affect (unless cold feet overwhelm a warm heart). Thus, not all stress comes from negative events.

Stress often reflects broader social and economic forces. Stress levels rise as unemployment levels rise, as do rates of child abuse, violence against spouses, alcoholism, suicide, and disease.

◆ INTERIM SUMMARY

Stress refers to a challenge to a person's capacity to adapt to inner and outer demands. Stress is a psychobiological process, with both physiological and psychological components and consequences. The **general adaptation syndrome** consists of three stages: alarm, resistance, and exhaustion. Stress is also a *transactional* process—a transaction between the individual and the environment, in which the individual perceives that demands of the environment tax or exceed her psychosocial resources. In a **primary appraisal** of the situation, the person decides whether the situation is benign, stressful, or irrelevant. During **secondary appraisal**, the person evaluates the options and decides how to respond.

Sources of Stress

Stress is an unavoidable part of life. *Events that often lead to stress* are called **stressors**. Stressors range from the infrequent, such as the death of a parent, to the commonplace, such as a demanding job or a noisy neighbor. Research on stressors has focused on life events, catastrophes, and daily hassles.

Life Events

One of the most significant sources of stress is change. Virtually any event that requires someone to make a readjustment can be a stressor. The Holmes–Rahe scale, a portion of which is reproduced in Table 11.2, measures stress related to 43 common

Table 11.2 ◆ Top 15 Stressors on the Holmes–Rahe Life Events Rating Scale		
Rank	Life Event	Mean Value
1	Death of spouse	100
2	Divorce	73
3	Marital separation	65
4	Jail term	63
5	Death of a close family member	63
6	Personal injury or illness	53
7	Marriage	50
8	Fired at work	47
9	Marital reconciliation	45
10	Retirement	45
11	Change in health in family member	44
12	Pregnancy	40
13	Sex difficulties	39
14	Gain of new family member	39
15	Business readjustment	39

Source: Holmes & Rahe, 1967.

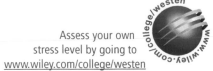

Assess your own stress level by going to www.wiley.com/college/westen and click on **Chapter 11: College Life Stressor Inventory.**

life events that require change and adaptation (Holmes & Rahe, 1967). An important feature of the Holmes–Rahe scale is that it includes both negative items (e.g., death of a spouse) and positive items (e.g., marriage) that can be stressful.

Although the Holmes–Rahe scale offers a good rough estimate of the amount of stress a person is encountering (by summing all the life change units experienced over the past 12 months), it does not take into account the meanings of various experiences for different individuals. Consequently, some researchers have turned, instead, to measures of *perceived stress*—that is, the extent to which people *consider* the experiences they have undergone stressful (Blascovich & Mendes, 2000).

Major Stressors   One of the most stressful events any individual can experience is the death of a spouse or child—a stress that can take its toll for many years afterward. For example, a study of people who lost a spouse or child in a car accident indicated that, for many bereaved persons, distress lasts as long as four to seven years after a sudden loss. Symptoms of prolonged distress included depression, sleep disturbances, fatigue, panic attacks, loneliness, and increased mortality rate. Additionally, parents who had unexpectedly lost a child were at substantially higher risk for divorce (Lehman et al., 1987).

Striking findings on the relation between loss and mortality emerged in a study of over 1 million people from Finland (Martikainen and Valkonen, 1996). The investigators charted the mortality rates of individuals who had lost a spouse over a five-year period. Those who lost a spouse were at substantially elevated risk for death by accident, violence, and alcohol. Deaths from heart disease doubled—perhaps confirming the popular view that people can "die of a broken heart." The relative risk of dying was particularly high within six months of the death of a spouse and was highest in younger people (Table 11.3). Other research finds that bereaved spouses displaying a higher proportion of "fake" smiles to "real" smiles are at greater risk for depression in the following years (Keltner & Bonanno, 1997; Keltner et al., 1999). Once again, suppressing genuine feelings does not appear to be a particularly healthy strategy, at least for dealing with loss.

Another major stressor, unemployment, can also impair physical and mental health, although the effects are generally not as dramatic as the death of a spouse (Jahoda, 1988; Kessler et al., 1987a). For example, another large Finnish study (the Finns seem to have cornered the market on stress) followed workers for several months after a plant lay-off (Viinamaeki et al., 1996). Those who remained unemployed were at increasing risk for depression, subjective distress, and stress-related illnesses as the months wore on.

Major stressors, such as loss of a loved one or unemployment, actually include many specific sources of stress. The effect on a given person depends on the individual's vulnerabilities to these specific stressors (Monroe & Simons, 1991). For example, unem-

Table 11.3 ◆ Relative Risk of Death Following Death of a Spouse							
	Cause of Death						
	Cancer	*Chronic Heart Disease*	*Alcohol- Related Illness*	*Motor Vehicle Accidents*	*Other Accidents and Violence*	*Suicide*	*All Causes*
Men	1.31	2.08	3.98	1.52	3.05	3.02	1.66
Women	1.04	1.71	2.91	1.52	2.45	2.30	1.25

Source: Adapted from P. Martikainen and T. Valkenen (1996). Mortality after the death of a spouse: Rates and causes of death in a large Finnish cohort. *American Journal of Public Health, 86,* 1090.

ployment can be devastating because of the financial strain on an individual or family. It can also lead to marital strain, forced relocation, and loss of social contact with friends from work (Bolton & Oakley, 1986; Kessler et al., 1989). Thus, even a person who has other sources of income, such as unemployment compensation or savings, may experience lowered self-esteem, loneliness, or anxiety following unemployment.

Acculturative Stress A severe stressor that is increasingly confronting people throughout the world is acculturative stress (Berry, 1989, Berry et al., 1997; Rogler et al., 1991). Acculturation means coming into contact with a new, typically dominant culture. Thus, **acculturative stress** refers to *the stress people experience in trying to adapt to a new culture.* Acculturative stress can occur whether people willingly emigrate for better opportunities or flee as refugees. Symptoms may include anxiety, depression, uncertainty and conflict about ethnic identity, and alcohol abuse.

Like other major life stresses, acculturative stress includes many specific stressors. People entering new cultures frequently encounter language difficulties, racial or ethnic prejudice, lower socioeconomic status (such as Russian doctors working in North America as paramedics because of licensing requirements), and separation from family. Immigrants also face conflicts over preserving their old values and beliefs and adapting to the mores of their new culture—conflicts often played out across the generations, as children shun their parents' Old World attitudes. Finally, many refugees must also come to terms with torture or with the torture or murder of loved ones back home.

Catastrophes

Catastrophes are *stressors of massive proportions.* Catastrophes may be caused by nature, such as the earthquakes that have struck Turkey and India in recent years, or by humans, such as the recent civil wars in Somalia, Rwanda, and the Balkans.

One natural catastrophe studied by psychologists was the 1980 eruption of the Mount St. Helens volcano, which spewed a heavy covering of ash over a large area of Washington State (Adams & Adams, 1984). Because the Mount St. Helens ash fall was predictable, researchers could compare people's predisaster and postdisaster functioning. In the small agricultural town of Othello, for example, emergency room visits, court cases, crisis hotline calls, and mental health appointments significantly increased for months after the eruption (Figure 11.12).

A man-made (and seldom woman-made) stress of catastrophic proportions, practiced by dozens of countries, is torture (Basoglu, 1997). In any given year, over 150

Making Connections

Catastrophes, such as the war in Bosnia, sometimes lead to post-traumatic stress disorder (PTSD). PTSD includes symptoms such as nightmares, flashbacks to the traumatic event, depression, and anxiety. Most severe life events, such as losses, actually do not elicit PTSD. The major exception is rape, which leads to PTSD 80 percent of the time (Chapter 15).

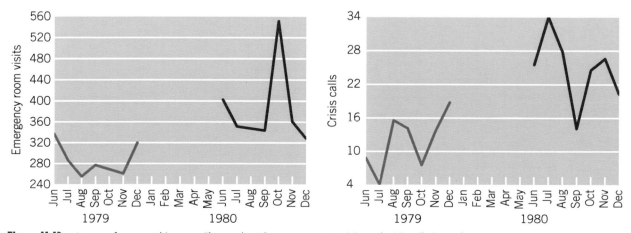

Figure 11.12 Impact of catastrophic stress. The number of emergency room visits and crisis calls jumped dramatically after the Mount St. Helens eruption, demonstrating the powerful effects of catastrophic stress. *Source:* Adams & Adams, 1984, p. 257.

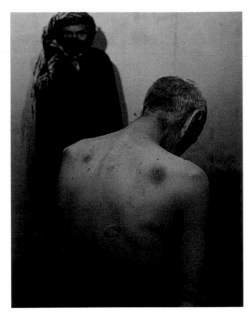

A Kurdish man tortured by the Iraqis.

*It's not the large things that
send a man to the
madhouse....
no, it's the continuing series
of small tragedies
that send a man to the
madhouse...
not the death of his love
but a shoelace that snaps
with no time left....*

C. BUKOWSKI,
"The Shoelace," 1980

countries in the world practice torture, and between 5 and 35 percent of the world's 14 million refugees have been subjected to at least one episode of torture. The most common psychological effects include anxiety and depression, social withdrawal, problems with memory and attention, sexual dysfunction, nightmares, insomnia, and personality changes. A study of torture victims in Turkey found that years later nearly half the survivors continued to suffer from nightmares and other symptoms of post-traumatic stress (Basoglu et al., 1994). The average subject was tortured 291 times over four years in captivity, with forms of torture including beating, electric shock, prevention of urination or defecation, rape, and twisting of the testicles.

Daily Hassles

Although the concept of stressors tends to bring to mind major events such as death, unemployment, and catastrophes, more mundane events can be important as well and are often central to the subjective experience of stress (Hahn & Smith, 1999). **Daily hassles** are *"the irritating, frustrating, distressing demands that to some degree characterize everyday transactions with the environment"* (Kanner et al., 1981, p. 3). Daily hassles range from interpersonal conflicts to commuting during rush hour. The most common daily hassles include concerns about weight, ill health of a family member, rising prices of common goods, home maintenance, too many things to do, and misplacing or losing things (Kanner et al., 1981).

◆ INTERIM SUMMARY

Events that often lead to stress are called **stressors**. Life events are stressors that require change and adaptation. Perceived stress refers to the extent to which people consider the experiences they have undergone stressful. **Acculturative stress** refers to the stress people experience in trying to adapt to a new culture. **Catastrophes** are stressors of massive proportions, including both natural and human-made disasters. **Daily hassles** are minor annoyances of everyday life that contribute to stress.

Stress and Health

Stressful events obviously can have a substantial impact on psychological well-being. They can also affect other psychological functions, such as memory. Anyone who has ever been in a frightening car accident, suddenly lost a loved one, or even "pulled an all-nighter" studying for a final exam knows that stress can impair the ability to focus and commit information to memory. Researchers are now beginning to unravel the reasons stressful events can affect memory.

As we saw in Chapter 6, the prefrontal cortex plays a particularly important role in working memory (e.g., momentarily holding in mind a phone number), and the hippocampus is involved in long-term memory (e.g., remembering the number over several weeks or years). Stress interferes with the functioning of both of these structures (Arnsten, 1998; McEwan, 1999). In fact, chronic stress leads to permanent cell death and a reduction in the size of the hippocampus (Bremner, 1999).

Thus, stress can alter the structure and function of the brain. It can also have a substantial effect on *physical* health and mortality (Kemeny & Laudenslager, 1999; O'Leary, 1997; Watkins & Maier, 2000). People under stress often suffer from headaches, depression, and other health problems such as influenza, sore throat, and backache (Cohen et al., 1991; DeLongis et al., 1988). Several studies have linked stress to vulnerability to cancer and have found that psychotherapy aimed at realistically but optimistically facing the cancer and maximizing social support may increase life expectancy in some cancer patients (Jacobs & Charles, 1980; Levenson & Bemis, 1991; Spiegel, 1999; Spiegel & Kato, 1996).

How does stress affect health? Stress can have a *direct* effect by decreasing the body's capacity to fight illness. It can also affect health *indirectly* by instigating behav-

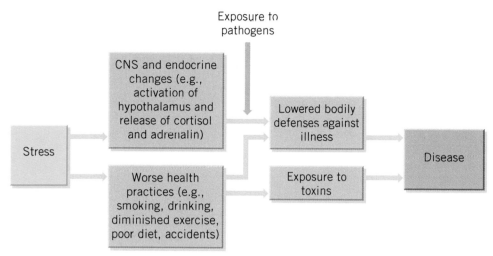

Figure 11.13 Pathways linking stress to infectious diseases. Stress can influence the onset of infectious disease in a number of ways. It can lead to CNS (central nervous system) and endocrine responses that diminish immune system functioning, leaving the person vulnerable to infection and illness from random exposure to pathogens such as airborne viruses. Alternatively, stress can lead to nonrandom exposure to toxins through poor health practices such as smoking. *Source:* Adapted from Cohen & Williamson, 1991, p. 8.

iors that weaken the body's defenses or lead to exposure to *pathogens*, toxic agents that can produce physical illness (Figure 11.13). People under stress tend to drink more alcohol, smoke more, sleep less, and exercise less than their peers (Cohen & Williamson, 1991; O'Leary, 1992).

Other variables can increase or decrease the impact of stress on health. Stress is more likely to affect people's health, for example, if they do not have adequate social support (Baron et al., 1990; Cohen & Williamson, 1991). Exercise can also reduce the impact of stress on health. One study compared the number of visits to the health clinic of college students who were either high or low in physical fitness (Brown, 1991). Physically fit participants made fewer visits even when reporting many negative life events. Participants who were less physically fit tended to become ill when stressed (Figure 11.14).

Stress and the Immune System

The **immune system** is *the body's "surveillance and security" system, which detects and eliminates disease-causing agents in the body such as bacteria and viruses.* Three important types of cells in the immune system are *B cells, T cells,* and *natural killer cells.*

B cells produce **antibodies**, *protein molecules that attach themselves to foreign invaders and mark them for destruction.* Some T cells search out and directly destroy invaders, while others (T-helper cells) stimulate immune functioning. T-helper cells are the primary target of HIV, the virus that causes AIDS. Natural killer cells fight viruses and tumors (Weisse, 1992). Both acute and chronic stress can affect the efficiency and availability of cells in the immune system and hence the body's capacity to fight off disease (O'Leary et al., 1997).

When a group of people are exposed to an infectious disease, such as respiratory illness, only some of them actually become sick. Consequently, one way to explore the effects of stress on the immune system is to see whether people under stress are more likely to suffer from infectious diseases. The evidence suggests that they are.

For example, one study (Jemmott et al., 1983) investigated the relationship between academic pressure and immunologic functioning (specifically, the secretion of an antibody called immunoglobulin A, or IgA). During periods of the academic calendar rated by both the researchers and participants as most stressful, the secretion rate of IgA was lower; that is, the immune response was reduced.

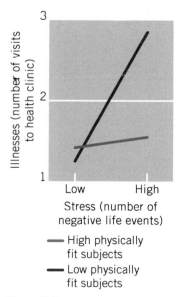

Figure 11.14 Interaction between stress and physical fitness. Students who were physically fit did not become sick when confronted with stress. Less fit participants, however, became ill when confronted with negative life events. *Source:* Brown, 1991, p. 559.

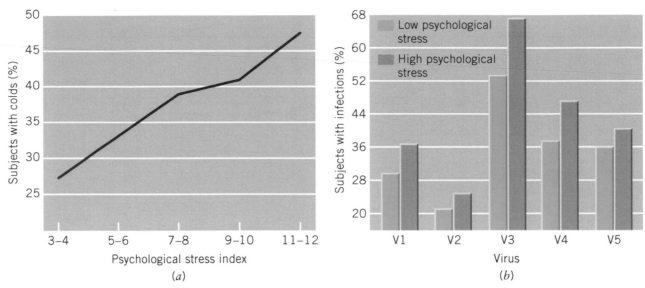

Figure 11.15　The relation between stress and illness following viral exposure. Part (*a*) shows the relation between the amount of self-reported psychological stress and the percentage of participants judged by a physician to have a clinical cold after exposure to a virus. As can be seen, the more stress, the more colds. Part (*b*) presents data from a biological test of participants' blood for presence of infection. For each of five viruses, participants reporting higher stress showed higher rates of infection. *Source:* Cohen et al., 1991, pp. 609–610.

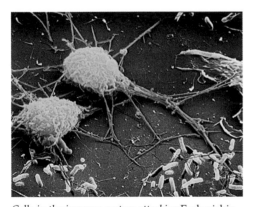

Cells in the immune system attacking Escherichia coli *bacteria.*

Perhaps the most conclusive study yet of the influence of stress on both immune functioning and illness assessed 394 healthy participants for degree of life stress and then administered nasal drops containing one of five different viruses (Cohen et al., 1991). Participants reporting higher stress showed greater rates of infection for all five viruses (Figure 11.15).

Stress and Health-Seeking Behavior

Stress can influence health in a more subtle way by influencing the way the person interprets bodily symptoms (Cameron et al., 1998; Leventhal & Leventhal, 1993). When symptoms are unambiguous and ominous, such as severe stomach pain accompanied by bloody stools, people tend to seek help immediately. Many symptoms, however, are ambiguous, and this ambiguity can lead to several alternative responses.

For example, a middle-aged man might ignore chest pains or take a "wait-and-see attitude" if they go away. This strategy may represent an effort to cope with the emotion he would likely feel (fear) if he took the symptom seriously. By deciding that "it's probably nothing," he may be trading short-term reassurance for long-term danger. People's appraisals of health risk also reflect their judgments about the context of the symptom, as when a person who experiences chest pain in the weeks following a job loss decides that "it's just stress."

At other times, and for other people, stress can have precisely the opposite effect, leading them to seek medical care for one minor complaint after another, fearing that each new symptom could be a sign of serious disease. In fact, people who are depressed, anxious, or recently stressed by experiences such as job loss tend not only to *have* more physical illnesses but also to *interpret* their illnesses more seriously and to experience the pain as greater (Leventhal & Leventhal, 1993). Thus, stress can lead people either to take their health too seriously or not to take it seriously enough.

Stress, Health, and Personality

Whether a person under stress remains healthy or becomes ill also depends on the person's enduring personality traits (O'Brien & DeLongis, 1996; Suls et al., 1996). Personality can influence stress and health through the motives people pursue, the way they tend to appraise circumstances (for example, easily becoming angry or sad), or the way they tend to cope with stress (such as through drinking, cigarette smoking, avoiding doctors, or suppressing emotions).

For example, in one study, participants kept a daily diary of their moods and the events of the day (Suls et al., 1998). The higher participants were in neuroticism—the tendency to experience negative emotions such as depression or anxiety (Chapter 12)—the more daily problems they reported, the more reactive they were to stressors, and the more they were distressed by bad things that happened to them.

A recent study powerfully demonstrates the impact of personality on both stress and health (Caspi, 2000). A team of investigators has been following a sample of about a thousand people born in Dunedin, New Zealand, during one year in the early 1970s. They have assessed the group repeatedly, beginning at age 3. At age 18, they assessed aspects of their personality. Then, three years later, they assessed four high-risk behaviors associated with stress and health: alcohol dependence, violent crime, unprotected sex with multiple partners, and dangerous driving habits.

Personality at age 18 was a powerful predictor of high-risk behaviors three years later: Those who tended to engage in all four behaviors were lower on traditionalism, concern about avoiding danger, ability to regulate impulses, and social closeness. They were also higher on aggression. Perhaps more striking, risk behaviors at age 21 were predictable from the initial assessment of participants at age 3. Those who were classified in preschool as undercontrolled—that is, impulsive, poorly behaved, and aggressive—were more likely to engage in all four high-risk behaviors than their better controlled (and particularly overcontrolled) peers.

Genetic factors affect stress as well, in two ways: by influencing the probability a person will place herself in stressful situations and by influencing her vulnerability to the stressors she encounters (Kendler, 1995). For example, studies comparing monozygotic and dizygotic twins have found that the likelihood of being robbed, assaulted, or confronted with financial difficulties is moderately heritable, with heritability estimated between 30 and 40 percent! The correlation between monozygotic (identical) twins' reports of financial difficulties is .44, whereas for dizygotic (fraternal) twins the correlation is only .12. As we will see (Chapter 12), the tendency to take risks is itself heritable, in large part because people who are fearful take fewer risks and those who are more pleasure-driven take more. Once a person experiences a stressful event, the tendency to experience negative affect, which is also heritable, can then amplify the individual's distress.

Type A Behavior Pattern and Hostility   One of the most thoroughly researched links between personality and health, which was first observed by two cardiologists and later corroborated by psychological research, is between heart disease and the **Type A behavior pattern**, *a personality style characterized by impatience, ambition, competitiveness, hostility, and a "hard-driving" approach to life* (Friedman & Rosenman, 1959). Type B individuals, on the other hand, are more relaxed, easy-going, and less easily angered.

One psychologist illustrated the differences between Type A and Type B behavior in describing a fishing trip he took with a colleague (Schwartz, 1987, p. 136):

> I baited the hook and dropped the line over in a relaxed fashion, watched the gulls, and swayed with the swells. But what really struck [my colleague] was my talking to the fish when they bit the hook: "That's nice" or "Take your time, I'm in no rush."

In contrast to his own Type B pattern, a man fishing in a boat nearby exhibited Type A behavior (p. 136):

> He was fishing with two poles, racing back and forth between them, and tangling his lines while cursing the fish that happened to be on the line beyond his reach.

Central Questions

■ When does thinking about our physical or psychological problems promote adaptation?

■ When does thinking about our problems turn into a problem itself—as when people ruminate or worry excessively?

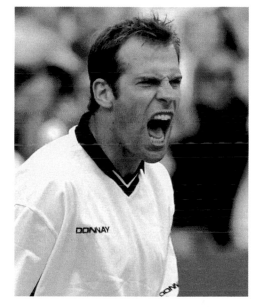

Type A and Type B behavior on the tennis court.

If the fish eluded him while others caught them, he would pull up the anchor in frustration, start the engine with a roar, and race to another part of the bay.

A comparison of bus drivers in North America and India suggests that these behavioral patterns occur cross-culturally, at least in some form (Evans et al., 1987). In both samples, Type A bus drivers reported greater job stress and had more accidents and absences per month than Type B drivers. In addition, in India, Type A bus drivers braked, blew their horns, and passed more frequently than Type B drivers.

More recent research suggests that subcomponents of the Type A pattern may be differentially related to heart disease (Dembroski & Costa, 1987; Siegman, 1994). In particular, hostility—or the combination of defensiveness, negative affect, and suppressed hostility—has been implicated in narrowing of the arteries leading to the heart. Angry people also tend to die slightly younger (Miller et al., 1996).

Optimism/Pessimism   Another personality dimension related to immune functioning and health is optimism/pessimism (Carver, 1998; Peterson, 1995). One study found that coronary artery bypass patients who reported higher levels of optimism on a questionnaire recovered more quickly and returned to normal life more easily than pessimistic participants (Scheier et al., 1989). Another found that college students with a pessimistic explanatory style (a tendency to explain bad events in negative, self-blaming ways; see Chapter 5) experienced more days of illness and visited physicians more frequently than other students (Peterson, 1988).

Even more striking results emerged in a 35-year study of 99 graduates of Harvard University. Participants with a pessimistic explanatory style at age 25 were more likely to be in poor health or dead at ages 45 to 50—even after controlling statistically for physical and mental health at age 25 (Peterson et al., 1988). People who are pessimistic do not take as good care of themselves, do not cope as well, and have poorer immune functioning, all of which lead to greater illness (Kamen & Seligman, 1987; Lin & Peterson, 1990).

◆ INTERIM SUMMARY

Stress can affect physical health in two ways: directly, by weakening the **immune system** (the system of cells that detects and destroys disease-causing agents), and indirectly, by leading to behaviors that weaken the body's defenses or lead to exposure to pathogens (toxic agents). Personality factors also affect stress levels and health, such as the tendency to experience negative affect (neuroticism), hostility and suppressed hostility, and pessimism.

◆ Coping

That people get sick or experience unpleasant emotions in response to stress should come as no surprise. What may seem more surprising is that most people who experience life crises remain healthy (Moos & Schaefer, 1986). This resiliency in the face of stress reflects *the ways people deal with stressful situations*, called ways of **coping** (or **coping mechanisms**).

Coping Mechanisms

Researchers often distinguish two or three basic types of coping strategies (Folkman & Lazarus, 1980; Folkman & Moskowitz, 2000; Moos & Billings, 1982). Strategies aimed at changing the situation producing the stress are called *problem focused*, because they try to deal with the stressor itself. Two other types of strategy—efforts to alter thoughts *about* the situation, and efforts to alter the unpleasant emotional consequences of

Apply & Discuss

■ Why do people engage in behaviors such as smoking and excessive drinking that increase the negative impact of stress on their health?

■ Why do people often fail to act in ways that promote health, such as exercising and getting prompt medical attention?

stress—are called *emotion focused*. Their aim is to regulate the emotions generated by a stressful experience. Thus, if a person cannot change a stressful situation directly, she can try to change her perception of it or the emotions it produces. Alcohol and drug use are common mechanisms for escaping emotional distress (Kushner et al., 2000).

Efforts to cope by changing the situation typically involve problem solving (Chapter 7). The individual may try to remove the stressor, plan ways of resolving the situation, seek advice or assistance from others to change the situation, or try to avoid the stressor altogether by planning ahead (Aspinwall & Taylor, 1997; Carver et al., 1989). Children whose mothers have a problem-focused coping style tend to be better adjusted and more socially skilled than their peers (Eisenberg et al., 1996).

A number of studies suggest that religious faith often helps people cope with stressful events, such as contracting a terminal disease or losing a child. Their beliefs allow them to ascribe meaning to the event or strengthen their sense of closeness to the divine (Pargament & Park, 1995). For example, one study found that people who used their religion to cope with a major life stress—a kidney transplant—tended to have better outcomes three and 12 months later, as did their significant others if they relied on their faith (Tix & Frazier, 1998).

Central Questions

■ To what extent is coping related to intelligence? Does general problem-solving ability make people better able to cope with social and emotional sources of stress?

The Impact of Culture on Coping Styles — A Global Vista

The way people respond to stress, as well as the situations they consider stressful, are in part culturally patterned. Relative to children in less technologically developed societies, such as Mexico, children in countries such as the United States and Canada tend to take a more active coping approach, directed at removing obstacles toward their goals (e.g., Diaz-Guerrero, 1979). This is not surprising in light of data showing that the emphasis on mastering the environment, characteristic of highly technologically developed societies, is relatively new in human history. Most cultures in human history have believed that humans should adjust to nature, not the other way around (Kluckhohn & Strodtbeck, 1961).

These findings suggest possible limits to Western theories and research linking an active coping style (characterized by a sense of mastery, self-efficacy, and control) to mental and physical health. In capitalist societies, which are based on entrepreneurship and personal initiative, an active coping style and a strong belief in one's own ability are highly adaptive traits. In societies organized around family, community, or tribal ties, such traits may be unrelated to mental and physical health. Coping is always relative to its cultural context, and coping strategies considered useful in one society (such as wailing at a funeral) may engender disapproval, and hence additional stress, in another.

Low-Effort Syndrome
Understanding patterns of culture and coping may also lead to a better understanding of dilemmas facing African-American and other minority adolescents in multicultural societies. For years, educators, social scientists, and policymakers have wrestled with the large gap between the educational performance of whites and some minority groups in the United States, such as African- and Latino-Americans, and the absence of such a gap for other immigrant groups, such as Arabs, Chinese, and West Indians.

John Ogbu (1991) argues that, throughout the world, minority groups who experience a ceiling on their economic prospects over several generations because of job discrimination develop a low-effort syndrome not seen in new immigrants who voluntarily move to a culture in search of a better life. **Low-effort syndrome**—*the tendency to exert minimal effort to escape stressful social and economic circumstances*—is an adaptive coping strategy when social barriers make effort and achievement fruitless and when hard work and academic success would only increase frustration and anger. The school performance of Koreans in Japan, who have been an underclass there for many years, is very poor, whereas Korean immigrants to North America tend to excel.

Making Connections

Efforts at achievement can sometimes lead to anxiety in even the most accomplished African-American students because of associations they, like their white peers, have formed over years between skin color and success. Simply filling out information on race or ethnicity before taking a standardized test like the SAT can prime negative associations, translating directly into lower test scores (Chapter 17).

Low-effort syndrome is an example of a coping strategy that solves one problem (minimizing frustration in the face of racism and barriers to success) but creates another, particularly if opportunities and social attitudes toward race change faster than coping styles developed over several generations. Because African-Americans for years faced impassable barriers to upward mobility, scholastic achievement became defined in many black communities as "white" behavior. Thus, for many black adolescents today the fear of being ridiculed for "acting white," together with a subcultural ambivalence toward achievement, inhibits scholastic achievement.

John Henryism

Low-effort syndrome among people who historically faced external limits on what they could hope to achieve can be understood as an adaptation to a social and political system that eliminated rewards for effort. Recent research suggests another way in which paradoxically low effort among African-Americans for years made adaptive sense: Those who tried harder died earlier.

A legend is told (and a song sung) of a "steel-drivin' man" named John Henry, a black man known among railroad workers in the late-nineteenth century for his tremendous strength and endurance. As the legend goes, in a famous steel-driving contest, after an extraordinary battle of man versus machine, Henry beat a mechanical steam drill with mighty blows from his nine-pound hammer. Moments later, however, he died from exhaustion (Sherman, 1994).

This may not have been an isolated incident. Physicians have been puzzled for years by the increased rate of high blood pressure in African-Americans, which is associated with greater rates of stroke. Genetics and food preferences may explain some of the difference between blacks and whites, but researchers have recently identified a coping style among some African-Americans that may also play a role, which researchers have called John Henryism (Sherman, 1994; Wright et al., 1996).

John Henryism is *the tendency among members of minority groups to work hard and cope actively despite difficult circumstances*. Individuals with this coping style show a single-minded determination to succeed despite the odds. Several studies show that individuals high in John Henryism are vulnerable to high blood pressure, particularly when they are black, and particularly when they are of low socioeconomic status. In some sense, low-effort syndrome may actually have been an adaptive solution to a system that psychologically put a noose around the neck of those who tried to better themselves. To what extent the physiological consequences of John Henryism will change as opportunities continue to expand for African-Americans is as yet unknown.

◆ INTERIM SUMMARY

Coping mechanisms are the ways people deal with stressful events. *Problem-focused coping* involves changing the situation. *Emotion-focused coping* aims to regulate the emotion generated by a stressful situation. The ways people respond to stress, as well as the situations they consider stressful, are in part culturally patterned. Members of minority groups who, for generations, experience a ceiling on their economic prospects because of discrimination sometimes develop a **low-effort syndrome** in which they seemingly stop making the kinds of active efforts that might alleviate some of their hardships. In African-Americans, **John Henryism**—the tendency to work hard and cope actively despite difficult circumstances—is associated with high blood pressure.

Social Support

An important resource for coping with stress is **social support**, *the presence of others in whom one can confide and from whom one can expect help and concern* (Strobe & Strobe, 1996). Social support is as important for maintaining physical as well as mental health (Salovey et al., 1998). A high level of social support is associated with protection against a range of illnesses, from hypertension and herpes to cancer and heart disease (Cohen & Herbert, 1996; Sarason et al., 1997; Spiegel & Kato, 1996).

The benefits of social support are apparent in humans as well as other social animals. In rhesus monkeys, immune functioning is suppressed when adult monkeys are separated from their social group but alleviated if they are given a companion (Gust et al., 1994; Laudenslager & Boccia, 1996). In humans, the number of social relationships a person has, and the extent to which the individual feels close to other people, is a powerful predictor of mortality (House et al., 1988a; J. Johnson et al., 1996). In fact, the evidence supporting the link between social relationships and health is as strong as the data linking smoking and ill health.

Two hypotheses have been advanced to explain the beneficial effects of social support, both of which have received empirical support (Cohen & Wills, 1985; Taylor, 1991). The *buffering hypothesis* proposes that social support is a buffer or protective factor against the harmful effects of stress during high-stress periods. In a classic study, urban women who experienced significant life stress were much less likely to become depressed if they had an intimate, confiding relationship with a boyfriend or husband (Brown & Harris, 1978).

Social support protects against stress and illness in humans and other animals.

An alternative hypothesis views social support as a continuously positive force that makes the person less susceptible to stress in the first place. In this view, people with supportive relationships are less likely to make a primary appraisal of situations as stressful, and they are more likely to perceive themselves as able to cope. For example, taking a new job is much more threatening to a person who has no one in whom to confide and no one to tell her, "Don't worry, you'll do well at it." Another important aspect of social support is the opportunity for emotional disclosure, which, as we have seen, strengthens the immune system.

The flipside of social support—loneliness—is a major source of stress in humans. Loneliness takes a physiological as well as a psychological toll, leading both to increased autonomic arousal during stressful situations and slower recovery from negative emotional states (Cacioppo et al., 2000).

The relationship between social support and stress is not, however, simple or uniform. For example, stress can erode social support, leading to a vicious cycle, particularly if the person under stress responds with anger or helplessness (Lane & Hobfoll, 1992). Severely stressful life events, such as getting cancer, can also overwhelm significant others, who may withdraw because they, too, feel helpless and distressed (Bolger et al., 1996).

Further high-conflict or unsupportive relationships can actually have detrimental effects on health and psychological well-being (e.g., Major et al., 1997).

◆ **INTERIM SUMMARY**

Social support refers to the presence of others in whom a person can confide and from whom the individual can expect help and concern. In humans and other primates, lack of social support predicts disease and mortality. The *buffering hypothesis* proposes that social support protects people against the harmful effects of acute stress. An alternative hypothesis suggests that social support is a continuously positive force that makes the person less susceptible to stress. Social support is not, however, uniformly beneficial. Bad relationships do not promote health, and significant others often have difficulty themselves being supportive at times of crisis.

◆ Central Questions: Thinking about Feeling

We began with two central questions. The first was about the adaptive function of emotion: When do emotions guide behavior in adaptive directions, and when do they lead us astray? The answer is not simple. Like other psychological functions, nature has endowed us with emotional responses "designed" to lead us to approach and avoid people, objects, and situations in ways that foster survival and reproduction. We tend to become happy when our goals are met, to be scared when we are in danger, to be anxious when danger could be around the corner, and to feel guilty when we have hurt others who matter to us or on whose good graces we rely.

Nothing guarantees, however, that we will draw the "right" emotional lessons from our experiences. People who have been rejected by someone they love may draw the conclusion, implicitly or explicitly, that they should avoid loving again, rather than that they should choose more wisely or maintain a realistic optimism, and hence deprive themselves of one of the greatest pleasures life affords. *In general*, emotions provide a compass for guiding our behavior, but sometimes we need to look at other psychological "instruments" to chart a more adaptive course.

The second question concerned the relation between cognition and emotion, a topic we have confronted before (Chapter 7). Cognition is central to virtually every aspect of emotion: Cognitive appraisals produce emotions and experiences of stress; cognitive interpretations are part of the subjective experience of emotion (particularly complex emotions, such as guilt); and cognitive processes can be essential for regulating stressful and painful experiences. At the same time, moods and emotions can influence cognition, which makes beliefs as fallible as emotions as guides for behavior. People who are depressed tend to see the glass as half empty and may have difficulty solving problems in ways that allow them to fill it the rest of the way. And as we have seen, people who cannot set aside their "reason" and follow their "gut" or who block off their access to emotion often suffer physical and psychological consequences.

In sum, we have both cognitions and emotions for a reason. Each serves a function that the other cannot replace. Perhaps Plato was right when he said that the key to "justice of the soul"—or what today we would call mental health—is a good balance between what we want and fear and what we think and know.

Summary

Emotion

1. **Emotion**, or **affect**, is an evaluative response (a positive or negative feeling state) that typically includes subjective experience, physiological arousal, and behavioral expression.

2. The **James–Lange theory** asserts that the subjective experience of emotion results from bodily experience induced by an emotion-eliciting stimulus. According to this theory, we do not run because we are afraid; we become afraid because we run (and our hearts pound). In contrast, the **Cannon–Bard** theory proposes that emotion-inducing stimuli simultaneously elicit both emotional experience and bodily responses. Although both theories have their strengths and limitations, recent research suggests that different emotions are, as James believed, associated with distinct, innate patterns of autonomic nervous system arousal.

3. **Emotional expression** refers to facial and other outward indications of emotion, such as body language and tone of voice. Many aspects of emotional expression, particularly facial expression, are innate and cross-culturally universal. Culturally variable patterns of regulating and displaying emotion are called **display rules**.

4. Psychologists have attempted to produce a list of basic emotions, emotions common to the human species from which all other emotions and emotional blends can be derived. Anger, fear, happiness, sadness, and disgust are listed by all theorists as basic. An even more fundamental distinction is between **positive affect** and **negative affect**.

5. Emotions are controlled by neural pathways distributed throughout the nervous system. The hypothalamus activates sympathetic and endocrine responses related to emotion. The limbic system, and particularly the amygdala, is part of an emotional circuit that includes the hypothalamus. The cortex plays several roles with respect to emotion, particularly in the appraisal of events.

6. The behaviorist perspective on emotion points to approach and avoidance systems associated with positive and negative affect, respectively. According to the psychodynamic perspective, people can be unconscious of their own emotional reactions, which can nonetheless influence thought, behavior, and health.

7. From a cognitive perspective, the way people respond emotionally depends on the **attributions** they make—that is, their infer-

ences about causes of the emotion and their own bodily sensations. According to the **Schachter–Singer theory**, emotion involves two factors: physiological arousal and cognitive interpretation of the arousal. Emotion and **mood** (relatively extended emotional states that, unlike emotions, typically do not disrupt ongoing activities) have an impact on encoding, retrieval, judgment, and decision making.

8. The evolutionary perspective on emotion derives from Charles Darwin's view that emotions serve an adaptive purpose. Emotion has both communicative and motivational functions.

Stress

9. **Stress** refers to a challenge to a person's capacity to adapt to inner and outer demands, which may be physiologically arousing and emotionally taxing and call for cognitive and behavioral responses. Stress is a psychobiological process that entails a transaction between a person and her environment. Selye proposed that the body responds to stressful conditions with a **general adaptation syndrome** consisting of three stages: alarm, resistance, and exhaustion.

10. From a psychological standpoint, stress entails a person's perception that demands of the environment tax or exceed his available psychosocial resources. Stress, in this view, depends on the meaning of an event to the individual. Lazarus's model identifies two stages in the process of stress and coping: **primary appraisal**, in which the person decides whether the situation is benign, stressful, or irrelevant, and **secondary appraisal**, in which the person evaluates the options and decides how to respond.

11. Events that often lead to stress are called **stressors**. Stressors include life events, catastrophes, and daily hassles.

12. Stress has a considerable impact on health and mortality, particularly through its effects on the **immune system**. Whether a person under stress remains healthy or becomes ill also depends in part on the person's enduring personality dispositions. **Type A behavior pattern**, and particularly its hostility component, has been linked to heart disease. Neuroticism (the tendency to experience negative affective states) and optimism/pessimism are other personality traits linked to stress and health.

Coping

13. The ways people deal with stressful situations are known as strategies for **coping**; these **coping mechanisms** are in part culturally patterned. People cope by trying to change the situation directly, changing their perception of it, or changing the emotions it elicits.

14. A major resource for coping with stress is **social support**, which is related to health and mortality.

Key Terms

acculturative stress 391
affect 368
antibodies 393
attributions 383
basic emotions 376
Cannon–Bard theory 370
catastrophes 391
coping 396
coping mechanisms 396
daily hassles 392
display rules 375
emotion 368
emotional expression 372
emotional forecasting 368
emotion regulation 381
immune system 393
James–Lange theory 369
John Henryism 398
low-effort syndrome 397
moods 381
negative affect 376
positive affect 376
primary appraisal 389
Schachter–Singer theory 383
secondary appraisal 389
social support 398
stress 388
stressors 389
Type A behavior pattern 395

Chapter 17

Attitudes and Social Cognition

Randy Stevens, *They're Here!*, 1995.

Whe people think of prejudice, they often think of apartheid in South Africa or Ku Klux Klan rallies. We think of racial and ethnic stereotypes as beliefs people overtly hold or express about other people based on arbitrary qualities such as the color of their skin. But recent research suggests that negative stereotypes can get *under* the skin in some subtle but powerful ways.

In a remarkable series of studies, Claude Steele (1997; Steele & Aronson, 1995) has demonstrated how racial stereotypes can affect even the people who are the targets of them. In one experiment, Steele and his colleagues presented black and white Stanford undergraduates—an elite group selected for their high achievement, who should have few doubts about their intellectual abilities—with difficult verbal items from the Scholastic Assessment Test (SAT) (Steele & Aronson, 1995). Black and

white students were matched in SAT scores, so that both groups were of similar intellectual ability. In one condition, students were told that the test did not measure anything significant about them. In the other condition, they were told that it measured their intellect.

Black and white students in the first condition performed equally well, as one would expect, since they had similar SAT scores before entering college. In the second condition, however, the performance of black students dropped substantially.

What happened? In the United States, blacks and whites are both exposed to negative stereotypes about the intellectual abilities of blacks. These stereotypes become part of their associative networks—their implicit understanding of race—even if they do not explicitly believe them. So when an African-American student takes a test believed to be diagnostic of his ability, these associations become active. Particularly if scholastic success is important to the student, stereotype activation will generate performance anxiety, which can in turn lead to diminished performance.

Just how much do these processes operate in real life? In a second experiment, Steele and his colleagues once again had black and white Stanford students answer difficult SAT items. The study had two conditions, with a seemingly minor difference between them: In the demographic questionnaire students filled out before taking the test, *race* was included in one condition but not the other. The results are depicted in Figure 17.1: Priming African-American students' racial associations simply by asking them to fill in their race led to a dramatic decline in their performance.

Steele suggests that the impact of processes of this sort are quite profound and likely extend to groups as diverse as the Maori minority in New Zealand and the

West Indian minority in Britain. They are also not limited to race: Steele and his colleagues have documented that activation of negative stereotypes about women's mathematical abilities similarly leads to declines in their performance on math tests. Over time, repeatedly feeling anxious or "choking" on tests can cause some students to distance themselves from school and stop trying, leading to further declines in performance. Based on his findings, Steele has begun testing a new intervention approach aimed at breaking this downward spiral, and initial results have been very promising.

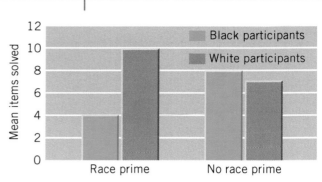

Figure 17.1   Performance on a difficult verbal test as a function of whether race was primed. *Source:* Steele, 1997, p. 521.

Steele's research is a classic example of **social psychology**, *which examines the influence of social processes on the way people think, feel, and behave* (Allport, 1968). Because almost everything people do is social, the subject matter is enormous and varied. In this chapter we focus on interpersonal thinking. We begin with a discussion of attitudes and how they change. This topic is of central concern to advertisers, who try to shape attitudes toward their products, as well as to politicians, who want to shape—and follow—public opinion. Next we examine the processes by which people make sense of each other, from the first impressions they form to enduring beliefs, including stereotypes. We conclude by considering the way people think about one of the major actors in their social worlds: themselves.

Throughout, we address one central question: To what extent do the principles of thought and memory discovered by cognitive scientists apply to *interpersonal* thought and memory? In other words, when we think about ourselves and others, do we use the same mechanisms as when we learn lists of words or theories of how chemicals combine to form molecules? Or are social thought and memory qualitatively different?

Central Questions

■ In what ways do social thought and memory differ from nonsocial cognition?

◆ Attitudes

Attitudes are probably the most fundamental concept in social psychology because they are involved in all social behavior, from political decisions to stereotyping and prejudice (Allport, 1935).

The Nature of Attitudes

An **attitude** is *an association between an act or object and an evaluation* (Eagly & Chaiken, 1992; Fazio, 1986). To put it another way, an attitude—whether toward Pepsi, Reebok, or Yassir Arafat—is a tendency to evaluate a person, concept, or group positively or negatively (Eagly & Chaiken, 1998). To say that alcohol (an attitude object) is a dangerous drug (evaluation) is to express an attitude. Some psychologists distinguish three components of an attitude: a *cognitive component* or belief (alcohol contributes to social problems such as traffic fatalities and child abuse); an emotional or *evaluative component* (alcohol is bad); and a *behavioral disposition* (alcohol should be avoided).

At first glance, attitudes seem relatively straightforward—a person is either for abortion or against it, favorable or unfavorable toward affirmative action, or more positive toward Nike than Reebok or vice versa. Recently, however, researchers have discovered a number of ways attitudes vary that make them far more complex (see Eagly & Chaiken, 1998).

Attitude Strength

One dimension on which attitudes vary is their strength. Personally, I like the Boston Red Sox, but as someone who is only minimally interested in baseball, my feelings toward the team are relatively weak. If they lose to the Yankees, I do not lose much sleep. Further, my beliefs about the team—the cognitive components of my attitude toward the Red Sox—also tend to sway in the wind. If my barber tells me they are going to be great next year, I am perfectly happy to believe him and will likely continue believing him until someone else informs me otherwise.

Attitude strength refers to *the durability and impact of an attitude* (Bassili & Krosnick, 2000; Petty & Krosnick, 1994). An attitude is durable if it tends to persist over time and is resistant to change. An attitude has impact if it affects behavior and influences the way the person thinks and feels. Using this definition, my attitude toward the Red Sox is very weak: It is highly unstable and has minimal impact on what I do on a Saturday afternoon or how I feel if the team loses. It also has little effect on whether I think an umpire made the right call at the plate.

Attitude Accessibility

Although attitudes may seem like stable "things" housed in a mental warehouse and hauled out of storage when someone asks to see them (as in political opinion polls), like all thoughts and memories, attitudes are constructed "on-line" at any given moment. Thus, the attitudes people report at any given time actually reflect a mixture of long-standing beliefs and feelings and current perceptions, thoughts, and emotional responses. A person who strongly believes that capital punishment is wrong may nevertheless construct the momentary attitude that a particular child molester deserves death after hearing the sordid details of the case. Or consider a person who strongly believes in free enterprise but also has strong feelings about protecting children. When asked about his attitudes toward regulating tobacco advertisements to minors, he may report very different attitudes if asked about the issue at a Chamber of Commerce meeting (a meeting of businesspeople) or a PTA meeting, simply because different values, feelings, and beliefs have been activated by the context. And when he reports the attitude, he is likely to believe that he has always held this attitude and have no idea how powerful situational forces were in determining his "current" belief (Bem & McConnell, 1970).

For an attitude (such as *free enterprise is good*) to have an impact on ongoing thought and behavior, it must be cognitively accessible, that is, readily accessed. **Attitude accessibility** refers to *the ease with which an attitude comes to mind* (Fazio, 1990, 1995). Highly accessible attitudes come to mind rapidly and automatically when primed by environmental events. For example, a person with positive attitudes toward women may have an immediate and positive initial reaction when the doctor at the clinic who comes out to examine her is female. The more accessible an attitude, the more likely it is to affect behavior.

Variation in accessibility makes sense from an adaptive (evolutionary) standpoint: The more frequently we encounter something, and the more its potential impact on our lives, the more quickly we should be able to react to it—and the more accessible our attitude toward it is likely to be. A downside of high accessibility, however, is its potential interference with our ability to detect changes in the attitude object (Fazio et al., 2000). A highly accessible attitude toward a politician may make a voter less likely to notice that the politician no longer votes the way he used to—and hence that the voter should reevaluate her attitude.

Implicit Attitudes

As with emotions, motives, and cognitions, social psychologists are increasingly recognizing the importance of distinguishing between explicit (conscious) attitudes and implicit attitudes—*associations between attitude objects and feelings about them that regulate thought and behavior unconsciously and automatically* (Greenwald & Banaji, 1995; Greenwald et al., 1998; Rudman et al., 1999). Someone who has just attended a lecture on alcohol-related fatalities is unlikely to stop at the bar on the way home because a conscious attitude is active. He may well, however, overindulge at a happy hour a few days later when his implicit attitudes toward alcohol—which reflect years of associations between drinking and enjoyment—become active. In fact, implicit attitudes of this sort play a more important role in predicting drug and alcohol use than people's conscious attitudes (Stacy, 1997).

Cognitive Complexity

The cognitive components of an attitude vary on a number of dimensions. For example, they can be relatively specific (a large tax cut right now would produce a budget deficit and hurt the economy) or general (tax cuts provide a strong stimulus for the economy in times of recession). An important dimension on which attitudes differ is their *cognitive complexity* (Bieri, 1966; Suedfeld & Granatstein, 1995). The beliefs of two people with equally positive attitudes toward a tax cut may have very different levels of complexity. One person might simply believe that "big government isn't the answer to our problems" and hence *always* favor tax cuts. Another might believe that large tax cuts foster investment and hence can stimulate a flagging economy. On a simple attitude rating of 1 to 5 (where 1 means the person is very unfavorable to a tax cut and 5 means very favorable), both people might nevertheless rate a 5.

Researchers have used some ingenious methods to assess the complexity of people's attitudes. For example, in one study, researchers read political speeches and coded them for the extent to which the thinking was complex (Tetlock, 1989). They found that people at both political extremes—far right and far left—tended to show less attitudinal complexity than people who were politically more moderate.

Attitudinal Ambivalence

Another dimension on which attitudes differ is the extent to which an attitude object is associated with conflicting feelings. For many years researchers measured attitudes by asking respondents to rate the extent to which they were for or against abortion, liked or disliked particular political candidates, and so forth. Periodically, however, attitude researchers have wondered whether this really captures the complexity of the *emotional* component of people's attitudes.

Researchers studying **attitudinal ambivalence**—*the extent to which a given attitude object is associated with conflicting evaluative responses*—argue that attitudes include two evaluative dimensions, positive and negative, that are relatively independent (Cacioppo & Gardner, 1999; Jonas et al., 1997; Priester & Petty, 1996). Each of these two components can be relatively weak or relatively strong. Low positive/low negative attitudes will have minimal impact on behavior because the person is indifferent (that is, does not care much either way) about the attitude object.

Weakly held attitudes of this sort are very different from highly ambivalent attitudes—high positive/high negative—but they often yield precisely the same (moderate) scores on bipolar attitude measures that assume that attitudes run from negative to positive. For example, one study compared people who were low on both positive and negative attitudes toward blood donation with those who were high on both. Those who were essentially indifferent were less willing to donate blood than those who were ambivalent, presumably because the latter were able to harness their social values (strong positive feelings) to overcome their squeamishness (strong negative feelings) (Gardner & Cacioppo, 1996; cited in Cacioppo et al., 1997).

Researchers have largely focused on positive and negative affect in attitudes, but it seems likely that attitudes also differ in the specific feelings associated with them. For a high-achieving African-American student, scholastic success may be associated not just with a mixture of positive and negative feelings but, more specifically, with a

Making Connections

Positive and negative affect are somewhat independent and rely on different neural circuits (Chapter 11). Thus, it is not surprising that a person could associate a single attitude object with both positive and negative feelings—such as mixed feelings toward an enticing sundae that could necessitate an extra trip to the gym.

combination of pride, happiness, anxiety, and shame (if the student's friends brand achievement as "white" behavior).

Coherence

A final dimension on which attitudes vary is **attitudinal coherence**—*the extent to which an attitude is internally consistent* (Eagly & Chaiken, 1998). Logically, the cognitive and emotional aspects of attitudes should be congruent because an emotional evaluation of an object should reflect a cognitive appraisal of its qualities. That is, we should like things we believe have positive consequences.

In fact, however, the beliefs and feelings comprising an attitude frequently develop separately and can change independently (see Petty & Cacioppo, 1981, 1986a; Edwards, 1991). A classic example occured in the U.S. presidential election in 2000. Many voters liked the policies of the Clinton administration, represented by Vice President Al Gore, but did not like Gore despite his policies. As political consultants well understand, the emotional component of a political attitude can be decisive in voting behavior and rests as much on implicit assessments of nonverbal gestures, likeability, and apparent sincerity as on the issues (Epstein, 1994).

◆ INTERIM SUMMARY

> An **attitude** is an association between an act or object and an evaluation. Attitudes can differ in a number of ways. **Attitude strength** refers to the durability and impact of an attitude on behavior. **Attitude accessibility** refers to the ease with which an attitude comes to mind. **Implicit attitudes** regulate thought and behavior unconsciously and automatically. Attitudes can also be either explicit or implicit. Attitudes vary in their degree of cognitive complexity as well as the extent to which the attitude object is associated with conflicting evaluative responses (**attitudinal ambivalence**). **Attitudinal coherence** refers to the extent to which an attitude (particularly its cognitive and evaluative components) is internally consistent.

Attitudes and Behavior

Logic would suggest that attitudes should predict behavior. For example, students' attitudes toward cheating should be closely related to how much they cheat. Once again, however, the empirical David is mightier than the logical Goliath: Broad attitudes predict behavior, but not very well (Ajzen, 1996; Fishbein & Ajzen, 1974). Students' attitudes toward cheating are not good predictors of the probability that they will cheat, any more than religious attitudes predict attendance at religious ceremonies (Wicker, 1969).

Why are attitudes and behaviors so imperfectly correlated, and what factors affect the link between what we think and feel and how we behave? First, people's attitudes *do* predict their actions if the attitude and action are both relatively specific (Ajzen & Fishbein, 1977; Kraus, 1995). Asking people their attitude toward protecting the environment does not predict whether they will recycle, but asking their attitude toward recycling does (Oskamp, 1991).

Second, and perhaps most importantly, people's attitudes are only one of many influences on what they do (Ajzen & Fishbein, 1977). From a behaviorist perspective, behavior is under the control of environmental consequences. An environmentally minded person who buys one small bag of groceries a week might re-use her own canvas shopping bag each week and thus contribute to the longevity of tropical rain forests. An equally environmentally conscious person who totes groceries for her family up six flights of stairs might find the convenience of plastic bags such overwhelming reinforcement that she contributes instead to the longevity of landfills.

Third, the recognition that attitudes vary along a number of dimensions points to some previously unrecognized complexities in the way attitudes affect behavior.

Making Connections

Because attitudes are only one of the factors that influence behavior, they may not be useful in predicting who a person will vote for in a *particular* election, but over the long run, they will in fact predict the party the individual tends to endorse at the ballot box. As we saw in Chapter 12, human behavior is so complex that a single variable—whether an attitude or a personality trait—is rarely likely to predict what a person will do in a specific circumstance. By aggregating (averaging) across behaviors, however, researchers get a clearer picture of a person's behavioral tendencies. Attitudes, like personality traits, predict behavior over the long run.

Much of behavior is controlled by implicit procedures (Chapter 6), or habits, that people develop through experience, rather than by their explicit (conscious) attitudes (Ouellette & Wood, 1997). Explicit attitudes predict some behaviors, particularly when people are consciously reflecting on them. Much of the time, however, implicit attitudes, which tend to be rapid and automatic, regulate people's actions and reactions, as when a white person who thinks she is unprejudiced makes less eye contact with black than white strangers.

Finally, the way attitudes are acquired influences their impact on behavior. Attitudes shaped by personal experience are especially likely to influence action (Fazio & Zanna, 1981; Smith & Swinyard, 1983). For example, one study examined students' attitudes toward a campus housing shortage that forced many to sleep on cots in makeshift quarters for weeks (Regan & Fazio, 1977). Both the affected students and their more comfortably housed peers had negative attitudes toward the situation, but those who were personally affected were much more likely to write letters and sign petitions.

◆ INTERIM SUMMARY

> The cognitive, evaluative, and behavioral components of an attitude may vary independently of each other. Although attitudes are generally believed to include a behavioral disposition, they often do not predict specific behaviors, for several reasons: The behavior and the attitude are often at different levels of generality; other variables influence behavior; and attitudes vary in different ways that make prediction complex, such as the extent to which they are implicit or explicit.

Persuasion

People often have a vested interest in changing others' attitudes, whether they are selling products, running for political office, or trying to convince a lover to reconcile one more time. **Persuasion** refers to *deliberate efforts to change an attitude*.

Central and Peripheral Routes

People sometimes change their attitudes after considerable conscious reflection. Other times they change their attitudes with little thought. Correspondingly, researchers have identified two routes through which people can be persuaded (Chen & Chaiken, 1999; Eagly & Chaiken, 1992; Petty & Cacioppo, 1981, 1986a; Petty & Wegener, 1998). The first, or **central route**, *involves inducing the recipient of a message to think carefully and weigh the arguments*. The second, or **peripheral route**, *appeals to less rational and thoughtful processes*. The peripheral route bypasses the cortex and often heads straight for points south, such as the limbic system, the heart, or the gut. Most beer commercials, for example, have little to offer in terms of rational persuasion. Were weekends really made for Michelob? When you say "Bud," have you *really* said it all?

The **elaboration likelihood model** *of persuasion posits that knowing how to appeal to people requires figuring out the likelihood that they will think much about (or elaborate on) the arguments* (Petty & Cacioppo, 1986b). Rational appeals are more likely to change the attitude of a person who both is *motivated* to think about a topic and has time to consider the arguments. In other words, when elaboration likelihood is high, appeals to logic are most likely to be persuasive.

Much of the time, however, people do not have the time, interest, or ability to weigh every argument about every possible attitude object that crosses their paths. Do I buy Green Giant string beans or Del Monte? If I am a true green bean devotee, I might spend the extra 30 seconds in the aisle at the grocery store pondering the merits of two brands (or walk over to the fresh produce aisle). However, as we have seen (Chapter 7), in everyday cognition people have to choose how to allocate their cognitive resources, because both working memory and time are limited commodities. People often use simple heuristics (cognitive shortcuts or rules of thumb) to make judgments

Apply & Discuss

Surprisingly, these people are not much more likely to recycle their glass and plastic at home than the average person.

■ Identify the basic dimensions on which attitudes toward the environment and recycling might vary?

■ Consider your own attitudes toward the environment and recycling. Where do they fall on each of these dimensions? For example, how complex are your feelings toward environmental protection in general, and recycling in particular?

■ What factors actually influence whether or not you recycle? How much do your attitudes determine your behavior on this issue?

about attitude objects. For example, they may simply follow the majority opinion (hence, laugh tracks on television shows, which tell people that the jokes are funny, in case they did not notice) or accept appeals to unknown experts (e.g., "nine out of ten dentists prefer …") (Chaiken, 1980; Chaiken et al., 1997).

The distinction between central and peripheral routes to attitude change parallels the distinction between explicit and implicit judgment and decision making (Chapter 7). Whereas explicit attitude change (the central route) requires conscious deliberation, implicit attitude change (the peripheral route) can occur in several ways. One is through classical conditioning of an object with an emotional response. Advertisers populate their commercials with beautiful women and virile men, subtly implying that using their product or drinking their beer will increase consumers' reproductive success (rather than their beer gut).

Another way to effect implicit attitude change is simply to repeat a message enough times that people start to believe it (Arkes et al., 1991). Politicians are well aware of this, which is why they often repeat inaccurate information if they can get away with it. Repetition has persuasive effects for several reasons: It produces familiarity, which tends to produce liking (Zajonc, 1968, 1998); it strengthens the association between the two pieces of information; and it capitalizes on the fact that, over time, people tend to forget the source of a message and assume that if they have heard it enough, it must have some credibility.

Changing someone's attitude, then, requires attention to several variables. If the attitude really matters to the person, if the recipient of the message is knowledgeable about the subject, if the recipient has time to evaluate the arguments, and if the attitude was initially generated rationally by weighing costs and benefits, then the best appeal is to the head (central processing). In this case, the persuader should avoid distractions (glitzy campaigns, jingles, and hoopla) that impede conscious, rational processing and annoy the receiver. If, however, the attitude is not strongly held and is based on minimal knowledge, the best route is usually to the heart or the gut—or, at any rate, as far from the frontal lobes as possible.

Components of Persuasion

Interest in persuasion has a venerable past. Long before modern psychology, Aristotle described *rhetoric*—the art of persuasive speaking—as a combination of *ethos* (characteristics of the speaker), *pathos* (the appeal of the message), and *logos* (the logic of the argument). Psychologists have expanded Aristotle's view to identify several components of persuasion, including the source, message, channel (the medium in which the message is delivered), context, and receiver (Lasswell, 1948; McGuire, 1985; Petty & Wegener, 1998). Attending to each of these aspects is crucial to the success of a persuasive appeal, whether the goal is to sell a car or get someone to agree to a date.

Source Speakers tend to be more persuasive when they appear credible (expert and trustworthy), attractive, likable, powerful, and similar to the recipient of the message (Chaiken, 1980; Simons et al., 1970). For politicians, particularly in countries such as the United States where presidential candidates must appeal directly to voters, winning votes is often a balancing act in which the successful candidate must seem likable but authoritative, powerful yet able to understand the concerns of everyday citizens.

Message   The type of appeal (e.g., presenting one side of the argument or both) and the way it is delivered also affect attitude change. As we have seen, the match between the recipient's willingness and ability to think about the message and the way the message is delivered is crucial for persuasion. A jingle about a low-fat margarine will not convince someone who has compared the fat content of multiple brands and cares about the difference.

Fear appeals—efforts to induce fear to try to change attitudes—can sometimes be effective, but they can backfire if they induce too much fear, leading people to stop attending to the message and instead to focus on managing their anxiety (Insko et al., 1965). For example, messages about AIDS may fall on deaf ears if they are so frightening that people simply deny the realities. Fear can, however, be useful in inducing attitude change if the recipients of the message believe the danger applies to them and that they can do something to avoid it (see Olson & Zanna, 1993).

Channel   The channel of persuasion is the means by which a message is sent—in words or images, verbally or nonverbally, in person or through media such as telephone or television. Choosing the right channel can be as important as selecting the right message. Turning someone down for a date is much more difficult face to face than on the telephone, so suitors of reluctant "targets" should make their pitch in person. Emotional appeals to contribute to emergency relief funds are more effective when the target of the communication can see starving children with distended stomachs rather than simply hear about their plight.

Context   The context in which a message is presented can also influence attitude change (Petty & Wegener, 1998). Soft music in the background may lead an ambivalent "recipient" to agree to a second date, and a roomful of cheering supporters can make a political message seem much more exciting. An important aspect of the context is the presence of competing messages. Things would be easier for Coke if Pepsi did not advertise, and vice versa.

Psychologists and advertisers have devised many methods to increase resistance to contrary appeals. One is to get there first: Being the first to make a pitch renders a persuasive appeal more effective (Insko, 1964; Miller & Campbell, 1959). Another method, called **attitude inoculation**, involves *building up the receiver's "resistance" to a persuasive appeal by presenting weak arguments for it or forewarning against it* (McGuire, 1961; McGuire & Papageorgis, 1962). Thus, much as a vaccine builds the body's defenses through exposure to small, inert amounts of a virus, weak and easily assailable arguments supporting the other point of view prompt the person to develop counterarguments that serve as attitudinal "antibodies." Salespeople frequently use this technique when they know a customer is about to visit a competitor ("He'll tell you Dell has a better customer service, but don't believe him").

Receiver   Receiver characteristics—qualities of the person the communicator is trying to persuade—also affect the persuasiveness of a communication. People with strong attitudes on a topic are obviously less likely candidates for attitude change, and some people are simply more difficult to persuade in general (see Haugtvedt & Petty, 1992; Hovland & Janis, 1959). Further, people bias their information processing in order to preserve attitudes they do not want to change (MacCoun, 1998). Coffee drinkers, for example, discount messages about the dangers of caffeine (Liberman & Chaiken, 1992).

Individuals also vary in the extent to which they are likely to attend to, elaborate, and reflect on careful arguments—that is, to rely on the central route to attitude formation and change (Jarvis & Petty, 1996). This does not mean, however, that people who focus on the substance of the arguments form "better" attitudes. People can exercise considerable effort in preserving their biases and carefully attacking arguments that do not support their position.

Behavioral Change   One of the most effective strategies for changing attitudes is inducing people first to change their behavior. As we saw in Chapter 16, convincing people with a snake phobia to get closer and closer to the slithery reptile can change their attitudes toward snakes (from intensely fearful to neutral) as well as toward themselves (inducing a greater sense of self-efficacy).

Another persuasive strategy that targets behavioral change is the **foot-in-the-door technique**, which operates on *the principle that once people comply with a small request, they are more likely to comply with a bigger one* (Beaman et al., 1983). In one classic study, experimenters posed as representatives of the Community Committee for Traffic Safety or the Keep California Beautiful Committee (Freedman & Fraser, 1966). They visited over 100 homes in Palo Alto, California, and asked residents to comply with one of two requests, either signing a petition or posting a small sign on their lawns reading, "Be a Safe Driver" or "Keep California Beautiful."

About two weeks later, the investigators visited the same homes as well as several others and made a larger request—to install a large "Drive Carefully" sign on their front lawn. Whereas over 55 percent of participants who had granted one of the small requests two weeks earlier complied, less than 20 percent of those who received only the second (large) request consented. The same principle may work in dating: If a potential date seems uncertain or ambivalent, suggest lunch (a much smaller investment) before proposing an entire evening out.

◆ INTERIM SUMMARY

Persuasion refers to deliberate efforts to change an attitude and can occur through a **central route**, inducing the message recipient to think about the argument, or a **peripheral route**, appealing to less thoughtful processes. According to the **elaboration likelihood model**, the central route to attitude persuasion is more effective when the person is both motivated and able to think about the arguments, whereas the peripheral route is more effective when the likelihood that the person will engage in high-effort cognitive processing is low. Characteristics of the source, message, channel, context, and receiver all affect the effectiveness of persuasive appeals. Getting people to change their behavior can also lead to attitude change.

Cognitive Dissonance

Although attitude change often involves deliberate efforts at persuasion, another path to attitude change is cognitive dissonance. According to Leon Festinger (1957, 1962), who developed cognitive dissonance theory, attitude change can occur when various objects of thought, which he called "cognitive elements," are logically inconsistent— that is, when they are *dissonant* with one another. These objects of thought can be attitudes, behaviors, new information—virtually anything a person can think about. **Cognitive dissonance** thus refers to *a perceived discrepancy between an attitude and a behavior or between an attitude and a new piece of information*. For example, if a person holds the belief that smoking is dangerous (element 1) but does not smoke (element 2), she does not experience dissonance; the two cognitive elements are consistent. If, on the other hand, she knows that smoking is dangerous (element 1) but also knows she smokes (element 2), she experiences a discrepancy between her beliefs and behavior.

According to Festinger, this kind of discrepancy leads to a state of psychological tension similar to anxiety. The tension, in turn, motivates the individual to change the attitude, the behavior, or the perception of the inconsistent information to eliminate

Central Questions

Advertisers are keenly interested in shaping attitudes toward brands, products, and political candidates.

■ To what extent can we use the same principles to understand attitudes toward cars and toward political figures?

■ Are advertisers wise to rely on the same principles to guide advertising campaigns for a brand of soda and a political candidate? If not, what should be different in persuading a consumer versus a voter?

unpleasant arousal or anxiety. For example, if the person knows that smoking is bad but smokes anyway, she may change the belief component of her attitude toward smoking ("it's not really that dangerous—I don't know anyone who has died of lung cancer from smoking"), or she may quit smoking. Alternatively, she may add some additional cognitive element that resolves the dissonance (e.g., "I don't plan to smoke that many years, so it won't hurt me").

Dissonance Reduction

Cognitive dissonance theory is essentially a drive-reduction theory (Chapter 10). That is, reducing an uncomfortable emotional state (a drive) reinforces an attitude change. Suppose, for example, Linda has been dating Justin for a few weeks. She was really interested in him when they began dating, but he has seemed somewhat unenthusiastic, often preferring to go out with his buddies on weekends. Whether Linda is free to date other people is ambiguous; they are involved enough to suggest otherwise, but Justin's level of commitment hardly seems to imply an exclusive relationship.

The plot thickens when Bob asks her out for Saturday night. Bob seems like a nice enough guy, and Linda has no intention of spending the evening at home while Justin spends another night out with the boys, so she accepts. Then she begins to worry whether she has made the right choice—a phenomenon called *postdecision regret*. The tension she experiences may lead her to convince herself that Bob is more attractive than he is—essentially justifying a choice she has made that is inconsistent with another choice, dating Justin. She may also talk with her friends about the situation in a way that solicits a particular answer—for example, talking only to friends who dislike the way Justin has treated her, or "talking up" Bob's virtues. These are examples of *postdecision dissonance reduction*—or dissonance reduction after the fact.

Cognitive dissonance can also arise when people carry out an act contrary to their attitudes. In a classic study, Festinger and Carlsmith (1959) had participants perform monotonous tasks for an hour. The experimenters told them that the aim of this procedure was to test their performance, but the actual purpose was to create a negative attitude toward the tasks. The investigators then asked some participants to tell the next "participant" (who was really a confederate of the experimenter) that the experiment was enjoyable. They paid the participants either $1 or $20 for their compliance.

One might expect that people who received $20 for hyping a boring task would feel more positive toward the task than those paid only $1. In fact, just the opposite occurred. Those who received only $1 rated the experimental tasks more enjoyable, and they more frequently agreed to participate in a similar experiment again. While these results seem counterintuitive, they exquisitely matched the predictions of dissonance theory: To say that a boring task is interesting for a meager payment creates considerable dissonance. Participants who received only $1 either had to change their attitude toward the task or face the dissonance associated with knowing that they had sold their souls rather cheaply. In contrast, those who received $20 reduced their dissonance and thus avoided the need to change their attitude because they could readily explain their behavior in terms of the payment, a considerable amount in the late 1950s.

In Festinger's terms, participants in both conditions (1$ and $20 payment) experienced a discrepancy between what they believed (cognitive element 1, "the task is boring") and what they did (cognitive element 2, "I told this poor sucker that the task is interesting"). When participants in the $1 condition tried to explain this to themselves, they had *insufficient justification* for their action, and hence had to change their attitude toward the task. In contrast, participants paid $20 could add a third cognitive element ("I told the guy it was interesting because they paid me a lot to do it"), which relieved the logical inconsistency between what they believed and what they said.

Two variables that influence the extent to which dissonance arises and requires resolution are the perception of choice and the size of rewards and punishments. A person with a gun to his head will not feel much pressure to cling to attitudes he publicly professed at the time. Coerced statements create little dissonance because they are uttered with minimal choice. Similarly, as in Festinger and Carlsmith's study, the smaller the reward or punishment, the greater the attitude change because larger incentives minimize dissonance.

To what extext is dissonance reduction a conscious process, whereby people change their attitudes or behaviors based on conscious reflection? Recent research with amnesics provides some important clues. If dissonance reduction requires conscious awareness of a discrepancy between present and past attitudes or behavior, then amnesics who cannot consciously recall their behavior should show little dissonance reduction when faced with dissonant information. In fact, however, amnesics show *more*, not less, dissonance reduction than people with intact memory (Lieberman et al., in press; see also Shultz & Lepper, 1995). This suggests that dissonance reduction occurs automatically, without conscious reflection.

Alternative Explanations

The original formulation of cognitive dissonance theory explained the results of these experiments in terms of the motivation to reduce dissonance. Not all researchers agree, however, that motivation is necessarily involved. An alternative nonmotivational explanation, derived from behaviorism, is self-perception theory. **Self-perception theory** holds that *individuals infer their attitudes, emotions, and other internal states by observing their own behavior* (Bem, 1967, 1972). Thus, if they see themselves telling someone that they like a task and they have only received $1 for doing so, they conclude that they must have liked it or they would not be saying so. According to self-perception theory, the attitudes people report depend on their behavior; as their behavior changes (because of changes in reinforcement contingencies), so again will their attitude. No motivation, tension, or perceived inconsistency is involved.

Other theories provide alternative motivational explanations of the results of dissonance experiments. For example, a *self-presentation* explanation suggests that what appear to be changes in attitudes in dissonance studies are really changes in *reported* attitudes. Because people want to present themselves as rational and do not want to look foolish by behaving inconsistently, they report attitudes they do not really hold. Still another motivational explanation maintains that people feel guilty, ashamed, or lacking in integrity after doing something that conflicts with their values, such as lying about a task. Thus, they change their attitudes to minimize their discomfort and preserve their self-esteem (see Abelson, 1983; Scher & Cooper, 1989; Steele, 1988).

Most likely, each of the explanations offered to explain the results of cognitive dissonance experiments is applicable at various times. When people do things that do not seem "like them" but that do not have unpleasant consequences for other people, simple self-perception processes may explain why they change their attitudes. However, experiments measuring physiological responses demonstrate that dissonant information *can* produce emotional arousal that people experience as uncomfortable and that these feelings can indeed be reduced by changing a belief—or by other emotion-regulation strategies (Chapter 11). For example, watching a funny movie, cleansing emotional wounds with alcohol, or misattributing the cause of discomfort to something irrelevant like a pill just taken can all reduce the need to change a dissonant belief (Fried & Aronson, 1995; Steele et al., 1991; Zanna & Cooper, 1974). Unpleasant feeling states are most likely to lead to attitude change when the person has done something that leads to shame, guilt, or anxiety, such as looking foolish to someone else or breaking a moral standard.

Culture and Dissonance

The extent to which cognitive dissonance is universal has recently come into question (Fiske et al., 1998). Research with Western subjects has shown that giving people positive feedback prior to a dissonance manipulation decreases dissonance-reduction motivation to reduce dissonance (because the person is less threatened about his self-worth). In contrast, negative feedback increases attitude change through disso-

Making Connections

Theories of cognitive dissonance that emphasize motivation resemble models of stress and coping and emotion regulation (Chapter 11). The person makes an appraisal of the situation as problematic—whether the problem is logical inconsistency, immorality, or the appearance of foolishness—which in turn leads to a negative or stressful emotional state. She then employs coping strategies (such as changing her attitude, changing her behavior, rationalizing her behavior by adding a third cognitive element, or changing the emotion directly by exercising, drinking, etc.) to reduce the unpleasant feeling.

nance reduction because it essentially heightens the person's sense of incompetence, immorality, lack of integrity, or similar feelings (Steele, 1988).

One study compared responses of Japanese and Canadian subjects to see if these findings would hold in a non-Western sample (Heine & Lehman, 1997). Participants were first given a fake "personality test" and told the results would be available shortly. Next, the investigators asked participants to choose 10 CDs from a list of 40 they would most like to own and to indicate how much they would like each CD by making a mark on an unmarked 118-mm line labeled "wouldn't like this CD at all" on the left and "would like this CD very much" on the right.

Immediately afterward, participants received the "results" of the personality test. Some received negative feedback, some positive, and some no feedback at all, after which they had a few minutes to ponder the results. Then the experimenter came back with subjects' fifth- and sixth-choice CDs and gave them a choice between them. After a few more minutes of filling out some irrelevant information (to give time for dissonance-reduction processes to occur), participants again rated each of the ten CDs using the same 118-mm line.

The results for Canadian participants were just as expected (Figure 17.2). Those who had received no feedback showed a substantial difference between their post-choice ratings of the two CDs; on the average, they preferred the one they had chosen by over 9 mm on a 118-mm line. Those who had been given positive feedback showed a much smaller effect, whereas those who had received negative feedback substantially changed their attitudes in favor of the CD they had chosen. No such effect occurred for the Japanese: They did not show a significant preference for the CD they had chosen under any condition.

Research with other Asian samples has produced similar findings. Why would this be? The authors suggest that the difference lies in the way Asians and North Americans view themselves. North Americans, like other people in the West, are individualistic and independent. To make a bad choice has strong implications for self-esteem, leading to attitude change in dissonance experiments. Asians, on the other hand, tend to be much more collectivist and interdependent in their views of themselves (Fiske et al., 1998; Markus & Kitayama, 1991). Their self-esteem rises and falls more with their ability to meet social expectations and maintain a sense of connection with those around them than it does with individual choices that indicate how smart or savvy they are.

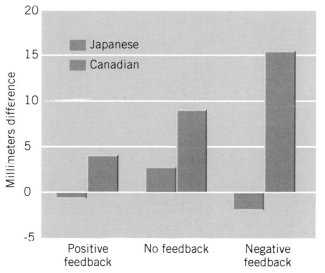

Figure 17.2 Dissonance reduction and culture. Canadian participants tended to reduce dissonance by increasing their relative preference for the CD they chose over the one they turned down, as assessed by the difference in the number of millimeters on a line on which they indicated their preference. This was particularly true under conditions of threat to their view of themselves (negative feedback). For Japanese participants, no dissonance reduction occurred under any of the three conditions. *Source:* Heine & Lehman, 1997, p. 396.

◆ **INTERIM SUMMARY**

Cognitive dissonance occurs when a person experiences a discrepancy between an attitude and a behavior or between an attitude and a new piece of information. This leads to a state of tension that can motivate attitude change. According to **self-perception theory**, attitudes change in dissonance experiments as people observe their own behavior. Other explanations emphasize self-presentation (trying to look good) or efforts to regulate unpleasant emotions such as guilt and shame. To some extent, cognitive dissonance may presume a particular way of thinking about and evaluating the self that is distinctively Western.

◆ Social Cognition

A friend has just told you she has the "perfect person" for you. She describes the individual as intelligent, witty, engaging, and articulate and thinks the two of you would make a great pair. You immediately form an impression of this person, which probably includes traits such as attractive, kind, outgoing, and generous. Now suppose instead your friend describes a potential date with precisely the same words—intelligent, witty, engaging, and articulate—but first warns that this person is a "real con artist." This time your impression probably includes less favorable traits, such as selfish, cold, and ruthless.

How does a simple phrase ("perfect for you" versus a "real con artist") change the meaning of a series of adjectives and lead to an entirely different impression? The answer lies in **social cognition**, *the processes by which people make sense of themselves, others, social interactions, and relationships*.

The study of social cognition has closely followed developments in cognitive science, which has provided many of its basic models and metaphors. Cognitive psychologists have proposed a number of different models of how information is represented in long-term memory (Chapters 6 and 7), which have guided research on social cognition (see Smith, 1998). Some emphasize principles of association, arguing that memories are stored as interconnected nodes on *networks of association*. Activation of one node in a network spreads activation to other nodes linked to it through experience.

Other models emphasize *schemas*, organized patterns of thought that direct attention, memory, and interpretation. Activation of a schema (such as a theater schema) makes a person more likely to hear the word "play" as referring to a theater production than as something children do in a schoolyard. Still other models focus on *concepts*, mental representations of categories, such as birds. In these models, categorizing a novel stimulus involves comparing it to an abstract prototype (a generalized image or idea of a class of stimuli), a set of defining features (such as a list of attributes common to all birds), or a salient example or exemplar (such as a robin).

More recently, connectionist models have proposed that representations are not so much "things" that are "stored" in the brain but patterns of activation in networks of neurons (Chapter 7). According to these models, when a person sees an object, multiple neural circuits are activated simultaneously (that is, in parallel). Somehow the system has to weed out less likely hypotheses about what the object is and settle on a solution. It does this by taking into account the multiple constraints imposed by the data.

Thus, the presence of wings on an animal in the garden activates multiple possible bird representations (robin, sparrow, etc.). At first, the brain automatically favors the most common birds, which begin with the highest level of activation because they are the most frequently encountered. However, if the bird's wings are flapping at an extremely rapid pace, this is inconsistent with the representation of garden-variety birds (at least in most parts of the world), so these representations are inhibited. The representation that is left "standing" at the end of this battle of competing networks is the one that receives the greatest activation: hummingbird.

These various models, or "languages," for speaking about representations all continue to be used in research on social cognition. Researchers are just beginning to sort out the extent to which they are compatible or incompatible and the conditions under which one model may be more accurate than another (Smith, 1998). As we will see, however, social psychologists are increasingly applying connectionist models to phenomena that have previously been understood using other models of representation, such as attitudes, social schemas, and stereotypes, which may actually reflect some similar principles (Kunda & Thagard, 1996; Read et al., 1997).

◆ **INTERIM SUMMARY**

Social cognition refers to the processes by which people make sense of themselves, others, social interactions, and relationships. Changing concepts of representation in cognitive science are beginning to lead to similar changes in the study of social cognition, such as the increasing use of connectionist models, which view representations as patterns of activation of networks of neurons operating in parallel.

Perceiving Other People

Social cognition is pervasive in everyday life, from the first impressions people form of other people to their more enduring knowledge about people, situations, and relationships.

First Impressions

Even before the field of social cognition emerged as a distinct discipline, psychologists interested in interpersonal perception studied **first impressions**, *the initial perceptions of another person that affect future beliefs about that person*. One early study demonstrated the power of first impressions. Participants read the two passages shown in Figure 17.3, but in different order (Luchins, 1957). The order of the material substantially influenced participants' evaluations of the person described: Seventy-eight percent of subjects who read paragraph A first considered Jim friendly, compared to only 18 percent who read paragraph B first.

A particularly salient characteristic of first impressions is physical appearance, particularly attractiveness. Individuals who are physically attractive benefit from the **halo effect**, *the tendency to assume that positive qualities cluster together*. Researchers have found halo effects for physical attractiveness across a wide array of situations. For example, more attractive people get lighter jury sentences and higher salaries (Hamermesh & Biddle, 1994; Landy & Aronson, 1969)! (Perhaps that explains my meager professor's salary….)

The positive glow of beauty, of course, has its limits (Eagly et al., 1991; Feingold, 1992; Larose & Standing, 1998). Not surprisingly, it is most powerful when people have minimal information about each other. It also extends to some traits more than to others. For example, people typically attribute greater sociability and social competence to attractive people, but they do not expect them to have more integrity, modesty, or concern for others.

An even more important variable than actual physical attractiveness, however, may be how attractive people *perceive* themselves to be. Individuals who perceive themselves as physically attractive report being more extroverted, socially comfortable, and mentally healthy than those less comfortable with their appearance (Feingold, 1992). Although they may simply be deluded in every realm of their lives, it is equally likely that seeing themselves as attractive produces a self-fulfilling prophecy, in which feeling attractive leads to behaviors perceived by others as attractive. In fact, research consistently finds that when people feel and act attractive, others are more likely to see them that way.

Schemas and Social Cognition

First impressions are essentially the initial schemas people form when they encounter someone for the first time. Schemas—the patterns of thought hypothesized to organize human experience (Chapters 4 and 6)—apply in the social realm as in other areas of life (see Fiske, 1993, 1995; Taylor & Crocker, 1980). We form schemas about specific people or types of people (e.g., extroverts, Hispanics, women); situations (e.g., how to behave in a classroom or restaurant); and roles and relationships (e.g., how a professor, student, parent, or friend is supposed to act) (Baldwin, 1992).

As in other cognitive domains, schemas guide information processing about people and relationships. They direct attention, organize encoding, and influence retrieval. For example, an employer who suspects that a job candidate may be exaggerating his accomplishments is likely to scrutinize his resume with special care and inquire about details that would normally not catch her eye. If later asked about the candidate, the first thing she may remember is that he described a part-time job as a courier at a radio station as a "communications consultant."

People are especially prone to recall *schema-relevant* social information—behaviors or aspects of a situation related to an activated schema (Higgins & Bargh, 1987).

Paragraph A

Jim left the house to get some stationery. He walked out into the sun-filled street with two of his friends, basking in the sun as he walked. Jim entered the stationery store, which was full of people. Jim talked with an acquaintance while he waited for the clerk to catch his eye. On his way out, he stopped to chat with a school friend who was just coming into the store. Leaving the store, he walked toward school. On his way out he met the girl to whom he had been introduced the night before. They talked for a short while, and then Jim left for school.

Paragraph B

After school Jim left the classroom alone. Leaving the school, he started on his long walk home. The street was brilliantly filled with sunshine. Jim walked down the street on the shady side. Coming down the street toward him, he saw the pretty girl whom he had met on the previous evening. Jim crossed the street and entered a candy store. The store was crowded with students, and he noticed a few familiar faces. Jim waited quietly until the counterman caught his eye and then gave his order. Taking his drink, he sat down at a side table. When he had finished his drink he went home.

Figure 17.3 First impressions. In this classic study, the order of presentation of two paragraphs had a substantial influence on the impression subjects formed of Jim. *Source:* Luchins, 1957, pp. 34–35.

For example, participants presented with a vignette about a librarian are likely a week later to remember information congruent with their librarian schema, such as a bun hairstyle and glasses. They are also prone to remember highly discrepant information, such as her tendency to go out dancing every night. If a librarian schema is active during encoding or retrieval, what people are *least* likely to remember are details irrelevant to the schema, such as her hair color.

◆ INTERIM SUMMARY

> **First impressions** can have an important influence on subsequent information processing. One of the features that strongly affects the way people perceive others upon first meeting is physical attractiveness. People process information about other people and relationships using schemas, which guide information processing by directing attention, organizing encoding, and influencing retrieval.

Stereotypes and Prejudice

"It required years of labor and billions of dollars to uncover the secret of the atom. It will take still a greater investment to gain the secrets of man's irrational nature. It is easier…to smash an atom than a prejudice."

GORDON ALLPORT (1954, P. XI)

Schemas are essential for social cognition. Without them, people would walk into every new situation without knowing how to behave or how others are likely to act. Schematic processing can go awry, however, when schemas are so rigidly or automatically applied that they preclude the processing of new information. This often occurs with **stereotypes**, *characteristics attributed to people based on their membership in specific groups*.

Stereotypes are often overgeneralized, inaccurate, and resistant to new information. Like other schemas and attitudes, however, they save cognitive "energy." In other words, they simplify experience and allow individuals to categorize others quickly and effortlessly (Allport, 1954; Hamilton & Sherman, 1994; Macrae et al., 1994).

Stereotypes are intimately related to prejudice. **Prejudice**, which literally means *pre-judgment*, involves *judging people based on (usually negative) stereotypes*. In attitude terms, stereotypes are the cognitive component, prejudice is the evaluative component, and **discrimination** is *the behavioral component of negative attitudes toward particular groups* (Fiske, 1998).

Racial, ethnic, and religious prejudice has contributed to more bloodshed over the past century than perhaps any other force in human history. Its path of destruction can be traced through the violence and institutionalized discrimination against blacks in the United States and South Africa, to the Holocaust, the Arab–Israeli conflict, the tension between Anglophones and Francophones in Quebec, the carnage in Northern Ireland, the tribal warfare and genocide in Rwanda and other African coun-

Apply & Discuss

Prejudice has a grim history, from cross-burnings and lynchings by the Ku Klux Klan (*a*) to concentration camps in Bosnia (*b*) that seemed eerily similar to the Nazi camps a half-century earlier.

■ Are some cultures more prone to prejudice than others, or is the belief that they are simply one more example of prejudice?

■ What social conditions give rise to prejudice, and what protects against it?

■ Is prejudice a personality trait? Would we all become prejudiced if our brother or sister were killed in a civil war based on ethnic or religious divisions?

(a)

(b)

tries, the civil war and atrocities in Bosnia, and the other civil wars that erupted after the breakup of the Soviet Union. The list is long and grim.

Since the 1930s, psychologists have proposed a number of explanations for prejudice, based on their answers to two central questions: Do the roots of prejudice lie in individual psychology (such as personality dynamics or cognition) or in social dynamics (the oppression of one group by another)? And are the causes of prejudice found in cognition or motivation—in the way people think or in the way they *want* to think? As we will see, the absence of a single widely accepted theory of prejudice probably reflects the fact that researchers have often tried to choose among these options (see Duckitt, 1992).

The Authoritarian Personality

Around the time of World War II, psychologists turned to psychodynamic theory to explain the racism that was devouring Europe and eating away at the United States. They noted that acts of racial violence increase in times of economic recession, as people search for scapegoats, or targets for displaced anger (Dollard et al., 1939). For example, the rate of lynchings in the southern United States was inversely correlated with the price of cotton: The harder the economic times, the more lynchings. According to this theory, prejudice is used defensively to avoid anxiety, anger, or feelings of low self-worth. More recent data support this hypothesis: Threatening participants' self-esteem through negative feedback increases their tendency to derogate members of stereotyped groups, which then leads to increases in their own self-esteem (Fein & Spencer, 1997).

According to a theory developed by a team of researchers who fled Nazi persecution in the middle of the last century, some people are likely to be attracted to racist ideology because of their personality characteristics. Theodore Adorno and his colleagues (1950) identified what they called the **authoritarian personality**, *characterized by a tendency to hate people who are different or downtrodden*. These individuals tended to have a dominant, stern, and sometimes sadistic father and a submissive mother—interestingly, like the family of origin of Adolph Hitler. According to the theory, children in such families fear and hate their fathers, but these feelings would be brutally punished if exposed, so they repress them. As adults, authoritarian individuals displace or project their rage onto groups such as Jews, blacks, homosexuals, or others who do not conform to social norms.

Adorno and colleagues thought (and hoped) that authoritarian personality dynamics were limited to, or especially common in, Nazi Germany. However, their research in the United States suggested otherwise. Despite criticism of Adorno's methodology, more recent work supports many of the original findings, such as the link between this personality style and harsh parenting requiring strict obedience (Christie, 1978; Snyder & Ickes, 1985).

Subtle Racism

Psychodynamic concepts of conflict, ambivalence, and unconscious processes (Chapter 12) actually dovetail with more recent cognitive approaches to prejudice. These approaches emerged from the observation that racism has changed in the last three decades, particularly in the United States. Today, overt racial discrimination against ethnic minorities is generally met with public disapproval. Gone are the days of separate buses, drinking fountains, and bathrooms for whites and blacks.

A Different Kind of Racism?   Several researchers contend, however, that new, more subtle kinds of racism exist in the wake of old-fashioned racism (Devine et al., 1991; Dovidio & Gaertner, 1993; Fiske, 1998). For example, many people claim not to be racist but in fact hold one after another attitude that "just happens" to be unfavorable to minorities, such as attitudes toward welfare or immigration (McConahay & Hough, 1976).

Another kind of subtle racism occurs in people who experience a conflict between two attitudes (Katz & Hass, 1988). On the one hand, they believe in what the sociologist Max Weber called the *Protestant work ethic*, the idea that hard work is the key to "making it," with the implication that people who are not successful have simply not applied themselves. On the other hand, they believe in equality of opportunity and recognize that all people in their society do not start out at the same place. This ambivalence can lead to extreme responses, both positive and negative, as they sometimes "land hard" on one side of the ambivalence or the other.

Implicit and Explicit Racism   Another form of conflict is between explicit and implicit attitudes toward members of minority groups. Like the African-American participants in Steele's studies described at the beginning of the chapter, who found themselves prey to their implicit associations, most white people have absorbed negative attitudes toward people of color over the course of their lives (Dovidio & Gaertner, 1993). They (or perhaps, more honestly, we) often express nonbigoted explicit attitudes, but when acting or responding without much conscious attention, unconscious stereotypes slip through the cracks. For example, in ambiguous situations, whites tend to be less helpful to blacks than to other whites, and they are more likely to impose stiffer penalties for black criminals.

In part, this discrepancy between what people say and what they do reflects a simple cognitive process. When people process information without much conscious thought, they are more likely to rely on stereotypes, to treat people as part of a category rather than as a specific individual (see Olson & Zanna, 1993). Negative stereotypes, like other attitudes, may thus be activated without awareness, as when a white man automatically checks his wallet after standing next to a young black man on the subway. Emotional arousal can also render people more susceptible to stereotypic thinking, in part because it draws limited attentional resources away from conscious reflection (Bodenhausen, 1993). The less people make conscious attributions, the more their unreflective, implicit attitudes prevail (Gilbert, 1995).

A growing body of research has begun to demonstrate just how different people's implicit and explicit racial attitudes can be (Dovidio et al., 2000; Greenwald et al., 1998; Kawakami et al., 2000). These studies have used priming procedures (Chapter 6), activating racial associations and then observing their effects on thought and behavior. In one of the first studies of this kind, the experimenter primed white subjects with words related to stereotypes of blacks, such as watermelon and Harlem (Devine, 1989). Subjects then read information about a fictional character. Simply activating stereotypes related to blacks led participants to rate the character more negatively (e.g., as more aggressive) than participants who were not primed with race-related words.

Another study found that people's implicit and explicit racial attitudes may be completely unrelated to each other—and may control different kinds of behavior (Fazio et al., 1995). To measure implicit attitudes, the investigators presented participants with a series of black and white faces followed by either a positive or a negative adjective. The participant's task was simply to press a key indicating whether the adjective was positive or negative. The theory behind the study was that negative attitudes are associatively connected to negative words (because they share the same emotional tone). Thus, the extent to which people have negative associations to blacks should be directly related to how quickly they recognize negative words after exposure to black faces. In other words, the speed with which participants respond to negative adjectives following priming with a black face can serve as a measure of their implicit attitudes toward blacks. The experimenters also measured *explicit* racial attitudes using self-report questionnaires asking about participants' beliefs about race-related issues and their attitudes about the Rodney King beating and the riots that followed acquittal of the police officers who beat him.

Implicit attitudes did not predict explicit attitudes. For example, many people who denied conscious, explicit racism showed substantial implicit racism as measured by their response to adjectives following black and white primes. But these implicit attitudes *did* predict something very important: subjects' behavior toward a black confederate of the experimenter who met them at the end of the study and simply rated the extent to which they seemed friendly and interested in what she had to say. Participants who had responded more quickly to negative adjectives after priming with black faces received lower ratings, regardless of what they believed explicitly.

Recent neuroimaging data suggest that implicit attitudes about race "run deep." Recall that the amygdala plays an important role in generating unpleasant emotions, particularly fear, in both rats and humans (Chapter 11). In a study just completed, the higher subjects scored on implicit racism, the more their brains showed activation of the amygdala as they looked at pictures of black faces (Phelps et al., in press).

A Connectionist Model of the Influence of Stereotypes on Judgments   Recently, researchers have applied connectionist models to social–cognitive and attitudinal phenomena such as stereotyping, demonstrating some of the ways implicit processes can affect ongoing thought and behavior (Kunda & Thagard, 1996). Consider what happens when a white person observes a white or black man shoving someone (Figure 17.4). The person could interpret the shove as an aggressive act (a violent push) or a playful, jovial shove. Because the person associates the category "black" with the trait "aggressive," activation spreads from "black" to "aggressive" to "violent push," and simultaneously inhibits interpretation of the action as a jovial shove. In contrast, because "white" is not associated one way or the other with "aggressive" (or may actually be slightly negatively associated with it), less activation spreads to the "violent push" interpretation (represented as a node in a network). Thus, in an ambiguous situation, satisfaction of multiple constraints can lead to inferences that are biased by stereotypes.

Suppressing Implicit Racism   Implicit racism (or sexism, which shows similar properties) may interact with motivational factors. No one wants to be a hypocrite. When conscious beliefs and values conflict with deep-seated, automatic negative stereotypes, people may alternate between extreme positions, either laying excessive blame at the feet of members of devalued groups or refusing to hold them accountable for their behavior. Alternatively, they may learn to recognize their unconscious tendencies toward

Making Connections

In several studies, people's explicit, conscious attitudes toward race have borne little or no relation to either their implicit attitudes or their behavior (for example, when talking with a black confederate of the experimenter). Conscious attitudes do, however, predict other conscious attitudes and beliefs, such as beliefs about what should happen to people who commit hate crimes. These findings directly parallel the results of studies distinguishing implicit motives, which predict long-term behavioral trends (such as success in business), from explicit motives, which control behavior only when people are consciously thinking about them (Chapter 10).

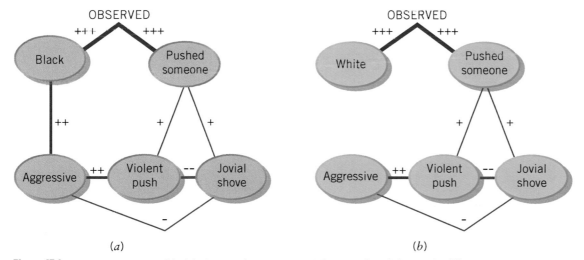

(a)   (b)

Figure 17.4   A connectionist model of the impact of stereotypes on inferences about behavior. The difference between the neural networks that lead to interpretation of an ambiguous shove by (*a*) a black man and (*b*) a white man lies in the weights that connect the nodes of the networks (the circles). Blue lines indicate positive weights, red lines indicate negative weights (inhibitory connections between nodes), and the thickness of the line indicates the strength of the connection (either positive or negative). *Source:* Adapted from Kunda & Thagard, 1996, p. 286.

racist thinking and perpetually monitor their reactions to try to prevent racist attitudes from coloring their actions (Devine & Monteith, 1993).

Researchers have begun examining the conditions under which people will express or suppress their stereotypes. In one series of studies, the investigators used a simple manipulation—the presence of a mirror—to heighten participants' focus on themselves while responding to a questionnaire about the acceptability of stereotypes (Macrae et al., 1998). The researchers hypothesized that under conditions of self-focus, people will be more likely to suppress stereotypic attitudes. That is precisely what they found: Participants in the mirror condition considered stereotyping less appropriate than control subjects without the mirror.

Suppressing a stereotype, however, can lead to rebound effects, in which the person later responds even more stereotypically. In another study, the investigators asked participants to evaluate a male hairdresser. After completing the task, the experimenter apologetically told them that some equipment had failed and asked them to do the task again, this time evaluating another male hairdresser. Some participants had the mirror in the room both times, others had the mirror initially but not while evaluating the second hairdresser, and some had no mirror on either occasion.

As predicted, those who had the mirror present initially produced less stereotypical descriptions of the first hairdresser. However, participants who had suppressed the stereotype the first time showed a substantial increase in stereotyping the second time if the mirror was removed (Figure 17.5). Thus, fighting a stereotype does not make it go away; in fact, it can intensify its expression when the person least expects it.

Can we fight stereotypes more effectively? This is the focus of some recent research. One method involves perspective taking: In a study of implicit attitudes toward the elderly (Chapter 14), individuals who were asked to imagine the world from the perspective of older people subsequently expressed fewer stereotypes both implicitly and explicitly (Galinsky & Moskowitz, 2000). Conscious efforts to combat stereotypes can also sometimes be effective in sensitizing people to their pervasive influence (Blair & Banaji, 1996; Kawakami et al., 2000). In fact, simply being aware of the labels one is using can reduce the impact of stereotypes. A recent neuroimaging study found reduced amygdala activation when participants intentionally thought of the stereotype label (e.g., "African-American") while viewing a face than when they saw the face without thinking of the label (Lieberman et al., in press).

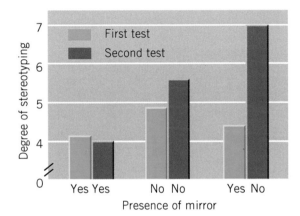

Figure 17.5 Stereotype suppression and rebound. Participants who initially suppressed their stereotype because of the presence of a mirror showed a rebound effect if the mirror was not present the second time. *Source:* Adapted from Macrae et al., 1998.

◆ INTERIM SUMMARY

Stereotypes are characteristics attributed to people based upon their membership in groups. **Prejudice** means judging people based on (usually negative) stereotypes. An early approach to prejudice focused on a personality style called the **authoritarian personality**, characterized by a tendency to project blame and rage onto specific groups. Cognitive researchers have focused on subtle forms of racism, many of which involve ambivalent attitudes. Of particular importance is implicit racism, which resides in the structure of people's associations toward members of minority groups rather than their explicit attitudes and often controls everyday behavior.

Prejudice and Social Conditions

In the late 1950s and 1960s, the civil rights movement in the United States was at its peak, and social scientists were optimistic about eradicating social evils such as poverty and racism. This optimism in part reflected research suggesting that the roots of prejudice lay less in personality dynamics than in social dynamics, particularly in socialization that teaches children racist attitudes (Duckitt, 1992; Pettigrew, 1958).

Prejudice is indeed transmitted from one generation to the next, and it takes hold early. In India, which has seen continued violence between Muslims and Hindus, children show signs of prejudice by age 4 or 5 (Saraswathi & Dutta, 1988). In multiethnic societies such as the United States, children from both minority and majority subcultures tend to express preferences toward the majority culture by the preschool years (see Spencer & Markstrom-Adams, 1990). Such culturally patterned associations can later make identity formation difficult for adolescent members of devalued groups, who must somehow integrate a positive view of themselves with negatives stereotypes others hold of them. And as Steele's research described at the opening of the chapter showed, these associations can also lead to self-fulfilling prophecies.

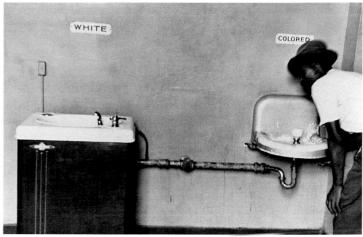

Scenes like this were commonplace in the American South just 40 years ago.

The roots of prejudice may lie in social conditions in yet another way. Many theorists, from Karl Marx to contemporary sociologists, have argued that prejudiced social attitudes serve a function: They preserve the interests of the dominant classes. Promulgating the view that blacks are inferior justifies a social order in which whites hold disproportionate power. Disparities in wealth and property ownership often create the fault lines along which societies crumble with ethnic strife because the haves and have-nots frequently differ in color, religion, or ethnicity.

Ingroups and Outgroups

Prejudice requires a distinction between **ingroups** and **outgroups**—*people who belong to the group and those who do not* (Brewer & Brown, 1998). The impact of ingroups and outgroups was demonstrated in a remarkable classroom experiment. Third-grade teacher Jane Elliott (1977), who taught in a rural, all-white community, one day announced that the brown-eyed children in her class were superior and the blue-eyed children, inferior. Soon the brown-eyed children refused to play with their blue-eyed classmates, and the blue-eyed children began to do poor work because they thought of themselves as stupid and bad.

Us and Them   Similar ingroup–outgroup behavior occurs with adults and is particularly powerful in naturally occurring groups such as families, clans, and communities. One process that intensifies stereotyping is that people tend to perceive members of outgroups as much more homogeneous than they really are and to emphasize the individuality of ingroup members (Moreland, 1985; Rothgerber, 1997). Thus, people of other races "all look alike," and members of other fraternities or sororities are seen to share many core traits—which is highly unlikely, given the tremendous differences in personality that exist within any group of people.

Based on something as simple as team affiliation, soccer fans can attack each other, demonstrating the power of ingroup–outgroup dynamics.

Interpretation of other people's behavior also depends on their ingroup–outgroup status. A set of studies with Hindu and Muslim students in Bangladesh showed that both groups attributed helpful behavior of ingroup members to their personal goodness and unhelpful behavior to environmental causes (Islam & Hewstone, 1993). The reverse applied to outgroup members, who did not similarly receive the benefit of the doubt.

Favoring the ingroup and denigrating the outgroup may at first appear to be polar opposites. However, as we have seen elsewhere in this book (Chapters 11, 14, and 15), research on a number of seemingly unrelated phenomena—positive and negative affect, parental acceptance and rejection, positive and negative interactions in couples, and positive and negative components of attitudes—has shown an interesting and counterintuitive phenomenon: What look like opposite ends of a single dimension are often actually separate dimensions. The same is true with positive feelings toward ingroups and negative feelings toward outgroups (Brewer & Brown, 1998). In most situ-

Apply & Discuss

At the beginning of the twentieth century, the United States was seen as a great melting pot, where people of many cultures could come and become "Americans." By the end of the century, a different attitude had emerged, emphasizing the multiethnic nature of the society and encouraging ethnic pride, leading people to define themselves as "hyphenated-Americans" (e.g., African-American, Asian-American).

■ Is fear of "the other"—particularly if the other speaks a different language, looks different, and has different values and beliefs—a tendency that is "built into" the human psyche, or is it entirely learned?

■ Is ethnic pride a threat to the ties that bind a multiethnic nation together? How can we maximize the conditions that allow people of different ethnicities to preserve their heritage without fostering ingroup–outgroup antagonism?

ations, ingroup favoritism is actually more common than outgroup derogation or devaluation. In fact, another form of subtle racism or group antagonism may lie less in the *presence* of hostile feelings than in the *absence* of the positive feelings that normally bind people together and lead them to help each other (Pettigrew & Meertens, 1995).

The readiness to create and act on ingroup–outgroup distinctions probably rests on both motivational and cognitive processes. From a motivational point of view, casting ingroup members in a positive light gives oneself a positive glow as a member of the group (Tajfel, 1981). In fact, one study showed that after watching their team win, basketball fans showed an increased belief in their abilities at an unrelated task (Hirt et al., 1992). From a cognitive perspective, ingroup effects reflect our continuous and automatic efforts to categorize and schematize information.

Reducing Group Antagonisms   Research on ingroups and outgroups inevitably led to interest in techniques for reducing group antagonisms. In a classic experiment, researchers created friction between two groups of boys, dubbed the Rattlers and the Eagles, at a Boy Scout summer camp (Sherif et al., 1961). Then the experimenters fostered strong ingroup sentiments by instructing the children to give their group a name, wear special clothes, and so forth. They also encouraged rivalries through competitive activities. Within a short time, the competition became so heated that it degenerated into overt hostility.

Initial attempts to defuse the hostility, such as bringing the groups together for pleasant activities, failed. Another approach was more successful: The experimenters contrived situations that created **superordinate goals**—*goals requiring the groups to cooperate for the benefit of all*. In one instance, the experimenters arranged for a truck transporting food for an overnight trip to stall. Eventually, both groups cooperated in pulling the truck with a rope. Similarly, when the camp's water supply stopped, both groups worked together to solve the problem.

The researchers concluded that contact alone is not enough to reduce conflict; the contact must also involve *cooperation* (see Sherif & Sherif, 1979). This finding has important implications for social policies such as school desegregation, because it suggests that simply placing children from two different races in the same school may not minimize animosities; it may in fact exacerbate them (Stephan, 1987). Compare this to sports teams, where black and white players work together for common goals and do not distinguish at the end of a winning game who they will throw their arms around based on race.

Other factors also influence whether contact leads to increased tolerance or animosity. First, individuals must have the opportunity to get to know one another on a one-to-one basis, as in sports teams and musical groups, and to have relatively equal status (Brewer & Brown, 1998). People from different groups also need to have enough shared values, beliefs, interests, culture, and skills so that their interactions dissolve stereotypes rather than confirm them. Unfortunately, members of cultures and subcultures often differ on precisely these things, which increases the need for superordinate goals and shared or complementary skills that deemphasize differences and emphasize commonalities.

◆ INTERIM SUMMARY

Prejudice lies not only in people's minds but also in social institutions and socialization practices that foster it. Prejudice requires a distinction between **ingroups** and **outgroups** (people who belong to the group and those who do not). People often attribute more homogeneity to outgroups than ingroups and make more positive interpretations of the behavior of ingroup members. Ingroup–outgroup distinctions probably reflect both motivational and cognitive factors. Contact between groups can decrease prejudice and hostility if it is accompanied by shared goals, personal acquaintance with members of the outgroup, relatively equal status, and enough shared values and culture to dissolve stereotypes.

Attribution

Whether trying to understand the causes of inner-city violence or a curt response from a boss, people are constantly thinking about the "whys" of social interaction. *The process of inferring the causes of one's own and others' mental states and behaviors* is called **attribution** (Gilbert et al., 1998). Attribution plays a central role in virtually every social encounter. For example, an attribution about why a friend did not call back when she said she would can affect the friendship, just as the attributions a student makes for a weak performance on a test can affect her self-esteem and motivation in the future.

Intuitive Science

People attribute causes by observing the *covariation* of situations, behavior, and specific people. In other words, they assess the extent to which the presence of one variable predicts the presence of another—that is, whether the two variables *co-vary* (Heider, 1958; Kelley, 1973, 1992). An employee who receives a terse response from his boss may have noticed that his boss is often brusque when she is stressed by approaching deadlines. Thus, he attributes her behavior to the situation rather than to her feelings about him.

According to one view, when people make attributions, they are like **intuitive scientists**: *They rely on intuitive theories, frame hypotheses, collect data about themselves and others, and draw conclusions as best they can based on the pattern of data they have observed* (Heider, 1958; Ross, 1977). In the language of connectionism, they are essentially trying to settle on a solution that takes into account as many constraints as possible.

Making Inferences

Understanding other people's behavior requires figuring out when their actions reflect demands of the situation, aspects of their personalities (often called personality *dispositions*), or interactions between the two (the ways specific people behave in particular situations). Thus, people sometimes make **external attributions**, or *attributions to the situation*, whereas other times they make **internal attributions**, *attributions to the person* (Chapter 5). Often they combine the two, as when the employee notices an interaction effect: that his boss tends to become tense and brusque (internal, or dispositional, attribution) when she is stressed by deadlines (external, or situational, attribution).

In making attributions, people rely on three types of information: consensus, consistency, and distinctiveness (Kelley, 1973, 1979). **Consensus** refers to *the way most people respond*. If everyone in the organization responds tersely to his questions, the employee might attribute his boss's brusque behavior to something situational (such as the organizational culture, or atmosphere of the company). **Consistency** refers to *the extent to which a person always responds in the same way to the same stimulus*. If the boss is frequently brusque, the employee will likely make an internal attribution about her personality. The **distinctiveness** of a person's action refers to *the individual's likelihood to respond this way to many different stimuli*. If the boss treats other people brusquely, the employee is likely to conclude that brusqueness is an enduring aspect of her personality, rather than a reflection of her attitude toward him. Consistency and distinctiveness are the intuitive scientist's versions of the concepts of consistency across time and consistency over situations debated by personality psychologists (Chapter 12).

Part of the difficulty in making accurate attributions is that most actions have multiple causes, some situational and some dispositional. In deciding how much to credit or blame a person, people generally adjust for the strength of situational demands through two processes, discounting and augmentation (Trope & Liberman, 1996). **Discounting** occurs when *people downplay (discount) the role of one variable*

Attributions are central to legal decision making. Suppose, for example, a person is charged with killing another person using a handgun.

■ What attributions lead to a charge of first-degree murder rather than a lesser charge, such as manslaughter?

■ What attributions affect the severity of the sentence once a person has been convicted?

Do we really know why we do what we do, or are our views of ourselves just theories? Go to www.wiley.com/college/westen and click on **Chapter 17: Self-Attribution: Making Inferences about Ourselves**

(such as personality, intelligence, or skill) because they know that others may be contributing to the behavior in question (Heider, 1958; McClure, 1998). For example, the employee may discount his boss's bad manners because she is under the strain of an approaching deadline, or because her father recently died. The opposite situation occurs with **augmentation**, which means *increasing (augmenting) an internal attribution for behavior that has occurred despite situational demands*. The employee may attribute particular coldness to his boss if she continues to respond tersely to his questions when the workload is low.

Making an attribution is typically a three-step process (Gilbert & Malone, 1995). First, people categorize the behavior they have observed (e.g., did the boss sound angry?). Then, based on the way they have interpreted the behavior, they categorize the person's personality (e.g., this is a hostile person). Finally, if the situation seems to have elicited or contributed to the behavior (e.g., the angry comment was provoked), they may discount the attribution of hostility. Experimental research supporting this theory shows that distracting participants while they are making attributions leads them to make automatic attributions to the person, which they would have discounted if they had had time to think about the situation. In other words, people first jump to conclusions about personality implicitly, and they correct these attributions if they have the time to think about it.

◆ INTERIM SUMMARY

Attribution is the process of inferring the causes of one's own and others' mental states and behaviors. People attribute causes by observing the covariation of social stimuli or events. People are like **intuitive scientists**, who use intuitive theories, frame hypotheses, and try to draw inferences from the data they have collected. They sometimes make **external attributions** (attributions to the situation), **internal attributions** (attributions to the person), or attributions that reflect the *interaction* of the two.

Biases in Social Information Processing

Although individuals in some sense act like intuitive scientists, their "studies" often have substantial methodological shortcomings. Indeed, rigorous application of the scientific method is so important in social psychology precisely because it prevents researchers from making the same kinds of intuitive errors we all make in everyday life.

Social psychologists have identified several biases in social information processing. Here we examine two of the most widely studied, and then explore the cognitive and motivational roots of biased social cognition.

Correspondence Bias

One of the most pervasive biases in social cognition, the **correspondence bias**, is *the tendency to assume that people's behavior corresponds to their internal states rather than external situations*—that is, to attribute behaviors to people's personalities and to ignore possible situational causes (Gilbert & Malone, 1995; Heider, 1958; Ross, 1977). A good illustration occurs while driving—which in the extreme case can turn into "road rage." In my clinical work, I tend to be very careful before drawing conclusions about a patient's personality and will usually take two or three sessions with a patient before coming to some tentative initial conclusions. I have no such caution on the road, however, where I seem to be able to diagnose other drivers with extraordinary speed and subtlety. I may, for example, draw highly sophisticated inferences about a person's character (e.g., "what a jerk!") from the fact that he is holding me up on my way to work by driving slowly—only to recognize when I see his license plate that he is from another state and probably has no idea where he is going.

Self-Serving Bias

Another pervasive bias in social cognition is the **self-serving bias**, in which *people tend to see themselves in a more positive light than others see them* (Baumeister, 1998; Epstein, 1992; Greenwald, 1980). The self-serving bias takes a number of forms. For example, a majority of people rate themselves as above average on most dimensions. This is, of course, statistically impossible (Taylor & Brown, 1988). People are also more likely to recall positive than negative information about themselves (Kuiper & Derry, 1982; Kuiper et al., 1985) and to see their talents as more striking and unusual than their deficiencies (Campbell, 1986). In addition, they attribute greater responsibility to themselves for a group product than other group members attribute to them (Ross & Sicoly, 1979) and assume that they are less driven by self-interest than those around them (Miller & Ratner, 1998).

Self-serving biases are not without their limits. Most people will not totally ignore reality (see Kunda, 1990), but they do differ tremendously in their tendency to let their needs for self-enhancement interfere with their objectivity. One study observed MBA students in simulated corporate decision-making meetings over a weekend (John & Robins, 1994). At the conclusion, participants ranked their own performance and that of their peers. The researchers also observed their behavior and ranked each participant.

Participants were fairly objective in ranking their peers' performance: Peer and psychologist rankings correlated at about .50. However, they were less objective about themselves. The correlation between self-rankings and psychologist rankings was only about .30. Moreover, 60 percent overestimated their own performance, suggesting a self-serving bias. And those who were rated as more narcissistic by the researchers showed the greatest biases of all! The data suggest that most people wear mildly rose-tinted glasses when they look in the mirror, but that people who are narcissistic keep a pair of opaque spectacles on hand in case the spotlight shines too brightly on their flaws (see also Epley & Dunning, 2000; Robins & Beer, 2001).

Like other biases in social cognition, the self-serving bias may depend in part on culture (Kitayama et al., 1998). This bias is pervasive in the West but much less so in Eastern and other collectivist cultures, in which people do not define themselves as much in terms of their individual accomplishments. When people in the United States describe themselves, they tend to list about five times as many positive as negative traits (Holmberg et al., 1995). This pattern is unheard of in cultures such as Japan and Korea, where people do not toot their horns so loudly, either in private or in public. Recent research suggests that as Asians become assimilated into Western culture, their conscious self-descriptions begin to show the Western bias; however, deeper, implicit processes (assessed, for example, by the speed with which they recognize the words *good* and *bad* after priming with the word *me*) may take a generation to change (Pelham et al., 1998, cited in Fiske et al., 1998).

Causes of Biases

What causes biases in processing social information? The answers appear to lie in both cognition and motivation.

Cognitive Biases Some of the errors people make reflect the same kinds of cognitive biases people display in nonsocial cognition (Chapter 7). For example, heuristics can lead to biases in social thinking, as when people assume that "all politicians are crooks" because of some salient examples that come to mind (the availability heuristic). In fact, one of the main reasons politicians often appear crooked is that their behavior—including their tax returns, business dealings, and so forth—is so closely scrutinized.

As in nonsocial cognition, heuristics can lead people awry, but they are essential to everyday functioning, because they allow us to make decisions and judgments rapidly

Most of these people believe they are smarter, more personable, and better looking than the person next to them.

Making Connections

People often see what they expect to see and fail to test alternative hypotheses, leading to false confirmation of schemas (Chapter 7). When a couple buys a car together, the salesperson often talks primarily to the man, assuming that the man knows more and is more interested in cars—and may not discover, for example, that the woman is more knowledgeable or making the decision. (My wife and I just had this experience: We were negotiating the price of a car with two dealerships, and although my wife would leave a message for the salespeople, they would invariably leave a return message on *my* voicemail.) Gender stereotypes of this sort are widespread and can be highly resistant to change (Chapter 14).

and without conscious reflection. People frequently lack the time or information they need to make accurate attributions, so they do the best they can. Often, these rapid, good-enough attributions are just that—good enough. On the other hand, phrases like "I had no idea he would turn out to be that way" or "I can't believe I didn't see that" express the regrets people feel when they discounted or failed to piece together some initial "clues" as they employed heuristics that turned out to be not quite good enough.

Motivational Biases   Other biases reflect motivation (Bruner & Tagiuri, 1954; Fiske, 1992; Kunda, 1990; Westen, 1991, 1998). Schemas and attributions are influenced by wishes, needs, and goals. For example, people who are currently involved in romantic relationships tend to perceive opposite-sex peers as less attractive and sexually desirable than people who are uninvolved (Simpson et al., 1990). This bias is useful because it makes maintaining a monogamous relationship easier.

Motivation can also influence the extent to which people think complexly about themselves and others. For example, one study compared people high in need for intimacy with those high in need for power (Woike & Aronoff, 1992). Participants were asked to evaluate potential research assistants by watching them interact with each other on videotape. In one condition, the investigators emphasized the need to be sensitive and empathic toward the applicant. In the other condition, the investigators stressed the importance of taking control of the situation and exercising decision-making power.

After watching the videotapes, the researchers instructed participants to describe the candidates and then coded the complexity of subjects' responses. The investigators reasoned that participants motivated by power would think more deeply and complexly when their power motives were activated, and those high in intimacy motivation would think more complexly when motivated by instructions emphasizing intimacy. The findings strongly supported the hypothesis (Figure 17.6), suggesting that the extent to which people think deeply about others depends on their motivation to do so.

Motivated biases can occur at the societal level as well as the personal, especially when nations are on the verge of war (Winter, 1987, 1993). One researcher studied the motives attributed by Northern and Southern newspapers to Abraham Lincoln and his Confederate counterpart, Jefferson Davis, following a series of speeches in 1861 (Winter, 1987). The Northern media saw Davis as power-hungry; the Southern media saw Lincoln as power-hungry. The Southern newspapers also saw Lincoln as low on the socially desirable motive, affiliation (which was rather ironic, since he was trying to keep the South from "disaffiliating" from the union!).

Interactions of Cognition and Motivation   Although social psychologists have spent many years debating whether particular biases are cognitive *or* motivational in origin, many biases probably reflect both (Tetlock & Levi, 1982). Consider the *confirmation bias*—the tendency to seek out information that confirms one's hypotheses. When presented with the task of finding out whether a target person is extroverted, subjects tend to ask the person questions that elicit extroverted responses and to fail to ask questions like "Do you enjoy spending time alone?" (Snyder & Cantor, 1979). People are more likely to commit the confirmation bias when they are not particularly motivated or when they lack the cognitive resources to do a more thorough assessment—for example, if they are distracted by a second task (Trope & Liberman, 1998).

Even more powerful biases can occur when individuals are motivated to come to a particular conclusion. For example, during the Lewinsky scandal in 1998, my colleagues and I found that, almost 90 percent of the time, we could predict six months in advance whether people would ultimately believe that President Clinton's actions met the criteria set forth in the Constitution for impeachable offenses ("high crimes and misdemeanors") based on their *feelings* about Clinton, Democrats and Republicans, feminism, and infidelity (Westen & Feit, 1999). These feelings appeared to lead people to listen to television commentators and read magazine articles that provided more data for their point of view and to weigh arguments in ways that would support their emotional prejudices. Similar findings emerged during the contested 2000 election: People's beliefs about whether hand or machine counting of votes produces more accurate results reflected a mixture of their feelings toward Gore, Bush, Democrats, and Republicans. Providing them with new data that seemed to prove the advantage of one or the other (an experimental manipulation) had little influence on their beliefs (Westen, Arkowitz, & Thagard, 2001.)

If people are intuitive scientists, then, research suggests that they could use a basic course in research design. Aside from cognitive errors, social perceivers have many goals besides the scientific objective of seeking truth, and these other agendas often influence their "findings." They are interested in looking good, maintaining positive feelings about themselves, believing good things will happen to them, protecting their idealized views of people they care about, and maintaining negative schemas of people (or groups) they dislike. Because motives play a fundamental role in attention, encoding, retrieval, and problem solving, social cognition is inherently intertwined with social motivation (see Fiske, 1993).

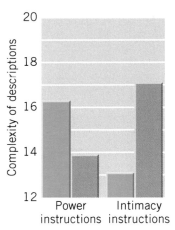

Figure 17.6 Motivation and the complexity of social cognition. When the instructions stressed power, participants high in power motivation showed greater cognitive complexity in describing potential research assistants. When the instructions stressed intimacy, participants high in intimacy motivation thought more complexly. *Source:* Woike & Aronoff, 1992, p. 102.

◆ **INTERIM SUMMARY**

The **correspondence bias** is the tendency to attribute behaviors to people's personalities and to ignore possible situational causes. The **self-serving bias** is the tendency to see oneself in a more positive light than one deserves. Biases in social cognition reflect both cognitive factors (such as the use of heuristics) and motivational factors (the impact of wishes, needs, and goals).

◆ The Self

Thus far, we have paid little attention to the social stimulus to which people attend more than any other: the self. The concept of self has a long and rather serpentine history in psychology, slithering in and out of vogue. In some eras, such as the present, psychologists have viewed the self as a central aspect of psychological functioning (Baumeister, 1998; Epstein, 1994; Markus & Cross, 1990). In others, particularly during the heyday of behaviorism, psychologists viewed the self as a fuzzy, mushy concept, unobservable and hence scientifically unknowable.

One of the greatest challenges in describing the self seems to be defining it. Many behaviorists have justifiably complained that psychologists have used the same word to denote dozens of discrete phenomena and hence have failed to provide a coherent, empirically valid construct of the self. For years, theorists of nearly every persuasion have defined the self as the self-concept—the way people see themselves. The problem with this definition is that it is logically impossible: If the self-concept is a concept of something, it must be a concept of the self. The self, then, cannot be a self-concept, or the self-concept becomes a person's concept of her self-concept! This is analogous to saying that a person's lamp and her concept of the lamp are the same thing.

The only logically sensible definition, then, is that the **self** is *the person, including mental processes, body, and personality characteristics*. From this definition several others logically follow. The **self-concept** is *the person's concept of himself*. It is a concept like any other (Chapter 7), such as squirrel, tree, or hairdresser. **Self-esteem** refers to *the degree to which the person likes and respects the self*.

Approaches to the Self

William James (1890) proposed a fundamental distinction between self as subject and self as object. The *self as subject* includes the person's experience of self as thinker,

Apply & Discuss

■ In what ways does cognition about ourselves follow similar principles to cognition about others? To what extent do similar principles of memory apply?

■ In what ways is cognition about ourselves different from cognition about others?

feeler, and actor. When I feel an emotion or think a thought, it is "I"—the self as subject—who is feeling or thinking. When I take an action, I have a sense that it is I who has made a choice about how to behave.

In contrast, the *self as object* is the person's view of the self. This is the self-concept on which people reflect when they take the self as an object of thought. The difference between self as subject and as object can be easily remembered grammatically: The self as subject, which James called the "I," is the subject who is capable of thinking about the self as object, the "me." Thus, the statement "I am thinking about me" contains both elements of self.

Two perspectives have recently given increasing prominence to the self: the psychodynamic and the cognitive (see Baumeister, 1998; Westen, 1992).

Psychodynamic Perspective

Contemporary psychodynamic thinking focuses on **self-representations**—*mental models or representations of the self.* Psychodynamic theories assert that people's representations of themselves and others play a key role in personality and psychopathology (Chapter 12). Patients with borderline personality disorder, for example, often view themselves as totally unlovable or evil to the core, which can make them vulnerable to suicide (Waldinger & Gunderson, 1984; Kernberg, 1975; Wixom et al., 1993).

Two characteristics distinguish psychodynamic views of self. First, they emphasize that people associate the self with many different positive and negative emotions, which are activated under different circumstances (Horowitz, 1988). Second, self-representations can be conscious or unconscious, explicit or implicit (Sandler & Rosenblatt, 1962). These representations can be at odds or even completely contradictory. For example, one patient with a narcissistic personality disorder was furious and deeply depressed when he was passed over for a supervisory position. At some level he worried that his own failings were the cause, but he convinced himself that the only reason he was passed over was because "mediocrity cannot appreciate true genius." This consciously grandiose representation seemed to mask a very different unconscious or implicit view of himself. Recent research from a cognitive perspective suggests, in fact, that implicit and explicit feelings about the self can often be very different and that implicit self-esteem, like implicit racism, can predict behavior in ways that explicit self-esteem cannot (Spalding & Hardin, 1999).

The psychodynamic view of self is thus converging in many respects with contemporary attitude research in emphasizing ambivalence (especially given all the ways we evaluate ourselves) and the distinction between implicit and explicit self-representations. In this sense, the self-concept is an *attitude* toward the self, which includes beliefs, feelings, and tendencies to behave toward oneself in particular ways.

Cognitive Perspective

Cognitive theorists focus on the way the self-concept shapes thought and memory (see Higgins, 1999; Markus & Cross, 1990). Extending the "intuitive scientist" view, one theorist has proposed that the self-concept is like a *theory* of oneself (Epstein, 1973, 1994). Other cognitive theorists propose that the self-concept is a **self-schema**—*a schema about the self that guides the way we think about and remember information relevant to ourselves* (Rogers et al., 1977; Markus, 1977; Markus & Wurf, 1987). Thus, a person who has a self-schema as incompetent is likely to remember times he failed in exquisite detail and to forget occasions in which he was successful.

Self-schemas may be hierarchically organized (Kihlstrom & Cantor, 1983). At the core of the broader self-schema are fundamental attributes of the self, such as the person's name, sex, physical appearance, relationships to family members, and salient personality traits. Below this general level in the hierarchy are schemas of the self in different situations or relationships (Figure 17.7). Each subschema is associated with its own attributes; a person may see herself as annoyed and anxious with her mother but comfortable with friends.

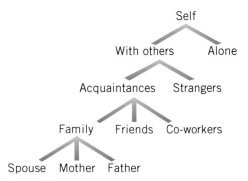

Figure 17.7 Hierarchical organization of a self-schema. Self-schemas may be organized hierarchically with multiple components, many defined by relationships, such as the self with family, friends, and co-workers. *Source:* Kihlstrom & Cantor, 1983.

People have schemas not only about the way they are but also about the way they *wish* they were or *fear* becoming (Markus & Nurius, 1986; Niedenthal et al., 1992). One theory distinguishes three kinds of self-concepts: actual, ideal, and ought (Higgins, 1987, 1999). The **actual self** refers to *people's views of how they actually are.* The **ideal self** refers to *the hopes, aspirations, and wishes that define the way the person would like to be.* The **ought self** includes *the duties, obligations, and responsibilities that define the way the person should be.*

Thus, a person may see himself as a moderately successful businessman (actual self) but hope to become the chief executive officer of a company (ideal self). At the same time, he may volunteer at a soup kitchen on Thanksgiving to satisfy a nagging sense that he is not contributing enough to his community (ought self). People have actual, ideal, and ought selves from a number of points of view, including their own and those of significant others. A person may feel she is meeting her "ought" standards for herself but that she has failed to meet her mother's expectations.

Discrepancies between these various self-schemas are associated with particular types of emotion (Higgins, 1987; Strauman, 1992). When people perceive a discrepancy between their actual self and their ideal self, they tend to feel emotions such as disappointment, dissatisfaction, shame, and embarrassment. These are characteristic feelings of individuals who are depressed, who feel their wishes and hopes are unfulfilled. People who experience a discrepancy between actual self and ought self feel emotions such as anxiety, fear, resentment, guilt, self-contempt, or uneasiness. These feelings are characteristic of anxious individuals, who believe they have failed to meet their obligations and hence may be punished.

Research suggests that these schemas may influence not only mood but physical health. As we have seen (Chapter 11), emotional distress can depress immune-system functioning, making a person vulnerable to ill health. Enduring ways of perceiving the self may thus lead to chronic feelings that increase vulnerability to illness.

One remarkable study demonstrated this by comparing people who were anxious, depressed, or neither (Strauman et al., 1993). The investigators asked participants to describe their actual, ideal, and ought selves, thanked them for their participation, and told them the experiment was over. Six weeks later, their research assistants, allegedly conducting a different experiment, primed discrepancies between actual and ideal self in depressed participants and between actual and ought self in anxious participants. They did this by exposing participants to words they had previously mentioned that were related to these discrepancies. For example, the investigators might ask an anxious subject who described his actual self as shy but his ought self as confident to think about the importance of being confident. (They also included words that were irrelevant to the person so that participants would not figure out what was happening.)

A week later, the experimenters exposed participants to a set of entirely irrelevant words (actually, taken from other participants), which they compared against the results of the previous session. Control subjects were similarly exposed one day to self-referential words (words taken from their first session) and another day to irrelevant words. After each session, the investigators took blood samples to ascertain levels of natural killer cells, a rough index of immune response.

The main findings are reproduced in Figure 17.8. The killer cell activity of control subjects, who were neither depressed nor anxious, went up slightly when they were exposed to self-referential words. Depressed subjects showed a slight decrease in killer cell activity when exposed to words related to their ideal-self discrepancies, al-

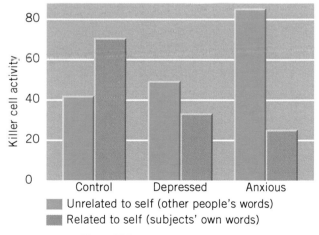

Figure 17.8 Self-schemas and immune functioning. Exposing nondepressed, nonanxious control subjects to words related to their ideal and ought selves led to a slight increase in killer cell activity—that is, to heightened immune functioning. For depressed and especially for anxious subjects, in contrast, exposure led to diminished immune functioning. *Source:* Adapted from Strauman et al., 1993, p. 1049.

though this was not statistically significant. The most striking finding was for anxious subjects, whose killer cell levels were significantly lower after being exposed to words related to their self-perceived failings (actual/ought discrepancies). Thinking about their unfulfilled obligations or unmet standards made them momentarily more vulnerable to illness. These findings are preliminary, but they suggest that chronic discrepancies between the way one believes one is and the way one ought or ideally should be might have a lasting impact on health.

◆ INTERIM SUMMARY

William James distinguished the self as subject, which includes the person's experience of self as thinker, feeler, and actor, and the self as object, or **self-concept** (the person's view or concept of self). Contemporary psychodynamic thinking focuses on **self-representations**, mental models or representations of the self that are typically associated with multiple emotional states and can be implicit or explicit. According to some cognitive theorists, the self-concept is a **self-schema**, or schema about the self, which may be hierarchically organized. People have schemas about not only the way they are but also the way they ideally would like to be and ought to be.

Self-Esteem

Individuals have multiple motives that guide the way they think about themselves, such as the motive to see themselves accurately (Baumeister, 1998). Another primary motive regarding the self, which often competes with accuracy motivation, is the motivation to maintain high self-esteem (Chapter 10). Just as individuals can conjure up a typical or prototypical self-concept, they have a core or global sense of self-esteem (Rosenberg, 1979), a usual way they feel about themselves. They also experience momentary fluctuations in self-esteem, depending on which self-schemas are currently active. An athlete who wins a competition sees herself as a winner and enjoys a momentary boost in self-esteem, regardless of whether being a winner is part of her prototypical self-concept.

Research with Western subjects suggests that self-esteem is hierarchically organized, presumably tied to a hierarchically organized view of the self. Thus, nested below a general level of self-esteem, people have feelings about themselves along specific dimensions, such as their morality, physical appearance, and competence (Coopersmith, 1967; Harter et al., 1998). A person with generally low esteem for his athletic prowess may nevertheless recognize himself to be a decent tennis player. People generally maintain positive self-esteem by giving greater emotional weight to areas in which they are more successful.

Although self-esteem often feels like something we "have," self-esteem reflects as much a dynamic set of skills for *maintaining* positive feelings about the self as it does the accessibility of positive attitudes toward the self. Individuals with high self-esteem think and behave in ways that lead to positive feelings. When experimentally forced into a bad mood, they tend to problem-solve and think positive thoughts, which in turn makes them feel better (and better about themselves). In contrast, people with low self-esteem tend to respond to bad moods with negative thoughts (Smith & Petty, 1995). Similarly, people with high, but not low, self-esteem are more likely to help someone out while in a negative mood, which then makes them feel better about themselves (Brown & Smart, 1991).

Self-Consistency

A less obvious motive toward the self is **self-consistency**, *the motive to interpret information to fit the way one already sees oneself and to prefer people who verify rather than challenge that view* (Lecky, 1945; Pinel & Swann, 2000; Swann, 1990). Most of the time, self-consistency and self esteem motives do not conflict; because most people hold relatively favorable views of themselves, they prefer positive information because it enhances self-esteem and bolsters their existing self-concept.

For people who do not like themselves, however, these two motives can lead in opposite directions. They want to feel better about themselves, but they also dislike evidence that contradicts their self-concept. Depressed people actually prefer to interact with others—including marital partners—who have a negative view of them (Chapter 15). Individuals who perceive themselves negatively appear to avoid people who give them feedback to the contrary for several reasons: They consider the feedback untrue, they feel that the relationship will be smoother and more predictable if the other person understands them, and they believe people who view them positively are less perceptive (Swann et al., 1992a).

<table>
<tr><td>Culture and Self</td><td>A Global Vista</td></tr>
</table>

The notion that people have a self-concept and some core of selfhood that distinguishes them from others seems intuitively obvious to people living in twentieth-century Western societies. This view would not, however, be commonsensical to people in most cultures in most historical epochs (Geertz, 1974; Markus & Kitayama, 1991; Shweder & Bourne, 1982). That the term "the individual" is synonymous with "the person" in contemporary usage demonstrates how the individualism of our culture is reflected in its language. Not coincidentally, the prefix "self-," as in "self-esteem" or "self-representation," did not evolve in the English language until around the time of the Industrial Revolution.

A Relational View of the Self

The contemporary Western view of "the person" is of a bounded individual, distinct from others, who is defined by more or less idiosyncratic attributes. In contrast, most cultures, particularly the nonliterate tribal societies that existed throughout the vast expanse of human history, view the person in her social and familial context, so that the self-concept is far less distinctly bounded.

When the Wintu Indians of North America described being with another person who was closely related or intimate with them, they would not use a phrase such as "John and I," but rather, "John we." They reserved "and" to signify distance between people with minimal relation. When anthropologist Dorothy Lee (1950) tried to elicit an autobiography from a Wintu woman, she received an extensive account of the lives of the woman's ancestors. Only with considerable prompting did the woman eventually discuss "that which was in my mother's womb." Cheyenne autobiographies similarly tend to begin with "My grandfather…" (Straus, 1982).

This relational view of selfhood is not confined to North American tribes. It is common among African groups (Comaroff, 1980) and has been observed in many Asian and Indo-Chinese cultures. For example, traditional Hindus in India frequently give their caste and village along with their name when they are asked to identify themselves (De Vos et al., 1985).

Why Does the Self Differ across Cultures?

Two factors seem to explain the differences between contemporary Western and other views of the self. First, some cultures are simply more group centered and others more individualistic (Fiske et al, 1998; Markus & Kitayama, 1991; Triandis, 1989). Because Japanese culture emphasizes cooperation rather than the Western ideal of autonomy, the Japanese experience the self less in terms of internal states than in terms of social relationships (Cousins, 1989; DeVos et al., 1985). Thus, for the Japanese, *sincerity* describes behavior that conforms to a person's role expectations (carrying out one's duties), whereas for North Americans it means behaving in accordance with one's inner feelings (DeVos et al., 1985). Sincere behavior in Japan may thus be very insincere to an American. In general, the Western self tends to be conceptualized as more independent, whereas the Asian self tends to be conceptualized as more *inter*dependent (Kitayama et al., 1998).

A second influence on conceptions of selfhood is technological development (Westen, 1985, 1991). Careful examination of historical documents suggests that only a few centuries ago the Western concept of self was much closer to the non-Western, group-centered view (Baumeister, 1986). The values, attitudes, and self-concepts of people in rural Greece, for example, resemble the collectivistic orientation one finds in China more than the individualism of contemporary Athens (see Triandis, 1989).

Ten thousand years ago, before the advent of agriculture, humans lived in bands (small groups). In these band societies, a concept of self distinct from other people and nature was generally absent, and moral values focused on the interests of the clan or band. With the rise of agriculture, which allowed accumulation of personal resources and led to social classes, people became more aware of individuality. At the same time, however, this awareness was countered by cultural proscriptions against it.

Around the time of the Industrial Revolution, something remarkable happened: The concept of the individual, free of attachments and duties, was born. And the individual has been born again wherever technological development has taken hold.

Technological development seems to facilitate individualism, and with it a more individuated sense of selfhood, for several reasons. The first is geographical mobility. People who remain in a small community, as their kin have before them, tend to view themselves in a different context than people who may relocate hundreds or thousands of miles away. In addition, changing work conditions, such as wage labor and work that is not performed communally with kin or clan, lead to a sense of individual competence.

Furthermore, in technologically developed societies people earn much of their status through their actions rather than their family affiliations. They also frequently take up occupations different from those of their parents. When a man is no longer a hunter or farmer like his father, his representations of self and father diverge. Literacy and education also personalize skills and competences, which are no longer experienced as collective knowledge because they may be learned through individual study.

In the late nineteenth century, Americans thought nothing of lending neighbors a hand for days or weeks to build a barn. This seems inconceivable just a century later, with the highly individualized sense of self associated with industrialization.

In addition, increased life span and higher standard of living make personal pleasures, desires, and interests more important. Factors such as family size and whether children have their own rooms probably have a subtle influence as well. Whether the cultural differences that now divide Japan and the West will remain despite the pressures of industrialization is a profound psychological question that will probably be resolved over the course of this next century.

◆ INTERIM SUMMARY

> The self-concept is shaped by at least three motives: accuracy, **self-esteem** (the need to view oneself positively), and **self-consistency** (the motive to interpret information to fit existing self-concepts). The contemporary Western view of self is of an independent, bounded, autonomous individual. This contrasts with other views of self, which are more group centered, collectivistic, and relational. Some of these differences reflect cultural factors. Others reflect the impact of technological development, which tends to promote individualism for a number of reasons, such as geographical mobility, less communal working conditions, literacy, and increased life span.

◆ Central Questions: Social and Nonsocial Cognition

We began this chapter with a fundamental question: To what extent are social and nonsocial cognition alike? Although social psychologists have followed developments in cognitive science closely and have borrowed many of their models from cognitive science, they also recognize a number of ways in which social cognition differs from nonsocial cognition (see Fiske, 1993, 1995; Markus & Zajonc, 1985). The differences are not black and white, but social and nonsocial cognition fall on opposite sides of a number of dimensions.

First, a person observing a social interaction is almost always missing the most relevant data: the unspoken intentions, thoughts, and feelings of the people involved. Because observers of a social interaction have access only to behaviors, they must infer what those behaviors mean. Ambiguity is thus the rule in social cognition, leaving substantial opportunities for error, bias, and idiosyncratic interpretation.

Second, social cognition is inherently intertwined with emotion. People either like or dislike their roommate; their psychology professor is either interesting or boring; the clerk is either courteous or rude. Thinking about chemical formulas, in contrast, may not engender quite so much feeling.

Third, although culture influences many cognitive processes, such as categorization, it plays a particularly important role in social cognition. An individual who is competitive and driven to accumulate wealth may appear perfectly normal in Western culture, and hence draw little attention. The same person may be classified as antisocial or self-centered in many other cultures. Social cognition is inherently infused with cultural value judgments because categories (such as men, nurses, or doctors) carry with them implications for how people who fit them *should* behave (Shweder, 1980).

Culture also influences the way people interpret interpersonal events by providing intuitive theories of personality and causality. When children and adults in the West explain their successes and failures, they rely on concepts such as skill, effort, and luck (Weiner, 1980). In contrast, Buddhist children from Sri Lanka sometimes attribute achievement and failure to good and bad deeds in past lives. Good deeds from another life lead to good karma, a positive moral force that guides one's fate (Little, 1988).

Finally, social cognition is reciprocal. The "object" being perceived in social cognition may respond to the perceiver—and change its actions based on how it believes it is being perceived. Getting annoyed at a textbook for being thick and boring does not change it. Getting annoyed at a professor for the same reasons, however, may well influence the way he lectures.

Understanding basic principles of thought and memory is thus necessary for understanding social thought and memory, but it is not sufficient. Humans are social animals, and this aspect of human nature has shaped the way we think about ourselves and others. In the next chapter, we turn to the way humans as social animals *behave*.

Summary

1. **Social psychology** examines the influence of social processes on the way people think, feel, and behave.

Attitudes

2. An **attitude** is an association between an object and an evaluation, which usually includes cognitive, evaluative, and behavioral components. These three components can, however, vary independently. Attitudes vary on a number of dimensions, such as their strength, accessibility, and complexity; whether they are implicit or explicit; and the extent to which they involve ambivalence. They also differ on their coherence (particularly the fit between cognitive and evaluative components). Broad attitudes tend not to be good predictors of behavior.

3. **Persuasion** refers to deliberate efforts to change an attitude. It can occur through either careful, explicit thought (the **central route**) or less explicit and rational processes (the **peripheral route**). The effectiveness of a persuasive appeal depends on a number of factors related to the source of the communication, the message, the channel (the means by which a message is sent), the context, and the receiver. Persuading people to change their behavior can also lead them to change their attitudes.

4. **Cognitive dissonance** occurs when a person experiences a discrepancy between an attitude and a behavior or between an attitude and a new piece of information that does not fit with it. Cognitive dissonance can motivate attitude change, although several distinct processes may underlie dissonance phenomena.

Social Cognition

5. **Social cognition** refers to the processes by which people make sense of others, themselves, social interactions, and relationships.

6. **First impressions** are the initial representations people form when they encounter someone for the first time. **Schemas**—patterns of thought that organize experience—guide attention, encoding, and retrieval of information about people, situations, and relationships.

7. **Stereotypes** are characteristics attributed to people based on their membership in specific groups. **Prejudice** refers to judging an individual based on (usually negative) stereotypes. Racial and ethnic prejudice has roots both in motivation and cognition, and in the person and the broader social system. Stereotypes can be implicit or explicit. Prejudice typically requires the distinction between **ingroups** and **outgroups**.

8. The process of making inferences about the causes of one's own and others' thoughts, feelings, and behavior is called **attribution**. People can make **external attributions** (attributions to the situation), **internal attributions** (attributions to the person), and attributions about interactions between the person and the situation. In making these attributions, they rely on three types of information: **consensus** (how everyone acts in that situation), **consistency** (how this person typically reacts in that situation), and **distinctiveness** (how this person usually reacts in different situations). **Discounting** occurs when people downplay the role of a variable that could account for a behavior because they know other variables may be contributing to the behavior in question. The opposite situation occurs with **augmentation**, which involves increasing an internal attribution for behavior that has occurred despite situational pressures.

9. Social cognition may be biased in a number of ways, including the tendency to attribute behavior to other people's dispositions even when situational factors could provide an explanation (the **correspondence bias**), and the propensity to see oneself in a more positive light than one deserves (the **self-serving bias**).

The Self

10. The **self** refers to the person. The *self as subject* refers to the individual's experience of self as thinker, feeler, and actor. The *self as object*, or **self-concept**, is the person's concept or view of the self.

11. Contemporary psychodynamic thinking focuses on mental representations of the self, or **self-representations**, which can be conscious or unconscious, and are typically associated with a variety of feelings. From a cognitive perspective, the self-concept is a **self-schema**, which guides thought, attention, and memory. **Self-esteem** refers to a person's feelings toward the self. People's views of themselves are motivated not only by the desire to perceive themselves accurately and by self-esteem motivation but also by the need for **self-consistency**, interpreting information to fit the way they already see themselves.

12. The contemporary Western view of the person is of a bounded individual, distinct from significant others, who is defined by more or less idiosyncratic attributes. In contrast, most cultures have understood the person in social and familial context. Technological development has fostered individualism.

13. Social cognition differs from nonsocial cognition in a number of ways, including its inherent ambiguity, its inseparability from emotion, its heavy cultural influence, and its reciprocal nature.

Key Terms

Chapter 18
Interpersonal Processes

Bill Jacklin, *Bathers IV, Coney Island*, 1992.

Samuel Oliner was 12 years old when the Nazis invaded the Jewish ghetto in Poland where he lived. His entire family was killed, but Samuel managed to escape. After two days of hiding, during which he witnessed a child bayoneted and a baby shot with a pistol, he found his way to the home of a Christian woman with whom his father had done business. She fed him and taught him how to pass for a Christian peasant, and he survived the war.

Years later, Oliner wrote a book about the small number of people who risked their lives and the lives of their families to protect Jews during the Holocaust (Oliner & Oliner, 1988). He and his research team interviewed over 400 rescuers and compared them with 72 individuals who neither helped nor hindered the Nazis. They sought to answer a simple question: What made the rescuers perform such extraordinary acts of **altruism**, that is, *helping another person with no apparent gain, and even potential cost, to oneself?*

The altruism of these individuals seems to defy theories of moral development (Chapter 14). For example, according to cognitive–social theories, reward, punishment, and expectancies control behavior. Everyone in Germany and the occupied countries during the war faced the same contingencies of reinforcement—to be caught rescuing Jews meant certain execution—but several thousand people did so nonetheless. According to cognitive–developmental theories, moral heroism should occur only among people with a high level of moral reasoning. Yet only about half of Oliner's rescuers referred to complex or abstract principles. In fact, several offered strikingly conventional reasons for their actions, such as, "I am an obedient Christian; the Lord wanted us to rescue those people and we did" (Oliner & Oliner, 1988, p. 155).

Rescuers differed from nonrescuers on both **situational variables** (*the situations in which people find themselves*) and **dispositional variables** (*their personalities and attitudes*). Perhaps surprisingly, one of the variables that distinguished the two groups was completely situational: Rescuers had more available rooms in their houses and were more likely to have a cellar. On the dispositional side, rescuers reported having come from closer knit families and having had parents who sometimes reasoned with them as a mode of discipline, rather than simply punishing them. Overwhelmingly, they reported being taught to treat people fairly regardless of their race, color, or class.

Understanding why some people risked their lives while others did nothing—and why still others have used ultranationalist ideology as an excuse to steal, rape, and murder—is the work of social psychologists. The previous chapter focused on the cognitive processes people use to try to understand themselves and others. This chapter addresses motives, emotions, and behaviors that emerge in social interaction.

We begin by examining interpersonal attraction and relationships, from brief encounters through long-term love relationships. We then turn to two very different forms of social interaction, which Oliner encountered in his childhood odyssey: altruism and aggression. Next we investigate the influence of other people on the way individuals behave, as they obey and conform, and consider what happens when individuals participate in groups. We conclude by placing the psychology of our era in its social and historical context and returning to some of the central themes with which we began in the opening chapter.

Throughout, we address a central question: To what extent does our behavior depend on the groups of which we are a part? In other words, do the same psychological principles apply when people are alone as when they are with groups? Can we understand social behavior through principles of individual psychology, or do people function differently when they are together? And how do social and cultural change affect individual psychology?

Central Questions

- To what extent does behavior depend on the groups of which people are a part?
- Can we understand individual psychology apart from social psychology?

◆ Relationships

People *affiliate*, or seek out and spend time with others, for many reasons. Sometimes they interact to accomplish instrumental goals, such as raising money for a charity or meeting over dinner to discuss a business deal. Other interactions reflect family ties, shared interests, desires for companionship, or sexual interest (Fiske, 1992; Mills & Clark, 1994). Here we focus on two lines of research, one that examines the factors that attract people to each other and another that explores a particular kind of attraction in enduring relationships: love.

Factors Leading to Interpersonal Attraction

Social psychologists have devoted considerable attention to **interpersonal attraction**, *the reasons people choose to spend time with other people*. What draws us to some people but not to others? Researchers have identified several factors.

Proximity

Sometimes the answer is as simple as proximity: Numerous studies have documented that people tend to choose their friends and lovers from individuals nearby. One study surveyed 44 Maryland State Police trainees who had been assigned rooms and classroom seats in alphabetical order (Segal, 1974). When the trainees were asked to name their three closest friends on the force, the closer together their surnames, the more likely they were to be friends.

Proximity plays an equally important role in romantic relationships. As one observer wryly commented, "Cherished notions about romantic love notwithstanding, the chances are about 50–50 that the 'one and only' lives within walking distance" (Eckland, cited in Buss & Schmitt, 1993, p. 205). Social–psychological research has repeatedly shown that situational influences such as proximity (or merely having a spare room in Nazi-occupied Germany) have a remarkably strong impact on behavior.

Of course, people neither become friends nor fall in love *simply* because the other person is within walking distance. Rather, proximity allows people to get to know one another. It also sets the stage for familiarity, and familiarity tends to breed affection (Zajonc, 1968, 1998). From an evolutionary perspective, the link between familiarity and liking may be part of our genetic endowment: People who are familiar are likely to be safe, and they are likely to be relatives or alliance partners. On the other hand, increased proximity and familiarity with someone initially disliked can lead to increasing dislike over time if nothing changes to "dislodge" the initial impression (Festinger et al., 1950; Klinger & Greenwald, 1994).

Interpersonal Rewards

A second factor that influences interpersonal attraction is the degree to which interaction with another person is rewarding. From a behaviorist point of view, the more people associate a relationship with reward, the more likely they are to affiliate (Byrne & Murnen, 1988; Clark & Pataki, 1995; Newcomb, 1956).

One ingenious experiment tested a classical conditioning theory of attraction: that children should prefer other children they meet under more enjoyable conditions (Lott & Lott, 1974). The investigators placed first and third graders in groups of three. They gave some of the children a chance to succeed on a task, rewarding them for it, and rigged the task so that others would fail. Later, they asked the children to name a classmate they would like to take on a family vacation. One out of four children in the success condition chose a child who had participated in the study with them, compared to only one in *20* children in the failure condition.

Social exchange theories, based on behaviorist principles, *consider reciprocal reward the foundation of relationships* (Homans, 1961). In this view, in the social as in the economic "market," people try to maximize the value they can obtain with their resources (Kenrick et al., 1993). Or to put it another way, choosing a relationship is like trying to get the best "bang for the buck." The resources (the "bucks") in social relationships are personal assets: physical attractiveness, wit, charm, intelligence, material goods, and the like. In romantic relationships, people tend to choose others of similar value (as culturally defined) because both partners are trying to maximize the value of their mate.

Similarity

A third factor that influences attraction is similarity. People tend to choose casual acquaintances, as well as mates and best friends, on the basis of shared attitudes, values, and interests. One study periodically assessed the attitudes and patterns of affiliation of incoming male college transfer students assigned to the same dormitory (Newcomb, 1961). Over the course of the semester, as the students had a chance to learn one another's attitudes, friendship patterns began to match initial attitude profiles. Surrounding oneself with like-minded others seems to be rewarding, leading to the kind of interpersonal reinforcement described by social exchange theorists.

Folk wisdom that "birds of a feather flock together" thus tends to have more than a grain of truth. So what do we make of the opposite adage, that "opposites attract"? Although people tend to like others who share their values and attitudes, they often prefer being with people whose resources, needs, or behavioral styles complement their own (Dryer & Horowitz, 1997; Pilkington et al., 1991). For example, dominant people tend to prefer to interact with others who are more submissive, and vice versa.

Physical Attractiveness

A final factor that influences interpersonal attraction is physical attractiveness (Chapter 17). Even in nonsexual relationships, physically attractive people are magnets (Eagly et al., 1991). Attractive children tend to be more popular among their peers and are treated more leniently by adults (Clifford & Walster, 1973; Dion & Berscheid, 1974). Attractive adults receive more cooperation and assistance from others (Sigall et al., 1971) and better job recommendations (Cash et al., 1977)

Not surprisingly, physical attractiveness tends to have a greater impact on romantic than nonromantic relationships (Fletcher et al, 1999). Attractiveness is a major, if not *the* major, criterion college students use in judging initial attraction (e.g., Curran & Lippold, 1975; Walster et al., 1966). One study asked students to indicate whether they were attracted to strangers pictured in photographs. The experimenters gave another group the same photographs but stapled them to surveys showing the strangers' attitudes. Information about the strangers' attitudes had virtually no effect (Byrne et al., 1968). At first meeting, attraction appears to be skin deep.

Given that only a small percentage of people can occupy the choice locations on the bell curve of attractiveness, how do the rest of us ever get a date? In reality, people tend to choose partners they perceive to be equally attractive to themselves, not necessarily the most beautiful or handsome (Berscheid et al., 1971). One set of studies clarified how and why this happens. In one condition, male participants were told that a number of different women would gladly date them; in the other condition, they were offered no such assurance. Men in the second condition chose less attractive partners. By doing so, they were apparently trying to maximize the beauty of their partner while minimizing their risk of rejection (see Huston, 1973).

Across a number of studies, the average correlation between rated attractiveness of members of a couple is around .50, suggesting that people do indeed tend to find someone of equivalent attractiveness. In economic terms, one of the major "assets" people take on the dating "market" is their appearance, and they tend to exchange "goods" of relatively equal value.

Standards of physical attractiveness vary tremendously from culture to culture (and from individual to individual). Nevertheless, views of beauty are not entirely culture specific. People across the world tend to rate facial attractiveness in similar ways (Cunningham et al., 1995; Wheeler & Kim, 1997), with correlations between raters across cultures generally exceeding .60 (which is close to the correlation between the speed at which people travel while driving and the speed limit—not a perfect correlation, but a very high one). Several studies have also found that infants in the West who have not yet been socialized to norms of physical beauty gaze longer at faces rated attractive by adults. This occurs whether the faces are of adults or infants, males or females, or blacks or whites (Langlois et al., 1991).

Just How Shallow Are We?

The research on interpersonal attraction described thus far suggests that we humans are a shallow lot indeed. What we most desire is someone a few doors down, who brings us a beer on a warm afternoon, reminds us of ourselves, and looks like Denzel Washington or Charlize Theron.

We may be shallow creatures, but probably not quite that shallow. An important caveat about this body of research is that most studies were conducted in brief laboratory encounters between college students who did not know each other. While all the factors identified are probably important, the extent to which each influences interpersonal attraction outside this special circumstance is not clear. People tend to emphasize physical attractiveness more during the late teens and early twenties than in any other life stage. Concerns about identity in late adolescence also probably promote a preference for peers who are similar because they reinforce the individual's sense of identity (Sears, 1986).

College students may not be representative for research on relationships for another reason: Few have had long-term relationships, simply by virtue of their age. The importance of various dimensions of attraction waxes and wanes at different points in a relationship. Studies using broader community samples find that marital satisfaction is typically high initially, lower during child-rearing years (especially when children are toddlers), and higher again once the children leave home, particularly during retirement (Sillars & Zietlow, 1993).

Love

Researchers aware of these limitations have turned their attention to long-term adult love relationships (Berscheid & Reis, 1998) in an attempt to convert this enigmatic experience from sonnets to statistics, or from poetry to p-values.

Making Connections

A defining feature of some severe personality disorders is indifference to social contact (Chapter 15).

■ Are humans "born to love"—that is, do we innately need other people?

■ Are people who do not seek relationships genuinely disordered, or is this simply a cultural value judgment?

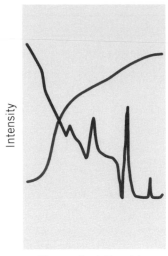

Years of relationship
— Passionate love
— Companionate love

Figure 18.1 Passionate and companionate love in a long-term relationship. The figure depicts the intensity of two kinds of love over time. Passionate love is high at the beginning of a relationship but tends to diminish over time, with periodic resurgences, or "peaks." Companionate love usually grows over time.

Classifying Love

At considerable risk to themselves from Cupid's arrows, some researchers have tried to classify love. One important distinction is between passionate and companionate love (Walster & Walster, 1978). **Passionate love** is a wildly emotional condition, *marked by intense physiological arousal and absorption in another person*. It is the stuff of Hollywood movies, sleepless nights, and daytime fantasies. In contrast, **companionate love** involves *deep affection, friendship, and emotional intimacy*. It grows over time through shared experiences and increasingly takes the place of passionate love—which, alas, does not last forever. However, the two kinds of love generally coexist (Figure 18.1), and people experience resurgences of passionate love throughout long relationships (Baumeister & Bratslavsky, 1999).

Another classification divides love into three components: *intimacy* (feelings of closeness), *passion* (sensual arousal), and *commitment* (dedication to the other person and to the relationship) (Sternberg, 1988, 1997b). According to this view, relationships can differ on the extent to which they are based in one component or another. Some, for example, are all passion with little intimacy or commitment. Others involve mixtures of all three.

An Evolutionary Perspective

From an evolutionary perspective, the feelings and behaviors we associate with the concept of love are evolved mechanisms that tend to lead to reproductive success (Buss & Kenrick, 1998). Caring for offspring (parental love), courtship, sexual intimacy, and concern for family all maximize the likelihood that we, and those related to us, will reproduce (and survive to reproduce in the future). Romantic love, in this view, is an adaptation that fostered the reproductive success of our ancestors by bonding two people likely to become parents of an infant who would need their reliable care (Hazan & Shaver, 1987).

Neither love nor lust, however, inevitably leads to monogamous marriage. In fact, a relatively permanent union of two individuals is just one mating strategy that occur across species. Even among humans, 80 percent of cultures have practiced polygyny, which permits men multiple wives or mistresses. In Western cultures, premarital sex is virtually ubiquitous, and roughly half of married people at some point have extramarital affairs (Buss & Schmitt, 1993).

Sexual Strategies Evolutionary psychologists have studied the **sexual strategies** (*tactics used in selecting mates*) people use in different kinds of relationships, from brief romantic liaisons to marriages (Buss & Kenrick, 1998; Buss & Schmitt, 1993). Where many researchers studying interpersonal attraction and relationships generalize across genders, evolutionary theorists argue that males and females face very different selection pressures and hence have evolved different sexual strategies. Because a man can have a virtually infinite number of offspring if he can obtain enough willing partners, he can maximize his reproductive success by spreading his seed widely, inseminating as many fertile females as possible. In contrast, women can bear only a limited number of children, and they make an enormous initial investment in their offspring during nine months of gestation. As a result, women should be choosier about their mating partners and select only those who can and will commit resources to them and their offspring.

From these basic differences ensues a battle of the sexes. Females maximize their reproductive success by forcing males with resources to commit to them in return for sexual access, and their short- and long-term mating strategies should be relatively similar. (Bear in mind that sexual strategies, like other

Is love unique to humans?

mechanisms for adaptation, were selected in an environment very different from our own, tens or hundreds of thousands of years ago, long before condoms and birth control pills. Changing conditions are likely to alter their expression but not eliminate them entirely.)

For males, in contrast, short- and long-term sexual strategies may be very different. In the short term, the female with the greatest reproductive value is one who is both fertile (young) and readily available for copulation. In the long run, committed relationships provide exclusive sexual access to a female, which allows the male to contribute resources to offspring without uncertainty about paternity (Chapter 1). Long-term relationships also bring potential alliances and resources from the woman's family. Thus, for long-term relationships, men should prefer less promiscuous partners who are young enough to produce many offspring and attractive enough to elicit arousal over time and increase the man's status. Men should also be choosier in long-term than in short-term encounters because the woman chosen for a long-term relationship will provide half the genes of the offspring in whom they invest.

"I dreamt I had a Harem, but they all wanted to talk about the relationship."

Aspects of this portrait of male and female sexual strategies probably sound familiar to anyone who has ever dated, although, of course, cultural and historical factors have substantial influences on sexual behavior as well (Chapter 10). Consider the Casanova who professes commitment and then turns out a few months later not to be ready for it; the man who gladly sleeps with a woman on a first date but then does not want to see her again, certainly not for a long-term relationship; or the woman who only dates men of high status and earning potential. From an evolutionary perspective, these are well-known figures because they exemplify common mating strategies.

The Empirical Evidence   How well do the data support these evolutionary predictions? Although the differences between the sexes are not always enormous, they tend to be consistent. For example, a study of 37 cultures found that in all but one, males tended to value the physical attractiveness of their mates more than females, whereas females were more concerned than males about the resources a spouse could provide (Buss & Angleitner, 1989). Males also consistently prefer females who are younger and hence have greater reproductive potential. Females prefer males who are older and hence are more likely to possess resources (Buss & Schmitt, 1993; Kenrick & Keefe, 1992; Kenrick et al., 1993). Figure 18.2 shows the results of some tests of evolutionary hypotheses in several cultures.

Studies of North American undergraduates also corroborate many evolutionary predictions about sexual strategies. For example, when males are asked to identify desired characteristics of potential partners, they prefer good-looking, promiscuous women for the short run, but they dislike promiscuity and pay somewhat less attention to physical appearance in the long run. In general, compared to women, men report a desire for a greater number of short-term sexual partners, a greater number of sexual partners in a lifetime, and a willingness to engage in intercourse after less time has elapsed (Buss & Schmitt, 1993).

Further, gender differences in reproductive strategies proposed by evolutionary psychologists may help explain some of the errors men and women make in "reading" each others' intentions. In trying to detect another person's sexual interest, everyone makes mistakes. According to evolutionary psychologists, men and women make *different* mistakes, which reflect gender-specific reproductive pressures (Haselton & Buss, 2000). Men tend to overestimate the sexual interest of women, whereas women tend to underestimate the commitment intentions of men. These errors fit with men and women's genetic "interests."

Apply & Discuss

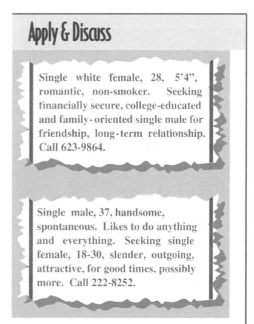

Single white female, 28, 5'4", romantic, non-smoker. Seeking financially secure, college-educated and family-oriented single male for friendship, long-term relationship. Call 623-9864.

Single male, 37, handsome, spontaneous. Likes to do anything and everything. Seeking single female, 18-30, slender, outgoing, attractive, for good times, possibly more. Call 222-8252.

Some researchers have examined the content of advertisements in "the personals" to test the evolutionary view of men as success objects and women as sex objects (Davis, 1990; Mills, 1995).

■ To what extent do personal ads support or not support evolutionary hypotheses? Would your own personal ad fit evolutionary theory?

■ How else could gender differences in ads be explained? What other factors affect the qualities potential suitors "advertise" and seek?

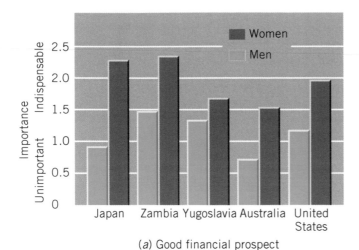

(a) Good financial prospect

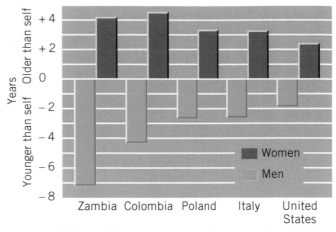

(b) Age difference preferred between self and spouse

Figure 18.2 Preferred characteristics of mates across cultures. Across cultures, financial prospects are more important to females than males in choosing a mate (a). Nearly everywhere, males prefer females who are younger, while females prefer males who are older (b). Source: Buss & Schmitt, 1993, pp. 204–232.

These evolutionary hypotheses are, of course, controversial. Some critics argue that they could be used to justify a double standard ("Honey, I couldn't help it, it's in my genes") or date rape (i.e., males have an "innate" tendency to see women as sexually more interested in them than they are). Others argue that the social learning of gender roles could produce similar results (see Chapter 14). From this point of view, increasing gender equality in a given culture should erode gender differences in mate preferences, a hypothesis that has received empirical support (Eagly & Wood, 1999). Further, evolutionary theory does not adequately explain the large numbers of extramarital affairs among females, the choice to limit family size or remain childless among couples with plenty of resources in cultures like our own, or homosexuality (although evolutionary theorists have attempted to offer explanations for all these apparently "maladaptive" phenomena). Nevertheless, evolutionary theory offers some very challenging explanations for phenomena that are not otherwise easily explained. When tempered by a recognition of the role of culture in channeling evolved reproductive tendencies, evolutionary theory provides a powerful source of testable hypotheses.

Romantic Love as Attachment

Another theory of love based on evolutionary principles comes from attachment theory. Romantic love relationships share several features with attachment relationships in infancy and childhood (Hazan & Diamond, 2000; Shaver et al., 1996). Adults feel security in their lover's arms, desire physical proximity to them, and experience distress when their lover is away for a considerable period or cannot be located (Shaver et al., 1988). Adults respond to wartime and job-related marital separations with much the same pattern of depression, anger, and anxiety observed in childhood separations, suggesting that attachment processes continue into adulthood (Vormbrock, 1993). Romantic love also brings security, contentment, and joy, like the satisfaction an infant feels in its mother's arms.

The bond between lovers does, of course, differ from infant attachment. Care for offspring and sexuality are components of adult romantic love absent from infant attachment. Nevertheless, the love between an infant and mother and between two lovers may have more in common than may first appear.

Attachment styles may be especially evident in adults when they are under stress because the attachment system is activated by threats to security. One study examined coping mechanisms among Israeli college students during the Gulf War, when Iraq

Making Connections

Attachment theorists argue that people pattern their adult love relationships on the mental models they constructed of earlier attachment relationships. Thus, the way individuals love as adults—particularly whether they are secure or insecure in their attachments—tends to reflect the way they loved and were loved as children (Chapter 14).

was bombarding civilian areas of Israel (Mikulincer et al., 1993). Subjects who lived in areas directly threatened by missile attacks differed from one another in the ways they coped with the danger. Securely attached subjects tended to seek support from others and generally experienced less distress from the bombings. Avoidantly attached people used distancing strategies (such as "I tried to forget about the whole thing"). Their distress was manifested primarily in physical symptoms, as might be expected given their difficulty experiencing emotional distress consciously. Ambivalently attached subjects used coping strategies aimed at calming themselves and quelling their emotions, which makes sense given their high level of conscious distress.

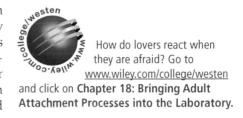

How do lovers react when they are afraid? Go to www.wiley.com/college/westen and click on **Chapter 18: Bringing Adult Attachment Processes into the Laboratory.**

Love in Cross-Cultural Perspective — A Global Vista

Western theorists were not the first to recognize a link between infant and adult love. The Japanese have a concept of love that combines the experience of attachment and dependence, called *amae*, derived from the word for "sweet" (Doi, 1992). *Amae* is both what infants desire with their mothers and what adults feel in the presence of their beloved.

Although adult romantic love may have its origins in the biological proclivity of infants to form attachments, by the time people have participated in relationships for 15 to 20 years, their manner of loving as adults is highly influenced by their culture (Dion & Dion, 1996). Many societies have arranged marriages, which are as much economic bonds linking families or clans as personal and sexual bonds between lovers. In parts of India where marriages have traditionally been arranged, people may experience passionate love, but they typically hide it (Traiwick, 1990). Public displays of affection are avoided, although they are tolerated more between an unmarried than a married couple. Patterns of marriage and intimacy also vary among castes. In one Untouchable caste, the Chuhras, even private expressions of affection and desire are limited, and spouses do not share sleeping quarters.

Chinese culture, too, has historically expected couples to consider their obligations to family in choosing a marriage partner: "An American asks, 'How does my heart feel?' A Chinese asks, 'What will other people say?'" (Hsu, 1981, p. 50). Indeed, in Chinese culture, love is so secondary to family obligations that the term *love* does not refer to a legitimate, socially sanctioned relationship between a man and a woman but connotes an illicit, shameful affair (see also Dion & Dion, 1988). In feudal China, passionate love was likely to constitute a reason why a couple should *not* marry. The female protagonist in Chinese love stories was more likely to be a concubine than a woman eligible for marriage. The marriage contract was signed by the fathers of the bride and groom; the engaged couple was not required to endorse the contract (Lang, 1946).

So does the passionate, romantic love seen on movie screens exist everywhere, or is it a Western (or Hollywood) creation? Romantic, passionate love probably does not exist *everywhere*, but it is common across cultures. A study using data from 42 hunter-gatherer societies from around the globe (gathered by anthropologists over the last century) found evidence of romantic love in 26 of them, or about 60 percent (Harris, 1995). Only six cultures allowed pure individual choice of marital partners, however; the other 36 required some degree of parental control, either in the form of veto power or arranged marriages.

Why is the concept of romantic love so central to contemporary Western culture that it fills our fairy tales (e.g., *Cinderella*, *Sleeping Beauty*) and movie screens? In a paradoxical way, the *individualism* of countries such as the United States or Australia may in part explain our preoccupation with passionate coupling. Contemporary Western culture is unique in its focus on individual satisfaction as a valued end (Chapter 17). This orientation extends into relationships, which are viewed as vehicles for personal gratification. Just 30 years ago, marriage in the West was something people entered and rarely exited. Today, if a marriage is unsatisfying, people often opt to leave and seek passion or satisfaction elsewhere. Romantic love may be a human potential, but cultures shape the ways we love—and leave.

Maintaining Relationships

Maintaining a relationship over time is no easy task. Oscar Wilde once quipped that the chains of matrimony are so heavy that it often takes three to carry them. Relationships pass through many phases (Borden & Levinger, 1991; Huston, 1994), and the majority of marriages in the United States and some other Western countries now end in divorce. The real question may not be what causes relationships to end but what allows some to last for 50 years or more!

In part, people decide whether to stay in a relationship by weighing its relative costs and benefits (Kelley & Thibaut, 1978; Levinger, 1976; Rusbult & Van Lange, 1996; Wieselquist et al., 1999). Whether a person remains committed over time depends on the balance of pleasure and discomfort it brings. Commitment to a relationship also depends on how much the person has invested in it and what the alternatives look like. People will tend to stay in a relatively unhappy marriage if they feel they have put so much into it that they cannot leave and if they do not think they can do any better.

Researchers interested in long-term relationships have attempted to track down the causes of marital satisfaction, dissatisfaction, and dissolution (Gottman, 1998). For example, people with successful relationships know how to stop spirals of *negative reciprocity*, in which one person's hostile or aversive behavior (e.g., sarcastic criticism) provokes a counterattack, leading to an escalation of conflict (Chapter 16). One of the most characteristic features of marriages that last is the ability to stop such cycles and to avoid the simmering feelings of hatred and disgust they tend to breed.

People in satisfying relationships also tend to make relatively benign attributions of their partners' actions, giving them the benefit of the doubt in difficult situations (Karney & Bradbury, 2000). People in satisfying relationships also frame their thinking about how to change the relationship in terms of how to approach a better relationship ("How can we become closer?") than how to escape a bad one ("How can we stop drifting apart?") (Gable & Reis, 1999). If anything unites these factors, it is probably the tendency both to accept the other person as he or she is, and to avoid repetitive and spiraling aversive encounters (L. Westen & Fruzetti, 2001).

People whose relationships are stable also tend to overlook or "reframe" each other's faults. Studies of both dating and married couples find that people report greater satisfaction with—and stay longer in—relationships when they have a somewhat idealized or moderately unrealistically positive perception of their partner (Murray & Holmes, 1997, 1999). (As a beneficiary of this defensive process, I support it wholeheartedly—as, I suspect, does my wife, whom I adore.) These findings make sense in light of research on "positive illusions," which suggests that people often enhance their sense of well-being by holding mildly positive illusions about who they are and what they can accomplish (Chapter 11).

Most people reap substantial rewards from their partners' slightly idealized views of them. However, people with low self-esteem (Chapter 17) have difficulty taking advantage of their partners' illusions. Despite the fact that their partners tend to hold idealized views of them, people with low self-esteem have difficulty basking in the warm glow of spousal unreality and instead assume that their own negative view of themselves is shared by their partner (Murray et al., 2000). When threatened, people with low self-esteem tend to doubt their partner's regard even more; in contrast, those with high self-esteem respond by inflating their beliefs about their partners' regard for them and hence use the relationship to insulate themselves from negative feelings, particularly about themselves (Murray et al., 1998).

Making Connections

Research across a number of areas consistently finds that negative and positive feelings not only are physiologically distinct but have independent effects on a variety of outcomes (Chapter 11). Parental warmth and hostility each have an impact on a growing child's self-esteem and psychological health, just as the tendency of spouses to display acceptance and warmth toward one another contributes to marital satisfaction *independently* of the extent to which the couple fights. Some couples with good marriages have "knock-down-drag-out" arguments but are genuinely loving toward each other most of the time. Others with bad marriages are too indifferent to one another to fight.

◆ INTERIM SUMMARY

Several factors lead to interpersonal attraction, including proximity, interpersonal rewards, similarity, and physical attractiveness. One taxonomy of love contrasts **passionate love** (intense physiological arousal and absorption in another person) with **companionate love** (love that involves deep affection and intimacy). Some theorists argue that romantic love is a continuation of attachment mechanisms that first emerge in infancy. Evolutionary theorists emphasize **sexual strategies**, tactics used in selecting mates, which reflect the different evolutionary selection pressures on males and females. Love appears to be rooted in attachment but is shaped by culture and experience. Maintaining relationships over time is a difficult task. People in satisfying long-term relationships tend to avoid negative spirals, give their partners the benefit of the doubt, and hold slightly idealized views of their partners.

◆ Altruism

Thus far, we have focused on the ties that bind. In this section, we examine another interpersonal process that brings people together: altruism. A person who donates blood, volunteers in a soup kitchen, or risks death (like the heroes of Oliner's World War II experience that opened this chapter) is displaying altruism. Many forms of altruistic behavior are so common that we take them for granted—holding open a door, giving a stranger directions, or trying to make someone feel comfortable during a conversation. Indeed, charitable contributions in the United States alone exceed $50 billion a year (Batson, 1995).

We begin this section by examining theories of altruism. We then consider experimental research on a particular form of altruism, bystander intervention.

Theories of Altruism

For centuries, philosophers have debated whether any prosocial act —no matter how generous or unselfish it may appear on the surface—is truly altruistic. When people offer money to a homeless person on the subway, is their action motivated by a pure desire to help, or are they primarily alleviating their own discomfort?

Ethical Hedonism

Many philosophers argue for **ethical hedonism,** *the doctrine that all behavior, no matter how apparently altruistic, is—and should be—designed to increase one's own pleasure or reduce one's own pain.* As one observer put it, "Scratch an 'altruist' and watch a hypocrite bleed" (Gheslin; cited in Batson, 1995).

People have many selfish reasons to behave selflessly (Batson, 1991, 1998). People are frequently motivated by their emotions (Chapter 11), and behaving altruistically can produce positive emotions and diminish negative ones. The overwhelming majority of Oliner's subjects who saved Jews from the Nazis reported that their emotions—pity, compassion, concern, or affection—drove them to help (Oliner & Oliner, 1988). Prosocial acts can also lead to material and social rewards (gifts, thanks, and the esteem of others) as well as to positive feelings about oneself that come from meeting ideal-self standards (Wedekind & Milinski, 2000).

Some theorists explain the motivation to act on another's behalf in terms of *empathic distress*: Helping relieves the negative feelings aroused through empathy with a person in distress (Hoffman, 1982). This mechanism does not appear to be unique to humans. In one study, researchers trained rhesus monkeys to pull a chain to receive food (Masserman et al., 1964). Once the monkeys learned the response, the investigators placed another monkey in an adjacent cage, who received an electric shock

Apply & Discuss

How might each of the following perspectives explain why some people give money to street beggars?

- Behaviorist
- Psychodynamic
- Cognitive
- Evolutionary

Did you never see little dogs caressing and playing with one another, so that you might say there is nothing more friendly? But that you may know what friendship is, throw a bit of flesh among them, and you will learn. Throw between yourself and your son a little estate, then you will know how soon he will wish to bury you and how soon you wish your son to die…. For universally, be not deceived, every animal is attached to nothing so much as to its own interest…. For where the I and Mine are placed, to that place of necessity the animal inclines.

EPICTETUS

How selfish soever man may be supposed, there are evidently some principles in his nature, which interest him in the fortune of others, and render their happiness necessary to him, though he derives nothing from it except the pleasure of seeing it. Of this kind is pity or compassion, the emotion which we feel for the misery of others, when we either see it, or are made to conceive it in a very lively manner.

ADAM SMITH, 1759
A Theory of Moral Sentiments

every time they pulled the chain. Despite the reward, the monkeys stopped pulling the chain, even starving themselves for days to avoid causing the other monkey to suffer.

Empathizing with others apparently does involve actually *feeling* some of the things they feel. In one experiment, participants watched videotaped interactions between spouses and were asked to rate the degree of positive or negative affect one of the spouses was feeling at each instant (Levenson & Ruef, 1992). To assess the accuracy of these ratings, the experimenters correlated participants' ratings with the spouses' own ratings of how they felt at each point. Participants who accurately gauged these feelings showed a pattern of physiology similar to the person with whom they were empathizing, such as a similar level of skin conductance—but only for unpleasant emotions. In other words, when people "feel for" another's pain, they do just that—feel something similar, if less intensely—and use this feeling to gauge the other person's feeling. With positive emotions, people apparently use their head instead of their gut.

Genuine Altruism

An alternative philosophical position is that people can be genuinely altruistic. Jean-Jacques Rousseau, the French Romantic philosopher, proposed that humans have a natural compassion for one another and that the only reason they do not always behave compassionately is that society beats it out of them. Adam Smith, an early capitalist economist, argued that people are generally self-interested but have a natural empathy for one another that leads them to behave altruistically at times.

Some experimental evidence suggests that Rousseau and Smith may have been right. People who have the opportunity to escape empathic distress by walking away, or who are offered rewards for doing so, still frequently choose to help someone in distress (Batson, 1991; Batson & Moran, 1999). People also may behave altruistically for the benefit of a group, usually one with which they identify themselves.

An Evolutionary Perspective

Evolutionary psychologists have taken the debate about altruism a step further by redefining self-interest as reproductive success. By this definition, protecting oneself and one's offspring is in an organism's evolutionary "interest."

Evidence of this type of altruistic behavior abounds in the animal kingdom. Some mother birds will feign a broken wing to draw a predator away from their nest, at considerable potential cost to themselves (Wilson, 1975). Chimpanzees "adopt" orphaned chimps, particularly if they are close relatives (Batson, 1995). If reproductive success is expanded to encompass inclusive fitness (Chapter 10), one would expect humans and other animals to care preferentially for themselves, their offspring, and their relatives. Organisms that paid little attention to the survival of related others, or animals that indiscriminately invested in kin and non-kin alike, would be less represented in the gene pool with each successive generation. The importance of these evolutionary mechanisms has been documented in humans, who tend to choose to help related others, particularly those who are young (and hence still capable of reproduction), in life-and-death situations (Burnstein et al., 1994).

Why, then, do people sometimes behave altruistically toward others unrelated to them? Was Mother Teresa an evolutionary anomaly? And why does a flock of black jackdaws swarm to attack a potential predator carrying a black object that resembles a jackdaw when it means some may be risking their feathers for a bird to which they are genetically unrelated?

To answer such questions, evolutionary theorists invoke the concept of **reciprocal altruism**, which holds that *natural selection favors animals that behave altruistically if the likely benefit to each individual over time exceeds the likely cost* (Caporael & Baron, 1997; Trivers, 1971). In other words, if the dangers are small but the gains in survival and reproduction are large, altruism is an adaptive strategy. For example, a jackdaw takes a slight risk of injury or death when it screeches or attacks a predator, but its action may save the lives of many other birds in the flock. If most birds in the flock warn one another, they are *all* more likely to survive than if each behaves "selfishly."

The same applies to humans. Social organization for mutual protection, food gathering, and so forth permits far greater reproductive success for each member on the average than a completely individualistic approach that loses the safety of numbers and the advantages of shared knowledge and culture.

◆ INTERIM SUMMARY

> **Altruism** refers to behaviors that help other people with no apparent gain or with potential cost to oneself. Philosophers and psychologists disagree as to whether an act can be purely altruistic or whether all apparent altruism is really intended to make the apparent altruist feel better (**ethical hedonism**). Evolutionary psychologists propose that people act in ways that maximize their inclusive fitness and are more likely to behave altruistically toward relatives than others. Natural selection also favors animals that behave altruistically toward unrelated others if the likely benefit to each individual over time exceeds the likely cost, a phenomenon known as **reciprocal altruism**.

Bystander Intervention

Although philosophers and evolutionists may question the roots of altruism, apparent acts of altruism are so prevalent that their *absence* can be shocking. A case in point was the brutal 1964 murder of Kitty Genovese in Queens, New York. Arriving home from work at 3:00 A.M., Genovese was attacked over a half-hour period by a knife-wielding assailant. Although her screams and cries brought 38 of her neighbors to their windows, not one came to her assistance or even called the police. These bystanders put on their lights, opened their windows, and watched while Genovese was repeatedly stabbed.

To understand how a group of law-abiding citizens could fail to help someone who was being murdered, social psychologists John Darley and Bibb Latane (1968) designed several experiments to investigate **bystander intervention**, or *helping a stranger in distress*. Darley and Latane were particularly interested in whether being part of a group of onlookers affects an individual's sense of responsibility to take action.

In one experiment, male college students arrived for what they thought would be an interview (Darley & Latane, 1968). While the students waited, either by themselves or in groups of three, the investigators pumped smoke into the room through an air vent. Students who were alone reported the smoke 75 percent of the time. In contrast, only 38 percent of the students in groups of three acted, and only 10 percent acted when in the presence of two confederates who behaved as if they were indifferent to the smoke.

This quiet street in New York was the scene of a brutal murder—and the impetus for research attempting to understand why Kitty Genovese's neighbors did nothing to help.

A Model of Bystander Intervention

Based on their experiments, Darley and Latane developed a multi-stage model of the decision-making process that underlies bystander intervention: Bystanders must *notice* the emergency, *interpret* it as one, *assume personality responsibility* to intervene, *decide how* to intervene, and then *actually intervene* (Figure 18.3). At any point in this process, a bystander may make a decision that leads to inaction.

This model helps explain why the presence of others can foster action or inaction. In the first two stages (noticing the emergency and interpreting it as one), other people serve as both a source of information ("Is there a crisis here or isn't there?") and a source of reassurance if they do not react strongly. At the next stage, the presence of others leads to a **diffusion of responsibility**—*a diminished sense of personal responsibility to act because others are seen as equally responsible*. At this point people also consider the consequences of action and are less willing to intervene (and more

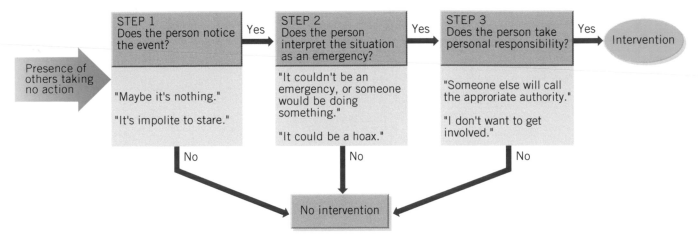

Figure 18.3   A decision-making model of bystander intervention. In the first stage, the bystander must notice the emergency. In stage 2, the bystander must interpret the incident as an emergency. In stage 3, the bystander must assume responsibility. Once the bystander accepts responsibility, he must then decide what to do and try to do it. Source: Adapted from Darley & Latane, 1968, pp. 70–71.

likely to justify inaction) if it jeopardizes their own safety or if they fear they might look foolish if they have misinterpreted the situation. Bystanders who are anonymous, like Kitty Genovese's neighbors and most German citizens during the reign of Nazism, are less likely to help.

The findings of these studies actually support a long tradition of sociological theory suggesting that the anonymity of city life reduces individuals' sense of personal responsibility for the welfare of others. Research comparing the responses of urban and rural subjects largely supports this view (see Solomon et al., 1982). Population density—the number of people crammed into a small urban space—also predicts rates of altruism: The more densely populated a city, the less people help (Levine et al., 1994).

How Bleak Is This Picture?

Most of the bystander studies described so far involved simulated emergencies in laboratory settings. Under other experimental conditions, however, the results are sometimes quite different. One study examined whether bystanders are more likely to respond to an emergency in a natural setting where their compatriots are friends rather than strangers. The investigators staged a rape in a campus parking lot (Harari et al., 1985). When unsuspecting male bystanders observed the female victim struggling with her attacker and heard her cries for help, 85 percent of those walking in groups of two or three responded, versus 65 percent of those walking alone. In this study, the presence of several people increased, rather than decreased, bystander intervention—probably because the naturalistic setting, the clarity of the victim's plight, and the ability of group members to see and talk to one another made intervention more likely.

◆ INTERIM SUMMARY

Researchers studying **bystander intervention** have found that individuals often do not help in a crisis in the presence of other people. To intervene, a person must notice the event, define it as an emergency, and assume personal responsibility for intervening. **Diffusion of responsibility**, a diminished sense of personal responsibility to act, is one important reason people do not intervene.

◆ Aggression

Although charitable contributions may exceed $50 billion a year in the United States, that is less than half the military budget. **Aggression**—*verbal or physical behavior aimed at harming another person or living being*—is at least as characteristic of human interaction as altruism.

Aggression is often elicited by anger, as when someone lashes out at a perceived injustice, but it can also be carried out for practical purposes without anger, as when a driver leans on the horn to protest reckless lane-changing that could cause an accident. *Calm, pragmatic aggression* is called **instrumental aggression** and is often used by institutions such as the judicial system to punish wrongdoers (Geen, 1990, 1998). Aggressive acts are also frequently mixed with other motives. The behavior of kamikaze pilots during World War II, terrorists who carry out suicide bombings, and many soldiers in wartime involve blends of aggression and altruism, depending upon one's point of view.

Violence and Culture

The prevalence and forms of aggression vary considerably across cultures. Among technologically developed countries, the United States has the highest rates of aggression. Indeed, violence has overtaken communicable diseases as the leading cause of death among the young. Homicide rates are up to 10 times higher in the United States than in Europe (see Lore & Schultz, 1993), and the murder rate in some major U.S. cities dwarfs the annual number of murders in all of Canada. In Canada, roughly 600 people a year die from homicides, compared with 24,000 in the United States. Taking into account the larger population in the United States, the murder rate is still over five times higher in the United States. Cross-cultural data have demonstrated that much of the difference in murder rates is attributable to the ready availability of firearms in the United States (Archer, 1994).

Across and within societies, cultural differences play an important role in violence and aggression. Psychologists have recently begun studying a cultural difference between men (particularly white men) from the northern and southern United States that is related to a tendency to behave violently (Cohen & Nisbett, 1997). Homicide rates are higher in the South, but not for crimes committed during felonies such as burglaries. The difference lies in the tendency of southern men to resort to violence in the midst of conflicts or arguments.

According to one explanation, the South is characterized by what anthropologists call a *culture of honor*, where small disputes between men can turn violent because they become contests of reputation and status. For reasons rooted in the ancestry, history, and economy of the South, to be dishonored—to show cowardice or a lack of "manliness" in the face of possible insult—is to lose face and status. Thus, southern men are more likely than northerners to respond with violence to insults or ambiguous situations that could suggest an insult.

Researchers demonstrated this in a fascinating study at the University of Michigan. In one condition, an associate of the experimenter bumped into northern and southern male students, called them an obscene name, and walked off into another room (Cohen et al., 1996). In the control condition, northern and southern participants received no such insult.

The researchers measured a number of variables, including observers' ratings of how amused versus angry participants appeared after the bump and how they completed a hypothetical scenario in which a woman complained to her boyfriend that a mutual male friend kept making passes at her. They also assessed participants' physiological stress during the incident by analyzing cortisol levels in their saliva (recall from Chapter 11 that cortisol is a hormone secreted during stress) and testosterone

Apply & Discuss

A soccer field in Bosnia converted to a cemetery. How would each of the following perspectives explain such bloodshed among presumably "civilized" people?

- Behaviorist
- Psychodynamic
- Cognitive
- Evolutionary

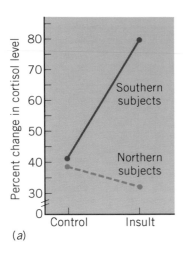

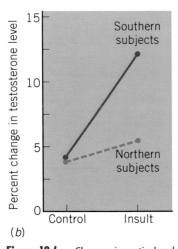

Figure 18.4   Changes in cortisol and testosterone levels for insulted and noninsulted southerners and northerners. In (a), cortisol levels (measured both before and after the experimental manipulation) showed dramatic increases for insulted southerners. In (b), the same was true for testosterone. *Source:* Cohen, et al., 1996.

What kind of men commit sexual violence? To find out, go to www.wiley.com/college/westen and click on **Chapter 18: Why Men Rape.**

levels before and after the incident (testosterone provides, among other things, a physiological index of readiness to fight).

The results were striking. The majority of northern students responded to the insult with more amusement than anger; in contrast, 85 percent of southerners displayed more anger than amusement. Roughly half the northerners who were insulted completed the scenario about the woman complaining to her boyfriend about their friend's inappropriate attention with a violent ending; the percentage who did so was similar in the experimental and control conditions. In contrast, 75 percent of southerners in the experimental condition (who received the insult) wrote a violent ending, compared with 20 percent of "unbumped" southerners. Southern men thus appeared to be gentlemen when they were not insulted but when primed with an insult were ready to act with aggression.

The biological findings led to precisely the same conclusion (Figure 18.4): Whereas northerners showed virtually no physiological reaction to the insult, both cortisol and testosterone levels jumped dramatically in Southern men who were insulted. Thus, cultural factors can influence not only how people feel, think, and act when confronted with a situation that could potentially lead to violence, but also how they respond physiologically.

Violence and Gender

Gender differences in aggression are highly consistent across cultures. In most societies, males commit the majority of criminal and aggressive acts. Male adolescents are particularly likely to be the perpetrators; in fact, fluctuations in crime rates in most countries can be predicted simply from the proportion of adolescent males in the population (see Segall, 1988).

Violence perpetrated by men against men has been so universal that until recently it drew little attention from either psychologists or policy makers (Goodman et al., 1993). The number of women battered by their male partners is unknown because many women do not report domestic violence, but the U.S. Department of Justice estimates that over 2 million women are battered each year in the United States alone (Frieze & Browne, 1989; Harway, 2000). Other estimates suggest that as many as 10 percent of marriages in the United States are marred by violent assaults, the most severe typically committed by the man (Dutton, 1996). Most batterers do not begin abusing their partners until the woman has made an emotional commitment to them, and attacks are most likely to occur during pregnancy or upon separation or divorce (Russell, 1991).

Sexual aggression against women is as old as the species. Men have traditionally viewed rape as one of the spoils of war. Some studies suggest that as many as 14 to 25 percent of women have been forced into sex by strangers, acquaintances, boyfriends, or husbands at some point in their lives (Goodman et al., 1993; Koss, 1993). A substantial percentage of women (27 percent) also report histories of childhood sexual abuse (as do 16 percent of men) (Finkelhor et al., 1990).

◆ INTERIM SUMMARY

Aggression refers to verbal or physical behavior aimed at harming another person or living being. Rates of violence vary cross-culturally, but across cultures, males tend to be more aggressive than females. Researchers are increasingly recognizing the prevalence of male violence perpetrated against women, including battering and rape.

The Roots of Violence

The universality of aggression and the individual differences seen in aggressive behavior have led to considerable controversy about its origins. Some theories maintain that the roots of aggression lie in biology and evolution; others look to the environment and social learning. In this section we explore psychodynamic, evolutionary, and cognitive–social approaches (which integrate cognitive and behavioral perspectives). We also examine the biopsychological processes that underlie aggressive behavior, and offer a tentative integration of multiple standpoints.

Psychodynamic Perspective

Freud viewed aggression as a basic instinct in humans (Chapter 10). Although most psychodynamic psychologists no longer accept this theory, they view aggression as an inborn behavioral potential that is usually activated by frustration and anger. In fact, in every human society ever observed, socialization to control aggressive impulses is one of the most basic tasks of parenting (see Whiting & Child, 1953). Infants and toddlers bite, scratch, and kick when they do not get what they want; as children get older, they show less overt aggression (Hartup, 1977, 1998). This suggests that societies have to teach children to *inhibit* aggression, rather than that aggression is primarily learned. (As we will see, other theories take the opposite perspective.)

Perhaps the most distinctive aspect of the psychodynamic approach to aggression regards the role of consciousness. From a psychodynamic perspective, aggressive motives may blend with other motives to produce behavior not consciously intended as sadistic, as in "good-humored" teasing among buddies, enjoyment of aggressive movies or sports, "forgetting" to pick up the dry cleaning after an argument with one's spouse (passive aggression), harsh parenting, or playful biting or pinching during sex. Aggressive motives may also blend with other motives, such as achievement or altruism, in choice of occupation, such as a career in the military (or the Internal Revenue Service!). The passion with which many journalists delve into other people's private lives and try to confront them publicly with anything that could be perceived as improper or humiliating has elements of sadism that most journalists would likely consciously deny.

The *triggers* for aggression can also be unconscious. For example, James Gilligan spent years working with violent prisoners and conducted extensive interviews with a sample of men incarcerated for violent crimes (Gilligan, 1996). Asked to tell the stories of the acts that landed them behind bars, one after another told stories in which they lashed out after feeling "dissed"—treated with perceived disrespect. Gilligan concluded that one of the major triggers for violence is the feeling of shame in individuals prone to feeling inadequate or disrespected.

Recent research points to the importance of *implicit* shame in activating aggression. One study compared the tendency to experience shame in men with histories of sexual abuse who either did or did not go on to perpetrate sexual violence themselves (Conklin, 1999). Those who became abusers reported minimal shame on self-report questionnaires—they were consciously *shameless*. But the stories they told in response to the Thematic Apperception Test (TAT), an instrument used to assess implicit motives and emotions (Chapter 10), told a different story: Their responses were filled with themes of shame. Men who went on to become perpetrators appeared to suffer from *unacknowledged* shame. A wide range of research suggests, more generally, that threats to self-esteem or valued views of the self can in fact trigger violence (Baumeister et al., 1996).

An Evolutionary Perspective

Aggression, including killing members of one's own species, occurs in all animals. From an evolutionary standpoint, the capacity for aggression evolved because of its value for survival and reproduction (Lore & Schultz, 1993). Males typically attack other males to obtain access to females and to keep or take over territory. In many animal species, including some lions and monkeys, a male who takes over a "harem" from another male kills all the infants so that the females will breed with him and devote their resources only to *his* offspring, maximizing his reproductive success. Females often try to fight back in these circumstances. Across species, overt female aggression is elicited largely by attacks on their young.

Apply & Discuss

■ Why are we so captivated by horror and violence in films? What psychological functions do scary or violent movies serve?

■ Is pleasure in watching violence in the movies a learned response? Or is fascination with violence part of our genetic heritage?

Wolves have innate mechanisms that can stop a confrontation from becoming lethal.

Contemporary evolutionary psychologists, like their psychodynamic colleagues, do not consider aggression a drive that builds up and requires discharge. Rather, many believe that humans, like other animals, have evolved aggressive mechanisms that can be activated when circumstances threaten their survival, reproduction, the reproductive success of their kin, or the survival of alliance partners. In this view, aggression is like a pilot light that is always on but can burst into flames if conditions threaten reproductive success (de Waal, 1989).

Although aggression is common to all animal species, the degree of violence toward members of their own species is remarkable in humans, who slaughter each other on a scale unimaginable to even the cruelest of beasts (see Lorenz, 1966). Other animals have evolved inhibitory mechanisms that stop them from ravaging their own. A wolf can call off the most vicious fight simply by rolling over and exposing his jugular. This typically leads the attacker to halt his aggression immediately—an innate mechanism especially prevalent in animals with built-in weaponry, such as powerful jaws.

Primates, including humans, have a variety of appeasement gestures to avoid violence, notably facial expressions, vocalizations, and gestures (de Waal, 1989; Krebs & Miller, 1985). Unfortunately, humans are unique in their capacity to override evolved mechanisms for inhibiting aggression, particularly when divided by nationality, ethnicity, or ideology. Furthermore, as Konrad Lorenz noted, humans have developed the ability to kill one another from a distance. Not seeing our victims suffer prevents activation of natural inhibitions against killing members of the species, such as empathic distress responses, which are probably involved in both inhibiting aggression and promoting altruism. We are not, sadly, as civilized as wolves.

From Brain to Behavior

Biological Foundations of Aggression

Psychodynamic and evolutionary psychologists presume that aggression is built into the human behavioral repertoire. If a tendency to behave aggressively is innate, it must be rooted in the nervous system and perhaps in the endocrine system as well. Mounting evidence in animals and humans supports this view.

Neural Systems

The neural systems that control aggression, like those involved in other forms of behavior, are hierarchically organized: Neurons in evolutionary primitive structures such as the hypothalamus are part of circuits regulated by more recent (in evolutionary time) structures, notably the cortex (Figure 18.5). As we have seen (Chapter 3, 10, and 11), the amygdala and hypothalamus are involved in emotional reactions and drive states (Chapter 3). When researchers electrically stimulate regions of the lateral hypothalamus of a normally nonpredatory cat or rhesus monkey, the animal immediately attacks (Egger & Flynn, 1963; Robinson et al., 1969). Similar results occur in humans when electrodes are implanted in the amygdala during surgery. With electrical stimulation, a normally submissive, mild-mannered woman became so hostile and aggressive that she tried to strike the experimenter—who was able to control the outburst by switching off the current (King, 1961). Lesioning parts of the midbrain can also eliminate an animal's ability to respond with species-typical aggressive motor movements (such as hissing and bared teeth in cats), suggesting a substantial role for midbrain structures in aggression (Carlson, 1999).

Although sensory information processed by the thalamus (e.g., a threatening gesture) can probably trigger responses directly, in humans, aggression is under substantial cortical control. Sophisticated processing at the cortical level can either inhibit or facilitate aggression. A threatening gesture, for example, can be interpreted as either an attack or a joke, and a person with intact frontal lobes (Chapters 3 and 6) can usually decide to "hold back" before lashing out physically or verbally.

Testosterone and Serotonin

Hormones play a substantial role in the tendency to behave aggressively. In species after species, males are more aggressive than females, and these sex differences appear linked to action of the hormone testosterone both before birth and during development (Archer & Lloyd, 1985). Recall that hormones both *organize* and *activate* neural circuits (Chapter 10). With respect to organizational effects (that is, influences on the development of the brain), female rats and monkeys that receive testosterone in utero exhibit increased play fighting after birth (Goy, 1968; Meaney & McEwen, 1986). Similarly, prenatal exposure to synthetic hormones can lead to increased aggression in childhood and adolescence (Reinisch, 1981).

With respect to activational effects (that is, direct influences of hormones on behavior), studies with rats find that the amount of aggressive behavior displayed by both sexes correlates with circulating blood testosterone levels (with additional hormones involved in females) (Albert et al., 1991). Testosterone does not, however, tend to cause aggression in the absence of environmental triggers, such as competition between males for females, or repeated exposure to unfamiliar members of the same species.

The data in humans are less definitive, but several studies provide suggestive evidence. One examined the relation between physical and verbal aggression and levels of testosterone in adolescent boys (Olweus et al., 1980). Participants with higher levels of testosterone tended to be more impatient and irritable. Men convicted of violent crimes also tend to have higher testosterone levels than nonviolent offenders and nonoffenders (see Archer, 1991). The dramatic increase in male aggression that occurs at sexual maturation (puberty) in many species and cultures is also likely related to a surge in testosterone levels (see Segall, 1988).

Testosterone is not the only hormone linked to aggression. A number of studies in humans and other animals implicate low serotonin levels (which are also associated with depression; Chapter 15) (Cleare & Bond, 1997; Suomi, in press). Serotonin and testosterone appear to regulate different aspects of aggression. Testosterone is linked to social dominance and thus leads to aggression in the service of maintaining status within a social hierarchy (Olweus, 1984). Serotonin is linked instead to impulsivity (acting without thinking) and thus leads to unprovoked and socially inappropriate forms of aggression (Higley et al., 1992).

Genetics

Genetic factors also contribute to individual differences in aggressive behavior. Successful attempts to breed highly aggressive strains of rats, mice, and rabbits demonstrate that among these animals, individuals can inherit an aggressive temperament (see Cologer-Clifford et al., 1992; Moyer, 1983). Questionnaire studies comparing monozygotic and dizygotic twin pairs find aggressive behavior, like other personality traits, to be heritable in humans (Caspi, 1998; Rushton, 1986). Researchers have recently focused attention on a gene on chromosome 11 that is involved in regulating serotonin in the brain (Nielsen et al., 1997). Presence of a particular allele at this level of the chromosome is associated with unprovoked aggression as assessed by self-report (Manuck et al., 1999).

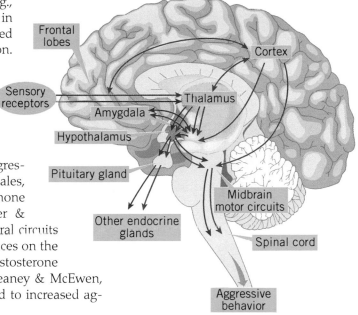

Figure 18.5 Areas of the brain involved in aggressive behavior. Stimulus information (e.g., a threatening gesture) is relayed via the thalamus to the amygdala and hypothalamus for immediate action. The information is also relayed from the thalamus to the cortex for more careful consideration. One or both of these pathways can generate an aggressive response, which may activate midbrain motor mechanisms involved in species-specific aggressive responses. Limbic structures, particularly the amygdala, assess the emotional significance of the stimulus and activate the hypothalamus. The hypothalamus then triggers endocrine responses, which in turn affect arousal and readiness for action. Limbic structures also activate the frontal lobes, which integrate cognitive and emotional responses to stimuli (Chapter 7).

Making Connections

Correlational studies show that higher levels of testosterone in men are associated with higher levels of aggression. However, these studies cannot definitively show whether circulating testosterone levels cause violent behavior or whether aggression leads to heightened testosterone levels. The reason is that correlation cannot demonstrate causation: When two variables correlate highly, one could cause the other, or some third variable could explain the link between them (Chapter 2).

◆ **INTERIM SUMMARY**

> Psychodynamic theorists view aggression as an inborn potential usually activated by frustration or anger. They argue that aggressive motives can blend with other motives and be triggered unconsciously. Evolutionary theorists similarly view aggression as an inborn human potential that gets activated under conditions that affect reproductive success, such as competing for territory or mates and protecting oneself and related others. The neural control of aggression is hierarchically organized, with the amygdala, hypothalamus, and cortex (particularly the frontal lobes) playing prominent roles. Aggression is also partially controlled by hormones, particularly testosterone and serotonin.

A Cognitive–Social Perspective

The capacity for aggression appears to be innate, but the activation and inhibition of aggression depends on culture and learning. Harsh parental discipline, for example, produces children who are more aggressive than children whose parents spare the rod (Weiss et al., 1992). According to cognitive–social theories, children and adults learn to behave aggressively through social rewards and punishments. They also learn through observational learning such as modeling. As Bandura (1967) demonstrated, children who watch adults abusing dolls are much more likely to do so themselves (Chapter 5). Cognitive processes, especially the attributions people make for the causes of their misfortunes, play a role in eliciting and controlling aggression as well. Individuals are more likely to become aggressive, for example, if they believe someone has willfully and knowingly inflicted harm (see Geen, 1995).

Research from a cognitive-social perspective has contributed to the public debate about the influence of television violence on aggressive behavior. (It is worth noting, however, that the most important modeling for aggression is closer to home than the television screen: Media violence pales as a predictor of aggressive behavior in comparison with violence witnessed in the family, in the schools, or in the streets; Gunter & McAleer, 1990.) To estimate the long-term effects of television violence on behavior is very difficult because people who are aggressive tend to seek out aggressive shows, and they do this from the time they are young. Experimental data show that in the short run, children and adolescents are in fact more likely to behave aggressively immediately after viewing violent television shows, particularly if they are provoked (Singer & Singer, 1981; Wood et al., 1991). This could occur because watching television violence increases arousal, decreases inhibition, provides aggressive models, or desensitizes children to violence by making violent acts seem commonplace (Gunter & McAleer, 1990).

The data are less conclusive for long-term effects (see Gadow & Sprafkin, 1993; McGuire, 1986). Rather than having a global effect on every child or adult, televised violence is likely to have a stronger impact on people who are already highly aggressive. In fact, experimental research suggests that people who test high in aggressiveness not only prefer violent films but become more angry after watching them and are more likely to behave aggressively after doing so (Bushman, 1995). Thus, the impact of televised aggression on violence likely reflects a person-by-situation interaction (Chapter 12)—that is, a tendency of certain people to behave in certain ways under certain conditions—rather than a general phenomenon.

Similar results emerge from research assessing the effects of pornography on sexual violence. Viewing pornography does not cause sexual violence, but viewing pornographic *aggression* appears to desensitize men to the brutality of rape and other sexual crimes against women (see Malamuth & Donnerstein, 1982). As with television violence, pornographic aggression may affect a person's emotional response to violence or slightly weaken inhibitions in deviant individuals with poor internal controls. Nonetheless, most people will not kill or rape after watching a violent or pornographic movie.

Toward an Integrated View of Aggression

In 1939, John Dollard, Neal Miller, and their colleagues at Yale University proposed the **frustration–aggression hypothesis**, which states that *when people are frustrated in achieving a goal, they may become aggressive*. The child who wants a cookie and is told to wait until after dinner may throw a tantrum or the college student who had his heart set on a particular graduate school and was rejected may become not only sad but furious.

This model is simple and intuitively appealing. It was initially hailed as a significant advance toward a comprehensive theory because it tied aggression to environmental events rather than solely to instincts. However, researchers soon realized that not all aggression results from frustration and not all frustration leads to aggression. Physical pain may cause aggression, and frustrated goals can lead one person to become aggressive, another to become depressed, and still another to become more determined.

A reformulated frustration–aggression hypothesis suggests that frustration breeds aggression to the extent that a frustrating event elicits an unpleasant emotion (Berkowitz, 1989). Blocked goals can be frustrating, as Dollard and his colleagues emphasized, but so can innumerable other unpleasant experiences. Air pollution, tobacco smoke, and other noxious odors have all been linked to increases in aggressive behavior (Rotton et al., 1979; Zillman et al., 1981).

The relation between heat and aggression is particularly well documented (Anderson, 1989; Rotton & Cohn, 2000). As temperature rises, so does temper. One study found a strong correlation between temperature and the incidence of riots in U.S. cities between 1967 and 1971 (Carlsmith & Anderson, 1979). Rape, murder, assault, and prison unrest all vary with the time of the year, peaking in the hot summer months (Figure 18.6). Within countries as diverse as Spain, Italy, France, and the United States, the southern regions typically have the highest rates of violent crime (Anderson, 1989). Even the number of batters hit by pitches in professional baseball varies with the temperature (Reifman et al., 1991)!

According to the reformulated frustration–aggression hypothesis, people respond to negative emotions with either aggression or withdrawal—fight or flight—depending on their genetic endowment, learning history, and the situation. Unpleasant thoughts, feelings, and behaviors are associatively connected in memory, so that activating one will activate the others. As a result, people can become angry and behave

I pray thee, good Mercutio, let's retire:
The day is hot, the Capulets abroad,
And, if we meet, we shall not 'scape a brawl;
For now, these hot days, is the mad blood stirring.

SHAKESPEARE,
Romeo and Juliet (III, i)

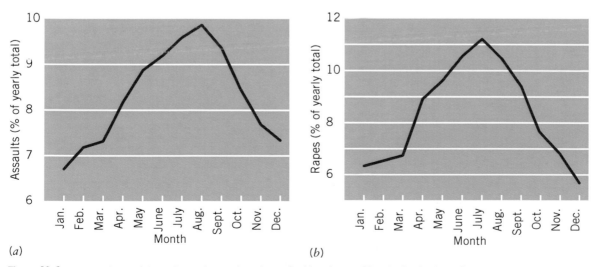

Figure 18.6 Aggression and time of year. The number of assaults (a) and rapes (b) varies by the time of year and is highest in the hottest months. Data were averaged across studies from North America and Europe over the last hundred years. *Source:* Anderson, 1989, pp. 85–86.

aggressively no matter how the underlying emotional state was elicited—whether through an insult, an uncomfortable temperature, or an unpleasant memory.

The reformulated frustration–aggression hypothesis points the way toward an integrative perspective on aggression that takes seriously both the role of biology and the influence of culture and experience. Although humans are not driven to act aggressively like they are driven to eat, children spontaneously behave aggressively, and humans are endowed with hormonal and neural mechanisms that mediate aggressive responses. Moreover, like other animals, humans (particularly males) compete for territorial resources and sexual partners, and they are omnivores who hunt prey. That natural selection would have failed to endow them with emotional and behavioral mechanisms that produce aggression under certain circumstances therefore seems unlikely.

Culture and learning, however, largely define those circumstances. Humans appear biologically constructed to behave aggressively when they feel hurt, deprived, or blocked from reaching their goals, but many goals, as well as strategies for dealing with frustration, reflect culture and learning. Prior experiences with aggressive behavior and its consequences, both direct and vicarious, also influence future tendencies to behave aggressively. Batterers who are arrested for their crimes re-victimize their spouse at a much lower rate than those who are not arrested, just as children who get a clear message that violence will not be tolerated tend to find other ways of resolving conflicts (Lore & Schultz, 1993). Because the potential for aggression is rooted in our biology, then, does not mean it is uncontrollable.

◆ INTERIM SUMMARY

According to cognitive–social theories, the roots of aggressive behavior lie in social rewards and punishments, cognitive processes such as attributions, and observational learning. The **frustration–aggression hypothesis** states that people may become aggressive when they are frustrated in achieving a goal. A reformulated hypothesis suggests that frustrating or unpleasant circumstances are likely to evoke aggression if they elicit unpleasant emotion. The capacity for aggression appears to be innate, but the activation and inhibition of aggression depends on culture and learning.

In 1991, the world was shocked by a home video of Los Angeles police officers beating black motorist Rodney King after a high-speed chase. When a jury at first acquitted the officers, the African-American community erupted in anger. Enraged mobs looted stores, pulled people from their vehicles and beat them senseless, set buildings and cars on fire, and attacked anyone whose race placed him in the wrong neighborhood at the wrong time. The riots left 54 people dead, over 2000 injured, and racial tensions burning like the streets of the city. Both the behavior of the officers and the behavior of the rioters raise questions about why people behave the way they do in "mobs."

◆ Social Influence

By the late nineteenth century, sociologists and philosophers had recognized that people behave differently in crowds than they do as individuals and that a crowd is more than the mere sum of its parts. In a classic book published in 1895, called *The Crowd*, Gustave Le Bon argued that people in a crowd may lose their personal identities and ability to judge right and wrong. They become anonymous and no longer consider themselves accountable for their behavior. Le Bon had in mind events of the eighteenth and nineteenth centuries, such as the frenzied mobs of the French Revolution, but his reflections could equally apply to the behavior of the police officers who beat Rodney King or the rioters who rampaged through Los Angeles after the officers' acquittal.

Since Le Bon's time, social psychologists have examined a number of forms of **social influence**, *effects of the presence of others on the way people think, feel, and behave*. Norman Triplett (1897) conducted one of the first experiments on social influence over a century ago, when he investigated how the mere presence of other people affects performance. Triplett asked 40 adolescents to wind a fishing reel as quickly as possible and found that they wound it faster when competing with others than when racing solely against the clock. Psychologists have observed *the performance-enhancing effect of the presence of others*, called **social facilitation**, in a wide variety of species, from cockroaches to humans (Buck et al., 1992; Zajonc, 1965).

Social influence processes can be remarkably subtle. For example, Robert Rosenthal and his colleagues discovered decades ago that teachers' expectations of students—their beliefs about their abilities—can have a profound impact on students' performance (Rosenthal & Jacobson, 1966). Teachers who are led to believe that a particular student is smarter than he appears will tend to behave in ways that lead the student to perform better. Similarly, teachers who hold negative implicit attitudes toward particular minority groups (Chapter 17) are likely to respond to student members of those groups in ways that lead them to underachieve.

The influence of implicit and explicit expectations of this sort provides the basis for **self-fulfilling prophecies**, in which *false impressions of a situation evoke behavior that, in turn, makes these impressions become true* (Merton, 1957). Mark Snyder and his colleagues (1977) conducted a classic study of self-fulfilling prophecies, in which pairs of male and female college students conversed from separate rooms through an intercom system. The students had never met, but the male students thought they knew what their partner looked like from a photograph

Actually, the photo was not of her: Half the participants received a picture of a college-age woman rated by other students as physically very attractive, and the other half received an unattractive mug-shot. Not surprisingly, males who believed their partners were attractive were more sociable and sexually warm toward them. The more interesting finding came from studying the responses of the females. Judges who listened to the taped conversation with the male's comments edited out rated the women in the attractive photograph condition more friendly, sociable, witty, and appealing. Conversely, women who were treated as if they were unattractive actually behaved unattractively.

In this section we focus on three forms of social influence that are pervasive in social life: obedience, conformity, and group processes.

Obedience

In 1978, in the small community of Jonestown, located in a Guyana jungle, over 900 members of the People's Temple cult drank cyanide-laced Kool Aid to commit mass suicide. The cult's leader, Jim Jones, told his people that a "revolutionary suicide" would dramatize their dedication. According to the few survivors, some people resisted, but most took their lives willingly, with mothers giving cyanide to their children and then drinking it themselves. Equally grizzly examples of misplaced obedience include the inferno in Waco, Texas, in which many Branch Davidian cult members lit their own compound ablaze under the leadership of David Koresh; and the mass suicide of California cult members who believed salvation was just around the corner with the arrival of the Hale–Bopp comet.

Psychological research on **obedience**, or *compliance with authority*, increased dramatically following World War II, primarily as an attempt to understand the horrors of the Third Reich. Many American social psychologists were refugees from the Nazis who presumed that the blind obedience they had witnessed was an aberration or anomaly caused by flaws in the German character or by the political, social, and economic upheaval that left Germany in ruin after World War I. Subsequent research on authoritarian personality dynamics in their new land (Chapter 17) led instead to a disquieting conclusion: Many people in the United States were also attracted to ideology glorifying blind obedience (Adorno et al., 1950).

The Milgram Experiments
In the 1960s, Stanley Milgram (1963, 1974) conducted a series of classic studies on obedience at Yale University that took many people, including psychologists, by surprise. The results of his investigations suggested that the philosopher Hannah Arendt may have been right when she said that the horrifying thing about the Nazis was not that they were so deviant but that they were "terrifyingly normal."

Central Questions

In the small South Vietnamese village of My Lai on March 16, 1968, at the height of the Vietnam War, three platoons of American soldiers massacred several hundred unarmed civilians, including children, women, and the elderly. The platoons had arrived in Vietnam only a month before but had sustained heavy casualties, leaving the surviving soldiers scared and vengeful. Any inhibitions the soldiers might have had against killing innocent civilians disappeared when their commander, Lt. William Calley, ordered them to shoot the villagers, whom he suspected of being enemy sympathizers. The issues raised by the My Lai massacre resurfaced recently when former U.S. Senator Bob Kerrey publicly described a massacre in which he participated during the Vietnam War, which left at least 13 unarmed women and children dead.

■ Do soldiers relinquish their ability—or duty—to judge right and wrong when receiving orders?

■ Can a military function if soldiers make independent moral judgments? How can the military maximize the likelihood that soldiers will both respect their commanders and respect human rights?

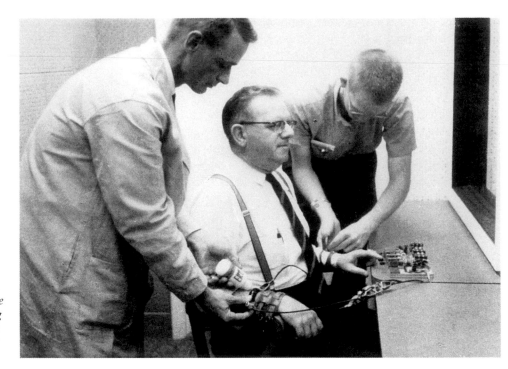

Milgram's research on obedience shocked both psychologists and the lay public, who never would have imagined that participants would have been willing to shock a stranger at the command of an authority who told them that he would take responsibility for their action.

Making Connections

Milgram's experiments drew storms of controversy from psychologists concerned that he did not safeguard the rights of his subjects, who were often visibly distressed by the experience. In fact, the Milgram studies played an important role in the development of institutional review boards that determine whether a study meets ethical standards (Chapter 2). Today, Milgram's studies could not be conducted.

■ Milgram debriefed his subjects at the end of the experiment to minimize any impact the experience might have had on them, and none reported regretting having participated. Did the knowledge generated by these experiments outweigh the costs to participants?

■ Could we possibly know what we now know had Milgram not performed his experiments? Could a different, less stressful, research design have led to such important results?

The basic design of the studies was as follows. The experimenter told subjects they were participating in an experiment to examine the effect of punishment on learning. Subjects were instructed to punish a "learner" (actually a confederate of the researcher) in the next room whenever the learner made an error, using an instrument they believed to be a shock generator. Panel switches were labeled from 15 volts (slight shock) to 450 volts (danger: severe shock). The experimenter instructed the subjects to begin by administering a slight shock and increase the voltage each time the learner made an error. The learner actually received no shocks, but subjects had no reason to disbelieve what they were told—especially since they heard protests and, later, screaming from the next room as they increased the punishment.

Milgram was not actually studying the impact of punishment on learning. Rather, he wanted to determine how far people would go in obeying orders. Before conducting the study, Milgram had asked various social scientists to estimate how many subjects would go all the way to 450 volts. The experts estimated that a very deviant subsample—well below 5 percent—might administer the maximum.

They were wrong. Approximately *two-thirds* of subjects administered the full 450 volts, even though the learner had stopped responding (screaming or otherwise) and was apparently either unconscious or dead. Many participants were clearly distressed by the experience, but each time they asked if they should continue to administer the shocks, the experimenter told them that the experiment required that they continue. If they inquired about their responsibility for any ill effects the learner might be experiencing, the experimenter told them that he was responsible, and that the procedure might be painful but it was not dangerous. The experimenter never overtly tried to coerce subjects to continue; all he did was remind them of their obligation.

To Milgram, the implications were painfully clear: People will obey, without limitations of conscience, when they believe an order comes from a legitimate authority (Milgram, 1974).

Factors That Influence Obedience

By varying the experimental conditions, Milgram discovered several factors that influence obedience. One is the proximity of the victim to the subject. Obedience declined substantially if the victim was in the room with the subject, if a voice replaced pounding on the wall, and if the subject had to force the victim's hand onto a shockplate to administer further punishments (see Figure 18.7). Proximity to the experimenter also affected the decision to obey. The closer the subject was to the experimenter, the more difficult was disobedience; when the experimenter sat in another room, obedience dropped sharply. More recent research implicates personality variables such as authoritarianism and hostility that can influence the likelihood of obedience as well (Blass, 1991, 2000).

The results of the Milgram studies are in sharp contrast to what most of us believe about ourselves, namely that we would never obey in such a situation. The disjunction between our beliefs about how we would behave and the way most of us would *actually* behave highlights a consistent finding in social psychology, namely our blindness to the power of situations over our own behavior. The effects of powerful situations tend to be implicit and hence to occur automatically and without conscious awareness (Epley & Gilovich, 1999; Wegner & Bargh, 1998). Thus, when we predict our own behavior, we tend to picture what we would *consciously* think and feel and to underestimate the power of implicit situational "pulls."

Conformity

Whereas obedience refers to compliance with the demands of an authority, **conformity** means *changing attitudes or behavior to accommodate the standards of peers or groups*. The pressure to conform can be immense, even if subtle. Wearing a thin tie when wide is in vogue makes many men uncomfortable, as does wearing the wrong brand of tennis shoes for many teenagers.

The Asch Studies

A series of classic studies by Solomon Asch (1955, 1956) documented the power of conformity, much as Milgram's studies established the power of obedience. Asch assembled groups of seven to nine college students and told them they were participating in an experiment on visual judgment. All but one of the students were actually confederates, so their responses were planned in advance.

The experimenter asked the "subjects" to match the lines on two white cards (Figure 18.8). The first card had one line printed on it; the second had three lines, one of which clearly matched the line on the first card in length. The subject's task was to select the line on the second card that matched the line on the first.

On the first and second trials, everyone—subject and confederates alike—gave the right answer. On subsequent trials, however, the confederates (who went first) unanimously chose a line that was obviously incorrect. Their answers placed the subject in the uncomfortable position of having to choose between publicly opposing the view of the group or answering incorrectly.

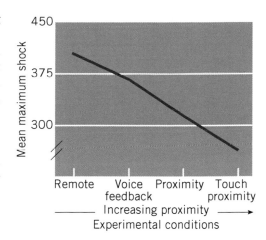

Figure 18.7 Effects of proximity on maximum shock delivered. Subjects in the Milgram experiments generally obeyed, but the closer they were to the victim, the less they tended to obey. *Source:* Milgram, 1965, p. 63.

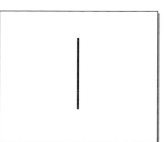 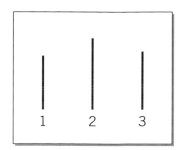

Figure 18.8 The Asch conformity experiments. Participants in Asch's experiments on conformity were asked which of the three lines in the box on the right matched the one on the left. Pressure to conform swayed their responses. *Source:* Asch, 1955, p. 193.

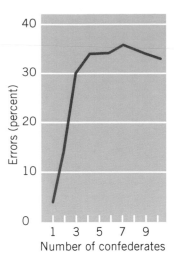

Figure 18.9 Effect of number of confederates on performance. Participants in Asch's experiments tended to conform when three or more confederates chose the wrong line. *Source*: Asch, 1955, p. 193.

Without peer pressure to conform, subjects chose the wrong line less than 1 percent of the time. However, when faced with a unanimous (but incorrect) opinion of the confederates, subjects made the same incorrect choice as the confederates 36.8 percent of the time. Up to a point, the more confederates, the greater the tendency to conform (Figure 18.9). Subjects only conformed, however, if the confederates all gave the same answer. If at least one confederate gave a different answer than the others, subjects followed their own judgment most of the time. Apparently, bucking the majority is extremely difficult without at least one other dissenter.

The Asch studies powerfully demonstrate the *power of situations* to influence behavior and attitudes. Personality factors, however, also influence the tendency to conform. Individuals with low self-esteem and those who are especially motivated by a need for social approval are more likely to conform (Crowne & Marlowe, 1964; Dittes, 1959; Moeller & Applezweig, 1957; Strang, 1972).

To what extent subjects actually alter their beliefs in the Asch studies rather than simply comply with situational demands to avoid disapproval is a matter of debate. Many of Asch's subjects reported that they believed their (incorrect) answers, perhaps because of cognitive dissonance or a desire not to look foolish. Nevertheless, the main implication of these studies is that many people will change at least the public expression of their beliefs when confronted with a group that disagrees with them.

Conformity and Culture

Conformity varies by culture and appears to be linked to the way people earn their livelihood (Price-Williams, 1985). People in hunter-gatherer societies exercise more independent judgments than people in agricultural societies (Berry, 1979). Agricultural societies depend heavily on communal organization and coordinated action; too much independent judgment can be counterproductive during planting and harvest times, when work needs to be done. Agricultural societies also have much higher population density, whereas hunter-gatherer societies are often highly dispersed across a territory and may thus require less compliance with social norms (see Barry et al., 1957).

In general, conformity is higher in collectivist than in more individualistic cultures (Bond & Smith, 1996). One study with an East Asian sample found that participants preferred to conform rather than to be different even when "independence" had no cost (Kim & Markus, 1999). When given a choice among pens, Americans overwhelmingly chose the one pen that was a different color from the others; East Asians preferred a pen of the same color as all the others (Kim & Markus, 1999).

Conformity also varies *within* cultures in systematic ways. In both North America and Australia, low-income and rural parents tend to emphasize obedience and conformity in their child-rearing practices as compared with urban and middle-class parents (Cashmore & Goodnow, 1986; Peterson & Peters, 1985). This finding, too, makes adaptive sense because parents typically prepare their children for work similar to their own (LeVine, 1982), and laborers have less autonomy than professionals.

◆ INTERIM SUMMARY

Social influence refers to the effects of the presence of others on the way people think, feel, and behave. **Obedience** refers to compliance with authority. The Milgram experiments demonstrated that most people will obey, without limitations of conscience, when they believe an order comes from a legitimate authority. **Conformity** means changing attitudes or behavior to accommodate the standards of peers or groups. The Asch experiments demonstrated that people tend to conform rather than be the lone dissenting voice. Conformity varies across and within cultures and tends to reflect economic and ecological demands.

Group Processes

The Asch conformity experiments illustrate just how powerful group processes can be. A **group** is *a collection of people whose actions affect the other group members*. When a collection of people congregate for even relatively short periods of time, their interactions tend to become patterned in various ways; the same is true of more enduring social institutions such as families and corporations. Features common to many groups include norms, status, roles, and leadership.

Norms

All groups develop **norms**, or *standards for behavior*. Norms guide thought, feeling, and behavior, from the way people dress to their attitudes about sex, Republicans, and lawyers. Sometimes norms are explicit (e.g., a written dress code), but much of the time they are implicit (men do not wear dresses; peers do not issue commands to each other). Different groups have different norms, and particularly in complex societies, people must pick and choose the norms to obey at any given moment because they belong to many groups, which may have conflicting norms. Adolescents, for example, frequently find themselves choosing between the norms of adults and peers.

The way people respond to norms depends on their attitude toward the groups with which the norms are associated. *Groups whose norms matter to an individual, and hence have an impact on the individual's behavior*, are known as **reference groups**. In other words, these are the groups to which a person *refers* when taking action.

A reference group can be positive or negative. A reference group is considered *positive* if the person tries to emulate its members and meet their standards. When a teenage boy gets drunk on weekends because his friends do, his friends are a positive reference group (but not necessarily a positive influence). A reference group is *negative* if a person rejects its members and disavows their standards. If a teenager gets drunk every weekend to establish his independence from his teetotaling parents, his parents are a negative reference group. In both cases, the reference group is influencing the teenager's behavior (which he might be loath to admit).

Status

Status *in a group reflects the amount of power a member holds*. Status distinctions emerge rapidly in many groups, and they become solidified over time in groups of longer duration such as families and organizations. Status distinctions emerge quickly in other primate groups as well, where power often reflects physical stature (de Waal, 1989). In many species, status distinctions arise through physical confrontations or threats of confrontation, which result in a pecking order that each partner in a potential conflict recognizes (or learns the hard way).

Humans, like other animals, usually have little difficulty reading signs of status and recognizing who defers to whom. People high in status in a group tend to talk more and are freer to interrupt. They also display their status nonverbally, by standing erect, maintaining eye contact longer, and generally displaying signs of confidence (Levine & Moreland, 1998).

Roles

Not only do members of a group vary in status, but they differ in the roles they play in the group. A **role** is *a position in a group that has norms specifying appropriate behavior for its occupants* (see Merton, 1957; Parsons, 1951). Roles are essentially norms that are specific to particular people or subgroups.

Roles reflect shared expectations about how particular members of a group are supposed to behave. They tend to be flexible, allowing the individual to make decisions about specific actions, much like roles in improvisational theater. A mother can decide how she will care for her child in a given circumstance, but her culture provides general guidelines for acceptable maternal behavior, such as whether she should stay home with her child or what forms of discipline she should employ.

Role theorists often use a theatrical metaphor: Roles are the parts individuals play in life's drama; society directs them until their time on the stage has passed and another actor takes their place. Individuals internalize roles as *role schemas*, which direct their behavior when they are in a particular role and lead them to expect certain responses from people with complementary roles (such as husband and wife, teacher and student).

The Influence of Roles on Behavior   Several roles routinely emerge in groups, even in brief, unstructured ones (see Bales, 1953). When strangers enter into groups in the laboratory and are asked to solve problems, *the group members who take responsibility for seeing that the group completes its tasks* are called **task leaders**, or *instrumental leaders*. Others, called **social–emotional leaders**, *try to keep the group working cohesively and with minimal animosity*. Sometimes a group member takes on a *tension-release* role, making jokes to relieve the pressure that builds as the group tries to accomplish its tasks. Although people in this role may appear at times to interfere with the group's progress, their presence in a jury room or corporate meeting can actually help the group function.

Because people often define themselves by their roles, roles can have a profound impact on attitudes. One classic study examined the way workers' attitudes changed as a result of job promotions (Lieberman, 1956). The researcher measured the attitudes of plant workers and then reassessed them after some were promoted to foreman (a management position) or shop steward (a union position). Not surprisingly, after their promotions, the foremen were more pro-company than they had been as workers, whereas the shop stewards were more pro-union. More interestingly, however, when the company later experienced financial problems and had to demote some of the foremen to their previous rank-and-file positions, they returned to their original attitudes.

Zimbardo's Prison Study   One of the most dramatic illustrations of the influence of roles on social behavior occurred in a study by Philip Zimbardo (1972, 1975). Twenty-two male college student volunteers played the roles of prisoners and guards in a simulated prison. To make the experiment as realistic as possible, students designated as prisoners were arrested at their homes and searched, handcuffed, fingerprinted, and booked at a police station. They were then blindfolded and driven to the simulated prison where they were stripped, sprayed with a delousing preparation (actually a deodorant spray), and told to stand alone naked in the cell yard. After a short time, they were given a uniform and placed in a cell with two other "prisoners." The guards received minimal instructions and were free to devise their own rules. The only prohibition was against physical punishment.

Soon after the experiment began, Zimbardo noted marked differences between the behavior of the guards and the prisoners. The guards became increasingly aggressive, treating the prisoners as less than human, seldom using their names (instead calling them by number, if referring to them as individuals at all), and subjecting them to roll calls that could last for hours. Many acted with clear sadistic pleasure.

The prisoners, for their part, initiated progressively fewer actions and appeared increasingly depressed. Half the prisoners (five participants) suffered such extreme depression, anxiety, or psychosomatic illness that they had to leave the experiment. The prisoners talked almost exclusively about prison life, maintaining the illusion of their roles. By the fifth day, those who remained were brought before a mock parole board, which would determine whether or not they would be released. Most were willing to forfeit all the money they had earned in the experiment if they could be released. When their requests for parole were denied, they obediently returned to their cells.

The study was originally designed to last two weeks, but the shocking results led Zimbardo to abort it after only six days. The study provides a powerful demonstration of the way roles structure people's behavior and ultimately their emotions, attitudes,

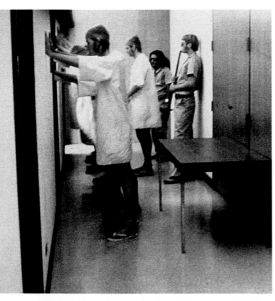

Zimbardo's prison study showed how powerful the demands of roles and situations can be on individual behavior.

and even their identities. Although participants were, in reality, college students randomly assigned to be prisoners or guards, within days they had *become* their roles—in action, thought, and feeling.

◆ INTERIM SUMMARY

A **group** is a collection of people whose actions affect the other group members. All groups develop **norms**, or standards for behavior. Members' **status** in a group reflects the amount of power they hold. People also frequently play particular roles in groups (positions in the group that have norms specifying appropriate behavior for their occupants). **Task leaders** take responsibility for seeing that the group completes its tasks; **social–emotional leaders** try to keep the group working cohesively and with minimal conflict. Roles can have a dramatic influence on attitudes and behaviors, as demonstrated in Zimbardo's prison experiment, which had to be aborted because people became immersed too deeply in their assigned roles.

Leadership

As we have seen, groups tend to have formal or informal **leaders**, *people who exercise greater influence than the average member.* A major initial impetus to research on leadership was Adolf Hitler. Social scientists were astonished that an individual so manifestly disturbed could arouse such popular sentiment and create such a well-oiled war machine. Could democratic forms of leadership be as effective or efficient?

Leadership Styles   In a classic study, Kurt Lewin and his colleagues (1939) randomly assigned ten-year-old boys to one of three groups for craft activities after school. Each group was led by an adult who took one of three leadership styles: He made all the decisions (an *autocratic* leadership style); involved himself in the group and encouraged members to come to decisions themselves (a *democratic* style); or simply let things happen, intervening as little as possible (a *laissez-faire* style).

Boys with an autocratic leader produced more crafts, but they were more likely to stray from the task when the leader left the room, and their products were judged inferior to those produced in the democratic condition. Boys in the democratic group expressed greater satisfaction and displayed less aggression than the others. Laissez-faire leadership led to neither satisfaction nor efficiency. Lewin and his colleagues concluded that autocratic leadership breeds discontent but can be efficient, whereas democratic leadership seems to be both efficient and motivating.

In recent years, industrial/organizational (I/O) psychologists have conducted much of the research on leadership, trying to translate theory and research on effective leadership into interventions to make organizations more efficient. Contemporary organizational psychologists emphasize two dimensions on which leaders vary: *task orientation* and *relationship orientation* (see Blake & Mouton, 1964; Hersey & Blanchard, 1982; Misumi & Peterson, 1985; Stogdill & Coons, 1957). In other words, leaders differ in the extent to which they focus on efficiency and on the feelings of their employees. The distinction is similar to the two major clusters of psychosocial motives found cross-culturally, agency and communion (Chapter 10.)

Cultural values and norms also guide leadership styles (see Gerstner & Day, 1994). Managers in traditional societies like Greece and India tend to prefer autocratic leadership styles with passive subordinates; by contrast, leaders in technologically developed societies like Japan, the United States, Canada, and England prefer subordinates who are active and participatory (Barrett & Franke, 1969; Negandhi, 1973). A study of managers in the United States, Hong Kong, and China found American managers more concerned with worker productivity and Chinese managers more concerned with maintaining a harmonious work environment (Ralston et al., 1992). Hong Kong managers expressed moderate concerns about both productivity and harmony, presumably reflecting Hong Kong's economic similarity to the United States and cultural similarity to China.

Central Questions

■ Why do people so readily slip into roles, such as prisoners and guards?

■ Why are social processes so compelling that they can seemingly override individuals' normal ways of behaving and responding morally?

Making Connections

Lewin's leadership categories parallel Diana Baumrind's findings on parenting styles (Chapter 14). Baumrind showed that authoritative parenting is more effective than either authoritarian (autocratic) or permissive (laissez faire) parenting. Authoritative parenting is not democratic, because it recognizes the limits of children's judgment, but it is participatory and allows input by "citizens" of the family.

Leadership style and effectiveness also depend on the leader's personality (Hogan et al., 1994). Research on the Five Factor model and similar dimensions of personality (Chapter 12) finds that successful leaders tend to be high on extroversion (including dominance, energy, and orientation toward status), agreeableness, and conscientiousness. Thus, effective leaders tend to be outgoing, energetic, powerful, kind, hard working, and attentive to the task at hand. Ineffective leaders tend to be perceived as arrogant, untrustworthy, selfish, insensitive, and overambitious—in a word, narcissistic.

These generalizations, however, require the same caveat as all generalizations about personality traits: They are more likely to apply in some situations than in others (Chapter 12). Situational factors that influence the effectiveness of a particular management style include the motivation and ability of employees, the extent to which tasks require autonomy and creativity, the leader's position in the organizational hierarchy, the degree of pressure to produce, the type of organization, and the extent to which the environment is competitive (Dipboye et al., 1997). A good leader is one who can adjust her leadership style to the context in which she leads—and, where appropriate, to adjust the context in the process of leading.

Charismatic Leaders A type of leader prevalent today, as in most periods of rapid social change, is the charismatic leader. A **charismatic leader** is *a leader who inspires obedience by the force of his or her personality* (House, 1977; Weber, 1924). Charismatic

Martin Luther King, Jr., was one of the most powerful charismatic leaders of the 20th century.

leaders from the last century range from Martin Luther King, Jr., John Kennedy, and Nelson Mandela, to Adolf Hitler. As this list suggests, leaders can harness charisma for good or for ill.

Charismatic leaders offer their followers a vision of a better life and redemption from suffering (House & Singh, 1987), which are particularly appealing to people who feel oppressed, humiliated, confused by rapid cultural change, or conflicted about their identity. Charismatic leaders capture the hearts of their followers because their political message is not merely pragmatic but infused with cultural or spiritual meaning. This infusion was especially evident in Gandhi's leadership of the Indian independence movement (Erikson, 1969). Gandhi's success as a leader lay in developing a strategy for political action—passive resistance—that was compatible with traditional Indian collectivistic and nonviolent values while fostering independence from British colonialism.

◆ **INTERIM SUMMARY**

Leaders are people who exercise greater influence than the average member of a group. Leaders tend to vary in the extent to which they are *task oriented* or *relationship oriented*. Leadership styles that are optimal or considered appropriate in one culture or setting may not be optimal in others. Leadership style (and effectiveness) differs across cultures as well as across individuals. At least in the West, effective leaders tend to be extroverted, agreeable, and conscientious. A **charismatic leader** is one who inspires obedience by the force of his personality.

◆ Central Questions: Individuals, Groups, and the Nature of Human Nature

We began this chapter with a central question: To what extent does our behavior depend on the groups of which we are a part? The data from a century of social–psychological research are clear: We are social animals. As we saw in the last chapter, the cultures, groups, and families of which we are a part get "under our skin"—they become part of the way we think, feel, and behave, from the attitudes we hold to the ways we view ourselves. And as we have seen in this chapter, the tendency to behave in groups in ways that seem "out of character" appears to be very much a part of our character. Much as we might look with horror and astonishment on the subjects in Milgram's studies, the only difference between them and us is that they know the truth about themselves.

In this sense, people's behavior in groups clearly differs qualitatively from their behavior when they are alone. A group is more than a sum of its parts. In another sense, however, we are never actually alone at all. We are always living with mental representations of the people who matter to us—people we love, hate, admire, and interact with every day. We are always in the presence of real or imagined others.

These are very special times to study psychology, because the cultures that get "under our skin" and so powerfully influence everything we do are so rapidly changing. In the twentieth century, we witnessed the most momentous period of social change in human history, as the vast majority of the world's people shifted from agricultural, nomadic, or hunter-gatherer societies to industrial nation-states. Not since the rise of agriculture thousands of years ago has the structure of human society changed so dramatically, and never as rapidly as in the present epoch. A century ago, most people lived with their extended families and believed in the values of their parents and ancestors. Within a few brief generations, traditional values and beliefs have broken down, and technology has advanced beyond anyone's wildest predictions.

People cope with social change in many ways. Some embrace new ideologies, technologies, and values. Others, coping with spiritual unease or feelings of envy, inferiority, and hatred of the dominant cultures that swept away their traditions, search for the future in the past, embracing fundamentalist ideologies that rigidly define good and evil, eliminate ambiguity, and offer a blueprint for how to live (Lifton, 1963). Another route to personal meaning lies in transferring loyalties from family and clan to large nation-states (see Geertz, 1963). Unfortunately, this process can produce the kind of fervent nationalism that left so many dead in the twentieth century, from Nazi Germany to Bosnia. Still another strategy for coping with social change is to synthesize the old and the new, to preserve a continuity with the past while somehow mooring one's identity in the future, as was Gandhi's path.

These psychological responses to the social and political realities of our age lie at the intersection of brain, behavior, and culture. The aggression that fuels conflicts between nations, like the powerful feelings of kinship and solidarity that unite people and give their lives meaning, springs from a brain constructed to make possible the passions that divide and unite. We all share a core of human nature rooted in biology. But the way that nature develops and expresses itself is as diverse as the cultures and individuals who populate the globe.

The twentieth century brought more dramatic social change than any other century in human history, presenting people everywhere with profound psychological challenges.

Summary

Relationships

1. Several factors lead to **interpersonal attraction**, including proximity, similarity, rewards, and physical attractiveness. **Social exchange theory** holds that the foundation of relationships lies in reciprocal rewards.

2. Psychologists studying love distinguish the factors that produce initial attraction from those that maintain or corrode relationships over time. Two kinds of love seen in long-term relationships are **passionate love** (marked by intense physiological arousal and absorption in another person) and **companionate love** (love that involves deep affection, friendship, and emotional intimacy).

3. Evolutionary theorists understand love in terms of contributions to reproductive success. From this point of view, romantic love

shares many features of attachment, and may have evolved to bind parents together to take care of their children. **Sexual strategies**, tactics used in selecting mates, vary by gender and reflect the different evolutionary selection pressures on males and females. The capacity for love is rooted in biology, but its specific nature is shaped by culture.

Altruism

4. **Altruism** means behaving in a way that helps another person with no apparent gain or with potential cost to oneself. Philosophers and psychologists disagree as to whether any act can be genuinely altruistic or whether all apparent altruism is really aimed at making the apparent altruist feel better (**ethical hedonism**). Altruistic behavior probably reflects a blend of selfish and unselfish motives.

5. Evolutionary psychologists propose that people act in ways that maximize their inclusive fitness and hence are most likely to behave altruistically toward their relatives. Natural selection favors animals that behave altruistically toward unrelated members of the species if the likely benefit to each individual over time exceeds the likely cost, a phenomenon known as **reciprocal altruism**.

6. Researchers studying **bystander intervention** have found that in the presence of other people who do not take action, people often do not help in a crisis. In part this reflects a **diffusion of responsibility** (a diminished sense of personal responsibility to act).

Aggression

7. **Aggression** refers to verbal or physical behavior aimed at harming another person or living being. Across cultures, males tend to be more aggressive than females. Researchers are increasingly recognizing the prevalence of male violence perpetrated against females, including battering and rape.

8. Psychodynamic and evolutionary psychologists view aggression as rooted in biology. The neural control of aggression is hierarchically organized, with the amygdala, hypothalamus, and frontal lobes playing prominent roles. Aggression is also partially controlled by hormones, particularly testosterone. Cognitive–social approaches explain aggressive behavior as a result of rewards and punishments, cognitive processes (such as attributions about people's intentions), and social learning (such as modeling).

9. The **frustration–aggression hypothesis** asserts that aggressive behavior arises from frustrated desires or needs. A reformulated version of this hypothesis suggests that frustrating or unpleasant circumstances are likely to evoke aggression if they elicit unpleasant emotion.

Social Influence

10. **Social influence** refers to the influence of the presence of other people on thought, feeling, and behavior. **Obedience** is a social influence process whereby individuals follow the dictates of an authority. The Milgram studies demonstrated that most people will obey without limitations of conscience if they believe the authority is legitimate.

11. **Conformity** is the process by which people change their attitudes or behavior to accommodate the standards of peers or groups. Asch's studies demonstrated that a substantial number of people will conform when confronted by a group with a consensus opinion, even if the opinion is manifestly wrong. Conformity is highest in agricultural societies with dense populations, where independence may be less adaptive than in hunter–gatherer or urban, technologically developed societies.

12. A **group** is a collection of people whose actions affect the other group members. Naturally occurring groups routinely have **norms** (standards for the behavior of group members), **status** systems (distributions of power within the group), **roles** (socially patterned positions within a group that define appropriate behavior for the people occupying them), and **leaders** (people who exercise greater influence than the average member).

13. People behave differently in the presence of others, although they also carry "others" with them all the time in the form of mental representations. The massive social changes in the last century, such as rapid technological development and the breakdown of traditional family structures and values, have created profound psychological changes and dilemmas for coping.

Key Terms

APPENDIX

Additional chapters excerpted from
Psychology in Action 6e

Karen Huffman
Palomar College

PSYCHOLOGY
IN ACTION
Sixth Edition

Karen Huffman
Palomar College

JOHN WILEY & SONS, INC.

New York | Chichester | Weinheim | Brisbane | Singapore | Toronto

Acquisitions Editor	Ellen Schatz
Developmental Editor	Johnna Barto/Harriett Prentiss
Editorial Assistant	Lilli DeGrasse
Marketing Manager	Kevin Molloy
Senior Production Editor	Sandra Russell
Senior Designer	Kevin Murphy
Interior Design	Lee Goldstein/Norm Chrisitansen
Cover Design	Suzanne Noli
Illustration Editor	Sandra Rigby
Photo Editors	Sara Wight/Hilary Newman
Production Management Services	Hermitage Publishing Services
Photo Researcher	Mary Ann Price
Cover Image	*"Lightbulb IV", 1992, by Paul Giovanopoulos*

This book was typeset in 10/12 Fairfield LH Medium by Hermitage Publishing Services and printed and bound by R.R. Donnelley (Willard). The cover was printed by Lehigh Press, Inc.

The paper in this book was manufactured by a mill whose forest management programs include sustained yield harvesting of its timberlands. Sustained yield harvesting principles ensure that the number of trees cut each year does not exceed the amount of new growth.

This book is printed on acid-free paper. ∞

Library of Congress Cataloging-in-Publication Data:

Huffman, Karen.
    Psychology in action/Karen Huffman.—6th ed.
        p. cm.
    Includes bibliographical references and indexes.
    ISBN 0-471-39495-5 (cloth: alk. paper)
      1. Psychology. I. Title.
  BF121 .H78 2001
  150—dc21   2001017673

Printed in the United States of America.

10 9 8 7 6 5 4 3 2 1

3A

Stress and Health Psychology

Core Learning Objectives

As you read Chapter 3, keep the following questions in mind and answer them in your own words:

▶ What is health psychology? Can health psychologists help with problems related to smoking, binge drinking, and chronic pain?

▶ What is stress and what are its major sources and results?

▶ How is stress related to serious illnesses like cancer and coronary heart disease?

▶ What techniques and resources are available to help people cope with stress?

College Life Stress Inventory

Copy the "stress rating" number into the last column for any event you have experienced in the last year. Then add up the ratings for your total stress score.

Event	Stress Rating	Your Items
1. Being raped	100	_____
2. Finding out that you are HIV-positive	100	_____
3. Being accused of rape	98	_____
4. Death of a close friend	97	_____
5. Death of a close family member	97	_____
6. Contracting a sexually transmitted disease (other than AIDS)	94	_____
7. Concerns about being pregnant	91	_____
8. Finals week	90	_____
9. Concerns about your partner being pregnant	90	_____
10. Oversleeping for an exam	89	_____
11. Flunking a class	89	_____
12. Having a boyfriend or girlfriend cheat on you	85	_____
13. Ending a steady dating relationship	85	_____
14. Serious illness in a close friend or family member	85	_____
15. Financial difficulties	84	_____
16. Writing a major term paper	83	_____
17. Being caught cheating on a test	83	_____
18. Drunk driving	82	_____
19. Sense of overload in school or work	82	_____
20. Two exams in one day	80	_____
21. Cheating on your boyfriend or girlfriend	77	_____
22. Getting married	76	_____
23. Negative consequences of drinking or drug use	75	_____
24. Depression or crisis in your best friend	73	_____
24. Difficulties with parents	73	_____
25. Talking in front of a class	72	_____
26. Lack of sleep	69	_____
27. Change in housing situation (hassles, moves)	69	_____
28. Competing or performing in public	69	_____
29. Getting in a physical fight	66	_____
30. Difficulties with a roommate	66	_____
31. Job changes (applying, new job, work hassles)	65	_____
32. Declaring a major or concerns about future plans	65	_____
33. A class you hate	62	_____
34. Drinking or use of drugs	61	_____
35. Confrontations with professors	60	_____
36. Starting a new semester	58	_____
37. Going on a first date	57	_____
38. Registration	55	_____
39. Maintaining a steady dating relationship	55	_____
40. Commuting to campus or work, or both	54	_____
41. Peer pressures	53	_____
42. Being away from home for the first time	53	_____
43. Getting sick	52	_____
44. Concerns about your appearance	52	_____
45. Getting straight A's	51	_____
46. A difficult class that you love	48	_____
47. Making new friends; getting along with friends	47	_____
48. Fraternity or sorority rush	47	_____
49. Falling asleep in class	40	_____
50. Attending an athletic event (e.g., football game)	20	_____
Total		_____

From Renner & Mackin, 1998.

Marriage as a stressor? Getting married is normally a very happy occasion; nevertheless the changes it brings can be stressful.

How did you do? Were you surprised that getting married or getting straight A's could be considered stressful? Michael Renner and Scott Mackin (1998) developed this scale on the basis of their research with college students, and they found that scores ranged between a low of 182 and a high of 2,571, with an average of 1,247. What was your total score? If you are a "typical" college student, 18 to 22 years of age, living on campus, and away from home for the first time, this scale may provide an accurate assessment of important stressors in your life. However, as an older returning student, a young student living at home, or a married person with small children, you have different stressors (such as divorce, unemployment, child care) and this scale would be inappropriate.

We use this scale as an introduction to the complex and fascinating world of health psychology. The topics of health and stress are a part of everyday conversation, with most people assuming that everyone shares the same definitions and life experiences. As you have just found with the college stress inventory, however, stress is highly individual. Stress is also a normal part of all our lives, but when it is chronic or severe, it can damage our health.

The well-established relationship between stress and physical illness takes us into a broader discussion of the psychology of health. In the first part of this chapter, we explore this field and three important health issues: smoking, binge drinking, and chronic pain. After that, we examine the numerous causes and results of stress, the role of stress in cancer and heart disease, and how people cope with stress. We end the chapter with specific tips to help you stay healthy.

HEALTH PSYCHOLOGY IN ACTION

What is health psychology? Can health psychologists help with problems related to smoking, binge drinking, and chronic pain?

Throughout most of history, the relationship between mind and physical health had been a widely accepted fact. However, in the late 1800s, the discovery of physiological causes for infectious diseases such as typhoid and syphilis led scientists to intensify the search for physiological causes of disease. As a result, medicine and public health made marked advances. Over the last century, life expectancy for Americans of all races and genders has steadily increased, and for those born in 1997 it is an all-time high of 76.5 years (National Center for Health Statistics, 2001).

Interestingly, the major causes of death have shifted from contagious diseases (pneumonia, influenza, tuberculosis, measles, and typhoid fever) to noncontagious diseases (cancer, heart and cardiovascular disease, chronic lung disease) (National Center for Health Statistics, 2001). Can you see how today's key health problems are strongly related to behavior and lifestyle? Scientists and medical experts are now reemphasizing the close relationship between psychological behavior and physical health and illness, with an emphasis on wellness and the prevention of illness. This is the heart (and definition) of **health psychology** (Baum & Posluszny, 2001).

What Health Psychologists Do: Research and Practice

Health psychologists study how people's lifestyles and activities, emotional reactions, ways of interpreting events, and personality characteristics influence their physical health and well-being. Some health psychologists are involved primarily in research, whereas others work directly with physicians and other health professionals to implement research findings.

As researchers, they have been particularly interested in the relationship between stress and the immune system. A normally functioning immune system helps detect and defend against disease, and a suppressed immune system leaves the body susceptible to any number of diseases. Today we know that stress plays a role

Health Psychology *The study of the relationship between psychological behavior and physical health and illness, with an emphasis on wellness and the prevention of illness.*

in suppressing the immune system and may make us more vulnerable to a host of modern illnesses and disease, including cancer, heart disease, AIDS (acquired immunodeficiency syndrome, and even the common cold (Cohen et al., 1998, 1999; Kiecolt-Glaser & Glaser, 2001; Leserman et al., 2000; Pratt et al., 1996). Until the 1970s, however, most experts believed the immune system was completely independent of the other body systems. As you will see in a later section, the scientific view of stress and the immune system has changed dramatically in the last few years.

As practitioners, health psychologists can work as independent clinicians or as consultants alongside physicians, physical and occupational therapists, and other health care workers. Their goal is to reduce psychological distress or unhealthy behaviors. They also help patients and families make critical decisions and prepare psychologically for surgery or other treatment.

In addition to their work as researchers and practitioners, health psychologists also educate the general public about health *maintenance*. They provide information about the effects of stress, smoking, alcohol, lack of exercise, and other health issues. In addition, health psychologists help people cope with chronic problems, such as pain, diabetes, and high blood pressure, as well as unhealthful behaviors, such as lack of assertiveness and anger expression (Davidson, MacGregor, Stuhr, Dixon, & MacLean, 2000; Haerenstam, Theorell, & Kaijser, 2000; Lepore, Ragan, & Jones, 2000). To illustrate the work of health psychologists, we begin this chapter discussing two of the most prevalent (and preventable) health problems in the United States — smoking and binge drinking.

Smoking: Hazardous to Your Health

> A custom loathsome to the eye, hateful to the nose, harmful to the brain, dangerous to the lungs, and in the black, stinking fume thereof, nearest resembling the horrible Stygian smoke of the pit that is bottomless.

This is what King James I wrote about smoking in 1604, shortly after Sir Walter Raleigh introduced tobacco to England from the Americas. Today, nearly 400 years later, many people would agree with the king's tirade against the practice.

According to the latest U.S. Public Health Service report, tobacco is the single most preventable cause of death and disease in the United States (Fiore, 2000). Smoking is a major risk factor for coronary heart disease and lung cancer and contributes to cancers of the mouth, larynx, throat, esophagus, bladder, and pancreas (Centers for Disease Control, 2001). Smoking also contributes to chronic bronchitis, emphysema, and ulcer disease. Moreover, smoking shortens life (Burns, 2000). This is true for both the smoker and those who breathe secondhand smoke.

What about all the new antismoking laws? Do they help? Ironically, the antismoking laws passed in the 1990s may have made quitting smoking even more difficult for some. First, the fact that smokers have to leave smoke-free environments and group together outdoors on the hottest summer days and the worst winter days to satisfy their habit creates a strong social bond: Together they will suffer the tyranny of nonsmoking laws. Cigarette companies play to this group loyalty (and the individual's "independence" and "perseverance") by showing smokers sitting high up on the ledges of office buildings and on the wings of airplanes in flight "going to any lengths" to have a cigarette. Second, when people cannot smoke in offices, on airplanes, in restaurants, or other public places, the interval between nicotine doses increases, which increases the severity of the withdrawal symptoms (Palfai, Monti, Ostafin, & Hutchinson, 2000). In effect, the smoker gets repeated previews of just how unpleasant quitting is going to be — and who wouldn't rather avoid something unpleasant?

Smoker's unite? Due to increased restrictions, many people are forced to go outside to smoke. Ironically, this may forge stronger bonds between smokers and make them even more resistant to quitting.

Most people know that smoking is bad for their health and that the more they smoke, the more at risk they are. It is therefore not surprising that most health psychologists and medical professionals are concerned with preventing smoking in the first place and getting those who already smoke to stop.

Smoking Prevention

The first puff on a cigarette is rarely pleasant. Why, then, do people ever start smoking? The answer is complex. First, smoking usually starts when people are young. The European School Survey Project on Alcohol and Other Drugs (ESPAD) (2001) reported that tobacco smoking was well established by the mid-teens in most European countries and showed few signs of diminishing since the previous ESPAD survey in 1995. A similar survey of U.S. middle schools, grades 6 to 8, found that one in eight students were experimenting with some form of tobacco, such as cigarettes, cigars, and chewing tobacco (Kaufman, 2000). There are many reasons people begin to smoke at such a young age, but peer pressure and imitation of role models (such as celebrities) are particularly strong factors. Young smokers want to look mature and be accepted by their social peers.

Secondly, regardless of the age at which a person begins smoking, once he or she begins to smoke, there is a biological need to continue because of the addictive effects of nicotine. The evidence clearly shows that nicotine is a powerful addictive drug, comparable to heroin, cocaine, and alcohol (Balfour & Ridley, 2000; Pahlavan, Bonnet, & Duda, 2000; Pich et al., 1997). In fact, when we inhale smoke, it takes only seconds for the nicotine to reach the brain, where it increases the release of the neurotransmitters acetylcholine and norepinephrine. Acetylcholine and norepinephrine, in turn, increase alertness, concentration, memory, and feelings of pleasure (McGaughy, Decker, & Sarter, 1999; Picciotto, 1998; Quattrocki, Baird, & Yurgelun-Todd, 2000). Several recent research projects have also indicated that nicotine stimulates the release of dopamine, the neurotransmitter most closely related to reward centers in the brain (Noble, 2000; Carboni, Bortone, Giua, & DiChiara, 2000). These neurotransmitters also decrease the symptoms of nicotine withdrawal, anxiety, tension, and pain, which come after a short period without tobacco.

Finally, social pressures and physical addiction combine to create additional benefits (Lazev, Herzog, & Brandon, 1999). For example, smokers learn to associate smoking with pleasant things, such as good food, friends, sex, and, not least, the high that nicotine gives them, so their smoking is rewarded. When smokers are deprived of cigarettes, they go through physical withdrawal with extremely unpleasant symptoms. When they get their next puff, the nicotine relieves the symptoms, so smoking is rewarded. It follows that the best way to reduce the number of smokers is to prevent people from taking their first puff.

Smoking as a "pediatric disease." Because many smokers take up the habit as adolescents or preteens, health psychologists recommend that antismoking programs begin in elementary school.

If most people begin smoking during adolescence, shouldn't prevention be aimed at this group? Prevention programs for teens face a tough uphill battle. For adolescents, the long-term health disadvantages of heart disease and cancer seem totally irrelevant, whereas smoking itself provides immediate short-term rewards from peers and the addictive, reinforcing properties of nicotine. Many smoking prevention programs therefore focus on immediate short-term problems with smoking, such as bad breath and interference with athletic performance.

Through films and discussion groups, teens also are educated about peer pressure and the media's influence on smoking, given opportunities to role-play refusal skills, taught general social and personal skills needed in decision making, and given strategies for coping with the stresses of adolescence and daily life (Worden, Flynn, Solomon, & Secker-Walker, 1996). Unfortunately, the research shows that the effect of psychosocial prevention programs is small (Baum & Posluszny, 1999). To have even a modest effect, these programs must begin early and continue for many years (Eckhardt, Woodruff, & Elder, 1997).

To reduce the health risk and help fight peer pressure, many schools ban smoking in college buildings and offer more smoke-free dormitories. Another possible deterrent to the college smoking trend results from expensive legal battles and settlements by the tobacco industry and the fact that these expenses are passed on to consumers in the form of higher prices for cigarettes. This increase, added to state and local taxes, brings the cost to over $4 per pack in most states. For a student who smokes a pack of cigarettes a day, the annual cost is nearly $1,500 — more than twice the cost of textbooks for an entire academic year.

Stopping Smoking

> To cease smoking is the easiest thing I ever did; I ought to know, for I have done it a thousand times.
>
> Mark Twain

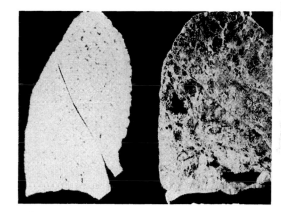

A hidden cost of smoking. Would people continue to smoke if they could see what it does to their lungs? Compare the healthy tissue of the lung of a non-smoker on the left to the blackened, unhealthy lung of the smoker on the right.

Unfortunately, Mark Twain was never able to quit for very long, and many ex-smokers say that stopping smoking was the most difficult thing they ever did. Although some people find the easiest way for them to cope with the physical withdrawal from nicotine is to suddenly and completely stop, the success rate for this "cold turkey" approach is extremely low. Even with medical aids, such as patches, gum, or pills, it is still very difficult to quit (Killen et al., 2000; Patten, 2000). Any program designed to help smokers break their habit must combat the social rewards of smoking as well as the physical addiction to nicotine.

Sometimes the best approach is a combination of cognitive and behavioral techniques and nicotine replacement therapy. Cognitively, smokers can learn to identify stimuli or situations that make them feel like smoking and then change or avoid them (Brandon, Collins, Juliano, & Lazev, 2000). They can also refocus their attention on something other than smoking or remind themselves of the benefits of not smoking (Taylor, Harris, Singleton, Moolchan, & Heishman, 2000). Behaviorally, they might cope with the urge to smoke by chewing gum, exercising, or chewing on a toothpick after a meal instead of lighting a cigarette.

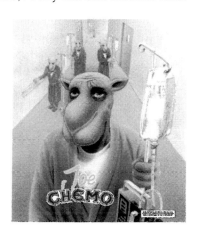

No program to quit smoking will work without a tremendous amount of personal motivation, but the payoffs can be just as tremendous: a more enjoyable and longer life. (See Wetter et al., 1998, for the Agency for Health Care Policy and Research's "Smoking Cessation Clinical Practice Guidelines.")

Antismoking ads. Because Joe Camel was once a popular icon that reportedly encouraged young children to smoke, antismoking activists created a "Joe Chemo" image to advertise the dangers of smoking.

Check & Review

WHAT HEALTH PSYCHOLOGISTS DO AND SMOKING

Health psychology is the study of the relationship between psychological behavior and physical health and illness, with an emphasis on wellness and the prevention of illness. As researchers, health psychologists study psychological issues that affect physical health and find ways to help patients cope with medical procedures and health problems. As practitioners, health psychologists work with patients alongside health care professionals to help reduce psychological distress and unhealthy behaviors and educate the general public about health risks and health maintenance.

Because smoking is the single most preventable cause of death and disease in the United States, prevention and cessation of smoking are of primary importance to all health practitioners, including health psychologists. Smoking prevention programs involve educating the public about short- and long-term consequences of smoking, trying to make smoking less socially acceptable, and helping nonsmokers resist social pressures to smoke. Most approaches to help people quit smoking

Health psychology in action. Your lifestyle and behavioral risk factors have a significant impact on your health and life expectancy (Gorman, 2001).

include cognitive and behavioral techniques to aid smokers in their withdrawal and nicotine replacement therapy (using patches, gum, and pills).

Questions

1. What is health psychology?
2. Since the late 1800s, major causes of death have shifted from _____ to _____ diseases.
3. Knowing smoking is very dangerous, why do many people find it so difficult to stop?
4. If you are mounting a campaign to prevent young people from taking up smoking, you are likely to get the best results if you emphasize the _____. (a) serious, unhealthy, long-term effects of tobacco use; (b) number of adults who die from smoking; (c) value of having a relatively healthy retirement; (d) short-term detrimental effects of tobacco use.

Answers to Questions can be found in Appendix B.

Binge drinking can be fatal. On many college campuses, it is a tradition to "drink your age" on your 21st birthday. Following this tradition, Bradley McCue, a University of Michigan Junior, drank 21 shots of alcohol plus three more to break his friends' record. He died on the morning of his 21st birthday from alcohol poisoning. For more information, contact www.BRAD.org.

Binge Drinking: A Growing Social Problem

Were you surprised by news reports of two freshmen at Massachusetts Institute of Technology who died from alcohol poisoning after binge drinking at fraternity parties? One of the students had a blood alcohol level of .5888 percent — the equivalent of more than 20 beers in 1 hour and over seven times the legal driving limit in most states. Unlike smoking, alcohol and other drugs can kill directly and immediately when they are taken in large amounts over a short period of time. They also impair the judgment and reaction times of the user, thus contributing to thousands of deaths and injuries from automobile accidents, rapes, and other assaults. (See Chapter 5 to review the short- and long-term health risks of alcohol.)

Binge drinking occurs when a man consumes five or more drinks in a row or a woman consumes four or more drinks at a time (Weingardt et al., 1998). Approximately 5.1 million Americans between the ages of 12 and 20 years are binge drinkers, and the greatest majority are college students (Wechsler, Lee, Kuo, & Lee, 2000). Binge drinking is a serious health problem for all college-age students, those who drink and those who don't.

What can be done about college binge drinking? Stopping students from binge drinking is very difficult. Students seem to think of it as part of the "college experience." Therefore, any real attack on binge drinking must approach the problem from many different directions. First, it is important to overcome the myths about college drinking and teach the facts. But just learning the facts does not stop people from drinking. The social rewards also must be reduced or removed.

So what are these misconceptions, and how do we reduce the social rewards? Henry Wechsler (1998), the first author of *The Harvard School of Public Health College Alcohol Study,* suggests the following:

- *Students who binge tend to think that they are just average or moderate drinkers.* We must make it clear to these students that binge drinking is not the norm. It is not normal or healthy to drink four or five drinks at a sitting, let alone to do that frequently.

- *Many students believe that binge drinking is harmless to the drinker and to college society.* But binge drinkers risk AIDS from unprotected sex and can be the victims or perpetrators of assault, rape, and car accident injuries.

- *Many students think that it's okay to binge-drink because the college administration looks the other way.* College administrations must enforce antidrinking rules and make a greater effort to help students who abuse alcohol. Strict penalties might help repeat offenders.

- *Members of fraternities and sororities seem to think that drinking is part of the Greek life.* College communities therefore have a responsibility to work with these organizations so that drinking is not central to social events.

- *When students see alumni drinking at tailgate parties and hear their stories of partying until dawn, they think that drinking is what alumni expect them to do at college.* Any alcohol-control measures directed at students must also apply to visiting alumni. Sporting events should be alcohol free, and colleges should avoid alcohol-related sports promotions.

GENDER & CULTURAL DIVERSITY

Binge Drinking Around the World

After reading the above section on binge drinking, you may think it is a problem unique to college students in the United States. Unfortunately, binge drinking is a worldwide problem.

- The European School Survey Project (2001) found an overall increase in binge drinking since 1995, especially in Britain, Denmark, Ireland, and Poland. More than 30 percent of school children in those countries reported binge drinking three or more times in the last month.

- In Mexico, a study of drinking patterns at 16 religious fiestas and 13 nonreligious fiestas in the community of Santa María Atzompa found that nearly all the men qualified as binge drinkers at every fiesta. Furthermore, the binge drinking contributed to several outbreaks of violence at the fiestas (Perez, 2000).

- A study in Spain and South America found that young men who reported binge drinking were more likely than others to behave aggressively toward people outside their family (Orpinas, 1999).

- Scientists in Denmark compared the drinking patterns of 56,970 men and women who prefer drinking beer, wine, or spirits (Gronbaek, Tjonneland, Johansen, Stripp, & Overvad, 2000). Results showed that beer drinkers were the least likely of the different types of drinkers to binge, whereas wine drinkers were the most likely to binge.

Alcohol is a global problem. Like the Octoberfest in Munich, Germany, many cultures use alcohol as a common part of holiday celebrations.

- Research on alcohol consumption in Russia shows that 44 percent of men are binge drinkers (Bobak, McKee, Rose, & Marmot, 1999).

- The lower rate of binge drinking in Japan has been linked to a genetic mutation that makes it difficult for many Japanese, and other Asians, to metabolize alcohol. Nearly half of the Japanese population is sensitive to alcohol owing to this genetic mutation. Research shows that Japanese who do not carry the mutation are much more likely to be binge drinkers than those who do not carry the mutation (Takeshita & Morimoto, 1999; Tu & Israel, 1995).

Chronic Pain: The Role of Psychologists in Helping Patients Cope

Pain is the most common reason why people seek medical attention. It is the major symptom reported in over 80 percent of all visits to physicians (Turk, 1994). Although we try to avoid pain, it is necessary for our survival. Pain alerts us to dangerous or harmful situations, and pain forces us to rest and recover from injury (Watkins & Maier, 2000). But **chronic pain**, pain that continues long past the healing of a wound or pain that is associated with a chronic disease, does not serve a useful function.

Chronic Pain *Continuous or recurrent pain over a period of 6 months or more.*

Although psychological factors rarely are the source of chronic pain, they can encourage and intensify it, and increase the related anguish and disability (Affleck, Tennen, & Apter, 2001; Fruehwald, Loffler, Eher, Saletu, & Baumhackl, 2001; Snow-Turek, Norris, & Tan, 1996). To treat chronic pain, health psychologist use specific treatment methods, such as behavior modification, biofeedback, and relaxation.

Behavior Modification

Chronic pain is a serious problem with no simple solution. For example, exercise is known to produce an increase in *endorphins,* naturally produced chemicals that attach themselves to nerve cells in the brain and block the perception of pain (Chapter 2). However, chronic pain patients tend to decrease their activity and exercise. In addition, well-meaning family members often ask chronic pain sufferers, "How are you feeling?" "Is the pain any better today?" Unfortunately, talking about pain focuses attention on it and increases its intensity (Harvey & McGuire, 2000). Furthermore, as the pain increases, anxiety increases, the anxiety itself then increases the pain, which further increases the anxiety, which further increases the pain!

To counteract these hidden personal and family problems and negative cycles, health psychologists may begin a behavior modification program for both the patient with chronic pain and his or her family. The effectiveness of such programs for treating chronic pain was first shown in the late 1970s (Cairns & Pasino, 1977). Researchers established individualized pain management programs, monitored each patient's adherence, and congratulated those who followed through with their pain treatment programs (daily exercise, use of relaxation techniques, and so on). Compared with a control group, patients who used these techniques experienced substantially reduced pain. Today, many pain control programs incorporate similar techniques for rewarding "well behaviors" (Kole-Snijders et al., 1999).

Biofeedback

In *biofeedback,* information about physiological functions, such as heart rate or blood pressure, is monitored, and the feedback helps the individual learn to control these functions. Such feedback about physiological processes helps reduce some types of chronic pain. Most biofeedback with chronic pain patients is done with the *electromyograph* (EMG). This device measures muscle tension by recording electrical activity in the skin. The EMG is most helpful when the pain involves extreme muscle tension, such as tension headache and lower back pain. Electrodes are attached to the site of the pain, and the patient is instructed to relax. When sufficient relaxation is achieved, the machine signals with a tone or a light. The signal serves as feedback to the patient.

Research shows that biofeedback is sometimes as effective as more expensive and lengthy forms of treatment (Newton-John, Spence, & Schotte, 1995). The reason for its success seems to be that it teaches patients to recognize patterns of emotional arousal and conflict that affect their physiological responses. This self-awareness, in turn, enables them to learn self-regulation skills that help control their pain (McKee, 1991).

Pain control through biofeedback. Using an electromyograph (EMG), muscular tension is recorded and the patient is taught specific relaxation techniques that reduce tension and help relieve chronic pain.

Relaxation Techniques

Because the pain always seems to be there, chronic pain sufferers tend to talk and think about their pain whenever they're not thoroughly engrossed in an activity. Watching TV shows or films, attending parties, or any activity that diverts attention from the pain seems to reduce discomfort. Attention might also be diverted with special *relaxation techniques* like those that are taught in so-called "natural childbirth" classes. These techniques focus the birthing mother's attention on breathing and relaxing the muscles, which helps distract her attention from the fear and pain of the birthing process. Similar techniques also can be helpful to chronic pain sufferers. Remember, though, that these techniques do not eliminate the pain; they merely allow the person to ignore it for a time. (Later in this chapter, you'll learn a relaxation technique that can be used for chronic pain and for everyday stress.)

Relaxation techniques. Massage is a healthy way to reduce stress and tension related pain.

Check & Review

BINGE DRINKING AND CHRONIC PAIN

Binge drinking is a serious problem that can lead to rape or assault, to death from alcohol poisoning, or automobile and other accidents. It occurs when a man has five or more drinks in a row and a woman has four or more. To reduce binge drinking, we must overcome the myths about drinking and teach the facts. We also must reduce or remove the social rewards.

Chronic pain is continuous or recurrent pain that persists over a period of six months or more.

Although psychological factors rarely are the source of chronic pain, they can encourage and intensify it. Increased activity, exercise, and dietary changes help to reduce chronic pain. Health psychologists also use behavior modification, biofeedback, and relaxation techniques to treat chronic pain.

Questions

1. What is binge drinking?
2. What are the 5 misconceptions about binge drinking, and how can we remove the social reinforcers?

3. Continuous or recurrent pain over a period of 6 months or more is known as _____.
4. An increase in activity and exercise levels benefits patients with pain because exercise increases the release of (a) endorphins; (b) insulin; (c) acetylcholine; (d) norepinephrine.

Answers to Questions can be found in Appendix B.

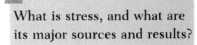

STRESS AND ITS ROLE IN HEALTH

Stress *A nonspecific response of the body to any demand made on it; the arousal, both physical and mental, to situations or events that we perceive as threatening or challenging.*

Eustress *Pleasant, desirable stress*

Distress *Unpleasant, objectionable stress*

Hans Selye (1974), a physiologist renowned for his research and writing in the area of stress since the 1930s, defines **stress** as the nonspecific response of the body to any demand made on it. When you play two nonstop tennis matches in the middle of a heat wave, your body responds with a fast heartbeat, rapid breathing, and an outpouring of perspiration. When you find out 10 minutes before class starts that the term paper you just started is due today rather than next Friday, your body has the same physiological stress response to a very different stressor. Stress reactions can occur to either internal, cognitive stimuli or external, environmental stimuli (Baum & Posluszny, 1999).

The body is nearly always in some state of stress, whether pleasant or unpleasant, mild or severe. *Anything* placing a demand on the body can cause stress. When stress is beneficial, such as moderate exercise, it is called **eustress** and when it is objectionable, as from chronic illness, it is called **distress** (Selye, 1974). The total absence of stress would mean the total absence of external stimulation, which would eventually lead to death. Because health psychology has been chiefly concerned with the negative effects of stress, we will adhere to convention and use the word "stress" to refer primarily to harmful or unpleasant stress (Selye's *distress*), even though there are some forms of beneficial *eustress*.

Sources of Stress: From Major Life Changes to Minor Hassles

Although stress is pervasive in our lives, some things cause more stress than others. The major sources of stress are life changes, chronic stressors, hassles, burnout, frustration, and conflict.

THE FAR SIDE® BY GARY LARSON

© 1985 FarWorks, Inc. All Rights Reserved/Dist. by Creators Syndicate

"The fuel light's on, Frank! We're all going to die! ... Wait, wait. ... Oh, my mistake— that's the intercom light."

Life Changes

The College Life Stress Inventory that you took at the beginning of the chapter is designed especially for college students. It is based on an earlier inventory developed for adults past college age by Thomas Holmes and Richard Rahe (1967) — the Social Readjustment Rating Scale (SRRS). The SRRS measures stress related to *life changes* brought about by major events, such as marriage, the death of a family member, moving to a new home, and getting (or losing) a job.

Such major changes disrupt our lives and cause more stress than normal. Holmes and Rahe believed that change, of any kind, that required some adjustment in behavior or lifestyle caused stress. Moreover, they believed that exposure to numerous stressful events within a short period of time could have a detrimental effect on health. Keep in mind, however, that Holmes and Rahe use the scientific definition of *stress*. Therefore, change can be anguishing, as with the loss of a parent or divorce, but it can also be joyous, as in the case of a marriage, or emotionally neutral, as with a change in work hours. The point is that all change causes stress. And too much stress can exceed the body's ability to cope, leading to moderate or serious illness.

In recent years, Mark Miller and Richard Rahe updated the original Holmes and Rahe SRRS. As you can see in Table 3.1, this scale is very similar to the one at the beginning of the chapter, but it is designed for older adults outside of college. These items are ranked according to their relative importance in contributing to health problems. Each event is assigned a numerical rating expressed in *life change units* (LCUs). To score yourself on this scale, add up the LCUs for all life events you have experienced during the last year and compare your score with the following standards: 0–150 = No significant problems, 150–199 = Mild life crisis (33 percent chance of illness), 200–299 = Moderate life crisis (50 percent chance of illness), 300 and above Major life crisis (80 percent chance of illness).

The SRRS scale is an easy and popular way to measure stress, and cross-cultural studies have shown that most people rank the magnitude of stressful events in similar ways (McAndrew, Akande, Turner, & Sharma, 1998). However, the SRRS is not foolproof. First, it only shows a *correlation* between stress and illness, and as you recall from Chapter 1, *correlation does not prove causation*. Like results on all correlational studies, stress could cause subsequent illnesses, but they could also be caused by other (yet unknown) factors.

In addition, as noted earlier, stress varies according to the individual. Any one event may be perceived as a stressful ordeal, a neutral occurrence, or an exciting opportunity. It depends on your personal interpretation and appraisal (Whelan & Kirkby, 2000). You might find moving to another state a terrible sacrifice and a tremendous stressor, whereas your friend might see the move as a wonderful opportunity and experience little or no stress. Furthermore, different people have differing abilities to deal with change, perhaps because of good coping skills, general physical health, healthier lifestyles, or even genetic predisposition.

Chronic Stressors

Not all stressful situations are single, short-term events such as a death or a birth. A bad marriage, poor working conditions, or an intolerable political climate can be *chronic stressors*. Even the stress of chronic aircraft noise is associated with measurable hormonal and cardiac changes (Evans et al., 1995). Our social lives also can be chronically stressful, because making and maintaining friendships involves considerable thought and energy (Griffith, Dubow, & Ippolito, 2000).

Perhaps the largest source of chronic stress is work. People often experience stress associated with keeping or changing jobs or with job performance (Steptoe, Cropley, & Joekes, 2000). However, the most stressful jobs are those that make great demands on performance and concentration but allow little creativity or opportunity for advancement (Parasuraman & Purohit, 2000). Assembly-line work ranks very high in this category.

Chronic stress? Although assembly line work might seem stress-free, the lack of creativity and little opportunity for advancement make this a highly stressful job.

TABLE 3.1 SOCIAL READJUSTMENT RATING SCALE

Life Events	Life Change Units
Death of spouse	100
Divorce	73
Marital separation	65
Jail term	63
Death of a close family member	63
Personal injury or illness	53
Marriage	50
Fired at work	47
Marital reconciliation	45
Retirement	45
Change in health of family member	44
Pregnancy	40
Sex difficulties	39
Gain of a new family member	39
Business readjustment	39
Change in financial state	38
Death of a close friend	37
Change to different line of work	36
Change in number of arguments with spouse	35
Mortgage or loan for major purchase	31
Foreclosure on mortgage or loan	30
Change in responsibilities at work	29
Son or daughter leaving home	29
Trouble with in-laws	29
Outstanding personal achievement	28
Spouse begins or stops work	26
Begin or end school	26
Change in living conditions	25
Revision of personal habits	24
Trouble with boss	23
Change in work hours or conditions	20
Change in residence	20
Change in schools	20
Change in recreation	19
Change in church activities	19
Change in social activities	18
Mortgage or loan for lesser purchase (car, major appliance)	17
Change in sleeping habits	16
Change in number of family get-togethers	15
Change in eating habits	15
Vacation	13
Christmas	12
Minor violations of the law	11

Source: Holmes & Rahe (1967).

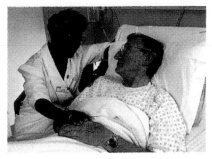

Is nursing a stressful career? People who think of their profession as a "calling" may lose their idealism when faced with the ongoing stresses and emotional turmoil. Over time they may suffer a type of mental and physical exhaustion known as "burn out."

Hassles *Little problems of daily living that are not significant in themselves but that accumulate and sometimes become a major source of stress*

Burnout *A state of physical, emotional, and mental exhaustion attributable to long-term involvement in emotionally demanding situations*

Researchers have documented that stress at work can also cause serious stress at home not only for workers but for other family members as well. And, of course, in our private lives, divorce, child and spouse abuse, alcoholism, and money problems can place severe stress on all members of a family (Grunberg, Moore, Anderson-Connolly, & Greenberg, 1999; Thompson & Kaslow, 2000; Tien, Sandler, & Zautra, 2000).

Hassles and Burnout

In addition to chronic stressors, a great deal of daily stress is in the form of **hassles**, little problems of daily living that are not significant in themselves but that pile up to become a major source of stress (Repetti, 1993). Some hassles tend to be shared by all: time pressures (getting to work or school on time, finding a parking place, fighting traffic jams), problems with family and coworkers (equitable sharing of work, scheduling conflicts, gossip), and financial concerns (competing demands for available funds, increasing prices). But our reactions to hassles may vary. For example, compared to women, men tend to have more impairment of their immune system and an increased heart rate in response to hassles (Delahanty et al., 2000; Scanlan, Vitaliano, Ochs, Savage, & Borson, 1998).

Some authorities believe hassles can be more significant than major life events in creating stress (Lazarus, 1999; Tien, Sandler, & Zautra, 2000). For example, divorce is extremely stressful, but it may so be because of the increased number of hassles — change in finances, child-care arrangements, longer working hours, and so on. Similarly, a move is a stressful life change, but preparing to move or having your house up for sale for an extended period of time can be more stressful than the actual move itself.

Persistent hassles in your work situation can lead to a form of physical, mental, and emotional exhaustion known as **burnout**. Although the term has become an overused buzzword, health psychologists use it to describe a specific syndrome that develops most commonly in idealistic people who are exposed to chronically stressful and emotionally draining professions (Alexander & Hegarty, 2000; Melamed et al., 1999). People who tend to think of their job as a "calling" tend to enter their careers with a high sense of motivation and commitment. But over

---

TRY THIS Yourself

Kanner and others developed a *Hassles Scale* to assess those everyday events on the job, at school, and in interpersonal relations that annoy, frustrate, and anger us (Kanner, Coyne, Schaefer, & Lazarus, 1981). Write down the top 10 hassles you most commonly experience and then compare your answers to the following list:

The 10 Most Common Hassles for College Students

	Percentage of Times Checked
1. Troubling thoughts about the future	76.6
2. Not getting enough sleep	72.5
3. Wasting time	71.1
4. Inconsiderate smokers	70.7
5. Physical appearance	69.9
6. Too many things to do	69.2
7. Misplacing or losing things	67.0
8. Not enough time to do the things you need to do	66.3
9. Concerns about meeting high standards	64.0
10. Being lonely	60.8

Source: Kanner, A. D., Coyne, J. C., Schaefer, C., & Lazarus, R. S. (1981). Comparison of two modes of stress measurement: Daily hassles and uplifts versus major life events. *Journal of Behavioral Medicine, 4,* 1–39.

time, some become emotionally drained and disillusioned and feel a loss of personal accomplishment — they "burn out." The result may be increased absences from work, a sharp downturn in productivity, and an increased risk of physical problems. Police officers, nurses, social workers, and teachers are particularly vulnerable.

Frustration

Frustration is a negative emotional state generally associated with a blocked goal such as not being accepted for admission to your first-choice college. The more motivated we are, the more frustration we experience when our goals are blocked. After getting stuck in traffic and missing an important appointment, we may become very frustrated. On the other hand, if the same traffic jam causes us to be five minutes late to a painful medical appointment, we may experience little or no frustration.

Frustration *An unpleasant state of tension, anxiety, and heightened sympathetic activity resulting from a blocked goal*

Conflicts

A final source of stress is **conflict,** which arises when people are forced to make a choice between at least two incompatible alternatives. The amount of stress produced by a conflict depends on the complexity of the conflict itself, and the difficulty involved in resolving it. There are three basic types of conflict: *approach–approach, avoidance–avoidance,* and *approach–avoidance.*

In an **approach–approach conflict,** a person must choose between two or more *favorable* alternatives. Thus, no matter what choice is made, the result will be desirable. At first it might seem that this type of conflict shouldn't create any stress, but consider this example. Suppose you have to choose between two summer jobs. One job is at a resort where you will meet interesting people and have a good time; the other will provide you with valuable experience and look impressive on your résumé. No matter which job you choose, you will benefit in some way. In fact, you would like to take both jobs, but you can't. The requirement to choose is the source of stress.

An **avoidance–avoidance conflict** involves making a choice between two or more unpleasant alternatives that will lead to negative results, no matter which choice is made. In the book (and film) *Sophie's Choice,* Sophie and her two children are sent to a German concentration camp. A soldier demands that she give up (apparently to be killed) either her daughter or her son, or they both will be killed. Obviously, neither alternative is acceptable; both will have tragic results. Although this is an extreme example, avoidance–avoidance conflicts can lead to intense stress.

An **approach–avoidance conflict** occurs when a person must choose between alternatives that will have both desirable and undesirable results. We have all been faced with such decisions as "I want to spend more time in a close relationship, but that means I won't be able to see as much of my old friends." This conflict thus leads to a great deal of ambivalence. In an approach–avoidance conflict, we experience both good and bad results from any alternative we choose.

The longer any conflict exists or the more important the decision, the more stress a person will experience. Generally, the approach–approach conflict is the easiest to resolve and produces the least stress. The avoidance–avoidance conflict, on the other hand, is usually the most difficult because all choices lead to unpleasant results. Approach–avoidance conflicts are somewhat less stressful than avoidance–avoidance conflicts and are usually moderately difficult to resolve.

Conflict *A negative emotional state caused by having to choose between two or more incompatible goals or impulses*

Approach Approach Conflict *Conflict in which a person must choose between two or more alternatives that will lead to desirable results*

Avoidance–Avoidance Conflict *Conflict in which a person must choose between two or more alternatives that will both lead to undesirable results*

Approach–Avoidance Conflict *Conflict in which a person must make a choice that will lead to both desirable and undesirable results*

TRY THIS
Yourself

One thing that seems to increase the hassles and frustration in our lives is the fact that technology is constantly changing. In their book *TechnoStress: Coping with technology @WORK @HOME @PLAY,* Michelle Weil and Larry Rosen (1997) discuss how emerging technologies can add stress to our lives.

Do any of the following situations sound familiar to you? Buying a new VCR that is (still!) impossible to program? Coming across yet another bug in your new word processing program that dumps your entire term paper? Playing endless phone tag with a professor whom you want to write a recommendation for you? Never getting your e-mail cleaned up because of endless ads and dumb jokes? Being stranded on the freeway because the computer that controls your car's engine malfunctions? These are examples of technostress.

Just as some handle generalized stress differently, people handle technostress in different ways. Weil and Rosen identify three techno-types. You can readily categorize yourself by answering the questions in the following techno-type quiz:

1. Suppose that for your birthday someone gives you a new electronic kitchen appliance (a coffeemaker, for example) that is completely computerized. Which of the following best describes how you would feel when you open the package?
   a. Thrilled, excited, and eager. Can't wait to give it a try.
   b. Hesitant and wondering if you really need it. The way you do it now works just fine. Maybe you'll just put it away for now.
   c. Upset, worried, or nervous. Unsure of your ability to use it correctly. Considering how you can return it for something a bit more practical.
2. When you want to record a TV show that airs while you are at work, what do you do?
   a. Quickly, confidently, and easily program the VCR to record the show.
   b. Ask your son, daughter, or spouse to set the VCR, or find the manual and try to figure out how to do it. You

know it's possible but are unsure that you'll be able to make it work.
   c. Squelch the thought, unless there is someone in the house to do it for you. After all, aren't VCRs just for playing rented movies?
3. Your friend calls and tells you that he just bought a new state-of-the-art, souped-up multimedia computer system and wants you to come see it. What's your response?
   a. Drop all your plans for the weekend, run right over, and play with the new toy for 8 hours.
   b. Murmur words of congratulations and promise to get over to see it as soon as your schedule clears.
   c. Pretend to listen, adding appropriately placed *oh*'s and *uh-huh*'s while clearly evading the request.

How did you do? If you answered *a* to two or three of the questions, chances are that you are what is called an *eager adopter.* If you mostly answered *B,* you, like most people, are most probably a *hesitant "prove it."* If you felt that *c* was the answer for you, you are a *resister.*

According to Weil and Rosen, eager adopters love technology. They make up only 10 to 15 percent of the population, but they consider technology fun and are the first to buy the latest gadget. Hesitant "prove its" account for one-half to two-thirds of the population, and they do not think technology is fun. They take a wait-and-see attitude, but once they are convinced that a new technology will make their life easier or is necessary, they will try to adopt it. Finally, the resisters avoid technology because they feel inadequate.

If you are an eager adopter, you are probably not stressed by technology. If you are one of the other types, consider this advice to relieve technostress: First, evaluate each new technology on its usefulness for you and your lifestyle. If something is useful, try to use it in the least stressful manner. Second, recognize that technology is here to stay, and you can learn to cope with technostress just as you do with other types of stress.

Check & Review

SOURCES OF STRESS

Stress is the body's arousal, both physical and mental, to situations or events that we perceive as threatening or challenging. A situation or event, either pleasant or unpleasant, that triggers arousal and causes stress is known as a stressor.

The major sources of stress are life changes, chronic stressors, hassles, burnout, frustration, and conflicts. Chronic stressors are ongoing events such as poor working conditions. **Hassles** are little everyday life problems that pile up to cause major stress. Persistent hassles and a loss of initial idealism in your work situation can lead to a form of physical, mental, and emotional exhaustion known as **burnout**. **Frustration** has to do with blocked goals, whereas conflict involves two or more competing goals. Conflicts can be classified as **approach–approach, avoidance–avoidance,** or **approach–avoidance.**

Questions

1. John was planning to ask Susan to marry him. When he saw Susan kissing another man at a party, he was quite upset. In this situation, John's seeing Susan kissing another man is _____, and it illustrates _____. (a) a stressor, distress; (b) eustress, a stressor; (c) distress, a stressor; (d) a stressor, eustress.

2. The Social Readjustment Rating Scale constructed by Holmes and Rahe measures the stress situation in a person's life on the basis of _____. (a) life changes; (b) stress tolerance; (c) daily hassles; (d) the balance between eustress and distress.

3. Frustration is a negative emotional state that is generally associated with _____, whereas _____ is a negative emotional state caused by an inability to choose between two or more incompatible goals or impulses.

4. Give an example for each of the 3 types of conflict: approach–approach, approach–avoidance, and avoidance–avoidance.

Answers to Questions can be found in Appendix B.

Results of Stress: How the Body Responds

When stressed either mentally or physically, your body undergoes several major and minor physiological changes, some of which we have already mentioned. The most significant changes are controlled by the autonomic nervous system (Chapter 2) and are particularly important because they can lower the body's resistance to disease.

Physiological Effects of Stress

Under normal, everyday low-stress conditions, the parasympathetic part of the autonomic nervous system tends to lower heart rate and blood pressure, while increasing muscle movement in the stomach and intestines. This allows the body to conserve energy, absorb nutrients, and maintain normal functioning. Under stressful conditions, the sympathetic part of the autonomic nervous system is dominant. It increases heart rate, blood pressure, respiration, and muscle tension; decreases the movement of stomach muscles; constricts blood vessels; and releases hormones such as epinephrine (adrenaline) and cortisol. These hormones in turn release fats and glucose into the bloodstream for energy.

Fight or Flight

There is a good reason for all this sympathetic activity. At the beginning of human evolutionary history, the autonomic nervous system served as the fight-or-flight system. Back then, when a person was under extreme stress — when she was confronted by a bear or he found big, strong strangers hunting in his territory — there were only two reasonable alternatives: fight or flight. Our ancestors, when faced with such stressors, needed the physiological boosts supplied by their sympathetic nervous system.

Today we have the same autonomic responses of our ancient ancestors, but our world is quite different. When we encounter stressful situations, we rarely jump into action. If we hear from our boss that we're being fired or that the stock market just dropped another 20 percent, we cannot "fight or flee." We have little need for the

Stress in ancient times. The automatic, "fight or flight" response was adaptive and necessary for early human survival. However, in modern society it occurs as a response to situations in which we cannot fight or flee, and is often detrimental to our health.

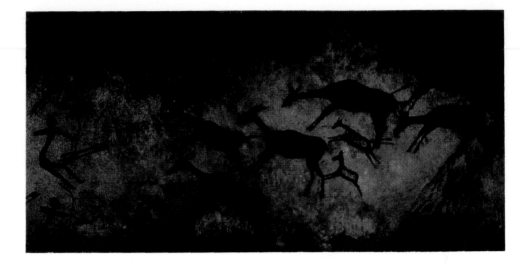

increased heart rate, blood pressure, and hormone levels produced by our autonomic nervous system. In fact, we are taught not to fight or to flee but to stay calm and resolve stressful situations rationally. When we comply with these cultural rules, we are left with all the arousal but no outlet for the physical changes caused by stressors. Thus, in modern times, the fight/flight response of the autonomic nervous system is less helpful than to our ancestors. It might even be maladaptive and dangerous (Arnsten, 1998).

Stress causes physiological changes that in the long run can be detrimental to health. Hans Selye, who was mentioned earlier in the chapter, described a generalized physiological reaction to severe stressors that he called the **general adaptation syndrome** (GAS) (1936). Figure 3.1 shows the three phases of this reaction. In the initial phase, called the *alarm reaction,* the body reacts to the stressor by activating the sympathetic nervous system (with increases in heart rate, blood pressure, secretion of hormones, and so on). The body has abundant energy and is alert and ready to deal with the stressor but is in a lowered state of resistance to illness.

If the stressor remains, the body enters the *resistance phase.* Now the alarm reaction subsides and the body adapts to the stressor, with resistance to illness increasing above normal levels. However, this adaptation and resistance phase is very taxing, and long-term exposure to the stressor may eventually lead to the *exhaustion phase* if the resistance is not successful. During this final stage, the signs of the alarm reaction reappear, resistance to illness decreases, all adaptation energy becomes depleted, and our susceptibility to illness increases. In severe cases, long-term exposure to stressors can be life threatening because we become vulnerable to serious illness such as heart attacks, stroke, and cancer.

General Adaptation Syndrome *As described by Hans Selye, a generalized physiological reaction to severe stressors consisting of three phases: the alarm reaction, the resistance phase, and the exhaustion phase*

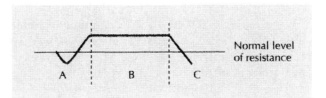

Normal level of resistance

A   B   C

Figure 3.1 *The general adaptation syndrome (GAS).* According to Hans Selye, when the body is exposed to severe, prolonged stress, it goes through three phases. During the initial phase, the alarm reaction (A), the body is in a lowered state of resistance to illness. If the stress continues, the body enters the resistance phase (B), when it is in a heightened state of resistance. After prolonged exposure to stress, the body enters the exhaustion phase (C), when resistance to illness decreases. Eventually this can lead to death.

Stress and the Immune System

A relatively new field, **psychoneuroimmunology**, studies the interactions of psychological factors (*psycho-*), the nervous and endocrine systems (*neuro-*), and the immune system (*immunology*). This interdisciplinary research has shown that the sympathetic nervous system is *directly* linked to virtually every part of the immune system and that physiological changes caused by stress (such as bereavement, surgery, sleep deprivation, or divorce) can suppress immune system functioning (De Moranville et al., 2000; Leonard, 2000; Miller & Cohen, 2001). Normal functioning of the immune system includes detecting and defending against disease. Therefore, a suppressed immune system leaves the body susceptible to illness. Changes in immune function have been linked to high levels of such stress-related hormones as epinephrine, norepinephrine, and cortisol in the bloodstream. Apparently, increases in these hormones often precede suppressed immune system function and the appearance of disease.

Psychoneuroimmunology [sye-koh-NEW-roh-IM-you-NOLL-oh-gee] *An interdisciplinary field that studies the effects of psychological factors on the immune system*

But how does something psychological, like bereavement, affect the cells of the immune system? Psychological factors do not directly affect cells of the immune system. Rather, a psychological stressor (such as death of a loved one) activates the autonomic fight-or-flight response. Autonomic functioning mobilizes the body's energy resources for immediate survival by releasing hormones, such as cortisol, that put all the body's long-term processes — tissue repair, immunity, digestion, reproduction — on hold, thus making more energy available to the brain and muscles. If the emergency lasts only a few minutes, this is a good solution to the fight–flight problem, and immune functioning soon resumes. But when a person is under prolonged stress, such as a difficult final exam schedule or a bad marriage that lasts for years, he or she is constantly in a state of heightened autonomic activation and may have reduced immune system response for an extended period.

Does this mean that I might get a cold or the flu just because I've been under a lot of stress? Sheldon Cohen and his colleagues (1998, 1999) have conducted studies that show stress does indeed have a small to moderate effect both on becoming infected with the cold virus and on exhibiting full-blown cold symptoms. It seems that stress suppresses the body's defenses that normally prevent the cold virus from multiplying and spreading throughout the body.

RESEARCH HIGHLIGHT

Procrastination, Performance, and Health

If your professor assigned a term paper for this class, have you already started working on it? Or are you putting it off until the last minute? Have you ever wondered if working continuously on a term paper from the first day of class until the paper is due might ultimately be more stressful than putting off the paper until the last minute?

To answer this question, Dianne Tice and Roy Baumeister (1997) at Case Western Reserve University assigned a term paper in their health psychology class at the beginning of the semester. Throughout the semester, they carefully monitored the stress, health, and procrastination levels of 44 student volunteers from the class. After the term papers were submitted at the end of the course, Tice and Baumeister found that procrastinators suffered significantly more stress and developed more health problems than nonprocrastinators. They

were also more likely to turn in their papers late and earn lower grades on those papers.

In the Tools for Student Success section in Chapter 1, you learned that research shows that spacing out your studying rather than cramming the night before produces higher scores on exams. Now you have additional research showing that distributed work also produces better grades on term papers — as well as less stress. The bottom line is this: *Don't procrastinate.* It can be hazardous to your health, as well as your grades.

Check & Review

RESULTS OF STRESS

When stressed, the body undergoes physiological changes. The sympathetic branch of the autonomic nervous system is activated, increasing heart rate and blood pressure. This sympathetic activation is beneficial if people need to fight or flee, but in today's world, it generally has negative consequences.

Hans Selye described a generalized physiological reaction to severe stressors, which he called the **general adaptation** syndrome (GAS). It has three phases: the alarm reaction, the resistance phase, and the exhaustion phase. Prolonged stress can suppress the immune system, which can render the body susceptible to a number of diseases.

Questions

1. How does the autonomic nervous system respond to stress?

2. The GAS consists of three phases: the _____ reaction, the _____ phase, and the _____ phase.

3. As Michael watches his instructor pass out papers, he suddenly realizes this is the first major exam and he is totally unprepared. Which phase of the GAS is the most likely experiencing? (a) resistance; (b) alarm; (c) exhaustion; (d) phaseout.

4. Why do students tend to get sick with a cold or flu during midterms or finals?

STRESS AND SERIOUS ILLNESS

How is stress related to serious illnesses like cancer and coronary heart disease?

We now know that many diseases far more serious than the common cold are either caused by or made worse by stress. Some of these are heart disease, cancer, rheumatoid arthritis, bursitis, migraine headache, asthma, and gastrointestinal conditions such as ulcers and colitis (Kiecolt-Glaser & Glaser, 2001; Matuszek, 2000; Sapolsky, 1999; Wu et al., 2000). In this section, we will explore how stress is related to two of our main killers — *cancer* and *coronary heart disease*.

Cancer: A Variety of Causes — Even Stress

The word *cancer* is frightening to nearly everyone, and for good reason: Cancer is among the leading causes of death for adults in the U.S. It occurs when a particular type of primitive body cell begins rapidly dividing, and then forms a tumor that invades healthy tissue. Unless destroyed or removed, the tumor eventually damages organs and causes death. To date, over 100 types of cancer have been identified. They appear to be caused by an interaction between environmental factors and inherited predispositions.

To understand how the environment contributes to cancer, it helps to know what normally happens to cancerous cells. Whenever cancer cells start to multiply, the immune system checks the uncontrolled growth by attacking the abnormal cells (see the accompanying photograph). This goes on constantly, with abnormal cells arising, and, in a healthy person, the immune system keeping cancer cells in check.

Something different happens when the body is stressed. As you read earlier, the stress response involves the release of adrenal hormones that suppress immune system functioning. The compromised immune system is less able to resist infection and cancer development. An experimental animal study found that stress inhibited immune system defenses against cancer and promoted tumor growth (Wu et al., 2000). Other research with humans suggests that stress can also directly affect lymphocytes, the main immune system cells that control cancer (Goebel & Mills, 2000).

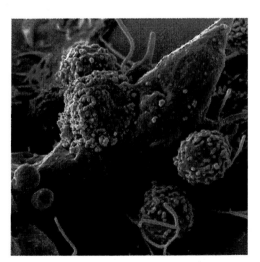

White blood cells and the immune system. The round structure near the left center of this photomicrograph is a T-lymphocyte, a type of white blood cell produced by the immune system. It has just killed a cancer cell, the sweet potato-shaped structure.

The good news is that we can substantially reduce our risk of cancer by making changes that reduce our stress level and enhance our immune system. For example, even mild sleep deprivation can affect the immune system. When researchers interrupted the sleep of 23 men and then measured their *natural killer cells* (a type of immune system cell), they found the killer cells were 28 percent below average (Irwin et al., 1994). Can you see how staying up late studying for an exam (or partying) can decrease the effectiveness of your immune system? Fortunately, these researchers also found that a normal night's sleep after the deprivation returned the killer cells to their normal levels.

Cardiovascular Disorders: The Leading Cause of Death in the United States

Cardiovascular disorders are the cause of over half of all deaths in the United States (Centers for Disease Control, 2001). Understandably, then, health psychologists are concerned because stress is a major contributor to these deaths. *Heart disease* is a general term for all disorders that eventually affect the heart muscle and lead to heart failure. *Coronary heart disease* results from *atherosclerosis,* a thickening of the walls of the coronary arteries that reduces or blocks the blood supply to the heart. Atherosclerosis causes *angina* (chest pain due to insufficient blood supply to the heart) or *heart attack* (death of heart muscle tissue). Controllable factors that contribute to heart disease include stress, smoking, certain personality characteristics, obesity, a high-fat diet, and lack of exercise (American Heart Association, 2000; Tennant, 1999).

How does stress contribute to heart disease? Recall that one of the major autonomic nervous system fight–flight reactions is the release of epinephrine and cortisol into the bloodstream. These hormones increase heart rate and release fat from the body's stores to give muscles a quickly available source of energy.

If no physical action is taken (and this is most likely the case in our modern lives), the fat released into the bloodstream is not burned as fuel and may become fatty deposits on the walls of blood vessels (Figure 3.2). These fatty deposits are a major cause of blood supply blockage that causes heart attacks. In other words, if stress causes blocked arteries and blocked arteries cause heart attacks, then people who are continually under a lot of stress are prone to heart attacks.

Personality Types

The effects of stress on heart disease may be amplified if an individual tends to be hard driving, competitive, ambitious, impatient, and hostile. People with such

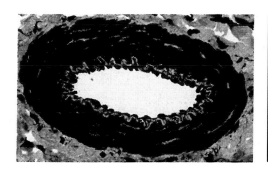 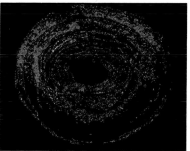

Figure 3.2 *Fatty deposits in arteries.* One major cause of heart disease is the blockage of arteries that supply blood to the heart. The artery at the left is normal; the one on the right is almost completely blocked. Reducing stress, exercising, and eating a low-fat diet can help prevent the buildup of fatty deposits in the arteries.

Type A Personality *Set of behavior characteristics that includes intense ambition, competition, drive, constant preoccupation with responsibilities, exaggerated time urgency, and a cynical, hostile outlook*

Type B Personality *Set of behavior characteristics consistent with a calm, patient, relaxed attitude toward life*

Type A personalities are chronically on edge, tend to talk rapidly, feel intense time urgency, and are preoccupied with responsibilities. The antithesis of the Type A personality is Type B. People with a **Type B personality** have a laid-back, calm, relaxed attitude toward life.

Two cardiologists, Meyer Friedman and Ray Rosenman (1959) were the first to identify and describe the Type A personality. The story goes that in the mid-1950s, an upholsterer who was recovering the waiting room chairs in Friedman's office noticed an odd wear pattern. He mentioned to Friedman that all the chairs looked like new except for the front edges, which were badly worn, as if all the patients sat only on the edges of the chairs. Initially, this didn't seem too important to Friedman. However, this chronic sense of time urgency and being literally "on the edge of your seat" was later believed to be a possible contributing factor to heart disease and the hallmark of the Type A personality.

Initial research into Type A behavior suggested Friedman and Rosenman were right, but more recent research has been less supportive. When researchers examined the relationship between characteristics of the Type A behavior pattern and heart disease, they found that the critical component and strongest predictor of heart disease was *hostility* (Fredrikson, Wik, & Fischer, 1999; Miller, Smith, Turner, Guijarro, & Hallet, 1996).

Actually, *cynical* hostility appears to be the most important factor in the Type A relationship to heart disease. Having a negative attitude toward the world means cynical people always expect problems. They are constantly alert and "on watch," trying to foresee problems and possibly avert them. This attitude produces a nearly constant state of stress, which translates physiologically into higher blood pressure, heart rate, and production of stress-related hormones. In addition, because of their hostile, suspicious, argumentative, and competitive style, these people tend to have more interpersonal conflicts (Friedman, Hawley, and Tucker, 1994). Constant interpersonal conflicts can lead to a loss of social support and heightened autonomic activation, which can then lead to increased risk of cardiovascular disease (Sher, 2000; Tennant, 1999).

Can people with a Type A personality change their behavior? Health psychologists have developed two types of behavior modification to help people with Type A personality — the *shotgun approach* and the *target behavior approach*. The *shotgun approach* aims to change all the behaviors that relate to the Type A personality. Friedman and his colleagues (1986) use the shotgun approach in their Recurrent Coronary Prevention Program. The program provides individual counseling, dietary advice, exercise, drugs, and group therapy to eliminate or modify Type A behaviors. Type A's are specifically encouraged to slow down and perform tasks incompatible with their personalities. For example, they might try to listen to other people without interrupting or stand in the longest supermarket line on purpose. The major criticism of the shotgun approach is that it eliminates desirable (ambitiousness and drive) as well as undesirable Type A traits (cynicism and hostility).

The alternative approach, the *target behavior approach,* focuses on only those Type A behaviors that are likely to cause heart disease — namely, cynical hostility. By modifying target behaviors, the person will likely reduce his or her risk of heart disease.

Hardiness

In addition to Type A and Type B personalities, there may be other personality patterns that affect the way we respond to stress. Have you ever wondered how some people survive in the face of great stress (repeated personal tragedies, demanding jobs, and even a poor home life) but others do not? Suzanne Kobasa was among the first to study this question (Kobasa, 1979, Pengilly & Dowd, 2000). Examining male executives with high levels of stress, she found that some people are more resistant to stress than others because of a personality factor called **hardiness**, a resilient type of optimism that comes from three distinctive attitudes:

Hardiness *A resilient personality characteristic based on three qualities: a commitment to personal goals, control over life, and viewing change as a challenge rather than a threat.*

1. ***Commitment.*** Hardy people feel a strong sense of commitment to both their work and personal life. They also make intentional commitments to purposeful activity and problem solving.

2. ***Control.*** These people also see themselves not as victims of whatever life brings but as personally in control.

3. ***Challenge.*** Finally, hardy people look at change as an opportunity for growth and improvement — not as a threat. Hardy people welcome challenges.

The important lesson from this research is that hardiness is a *learned behavior* — not luck or genetics. If you're not one of the *hardy* souls, you can develop the trait. The next time you face a bad stressor, such as four exams in one week, try using the 3 C's: "I am fully *committed* to my college education." "I can *control* the number of tests by taking one or two of them earlier than scheduled, or I can rearrange my work schedule." "I welcome this *challenge* as a final motivation to enroll in those reading improvement and college success courses I've always planned to take."

Before we go on, it's also important to note that Type A personality and lack of hardiness are not the only controllable risk factors associated with heart disease. Smoking, obesity, and lack of exercise are very important factors. Smoking restricts blood circulation, and obesity stresses the heart by causing it to pump more blood to the excess body tissue. A high-fat diet, especially one high in cholesterol, contributes to the fatty deposits that clog blood vessels. Lack of exercise contributes to weight gain and prevents the body from obtaining important exercise benefits, including strengthening heart muscle, increasing heart efficiency, and releasing hormones such as serotonin that alleviate stress and promote well-being.

Check & Review

STRESS AND SERIOUS ILLNESS

Cancer appears to result from an interaction of heredity, environmental insults (such as smoking), and immune system deficiency. Stress may be an importnat cause of decreased immunity. During times of stress, the body may be less able to check cancerous tissue growth because the immune system is suppressed.

The leading cause of death in the United States is heart disease. Risk factors in heart disease include smoking, stress, obesity, a high-fat diet, lack of exercise, and **Type A personality** (if it includes cynical hostil-

ity). The two main approaches to modifying Type A behavior are the shotgun approach and the target behavior approach. People with psychological **hardiness** are less vulnerable to stress because of three distinctive personality characteristics — commitment, control, and challenge.

Questions

1. Stress can contribute to heart disease by releasing the hormones _____ and _____, which increase the level of fat in the blood.

2. Which of the following is *not* among

the characteristics associated with Type A personality? (a) time urgency; (b) patience; (c) competition; (d) hostility.

3. The two major approaches to modifying Type A behavior are the _____ approach and the _____ approach. Which one do you think would work best for you, and why?

4. Explain how the three characteristics of the hardy personality help reduce stress.

Answers to Questions can be found in Appendix B.

COPING WITH STRESS

It would be helpful if we could avoid all negative stressful situations, but this is impossible. Everyone encounters pressure at work, long lines at the bank, and the death of a family member. Because we can't escape stress, we need to learn how to effectively cope with it. Lazarus and Folkman (1984) defined *coping* as "constantly changing cognitive and behavioral efforts to manage specific external and/or internal demands that are appraised as taxing or exceeding the resource of the person." In simpler terms, coping is an attempt to manage stress in some effective way. It is not one single act but a process that allows us to deal with various stressors. The coping process can focus on the emotional effects of the stressor or on solving the problem causing the stress.

What techniques and resources are available to help people cope with stress?

Emotion-Focused Forms of Coping: Reappraising the Situation

Emotion-focused forms of coping are emotional or cognitive strategies that change how we view a stressful situation. Suppose you are refused a highly desirable job or rejected by a desired lover. You might reappraise the situation and decide that the job or lover might not have been the right match for you or that you weren't really qualified or ready for that specific job or relationship.

One of the most common forms of emotion-focused coping is the use of **defense mechanisms**, unconscious strategies that protect the ego and avoid anxiety by distorting reality (Chapter 13). The use of defense mechanisms reduces anxiety and often helps us cope with unavoidable stress. For instance, *fantasizing* about what you will do once you graduate from college can motivate you to study for exams.

On the other hand, defense mechanisms can sometimes be destructive. You might decide you didn't get the job or the lover because you didn't have the right "connections" or "the perfect body." This is known as *rationalization*, fabricating excuses when frustrated in attaining particular goals. Not seeing the situation more clearly and realistically might prevent you from developing skills or qualities that could get you a desirable job or lover in the future.

In sum, emotion-focused forms of coping that are accurate reappraisals of stressful situations and do not distort reality may alleviate stress in some situations (Burke & Greenglass, 2000; Gold & Friedman, 2000). Many times, however, it is necessary and more effective to confront the stressor directly.

Emotion-Focused Forms of Coping *Coping strategies based on changing one's perceptions of stressful situations*

Defense Mechanisms *Unconscious strategies used to distort reality and relieve anxiety and guilt*

Problem-Focused Forms of Coping: Putting Problem-Solving Skills to Work

Problem-focused forms of coping deal directly with the situation or the stressor to eventually decrease or eliminate it (Bond & Bunce, 2000). Generally, these approaches are the same as problem-solving strategies discussed in Chapter 8. Thus, the better a person is at solving problems, the more likely he or she will develop effective strategies. These strategies include identifying the stressful problem, generating possible solutions, selecting the appropriate solution, and applying the solution to the problem — thus eliminating the stress.

To illustrate the difference between the two forms of coping, let's suppose that you are flying to Denver to be in your best friend's wedding. You have an exam that lets out at 10:00 and your plane leaves at noon; the wedding is at 4:00. It will be tight, but you can make it. Unfortunately, on the way to the airport, the taxi has a flat tire. You can cognitively evaluate the situation and tell yourself that because this is your best friend, he'll understand that you did everything you could to be there; it

Problem-Focused Forms of Coping *Coping strategies based on using problem-solving strategies to decrease or eliminate the source of stress*

wasn't your fault that the taxi had a flat (emotion-focused approach). Or, you could ask the driver to immediately call for another taxi to come and take you to the airport (problem-centered approach).

In general, the better a person is at solving problems, the more likely he or she will develop effective problem-focused coping strategies, including identifying the stressful problem, generating possible solutions, selecting the appropriate solution, and applying the solution to the problem.

Can people use both forms of coping strategies at once? Yes, most stressful situations are complex, and people often combine problem-focused and emotion-focused coping strategies. Furthermore, as you know from your own life, stressful situations change and the type of strategy we use depends not only on the stressor but also the changing nature of the stressor. In some situations, we may first need to use an emotion-focused strategy, which allows a step back from an especially overwhelming problem. Then, later on, when we have our emotional strength and our feet on the ground, we can reappraise the situation and use the problem-solving approach to look for solutions.

critical thinking

Active Learning

Is Your Job Stressful?

An important component of critical thinking is the ability to *define problems accurately*. By carefully identifying the problem in clear and concrete terms, critical thinkers prevent confusion and lay the foundation for gathering relevant information. Health psychologists (and industrial/organizational psychologists) have studied numerous factors in job-related stress. Their findings suggest that one way to prevent these stresses is to gather lots of information before making a career decision.

If you would like to apply this to your own career plans, start by identifying what you like and do not like about your current (and past) jobs. With this information in hand, you are then prepared to research jobs that will better suit your interests, needs, and abilities and avoid the stress caused by jobs failing to meet this criteria. To help your analysis, answer yes or no to these questions:

1. Is there a sufficient amount of laughter and sociability in your workplace?
2. Does your boss notice and appreciate your work?
3. Is your boss understanding and friendly?
4. Are you embarrassed by the physical conditions of your workplace?

5. Do you feel safe and comfortable in your place of work?
6. Do you like the location of your job?
7. If you won the lottery and were guaranteed a lifetime income, would you feel truly sad if you also had to quit your job?
8. Do you watch the clock, daydream, take long lunches, and leave work as soon as possible?
9. Do you frequently feel stressed and overwhelmed by the demands of your job?
10. Compared to others with your qualifications, are you being paid what you are worth?
11. Are promotions made in a fair and just manner?
12. Given the demands of your job, are you fairly compensated for your work?

Now score your answers. Give yourself one point for each answer that matches the following: 1. No; 2. No; 3. No; 4. Yes; 5. No; 6. No; 7. No; 8. Yes; 9. Yes; 10. No; 11. No; 12. No.

The questions you just answered are based on four factors that research shows are conducive to increased job satisfaction

and reduced stress: supportive colleagues, supportive working conditions, mentally challenging work, and equitable rewards (Robbins, 1996). Your total score reveals your overall level of dissatisfaction, whereas a look at specific questions can help identify which of these four factors is most important to your job satisfaction — and most lacking in your current job.

Supportive colleagues (items 1, 2, 3): For most employees, work fills important social needs. Therefore, having friendly and supportive colleagues and superiors leads to increased satisfaction.

Supportive working conditions (items 4, 5, 6): Not surprisingly, studies find most employees prefer working in safe, clean, and relatively modern facilities. They also prefer jobs close to home.

Mentally challenging work (items 7, 8, 9): Jobs with too little challenge create boredom and apathy, whereas too much challenge creates frustration and feelings of failure.

Equitable rewards (items 10, 11, 12): Employees want pay and promotions based on job demands, individual skill levels, and community pay standards.

We may also use one coping strategy to prepare us to use the other. For example, humor is an emotion-focused coping strategy that is highly effective in altering negative moods. Also, in many situations, dealing with emotions helps us problem-solve (Keltner & Bonanno, 1997; Moran & Massam, 1999). Imagine that you are about to take your first exam in a difficult course. You are naturally very anxious: To calm yourself, you can first take an emotion-focused approach. You might say to yourself, "Relax and take a deep breath; it can't be as bad as you imagine." With reduced anxiety, you can then use problem-focused coping techniques and concentrate on answering the questions on the test.

Resources for Effective Coping: From Good Health to Money

A person's ability to cope effectively depends on the stressor itself — its complexity, intensity, and duration — and on the type of coping strategy used. It also depends on available resources. Researchers have identified several important coping resources:

1. *Health and energy.* All stressors cause physiological changes. Therefore, an individual's health significantly affects his or her ability to cope. Look again at Figure 3.1 on the GAS: The resistance stage is the coping stage. The stronger and healthier people are, the better they cope and the longer they stay in the resistance stage without entering the exhaustion stage.

2. *Positive beliefs.* A positive self-image and a positive attitude can be especially significant coping resources. Research shows that even temporarily raising self-esteem reduces the amount of anxiety caused by stressful events (Greenberg et al., 1993). Also, hope can sustain a person in the face of severe odds, as is often documented in news reports of people who have triumphed over seemingly unbeatable circumstances. According to Lazarus and Folkman, hope can come from a belief in oneself, which can enable us to devise our own coping strategies; a belief in others, such as medical doctors who we feel can effect positive outcomes; or a belief in a just and helpful God.

3. *Social skills.* Social situations — meetings, discussion groups, dates, parties, and so on — are often a source of pleasure, but they can also be a source of stress. Merely meeting someone new and trying to find something to talk about can be very stressful for some people. Therefore, people who acquire social skills (know appropriate behaviors for certain situations, have conversation-starters "up their sleeves," and express themselves well) suffer less anxiety than people who do not. In fact, people lacking social skills are more at risk for developing illness (Cohen & Williamson, 1991).

Social skills help us not only interact with others but also communicate our needs and desires, enlist help when we need it, and decrease hostility in tense situations. If you have weak social skills, you may find it worth the effort to learn how to act in a variety of social situations. Observe others and ask people with good social skills for advice. You can also practice your new skills by role-playing before applying them in real life.

People need people. These recently widowed women realize that an important resource for coping with stress is social support from friends, families, and support groups.

4. *Social support.* Having the support of others helps offset the stressful effects of divorce, loss of a loved one, chronic illness, pregnancy, stressful work training, job loss, and work overload (Frazier, 2000; Gold & Friedman, 2000). When we are faced with stressful circumstances, our friends and family often help us take care of our health, listen and "hold our hand," make us feel important, and provide stability to offset the changes in our lives (D'Imperio, Dubow, & Ippolito, 2000; Lohman & Jarvis, 2000).

For people with specific problems, support and self-help groups can be very helpful. There are groups for alcoholics and families of alcoholics, for former drug addicts, for divorced people, for single parents, for cancer patients, for parents who have had a young child die, and so on. Support groups help people cope not only because they provide other people to lean on but also because people can learn techniques for coping from others with similar problems (see Chapter 15).

5. *Material resources.* We've all heard the saying "Money isn't everything," but when it comes to coping with stress, money and the things that money can buy can be very real resources. Money increases the number of options available to eliminate sources of stress or reduce the effects of stress. When they are faced with the minor hassles of everyday living, with chronic stressors, or with major catastrophes, people with money who have the skills to effectively use that money generally fare much better and experience much less stress than people without money (Chi & Chou, 1999; Ennis, Hobfoll, & Schroeder, 2000).

6. *Personal control.* Do you believe that what happens to you is primarily the result of your own actions? That success is mostly a matter of hard work versus luck? Our sense of controlling our environment, rather than feeling helpless, is an important resource in effective coping. This perception of personal **locus of control** over the events in one's life tends to make people more sensitive to health messages and more likely to take actions to improve their health. It also buffers the negative effects of stress. In fact, one of the greatest threats to well-being occurs when people feel caught in a situation and unable to control their circumstances.

People with an *external locus of control* are more likely to believe in bad luck or fate. They feel powerless to change their circumstances and are less likely to make healthy changes, follow treatment programs, or positively cope with the situation. Conversely, people with an *internal locus of control* believe they are in charge of their own destiny and tend to adopt more positive coping strategies. For example, internals who believe their heart attacks happened because of their unhealthy choices, such as smoking or having a stressful job, are more likely to change their unhealthy behaviors and recover more quickly (Ewart & Fitzgerald, 1994). Studies in China (Hamid & Chan, 1998), Taiwan, and the UK (Lu, Kao, Cooper, & Spector, 2000) found that those who had a higher internal locus of control experienced less psychological stress than did those with a higher external locus of control.

Locus of Control *The belief that life's circumstances are under personal, internal control or outside, external factors*

Active Coping Strategies: Taking Action Against Stress

In addition to coping styles and resources that rely primarily on cognitive and emotional strategies, there are other more direct, action-oriented approaches. Active coping methods "provide more direct and deliberate means of controlling and reducing the impact of stress ... [and] prepare us to deal with unexpected stress and keep us in stress-ready condition" (Gill, 1983, p. 84). The two major active methods are exercise and relaxation.

Exercise

If you exercise and keep yourself physically fit, you will probably experience less anxiety, depression, and tension than do people who do not exercise or who are less fit. Moreover, researchers have found that people engaging in strenuous exercise experienced greater reductions in anxiety than did those in moderate programs (Hong, 2000; Katula, Blissmer, & McAuley, 1999; McEntee & Halgin, 1999).

Exercise reduces the negative effects of stress in several ways. First, it uses up the hormones secreted into the bloodstream during stress, thereby helping the immune system return to normal functioning sooner. Second, exercise can help

Coping with stress. Exercise and friends are important resources for effective stress reduction. "I get by with a little help from my friends." John Lennon and Paul McCartney, Sgt. Pepper's Lonely Hearts Club Band, 1967.

work out tension that has built up in muscles. Third, exercise increases strength, flexibility, and stamina for encountering future stressors and increases the efficiency of the cardiovascular system. The best exercise for all these purposes is aerobic exercise — regular strenuous activity that heightens cardiovascular functioning, such as brisk walking, jogging, bicycling, swimming, dancing, and so on.

Relaxation

One of the most effective means of dealing with physical stress reactions is to make a conscious decision to relax during the stressful situation (Matuszek, 2000; Robert-McComb, 2001). There are a variety of relaxation techniques. Earlier, we discussed the use of biofeedback with chronic pain, but it is also extremely helpful in teaching people to relax and manage their stress. Progressive relaxation is also very helpful in reducing or relieving the muscular tension commonly associated with stress. Using this technique, patients first tense and then relax specific muscles, such as in the neck, shoulders, and arms. This technique teaches people to recognize the feel of tense and relaxed muscles.

A Final Note

You are the one who is ultimately responsible for your own health and well-being. Although doctors, nurses, and other health professionals are there for you if you become ill, it is best to do all you can to prevent disease in the first place. By minimizing the harmful effects of stress in our lives, we help our bodies stay well and fight off disease.

TRY THIS
Yourself

You can use the following progressive relaxation technique anytime and anywhere you feel stressed, such as while waiting for an exam to begin. Here's how:

1. Sit in a comfortable position, with your head supported.
2. Start breathing slowly and deeply.
3. Let your entire body go limp — let go of all tension. Try to visualize your body getting more and more relaxed.
4. Systematically tense and release each part of your body, beginning with your toes. Focus your attention on your toes and try to visualize what they are doing. Curl them tightly, while counting to 10, then release them and feel the difference between the tense state and the relaxed state. Next, tense your feet to the count of 10, then relax them and feel the difference between the two states. Continue with your calves, thighs, buttocks, abdomen, back muscles, shoulders, upper arms, forearms, hands and fingers, neck, jaws, facial muscles, and forehead.

Try practicing progressive relaxation twice a day for about 15 minutes. You will be surprised at how quickly you can learn to relax — even in the most stressful situations.

Check & Review

COPING WITH STRESS

The two major forms of coping with stress are **emotion-focused** and **problem-focused**. Emotion-focused coping change how we view stressful situations. Problem-focused coping deal directly with the situation or the factor causing the stress so as to decrease or eliminate it. The ability to cope with a stressor also depends on the resources available to a person. Resources include health and energy, positive beliefs, social skills, social support, material resources, and personal control. Exercise and relaxation are active methods people can use to cope with stress.

Questions

1. Which form of coping is being used in the following reactions to forgetting your best friend's birthday? (a) "I can't be expected to remember everyone's birthday"; (b) "I'd better put Cindy's birthday on my calendar so this won't happen again."

2. What are two common defense mechanisms, and why should people avoid using them?

3. People with a(n) _____ locus of control are better able to cope with stress.

4. What are the six major resources for coping with stress? Which resource is most helpful for you? Least helpful?

Answers to Questions can be found in Appendix B.

KEY TERMS

Health Psychology in Action
health psychology (p. 88)
Stress and Its Role in Health
approach–approach conflict (p. 99)
approach–avoidance conflict (p. 99)
avoidance–avoidance conflict (p. 99)
burnout (p. 98)
chronic pain (p. 94)
conflict (p. 99)
distress (p. 96)

eustress (p. 96)
frustration (p. 99)
general adaptation syndrome (GAS) (p. 102)
hassles (p. 98)
psychoneuroimmunology [sye-ko-NEW-ro-IM-you-NOLL-oh-gee] (p. 103)
stress (p. 96)
Stress and Serious Illness
hardiness (p. 107)

Type A personality (p. 106)
Type B personality (p. 106)
Coping with Stress
defense mechanisms (p. 108)
emotion-focused forms of coping (p. 108)
locus of control (p. 111)
problem-focused forms of coping (p. 108)

Visual Summary for Chapter 3

Health Psychology in Action

Health Psychology: Studies relationship between psychological behavior and physical health and illness.

What Health Psychologists Do

- Research issues that affect physical health and methods for improving health.
- Work in the health field to reduce distress and unhealthy behaviors.

Smoking

- *Why do people smoke?* Peer pressure; imitation of role models; addiction (nicotine increases release of neurotransmitters that increase alertness, memory, and well being and decrease anxiety, tension, and pain); learned associations with positive results.
- *Prevention?* Educate about short- and long- term consequences, make smoking less socially acceptable, and help nonsmokers resist social pressures.
- *Stopping?* Use cognitive and behavioral techniques to deal with withdrawal; supplement with nicotine replacement therapy (patches, gum, and pills).

Binge Drinking

Binge drinking: When a man consumes 5 or more drinks in a row, or a woman consumes 4 or more.
How to reduce?
- Overcome the myths and teach facts.
- Reduce or remove social rewards.

Chronic Pain

Chronic pain: Pain lasting over 6 months.
How to reduce?
- Increase activity, exercise, and dietary changes.
- Use behavior modification strategies to reinforce changes.
- Employ *biofeedback* with *electromyograph (EMG)* to reduce muscle tension.
- Use relaxation techniques and practice distraction.

Stress and Its Role in Health

Stress: Body's nonspecific response to any demand made on it.

Sources of Stress

- *Life changes*: Holmes and Rahe Scale measures stress caused by adaptations to important life events.
- *Chronic stressors*: Ongoing, long term stress related to political world, family, work, etc.
- **Hassles**: Small, everyday problems that accumulate.
- **Burnout**: Exhaustion resulting from emotionally demanding situations.
- **Frustration**: Negative emotional state from blocked goals.
- **Conflict**: Negative emotional state from 2 or more incompatible goals.

There are 3 types of conflict

Approach-approach conflict: Two or more desirable goals

Avoidance-avoidance conflict: Two or more undesirable goals

Approach-avoidance conflict: Both desirable and undesirable goals

Stress and Its Role in Health (cont).

Results of Stress

- *Sympathetic nervous system activation* increases heart rate, blood pressure, respiration, and muscle tension and releases stress hormones.
- *Fight/flight system* frequently engaged but generally overused and harmful in modern times.
- *Suppressed immune system* leaves body vulnerable to disease.

- **General adaptation syndrome** is a 3-phase generalized physiological that develops in response to severe stressors:
1. Alarm reaction ➜ 2. Resistance phase ➜ 3. Exhaustion

Stress and Serious Illness

Cancer
- Occurs when cells replicate beyond control.
- Caused by hereditary dispositions and environmental factors that lead to changes in body chemistry and the immune system

Cardiovascular Disorders
Heart disease: All disorders that affect the heart muscle and lead to heart failure.
Contributing Factors:

↓	↓	↓
Stress related hormones, which release fat into bloodstream that later attaches to the walls of blood vessels.	**Type A personality** with high ambition, time worries, anger, and hostility is at increased risk; whereas, the personality factor of **hardiness** decreases risk.	Behaviors such as smoking, stress, lack of exercise, obesity, and high-fat diet.

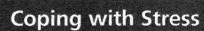

Coping with Stress

Emotion-Focused Forms of Coping	**Problem-Focused Forms of Coping**	**Resources for Effective Coping**	**Active Coping Strategies**
Emotional and cognitive strategies that change how one appraises a stressful situation. **Defense mechanisms** are unconscious strategies that protect the ego and avoid anxiety by distorting reality.	Strategies that deal directly with the stressful situation by applying problem-solving techniques to decrease or eliminate it.	Good health, energy, positive beliefs, social skills, social support, material resources, and personal control (e.g., internal **locus of control**) all reduce stress.	Exercise and relaxation techniques directly reduce stress.

11A Gender and Human Sexuality

t was an unusual circumcision. The identical twin boys were already 8 months old when their parents took them to the doctor to be circumcised. For many years in the United States, most male babies have had the foreskin of their penis removed during their first week of life, when it is assumed they will experience less pain. The most common procedure is cutting or pinching off the foreskin tissue. In this case, however, the doctor used an electrocautery device, which is used to burn off moles or small skin growths. The electrical current used for the first twin was too high, and the entire penis was accidentally ablated, or removed. (The parents did not let the physician try to circumcise the other twin.)

In anguish over the tragic accident, the parents sought advice from medical experts. Following discussions with John Money and other specialists at John Hopkins University, the parents and doctors made an unusual decision — the twin with the destroyed penis would be raised as a girl.

The first step in the reassignment process occurred at age 17 months, when the child's name was changed — Bruce became "Brenda" (Colapinto, 2000). Brenda was dressed in pink pants and frilly blouses and "her" hair was allowed to grow long. At 21 months, plastic surgery was performed to create external female genital structures. Further plastic surgery to create a vagina was planned for the beginning of adolescence, when the child's physical growth would be nearly complete. At this time she would also begin to take female hormones to complete the boy-to-girl transformation.

According to John Money (Money & Ehrhardt, 1972), the children's mother was surprised and pleased by the striking differences that developed in her two children. The case of "John/Joan" (pseudonyms) was reported in the medical literature as an unqualified success. By age three, the "female" twin wore nightgowns and dresses almost exclusively and liked bracelets and hair ribbons. During the preschool years, the girl reportedly preferred playing with "girl-type" toys and asked for a doll and carriage for Christmas. Her brother

asked for a garage with cars, gas pumps, and tools. By age 6, the brother was accustomed to defending his sister if he thought someone was threatening her. The daughter copied the mother in tidying and cleaning up the kitchen, whereas the boy did not. The mother agreed that she encouraged her daughter when she helped with the housework and expected the boy to be uninterested.

What first looked like a success was, in fact, a dismal failure. Follow-up studies report that the child never really adjusted to her assigned gender (Diamond & Sigmundson, 1997). In spite of being raised from infancy as a girl, she did not feel like a girl and avoided most female activities and interests. By age 14, she was so unhappy that she contemplated suicide. The father then tearfully explained what had happened earlier. For the child, "All of a sudden everything clicked. For the first time things made sense, and I understood who and what I was" (Thompson, 1997, p. 83).

What do you think about the parents' and experts' solution to this terrible accident? Is it possible that what makes some children prefer "girl-type" toys and clothes is how parents or others treat them? Or is biology the predictor of our gender-related behaviors? The concepts of sex, gender, attraction, and maleness and femaleness are not simple. You will learn more about "Brenda" and your own gender development and sexuality in the first section of this chapter. Then we introduce four pioneers in sex research and discuss cultural differences in sexual practices and attitudes. In the third section, we describe sexual arousal, response, and orientation. Finally, we look at sexual dysfunction and sexually transmitted infections, including AIDS (acquired immunodeficiency syndrome).

SEX AND GENDER

Why is it that the first question most people ask after a baby is born is "Is it a girl or a boy?" What would life be like if there were no divisions according to maleness or femaleness? Would your career plans or friendship patterns change? These questions reflect the importance of *sex* and *gender* in our lives. This section begins with a look at the various ways sex and gender can be defined, followed by a discussion of gender role development and sex and gender differences.

> How are sex and gender defined, and how do we develop our gender roles? What are the major sex and gender differences between men and women?

Problems with Definition: What Is "Maleness" or "Femaleness"?

When people ask if a newborn is a girl or boy, they're typically thinking of standard biological differences as seen in Figure 11.1. But when they buy gifts for children, they frequently demonstrate their expectations of *femininity* ("She'll like this pretty doll") versus *masculinity* ("This fire truck is perfect for him"). In the case of the male twin who was reassigned as a female, do you still think of "her" as basically male? Is

Figure 11.1 *Male and female internal and external systems.* (a) The internal and external sex organs of the male. (b) The internal and external sex organs of the female.

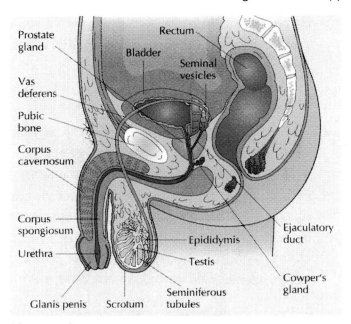

(a)

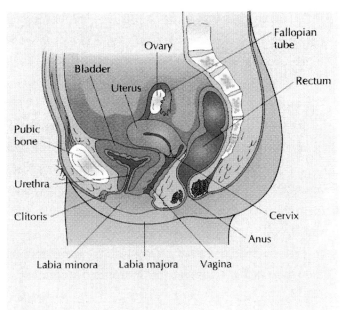

(b)

a man who cross-dresses female? The question of what is "male" and "female" can be confusing.

In recent years, researchers have come to use the term **sex** to refer to the biological elements of maleness and femaleness (such as having a penis or vagina), or physical activities (such as masturbation and intercourse). **Gender**, on the other hand, encompasses the psychological and sociocultural meanings added to biological maleness or femaleness (such as "Men should be aggressive" and "Women should be nurturing"). There are at least seven dimensions or elements of *sex* and two of *gender* (Table 11.1).

If you apply the dimensions of sex and gender that are presented in Table 11.1 to the case of the reassigned twin, you can see why it is a classic in the field of human sexuality. Although born a chromosomal male, the child's genital sex was first altered by the doctor who accidentally removed the penis and later by surgeons who created female genitals. The question was whether surgery, along with female hormones and "appropriate" gender role expectations of the parents, would be enough to create a stable female **gender identity**. Would the child accept the sex reassignment and identify herself as female?

At first, it appeared that Brenda's reassignment was successful, and psychology and sociology texts cited this case as evidence of the environment's predominant role in creating gender identity. As she entered adolescence, however, the early "success" began to be questioned. Her appearance and masculine gait led classmates to tease her and call her "cave woman." At this age, she also expressed thoughts of becoming a mechanic, and her fantasies reflected discomfort with her female role. She even tried urinating in a standing position. By age 14, she insisted she wanted to live as a boy (Diamond & Sigmundson, 1997).

Brenda was later surgically changed back to a man, with a new name, David. At age 25, he married a somewhat older woman and adopted her children. Although David now says, "I don't blame my parents," they still feel extremely guilty about their participation in the reassignment. David, his twin brother, and parents all suffered tremen-

Sex *Biological maleness and femaleness, including chromosomal sex, gonadal sex, hormonal sex, external genitals, and internal accessory organs; also, activities related to sexual behaviors, such as masturbation and intercourse*

Gender *The psychological and sociocultural meanings added to biological maleness or femaleness*

Gender Identity *How one psychologically perceives oneself as either male or female*

TABLE 11.1 DIMENSIONS OF SEX AND GENDER

	Male	Female
Sex Dimensions		
1. Chromosomes	XY	XX
2. Gonads	Testes	Ovaries
3. Hormones	Androgens	Estrogens
4. External genitals	Penis, scrotum	Labia majora, labia minora, clitoris, vaginal opening
5. Internal accessory organs	Prostate gland, seminal vesicles, vas deferens, ejaculatory duct, Cowper's gland	Vagina, uterus, fallopian tubes, cervix
6. Secondary sex characteristics	Beard, lower voice, wider shoulders, sperm emission	Breasts, wider hips, menstruation
7. Sexual orientation	Heterosexual, gay, bisexual	Heterosexual, lesbian, bisexual
Gender Dimensions		
8. Gender identity (self-definition)	Perceives self as male	Perceives self as female
9. Gender role (societal expectations)	Masculine ("Boys like trucks and sports")	Feminine ("Girls like dolls and clothes")

Why do some men cross-dress? Those who are transvestites dress like women to release sexual tension and enjoy the other sex's gender role. Contrary to common believe, gay men seldom cross-dress.

Sexual Orientation *An individual's primary erotic attraction can be toward members of the same sex (homosexual, gay or lesbian), both sexes (bisexual), or other sex (heterosexual)*

dously from the tragic accident and the no less tragic solution. The family members have since reconciled, but David is no longer in contact with the doctor, John Money.

[A similar botched circumcision occurred in 1985, exactly 20 years after David and his twin brother were born. Although David had announced his decision to live as a male 5 years earlier, "Baby Doe" was also surgically altered and reassigned as a female. The current status of this child is carefully guarded, but limited facts point to a similarly unhappy outcome (Colapinto, 2000). The consulting specialist was John Money.]

The fact that David ultimately rejected his assigned female gender despite strong pressure from his family and doctors indicates that the most important factor in gender identity may be biological. A recent longitudinal study offers additional evidence of a biological link. Researchers at Johns Hopkins Hospital tracked the development of 27 normal boys, born without a penis, a rare defect known as *cloacal exstrophy*. Twenty-five of these boys were castrated at birth and raised as girls, yet researchers observed many signs of masculine behavior, including lots of "typical" male "rough-and-tumble" play. Fourteen of the children, currently ranging in age from 5 to 16 years, have recently rejected their female reassignment and declared themselves to be boys (Hettena, 2000).

In addition to the gender difficulties involved in David's case and the cases of the boys born without a penis, other gender problems may develop when a person expresses persistent discomfort about his or her gender and repeatedly expresses a wish to be a member of the other sex. This is known as *transsexualism* (having a gender identity opposite to biological sex). Although some may see the case of Brenda/Bruce/David as a form of transsexualism, "true" transsexuals are not the result of botched circumcisions. They are born chromosomally and anatomically one sex, but their **gender identity** is that of the other sex. Thus, an anatomically male transsexual feels he is the victim of a "birth defect" and often seeks corrective reassignment surgery (Bower, 2001). At one time, the number of men seeking reassignment was much higher than the number of women who wished to be men, but the ratio has narrowed considerably in recent years (Landen, Walinder, & Lundstrom, 1998).

Is a transsexual the same as a transvestite? No, *transvestism* involves individuals (almost exclusively men) who become sexually aroused or gratified by wearing the clothes stereotypical of the other sex (cross-dressing) (Allgeier & Allgeier, 2000). Transsexuals, however, feel that they are really members of the opposite sex imprisoned in the wrong body — their gender identity does not match their gonads, genitals, or internal accessory organs. Transsexuals may also cross-dress, but their motivation is to look like the "right" sex rather than to obtain sexual arousal. Transvestites can also be distinguished from female impersonators (who cross-dress to entertain) and from gay men who occasionally "go in drag" (cross-dress).

Are transvestites and transsexuals also homosexual? When a person is described as *homosexual*, it is because of a **sexual orientation** toward the same sex. (The preferred terms today are *gay* and *lesbian* rather than *homosexual*.) Transvestites are usually heterosexual (Bullough & Bullough, 1997). Transsexuality, on the other hand, has nothing to do with sexual orientation. In fact, a transsexual can be heterosexual, gay, lesbian, or *bisexual* (being sexually attracted to both males and females).

The confusion between homosexuality and transsexuality can be avoided if you remember that sexual orientation and gender identity are two different things. For example, a male transsexual's attraction to a male sex partner might appear to be a case of homosexuality. But after sex-change surgery, this same sexual orientation would logically be classified as heterosexual. Also, some male transsexuals are married to or sexually attracted to females before the sex-change operation and continue to prefer female partners after their bodies have been changed to females.

Gender Role Development: Two Major Theories

With a basic understanding of sexual orientation and problems with gender identity, let's look at **gender roles** — societal expectations for normal and appropriate female and male behavior. Gender roles influence our lives from the moment of birth (when we are wrapped in either a pink or blue blanket) until the moment of death (when we are buried in either a dress or a dark suit). By age two, children are well aware of gender roles. They recognize that boys "should" be strong, independent, aggressive, dominant, and achieving, whereas girls "should" be soft, dependent, passive, emotional, and "naturally" interested in children (Kimmel, 2000; Witt, 1997). The gender role expectations learned in childhood apparently influence us throughout our life.

How do we develop our gender roles? There are currently two major theories of gender role development: *social learning* and *cognitive developmental*.

Social Learning Theory

Social-learning theorists emphasize the power of the immediate situation and observable behaviors on gender role development. They suggest girls learn how to be "feminine" and boys learn how to be "masculine" in two major ways: (1) They receive rewards or punishments for specific gender role behaviors and (2) they watch and imitate the behavior of others — particularly the same-sex parent (Bandura, 1989, 2000; Leaper, Anderson, & Sanders, 1998; Ruble & Martin, 1998). A boy who puts on his father's tie or baseball cap wins big, indulgent smiles from his parents. But can you imagine what would happen if he put on his mother's nightgown or lipstick? Parents, teachers, and friends generally reward or punish behaviors according to traditional boy/girl gender role expectations. Thus, a child "socially learns" what it means to be male or female.

Cognitive Developmental Theory

Cognitive-developmental theorists acknowledge that social learning is part of gender development, but, they argue, the social learning model sees gender development as a passive process. Cognitive developmentalists point out that children also actively observe, interpret, and judge the world around them (Bem, 1981, 1993; Liben & Signorella, 1993; Welch-Ross & Schmidt, 1996). As children process this information, they create internal rules governing correct behaviors for boys versus girls. On the basis of these rules, they form *gender schemas* (mental images) of how

Gender Role *The societal expectations for normal and appropriate male and female behavior; when these expectations are based on exaggerated and biased beliefs about differences between the sexes and are rigidly applied to all members of each sex, they are known as gender role stereotypes*

Early gender role conditioning. What are the long-term effects of this type of gender role training on young boys and girls?

they should act. (Recall from the discussion of Piaget in Chapter 9 that a schema is a cognitive structure, a network of associations, that guides perception.)

Thus, a little boy plays with fire trucks and building blocks because his parents smiled approvingly in the past and because he has seen more boys than girls playing with these toys. But his internal thought processes also contribute to his choice of "masculine" toys; he realizes he is a boy, and he has learned that boys "should" prefer fire trucks to dishes and dolls.

Sex and Gender Differences: Nature Versus Nurture

Now that we have looked at the different dimensions of sex and gender and examined gender role development, let's turn our attention to sex and gender differences between males and females.

Sex Differences

Physical anatomy is the most obvious biological difference between males and females. As we discussed in Chapter 9, males and females differ in their secondary sex characteristics (facial hair, breasts, and so on), their signs of reproductive capability (the menarche for girls and the ejaculation of sperm for boys), and their physical reactions to middle age or the end of reproduction (the female menopause and male climacteric). The average man is also taller, heavier, and stronger than the average woman, but he is also more likely to be bald and color-blind.

There are also important functional and structural differences in the brains of human females and males. These differences result, at least in part, from prenatal sex differentiation and are most apparent in the *hypothalamus, corpus callosum,* and *cerebral hemispheres* (Diamond & Sigmundson, 1997; Dorion et al., 2000; Gur et al., 1995; Reiner, 1997). During puberty, a female's hypothalamus directs her pituitary gland to release hormones in a cyclic fashion, known as the menstrual cycle, whereas the male's hypothalamus directs a *relatively* steady production of sex hormones. Researchers have also documented differences in the cerebral hemispheres of men and women that may account for differences in verbal and spatial skills (Castle, 2000; Joseph, 2000; Shaywitz, 1996; Wisniewski, 1998).

Gender Differences

Do you think there are inborn psychological differences between women and men? Do you believe that women are more emotional and more concerned with aesthetics, whereas men are naturally more aggressive and competitive? Scientists have researched questions such as these; their major findings on gender differences are summarized in Table 11.2. In this section, we will focus on two of their most important findings — regarding cognitive abilities and aggression. We will also explore one way to minimize gender differences, through androgyny.

1. *Cognitive abilities.* For many years, researchers have noted that females tend to score higher on tests of verbal skills, whereas males score higher on math and visuospatial tests (Gallagher et al., 2000; Ruble & Martin, 1998). As mentioned earlier, some researchers suggest that these differences may reflect biology — that is, structural differences in the cerebral hemispheres, hormones, or in the degree of hemispheric specialization.

One very strong argument against such a biological model, however, is that cognitive gender differences have dramatically declined in recent years (Brown & Josephs, 1999; Halpern, 1997, 2000). By comparing a large number of studies, Hyde and her colleagues (1988, 1990) found a significant reduction in male–female differences in verbal ability scores and math scores. The major exception in this trend of vanishing gender differences is found in a small segment of the population,

TABLE 11.2   RESEARCH-SUPPORTED SEX AND GENDER DIFFERENCES

Type of Behavior	More Often Shown by Men	More Often Shown by Women
Sexual	Begin masturbating sooner in life cycle and have higher overall occurrence rates. Start sexual life earlier and have first orgasm through masturbation. Are more likely to recognize their own sexual arousal. Experience more orgasm consistency in their sexual relations.	Begin masturbating later in life cycle and have lower overall occurrence rates. Start sexual life later and have first orgasm from partner stimulation. Are less likely to recognize their own sexual arousal. Experience less orgasm consistency in their sexual relations.
Touching	Are touched, kissed, and cuddled less by parents. Exchange less physical contact with other men and respond more negatively to being touched. More likely to initiate both casual and intimate touch.	Are touched, kissed, and cuddled more by parents. Exchange more physical contact with other women and respond more positively to being touched. Less likely to initiate either casual or intimate touch.
Friendship	Have larger number of friends and express friendship by shared activities.	Have smaller number of friends and express friendship by shared communication about self.
Personality	Are more aggressive from a very early age. Are more self-confident of future success. Attribute success to internal factors and failures to external factors. Achievement is task oriented; motives are mastery and competition. Are more self-validating Have higher self-esteem.	Are less aggressive from a very early age. Are less self-confident of future success. Attribute success to external factors and failures to internal factors. Achievement is socially directed with emphasis on self-improvement; have higher work motives. Are more dependent on others for self-validation Have lower self-esteem.
Cognitive Abilities	Are slightly superior in mathematics and visospatial skills.	Are slightly superior in grammar, spelling, and related verbal skills.

Sources: Allgeier & Allgeier, 2000; Baldwin & Baldwin, 1997; Crooks & Bauer, 1999; Hyde & Plant, 1995.

the brightest of the bright. Males in this group tend to score significantly higher in SAT math scores.

2. Aggression. One of the clearest and most consistent findings in gender studies is greater physical aggressiveness in males. From an early age, boys are more likely to engage in mock fighting and rough-and-tumble play (Hettena, 2000; Niehoff, 1999; Reed & Brown, 2001). As adults, they are also more likely to commit aggressive crimes. But gender differences are clearer for physical aggression (like hitting) than for other forms of aggression (Zurbriggen, 2000). Although early research suggested females were more likely to engage in more indirect and relational forms of aggression, such as spreading rumors, ignoring, or excluding someone (Bjorkquist, 1994; Crick, 1996). But later research has not found such clear differences (Pakaslahti & Keltikangas-Jaervinen, 2000; Richardson & Green, 1999).

What causes these gender differences in aggression? Nativists generally cite biological factors. For example, several studies have linked the male gonadal hormone testosterone to aggressive behavior (Boyd, 2000; Dabbs & Dabbs, 2000; Sanchez-Martin et al., 2000). Other studies have found that men have lower levels of serotonin, a neurotransmitter found to be inversely related to aggression (Berman, Tracy, & Coccaro, 1997; Holtzworth-Munroe, 2000). In addition, studies on identical twins find that genetic factors account for about 50 percent of aggressive behavior (Cadoret, Leve, & Devor, 1997; Segal & Bouchard, 2000).

Nurturists typically point to environmental pressures that encourage "sex-appropriate" behaviors and skills. For example, children's picture books, video games, and TV programs and commercials frequently present women and men in stereotypical gender roles — men as pilots and doctors, women as moms and nurses (Dietz, 1998; Kimmel, 2000).

What if we don't like this part of gender roles? What can we do?

Androgyny [an-DRAW-juh-nee]
Combining characteristics considered typically male (e.g., assertive, athletic) with characteristics considered typically female (e.g., yielding, nurturant); from the Greek andro, meaning "male", and gyn, meaning "female."

Androgyny

One way to overcome gender role stereotypes is to encourage **androgyny**, expressing both the "masculine" and "feminine" traits found in each individual. Rather than limiting themselves to rigid gender-appropriate behaviors, androgynous men and women can be assertive and aggressive when necessary, but also gentle and nurturing.

Although some people think *androgyny* is a new term for asexuality or transsexualism, the idea of androgyny has a long history referring to positive combinations of gender roles, like the yin and yang of traditional Chinese religions. Carl Jung (1946, 1959), an early psychoanalyst, described a woman's natural masculine traits and impulses as her "animus" and feminine traits and impulses in a man as his "anima." Jung believed we must draw on both our masculine and feminine natures to become fully functioning adults.

Using personality tests and other similar measures, modern researchers have found that masculine and androgynous individuals generally have higher self-esteem, are more socially competent and motivated to achieve, and exhibit better overall mental health (Gianakos, 2000; Courtenay, 2000; Stake, 1997). It seems that androgyny and masculinity are adaptive for both sexes.

Androgeny in action. Combining the traits of both genders helps many couples meet the demands of modern life.

How can you explain this? The most likely explanation is that traditional masculine characteristics (analytical, independent) are more highly valued than traditional feminine traits (affectionate, cheerful). In fact, when college students in 14 different countries were asked to describe their "current self" and their "ideal self," the ideal self-descriptions for both men and women contained more masculine qualities than feminine (Williams & Best, 1990).

This shared preference for male traits also explains why extensive observation of children on school playgrounds has found that boys who engage in feminine activi-

Would you like to see how androgynous you are? Social psychologist Sandra Bem (1974, 1993) developed a personality measure that has been widely used in research. You can take this version of Bem's test by rating yourself on the following items. Give yourself a number between 1 (never or almost never true) and 7 (always or almost always true):

1. ____ Analytical
2. ____ Affectionate
3. ____ Competitive
4. ____ Compassionate
5. ____ Aggressive
6. ____ Cheerful
7. ____ Independent
8. ____ Gentle
9. ____ Athletic
10. ____ Sensitive

Now add up your points for all the odd-numbered items; then add up your points for the even-numbered items. If you have a higher total on the odd-numbered items, you are "masculine." If you scored higher on the even-numbered items, you are "feminine." If your score is fairly even, you may be androgynous.

ties (like skipping rope or playing jacks) lose status. The reverse of this is not true for girls (Leaper, 2000). Even as adults, it is more difficult for males to express so-called female traits like nurturance and sensitivity than for women to adopt traditionally male traits of assertiveness and independence (Kimmel, 2000; Christensen, Hebl, Rothgerber, & Wood, 1997). In short, most societies prefer "tomboys" over "sissies."

Recent studies show that gender roles in our society are becoming less rigidly defined (Kimmel, 2000; Loo & Thorpe, 1998). Asian American and Mexican American groups show some of the largest changes toward androgyny, and African Americans remain among the most androgynous of all ethnic groups (Espin, 1993; Harris, 1996; Huang & Ying, 1989).

But in spite of positive trends in gender roles, behavior in some areas — especially dating — is difficult to understand. Although most couples still follow the unspoken gender rule that men should make the first approach, how does the man know if the woman is interested? Researchers have found some very interesting answers; see the accompanying Research Highlight.

Check & Review

SEX AND GENDER

The term **sex** is differentiated along seven dimensions: chromosomal sex, gonadal sex, hormonal sex, external genitals, internal accessory organs, secondary sex characteristics, and sexual orientation. **Gender**, on the other hand, is differentiated according to **gender identity** and **gender role**. Transsexualism is a problem with gender identity; trans-vestism is cross-dressing for sexual arousal. **Sexual orientation** (gay, lesbian, bisexual, or heterosexual) is unrelated to both transsexualism and trans-vestism. There are two main theories of gender role development: Social-learning theorists focus on rewards, punishments, and imitation, whereas cognitive-developmental theorists emphasize the active, thinking processes of the individual.

Studies of male and female sex differences find several obvious physical differences, such as height, body build, and reproductive organs. There are also important functional and structural sex differences in the brains of human females and males. Looking at gender differences, studies find some differences (such as in aggression and verbal skills), but the cause of these differences (either nature or nurture) is still being debated.

Questions

1. Match the following dimensions of gender with their appropriate meaning:

____ Chromosomal sex

____ Gender identity

____ Gonadal sex

____ Gender role

____ Hormonal sex

____ Secondary sex characteristics

____ External genitals

____ Sexual orientation

____ Internal accessory organs

a. Ovaries and testes

b. XX and XY

c. Estrogens and androgens

d. One's perception of oneself as male or female

e. Breasts, beards, menstruation

f. Uterus, vagina, prostate gland, vas deferens

g. Labia majora, clitoris, penis, scrotum

h. Homosexual, bisexual, heterosexual

i. Differing societal expectations for appropriate male and female behavior

2. Individuals who have the genitals and secondary sex characteristics of one sex but feel as if they belong to the other sex are known as _____ . (a) transvestites; (b) heterosexuals; (c) gays or lesbians; (d) transsexuals

3. Briefly summarize the two major theories of gender role development.

4. A combination of both male and female personality traits is called _____.
(a) heterosexuality; (b) homosexuality; (c) transsexualism; (d) androgyny

Answers to Questions can be found in Appendix B.

RESEARCH HIGHLIGHT

The Art and Science of Flirting

Pretend for the moment that you are watching a man (Tom) and woman (Kaleesha) at a singles bar. As Tom approaches the table, Kaleesha sits up straighter, smiles, and touches her hair. Tom asks her to dance, and Kaleesha quickly nods and stands up while smoothing her skirt. During the dance, she smiles and sometimes glances at him from under her lashes. When the dance finishes, Kaleesha waits for Tom to escort her back to her chair. She motions him to sit in the adjacent chair and they engage in a lively conversation. Kaleesha allows her leg to graze his briefly. When Tom reaches for popcorn from the basket in front of Kaleesha, she playfully pulls it away. This surprises Tom and he frowns at Kaleesha. She quickly turns away and starts talking to her friends. Despite his repeated attempts to talk to her, Kaleesha ignores him.

What happened? Did you recognize Kaleesha's sexual signals? Did you understand why she turned away at the end? If so, you are skilled in the art and science of flirting. If not, you may be very interested in the work of Monica Moore at the Uni-

versity of Missouri (1998). As a scientist interested in describing and understanding flirting and the role it plays in human courtship, Moore has observed and recorded many scenes — in singles bars and shopping malls — like the one with Tom and Kaleesha. Although she prefers the term *nonverbal courtship signaling*, what Moore and her colleagues have spent thousands of hours secretly observing is flirting behavior.

From these naturalistic observations, we know a great deal more about what works and doesn't work in courtship. First of all, though both men and women flirt, women generally initiate a courtship. The woman signals her interest with glances that may be brief and darting, or direct and sustained. Often she smiles at the same time she gestures with her hands — often with an open or extended palm. Primping (adjusting clothing or patting hair) is also

common. A flirting woman will also make herself more noticeable by sitting straighter, with stomach pulled in and breasts pushed out.

Once contact is made and the couple is dancing or sitting at a table, the woman increases the level of flirting. She orients her body toward his, whispers in his ear, and frequently nods and smiles in response to his conversation. Most significant, she touches the man or allows the man to touch her. Like Kaleesha with Tom, allowing her leg to graze his is a powerful indication of her interest.

Women also use play behaviors to flirt. They tease, mock-hit, and tell jokes, not only to inject humor but also to test the man's receptivity to humor. As in the case of Tom's reaction to the popcorn tease, when a man doesn't appreciate the playfulness, a woman often uses rejection signals to cool or end the relationship. Other studies confirm Moore's description of women's nonverbal sexual signaling (Lott, 2000).

Now that you know what to look for, watch for flirting behavior in others — or perhaps in your own life. According to Moore and other researchers, flirting may be the single most important thing a woman can do to increase her attractiveness. Because the burden of making the first approach is usually the man's, men are understandably cautious and welcome a woman who clearly signals her interest.

Two cautions are in order, however. First, signaling interest does not mean that the woman is ready to have sex with the man. She flirts because she wants to get to know the man better; later, she'll decide whether she wants to develop a relationship (Allgeier & Allgeier, 2000). Second, Moore reminds women to "use their enhanced flirting skills only when genuinely interested" (1997, p. 69). Being aware of sexual signals can benefit both men and women, but flirting should be reserved for times when you genuinely want to attract or keep the attention of a particular partner.

THE STUDY OF HUMAN SEXUALITY

Sex is used and abused in many ways: as a theme in literature, movies, and music; to satisfy sexual desires; to gain love and acceptance from partners and peer groups; as a way of expressing love or commitment in a relationship; as a way of ending relationships through affairs with others; to dominate or hurt others; and, perhaps most conspicuously, to sell products.

People have probably always been interested in understanding their sexuality, but cultural forces have often suppressed and controlled this interest. During the nineteenth century, for example, polite society avoided mention of all parts of the body covered by clothing. The breast of chickens became known as "white meat," female patients were examined by male doctors in totally dark rooms, and some

How do scientists study a sensitive topic like sex?

TRY THIS
Yourself

Before we begin our study of human sexuality, try this quiz. The answers are at the bottom, and expanded explanations are found throughout this chapter.

Which of the following statements are true and which are false?

1. The breakfast cereal Kellogg's Corn Flakes was originally developed to discourage masturbation.
2. Nocturnal emissions and masturbation are signs of abnormal sexual adjustment.
3. The American Academy of Pediatrics (AAP) no longer recommends routine circumcision for male babies.
4. The American Psychiatric Association and the American Psychological Association (APA) consider homosexuality a type of mental illness.
5. Sexual skill and satisfaction are learned behaviors that can be increased through education and training.
6. If you're HIV positive (have human immunodeficiency virus) you cannot infect someone else; only if you have AIDS (acquired immunodeficiency syndrome) can you spread the disease.
7. Women cannot be raped against their will.

Answers: 1. T   2. F   3. T   4. F   5. T
6. F   7. F

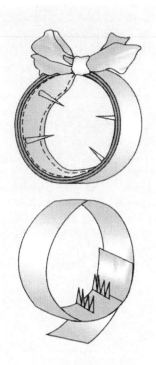

Figure 11.2 *Victorian sexual practice.* During the nineteenth century, men were encouraged to wear spiked rings around their penises at night to avoid nocturnal emissions (wet dreams). If the man had an erection, the spikes would cause pain and awaken him.

The first sex scientist. Havelock Ellis was one of the first sex researchers to celebrate eroticism and acknowledge female sexuality.

people even covered piano legs for the sake of propriety (Allen, 2000; Gay, 1983; Money, 1985a).

During this same Victorian period, medical experts warned that masturbation led to blindness, impotence, acne, and insanity (Allen, 2000; Michael, Gagnon, Laumann, & Kolata, 1994). Believing a bland diet helped suppress sexual desire, Dr. John Harvey Kellogg and Sylvester Graham developed the original Kellogg's Corn Flakes and Graham crackers and marketed them as foods that would discourage masturbation (Money, Prakasam, & Joshi, 1991). One of the most serious concerns of many doctors was nocturnal emissions (wet dreams), which were believed to cause brain damage and death. Special devices were even marketed for men to wear at night to prevent sexual arousal (Figure 11.2).

In light of modern knowledge, it seems hard to understand these strange Victorian practices and outrageous myths about masturbation and nocturnal emissions. One of the first physicians to explore and question these beliefs was Havelock Ellis (1858–1939). When he first heard of the dangers of nocturnal emissions, Ellis was frightened — he had personal experience with the problem. His fear led him to frantically search the medical literature, but instead of a cure, he found predictions of gruesome illness and eventual death. He was so upset, he contemplated suicide.

Ellis eventually decided he could give meaning to his life by keeping a detailed diary of his deterioration. He planned to dedicate the book to science when he died, but after several months of careful observation, he realized the books were wrong. He wasn't dying. He wasn't even sick. Angry that he had been so misinformed by the "experts," he spent the rest of his life developing reliable and accurate sex information. Today, Havelock Ellis is acknowledged as one of the most important early pioneers in the field of sex research.

The second major contributor to sex research was Alfred Kinsey and his colleagues (1948, 1953). Kinsey and his coworkers personally interviewed over 18,000 participants, asking detailed questions about their sexual activities and preferences. Given that most research participants were young, single, urban, white, and middle class, Kinsey's sampling and methodology were heavily criticized. But Kinsey's work is still widely respected, and his data are frequently used as a *baseline* for modern research. In recent years, hundreds of similar sex surveys and interviews have been conducted on such topics as contraception, abortion, premarital sex, and rape (Brannigan, Allgeier, & Allgeier, 1998; Janus & Janus, 1993; Laumann, Gagnon, Michael, & Michaels, 1994). By comparing Kinsey's data to the responses found in later surveys, we can see how sexual practices have changed over the years.

In addition to surveys, interviews, and case studies, some researchers have employed direct laboratory experimentation and observational methods. To document the physiological changes involved in sexual arousal and response, William Masters and Virginia Johnson (1961, 1966, 1970) and their research colleagues enlisted several hundred male and female volunteers. Using intricate physiological measuring devices, the researchers carefully monitored participants' bodily responses as they masturbated or engaged in sexual intercourse. Masters and Johnson's research findings are hailed as a major contribution to our knowledge of sexual physiology. Some of their results are discussed in later sections.

GENDER & CULTURAL DIVERSITY

A Cultural Look at Sexual Behaviors

Sex researchers interested in both universalities and variations in human sexual behavior conduct cross-cultural studies of sexual practices, techniques, and attitudes (Bhugra, 2000; Beach, 1977; Brislin, 1993, 2000; Mackay, 2001). Their stud-

ies of different societies put sex in a broader perspective and help counteract *ethnocentrism*, the tendency people have to judge their own cultural practices as "normal" and preferable to those of other groups.

For example, do you know that kissing is unpopular in Japan and unknown among some cultures in Africa and South America? Do you find it strange that Apinaye women in Brazil often bite off pieces of their mate's eyebrows as a natural part of sexual foreplay (Goldstein, 1976)? Does it surprise you that members of Tiwi society, off the northern coast of Australia, believe that young girls will not develop breasts or menstruate unless they first experience intercourse (Goodall, 1971)? Did you know that the Sambia of New Guinea believe that young boys must swallow semen to achieve manhood (Herdt, 1981)? And that adolescent boys in Mangaia, a small island in the South Pacific, routinely undergo superincision, a painful initiation rite in which the foreskin of the penis is slit and folded back (Marshall, 1971)? Table 11.3 gives other examples of cultural variation in sexuality.

Although other cultures' practices may seem unnatural and strange to us, we forget that our own sexual rituals may appear equally curious to others. If the description of the Mangaian practice of superincision bothered you, how do you feel about our culture's routine circumcision of infant boys? Before you object that infant circumcision in the United States is "entirely different" and "medically safe and necessary," you might want to consider the position now taken by the American Academy of Pediatrics (AAP). In 1999, they decided the previously reported medical benefits of circumcision were so statistically small that the procedure should *not* be routinely performed. The AAP does consider it legitimate for parents to take into account cultural, religious, and ethnic traditions in deciding whether to circumcise their sons.

If the controversy over infant male circumcision surprises you, so, too, may information about female genital mutilation. Throughout history and even today in parts of Africa, the Middle East, and Asia, young girls undergo several types of genital mutilation: circumcision (removal of the clitoral hood), *clitoridectomy* (removal of the clitoris), and *genital infibulation* (removal of the clitoris and labia and stitching together of the remaining tissue to allow only a small opening for urine and menstrual flow (McConville, 1998; Barstow, 1999; Stewart, 1997). In most countries, the surgeries are performed on girls between ages 4 and 10 and often without anes-

Circumcision and religion. Although circumcision is an important part of some religions, it is relatively rare in most parts of the world.

TABLE 11.3 SEXUAL BEHAVIORS ACROSS CULTURES

	Childhood Sexuality	Adult Sexuality
Mangaia (Polynesian Island)	Children readily exposed to sex. Adolescents are given direct instruction in techniques for pleasuring their sexual partners, and both boys and girls are encouraged to have many partners.	After marriage, three orgasms per night are not uncommon for men, and they are encouraged to "give" three orgasms to their female partner for every one of their own. Adults practice a wide range of sexual behaviors.
Yolngu (Island Near Australia)	Permissive attitude toward childhood sexuality. Parents soothe infants by stroking their genitals. Nudity accepted from infancy through old age.	Men can have many wives and are generally happy with their sex life. Women are given no choice in marital partner and little power in the home. Women are apathetic about sex, seldom orgasmic, and generally unhappy.
Inis Beag[a] *(Irish Island)*	Sexual expression is strongly discouraged. Children learn to abhor nudity and are given no information about sex. Young girls are often shocked by their first menstruation.	Little sex play before intercourse. Female orgasm is unknown or considered deviant. Numerous misconceptions about sex (e.g., intercourse can be debilitating, menopause causes insanity).

[a] Inis Beag is a pseudonym used to protect the privacy of this Irish island.

Sources: Crooks & Baur, 1999; Ford & Beach, 1951; Marshall, 1971; Money et al., 1991; Ortner & Whitehead, 1981.

thesia or antiseptic conditions (Abusharaf, 1998). The young girls suffer numerous health problems because of these practices — the most serious from genital infibulation. Risks include severe pain, bleeding, chronic infection, and menstrual difficulties. As adults, these women frequently experience serious childbirth complications or infertility (Ortiz, 1998).

What is the purpose of these procedures? The main objective is to ensure virginity before marriage (Orubuloge & Caldwell, 1997). Without these procedures, young girls are considered unmarriageable and without status. As you may imagine, these practices create serious culture clashes. For example, physicians in Western societies are currently being asked by immigrant parents to perform these operations on their daughters. What should the doctor do? Should this practice be forbidden? Or would this be another example of ethnocentrism?

As you can see, it is a complex issue. Canada was the first nation to recognize female genital mutilation as a basis for granting refugee status, and the United Nations has suspended its regular policy of nonintervention in the cultural practices of nations. The World Health Organization (WHO) and the United Nations International Children's Emergency Fund (UNICEF) have both issued statements opposing female genital mutilation and have developed programs to combat this and other harmful practices affecting the health and well-being of women and children.

Check & Review

THE STUDY OF HUMAN SEXUALITY

Although sex has always been an important part of human interest, motivation, and behavior, it received little scientific attention before the twentieth century. Havelock Ellis was among the first to study human sexuality despite the repression and secrecy of nineteenth-century Victorian times.

Alfred Kinsey and his colleagues were the first to conduct large-scale, systematic surveys and interviews of the sexual practices and preferences of Americans during the 1940s and 1950s. The research team of William Masters and Virginia Johnson pioneered the use of actual laboratory measurement and observation of human physiological response during sexual activity. Cultural studies are also important sources of scientific information on human sexuality.

Questions

1. During earlier times, it was believed that _____ led to blindness, impotence, acne, and insanity, whereas _____ caused brain damage and death. (a) female orgasms, male orgasms; (b) masturbation, nocturnal emissions; (c) menstruation, menopause; (d) oral sex, sodomy

2. Match the following researchers with their contributions to the study of human sexuality:

   a. Havelock Ellis   _____ Based his/their groundbreaking research into human sexuality on personal diaries

   b. William Masters   _____ Popularized the use of the survey method in
      and Virginia Johnson   studying human sexuality

   c. Alfred Kinsey   _____ Pioneered the use of direct observation and physiological measurement of bodily responses during sexual activities

3. What are the advantages of cultural studies in sex research?

4. Viewing one's own ethnic group (or culture) as central and "correct" and then judging the rest of the world according to this standard is known as _____. (a) standardization; (b) stereotyping; (c) discrimination; (d) ethnocentrism

Answers to Questions can be found in Appendix B:

SEXUAL BEHAVIOR

Are women and men fundamentally alike in their sexual responses? Or are they unalterably different? What causes a gay or lesbian sexual orientation? What is sexual prejudice? These are some of the questions we will explore in this section.

Sexual Arousal and Response: Gender Differences and Similarities

To understand differences and similarities in male and female sexual behavior, it helps to begin with Masters and Johnson's (1966) four-stage **sexual response cycle** (Figure 11.3):

Stage 1: In the **excitement phase**, which can last from a few minutes to several hours, arousal is initiated through physical factors, such as touching or being touched, or through psychological factors, such as fantasy or erotic stimuli. During this stage, heart rate and respiration increase and blood flows to the pelvic region, causing engorgement of the penis and clitoris. Both males and females may have nipples becoming erect, and both may experience a *sex flush*, or reddening of the upper torso and face.

Stage 2: If stimulation continues, the **plateau phase** begins and heartbeat, respiration rate, and blood pressure stabilize or level off at a heightened rate. In the man, the penis becomes more engorged and erect while the testes swell and pull up closer to the body. In the woman, the clitoris pulls up under the clitoral hood and the entrance to the vagina contracts while the uterus rises slightly. This movement of the uterus causes the upper two-thirds of the vagina to balloon, or expand. As

What is the latest research on sexual orientation? How are men and women alike and different in sexual arousal and response?

Sexual Response Cycle *William Masters and Virginia Johnson's description of the bodily response to sexual arousal; the four stages are excitement, plateau, orgasm, and resolution*

Excitement Phase *First stage of the sexual response cycle, characterized by increasing levels of arousal and increased engorgement of the genitals.*

Plateau Phase *Second stage of the sexual response cycle, characterized by a leveling off of high arousal.*

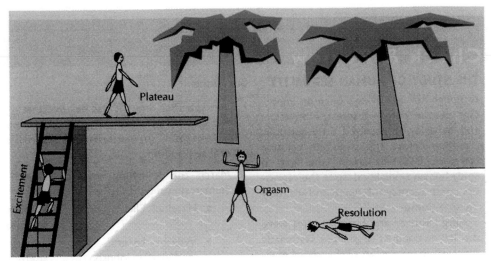

Figure 11.3 *Masters and Johnson's sexual response cycle.* One way to visualize (and remember) the four stages of the sexual response cycle is to compare it to diving off a high diving board. During the *excitement phase* (climbing up the ladder), both men and women become progressively more aroused and excited, resulting in penile and clitoral erection, and vaginal lubrication in women. In the *plateau phase* (walking across the diving board), sexual and physiological arousal "level off" at a heightened state. The *orgasm phase* (jumping off the diving board) involves rhythmic muscle contractions in both men and women and ejaculation of sperm in men. During the final *resolution phase* (resting and swimming back to shore), physiological responses return to normal.

Orgasm Phase *Third stage of the sexual response cycle when pleasurable sensations peak and orgasm occurs.*

Resolution Phase *Final stage of the sexual response cycle when the body returns to its unaroused state.*

Refractory Period *Phase following orgasm during which further orgasm is considered physiologically impossible.*

excitement reaches its peak, some fluid, which often contains sperm, may seep out of the opening of the penis and both sexes may experience a feeling that orgasm is imminent and inevitable.

Stage 3: During the **orgasm phase**, the individual experiences a highly intense and pleasurable release of tension. In the woman, muscles around the vagina squeeze the vaginal walls in and out and the uterus pulsates. Muscles at the base of the penis contract in the male, causing *ejaculation*, the discharge of semen or seminal fluid.

Stage 4: Both male and female bodies gradually return to their preexcitement state during the **resolution phase**. After one orgasm, most men enter a **refractory period**, during which further excitement to orgasm is considered impossible. Many women (and some men), however, are capable of multiple orgasms in fairly rapid succession.

GENDER & CULTURAL DIVERSITY

Are There Evolutionary Advantages to *Female* Nonmonogamy?

In many ways, women and men are similar in their general sexual responses. But it is our differences that attract the most attention. For example, have you heard that men have more sexual drive, interest, and activity than women do? How do we explain these differences? There are two major perspectives — evolutionary and social role.

The *evolutionary perspective*, emphasizing genetic and biological forces, suggests that sexual differences (such as men having more sexual partners) evolved from ancient mating patterns that helped the species survive (Buss, 1989, 1999, 2000; Fischman, 2000; Low, 2000). According to this *sexual strategies theory* (SST), men have a greater interest in sex and multiple partners and are sexually jealous and controlling because these behaviors maximize their chances for reproduction. Women, on the other hand, seek a good protector and provider to increase their chances for survival, as well as their offspring's. Ultimately, both male and female strategies serve to pass along their genes and ensure the survival of the species.

Although the evolutionary perspective suggests that only men have a biological advantage to multiple sex partners, it is important to note that in at least 18 societies around the world it is *female nonmonogamy* (women having multiple sex partners) that offers survival value to women and children (Beckerman et al., 1999). People in these cultures believe in *partible paternity* (one child having more than one biological father), and pregnant women openly acknowledge their extramarital lovers as "secondary fathers."

Believing that multiple men contribute to the initial impregnation and later "building of the child" seems to benefit both the pregnant woman and her children. Among the Bari of Venezuela and Colombia, Beckerman and his colleagues found that pregnant women with lovers were less likely to miscarry, possibly because of courtship gifts that boosted their nutrition. In addition, 80 percent of children with "extra" fathers lived to age 15, in contrast to 64 percent of children with lone dads.

In contrast to the evolutionary perspective with its biological emphasis, the *social role approach* suggests that gender differences in sexual behavior result from the roles that men and women internalize from their society (Eagly, 1997). For instance, in traditional cultural divisions of labor, women are child bearers and homemakers whereas men are providers and protectors. But as women gain more reproductive freedom and educational opportunities, they also acquire more personal resources and status through means other than mates.

This hypothesis is directly supported by a recent reanalysis of Buss's original data collected from 37 cultures (Buss et al., 1990). Kasser and Sharma (1999) found that women did indeed prefer resource-rich men, but only when the women lived in cultures with little reproductive freedom and education equality. Therefore, say Kasser and Sharma, the conflict between the evolutionary and social role perspectives may be resolved by examining patriarchal cultural systems that limit women's choices.

If strong patriarchies existed during the Pleistocene epoch, enough time may have passed for psychological mechanisms to evolve in reaction to such environments (Smuts, 1995). If, however, patriarchy emerged only in the past 10,000 years, with the advent of agriculture (Miller & Fishkin, 1997), the time span is too short for evolutionary changes, and the social role explanation may be the best. Kasser and Sharma's theory is intriguing, but further research is necessary.

Sexual Orientation: Contrasting Theories and Myths

What causes homosexuality? What causes heterosexuality? Many have asked the first question, but few have asked the second. As a result, the roots of sexual orientation are poorly understood. However, research has identified several widespread myths and misconceptions about homosexuality (Bell, Weinberg, & Hammersmith, 1981; Fone, 2000; Golombok & Tasker, 1996; Lamberg, 1998; Parks, 1998). Every one of the following popular beliefs is false:

- *Seduction theory.* Gays and lesbians were seduced as children by adults of their own sex.

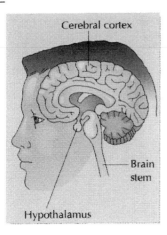

Figure 11.4 *The hypothalamus and sexual orientation.* Researcher Simon LeVay found that an area of the hypothalamus was smaller among gay men compared to the same area in men he assumed were heterosexual.

Hate crimes. The vicious beating and muder of Mattew Shepard in 1998 is a tragic reminder of the costs of sexual prejudice.

Sexual Prejudice *Negative attitudes toward an individual because of her or his sexual orientation*

- *"By default" myth.* Gays and lesbians were unable to attract partners of the other sex or had unhappy heterosexual experiences.
- *Poor parenting theory.* Sons become gay because of domineering mothers and weak fathers, whereas daughters become lesbians because their fathers were their primary role model.
- *Modeling theory.* Children raised by gay and lesbian parents usually end up adopting their parents' sexual orientation.

It is important to remember that all of these popular beliefs have been shown to be *false* and that the causes of sexual orientation are still unknown. At this point, however, most studies suggest that genetics and biology play the dominant role in sexual orientation (Bailey, Dunne, Martin, 2000; Hamer & Copeland, 1999; Hershberger, 1997; LeVay, 1996; Williams et al., 2000).

For example, a genetic predisposition toward homosexuality is supported by studies on identical male and female twins, fraternal twins, and adopted siblings (Kirk, Bailey, Dunne, & Martin, 2000; Pillard & Bailey, 1995). These studies found that if one identical twin was gay, about 48 to 65 percent of the time so was the second twin. (Note that if the cause were totally genetic, the percentage would be 100.) The rate for fraternal twins was 26 to 30 percent and 6 to 11 percent for adopted brothers or sisters. Estimates of homosexuality in the general population run between 2 and 10 percent.

Some researchers have also hypothesized that prenatal hormone levels affect fetal brain development and sexual orientation. Animal experiments have found that administering male hormones prenatally can cause female sheep to engage in the mounting behavior associated with male sheep (Bagermihl, 1999). Because it is obviously unethical to experiment with human fetuses, we cannot come to any meaningful conclusions about the effect of hormones on fetal development. Furthermore, no well-controlled study has ever found a difference in adult hormone levels between heterosexuals and gays and lesbians (Banks & Gartrell, 1995; Le Vay, 1996).

The possibility of structural brain differences received support (and wide media attention) when Simon LeVay (1991, 1996) found that the front part of the hypothalamus (Figure 11.4) was smaller among gay men than among those he assumed were heterosexuals. Because we know the hypothalamus influences sexual behavior, LeVay's findings may help explain differences in sexual orientation. However, it is impossible to determine whether the brain differences were a cause or result of sexual orientation.

Although the origin of sexual orientation remains a mystery, the fact of being gay or lesbian brings certain difficulties and challenges. Gays and lesbians endure verbal and physical attacks; disrupted family and peer relationships; and high rates of anxiety, depression, and suicide (Fone, 2000; Herek, 2000; Lock & Steiner, 1999; Rottnek, 1999). Some of the hostility supposedly stems from an irrational fear of homosexuality in oneself or others, which Martin Weinberg labeled *homophobia* in the late 1960s. However, this term is too limited and not scientifically acceptable: It implies that antigay attitudes are limited to individual irrationality and pathology. Psychologist Gregory Herek (2000) proposes the term **sexual prejudice** instead, to emphasize multiple causes and to allow researchers to draw on the rich scientific research on prejudice (Chapter 16).

Despite the acknowledgment in 1973 by both the American Psychiatric Association and the American Psychological Association that homosexuality is not a mental illness, it continues to be a divisive societal issue in the United States. Seeing *sexual prejudice* as a socially reinforced phenomenon rather than an individual pathology, coupled with political action by gays and lesbians, may help fight discrimination and hate crimes.

Fighting back against sexual prejudice. These protesters are working to increase public awareness of and acceptance of different sexual orientations.

Check & Review

SEXUAL BEHAVIOR

William Masters and Virginia Johnson identified a four-stage **sexual response cycle** during sexual activity — *excitement, plateau, orgasm,* and *resolution.* There are numerous similarities and differences between the sexes in this cycle, but differences are the focus of most research. According to the *evolutionary perspective,* men engage in more sexual behaviors with more sexual partners because it helps the species survive. The *social role approach* suggests this difference results from traditional cultural divisions of labor.

Although researchers have identified several myths concerning the causes of homosexuality, the origins remain a puzzle. In recent studies, the genetic and biological explanation has gained the strongest sup-

port. Despite increased understanding, sexual orientation remains a divisive issue in the United States.

Questions

1. Briefly describe the four stages of Masters and Johnson's sexual response cycle.

2. How do the evolutionary and social role perspectives explain male and female differences in sexual behavior?

3. The genetic influence on sexual orientation has been supported by research reporting that_____.

   a. among identical twins, if one brother is gay, the other brother has a 52 percent chance of also being gay

   b. gay men have fewer chromosomal pairs than straight men, whereas

lesbians have larger areas of the hypothalamus than straight women

   c. among adoptive pairs of brothers, if one brother is gay, the other brother has an increased chance of also being gay

   d. parenting style influences adult sexual orientation for men but not for women

4. A homosexual orientation appears to be the result of_____.

   a. seduction during childhood or adolescence by an older homosexual

   b. a family background that includes a dominant mother and a passive, detached father

   c. a hormonal imbalance

   d. unknown factors

Answers to Questions can be found in Appendix B.

SEXUAL PROBLEMS

When we are functioning well sexually, we tend to take this part of our lives for granted. But what happens when things don't go smoothly? What causes normal sexual functioning to stop for some people and never begin for others? What are the major diseases that can be spread through sexual behavior? We will explore these questions in the following section.

What factors contribute to sexual dysfunction and sexually transmitted diseases?

Sexual Dysfunction: The Role of Biology and Learning

Sexual Dysfunction *Impairment of the normal physiological processes of arousal and orgasm*

There are many forms of **sexual dysfunction**, or difficulty in sexual functioning, and their causes are complex (Table 11.4). In this section, we will discuss how biology and learning both contribute to sexual problems.

Biological Factors

Although many people may consider it unromantic, a large part of sexual arousal and behavior is clearly the result of biological processes (Meston, 2000). *Erectile dysfunction* (the inability to get or maintain an erection firm enough for intercourse) and *orgasmic dysfunction* (the inability to respond to sexual stimulation to the point of orgasm) often reflect medical conditions such as diabetes, alcoholism, hormonal deficiencies, circulatory problems, and reactions to certain prescription and non-prescription drugs. Hormones also affect sexual drives and behaviors. Testosterone has a clear effect on sexual desire in both men and women, but otherwise, the precise role of hormones in human sexual behavior is not well understood.

In addition to problems resulting from medical conditions, sexual responsiveness can be affected by inappropriate activation of the spinal cord and sympathetic nervous system. As we discussed in Chapter 2, some aspects of human behavior are reflexive — that is, unlearned, automatic, and occurring without conscious effort or motivation. Sexual arousal for both men and women is partially reflexive and somewhat analogous to simple reflexes like the eye blink response to a puff of air. Just as the puff of air produces an automatic closing of the eye, certain stimuli, such as stroking of the genitals, can lead to automatic arousal. In both situations, nerve impulses from the receptor site travel to the spinal cord, which responds by sending messages to target organs or glands. Normally the blood flow into organs and tissues through the arteries is balanced by an equal outflow through the veins. During sexual arousal, however, the arteries dilate beyond the capacity of the veins to carry the blood away. This results in erection of the penis in men and an engorged clitoris and surrounding tissue in women.

If this is so automatic, why do some people have difficulty getting aroused? Unlike simple reflexes such as the eye blink, negative thoughts or high emotional states may block sexual arousal. Recall from Chapter 2 that the autonomic nervous system (ANS) is intricately involved in emotional (and sexual) responses. The ANS is composed of two subsystems: the sympathetic, which prepares the body for "fight or flight," and the parasympathetic, which maintains bodily processes at a steady, even balance. The parasympathetic branch is dominant during sexual arousal (the body must be relaxed to allow blood flow to the genital area), and the sympathetic branch is dominant during ejaculation and orgasm.

Problems with arousal are sometimes explained by the fact that strong emotions, like fear or anxiety, place the individual in sympathetic dominance, which blocks the initial arousal. Fear and anxiety also explain why young women often have difficulty with sexual arousal. The secretive and forbidden conditions of many early sexual experiences create strong anxieties and fear of discovery, fear of loss of respect, and fear of unwanted pregnancy. Many women discover that they need locked doors, committed relationships, and reliable birth control to enjoy sexual relations.

Performance Anxiety *A fear that one will be unable to meet the expectations, of oneself or one's partner, for sexual "performance"*

What about men? Men often have difficulty with arousal if they drink too much alcohol or are simply fatigued. Some men also experience **performance anxiety**, in which they fear they may not meet their partner's or their own expectations, and this anxiety creates problems with arousal. These same factors affect female arousal, and many men also share women's desire for privacy, commitment, and freedom from pregnancy concerns.

TABLE 11.4 THE MAJOR MALE AND FEMALE SEXUAL DYSFUNCTIONS

Type of Dysfunction	Description	Causes
Male		
Erectile dysfunction (impotence)	Inability to have or maintain an erection firm enough for intercourse	Physical — diabetes, circulatory conditions, heart disease, drugs, extreme fatigue, alcohol consumption, hormone deficiencies
Primary erectile dysfunction	The man has never been able to have sexual intercourse	Psychological — performance anxiety, guilt, difficulty in expressing desires to partner,
Secondary erectile dysfunction	Erection problems occurring in at least 25 percent of sexual encounters	severe antisexual upbringing
Premature ejaculation	The rapid ejaculation that is beyond the man's control, and his partner is nonorgasmic in at least 50 percent of their intercourse episodes	Almost always psychological — the man has learned to ejaculate quickly due to guilt, fear of discovery while masturbating, hurried experiences in cars or motels, and so on
Both male and female		
Dyspareunia	Painful intercourse more frequent in women but also occurs in men	Primarily physical — irritations, infections, or disorders of the internal or external genitals
Inhibited sexual desire (sexual apathy)	Lack of willingness to participate in sexual relations due to disinterest	Physical — hormone deficiencies, alcoholism, drugs, chronic illness Psychological — depression, prior sex trauma, relationship problems, anxiety
Sexual aversion	Lack of participation in sex due to overwhelming fear or anxiety	Psychological — severe parental sex attitudes, prior sex trauma, partner pressure, gender indentity confusion
Female		
Orgasmic dysfunction (anorgasmia, frigidity)	Inability or difficulty in reaching orgasm	Physical — chronic illness, diabetes, extreme fatigue, drugs, alcohol consumption, hormone deficiencies, pelvic disorders, lack of appropriate or adequate stimulation
Primary orgasmic dysfunction	The woman has never had an orgasm	Psychological — fear of evaluation, poor body image, relationship problems, guilt,
Secondary orgasmic dysfunction	The woman was regularly orgasmic at one time, but no longer is	anxiety, severe antisexual upbringing, difficulty in expressing desires to partner,
Situational orgasmic dysfunction	Orgasms occur only under certain circumstances	prior sexual trauma, childhood sexual abuse
Vaginismus	The muscles around the outer one-third of the vagina have involuntary spasms, and penile insertion is impossible or difficult and painful	Primarily psychological — the woman has learned to associate pain or fear with intercourse, owing to prior sexual trauma, severe antisexual upbringing, guilt

Sources: Adapted from Allgeier & Allgeier, 2000; Crooks & Baur, 1999; Masters et al., 1995.

The Role of Learning

Our bodies may be biologically prepared to become aroused and respond to erotic stimulation, but learning also plays a role. As we have just seen, fear of evaluation or of the consequences of sexual activity and performance anxiety are all learned, psychological factors that contribute to both male and female sexual dysfunction. *Gender role training*, the *double standard*, and *sexual scripts* are also important contributors.

Gender role socialization begins at birth and significantly influences all aspects of our life, as the story of "Brenda/David" from the beginning of this chapter shows.

"Now, that's product placement!"

Double Standard *The beliefs, values, and norms that subtly encourage male sexuality and discourage female sexuality*

Can you imagine how traditional male gender roles — being dominant, aggressive, independent — could lead to different kinds of sexual thoughts and behaviors than traditional female gender roles — being submissive, passive, and dependent? These gender role differences have led to a **double standard**, where men are generally encouraged to explore their sexuality and bring a certain level of sexual knowledge into the relationship, whereas women are expected to stop male advances and refrain from sexual activity until marriage.

Although overt examples of the double standard are less evident in modern times, covert or hidden traces of this belief still cause many problems. After examining the gender differences in Table 11.5, can you see how items like men wanting women to "initiate sex more often" or women wanting men "to talk more lovingly" might be related to the double standard?

In addition to gender role training and the double standard, we also learn explicit **sexual scripts** that teach us "what to do, when, where, how, and with whom" (Gagnon, 1990). During the 1950s, societal messages said the "best" sex was at night, in a darkened room, with a man on top and a woman on the bottom. Today, the messages are more bold and varied, partly because of media portrayals. Compare, for example, the sexual scripts portrayed in Figure 11.5.

Sexual Scripts *Socially dictated descriptions of the sequences of behavior that are considered appropriate in sexual interactions*

Sexual scripts, gender roles, and the double standard may all be less rigid today, but a major difficulty remains. Many people and sexual behaviors do not fit society's scripts and expectations. Furthermore, we often "unconsciously" internalize societal messages and then fail to realize how they affect our values and behaviors. For example, modern men and women generally say they want equality, yet both may feel more comfortable if the woman is a virgin and the man has had many partners. Sex therapy encourages partners to examine and sometimes modify inappropriate sexual scripts, gender roles, and beliefs in the double standard.

How do therapists work with sex problems? Clinicians usually begin with interviews and examinations to determine whether the problem is organic, psychological, or, more likely, a combination of both (Knoll & Abrams, 1998; Lefebvre, 1997). Organic causes of sexual dysfunction include medical conditions (such as diabetes mellitus), medications (such as antidepressants), and drugs (such as alco-

TABLE 11.5 WHAT MEN AND WOMEN WISH THEY HAD MORE OF IN THEIR SEXUAL RELATIONSHIPS

Dating Couples

Men wish Their Partners Would:	Women Wish Their Partners Would:
Be more experimental	Talk more lovingly
Initiate sex more often	Be more seductive
Try more oral-genital sex	Be warmer and more involved
Give more instructions	Give more instructions
Be warmer and more involved	Be more complimentary

Married Couples

Men Wish Their Partners Would:	Women Wish Their Partners Would:
Be more seductive	Talk more lovingly
Initiate sex more often	Be more seductive
Be more experimental	Be more complimentary
Be wilder and sexier	Be more experimental
Give more instructions	Give more instructions
	Be warmer and more involved

Source: Based on Hatfield & Rapson, 1996, p. 142.

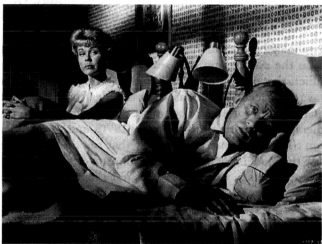

Figure 11.5 *Changing sexual scripts.* In the 1950s and 60s, television and movies generally showed only married couples sleeping in long pajamas in separate twin beds. Contrast this with today's common portrayal of unmarried couples with minimal clothing "actively engaged" on one bed. Also compare the clothes and body postures in beach scenes from 1960 and today.

TABLE 11.6 SEXUAL EFFECTS OF COMMONLY ABUSED AND ILLICIT DRUGS

Drugs	Effects
Alcohol	Chronic abuse causes hormonal alterations (reduces size of testes and suppresses hormonal function) and permanently damages the circulatory and nervous systems
Tobacco	Decreases the frequency and duration of erections and vaginal lubrication
Cocaine	Causes erectile dysfunction, inhibits orgasm, and lowers sperm count
Amphetamines	High doses and chronic use result in inhibition of orgasm and decrease in erection and lubrication
Barbiturates	Cause decreased desire, erectile disorders, and delayed orgasm
Marijuana	Reduces testosterone levels and decreases sexual desire

Source: Abadinsky, 2001; Doweiko, 1999; Julien, 2000.

hol and tobacco — see Table 11.6). Erectile disorders are the problems most likely to have an organic component. In 1998, a medical treatment for erectile problems, *Viagra*, quickly became the fastest-selling prescription drug in U.S. history. Other medications for both men and women are currently being tested (Becker et al., 1998; Mann, 1998).

Years ago, the major psychological treatment for sexual dysfunction was long-term psychoanalysis, based on the assumption that sexual problems resulted from deep-seated personality conflicts that originated in childhood. During the 1950s and 1960s, behavior therapy was introduced; it was based on the idea that sexual dysfunction was learned. (See Chapter 14 for a more complete description of both psychoanalysis and behavior therapy). It wasn't until the early 1970s and the publication of Masters and Johnson's *Human Sexual Inadequacy* that sex therapy gained national recognition. Because the model that Masters and Johnson developed is still popular and used by many sex therapists, we will use it as our example of how sex therapy is conducted.

Masters and Johnson's Sex Therapy Program

Masters and Johnson's approach is founded on four major principles:

1. *A relationship focus.* Unlike forms of therapy that focus on the individual, Masters and Johnson's sex therapy focuses on the relationship between two people. To counteract any blaming tendencies, each partner is considered fully involved and affected by sexual problems. Both partners are taught positive communication and conflict resolution skills.

2. *An integration of physiological and psychosocial factors.* Because medication and many physical disorders can cause or aggravate sexual dysfunctions, Masters and Johnson emphasize the importance of medical histories and exams. They also explore psychosocial factors, such as how the couple first learned about sex and their current attitudes, gender role training, and sexual scripts.

3. *An emphasis on cognitive factors.* Recognizing that many problems result from fears of performance and *spectatoring* (mentally watching and evaluating responses during sexual activities), couples are discouraged from goal setting and judging sex in terms of success or failure.

Experiments in sex? William Masters and Virginia Johnson were the first researchers to use direct laboratory experimentation and observation to study human sexuality.

If you would like to improve your own or your children's current or future sexual functioning, sex therapists would recommend the following:

- *Begin sex education as early as possible.* Children should be given positive feelings about their bodies and an opportunity to discuss sexuality in an open, honest fashion.
- *Avoid goal- or performance-oriented approaches.* Therapists often remind clients that there really is no "right" way to have sex. When couples or individuals attempt to judge or evaluate their sexual lives or to live up to others' expectations, they risk making sex a *job* rather than pleasure.
- *Communicate openly with your partner.* Mind reading belongs onstage, not in the bedroom. Partners need to tell each other what feels good and what doesn't, and sexual problems should be openly discussed without blame, anger, or defensiveness. If the problem does not improve within a reasonable time, consider professional therapy.

4. *An emphasis on specific behavioral techniques.* Couples are seen in an intensive 2-week counseling program. They explore their sexual values and misconceptions and practice specific behavioral exercises. "Homework assignments" usually begin with a *sensate focus* exercise in which each partner takes turns gently caressing the other and communicating what is pleasurable. There are no goal or performance demands. Later exercises and assignments are tailored to the couple's particular sex problem.

Sexually Transmitted Infections: The Special Problem of AIDS

Early sex education and open communication between partners are not only important for full sexual functioning; they are also key to avoiding and controlling sexually transmitted infections (STIs), formerly called sexually transmitted diseases (STDs), venereal disease (VD), or social diseases. *STI* is the term used to describe the disorders caused by more than 25 infectious organisms transmitted through sexual activity.

Each year, millions of North Americans contract one or more STIs, and more than two-thirds of them are under age 35 (CDC, 2000; Gilbert & Alexander, 1998; Loay & Loay, 2000). Also, as Figure 11.6 shows, women are at much greater risk than men of contracting major STIs. It is extremely important for sexually active people to get medical diagnosis and treatment for any suspicious symptoms and to inform their partners. If left untreated, many STIs can cause severe problems, including infertility, ectopic pregnancy, cancer, and even death.

The good news is that most STIs are readily cured in their early stages. See Table 11.7 for an overview of the signs and symptoms of the most common STIs. As you read through this table, remember that many infected people are *asymptomatic,* meaning lacking obvious symptoms. You can have one or more of the diseases without knowing it, and it is often impossible to tell if a sexual partner is infectious.

Although STIs such as genital warts and chlamydial infections have reached epidemic proportions, **AIDS (acquired immunodeficiency syndrome)** has received the largest share of public attention. AIDS results from infection with *human immunodeficiency virus (HIV)*. A standard blood test can determine if someone is

AIDS (Acquired Immunodeficiency Syndrome) *A catastrophic illness in which human immunodeficiency viruses (HIVs) destroy the immune system's ability to fight disease, leaving the body vulnerable to a variety of opportunistic infections and cancers*

Figure 11.6 *Male–female differences in susceptibility to sexually transmitted infections (STIs).* These percentages represent the chances of infection for men and women after a single act of intercourse with an infected partner. Note that women are at much greater risk than men for four of these six STIs. This is partly because female genitals are more internal.

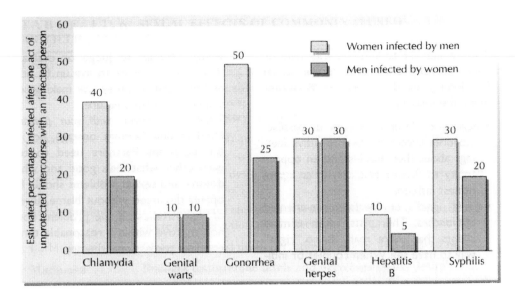

HIV Positive *Being infected by the human immunodeficiency virus (HIV)*

HIV positive, which means the individual has been infected by one or more of the HIV viruses. Being infected with the HIV virus, however, is not the same as having AIDS. AIDS is the final stage of the HIV infection process.

In the beginning of the infection process, the HIV virus replicates rapidly. It is important to know that newly infected individuals are 100 to 1,000 times more infectious than they are throughout the remainder of the disease (Royce, Sena, Cates, & Cohen, 1997). This is especially troubling because most infected people are likely to remain symptom free for months or even years, yet during this time, they can spread the disease to others — primarily through sexual contact.

TABLE 11.7 COMMON SEXUALLY TRANSMITTED INFECTIONS (STIs)

Danger Signs	Could Be	Complications
Male Signs Unusual discharge from penis Soreness inside penis	Chlamydia Gonorrhea Nongonococcal urethritis (NGU)	Untreated gonorrhea can cause prostatitis, sterility, arthritis, and heart trouble. Repeated infections can cause partial or complete blockage of penis or cause abscesses in the genital area or elsewhere.
Female Signs Unusual vaginal discharge Out-of-cycle abdominal pain Unusual vaginal bleeding	Chlamydia Gonorrhea Monilia (yeast) Trichomoniasis Vaginitis	Untreated gonorrhea or chlamydia can cause pelvic inflammatory disease (PID), which can resemble appendicitis. PID causes severe pain, fever, and sterility. Untreated gonorrhea in the birth canal can cause blindness in the newborn
Signs for Both Sexes Painful intercourse Diarrhea Painless sore on penis or vagina Painful sore or blisters on or around genital area Rash on hands and feet or entire body Painful urination Small, pink cauliflower growths on or around sex organs Intense itching Flulike feeling Swollen glands in groin Sore throat	Acquired immunodeficiency syndrome (AIDS) Crabs Genital warts Hepatitis Herpes Scabies Syphilis	Untreated syphilis can cause brain and other organ damage, paralysis, blindness, heart disease, or death. The most severe complication of herpes genitalis is infection of the newborn during birth. Can be fatal to the baby. Presently, there is no demonstrated cure for herpes. (Refer to text of this chapter for more information on AIDS.)

You may have an STI without any of the danger signs but still acquire the complications. Seek medical attention if you suspect that you have come in contact with any of the infections! Follow all medical recommendations. This may include returning for a checkup to make sure you are no longer infected. Take only medications prescribed by your doctor, and take all of them as directed. Don't share them.

Sources: Adapted from Allgeier & Allgeier, 2000; Crooks & Baur, 1999; Kelley & Byrne, 1998.

As the initial HIV infection advances to AIDS, the virus progressively destroys the body's natural defenses against disease and infection. The victim's body becomes increasingly vulnerable to opportunistic infections and cancers that would not be a threat if the immune system were functioning normally. The virus may also attack the brain and spinal cord, creating severe neurological deterioration. The official term *full-blown AIDS* includes anyone infected with HIV who also has a CD4 count of 200 cells per cubic millimeter of blood or less. (The HIV virus destroys CD4 lymphocytes, also called T-cells, which coordinate the immune system's response to disease.)

AIDS is considered one of the most catastrophic diseases of our time. An estimated 1 million people in the United States and 31 million people worldwide are infected with HIV (Crooks & Baur, 1999). Recent advances in the treatment of AIDS have increased the survival time of victims, but for almost everyone, AIDS remains an ultimately fatal disorder, and some researchers doubt that a 100 percent effective vaccine will ever be developed. Despite the severity of this disease, there are signs of public complacency due to the false notion that drugs can now cure AIDS and to a reduced emphasis on prevention and education (Boyce, 2001; Vanable, Ostrow, McKirnan, Taywaditep, & Hope, 2000).

Reflecting cutbacks in AIDS education, myths are widespread. For instance, many people still believe AIDS can be transmitted through casual contact, such as a sneeze, handshake, sharing drinking glasses or towels, social kissing, sweat, or tears. Some also think it is dangerous to donate blood, and others are paranoid about gays, because male homosexuals were the first highly visible victims. All of these are false beliefs.

Infection by HIV spreads only by direct contact with bodily fluids — primarily blood, semen, and vaginal secretions. Blood *donors* are at *no* risk whatsoever. Furthermore, AIDS is not limited to the homosexual community. In fact, the AIDS epidemic is now spreading most quickly among heterosexuals, women, African Americans, Hispanics, and children (CDC, 2000).

Protecting Yourself Against AIDS and Other STIs

The best hope for curtailing the HIV/AIDS epidemic is through education and behavioral change. The following "safer sex" suggestions are not intended to be moralistic — but only to help reduce your chances of contracting both HIV/AIDS and other STIs:

1. Remain abstinent or have sex with one mutually faithful, uninfected partner. Be selective about sexual partners and postpone physical intimacy until laboratory tests verify that you are both free of STIs.

2. Do not use intravenous illicit drugs or have sex with someone who does. If you use intravenous drugs, do not share needles or syringes. If you must share, use bleach to clean and sterilize your needles and syringes.

---

critical thinking ▶▶▶▶▶▶▶▶▶▶▶▶▶▶▶▶▶▶▶▶   **Active Learning**

Rape Myths and Rape Prevention

Sexuality can be a source of vitality and tender bonding, but it can also be traumatizing if one of the partners is unwilling. Rape is "oral, anal, or vaginal penetration forced on an unconsenting or unwilling victim" (Denney & Quadagno, 1998). As clear-cut as the definition seems, many people misunderstand what constitutes rape. To test your own knowledge, answer true or false to the following:

1. Women cannot be raped against their will.

2. A man cannot be raped by a woman.

3. If you are going to be raped, you might as well relax and enjoy it.

4. All women secretly want to be raped.

5. Male sexuality is biologically overpowering and beyond a man's control.

As you might have expected, all of these statements are false. Tragically, however, these myths are believed by a large number of men and women (Drieschner & Lange, 1999; Hall & Barongan, 1997; Reppucci, Woolard, & Fried, 1999). Using your critical thinking skills, can you explain how each of the following factors might contribute to rape myths?

• Gender role conditioning

• The double standard

• Media portrayals

• Lack of information

If you would like to compare your answers to ours or would like specific information regarding rape prevention, see Appendix B.

3. Avoid contact with blood, vaginal secretions, or semen. Using latex condoms and a spermicide containing nonoxynol 9 is the best way to avoid contact.

4. Avoid anal intercourse, with or without a condom. This is the riskiest of all sexual behaviors.

5. Do not have sex if you or your partner are impaired by alcohol or other drugs. The same is true for your friends. "Friends don't let friends drive [or have sex] drunk."

Check & Review

SEXUAL PROBLEMS

Many people experience **sexual dysfunction**. They often fail to recognize the role of biology in both sexual arousal and response. Ejaculation and orgasm are partially reflexive. And the parasympathetic nervous system must be dominant for sexual arousal, whereas the sympathetic nervous system must dominate for orgasm to occur. Several aspects of sexual arousal and response are also learned. Early *gender role training*, the **double standard**, and **sexual scripts** teach us what to consider the "best" sex.

Many sexual problems can be helped with sex therapy. William Masters and Virginia Johnson emphasize the couple's relationship, combined physiological and psychosocial factors, cognitions, and specific behavioral techniques. Professional sex therapists offer important guidelines for everyone: Sex education should be early and positive, avoid a goal or performance orientation, and keep communication open.

The most publicized sexually transmitted infection (STI) is **AIDS (acquired immunodeficiency syndrome)**. Although AIDS is transmitted only through sexual contact or exposure to infected bodily fluids, many people have irrational fears of contagion. At the same time, an estimated 1 million North Americans are **HIV positive** and therefore carriers.

Questions

1. Briefly explain the roles of the sympathetic and parasympathetic nervous systems in sexual response.

2. Sexual learning that includes "what to do, when, where, how, and with whom" is known as _____. (a) appropriate sexual behavior; (b) sexual norms; (c) sexual scripts; (d) sexual gender roles

3. What are the four principles of Masters and Johnson's sex therapy program?

4. What are five "safer sex" ways to reduce the chances of AIDS and other STIs?

Answers to Questions can be found in Appendix B.

KEY TERMS

Sex and Gender
androgyny [an-DRAW-jah nee] (p. 386)
gender (p. 381)
gender identity (p. 381)
gender role (p. 383)
sex (p. 381)
sexual orientation (p. 382)

Sexual Behavior
excitement phase (p. 393)
orgasm phase (p. 394)
plateau phase (p. 393)
refractory period (p. 394)
resolution phase (p. 394)
sexual prejudice (p. 396)
sexual response cycle (p. 393)

Sexual Problems
AIDS (acquired immunodeficiency syndrome) (p. 403)
double standard (p. 400)
HIV positive (p. 404)
performance anxiety (p. 398)
sexual dysfunction (p. 398)
sexual scripts (p. 400)

Visual Summary for Chapter 11 ----

Sex and Gender

Definitions

Sex: Biological dimensions of maleness or femaleness, and physical activities (such as intercourse).

Gender: Psychological and sociocultural meanings of maleness and femaleness.

Gender Role Development

Gender role: Social expectations for appropriate male and female behavior.

Two major theories:

Social learning (reward, punishment, and imitation).

Cognitive Developmental (active thinking processes).

Sex and Gender Differences

Sex differences: Physical differences (like height) and brain differences (function and structure).

Gender differences: Females tend to score somewhat higher in verbal skills. Males score somewhat higher in math and are more physically aggressive.

Androgyny: Combination of masculine and feminine personality traits.

Study of Human Sexuality

Havelock Ellis

Based his research on personal diaries.

Kinsey & Colleagues

Popularized the use of surveys and interviews.

Masters and Johnson

Used direct observation and measurement of human sexual response.

Cultural Studies

Provide insight into universalities and variations in sexual behavior across cultures.

Sexual Behavior

Sexual Arousal and Response

Masters and Johnson's **sexual response cycle: excitement, plateau, orgasm,** and **resolution.** There are numerous similarities of the sexes in this cycle, but differences are the focus of most research. According to the *evolutionary perspective*, males engage in more sexual behaviors with more sexual partners because it helps the species survive. The *social role approach* suggests this difference results from traditional cultural divisions of labor.

Sexual Orientation

Two major theories   *Genetic/biological* (genetic, prenatal biasing of the brain, and brain differences).

Psychosocial ("disturbed family," inability to attract opposite sex, and seduction—all unsupported by research).

Sexual Problems

Sexual Dysfunctions

Possible causes:

Biological: Anxiety blocks arousal. Parasympathetic nervous system must dominate for sexual arousal to occur, whereas sympathetic nervous system must dominate for orgasm to happen.

Psychological:
- Negative gender role training
- Unrealistic **sexual scripts**
- **Double standard** encourages male sexuality but discourages female's
- **Performance anxiety**, fearing one will not meet partner's sex expectations

Treatment: Masters and Johnson emphasize couple's relationship, combined physiological and psychosocial factors, cognitions, and specific behavioral techniques.

Sexually Transmitted Infections (STIs)

Most publicized STI is **AIDS.** AIDS transmitted only through sexual contact or exposure to infected bodily fluids, but irrational fears of contagion persist. An estimated one million in the U.S. are **HIV positive** and therefore carriers.

PSYCHOLOGY IN ACTION

Sixth Edition

Karen Huffman

Palomar College

JOHN WILEY & SONS, INC.

New York | Chichester | Weinheim | Brisbane | Singapore | Toronto

Chapter 17A

Industrial/ Organizational Psychology

Outline

Learning Objectives

As you read Chapter 17, keep the following questions in mind and answer them in your own words:
- How has I/O psychology evolved from the early 1900s to the present day?
- What is human factors psychology?
- Why is personnel psychology important?
- What does organizational psychology encompass?

This is your first day as a car washer at an automobile dealership. Your boss points to a new, and very expensive, white car and tells you to clean and prepare it for delivery to a customer. He asks you to move it from the display lot to the washing facility in the back. You get the keys, unlock the door, get in, fasten your seatbelt, insert the key, and start the car. After shifting into reverse and turning around to check behind you, you begin backing up. Suddenly the car begins to accelerate. You jam on the brakes, but the car does not stop. You push even harder on the brake pedal, but the car goes faster and faster. You crash into another new car parked behind you. As your co-workers rush to help, you're physically okay, but you feel confused and shocked. Two very expensive cars are badly damaged.

How could this have happened? You were sure your foot was on the brake pedal, but the car kept accelerating out of control. Did the brakes malfunction? The transmission? The engine? Could you have made some terrible mistake?

Describing the accident, you assure the manager of the dealership you definitely had your foot on the brake the entire time. However, he insists the car was thoroughly inspected by a service technician just that morning, and the steering, brakes, engine controls, and computer were all functioning perfectly. To make matters worse, when the car was reinspected after the accident, the technician could find no mechanical or computer failure. How to solve this puzzle? Perhaps Sherlock Holmes suggested an answer when he said in *The Sign of the Four*, "When you have eliminated the impossible, whatever remains, however improbable, must be the truth"

(Doyle, 1889).

Assuming that the technician was competent and honest, a mechanical failure was unlikely. Most researchers who study unintended acceleration accidents believe they are the result of driver error, not a mechanical malfunction of the automobile (Vernoy and Tomerlin, 1989). As the car washer, you must have actually had your foot on the gas pedal when you thought it was on the brake. This phenomenon, called "unintended acceleration," is relatively rare, but it has resulted in several lawsuits against automobile manufacturers.

Industrial/Organizational (I/O) Psychology
The study of how individual behavior affects, and is affected by, the physical environment and the organizational culture of the workplace.

*A*nytime a person makes a movement or a decision, there is possibility of error. Most errors such as spilling your milk, hitting the wrong key on your word processor, or betting on the Buffalo Bills, do not result in serious physical injury or property damage. However, if a manager makes a wrong decision in filling a key job or a designer misreads the market for a new line of clothing, a company may lose profits because of lack of productivity or low sales. Similarly, if a worker hits the wrong button at a nuclear power plant, the mistake can damage expensive machinery, seriously damage the environment, and possibly kill or injure thousands of people.

Reducing human error in the workplace involves many factors, including equipment design, selection and training of personnel, design of the work environment, and organizational and decision-making strategies. **Industrial/Organizational (I/O) psychology** studies how individual behavior affects and is affected by the physical environment and the organizational culture of the workplace.

With the possible exception of sleeping, a person spends more time at work than at any other single activity. Thus, finding ways to make our jobs safer and more fulfilling is essential, and perhaps even urgent. You have undoubtedly heard of cases where disgruntled workers attack their bosses or co-workers in a fit of job-related rage. We even have a new term for this behavior, coined as a result of several well publicized cases involving postal workers: "going postal." Reducing the number of workers who "go postal" is one job of the I/O psychologist.

I/O psychologists are frequently employed by business, industry, and the government. Their focus is in three major areas: (1) *human factors psychology* (improving the design and function of machines and the work environment); (2) *personnel psychology* (recruitment, testing, training, placement, and evaluation of workers); and (3) *organizational psychology* (managerial style, worker motivation, and job satisfaction). (See

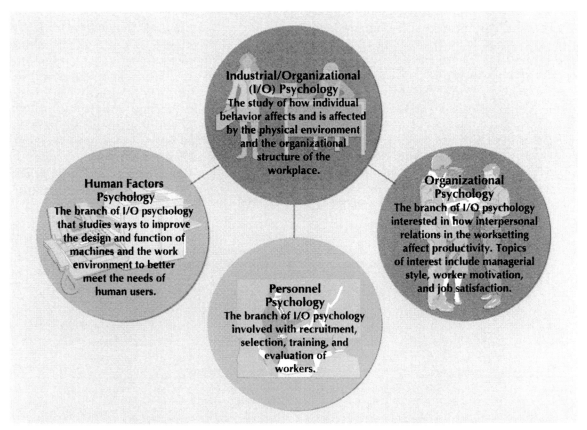

*Figure 17.1 **Specialties within industrial/organizational psychology**.* There are three primary areas of interest for I/O psychologists: human factors psychology, personnel psychology, and organizational psychology.

Figure 17.1.) We discuss each of these major areas, but to set the stage we begin with a look at the historical development of I/O psychology.

THE DEVELOPMENT OF I/O PSYCHOLOGY

The formal study of psychology is relatively short, spanning a mere 125 years or so. The study of I/O psychology is even shorter, originating with the work of Walter Dill Scott, Frederick W. Taylor, and Hugo Munsterberg at the beginning of the twentieth century.

> How has I/O psychology evolved from the early 1900s to the present day?

The Beginnings: Applying Psychology to Sales and Worker Efficiency

On December 20, 1901, Walter Dill Scott, a psychology professor at Northwestern University, addressed a group of advertising professionals. In his talk, he proposed an interesting idea: Using psychological principles in the field of advertising. Instead of merely exhibiting a product and hoping that customers would realize their need for it, he thought advertisers could aggressively influence customers by *suggesting* they buy it or by *arguing* and *debating* the undeniable merits of the purchase. In other words, use persuasion and argumentation to *sell*.

Scott also proposed several other ideas, radical at the time, but taken for granted today. He suggested imitating other companies' successful products, advertising, and production policies; encouraging competition among companies producing similar goods; building loyalty between producers and suppliers; and creating specialized products for markets (Muchinsky, 1993).

Walter Dill Scott

Other Major Figures

Frederick W. Taylor, the next major figure in I/O psychology, emphasized the value of designing the work situation to increase worker output. He correctly surmised that if workers performed their jobs more efficiently, the company would increase profits and workers' wages would go up. In his book *The Principles of Scientific Management* (1911), Taylor formulated four principles for increasing the efficiency and profitability of any organization: (1) scientifically design work methods for greater efficiency; (2) select the best workers and train them in new methods; (3) develop a cooperative spirit between managers and workers; and (4) encourage cooperation between workers and management to improve the work environment.

A particular story is often told about Taylor's attempt to increase the efficiency of workers who shoveled heavy pig iron. Each man moved an average of 12.5 tons of pig iron per day, which to most of us, sounds like a lot. But by allowing the men to rest at scientifically determined periods, and designing new shovels to better match the material being moved, Taylor increased each man's output to 47 *tons* per day! This incredible increase in efficiency resulted in less fatigue and increased wages for the worker, and increased profit for the company (Muchinsky, 1993). Taylor was not a psychologist, but he is nevertheless considered one of the founders of human factors psychology.

Like Scott, Hugo Munsterberg was an early psychologist interested in applying psychology to the workplace. His book *Psychology and Industrial Efficiency* (1913) covered three topics: (1) selecting workers, (2) designing work situations, and (3) using psychology in sales. Munsterberg was most influential in the area of personnel selection and training, and his best known research was a study of streetcar operators, where he created laboratory simulation of an actual streetcar. This research allowed Munsterberg to develop personnel selection criteria and training procedures that eventually led to better street car operators (Muchinsky, 1993).

Although Scott, Taylor, and Munsterberg all demonstrated the importance of applying psychology in the workplace, for many people in industry it took World

Frederick W. Taylor

Hugo Munsterberg

War I to give I/O psychology real respectability. At the beginning of the war, the American Psychological Association, led by President Robert Yerkes, approached Army officials and proposed that psychological testing be used to evaluate the mental ability of recruits. The results could then help establish criteria for assigning recruits to appropriate military jobs.

The Army agreed and Yerkes and a group of psychologists were assigned to develop the first group intelligence test, the *Army Alpha*. Finding that approximately 30 percent of the World War I recruits were functionally illiterate, they later developed the first nonverbal intelligence test, the *Army Beta*.

Walter Dill Scott, mentioned earlier for his advertising ideas, also contributed to the effort to classify and place soldiers in jobs according to their abilities. He is credited with developing job descriptions for over 500 military jobs. Although plans for complete testing of all recruits were never fully implemented, World War I saw a significant expansion of I/O psychology.

The Hawthorne Effect

During the period between World War I and World War II, I/O psychology continued to grow. Many companies added human resource departments for the first time, and a number of colleges and universities began to offer training in I/O psychology (Miner, 1992). Considerable research also was being conducted on advertising, personnel selection, and worker training, but the focus of most I/O research during this period was on testing. Rather than individual testing in the laboratory or in the military, however, workers were now tested in the workplace. In 1924, the most extensive—and by far the most famous—of these workplace projects was begun at the Hawthorne Works of the Western Electric Company, just outside Chicago.

In the original study, researchers from Harvard University installed lights of varying brightness levels in different workrooms where electrical equipment was assembled. The light in some rooms was intense, while as subdued as moonlight in others. The object was to study the relationship between worker efficiency and lighting. The results were quite surprising.

Psychologists, led by Robert Yerkes, developed the Army Alpha, *the first group IQ test. The* Army Alpha, *and later the* Army Beta, *were used to test and classify World War I recruits.*

The Western Electric Hawthorne Works was the site of a famous study of workplace behavior conducted between World War I and World War II.

Researchers found that worker productivity had little or nothing to do with the lighting level. Productivity improved under both *increased* and *decreased* brightness! Even more surprising, when the brightness level remained *unchanged*, productivity still increased. Simply knowing they were being used as research participants apparently improved worker performance. This is known as the **Hawthorne effect,** when people change their behavior because of the novelty of the research situation or because they know they are being observed.

Hawthorne Effect
The phenomenon that occurs when people change their behavior because of the novelty of the research situation or because they know they are being observed.

You may have observed the Hawthorne effect in everyday life. When you walk down the sidewalk singing and suddenly notice other people looking at you, you probably stop singing. Similarly, students taking a test are less likely to cheat if they know the professor is watching them, and people are more likely to wash their hands after using a public restroom when others are watching. Little Leaguers also pay more attention to the game when the coach yells their name. In each of these cases, behavior is changed as a result of being observed.

Because of the remarkable findings from the lighting tests, the Hawthorne project was expanded to investigate many other topics, including pre-employment testing, interviewing techniques, and personnel counseling. Various studies continued for over 10 years, ending just as World War II was beginning. The major contribution of the Hawthorne studies was to document the fact that a worker's behavior was influenced not only by the physical setting, but also by social factors in the workplace. That is, the workplace is a social system as well as a system for producing goods and services.

Try This Yourself

You can easily do a mini study on the Hawthorne effect. Choose a good friend—let's say your friend is a male—and (without his knowledge) observe him studying or watching television for about five minutes. Write down in detail what he is doing. Document how many times he looks up from his book, changes channels on the television, and so on.

At the end of five minutes, tell him you need to observe his behavior for five minutes as part of a psychology assignment. Now record the same behaviors. Does his behavior change? Does he look up from his studies more often? Less often? Does he do more or less "channel surfing" while watching television? If his behavior changes, you will have observed the *Hawthorne effect.* ■

Modern Times: Expanding the Role of I/O Psychology

By the beginning of World War II, I/O psychology had begun to mature. Many companies now had personnel offices that routinely tested and placed employees. They also implemented scientifically designed worker-training programs to improve productivity. Researchers were beginning to conduct studies in human factors psychology, as machines in the workplace became more complicated.

Many of these advances were applied to the war effort. The first contribution from I/O psychology was the development of the *Army General Classification Test* (AGCT). The AGCT made it possible to classify new recruits into a few broad categories based on their ability to learn the duties and responsibilities of a soldier. Psychologists also helped develop situational stress tests to select and train candidates for military intelligence units (spies). In addition, they developed tests for selecting aircraft pilots and training them more rapidly and safely.

Human factors psychology also contributed greatly to the operational safety of airplanes by designing better control panels. For example, at the beginning of the war many planes and pilots were lost because, when preparing for landing, pilots tended to mistake the landing gear control for the wing flap control. Consequently, pilots tried to land planes with the wheels up or with the wing flaps in the wrong position, providing insufficient lift.

The human factors solution to this problem was simple: design the controls to correspond to their function. Consequently, they redesigned the landing gear controls to look and feel like wheels, and they redesigned the wing flap controls to look and feel like a wing. The result: greatly reduced landing errors! These World War II airplane design changes are still used on contemporary aircraft.

Early I/O psychology was, in effect, industrial psychology, focusing on worker efficiency and productivity. During World War II, however, personnel psychology had emerged as a major subspecialty, and many researchers began to shift their attention from the manufacturing floor to the executive management offices. They thereby created organizational psychology and put the "O" in I/O psychology. Organizational psychologists studied companies with the goal of improving administration and productivity.

The civil rights movement of the late 1950s and early 1960s culminated in the Civil Rights Act of 1964. Among other things, it mandated the creation of employment tests, training programs, and recruitment programs that were fair to all job applicants regardless of ethnicity, religion, or gender. Tests given to screen job appli-

This photograph of a World War II bomber cockpit shows how human factors psychologists made flying safer and easier. Notice how the controls for the landing gear are designed to look and feel like the function they perform. The landing gear controls are round like a wheel (as shown in box).

cants had to be valid predictors of job performance. For example, general IQ tests could no longer be used to screen applicants at the Telephone Company for the job of directory assistance operator; instead, the Telephone Company might administer a spelling and reading comprehension test.

The Civil Rights Act of 1964 also forced a radical change in corporate recruitment and hiring policies that resulted in opening many previously unobtainable jobs to ethnic minority and women job applicants. Hence, I/O psychology was now responsible not only to corporate management, but to the federal government as well.

In the next section we will introduce you to human factors psychology in which I/O psychologists study how to make humans and machines work together.

CHECK AND REVIEW

Development of I/O Psychology

Industrial/organizational (I/O) psychology is the study of how individual behavior affects and is affected by the physical environment and the organizational structure of the workplace. Major founding figures were Walter Dill Scott, Fredrick W. Taylor, and Hugo Munsterberg.

The personnel needs of World War I gave the I/O field respectability. Based on newly developed group IQ tests, Walter Dill Scott developed a program to place recruits in jobs that suited their abilities.

Among important I/O research findings during this period was a phenomenon termed the Hawthorne effect, when people change their behavior because of the novelty of a research situation or because they know that they are being observed.

World War II led to scientifically designed worker training programs to improve productivity for the war effort. After the war, many I/O psychologists turned their attention from the manufacturing floor to the executive management offices, thereby creating organizational psychology.

The Civil Rights Act of 1964 required I/O psychology to create employment tests, training programs, and recruitment programs that were fair to all job applicants regardless of ethnicity, religion, age, or gender.

QUESTIONS

1. Match the founders of I/O psychology (Scott, Taylor, Munsterberg) with their major contribution:
    (a) Pioneered methods leading to improved personnel selection and training.
    (b) Developed principles companies could use to increase worker efficiency and company profit.
    (c) First to apply psychological principles to advertising

2. Hui-Ching is a consultant who is hired by a large law firm to study worker motivation and job satisfaction. Hui-Ching is part of which branch of I/O psychology? (a) consulting; (b) organizational; (c) personnel; (d) human factors.

3. The _____ occurs when a research participant changes his or her behaviors because they know they are being observed. (a) halo effect; (b) observational bias; (c) Hawthorne effect; (d) spectator bias.

4. How did the Civil Rights Act of 1964 influence I/O psychology?

Answers to Questions can be found in Appendix B.

HUMAN FACTORS PSYCHOLOGY

How has I/O psychology evolved from the early 1900s to the present day?

Human Factors Psychology
The branch of I/O psychology that studies ways to improve the design and function of machines and the work environment to better meet the needs of human users.

An automatic teller machine (ATM) is obviously more complicated than a videocassette recorder (VCR). However, most people find it much easier to get $20 out of their local ATM than to program their VCR to record "Ally McBeal" on Monday night. Why is the more complicated machine easier to use? At least part of the answer is in human factors.

Human factors psychology is the branch of I/O psychology that studies ways to improve the design and function of machines and the work environment to better meet the needs of human users. Thousands of hours of human factors research went into making your ATM easy to use. To get your money, all you need is a plastic card, a personal identification number, and the ability to read a few simple commands. To program your VCR, however, you must read a 20-page booklet. In this case, human factors research has been largely ignored.

The Human–Machine System: How to Get People and Machines to Mix

Human–Machine System
An arrangement of people and machines, tools, and other devices that produce a product or service.

Displays
Devices such as gauges and video monitors that form the machine output in the human—machine system.

Controls
Devices such as wheels, levers, and knobs that are the input for the machine in the human–machine system.

The problem with machines is that ordinary people run them. It is not difficult for an engineer to design a machine that functions efficiently by itself or when operated by an engineer. The difficulty arises when someone other than an engineer and the machine must work together as one unit to become a *human–machine system* (Oborne, 1995). A **human–machine system** is an arrangement of people and machines, tools, and other devices that produce a product or service. The basic components of the human–machine system are illustrated in Figure 17.2.

As Figure 17.2 shows, the machine side of the system consists of **displays** (the machine output) and **controls** (the machine input). The human side of the system consists of sensory functions (the human input), cognitive functions, and motor functions (the human output). The machine's displays provide the sensory input for the human, and the human's motor responses provide the control input for the machine.

Why is it so much easier to use an ATM machine than to program your VCR? The answer comes from human factors research.

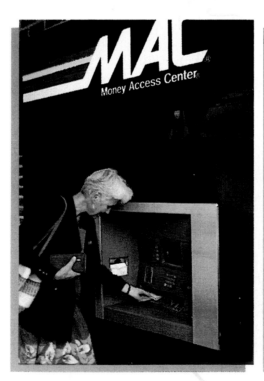
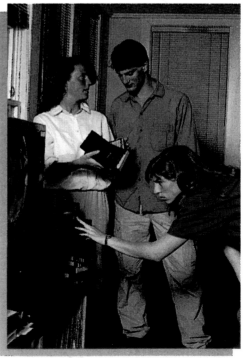

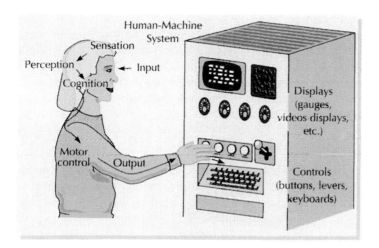

Human-Machine
System

Sensation

Perception ← Input

Cognition

Motor
control   Output

Displays
(gauges,
videos displays,
etc.)

Controls
(buttons, levers,
keyboards)

Figure 17.2 ***The human–machine system.*** In a human–machine system, a human and machine work as a unit to produce a product or service. The machine displays, such as gauges and video monitors, output information about the status of the machine to the sensory receptors of the human, which serve as the input for the human part of the system. Sensory information from the eyes or other sensory organs is processed by the brain of the human, and adjustments to the machine are communicated to the machine controls via the human's muscles and voice commands.

It is an interdependent system, where neither the human nor the machine can produce the product or service without the other.

Once the machine is running, the human needs the display data from the machine to determine whether corrections need to be made, and the machine needs the human to input the necessary corrections via the controls. In this way, machines can do the tedious precision tasks that are difficult for humans, and humans can do the cognitive tasks involving judgments and corrections that are impossible for the machine to do.

A driver and automobile are a good example of a human–machine system. The driver has the cognitive ability to guide the car to its intended destination, and the automobile has the power to move the driver at relatively great speeds over large distances. When you are driving, you and the car act as one unit, a human–machine system. You use your sensory systems to collect and monitor information about the operation of the machine. You read the speedometer, the tachometer, and other gauges; you listen and feel for (hopefully!) normal functioning of the engine, body, and tires; and you even use your sense of smell if a strange odor suggests a problem. Using this varied input, you adjust the machine by pressing harder on the accelerator, adding oil, or stopping to change a flat tire. Once in a while, the human–machine system fails to perform properly—the car runs out of gas, or you step on the accelerator instead of the brake pedal.

Human factors psychologists help design the controls and displays in automobiles.

Designers can make the human–machine system more reliable in two ways: They can better train the people using it, or they can modify the machine. Because modifying the machine is easier than modifying people (it is much easier to make a display larger than to make a person's vision more acute), human factors psychology generally focuses on improving the design of the controls and displays on machines. Improving the design of a machine translates to matching its displays and controls to human sensory and motor skills.

Displays: How the Machine Talks to You

Displays providing data about the machine's operation form the input for the human side of the human–machine system. Or, to put it simply, the machine talks to you through its displays; video monitors, gauges, bells, and blinking lights. A good display design must recognize how people sense and perceive their world, as well as how people think. Therefore, a human factors psychologist must have a thorough knowledge of human sensation, perception, and cognition.

Failure to understand the limits of human sensory capabilities can have disastrous results (Aberg and Rimmoe, 1998; Shappell and Wiegmann, 1997). If the beeping sound accompanying the lowering of a heavy motor cannot be heard above background noise, a dangerous accident might occur on the automotive assembly line. If a gauge has lettering that is too small to read, a machine could overheat, requiring costly repairs. If a warning light does not get the machine operator's attention, the nuclear reactor core could be damaged.

Suppose you are hired to monitor several machines in a factory. Your supervisor explains that the machines' display panel was designed so that an uninterrupted line of green lights indicates normal operation. If any component malfunctions, its corresponding light on the display panel turns red. When you notice a red light, you are told to refer to the manual and make the indicated adjustments to bring the machine back into proper working order.

But, you tell the supervisor, you are red/green color defective and cannot tell the difference between red and green lights. She smiles and tells you not to worry: Human factors psychologists helped design these machines. Because they were aware of color deficiencies, they made sure that the red warning lights would blink instead of remaining lit like the green lights, so that any sighted person would be sure to detect a malfunction. (Of course, the blink rate of the light must not be too slow or too fast. But that is a different perceptual/human factors problem.)

Control panels of large complicated machines, such as this automated can maker, use color-coded lights, dials, gauges, and displays to lessen the chance for human error.

In addition to knowing about human sensory abilities, human factors psychologists also need to be aware of the cognitive abilities and limits of the people who will be part of the human–machine system (Reinach et al., 1997; Sterns and Camp, 1998). Suppose you want to design a display that indicates speed of a car to the driver. You have the three options displayed in Figure 17.3. The first option, Figure 17.3a, is a typical circular speedometer scaled in one-mile-per-hour increments. The second option, a digital speedometer, also gives the reading in one-mile per hour increments (see Figure 17.3b). The third option, Figure 17.3c, is a continually changing bar graph that shows changes in increments of one mile per hour. Which one of these speedometers can be most quickly and accurately read by a typical driver? If you picked Figure 17.3b, you were right. People can read the exact speed more quickly and more accurately off a digital display than any other type.

But is speed the only information a speedometer is designed to display to a driver? The answer is no. Speedometers also give information about acceleration, the rate of change in speed. If you had to pick the speedometer that best indicates acceleration, you should choose the circular speedometer, Figure 17.3a because it takes very little cognitive processing to determine the direction of the needle's movement. Each of these types of speedometers has been tested in actual automobiles, but as human factors psychologists have found, the circular display is still the best design for relaying both speed and acceleration of the automobile.

Controls: How You Talk to the Machine

When someone decides to change a machine's functioning, they must input instructions via the machine controls. These controls can be as simple as a dial, a wheel, or a switch, or as complicated as a keyboard. The design of any control device must reflect the capabilities of both machine and human. If the machine demands input beyond the cognitive or motor abilities of the human, the system will fail or function at a suboptimal level. Human factors psychologists study variables like workers' strength, endurance, speed, and accuracy of movement.

Let's explore the topic of accuracy of movement. When you reach for a can of soda, you usually pick it up with no trouble. But once in a while, you bump and spill it. This is an example of a motor control error, an error everyone makes at one time or another—even Kobe Bryant misses a slam-dunk once in a while. Missing a shot in basketball is not life threatening, however. Hitting the wrong pedal in your car, could be.

As mentioned in the opening section, the most probable cause of unintended acceleration accidents was driver error. The driver, thinking he or she is stepping on the brake pedal, actually slams on the accelerator. Mark Vernoy and George Tomerlin (1989, 1990) investigated pedal errors in various types of cars using hundreds of licensed drivers as participants. They asked drivers to sit in cars, shift the transmission into park, reverse, or drive, step on the gas pedal, and step on the brake pedal. At an unexpected point in the experiment, participants were commanded to: "Stop! Step on the brake!"

The movement and placement of the participant's feet during this surprise braking were videotaped and later analyzed for errors. On several trials, participants failed to hit the brake, and hit the accelerator pedal instead. Thus, Vernoy and Tomerlin documented the role of human error in these instances of unintended acceleration. Because it is impossible to train a driver to be totally free from this type of pedal error, carmakers could modify the automobile controls to either reduce or eliminate this error.

Why not try to place the pedals as far apart as possible in order to minimize confusion between the brake and the gas? This is a possible solution, except increasing the distance between the pedals also increases the time needed to move the foot from the gas pedal to the brake. At 60 miles per hour, a delay of one-tenth of a second causes the car to travel an additional 8.8 feet before the brake is applied. Pedals that are farther apart might decrease pedal errors, but the overall number and severity of accidents might increase because the cars would take longer to stop.

Figure 17.3   Three different types of automobile speedometers. Which of these would be the easiest to read if you wanted to know only the speed of the automobile? Which of these would be the best if you wanted to know both the speed and acceleration of the automobile?

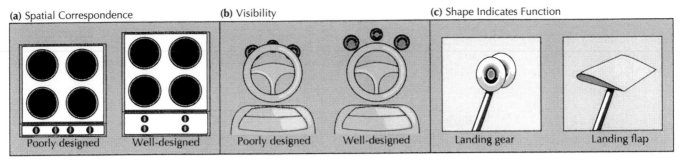

(a) Spatial Correspondence **(b)** Visibility **(c)** Shape Indicates Function

Poorly designed | Well-designed | Poorly designed | Well-designed | Landing gear | Landing flap

Figure 17.4 *Human factors design and the real world.* Well-designed appliances and machinery are easily understood and operated. (a) The controls for stovetops should be arranged in a pattern that corresponds to the placement of the burners. (b) In an automobile, gauges for fuel, oil, and speed should be easily visible to the driver. (c) Controls and knobs are easier and safer to use if their shape corresponds to their function.

What is the solution? Nearly all cases of severe unintended acceleration happen when people are *backing up* in a new or relatively unfamiliar car. If drivers first had to brake to unlock the transmission before they could shift into reverse, they would be less likely to mistake the brake pedal for the accelerator (Vernoy and Tomerlin, 1989). Such a simple correction would also have prevented the accident described in our chapter opener.

Figure 17.4 offers additional examples showing how a well-designed human–machine system can accomplish its task quickly, accurately, and safely.

 CHECK AND REVIEW

Human Factors Psychology

Human factors psychology is a branch of I/O psychology that studies ways to improve the design and function of machines and the work environment to better meet the needs of human users.

Researchers consider humans and the machines they use a human–machine system, an arrangement of people and machines, tools, and other devices that produce a product or service. The human side of the system consists of sensory functions (input) and cognitive and motor functions (output); the machine side consists of displays (output) and controls (input)

QUESTIONS

1. The improvement of the design and function of machines and the work environment to meet the needs of human users is studied by _____ psychology. (a) personnel; (b) human factors; (c) organizational; (d) technology.

2. When the human's motor responses provide the control input, while the machine's displays provide the sensory input, this is an example of _____.

3. What is the difference between a display and a control?

4. The keys of the first manual typewriters were not arranged alphabetically, but in a pattern that prevented fast typists from jamming the keys. This is an example of a good _____. (a) human-machine system; (b) operator/machine team; (c) man versus machine problem; (d) human factors analysis.

Answers to Questions can be found in Appendix B.

PERSONNEL PSYCHOLOGY

At the beginning of this chapter, we said that with the possible exception of sleeping, a person spends more time at work than at any other single activity. Think about that again: In your lifetime, you will spend at least twice as much time at work as you will with your friends and family. In other words, the quality of your life is directly related to the satisfaction you receive from your work. The importance of your career choice cannot be overestimated. And just as you need a job that maximizes your skills and satisfaction, business and industry need employees who have the skills and motivation to maximize productivity.

Personnel psychology plays an important role in locating the "right person for the right job" (Smith and Sutherland, 1996). In addition to (1) recruitment and selection, personnel psychologists also become involved in (2) employee training, and (3) developing objective criteria for evaluating employee performance. In this section, we will discuss each of these three elements. We will also explore the special problem of sexual harassment.

Recruitment and Selection: Finding the Right Person for the Right Job

Personnel recruitment and selection begins with **job analysis,** a detailed description of the skills, knowledge, and activities required by a particular job (Borman et al., 1997). Let's apply this definition to something that may be of interest to you as a student — the work of college instructors. They are primarily responsible for education and research, while administration (president, deans, etc.) and support staff (office personnel, custodians, directors) assume responsibility for running the college (funding, buildings, and maintenance).

While the knowledge, skills, and abilities necessary to perform as a successful college instructor vary according to academic discipline (psychology, math, physical education, etc.), all instructors share similar tasks: Teaching assigned classes, maintaining required office hours, preparing and grading exams and papers, attending department meetings, and serving on college committees. In addition, many colleges and universities expect professors to conduct research and to publish in professional journals.

If a college wanted to hire a new college instructor, they would begin with a job analysis like this, followed by the selection of a large, field of candidates. The next step — for any job — is to choose the one most qualified candidate. The number of candidates may be narrowed through applications, questionnaires, interviews, observations, standardized psychological tests, knowledge and skills tests, performance tests, and *biodata* (detailed biographical information).

Of all the selection devices, the interview continues to be the most popular — and to carry the most weight (Dipboye, 1992). Interviews can be *structured* or *unstructured*. Structured interviews involve a set of preplanned questions that are asked of every person who is interviewed and a standardized rating of the applicant's qualifications. This reduces several biases associated with unstructured interviews, which tend to be casual, short, and made up of random questions. As expected, structured interviews are much better predictors than unstructured interviews (Campion et al., 1999; Clarke et al., 1998; Rogers et al., 1997).

A personal interview involves questioning job applicants to learn their qualifications and to get an impression of their personalities (Borman et al., 1997). If you perform poorly at this stage, you are not likely to be hired, regardless of your experience, test scores, or letters of recommendation. Therefore, let's spend some time talking about interviewing.

If you are asked to come in for an interview, you can expect a face-to-face meeting with one or more interviewers. They may be using the interview as an alternative or adjunct to the application form. Questions are designed to measure your attitudes

Why is personnel psychology important?

Personnel Psychology
The branch of I/O psychology involved with recruiting, selecting, training, and evaluating workers.

Job Analysis
A detailed description of the skills, knowledge, and activities required by a particular job.

Table 17.1	WHY MOST PEOPLE HATE BEING INTERVIEWED
Problems	
"First date" syndrome	In initial meetings with important, but unstated, outcomes both parties behave with artificial care and skill.
Nervousness	Applicants know they are being evaluated and compared to others, and they are typically in a "one-down" position (they need what the employer has to give). Thus, most interviewees are tense and anxious.
Subjectivity	When one person meets another, impressions tend to be formed immediately—sometimes due to nothing more than clothes or facial appearance. These first impressions are often resistant to change.

Source: Auerbach, 1996.

("Did you like your last job?" "Do you prefer working in groups or alone?"), job experiences ("What did you do in your last job?"), and personal background ("What was your college major?"). Interviewers also use this face-to-face meeting to assess your communication and interpersonal skills. Successful applicants are typically friendly (but not overly so), eager (but not desperate), and assertive (but not aggressive).

Is interviewing really that complicated? I'm getting nervous just reading about this. Most interviewees tend to be anxious, and that is perfectly normal (Table 17.1). But there are also reasons to look forward to interviews. First, interviews allow for longer and more detailed answers than application forms, and most people find it easier to talk than to write. In addition, both parties have the opportunity to ask questions and to clarify exactly what the job requires. In effect, you are interviewing the company as much as it is interviewing you.

Try This Yourself

If you would like to improve your interviewing skills, try the following:

1. *Research* Before your interview, research the company, employer, supervisors, and all available positions. The information you gather can be invaluable in helping you respond to interview questions. Also, simply knowing the history and size of the company will show the interviewer that you are serious about your job search. Research can also help you decide if you really want to work for this company.

2. *Role playing* Ask someone to help you practice playing both interviewer and interviewee. Encourage honest feedback about verbal and nonverbal habits that may affect your interview. For example, do you nervously jiggle your feet or avoid eye contact? Also, brainstorm ahead of time about potential questions and good responses.

3. *Personality* Interviewers generally like friendly, eager, and assertive applicants. These are basic personality traits you've undoubtedly used before, when meeting new friends or on a first date, for example. Recognizing you've used these skills in the past, may help you relax in the interview and "be yourself."

(On the other side, if you become an interviewer, you can make the interview process more comfortable—and therefore more productive—in several ways. Most important, recognize that the applicant is tense. Begin by introducing yourself. Be relaxed and friendly, and briefly describe what the interview will be like. Tell how long it will take and what topics will be discussed. Finally, encourage the interviewee to ask questions.)

Employee Training: Objectives and Methods

After applicants are tested and interviewed and the best candidate is hired, the personnel psychologist helps train the new employee. Research shows training not only provides workers with appropriate skills for the assigned job, it also reduces frustration and stress (Aamodt, 1999; Saal and Knight, 1988).

Training typically begins with some form of *orientation*. Just as you may have had a college orientation designed to introduce the educational organization, new employees are usually given either a formal or informal introduction to the business setting. Pay close attention. The orientation is designed to "clue in" new employees. You are being taught the facts of organizational structure and operations as well as appropriate attitudes and allegiances.

Every organization has its shared pattern of thought and action, an **organizational culture.** This culture arises from each group's history and involves group identity, policies, and rituals. For example, organizations typically develop characteristic attitudes toward diversity, creativity, attention to detail, team versus individual orientation, and stability versus innovation (Hurley and Hult, 1998; Miller, 1998; Tesluk et al., 1997; Wilpert, 1995). Fitting into an organization means fitting into its culture.

Organizational Culture
A group's shared pattern of thought and action; a common perception held by the organization's members.

Personnel psychologists are also involved with training and upgrading skills for new and existing employees. Skill training can be technical and highly job specific. You might be taught how to sell or service the company's product, or how to operate the communication system and other machines. General training may also be offered for interpersonal skills, including effective listening, communication, and how to be a "team player."

One of the fastest growing areas of interpersonal skill development is diversity training, learning to work with individuals from various cultural backgrounds (Aamodt, 1999; Haggerty, 1993). Even the smallest of U.S. businesses may now compete globally and employees and managers need to adjust their style to conduct business all over the world.

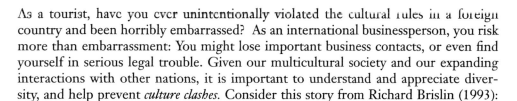

Gender and Cultural Diversity

WHAT HAPPENS TO BUSINESS WHEN CULTURES CLASH?

As a tourist, have you ever unintentionally violated the cultural rules in a foreign country and been horribly embarrassed? As an international businessperson, you risk more than embarrassment: You might lose important business contacts, or even find yourself in serious legal trouble. Given our multicultural society and our expanding interactions with other nations, it is important to understand and appreciate diversity, and help prevent *culture clashes*. Consider this story from Richard Brislin (1993):

> Kiyoshi, a Japanese executive, was visiting an automobile plant in the American Midwest to explore a possible joint venture in manufacturing a new model of car. Hank, an executive at the plant, invited Kiyoshi and his wife to dinner at his house. They arrived at the agreed upon time of 6:00 P.M. and the group enjoyed pleasant conversation over soft drinks ("No one drinks hard liquor any more!" Hank thought). Dinner was served at 7:00 P.M. and dessert at about 8:15 P.M. After finishing their dessert, Kiyoshi and his wife quickly thanked Hank and then quickly left. Hank thought something was wrong, either with himself or with Kiyoshi's manners. What went wrong? Why did Kiyoshi and his wife leave so quickly? (p. 98)

You may be surprised to see how differing cultural expectations help explain this awkward and confusing *culture clash*. The norms in Hank's culture require guests to engage in pleasant conversation after dessert, and if people leave early it is consid-

Table 17.2   DOING BUSINESS IN CANADA

Canadian V-for-Victory gesture

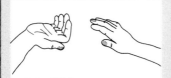

Canadian beckoning and waving gestures

Appointments

French-speaking areas of Canada may be more casual about time, but, as a foreigner, it is always good manners to be prompt. While business lunches are popular in Canada, dinners have traditionally been social occasions—if business is discussed at all, it is at the end of the meal. This is changing, but to be safe, allow your Canadian counterpart to bring up business first.

Negotiating

Although styles are similar, many Canadians think U.S. business people "hype" their products. Never inflate your product's benefits. English and French are the official languages, but in Quebec there are very stringent rules—French is the only legal language in which to conduct business.

Gestures

To beckon someone wave all the fingers in a scooping motion with the palm facing up. To wave good-bye, move your entire hand, facing outward. The "V-for-victory" sign is done with the palm facing out—it may be taken as an insult when done with the palm inward.

Gifts

Business gifts should be modest—Canadians tend to frown on ostentation. When visiting a home, it is customary to take flowers, candy, or liquor.
French–Canadian homes may be divided into "public" rooms that visitors may enter and "private" rooms where visitors may enter only when asked. The kitchen is often a private room—do not enter unless asked.

Source: Adapted from *Kiss, Bow, or Shake Hands* by T. Morrison, W. A. Conaway, and G. A. Borden, 1994. Adams Media Corp.

ered an insult. However, in Kiyoshi and his wife's culture, remaining after dinner is a sign that you are still hungry, and the host would be expected to offer more food! If you think differences exist mainly between Eastern and Western cultures, see Table 17.2, which outlines small, subtle differences between very similar nations, the United States and Canada.

While some clashes between cultures are inevitable, there are ways to minimize misunderstandings (adapted from Brislin, 1993, Dresser, 1996):

1. *Examine your thought processes*   Because norms are generally covert and unexamined, it is easy to mistakenly assume that our rules for conducting business or social interactions are the same as others'. One way to prevent misunderstandings like Hank and Kiyoshi's, is to become aware of your own cultural rules, and then learn the norms of your business client's country.

2. *Adjust your behaviors to match the other culture*   If you are doing business in Quebec, for example, use French in your transactions or ask for a French-speaking assistant to translate for you. At the least, apologize for not knowing the official language. Adjusting your behavior demonstrates that you recognize diversity and respect the other person's culture. Even within the United States, it can be helpful to adjust your behavior. For example, many Native Americans prefer more silence in their communications than Anglo Americans, who usually interpret silence as a sign that interactions are not going well. An Anglo American who understands this cultural difference will refrain from rushing to fill any silence when doing business with a Native American.

3. *Recognize that culture clashes are emotionally stressful*   When people interact with unfamiliar people in unfamiliar circumstances, stress is inevitable. It is frustrating not to be able to easily communicate with others and to find that familiar ways of behaving do not work in other cultures. For example, in the United States during informal entertaining, dinner guests often gather in the kitchen while the host finishes preparing the food. After dinner, guests often help clear the table and perhaps even put leftovers in the refrigerator. In French-Canadian homes, however, the kitchen is generally considered a "private" room that guests should not enter. Simply recognizing that some culture clashes are inevitable, may help reduce your stress.

CHECK AND REVIEW

Recruiting, Selecting, and Training Employees

Personnel psychology involves recruiting, selecting, training, and evaluating workers. Recruitment begins with a job analysis, which is a detailed description of skills, knowledge, and activities required in a particular job. Interviews are the most popular method of choosing the most qualified candidate. Structured interviews are better predictors of future job performance than unstructured interviews.

Prepare for an interview by doing research on the company, role playing with a friend, and emphasizing desirable personality traits.

Employee training typically begins with an orientation program. One of the major unstated goals of orientation is transmitting the organizational culture—the group's shared pattern of thought and action.

QUESTIONS

1. The branch of I/O psychology involved with recruiting, selecting, training, and evaluating workers is known as _____psychology. (a) human factors; (b) engineering; (c) social; (d) personnel.

2. When choosing a candidate for a job, the _____ is the most popular and most heavily weighted of all selection devices.

3. What are the three basic personality traits that most appeal to interviewers?

4. A group's shared pattern of thought and action is known as _____. (a) the organizational culture; (b) personality/job-fit theory; (c) the Hawthorne effect; (d) the organizational structure.

Answers to Questions can be found in Appendix B.

Evaluating Workers: Measuring Job Performance

After an employee has been in a job for awhile, his or her performance is then evaluated. **Performance evaluation** is the formal procedure an organization uses to assess the multidimensional job performance of employees (Arvey and Murphy, 1998). Organizations use performance evaluations for a number of purposes. One of the most important is providing feedback to the employee on how the organization views his or her performance. Employees need to know when they are doing well (so they can keep on doing well), and when they are not (so they can change). Research shows that employees fare better when their work is evaluated, when reinforcers are closely related to job performance, and when criticism is delivered constructively (Baron, 1990; Locke and Latham, 1990).

Performance Evaluation
The formal procedure used by an organization to assess job performance of employees.

Performance evaluations are also useful for identifying training and development needs. Does the employee need upgrading of skills or retraining? In addition, management uses performance evaluations for decisions on promotions, transfers, and termination.

A performance evaluation may be *objective* or *subjective*. Objective measures include such things as the number of sales for a salesperson or the number of publications for a college instructor. Many jobs (like management and support services), however, do not have an easily identifiable and objective product, and in some cases objective measures may not be appropriate. For example, how do you identify the *product* of a college instructor? The effect of one college instructor on any one student is difficult to measure objectively. Furthermore, benefits from a college instructor or a college degree are sometimes years away.

Subjective measures avoid some of these problems (but introduce others, as you will shortly see). Subjective ratings by supervisors or others who are familiar with the employee's job performance are the most common form of performance evaluation. Despite their popularity, subjective methods suffer from serious rater biases and other human errors (Arvey and Murphy, 1998). One of the most widely researched problems is the tendency to rate individuals either too high or too low based on one outstanding trait, the **halo effect.** If a person is rated "exceptional" in one area, he or she tends to be rated "exceptional" in all areas. The same thing occurs when someone is rated "poor" in one area.

The halo effect is a significant problem. If a supervisor happens to value friendliness, will he or she overrate an employee who smiles a lot? Also, how can we differentiate between what might be termed a *legitimate* halo—an employee who *does* perform well on all dimensions—and bias caused by the undue influence of one characteristic? Preventing and minimizing the halo effect is a major research topic in personnel psychology (Larose and Standing, 1998; Murphy, Jako, and Anhalt, 1993; Solomonson and Lance, 1997).

To offset problems with the halo effect and other evaluation biases, some organizations have recently turned to "360-degree" performance measures, which include evaluations from supervisors, peers, subordinates, and even customers. These multisource measures are useful for both feedback and personnel decisions (Arvey and Murphy, 1998).

Organizations may also use specially designed rating scales, where the supervisor evaluates an employee in certain critical areas by assigning a numerical rating. As Figure 17.5 shows, your job as student could be evaluated with this type of rating

Halo Effect
The tendency to rate individuals either too high or too low based on one outstanding trait. The halo effect is a characteristic defect in rating scales.

"He's not a perfect boss, but he *does* give you plenty of feedback."

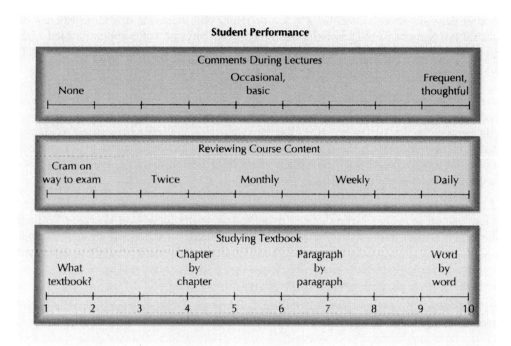

Figure 11.5 A possible rating scale for students. How would you score on this rating scale? Would you like this kind of performance evaluation or do you prefer the traditional rating scale, known as "grades"?

scale. The idea is that raters will be more accurate if they focus on specific *behaviors* rather than *traits*, such as friendliness.

Although rating scales are helpful, they also have drawbacks. As you know, some college instructors can be hard graders, while others may be easy. Supervisors in the work world can be similarly tough or lenient raters. In addition, research shows that supervisors like employees who perform well (Robbins and DeNisi, 1994), and that they do, in fact, give higher ratings to employees they like (Ferris et al., 1994).

Sexual Harassment: An Abuse of Power

What happens to the evaluation process when a supervisor says, "Let's go to the Holiday Inn and negotiate your raise"? Historically, personnel psychologists have been involved with recruitment and selection, training, and evaluation of workers; but today, they are also involved with problems of sexual harassment. The legal definition of **sexual harassment** is unwelcome sexual advances, requests for sexual favors, and other unwelcome verbal or physical conduct of a sexual nature.

A federal study defined three levels of sexual harassment: *less severe* (e.g., sexual teasing, suggestive gestures, sexual remarks), *severe* (e.g., pressure for dates or sexual favors, touching, letters, telephone calls), and *criminal* (sexual assault, attempted rape, and rape). The point is that any pattern of unwelcome sexual behavior may constitute sexual harassment (Egler, 1995). The suggestion to negotiate a raise at a motel was part of an actual court case, and the court ruled that this, and similar behavior, was sexual harassment. The plaintiff was awarded significant damages (Harris v. Forklift Systems, 1993; cited in Aamodt, 1999).

Sexual Harassment
Unwelcome sexual advances, requests for sexual favors, and other unwelcome verbal or physical conduct of a sexual nature.

Myths about Sexual Harassment

There are at least three major misconceptions about sexual harassment.

1. "It's a minor problem." Law Professor Anita Hill's charge that Supreme Court Justice Clarence Thomas sexually harassed her, the U.S. Navy's Tailhook convention, and the Army's Aberdeen scandal all brought national attention to the issue of sexual harassment (Healy, 1998; Shenon, 1997). The most recent case to make the headlines was Paula Jones' sexual harassment lawsuit against President Clinton. Despite such high profile cases, most people still underestimate the prevalence of occupational

Paula Jones's suit against President Clinton brought renewed debate and attention to the topic of sexual harassment.

sexual harassment and consider it a minor issue. One measure of the prevalence of sexual harassment in the United States may be the number of complaints filed with the EEOC (Equal Employment Opportunity Commission), which rose from 6,000 in 1990 to 15,300 in 1996 (Kaufman, 1997).

In addition to these business settings, sexual harassment also seems to be a major problem in the academic world. A recent survey of more than 1,000 Canadian female students reported that over 23 percent had experienced at least one episode of sexual harassment in the last six months (Bagley et al., 1997). Power is misused to coerce students into sexual acts. Students comply with the perpetrator's demands out of fear of academic repercussions, a need for a letter of recommendation, or desire for a research or work opportunity (Riger, 1991).

2. "It's overreported." Contrary to misperceptions that charges of sexual harassment are often made for the slightest provocation, a survey by The Working Women United Institute found that when women were harassed 75 percent ignored the harassment. Only 18 percent reported the harassment! Those who did not complain believed nothing would be done. They also worried that they might be blamed and would suffer negative repercussions.

3. "It's an expression of sexual desire." While the harasser *may* sometimes be attracted to the victim, the harassment is primarily an assertion and abuse of power (Cleveland and Kerst, 1993). Because of the misperception of sexual desire, older or less attractive women who complain of sexual harassment are often ignored or ridiculed ("Don't flatter yourself"). On the other hand, when the victim is young and attractive she is accused of "inviting" a sexual approach. Like other victims of sexual abuse, those who are harassed are often accused of "asking for it."

Sexual harassment is a serious issue. Victims often face severe financial difficulties, such as unemployment, demotion, or loss of promotions if they resist the harassment. On a psychological level, victims also suffer various physical and psychological effects, including nervousness, loss of motivation, sleeplessness, guilt, shame, anger, depression, and helplessness (Charney and Russell, 1994; Rhode, 1997).

Harassment also affects business and academic institutions. It causes stress, poor work or academic performance, absenteeism, and high turnover. The cost of sexual harassment averages at least $6 million a year for a Fortune 500 company (Rhode, 1997).

Recent court cases awarding large sums of money to victims have increased the cost of sexual harassment. Title VII of the 1964 Civil Rights Act imposes liability on companies for sexual harassment and the U.S. Department of Education guidelines can deny federal funds to schools that do not take measures to remedy the situation (Scher, 1997).

Preventing Sexual Harassment

There are several, specific steps that can be taken to reduce the likelihood of sexual harassment and an organization's potential legal liability:

1. All complaints, no matter how trivial or farfetched they appear, must be investigated.

2. Complaints must be kept confidential to protect both the accused and the complainant.

3. Action must be taken to protect the complainant from possible retaliation by the accused.

4. Both the accused and complainant must be given due process, and results of the investigation must be communicated in writing to both parties.

5. The severity of any punishment must match the severity of the violation.

(*Based on:* Bloch, 1995; and Robinson et al., 1993)

What can the victim or target of sexual harassment do to stop the abuse?   Here are several suggestions (Crooks and Baur, 1999):

1. If a professor or an employer harasses you, make your objections clear. A firm "no" is an important first step.

2. Discuss the problem with fellow students or employees. Identifying other victims bolsters your case and provides social and emotional support

3. If the problem continues, keep a detailed record (noting times, dates, locations, possible witnesses, and precisely what was said or done). In addition, contact authorities on the campus or at work. You might begin by consulting another professor or supervisor, whom you trust, to help you determine the appropriate officials and channels for complaints.

4. If the harassment continues and your grievances are not acted upon, you may want to contact your state's civil rights commission and file a formal grievance. Current affirmative action regulations protect those who file harassment complaints from instructor retaliation and from job demotion or firing.

CHECK AND REVIEW

Evaluating Workers, Sexual Harassment

Performance evaluation is the formal procedure an organization uses to assess the job performance of employees. Evaluations can be objective or subjective.

The subjective method is the most popular, but the halo effect (the tendency to rate individuals too high or too low based on one outstanding trait) can create a major problem. To overcome the halo effect, some organizations use "360-degree" multisource measures and special rating scales.

Sexual harassment involves sexual advances, requests for sexual favors, and other unwelcome verbal or physical conduct of a sexual nature. Most sexual harassment is an assertion or abuse of power, not an expression of sexual desire. Victims of sexual harassment often suffer financial losses and psychological difficulties.

QUESTIONS

1. The formal procedure an organization uses to assess the job performance of employees is known as _____. (a) job analysis; (b) the Hawthorne effect; (c) performance evaluation; (d) knowledge and skills evaluation.

2. What are the two major functions of performance evaluations?

3. What is the halo effect?

4. Sexual harassment is primarily _____ and not an expression of sexual desire.

Answers to Questions can be found in Appendix B.

ORGANIZATIONAL PSYCHOLOGY

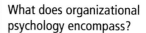

What does organizational psychology encompass?

When it comes to work, most people are social animals—they generally prefer to work with others. **Organizational psychologists** are interested in how interpersonal relations in the work setting affect productivity. In this section, we discuss three topics of special interest to organizational psychologists: managerial style, worker motivation, and job satisfaction.

Organizational Psychology
The branch of I/O psychology interested in how interpersonal relations in the work setting affect productivity. Topics of interest include managerial style, worker motivation, and job satisfaction.

DILBERT. Reprinted by permission of United Features Syndicate, Inc.

Theory X
The proposal that employees dislike working, are lazy, avoid responsibility, and must be prodded or manipulated to perform.

Theory Y
The proposal that employees like to work, are industrious, seek responsibility, and can exercise self-direction.

Participative Decision Making
A decision-making model in which the people involved in implementing a decision are also involved in making it.

Quality Circles
A form of participative decision making involving regular meetings of supervisors and employees to discuss improvement of product or service.

Managerial Style: Theory X and Theory Y

Douglas McGregor (1960) identified two types of managers, each with very different assumptions about human nature—one negative and the other positive. **Theory X** managers believe that employees dislike work, are lazy, avoid responsibility, and must be prodded or manipulated into being productive. Therefore, they believe in close supervision and extrinsic rewards, such as work quotas, bonuses, and commissions to motivate their workers. **Theory Y** managers believe that employees like work, are industrious, seek responsibility, and can exercise self-direction. They do not believe employees need close supervision because they are self-motivated by intrinsic rewards, such as personal feelings of achievement and satisfaction.

Which style do you endorse? McGregor himself favored Theory Y. As business and industry come to recognize that a worker's self-esteem and satisfaction are important to job efficiency, Theory Y is becoming increasingly popular.

An essential part of Theory Y management is **participative decision making**, in which the people involved in implementing a decision are also involved in making it. Theory Y managers realize that participative decision making promotes teamwork and avoids an adversarial relationship between management and employees. In comparison, Theory X managers typically make all decisions and tell employees what to do. Studies support Theory Y. When workers are given a greater voice in how their work will be accomplished, both efficiency and job satisfaction are improved (Ali et al., 1997; Farson, 1996; Greller, 1998; Harrison and Pietri, 1997).

Quality circles are a well-known form of participative decision making in some countries. Employees and employers meet regularly to discuss quality problems, investigate causes, recommend solutions, and take corrective action. The concept of the quality circle originated in Japanese car assembly plants. At the end of the work day or work week, some of the workers from each line meet with their supervisors in a circle (implying equal contributions) to discuss ways to improve efficiency and employee satisfaction (Chaffins et al., 1998; Jewell, 1990; Matsui and Onglatco, 1990).

As implemented in the United States (Figure 17.6), both management and employees initially discuss company problems. Then the circle team members choose which problem to address, and generate and evaluate their own feedback. Management typically retains control over the final decision.

When the San Diego Zoo reorganized animal exhibits into separate, cage free areas that resemble natural habitats, they also instituted participative decision making. Employees formed teams that assumed responsibility for operating and maintaining specific exhibits. For example, the Tiger River exhibit pictured here is self-managed by a team of horticulturists, mammal and bird specialists, and maintenance and construction workers.

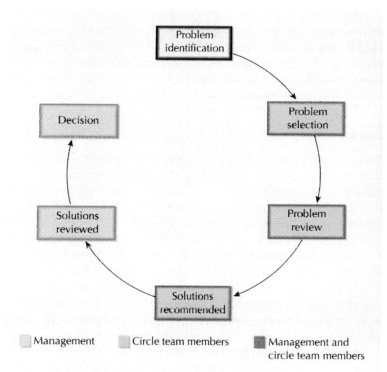

Figure 17.6 *A typical quality circle in the United States.* Note that management and employees begin by identifying problems. The quality circle (composed of employees) then selects which problem to work on, reviews it, and recommends solutions. Management reviews the solutions and makes the final decision. Most quality circles have been discontinued in the United States because management and employees tend to be more adversarial than loyal and trusting.

Do quality circles really work? Quality circles have not always worked well outside of Japan. In the United States, they seem to improve productivity, but have little or no effect on employee satisfaction, and have been mostly discontinued (Cotton, 1993). Their continued popularity in Japan may reflect Japanese organizational culture, which is based on lifetime employment, mutual respect between employer and employee, use of broad-based consensus to reach decisions, and fierce loyalty and devotion to the company by all employees (Chaffins et al., 1998; Ouchi, 1981). The U.S. organizational culture is quite different.

Worker Motivation: Goal-Setting, Equity, and Expectancy

Why do some workers put in long hours even when they are not being directly compensated, while others arrive late, do the minimum, and leave early if the boss isn't looking? You may have some answers after reading about personality differences and motivation and reinforcement in earlier chapters. In this section, we will explore three theories I/O psychologists have developed about what motivates workers: goal-setting theory, equity theory, and expectancy theory.

Goal-Setting Theory

Did your parents ever tell you to "just do your best?" What does this mean? How do you know when you have succeeded and can quit trying? Research on **goal-setting theory** suggests that setting *specific* and *difficult* goals leads to higher performance (Locke, 1968, 1996).

Goal-Setting Theory
The proposal that having specific and difficult goals leads to higher performance.

Under Detroit Edison's goals, measures, and targets (GMT) program, teams of employees define their joint and individual goals and performance measures. This photo shows a welder replacing boiler tubes at one of the company's power plants. Employees generated this cost-reduction project, which saved Detroit Edison $200,000 over the lowest bid from outside contractors. The savings were passed on to employees.

Equity Theory
The idea that individuals are driven by a need to maintain equilibrium or balance. In a work setting, employees prefer jobs in which the output is equal to the input. If imbalances occur, workers adjust their input, output, or their psychological perceptions.

Expectancy Theory
The idea that expectancy of outcomes, their desirability, and the effort needed to achieve them all determine worker motivation.

All things being equal, a person with specific goals will outperform someone without goals or with only a generalized "do my best" goal. For instance, when a sales representative commits to making 20 new contacts per week, he or she is setting a specific objective or goal. Also, the more difficult the goal (as long as it remains within reach), the greater the motivation. This theory enjoys wide support (Durham et al., 1997; Gilbourne and Taylor, 1998; Lee et al., 1997).

Equity theory

Have you ever worked for an employer who regularly asked for special favors, such as coming in on your day off? How would you respond if this same employer later refused to let you rearrange your lunch hour for a doctor's appointment? According to **equity theory,** we are strongly motivated to maintain a state of equilibrium or balance. We not only compare our contributions to that of our employer, we also compare our job's rewards and compensations with those of others (friends, neighbors, coworkers, colleagues in other organizations) and previous jobs (Beckett-Camarata et al., 1998; van Dierendonck et al., 1998; Wilpert, 1995).

If we compare our job contributions and job rewards and detect an imbalance (we're giving more than we're getting in return), we may quit or decrease our efforts in an effort to restore balance. If this doesn't work, we may change our psychological perceptions, by focusing on other compensations such as time off, ease of work, and so on. Balance is very important to workers, according to equity theory. If perceived *job input* (contributions) matches perceived *job outcome* (rewards), balance (or equity) is achieved and the worker goes home happy.

When an imbalance exists (the employer asks for extra consideration but is unwilling to return the favor), the worker is motivated to rebalance the relationship by altering inputs and outcomes or by psychologically adjusting his or her perception of the gains and losses. We can give the employer less, ask for more, or alter our thinking, e.g., "the boss would let me rearrange lunch if it were possible."

Expectancy Theory

One of the most popular theories of worker motivation is **expectancy theory,** the idea that workers perform in line with their expectancy of outcomes, the desirability of those outcomes, and the effort needed to achieve them. Before deciding to work hard (or not to work hard), individuals supposedly ask themselves three questions:

1. *What can I reasonably expect from my efforts?*   If employees perceive that rewards such as salary increases, bonuses, and promotions are based on hard work, they will work hard. On the other hand, if workers believe rewards are based on factors such as seniority or politics, both motivation and morale will be extremely low.

2. *Do I really want the rewards offered by management?*   If you've been working hard hoping for a salary increase, but are offered a promotion with increased responsibility and only a small bonus, you will obviously be disappointed. Similarly, if you had put in long hours hoping for a transfer to the West Coast office, but instead were offered the East Coast, you would be very disappointed. Managers should recognize that individual workers have different ideas of what is rewarding.

3. *If I give maximum effort, will it be reflected in my job evaluation?*   For some employees, the answer is too often no. If you lack the training or necessary skill level for a particular job, you are unlikely to be a high performer, no matter how hard you try. On the other hand, some workers are qualified but their supervisors may be unfair or may not like them. Regardless of their efforts, these external situations may block them from getting a good evaluation.

Try This Yourself

If you are a manager interested in increasing worker motivation (or someday hope to be), here are three ways you (and your employees) can benefit from expectancy theory:

1. *Clarify the route to rewards.* Be sure that promotions, salary increases, and bonuses are based on clear, definable measures of performance. Communicate these measures to your employees and give them frequent feedback on their efforts.

2. *Personalize the payoffs.* Ensure the rewards you've chosen for good performance are meaningful or val-

ued by your employees. Ask employees to help design payoffs that fit their personal goals and expectations.

3. *Reward maximum effort.* Begin by establishing a good fit between employees and their job assignments, and then ensure that employees are well trained. Once established in the work position, provide employees frequent evaluation on their work, including feedback on how their current performance level will affect their long-term job promotions and raises.

In sum, general knowledge of the three major worker motivation theories (goal-setting, equity, and expectancy) and implementation of this knowledge can help improve your own job performance and your management of others.

Job Satisfaction: What are the Important Factors?

What is the worst job you have ever had? What made it so bad? Was it the working conditions or low pay? Perhaps it was the work itself. Or maybe you just hated sitting at a desk for eight hours. Job satisfaction research is a high priority for I/O psychologists. In this section, we examine why managers should be concerned about employee job satisfaction (benefits to management and employees), and what factors determine worker satisfaction (personality/job factors).

Benefits to Management and Employees

Workers obviously prefer jobs that are rewarding and satisfying. But why should managers or business owners care if their employees are satisfied or not? According to research, there are several reasons:

1. **Decreased resignations**   Dissatisfied workers are more likely to resign or be absent from work (Tharenou, 1993). Because turnover and absenteeism are expensive, managers generally try to reduce them (Hellman, 1997; O'Quin and LoTempio, 1998).

2. **Increased productivity**   Research shows that job satisfaction leads to increased productivity (Ostroff, 1992; Wilk and Redmon, 1998). Although some early studies questioned this assumption, (e.g., Brayfield and Crockett, 1988), when satisfaction and productivity data are gathered for the organization as a whole rather than at the individual level, Ostroff found that organizations with more satisfied employees tend to be more effective.

3. **Employee health**   Studies show that satisfied workers have less stress, less "burnout," and better physical and psychological health (Bhatt, 1997; Pearson, 1998; Siu et al., 1997; Tang, 1998). In addition, satisfaction on the job apparently carries over to the employee's life outside the office. Job satisfaction not only contributes to overall quality of life, but it may be a better predictor of length of life than physical condition or tobacco use (Judge and Watanabe, 1993).

Why should employers care if workers are happy? Job satisfaction research shows important benefits to both employer and employee.

Personality/Job Factors

Now that we know that job satisfaction is important to both employer and employee, how do we discover what determines job satisfaction? One of the most interesting

"All work and no play makes you a valued employee."

Personality-Job Fit Theory
This theory identifies six personality types and proposes that a "good fit" between personality type and occupation determines job satisfaction.

and influential answers comes from John Holland (1985, 1994). According to Holland's **personality-job fit theory,** a match (or "good-fit") between a person's personality and occupation is a major factor in job satisfaction.

Holland developed a *Self-Directed Search* questionnaire that scores each person on six personality types and then matches them with various occupations. By matching personality types to appropriate occupations, Holland believes workers will bring the right interests and abilities to a job's demands. This "good fit" match between personality and occupation ensures success on the job and a higher level of job satisfaction (people tend to like what they are good at). Studies generally support Holland's theory (Hesketh and Myors, 1997; Judge and Cable, 1997; Maurer and Tarulli, 1997; Young et al., 1998).

Try This Yourself

Would you like to know which occupations might best match your own personality? Choose which of the personality descriptions on the left that most closely describes you, and then check the column on the right that lists matching/congruent occupations.

Personality Characteristics	*Holland's Six Types*	*Matching/Congruent Occupation*
Shy, genuine, persistent, stable, conforming, practical	1. Realistic: Prefers physical activities that require skill, strength, and coordination	Mechanic, drill press operator, assembly-line worker, farmer

Personality Characteristics	*Holland's Six Types*	*Matching/Congruent Occupation*
Analytical, original, curious, independent	2. Investigative: Prefers activities that involve thinking, organizing, and understanding	Biologist, economist, mathematician, news reporter
Sociable, friendly, cooperative, understanding	3. Social: Prefers activities that involve helping and developing others	Social worker, counselor, teacher, clinical psychologist

Personality Characteristics	Holland's Six Types	Matching/Congruent Occupation
Conforming, efficient, practical, unimaginative, inflexible	4. Conventional: Prefers rule regulated, orderly, and unambiguous activities	Accountant, bank teller, file clerk, corporate manager
Imaginative, disorderly, idealistic, emotional, impractical	5. Artistic: Prefers ambiguous and unsystematic activities that allow creative expression	Painter, musician, writer, interior decorator

Personality Characteristics	Holland's Six Types	Matching/Congruent Occupation
Self-confident, ambitious, energetic, domineering	6. Enterprising: Prefers verbal activities where there are opportunities to influence others and attain power	Lawyer, real estate agent, public relations specialist, small business manager

(*Source:* Adapted from *You and Your Career* by J. L. Holland, 1985).

R ESEARCH HIGHLIGHT

Job Satisfaction And Psychotherapy

Have you ever wondered about the work life of a psychotherapist? Is this a satisfying career? What are the most significant stressors and rewards? How do therapists cope when they have work-related problems?

Psychotherapy has always been a complex and demanding job, and earlier surveys documented numerous occupational hazards (Deutsch, 1985; Farber and Heifetz, 1981; Nash et al., 1984). These hazards could be categorized as (1) business-related problems (economic uncertainty, record keeping), (2) client-related issues (suicidal threats), (3) personal challenges of the psychotherapist (constant giving), (4) setting-related stressors (excessive workload), and (5) evaluation-related problems (difficulty evaluating client progress).

To add to this list, modern therapists also face problems from an increasingly litigious society and the expansion of managed care (Coster and Schwebel, 1997). With everyone more willing to sue these days, therapists must keep more detailed records. Expanded managed care creates even more paperwork, and its bureaucracy reduces the therapist's independence.

Which of these hazards is most stressful? Researchers Barbara Kramen-Kahn and Nancy Downing Hansen (1998) recently surveyed over 200 psychotherapists to identify their top occupational hazards, as well as, their personal coping strategies.

Their respondents rated business and economic demands and uncertainties, along with time and workload pressures as their top stressors. The most frequent coping methods were a sense of humor, freely consulting with other therapists, participating in leisure activities to balance work stresses, attending continuing education seminars, perceiving client problems as interesting, and using interpersonal supports.

Are there rewards in psychotherapy that offset the stress? According to the survey participants, the greatest rewards are seeing clients improve and grow, their own opportunities for self-growth, challenging and diverse tasks, and professional autonomy. It is interesting that female thera-pists reported greater occupational rewards and use of coping strategies than male therapists. Kramen-Kahn and Hansen suggest that this gender difference may reflect the fact that women are generally more relational than men (Jordan et al., 1991), and that therapy is an essentially relational occupation.

What can we learn from this research? Therapists should obviously try to reduce their perceived hazards, increase the rewards, and use more coping strategies. There is also a lesson for all of us in this research. Given the human tendency to react more strongly to (and perhaps have a longer memory for) aversive events—especially interpersonal ones (Rook, 1984), we might try to ignore the problems of our work and actively search for possible overlooked rewards. We could also emulate the therapists' most successful coping strategies. Developing a sense of humor and balancing work and leisure are important life skills for everyone.

CHECK AND REVIEW

Organizational Psychology

Organizational psychologists study how interpersonal relations affect productivity. Theory X managers take a negative approach, believing employees need close supervision and extrinsic rewards for motivation. Theory Y managers are positive and believe employees are self-motivated. Theory Y managers often use participative decision making, such as quality circles—groups of employees who meet regularly with supervisors to solve problems.

Goal setting is one major way to motivate workers; having specific and difficult goals improves performance. Equity theory says workers are motivated if they perceive that their job inputs match the perceived rewards. Expectancy theory, on the other hand, maintains that employees are motivated to work according to their expectancy of outcomes, the desirability of those outcomes, and the effort needed to achieve them.

Job satisfaction is important to both employer and employee. Employers gain because they save money (lower absenteeism and fewer resignations) and increase productivity. Employees gain because they are under less stress, enjoy better physical health, and have an improved overall quality and length of life.

According to personality-fit theory, job satisfaction results from a match between personality and occupation. Supportive colleagues, supportive working conditions, mentally challenging work, and equitable rewards are also important.

QUESTIONS

1. Briefly explain participative decision making, and why quality circles have been less successful in the United States than in Japan.

2. Identify the worker motivation theory that best explains the following situations:
   (a) Seong enjoys assignments that are difficult but attainable.
   (b) Denise avoids work and responsibility, but does not fear being fired because she is best friends with the boss and enjoys high seniority.
   (c) Juan, a salaried employee, feels he is being underpaid so he decides to cut back on his hours at work.

3. How does management benefit when employees have job satisfaction? What are the major benefits of job satisfaction to employees?

4. The theory that a match between a person's personality and occupation results in increased job satisfaction is known as _____. (a) expectancy theory; (b) the halo effect; (c) participative decision making; (d) personality job-fit theory.

Answers to Questions can be found in Appendix B.

Are You In The Right Job?

An important component of critical thinking is the ability to *define problems accurately*. By carefully identifying the problem in clear and concrete terms, critical thinkers prevent confusion and lay the foundation for gathering relevant information. For example, in choosing a career, first identify what you like and do not like about your current (and past) jobs. With this information in hand, you are then prepared to research jobs that will better suit your interests, needs, and abilities. To help your analysis, answer "Yes" or "No" to these questions:

_____ 1. Is there a sufficient amount of laughter and sociability in your workplace?

_____ 2. Does your boss notice and appreciate your work?

_____ 3. Is your boss understanding and friendly?

_____ 4. Are you embarrassed by the physical conditions of your workplace?

_____ 5. Do you feel safe and comfortable in your place of work?

_____ 6. Do you like the location of your job?

_____ 7. If you won the lottery and were guaranteed a lifetime income, would you feel truly sad if you also had to quit your job?

_____ 8. Do you watch the clock, daydream, take long lunches, and leave work as soon as possible?

_____ 9. Do you frequently feel stressed and overwhelmed by the demands of your job?

_____10. Compared to others with your qualifications, are you being paid what you are worth?

_____11. Are promotions made in a fair and just manner?

_____12. Given the demands of your job, are you fairly compensated for your work?

Now score your answers. Give yourself one point for each answer that matches the following: 1. No; 2. No; 3. No; 4. Yes; 5. No; 6. No; 7. No; 8. Yes; 9. Yes; 10. No; 11. No; 12. No.

The questions you just answered are based on four factors that research shows are conducive to job satisfaction: supportive colleagues, supportive working conditions, mentally challenging work, and equitable rewards (Robbins, 1996). Your total score reveals your overall level of dissatisfaction, while a look at specific questions can help identify which of these four factors is most important to your job satisfaction—and most lacking in your current job.

Supportive Colleagues (Items 1, 2, 3). For most employees, work fills important social needs. Therefore, having friendly and supportive colleagues and superiors leads to increased satisfaction.

Supportive Working Conditions (Items 4, 5, 6). Not surprisingly, studies find most employees prefer working in safe, clean, and relatively modern facilities. They also prefer jobs close to home.

Mentally Challenging Work (Items 7, 8, 9). Jobs with too little challenge create boredom and apathy, while too much challenge creates frustration and feelings of failure.

Equitable Rewards (Items 10, 11, 12). Employees want pay and promotions based on job demands, individual skill levels, and community pay standards.

KEY TERMS

The Development of I/O Psychology
Hawthorne Effect (p. 609)
Industrial/Organizational (I/O) Psychology (p. 606)
Human Factors Psychology
Controls (p. 612)
Displays (p. 612)
Human Factors Psychology (p. 612)
Human–Machine System (p. 612)

Personnel Psychology
Halo Effect (p. 622)
Job Analysis (p. 617)
Organizational Culture (p. 619)
Performance Evaluation (p. 621)
Personnel Psychology (p. 617)
Sexual Harassment (p. 623)
Organizational Psychology
Equity Theory (p. 628)
Expectancy Theory (p. 628)

Goal-Setting Theory (p. 627)
Organizational Psychology (p. 625)
Participative Decision making (p. 626)
Personality-Job Fit Theory (p. 630)
Quality Circles (p. 626)
Theory X (p. 626)
Theory Y (p. 626)

Visual Summary for Chapter 17

The Development of I/O Psychology

Industrial/Organizational (I/0) Psychology: studies how individual behavior affects and is affected by the physical environment and the organizational culture of the workplace.

The Beginnings

- Scott, Taylor, and Munsterberg were major founding contributors to I/0 psychology.

- World War I: Personnel needs gave **I/0** respectability. Based on newly developed group IQ tests, Scott developed a program to place recruits in jobs suiting their abilities. **Hawthorne effect:** people change their behavior because of the novelty of a research situation or because they know they're being observed.

Modern Times

- World War II: led to scientifically designed worker training programs to improve productivity for the war effort. After the war, many I/0 psychologists turned from manufacturing to management, thus creating *organizational psychology*.

- Civil Rights Act of 1964: **I/0** psychology's creation of employment tests, training programs, and recruitment programs that ignored ethnicity, religion, age, or gender.

Human Factors Psychology

Human factors psychology studies ways to improve the design and function of machines and the work environment to better meet the needs of human users.

Human-machine system: an arrangement of people and machines, tools, and other devices that produce a product or service. Human: sensory functions (input) and cognitive and motor functions (output). Machine: **displays** (output) and **controls** (input). The Human-Machine System:

Displays: Machines "talk" to human operators through their displays (video monitors, gauges, bells, and blinking lights).

Controls: Humans "talk" to machines by inputting instructions via machine controls (dial, wheel, switch, and keyboard).

Personnel Psychology

Personnel psychology: involved with recruiting, selecting, training, and evaluating workers.

Recruitment and Selection

Recruitment begins with a **job analysis,** a detailed description of the skills, knowledge, and activities required in a particular job. Selection often based on interviews. Structured (vs. unstructured) interviews are better predictors of future job performance. Prepare for an interview by doing research on the company, role playing, and emphasizing desirable personality traits.

Employee Training

Orientation programs transmit **organizational culture**, group's shared pattern of thought and action.

Personnel Psychology (cont.)

Evaluating Workers

Performance evaluation: formal procedure used to assess employee job performance. Evaluations can be objective or subjective. Subjective method most popular, but the **halo effect** (tendency to rate individuals too high or too low based on one outstanding trait) can be a problem. New techniques include "360-degree" multisource measures and special rating scales.

Sexual Harassment

Sexual harassment: sexual advances, requests for sexual favors, and other unwelcome verbal or physical conduct of a sexual nature. Most sexual harassment is an assertion or abuse of power, not sexual desire. Victims often suffer financial losses and psychological difficulties.

Organizational Psychology

Organizational psychology studies how interpersonal relations affect productivity.

Managerial Style: Two Theories

Theory X: negative approach (believing employees dislike work, thus need close supervision and extrinsic rewards for motivation).

Theory Y: positive approach (believing employees like work and are self-motivated).

Theory Y managers often use **participative decision making**, such as **quality circles**—groups of employees who meet regularly with supervisors to solve problems.

Worker Motivation: Three Major Theories

Goal setting theory: setting specific and difficult goals improves performance.

Equity theory: workers are better motivated if they perceive a balance between their job inputs and their perceived rewards.

Expectancy theory: employees perform according to the likely outcomes, the desirability of those outcomes, and the effort needed to achieve them.

Job Satisfaction: Importance of Job Satisfaction

Employees have less stress, better physical health, improved quality and length of life.

Employers save money from lower absenteeism, less turnover, increased productivity.

According to **personality-job fit theory**, job satisfaction comes from a match (or "good-fit") between personality and occupation.

Glossary

A

ABC theory of psychopathology Albert Ellis's theory of psychopathology, in which A refers to activating conditions, B to belief systems, and C to emotional consequences. (p. 570)

absolute threshold The minimum amount of physical energy (stimulation) needed for an observer to notice a stimulus. (p. 106)

absorptive phase The phase of metabolism during which a person is ingesting food. (p. 348)

accommodation In vision, the changes in the shape of the lens that focus light rays; in Piaget's theory, the modification of schemas to fit reality. (pp. 113, 456)

acculturative stress The stress people experience while trying to adapt to a new culture. (p. 391)

acetylcholine (ACh) A neurotransmitter involved in muscle contractions, learning, and memory. (p. 73)

action potential A temporary shift in the polarity of the cell membrane, which leads to the firing of a neuron. (p. 69)

activational effects Effects of hormones activating brain circuitry to produce psychobiological changes. (p. 358)

actualizing tendency The primary motivation in humans, according to Carl Rogers, which includes a range of needs that humans experience, from the basic needs for food and drink to the needs to be open to experience and express one's true self. (p. 430)

actual self People's views of how they actually are. (p. 619)

adaptive A term applied to traits that help organisms adjust to their environment. (p. 19)

adrenal glands Endocrine glands located above the kidneys that secrete adrenaline and other hormones during emergency situations. (p. 75)

adrenaline A hormone that triggers physiological arousal, particularly in potential danger situations. (p. 74)

adult attachment Patterns of mental representation, emotion, and proximity-seeking in adults related to childhood attachment patterns. (p. 480)

affect A positive or negative feeling state that typically includes arousal, subjective experience, and behavioral expression; a synonym for emotion. (p. 368)

affiliation motive A need for some kind of satisfying interaction with others. (p. 362)

ageism A form of prejudice against old people comparable to racism and sexism. (p. 451)

agency motives Motives for achievement, mastery, power, autonomy, and other self-oriented goals. (p. 361)

aggression Verbal or physical behavior aimed at harming another person or living being. (p. 639)

agoraphobia The fear of being in places or situations from which escape might be difficult. (p. 545)

alcoholism The tendency to use or abuse alcohol to a degree that leads to social or occupational dysfunction. (p. 531)

algorithm A systematic problem-solving procedure that inevitably produces a solution. (p. 246)

altered states of consciousness Deviations in subjective experience from a normal waking state. (p. 323)

altruism Behaving in a way that helps another person with no apparent gain, or with potential cost, to oneself. (p. 626)

Alzheimer's disease A progressive and incurable illness that destroys neurons in the brain, causing severe impairment of memory, reasoning, perception, language, and behavior. (p. 470)

ambivalence Conflicting feelings or intentions. (p. 405)

ambivalent attachment style Response to separation in which infants who are angry and rejecting simultaneously indicate a clear desire to be close to the mother. (p. 477)

amplitude The difference between the minimum and maximum pressure levels in a sound wave, measured in decibels; amplitude corresponds to the psychological property of loudness. (p. 125)

amygdala A brain structure associated with the expression of rage, fear, and calculation of the emotional significance of a stimulus. (p. 86)

analogical reasoning The process by which people understand a novel situation in terms of a familiar one. (p. 244)

anal stage The psychosexual phase occurring roughly around ages 2 to 3, which is characterized by conflicts with parents over compliance and defiance. (p. 408)

analysis of variance (ANOVA) A statistic that assesses the likelihood that mean differences between groups occurred by chance. (p. 61)

androgen insensitivity syndrome A condition in which androgens are secreted in utero, but a genetic defect leads to an absence of androgen receptors, so that a genetic male develops female genitalia. (p. 358)

anorexia nervosa An eating disorder in which a person refuses to eat, starving herself to the point that physical complications and sometimes death may occur. (p. 549)

antibodies Protein molecules that attach themselves to foreign agents in the body, marking them for destruction. (p. 393)

antidepressant medication Biological treatment of depression that increases the amount of norepinephrine and/or serotonin available in synapses. (p. 581)

antipsychotic medication Medication used to treat schizophrenia and other psychotic states, which has sedating effects and reduces positive symptoms such as hallucinations and delusions. (p. 581)

antisocial personality disorder A personality disorder marked by irresponsible and socially disruptive behavior in a variety of areas. (p. 552)

anxiety disorder A disorder characterized by intense, frequent, or continuous anxiety, which may lead to disruptive avoidance behavior. (p. 544)

assimilation The interpretation of actions or events in terms of one's present schemas. (p. 456)

association areas The areas of cortex involved in putting together perceptions, ideas, and plans. (p. 88)

attachment Enduring affectional ties that children form with their primary caregivers and become the basis for later love relationships. (p. 475)

attachment motivation The desire for physical and psychological proximity to an attachment figure. (p. 362)

attention The process of focusing consciousness on a limited range of experience. (p. 305)

attention-deficit hyperactivity disorder (ADHD) A disorder characterized by age-inappropriate inattention, impulsiveness, and hyperactivity. (p. 529)

attitude An association between an action or object and an evaluation. (p. 593)

attitude accessibility The ease with which an attitude comes to mind or is activated. (p. 594)

attitude innoculation Building up a receiver's resistance to an opposing attitude by presenting weak arguments for it or forewarning of a strong opposing persuasive appeal. (p. 599)

attitude strength The durability of an attitude (its persistence and resistance to change) and its impact on behavior. (p. 594)

attitudinal ambivalence A condition in which an attitude object is associated with conflicting evaluative responses. (p. 595)

attitudinal coherence The extent to which an attitude is internally consistent. (p. 596)

attribution The process of making inferences about the causes of one's own and others' thoughts, feelings, and behavior. (pp. 383, 613)

audition Hearing. (p. 124)

auditory nerve The bundle of sensory neurons that transmit auditory information from the ear to the brain. (p. 127)

augmentation Attributional phenomenon in which people emphasize an internal explanation for a behavior because it occurred despite situational pressures. (p. 614)

authoritarian parenting style A way of parenting that places high value on obedience and respect for authority. (p. 484)

authoritarian personality A personality type that is prone to hate people who are different or downtrodden. (p. 607)

authoritative parenting style A way of parenting that sets standards for children and firmly enforces them but also provides explanations for the parents' actions and encourages verbal give-and-take. (p. 484)

automatic thoughts The things people say spontaneously to themselves, which can lead to irrational feelings and behaviors. (p. 569)

automatization The process of executing mental processes with increasing efficiency, so that they require less and less attention. (p. 462)

autonomic nervous system The part of the peripheral nervous system that serves visceral or internal bodily structures connected with basic life processes, such as the beating of the heart and breathing. It consists of two parts: the sympathetic nervous system and the parasympathetic nervous system. (p. 76)

autonomy versus shame and doubt In Erikson's theory, the stage in which children begin to walk, talk, and get a sense of themselves as independent sources of will and power. (p. 507)

availability heuristic A strategy that leads people to judge the frequency of a class of events or the likelihood of something happening on the basis of how easy it is to retrieve from explicit memory. (p. 250)

avoidance learning A negative reinforcement procedure in which the behavior of an organism is reinforced by the prevention of an expected aversive event. (p. 173)

avoidant attachment style Response to separation in which infants ignore the mother when she returns. (p. 477)

axon The long extension from the cell body of a neuron through which electrical impulses pass. (p. 67)

B

babbling A child's earliest language utterances that are spontaneous and incomprehensible. (p. 271)

bad faith a form of self-deception in which people convince themselves that their actions are determined, which allows them to escape the anxiety of free choice. (p. 431)

basal ganglia A set of structures located near the thalamus and hypothalamus involved in the control of movement and in judgments that require minimal conscious thought. (p. 87)

basic emotions Feeling states common to the human species from which other feeling states are derived. (p. 376)

basic level The level of categorization to which people naturally go; the level at which objects share distinctive common attributes. (p. 239)

basic trust versus mistrust In Erikson's theory, the stage in which infants come to trust others or to perceive the social world as unfriendly or unreliable. (p. 507)

beeper studies An experience-sampling technique where participants carry pagers and report their experience when "beeped" at various points during the day. (p. 307)

behavioral analysis In cognitive-behavior therapy, the process of assessing the symptom and the stimuli or thoughts associated with it. (p. 565)

behavioral approach system (BAS) The anatomical system that is associated with pleasurable emotional states and is responsible for approach-oriented operant behavior. (p. 183)

behavioral genetics A field that examines the genetic and environmental bases of differences among individuals on psychological traits. (p. 20)

behavioral inhibition system (BIS) The anatomical system that is associated with anxiety and avoidance behavior. (p. 183)

behavioral neuroscience A field of investigation that examines the physical basis of psychological phenomena such as motivation, emotion, and stress; also called biopsychology. (p. 4)

behaviorist perspective The perspective pioneered by John Watson and B. F. Skinner, which focuses on the relation between observable behaviors and environmental events or stimuli; also called behaviorism. (p. 12)

behavior-outcome expectancy Belief that a certain behavior will lead to a particular outcome. (p. 419)

benzodiazepines Antianxiety medications that indirectly affect the action of norepinephrine. (p. 587)

binocular cells Neurons that receive information from both eyes. (p. 143)

binocular cues Visual input integrated from two eyes that provides perception of depth. (p. 143)

biofeedback A procedure for monitoring autonomic physiological processes and learning to alter them at will. (p. 186)

biopolar cells Neurons in the retina that combine information from many receptors and excite ganglion cells. (p. 114)

bipolar disorder A psychological disorder marked by extreme mood swings; also called manic-depression. (p. 540)

biopsychology The field that examines the physical basis of psychological phenomena such as motivation, emotion, and stress; also called behavioral neuroscience. (p. 4)

blindsight A phenomenon in which individuals with cortical lesions have no conscious visual awareness but can make discriminations about objects placed in front of them. (p. 119)

blind spot The point on the retina where the optic nerve leaves the eye and which contain no receptor cells. (p. 114)

blind studies Studies in which subjects are kept unaware of or "blind" to important aspects of the research. (p. 38)

blocking When a stimulus fails to elicit a conditioned response because it is combined with another stimulus that already elicits the response. (p. 167)

borderline personality disorder A personality disorder characterized by extremely unstable interpersonal relationships, dramatic mood swings, an unstable sense of identity, intense fears of abandonment, manipulativeness, and impulsive behavior. (p. 551)

bottom-up processing Perceptual processing that starts with raw sensory data that feed "up" to the brain; what is perceived is determined largely by the features of the stimuli reaching the sense organs. (p. 151)

bounded rationality The notion that people are rational within constraints imposed by their environment, goals, and abilities. (p. 251)

Broca's area A brain structure located in the left frontal lobe at the base of the motor cortex, involved in the movements of the mouth and tongue necessary for speech production and in the use grammar. (p. 90)

bulimia A disorder characterized by a binge-and-purge syndrome in which the person binges on food and then either induces vomiting or uses laxatives to purge. (p. 549)

bystander intervention A form of altruism involving helping a person in need. (p. 637)

C

Cannon-Bard theory A theory of emotion that asserts that emotion-inducing stimuli elicit both emotional experience and bodily response. (p. 370)

Cartesian dualism The doctrine of dual spheres of mind and body. (p. 13)

case study In-depth observation of one subject or a small group of subjects. (p. 41)

castration complex In Freud's theory, the fear the boy has in the phallic stage that his father will castrate him for his wishes toward his mother. (p. 409)

catastrophes Rare, unexpected disasters such as earthquakes, floods, and other traumatic events that affect a group of people. (p. 391)

categorical variable A variable comprised of groupings, classifications, or categories. (p. 31)

categorization The process of identifying an object as an instance of a category, recognizing its similarity to some objects and dissimilarity to others. (p. 237)

category A grouping based on a common property (p. 237)

cell body The part of the neuron which includes a nucleus containing the genetic material of the cell (the chromosomes), as well as other microstructures vital to cell functioning. (p. 67)

central nervous system (CNS) The brain and spinal cord. (p. 75)

central route to persuasion A method of persuasion that involves inducing the recipient of a message to think carefully and weigh the arguments. (p. 597)

cerebellum A large bulge in the dorsal or back area of the brain, responsible for the coordination of smooth, well-sequenced movements as well as maintaining equilibrium and regulating postural reflexes. (p. 83)

cerebral cortex The many-layered surface of the cerebrum, which allows complex voluntary movements, permits subtle discriminations among complex sensory patterns, and makes possible symbolic thinking. (p. 88)

cerebral hemispheres The two halves of the cerebrum. (p. 88)

cerebrum The "thinking" center of the brain, which includes the cortex and subcortical structures such as the basal ganglia and limbic system. (p. 80)

chaining A process of learning in which a sequence of already established behaviors is reinforced step by step. (p. 180)

charismatic leader A leader who inspires obedience by the force of his or her personality. (p. 654)

chi-square (χ^2) test Inferential statistic that compares the observed data with the results one would expect by chance and tests the likelihood the differences between observed and expected are accidental. (p. 60)

chromosomes Strands of DNA arranged in pairs. (p. 96)

chunking The process of organizing information into small, meaningful bits to aid memory. (p. 206)

circadian rhythms Biological rhythms that evolved around the daily cycles of light and dark. (p. 316)

classical conditioning A procedure by which a previously neutral stimulus comes to elicit a response after it is paired with a stimulus that automatically elicits that response; the first type of learning to be studied systematically. (p. 162)

client-centered therapy A therapeutic approach developed by Carl Rogers, based on the assumption that psychological difficulties result from incongruence between one's concept of self and one's actual experience, and that empathy is curative. (p. 572)

clinical syndrome A constellation of symptoms that tend to occur together. (p. 527)

closure A Gestalt rule of perception which states that people tend to perceive incomplete figures as complete. (p. 140)

cochlea The three-chambered tube in the inner ear in which sound is transduced. (p. 127)

cognition Thought and memory. (p. 15)

cognitive-behavioral Approach in clinical psychology in which practitioners integrate an understanding of classical and operant conditioning with a cognitive-social perspective. (p. 521)

cognitive-behavioral therapy Psychotherapy that uses methods derived from behaviorist and cognitive learning theories. (p. 565)

cognitive dissonance A phenomenon in which a person experiences a discrepancy between an attitude and a behavior or between an attitude and a new piece of information incongruent with it, which leads to a state of tension and a subsequent change in attitude, behavior, or perception. (p. 600)

cognitive distortions Cognitive mechanisms by which a depressed person transforms neutral or positive information in a depressive direction. (p. 542)

cognitive maps Mental representations of visual space. (p. 184)

cognitive perspective A psychological perspective that focuses on the way people perceive, process, and retrieve information. (p. 15)

cognitive social theory A theory of learning that emphasizes the role of thought and social learning in behavior. (p. 184)

cognitive therapy A psychological treatment that focuses on the thought processes that underlie psychological symptoms. (p. 569)

cognitive unconscious Information processing mechanisms that operate outside of awareness, such procedural memory and implicit associative processes, as opposed to the psychodynamic unconscious, which includes information the person is motivated to keep from awareness. (p. 310)

cohort effects Differences among age groups associated with differences in the culture. (p. 444)

color constancy The tendency to perceive the color of objects as stable despite changing illumination. (p. 147)

common factors Shared elements in psychotherapies that produce positive outcomes. (p. 586)

companionate love Love that involves deep affection, friendship, and emotional intimacy. (p. 630)

competence Skills and abilities used for solving problems. (p. 419)

complexity The extent to which a sound wave is composed of multiple frequencies. (p. 125)

compromise formations A single behavior, or a complex pattern of thought and action, which typically reflects compromises among multiple (and often conflicting) forces. (p. 406)

compulsion An intentional behavior or mental act performed in a stereotyped fashion. (p. 546)

computerized axial tomography (CT scan) A brain scanning technique used to detect lesions. (p. 47)

concept A mental representation of a category of objects, ideas, or events that share common properties. (p. 237)

concrete operational stage Piaget's third stage of cognitive development, in which children are capable of mentally manipulating internal representations of concrete objects in ways that are reversible. (p. 459)

conditioned response In classical conditioning, a response that has been learned. (p. 162)

conditioned stimulus A stimulus that the organism has learned to associate with the unconditioned stimulus. (p. 162)

conditioning A form of learning. (p. 162)

conditions Values or versions of the independent variable that vary across experimental groups. (p. 35)

conditions of worth In Carl Rogers' theory, standards children internalize that they must meet in order to esteem themselves. (p. 430)

conduct disorder A childhood disorder in which a child persistently violates the rights of others as well as societal norms. (p. 530)

cones One of two types of photoreceptors, which are specialized for color vision and allow perception of fine detail. (p. 114)

confirmation bias The tendency for people to

search for information that confirms their expectations. (p. 247)

conflict A battle between opposing motives. (p. 405)

conflict model Theoretical model of adolescence that holds that conflict and crisis are normal in adolescence. (p. 509)

conformity The process of changing attitudes or behavior to accommodate the standards of a group. (p. 649)

confounding variable A variable that produces effects of independent variables. (p. 39)

congenital adrenal hyperplasia A disorder in which the adrenal glands secrete too much androgen, thus masculinizing the genitals in females. (p. 358)

connectionism A model of human cognitive processes in which many cognitive processes occur simultaneously so that a representation is spread out (i.e., distributed) throughout a network of interacting processing units; also called parallel distributed processing (PDP). (p. 254)

conscious mental processes Processes that involve a subjective awareness of stimuli, feelings, or ideas (pp. 308, 405)

consciousness The subjective awareness of mental events. (p. 303)

consensus In attribution theory, a normative response in a social group. (p. 613)

conservation Recognition that basic properties of an object remain stable even though superficial properties may change. (p. 459)

consistency In attribution theory, the extent to which a person always responds in the same way to the same stimulus. (p. 613)

constraint satisfaction The tendency to settle on a cognitive solution that satisfied as many constraints as possible in order to achieve the best fit to the data. (p. 256)

context of discovery The part of the scientific process in which phenomena are observed, hypotheses are framed, and theories are built. (p. 53)

context of justification The part of the scientific process in which hypotheses are tested. (p. 53)

continuity model The theoretical model that holds that adolescence for most individuals is essentially continuous with childhood and adulthood and not distinguished by turbulence. (p. 510)

continuous reinforcement schedule When the environmental consequences are the same each time an organism emits a behavior. (p. 176)

continuous variable A variable that can be placed on a continuum, from none or little to much. (p. 31)

control group Subjects in an experiment who receive a relatively neutral condition to serve as a comparison group. (p. 38)

conventional morality The level of morality in which individuals define what is right by the standards they have learned from other people, particularly respected authorities. (p. 500)

coping The ways people deal with stressful situations; also called *coping mechanisms*. (p. 396)

cornea The tough, transparent tissue covering the front of the eyeball. (p. 113)

corpus callosum A band of fibers that connect the two hemispheres of the brain. (p. 88)

corrective mechanisms Processes that restore a homeostatic system to its set-point (p. 349)

correlate In research, to assess the extent to which the measure of one variable predicts the measure of a second variable. (p. 44)

correlational research Research that assesses the degree to which two variables are related, so that knowing the value of one can lead to prediction of the other. (p. 44)

correlation coefficient An index of the extent to which two variables are related. (p. 44)

correlation matrix A table presenting the correlations among several variables. (p. 46)

correspondence bias The tendency to assume that people's behavior corresponds to their internal states rather than external situations. (p. 614)

cortex See cerebral cortex. (p. 80)

couples therapy Psychotherapy that treats a couple; also called marital therapy. (p. 574)

creativity The ability to produce valued outcomes in a novel way. (p. 286)

critical period A period of special sensitivity to specific types of learning that shapes the capacity for future development. (p. 442)

cross-cultural psychology The field that attempts to test psychological hypotheses in different cultures. (p. 6)

cross-sectional studies The type of research that compares groups of different-aged subjects at a single time to see whether differences exist among them. (p. 444)

crystallized intelligence People's store of knowledge. (p. 290)

cultural models Shared cultural concepts, which organize knowledge and shape the way people think and remember (p. 222)

culture pattern approach An approach to personality and culture that views culture as an organized set of beliefs, rituals, and institutions that shape individuals to fit its patterns. (p. 434)

cycle A single round of expansion and contraction of the distance between molecules of air in a sound wave. (p. 125)

D

daily hassles The small, but irritating demands that characterize daily life. (p. 392)

daydreaming The part of the flow of consciousness in which attention turns from external stimuli to internal thoughts. (p. 307)

decay theory The notion that memories are lost as a result of a fading of the memory trace. (p. 226)

decibel (dB) The unit of measure of amplitude (loudness) of a sound wave. (p. 125)

decision making The process by which people weigh the pros and cons of different alternatives in order to make a choice among two or more options. (p. 248)

declarative memory Knowledge that can be consciously retrieved and "declared." (p. 207)

deductive reasoning The process of reasoning that draws logical conclusions from premises. (p. 242)

defense mechanisms Unconscious mental processes aimed at protecting a person from experiencing unpleasant emotions, especially anxiety. (p. 411)

defining features Qualities that are essential, or necessarily present, in order to classify an object as a member of a category. (p. 237)

degree of relatedness The probability that two people share any particular gene. (p. 96)

delusion A false belief firmly held despite evidence to the contrary. (p. 534)

demand characteristics The influence of subjects' perception of the researchers' goals on subjects' behavior. (p. 38)

dementia A disorder marked by global disturbance of higher mental functions. (p. 469)

dendrites Branch-like extensions of the neuron that receive information from other cells. (p. 67)

denial A defense mechanism in which the person refuses to acknowledge external realities or emotions. (p. 411)

dependent variables Subjects' responses in a study, hypothesized to depend on the influence of the independent variables. (p. 35)

depressant A drug that slows down the nervous system. (p. 327)

depth perception The organization of perception in three dimensions; also called distance perception. (p. 143)

descriptive diagnosis A classification of mental disorders in terms of clinical syndromes. (p. 527)

descriptive research Research methods that cannot unambiguously demonstrate cause and effect, including case studies, naturalistic observation, survey research, and correlational methods. (p. 41)

descriptive statistics Numbers that describe the data from a study in a way that summarizes their essential features. (pp. 39, 55)

developmental model Freud's model of how children develop, defined by his psychosexual stages. (p. 407)

developmental psychology The field that studies the way thought, feeling, and behavior develop through the lifespan. (p. 440)

developmental task Challenge that is normative for a particular period of life. (p. 507)

Diagnostic and Statistical Manual of Mental Disorders-IV **(DSM-IV)** The manual of clinical syndromes published by the American Psychiatric Association and used for descriptive diagnosis. (p. 527)

diathesis-stress model The model of psychopathology that proposes that people with an underlying vulnerability (also called a diathesis) may develop a disorder under stressful circumstances. (p. 523)

dichotic listening A procedure in which different information is presented to the left and right ears simultaneously. (p. 306)

difference threshold The smallest difference in intensity between two stimuli that a person can detect. (p. 108)

diffusion of responsibility The phenomenon in which the presence of other people leads to a diminished sense of personal responsibility to act. (p. 637)

direct perception A theory which states that sensory information intrinsically carries meaning. (p. 150)

discounting The attributional phenomenon in which people downplay the role of one variable that might explain a behavior because they know another may be contributing. (p. 613)

discourse The way people ordinarily speak, hear, read, and write in interconnected sentences. (p. 264)

discrimination The behavioral component of prejudiced attitudes. (p. 606)

discriminative stimulus A stimulus that signals that particular contingencies of reinforcement are in effect. (p. 178)

disorganized attachment style Response to separation in which infants behave in contradictory ways, indicating helpless efforts to elicit soothing responses from the attachment figure. (p. 477)

display rules Patterns of emotional expression that are considered acceptable in a given culture. (p. 375)

dispositional variables Personalities and attitudes. (p. 626)

dissociation A disturbance in memory and consciousness in which significant aspects of experience are kept separate and distinct (or dis-associated). (p. 550)

dissociative disorders Disorders characterized by disruptions in consciousness, memory, sense of identity, or perception of the environment. (p. 550)

dissociative identity disorder The most severe dissociative disorder; also known as multiple personality disorder. (p. 551)

divergent thinking The ability to generate multiple possibilities in a given situation. (p. 286)

distinctiveness In attribution theory, the extent to which an individual responds in a particular way to many different stimuli. (p. 613)

divided attention The process by which attention is split between two or more sets of stimuli. (p. 306)

dizygotic (DZ) twins Fraternal twins who, like other siblings, share only about half of their genes, having developed from the union of two sperm with two separate eggs. (p. 97)

dopamine A neurotransmitter with wide-ranging effects in the nervous system, involved in thought, feeling, motivation, and behavior. (p. 73)

dopamine hypothesis Hypothesis that implicates an imbalance in the neurotransmitter dopamine in schizophrenia. (p. 536)

dorsolateral prefrontal cortex An area in the brain that plays a central role in working memory and explicit manipulation of representations. (p. 257)

double-blind study A study in which both subjects and researchers are blind to the status of subjects. (p. 38)

drive According to Freud, an internal tension state that builds up until satisfied; according to behaviorist theory, an unpleasant tension state that motivates behavior, classified as either primary or secondary (acquired). (pp. 182, 339)

drive model Freud's theory of motivation, which held that people are motivated by sexual and aggressive instincts or drives. (p. 406)

drive-reduction theories Mid-twentieth century behaviorist theories which proposed that motivation stems from a combination of drive and reinforcement, in which stimuli become reinforcing because they are associated with reduction of a state of biological deficit. (pp. 182, 341)

dysthmymia Chronic low-level depression of more than two years' duration, with intervals of normal moods that never last more than a few weeks or months. (p. 539)

E

eardrum The thin, flexible membrane that marks the outer boundary of the middle ear; the eardrum is set in motion by sound waves and in turn sets in motion the ossicles; also called the tympanic membrane. (p. 126)

echoic storage An auditory sensory registration process by which people retain an echo or brief auditory representation of a sound to which they have been exposed. (p. 198)

effectiveness studies Studies that assess the outcome of psychotherapy as it is practiced in the field rather than in the laboratory. (p. 587)

efficacy studies Studies that assess psychotherapy outcome under highly controlled conditions, such as random assignment of patients to different treatment or control groups, careful training of therapists to

adhere to a manual, and standardized length of treatment. (p. 587)

ego The structure in Freud's model of the mind that must somehow balance desire, reality, and morality. (p. 410)

egocentric Being thoroughly embedded in one's own point of view. (p. 458)

elaboration likelihood model The model of persuasion that proposes that knowing how to appeal to a person requires figuring out the likelihood that he or she will think much about (or elaborate on) the arguments. (p. 597)

elaborative rehearsal An aid to long-term memory storage that involves thinking about the meaning of information in order to process it with more depth; see also depth of processing. (p. 199)

electroconvulsive therapy (ECT) A last-resort treatment for severe depression, in which an electric shock to the brain is used to induce a seizure. (p. 583)

electroencephalogram (EEG) A record of the electrical activity toward the surface of the brain, used especially in sleep research and diagnosis of epilepsy. (p. 47)

emotion A positive or negative feeling state that typically includes arousal, subjective experience, and behavioral expression; also called affect. (p. 368)

emotional expression The variety of models (e.g., facial expression, posture, hand gestures, voice tone) through which people express feelings. (p. 372)

emotional forecasting Predicting emotional reactions to future events (p. 368)

emotional regulation Efforts to control emotional states; also called affect regulation. (p. 381)

empathic distress Feeling upset for another person. (p. 503)

empathy Feeling for another person who is hurting, which includes a cognitive component (understanding what the person is experiencing) and an emotional component (experiencing a feeling of empathic discomfort; in Rogers's theory of personality, the capacity to understand another person's experience cognitively and emotionally. (pp. 430, 503)

empiricism The belief that the path to scientific knowledge is systematic observation and, ideally, experimental observation. (p. 24)

empty chair technique A technique associated with Gestalt therapy, in which clients practice emotional expression by imagining that the person to whom they would like to speak is seated in the chair. (p. 571)

encoded Refers to information that is cast into a representational form or "code," so that it can be readily accessed from memory. (p. 213)

encoding specificity principle The notion that the match between the way information is encoded and the way it is retrieved is important to remembering. (p. 214)

endocrine system The collection of ductless glands that secrete hormones into the bloodstream and control various bodily and psychological functions. (p. 74)

endorphins Chemicals in the brain similar to morphine that elevate mood and reduce pain (p. 74)

episodic memory Memories of particular episodes or events from personal experience. (p. 207)

equilibration According to Piaget, a balancing of assimilation and accommodation in trying to adapt to the world. (p. 457)

ERG theory A theory of worker motivation distinguishing existence, relatedness, and growth needs. (p. 345)

error That part of a subject's score on a test that is unrelated to the true score. (p. 34)

escape learning A negative reinforcement procedure in which the behavior of an organism is reinforced by the cessation of an aversive event that already exists. (p. 173)

estrogens Hormones produced by the female gonads, the ovaries, which control sex drive as well as the development of secondary sex characteristics. (p. 75)

ethical hedonism The school of philosophical thought that asserts that all behavior, no matter how apparently altruistic, is and should be designed to increase one's own pleasure or reduce one's own pain. (p. 635)

ethology The field that studies animal behavior from a biological and evolutionary perspective. (p. 20)

etiology Causes of a disorder. (p. 520)

everyday memory Memory as it occurs in daily life. (p. 211)

evolutionary perspective The viewpoint built on Darwin's principle of natural selection that argues that human behavioral proclivities must be understood in the context of their evolutionary and adaptive significance. (p. 18)

existential dread The recognition that life has no absolute value or meaning, that any meaning that does exist we create for ourselves, and that ultimately, we all face death. (p. 432)

existentialism A school of modern philosophy that focuses on each individual's subjective existence or phenomenology and on the way the individual comes to terms with basic issues such as meaning in life and mortality. (p. 431)

expectancies Expectations relevant to desired outcomes. (pp. 186, 418)

expected utility A combined assessment of the value and probability of different options. (p. 249)

experience sampling A method in which participants report on the contents of consciousness at specified times, as when researchers beep them at regular or irregular intervals over the course of a week. (p. 307)

experimental research A research design in which investigators manipulate some aspect of a situation and examine the impact of this manipulation on the way subjects respond. (p. 35)

explanatory style The way people make sense of events or outcomes, particularly aversive ones. (p. 187)

explicit cognition Thinking that involves conscious manipulation of representations. (p. 250)

explicit memory The conscious recollection of facts and events. (p. 208)

exposure techniques Behavior therapy techniques based on classical conditioning in which the patient is confronted with the actual phobic stimulus. (p. 567)

expressed emotion The tendency of family interactions to be characterized by criticism, hostile interchanges, and emotional overinvolvement or intrusiveness by family members, implicated in the etiology and maintenance of schizophrenia and other disorders. (p. 538)

external attribution An explanation of behavior that attributes the behavior to the situation rather than the person. (p. 613)

external locus of control The belief that one's life is determined by forces outside (external to) oneself. (p. 186)

external validity The extent to which the findings of a study can be generalized to situations outside the laboratory. (p. 31)

extinction In classical conditioning, the process by which a conditioned response is weakened by presentation of the conditioned stimulus without the unconditioned stimulus; in operant conditioning, the process by which the connection between an operant and a reinforcer or punishment is similarly broken. (p. 166)

extroversion The tendency to be sociable, active, and willing to take risks. (p. 422)

F

factor analysis A statistical technique for identifying common factors that underlie performance on a wide variety of measures. (p. 289)

factors Common elements that underlie performance across a set of tasks. (p. 289)

false self A condition in which people mold themselves to other people's expectations and to the demands of the roles they play. (p. 430)

family alliances Patterns of taking sides in family conflicts. (p. 525)

family boundaries In family systems theory, the physical and psychological limits of a family or system. (p. 524)

family homeostatic mechanisms Methods members use to preserve equilibrium in a family. (p. 524)

family roles Parts individuals play in repetitive family interaction patterns. (p. 524)

family systems model The model of psychopathology which suggests that an individual's symptoms are really symptoms of dysfunction in a family. (p. 524)

family therapy A psychological treatment that attempts to change maladaptive interaction patterns among members of a family. (p. 574)

fasting phase The second stage of metabolism, when the body converts glucose and fat into energy. (p. 348)

feature detector A neuron that fires only when stimulation in its receptive field matches a particular pattern or orientation. (p. 120)

Fechner's law The law of psychophysics proposed by Gustav Fechner, that the subjective magnitude of a sensation grows as a proportion of the logarithm of the stimulus. (p. 109)

feedback Information about the extent to which a system is meeting a goal. (p. 349)

feedback mechanisms Processes that provide information regarding the state of a homeostatic system with regard to its set-point or steady-state. (p. 349)

fight-flight system Anatomical system associated with unconditioned escape and defensive aggression and the emotions of terror and rage. (p. 183)

figure-ground perception A fundamental rule of perception described by Gestalt psychology which states that people inherently differentiate between figure (the object they are viewing, sound to which they are listening, etc.) and ground (background). (p. 140)

first impressions Initial perceptions of another person that can be powerful in shaping future beliefs about the person. (p. 605)

Five Factor Model (FFM) A trait theory which asserts that personality consists of five traits (openness to experience, conscientiousness, extroversion, agreeableness and neuroticism.). (p. 423)

fixations In psychoanalytic theory, prominent conflicts and concerns focused on wishes from a particular period. (p. 407)

fixed-interval (FI) schedules of reinforcement When the organism receives rewards for its responses only after a fixed amount of time. (p. 177)

fixed-ratio (FR) schedules of reinforcement When the organism receives reinforcement at a fixed rate, according to the number of responses emitted. (p. 177)

flashbulb memories Especially vivid memories of exciting or highly consequential events. (p. 224)

flooding Cognitive-behavioral technique designed to eliminate phobias, in which the patient confronts the real phobic stimulus all at once. (p. 567)

fluid intelligence Intellectual capacities that have no specific content but are used in processing information. (p. 290)

foot-in-the-door technique Persuasive technique often used by salespeople, which involves getting people to comply with a small request in order to induce their compliance with a larger request. (p. 600)

forebrain In humans, the most evolutionary recent part of the brain, which allows complex emotional reactions, thought processes, and movement patterns; consists of the hypothalamus, thalamus, and cerebrum. (p. 84)

forgetting The inability to retrieve memories. (p. 223)

form perception The organization of sensations into meaningful shapes and patterns. (p. 139)

formal operational stage Piaget's fourth stage of cognitive development, which begins at about age 12 to 15, and is characterized by the ability to manipulate abstract as well as concrete objects, events, and ideas mentally. (p. 460)

fovea The central region of the retina, where light is most directly focused by the lens. (p. 114)

free association The therapeutic technique for exploring associational networks and unconscious process involved in symptom formation. (p. 561)

free will versus determinism The philosophical question of whether people act on the basis of their freely chosen intentions, or whether their actions are caused or determined by physical processes in their bodies or in the environment in which they live. (p. 7)

frequency In a sound wave, the number of cycles per second, expressed in hertz and responsible for subjective experience of pitch. (p. 125)

frequency distribution A way of organizing data to show how frequently subjects received each of the many possible scores. (p. 55)

frequency theory The theory of pitch that asserts that perceived pitch reflects the rate of vibration of the basilar membrane. (p. 129)

frontal lobes Brain structures involved in coordination of movement, attention, planning, social skills, conscience, abstract thinking, memory, and aspects of personality. (p. 90)

frustration-aggression hypothesis The hypothesis that when people are frustrated in achieving a goal, they may become aggressive. (p. 645)

functional fixedness The tendency to ignore other possible functions of an object when one already has a function in mind. (p. 247)

functional magnetic resonance imaging (fMRI) A brain scanning technique used as an individual carries out tasks. (p. 47)

functionalism An early school of thought in psychology influenced by Darwinian theory that looked for explanations of psychological processes in terms of their role, or function, in helping the individual adapt to the environment. (p. 9)

G

GABA Acronym for gamma-aminobutyric acid, one of the most widespread neurotransmitters in the nervous system, which largely plays an inhibitory role in the brain. (p. 73)

galvanic skin response An electrical measure of the amount of sweat on the skin that is produced during states of anxiety or arousal; also called skin conductance or electrodermal activity (EDA). (p. 166)

ganglion cells Nerve cells in the retina that integrate information from multiple bipolar cells, the axons of which bundle together to form the optic nerve. (p. 114)

gate-control theory The theory of pain perception which proposes that cells in the spinal cord act as neurological "gates," allowing some pain signals through while blocking others. (p. 136)

gender The psychological meaning of being male or female. (p. 487)

gender constancy The recognition that people's gender cannot be altered by changes in appearance or activities. (p. 495)

gender identity The categorization of oneself as either male or female. (p. 494)

gender roles The range of behaviors considered appropriate by society for males and females. (p. 486)

gender schemas Representations that associate psychological characteristics with one sex or the other. (p. 495)

gender stability The understanding that one's gender remains constant over time. (p. 494)

gene The unit of hereditary transmission. (p. 96)

generalizability The applicability of a study's finding to the entire population of interest. (p. 31)

generalized anxiety disorder Persistent anxiety at a moderate but disturbing level. (p. 545)

generalized expectancies Expectancies that influence a broad spectrum of behavior. (p. 186)

generativity A concern for the next generation as well as an interest producing something of lasting value to society. (p. 508)

generativity versus stagnation In Erikson's theory, the stage in which people in mid-adulthood experience concern for the next generation as well as an interest in producing something of lasting value to society. (p. 508)

generic memory General world knowledge or facts; also called semantic memory. (p. 207)

genital stage In Freudian theory, psychosexual stage that occurs at approximately age 12 and beyond, when conscious sexuality resurfaces after years of repression. (p. 409)

genogram A map of a family over three or four generations, drawn by a therapist to explore possible similarities between current difficulties and the family's past. (p. 574)

Gestalt psychology A school of psychology that holds that perception is an active experience of imposing order on an overwhelming panorama of details by seeing them as parts of larger whole (or gestalts). (pp. 25, 571)

Gestalt therapy A psychological treatment based on the assumption that psychological distress results from losing touch with one's emotions and one's authentic inner voice, and that focusing on the "here and now" is curative. (pp. 25, 571)

g-factor The general intelligence factor that emerges through factor analysis of IQ tests. (p. 289)

Gf-Gc theory A hierarchical model of intelligence that argues for the presence of two overarching types of intelligence-fluid intelligence and crystallized intelligence, as well as more specific intellectual skills, such as short-term memory. (p. 290)

gifted Exceptionally talented. (p. 285)

glutamate One of the most widespread neurotransmitters in the nervous system, which largely plays an excitatory role; also called glutamic acid. (p. 72)

goal A desired outcome established through social learning. (p. 342)

goal-setting theory The theory of motivation that suggests that conscious goals regulate much human action, particularly performance tasks. (p. 343)

gonads Endocrine glands that influence much of sexual development and behavior. (p. 75)

good continuation A Gestalt rule of perception which states that, if possible, the brain organizes stimuli into continuous lines or patterns rather than discontinuous elements. (p. 140)

graded exposure A modified version of the behaviorist flooding technique for treating anxiety, in which stimuli are real but are presented to the patient in a gradual manner. (p. 567)

graded potential A spreading voltage change that occurs when the neural membrane receives a signal from another cell. (p. 69)

grammar A system of rules for generating understandable and acceptable language utterances. (p. 263)

group A collection of people whose actions affect the other group members. (p. 651)

group process The interactions among members of a group. (p. 573)

group therapy A treatment method in which multiple people meet together to work toward therapeutic goals. (p. 573)

gustation Taste. (p. 132)

H

habituation The decreasing strength of a response after repeated presentations of the stimulus. (p. 160)

hair cells Receptors for sound attached to the basilar membrane. (p. 127)

hallucinations Sensory perceptions that distort, or occur without, an external stimulus. (pp. 329, 534)

hallucinogen A drug that produces hallucinations. (p. 329)

halo effect A tendency to attribute additional positive characteristics to someone who has one salient quality, such as physical attractiveness. (p. 605)

heritability The extent to which individual differences in phenotype are determined by genetic factors or genotype. (p. 97)

heritability coefficient The statistic that quantifies the degree to which a trait is heritable. (p. 97)

hertz (Hz) The unit of measurement of frequency of sound waves. (p. 125)

heuristics In problem solving, cognitive shortcuts or rules of thumb. (p. 250)

hierarchy of needs. Maslow's theory that needs are arranged hierarchically, from physiological needs, safety needs, belongingness needs, and esteem needs, through self-actualization needs. (p. 344)

hindbrain The part of the brain above the spinal cord that includes the medulla, cerebellum, and parts of the reticular formation. (p. 82)

hippocampus A structure in the limbic system involved in the acquisition and consolidation of new information in memory. (p. 86)

histogram A graph that plots ranges of scores along the x axis and the frequency of scores in each range on the y axis. (p. 55)

homeostasis The body's tendency to maintain a relatively constant state that permits cells to live and function. (p. 348)

hormone A chemical secreted directly into the bloodstream by the endocrine glands. (p. 74)

hue The sensory quality people normally consider color. (p. 121)

humanistic theories of personality Theories that focus on aspects of personality that are distinctly human, not shared by other animals, such as how to find meaning in life and how to be true to oneself. (p. 430)

humanistic therapies Psychological treatments that focus on the patient's conscious or lived experience and on the way each person uniquely experiences relationships and the world. (pp. 430, 571)

hypnosis An altered state of consciousness characterized by deep relaxation and suggestibility which a person voluntarily enters through the efforts of a hypnotist. (p. 323)

hypnotic susceptibility The capacity to enter into deep hypnotic states. (p. 324)

hypothalamus The brain structure situated directly below the thalamus involved in the regulation of eating, sleeping, sexual activity, movement, and emotion. (p. 85)

hypothesis A tentative belief or educated guess that purports to predict or explain the relationship between two or more variables. (p. 30)

I

iconic storage A visual sensory registration process by which people retain an afterimage of a visual stimulus. (p. 197)

id In Freudian theory, the reservoir of sexual and aggressive energy, which is driven by impulses and is characterized by primary process thinking. (p. 410)

ideal self A person's view of what she/he should be like. (pp. 430, 619)

identification Making another person part of oneself by imitating the person's behavior, changing the self-concept to see oneself as more like that person, and attempting to become more like the person by accepting his or her values and attitudes. (p. 408)

identity A stable sense of knowing who one is and what one's values and ideals are. (p. 508)

identity confusion A condition in which the individual fails to develop a coherent and enduring sense of self, and has difficulty committing to roles, values, people, and occupational choices in his or her life. (p. 508)

identity versus identity confusion In Erikson's theory, stage in which adolescents develop a stable sense of who they are and a stable set of values and ideals. (p. 508)

ill-defined problem A situation in which both the information needed to solve a problem and the criteria that determine whether the goals are attained are vague. (p. 245)

immune system A system of cells throughout the body that fights disease. (pp. 165, 393)

implicit attitudes Attitudes that regulate thought and behavior unconsciously and automatically. (p. 595)

implicit cognition Thinking that occurs outside awareness. (p. 252)

implicit memory Memory that cannot be brought to mind consciously but can be expressed in behavior. (p. 208)

implicit motives Motives that can be activated and expressed outside of awareness. (p. 344)

imprinting The tendency of young animals of certain species to follow an animal to which they were exposed during a sensitive period early in their lives. (p. 476)

incentive An external motivating stimulus (as opposed to an internal need state). (p. 342)

inclusive fitness The notion that natural selection favors organisms that survive, reproduce, and foster the survival and reproduction of their kin. (p. 21)

independent variable The variable an experimenter manipulates, or whose effects the experimenter assesses. (p. 35)

individual differences The way people resemble and differ from one another in personality or intelligence. (p. 403)

inductive reasoning The process of reasoning from specific observations to generate propositions. (p. 242)

industry versus inferiority In Erikson's theory, the stage in which children develop a sense of competence as they begin to practice skills they will use in productive work. (p. 507)

infantile amnesia The inability to recall early childhood memories. (p. 454)

inferential statistics Procedures for assessing whether the results obtained with a sample are likely to reflect characteristics of the population as a whole. (pp. 39, 55)

information processing The transformation, storage, and retrieval of environmental inputs through thought and memory. (p. 16)

informed consent A subject's ability to agree to participate in a study in an informed manner. (p. 50)

ingroup People perceived as belonging to a valued group. (p. 611)

initiation rites Ceremonies such as the rites found in many cultures in adolescence, which initiate a person into a new social role, such as adulthood. (p. 508)

initiative versus guilt In Erikson's theory, the stage in which children develop a sense of planfulness and responsibility. (p. 507)

insight In learning theory, the ability to perceive a connection between a problem and its solution; in psychodynamic treatments, the understanding of one's own psychological processes. (pp. 186, 560)

insomnia The inability to sleep. (p. 317)

instinct A relatively fixed pattern of behavior that animals produce without learning. (p. 336)

instinct model Freud's theory of motivation, which held that people are motivated by sexual and aggressive instincts or drives. (p. 406)

instrumental aggression Calm, pragmatic aggression that may or may not be accompanied by anger. (p. 639)

integrity versus despair In Erikson's theory, stage in which older people look back on their lives with a sense of satisfaction that they have lived it well, or with despair, regret, and loss for loved ones who have died. (p. 509)

intelligence The application of cognitive skills and knowledge to learn, solve problems, and obtain ends that are valued by an individual or culture. (p. 280)

intelligence quotient (IQ) A score originally derived by dividing mental age and chronological age and multiplying by 100, but now generally established by comparing the individual's performance to norms of people his or her own age. (p. 282)

intelligence test A measure designed to assess an individual's level of cognitive capabilities compared to other people in a population. (p. 281)

interactionist approaches Multidirectional view of personality which asserts that personality is shaped by economic and cultural demands but that cultural and economic processes themselves are in part created to fulfill psychological needs. (p. 435)

interference The intrusion of similar memories on one another. (p. 226)

intermittent schedule of reinforcement An operant procedure in which an organism is reinforced only some of the time it emits a behavior; also called partial schedule of reinforcement. (p. 176)

intermodal processing The capacity to associate sensations of an object from different senses, or to match one's own actions to behaviors that are observed visually. (p. 453)

internal attribution An explanation of behavior that attributes it to the person rather than the situation. (p. 613)

internal consistency A type of reliability that assesses whether the items in a test measure the same construct. (p. 33)

internal locus of control The belief that one is the master of one's fate. (p. 186)

internal validity The extent to which a study is methodologically adequate. (p. 31)

internal working model A mental representation of the attachment relationship, which forms the basis for expectations in close relationships. (p. 478)

interneuron A neuron that connects other neurons to each other, found only in the brain and spinal cord. (p. 66)

interpersonal attraction The factors that lead people to choose to spend time with other people. (p. 627)

interpretation A therapeutic technique whereby the therapist helps the patient understand his or her experiences in a new light. (p. 562)

interrater reliability A measure of the similarity with which different raters apply a measure. (p. 33)

interstimulus interval The duration of time between presentation of the conditioned stimulus and the unconditioned stimulus. (p. 167)

interval schedules of reinforcement Operant conditioning procedures in which rewards are delivered according to intervals of time. (p. 177)

interview A research tool in which the investigator ask the subject questions. (p. 43)

intimacy A kind of closeness characterized by self-disclosure, warmth, and mutual caring. (p. 362)

intimacy versus isolation In Erikson's theory, the stage in which young adults establish enduring, committed friendships and romantic relationships. (p. 508)

intrinsic motivation The motivation to perform a behavior for its own sake, rather than for some kind of external (or extrinsic) reward. (p. 343)

introspection The method used by Wundt and other structuralists in which trained subjects verbally reported everything that went through their minds when presented with a stimulus or task; more generally, refers to the process of looking inward at one's own mental contents or process. (p. 8)

intuitive scientist The conception of people as lay scientists who use intuitive theories, frame hypotheses, collect data about themselves and others, and examine the impact of various experimental manipulations when trying to understand themselves and others; also called intuitive psychologist. (p. 613)

iris The ring of pigmented tissue that gives the eye its blue, green, or brown color; its muscle fibers cause the pupil to constrict or dilate. (p. 113)

J

James-Lange theory A theory of emotion that asserts that emotion originates with peripheral arousal, which people then label as an emotional state. (p. 369)

John Henryism The tendency among members of minority groups to work hard and cope actively despite difficult circumstances. (p. 398)

just noticeable difference (jnd) The smallest difference in intensity between two stimuli that a person can detect. (p. 108)

K

kinesthesia The sense that provides information about the movement and position of the limbs and other parts of the body; receptors in joints transduce information about the position of the bones, and receptors in the tendons and muscles transmit messages about muscular tension. (p. 138)

knowledge base Accumulated information stored in long-term memory. (pp. 292, 462)

L

labeling theory The theory that psychiatric diagnosis is a way of labeling individuals a society considers deviant. (p. 517)

language The system of symbols, sounds, meanings, and rules for their combination that constitutes the primary mode of communication among humans. (p. 260)

language acquisition device (LAD) The prewired, innate mechanism that allows for the acquisition of language hypothesized by Noam Chomsky. (p. 267)

latency stage The psychosexual phase that occurs roughly around ages 6 to 11, when children repress their sexual impulses. (p. 409)

latent content According to Freud's dream theory, the meaning that underlies the symbolism in a dream. (p. 321)

latent inhibition A phenomenon in classical conditioning in which initial exposure to a neutral stimulus without a UCS slows the process of later learning the CS-UCS association and developing a CR. (p. 167)

latent learning Learning that has occurred but is not currently manifest in behavior. (p. 185)

lateralized Localized on one or the other side of the brain (p. 92)

law of effect Law proposed by Thorndike which states that the tendency of an organism to produce a behavior depends on the effect the behavior has on the environment. (p. 171)

laws of association First proposed by Aristotle, basic principles used to account for learning and memory, which describe the conditions under which one thought becomes connected, or associated, with another. (p. 161)

leader A person who exercises greater influence than the average member of a group. (p. 653)

learned helplessness The expectancy that one cannot escape from aversive events. (p. 187)

learning Any relatively permanent change in the way an organism responds based on its experience. (p. 160)

lens The disc-shaped, elastic structure of the eye that focuses light. (p. 113)

lesions Damaged areas. (p. 3)

level of processing The degree to which information is elaborated, reflected upon, or processed in a meaningful way during encoding of memory. (p. 213)

libido In Freudian theory, the human sexual drive, which refers as much to pleasure-seeking and love as to sexual intercourse. (p. 406)

life history method A method of personality assessment whose aim is to understand the whole person in the context of his or her life experience and environment. (p. 413)

life tasks The conscious, self-defined problems people attempt to solve. (p. 418)

limbic system Subcortical structures responsible for emotional reactions, many motivational processes, learning, and aspects of memory. (p. 85)

lithium The drug treatment of choice for bipolar disorder. (p. 582)

localization of function The extent to which different parts of the brain control different aspects of functioning. (p. 4)

locus of control of reinforcement Generalized expectancies people hold about whether or not their own behavior will bring about the outcomes they seek. (p. 186)

longitudinal study Type of research that follows the same individuals over time. (p. 444)

long-term memory (LTM) Memory for facts, images, thoughts, feelings, skills, and experiences that may last as long as a lifetime. (p. 199)

long-term potentiation The tendency of a group of neurons to fire more readily after consistent stimulation from other neurons. (p. 170)

loosening of associations A tendency common in individuals with schizophrenia, in which conscious thought is directed along associative lines rather than by controlled, logical, purposeful processes. (p. 534)

loudness The psychological property corresponding to a sound wave's amplitude. (p. 125)

low-effort syndrome The tendency to exert minimal effort to escape stressful social and economic circumstance (p. 397)

M

magnetic resonance imaging (MRI) Brain scanning technique. (p. 47)

maintenance rehearsal The process of repeating information over and over to maintain it momentarily in STM. (p. 198)

major depressive disorder A form of psychopathology, characterized by depressed mood, loss of interest in pleasurable activities, and disturbances in appetite, sleep, energy level, and concentration. (p. 539)

mania A period of abnormally euphoric, elevated, or expansive mood. (p. 540)

manic Relating to a mood disturbance in which people feel excessively happy or euphoric and believe they can do anything. (p. 539)

manifest content The obvious storyline of a dream. (p. 321)

MAO inhibitors Antidepressant medication that keeps the chemical MAO from breaking down neurotransmitter substances in the presynaptic neuron, which makes more neurotransmitter available for release into the synapse. (p. 581)

marital therapy Psychotherapy that treats a couple; also called couple therapy. (p. 574)

mastery goals Motives to increase one's competence, mastery, or skill. (p. 363)

maturation Biologically based development. (p. 441)

mean The statistical average of the scores of all subjects on a measure. (p. 56)

measure A concrete way of assessing a variable. (p. 32)

measures of central tendency Statistical concepts that provide an index of the way a "typical" subject responded on a measure. (p. 56)

median The score that falls in the middle of the distribution of scores, with half of subjects scoring below it and half above it. (p. 56)

meditation A relaxation practice, often associated with religion, characterized by a state of tranquility. (p. 323)

medulla An extension of the spinal cord, essential to life, controlling such vital physiological functions as heartbeat, circulation, and respiration. (p. 82)

memory systems Discrete but interdependent processing units responsible for different kinds of remembering. (p. 200)

mental age (MA) The average age at which children can be expected to achieve a particular score on an intelligence test. (p. 281)

mental image A visual representation of a stimulus. (p. 235)

mental models Representations that describe, explain, or predict the way things work. (p. 236)

mental retardation Significantly subaverage general intellectual functioning, existing concurrently with deficits in adaptive behavior and manifested during childhood. (p. 284)

mental simulation A problem-solving strategy in which people imagine the steps to problem solving mentally before actually undertaking them. (p. 246)

meta-analysis A statistical technique that allows researchers to combine findings from various studies and make comparisons between the effects of treatment and no treatment. (p. 585)

metabolism The processes by which the body transforms food into energy. (p. 348)

metacognition People's understanding of the way they perform cognitive tasks such as remembering, learning, or solving problems. (p. 463)

method of loci A memory aid or mnemonic device in which images are remembered by fitting them into an orderly arrangement of locations. (p. 216)

midbrain The section of the brain above the hindbrain involved in some auditory and visual functions, movement, and conscious arousal and activation. (p. 84)

mind-body problem The question of how mental and physical events interact. (p. 7)

mnemonic devices Systematic strategies for remembering information. (p. 216)

mode The most common or most frequent score or value of a variable observed in a sample. (p. 56)

modeling A social learning procedure in which a person learns to reproduce behavior exhibited by a model. (p. 189)

monocular cues Visual input from a single eye alone that contributes to depth perception. (p. 143)

monozygotic (MZ) twins Twins identical in their genetic makeup, having developed from the union of the same sperm and egg. (p. 97)

mood Relatively extended emotional states that do not shift attention or disrupt ongoing activities. (p. 381)

mood disorder A disorder characterized by disturbances in emotion and mood. (p. 539)

morality of constraint According to Piaget's theory of moral development, the first stage of moral judgment, in which children believe that morals are absolute. (p. 499)

morality of cooperation According to Piaget's theory of moral development, the stage at which moral rules can be changed if they are not appropriate to the occasion as long as the people involved agree to do so. (p. 499)

morpheme In language, a basic unit of meaning. (p. 262)

motion detectors Ganglion cells that are particularly sensitive to movement. (p. 144)

motion parallax A monocular depth cue involving the relative movements of retinal images of objects; nearby objects appear to speed across the field of vision, whereas distant objects barely seem to move. (p. 144)

motion perception The perception of movement in objects. (p. 144)

motivated forgetting Forgetting for a reason, which leads to inhibition of retrieval. (p. 226)

motivation The moving force that energizes behavior. (p. 335)

motor cortex The primary zone of the frontal lobes responsible for control of motor behavior. (p. 90)

motor neuron A neuron that transmits commands from the brain to the glands or musculature of the body, typically through the spinal cord; also called efferent neuron. (p. 66)

Müller-Lyer illusion A perceptual illusion in which two lines of equal length appear different in size. (p. 148)

multiaxial system of diagnosis The system used in DSM-IV that places mental disorders in their social and biological context, assessing the patient on five axes. (p. 528)

myelin sheath A tight coat of cells composed primarily of lipids, which serves to insulate the axon from chemical or physical stimuli that might interfere with the transmission of nerve impulses and speeds neural transmission. (p. 67)

N

natural selection A theory proposed by Darwin which states that natural forces select traits in organisms that help them adapt to their environment. (p. 19)

naturalistic observation The in-depth observation of a phenomenon in its natural setting. (p. 42)

nature-nurture controversy The question of

degree to which inborn biological processes or environmental events determine human behavior. (p. 18)

need for achievement A motive to do well, to succeed, and to avoid failure. (p. 362)

negative affect A general category of emotions related to feeling bad. (p. 376)

negative correlation A relation between two variables in which the higher one is, the lower the other tends to be. (p. 45)

negative identity Taking on a role that society defines as bad but that nevertheless provides one with a sense of being something. (p. 508)

negative reciprocity The tendency of members of a couple to respond to negative comments or actions by their partner with negative behaviors in return. (p. 575)

negative reinforcement The process whereby a behavior is made more likely because it is followed by the removal of an aversive stimulus. (p. 173)

negative reinforcer An aversive or unpleasant stimulus that strengthens a behavior by its removal. (p. 173)

negative symptoms Symptoms of schizophrenia such as flat affect, socially inappropriate behavior, and intellectual impairments that reflect a deficit or a loss of something that was once present or should be present. (p. 534)

negative triad In Beck's cognitive theory of depression, negative outlook on the world, the self, and the future. (p. 542)

neglected children Children who are ignored by their peers. (p. 489)

neo-Piagetian theories Theories that attempt to wed a stage model of cognitive development with research on information processing and domain-specific knowledge. (p. 464)

nervous system The interacting network of nerve cells that underlies all psychological activity. (p. 66)

network of association A cluster of interconnected information stored in long-term memory. (p. 217)

neuroimaging techniques Methods for studying the brain that use computer programs to convert the data taken from brain scanning devices into visual images (p. 47)

neurons Cells in the nervous system. (p. 66)

neuroses Problems in living, such as phobias, chronic self-doubts, and repetitive interpersonal problems. (p. 519)

neuroticism A continuum from emotional stability to emotional instability. (p. 422)

neurotransmitter Chemical that transmits information from one neuron to another. (p. 70)

node A cluster or piece of information along a network of association. (p. 217)

non-REM (NREM) sleep States of sleep in which rapid eye movements (REM sleep) are not present. (p. 318)

nonverbal communication Mode of communication that relies on gestures, expressions, intonation, body language, and other unspoken signals. (p. 265)

normal distribution A frequency distribution in which most subjects' scores fall in the middle of the bell-shaped distribution, and progressively fewer subjects have scores at either extreme. (p. 57)

noradrenaline A hormone that triggers physiological arousal, particularly in potential danger situations. (p. 74)

norms Standards for the behavior of group members. (p. 651)

O

obedience Overt compliance with authority. (p. 647)

obesity A condition characterized by a body weight over 15 percent above the ideal for one's height and age. (p. 352)

object permanence In Piaget's theory, the recognition that objects exist in time and space independent of one's actions on, or observation of, them. (p. 458)

object relations Behavioral patterns in intimate relationships and the motivational, cognitive, and affective processes that produce them. (p. 412)

observational learning Learning that occurs by observing the behavior of others. (p. 189)

obsessions Persistent unwanted thoughts or ideas. (p. 546)

obsessive-compulsive disorder A disorder characterized by recurrent obsessions and compulsions that cause distress and significantly interfere with an individual's life. (p. 546)

occipital lobes Brain structures located in the rear portion of the cortex, involved in vision. (p. 88)

Oedipus complex In Freudian theory, process that occurs during the phallic stage of development when the child desires an exclusive, sensual/sexual relationship with the opposite sex parent. (p. 408)

olfaction Smell. (p. 130)

olfactory epithelium Thin pair of structures in which transduction of smell occurs. (p. 131)

olfactory nerve The bundle of axons from sensory receptor cells that transmits information from the nose to the brain. (p. 132)

operant A behavior that is emitted by the organism rather than elicited by the environment. (p. 172)

operant conditioning Learning that results when an organism associates a response that occurs spontaneously with a particular environment effect; also called instrumental conditioning. (p. 172)

operation In Piagetian theory, a mental action that the individual can use to manipulate, transform, and return an object of thought to its original state. (p. 459)

operationalizing Turning an abstract concept or variable into a concrete form that can be defined by some set of operations or actions. (p. 37)

opponent-process theory A theory of color vision that proposes the existence of three antagonistic color systems: a blue-yellow system, a red-green system, and a black-white system; according to this theory, the blue-yellow and red-green systems are responsible for hue, while the black-white system contributes to perception of brightness and saturation. (p. 123)

optic nerve The bundle of axons of ganglion cells that carries information from the retina to the brain. (p. 114)

oral stage In Freudian theory, the psychosexual phase occurring roughly in the first year of life, when children explore the world through their mouths. (p. 407)

organizational effects Effects of hormones that influence the structure of the brain. (p. 357)

ought self The duties, obligations, and responsibilities that define the way the person should be. (p. 619)

outgroup People perceived as not belonging to a valued group. (p. 611)

P

panic disorder A disorder characterized by attacks of intense fear and feelings of doom or terror not justified by the situation. (p. 545)

paradigm A broad system of theoretical assumptions employed by a scientific community to make sense out of a domain of experience. (p. 10)

parallel distributed processing (PDP) A model of human cognitive processes in which many cognitive processes occur simultaneously (i.e., in parallel), so that a representation is spread out (i.e., distributed) throughout a network of interacting processing units; also called connectionism. (p. 254)

parasympathetic nervous system The part of the autonomic nervous system involved in conserving and maintaining the body's energy resources. (p. 76)

parietal lobes Brain structures located in front of the occipital lobes, involved in a number of functions, including sense of touch and the experience of one's own body in space and in movement. (p. 89)

Parkinson's disease A disorder characterized by uncontrollable tremors, repetitive movements, and difficulty in both initiating behavior and stopping movements already in progress. (p. 73)

partial schedule of reinforcement An operant procedure in which an organism is reinforced only some of the time it emits a behavior; also called intermittent schedule of reinforcement. (p. 176)

participants The individuals who participate in a study; also called subjects. (p. 31)

participatory modeling A cognitive-behavioral technique in which the therapist models desired behavior and gradually induces the patient to participate in it. (p. 568)

passionate love A highly emotional form of love marked by intense physiological arousal and absorption in another person. (p. 630)

passive aggression The indirect expression of anger toward others. (p. 412)

penis envy In Freudian theory, feeling of envy that emerges in girls, who feel that because they lack a penis they are inferior to boys. (p. 409)

percentile scores A method of representing subjects' scores on a variable that shows the percentage of scores that fall below a score. (p. 58)

perception The process by which the brain selects, organizes, and interprets sensations. (p. 102)

percepts Meaningful perceptual units, such as images of particular objects. (p. 139)

perceptual constancy The organization of changing sensations into percepts that are relatively stable in size, shape, and color. (p. 146)

perceptual illusions Perceptual misinterpretations produced in the course of normal perceptual processes. (p. 142)

perceptual interpretation The process of generating meaning from sensory experience. (p. 149)

perceptual organization The process of integrating sensations into meaningful perceptual units. (p. 139)

performance-approach goals Goals that center on approaching or attaining a standard. (p. 363)

performance-avoidance goals Goals that center on avoiding failure, particularly publicly observable failure. (p. 363)

performance goals Motives to achieve at a particular level, usually one that meets a socially defined standard. (p. 363)

peripheral nervous system (PNS) A component of the nervous system that includes neurons that travel to and from the central nervous system; includes the somatic nervous system and the autonomic nervous system. (p. 75)

peripheral route to persuasion A method of persuasion that appeals less to rational and thoughtful processes than to automatic or emotional ones. (p. 597)

permissive parenting style A way of parenting that imposes few controls on children, allowing the children to make their own decisions whenever possible. (p. 484)

personal constructs Mental representations of the people, places, things, and events that are significant in a person's life. (p. 418)

personality The enduring patterns of thought, feeling, and behavior that are expressed by individuals in different circumstances. (p. 403)

personality disorder A chronic and severe disorder that substantially inhibits the capacity to love and to work. (p. 520)

personal value The importance individuals attach to various stimuli and to the outcomes they expect as a result of their behavior. (p. 418)

person-by-situation interaction Process by which some personality dispositions are activated only under certain circumstances. (p. 428)

person-centered approach Carl Rogers' theory of personality, which focuses on understanding the individual's phenomenal world. (p. 430)

perspectives Broad ways of understanding psychological phenomena, including theoretical propositions, shared metaphors, and accepted methods of observation. (p. 10)

perspective taking The ability to understand other people's viewpoints or perspectives. (p. 492)

persuasion Deliberate efforts to induce attitude change. (p. 597)

pessimistic explanatory style A tendency to explain bad events that happen in a self-blaming manner, viewing their causes as global and stable. (p. 187)

phallic stage In Freudian theory, the psychosexual phase occurring roughly around ages 4 to 6, when children discover that they can get pleasure from touching their genitals. (p. 408)

phantom limbs Misleading "sensations" from missing limbs (p. 134)

phenomenal experience The way individuals conceive of reality and experience themselves and their world. (p. 430)

pheromone A chemical secreted by organisms in some species that allow communication between organisms. (p. 131)

phobia An irrational fear of a specific object or situation. (pp. 165, 545)

phoneme The smallest unit of speech that distinguishes one linguistic utterance from another. (p. 262)

phrase A group of words that act as a unit and convey a meaning. (p. 262)

pitch The psychological property corresponding to the frequency of a sound wave; the quality of a tone from low to high. (p. 125)

pituitary gland Often referred to as the "master gland" of the endocrine system because many of the hormones it releases stimulate and thus regulate the hormonal action of other endocrine glands. (p. 75)

place theory A theory of pitch which proposes that different areas of the basilar membrane are maximally sensitive to different frequencies. (p. 128)

placebo effect A phenomenon in which an experimental intervention produces an effect because subjects believe it will produce an effect. (p. 38)

plasticity The flexibility of the brain to adapt to changing circumstances or damage. (p. 447)

population A group of people or animals of interest to a research from which a sample is drawn. (p. 31)

positive correlation A relation between two variables in which the higher one is, the higher the other tends to be. (p. 45)

positive affect A general category of emotions related to feeling good. (p. 376)

positive reinforcement The process by which a behavior is made more likely because of the presentation of a rewarding stimulus. (p. 172)

positive reinforcer A rewarding stimulus that strengthens a behavior when it is presented. (p. 172)

positive symptoms Symptoms of schizophrenia such as delusions and hallucinations that reflect the presence of something that was not there previously and is not normally present. (p. 534)

positron emission tomography (PET) A computerized brain scanning technique that allows observation of the brain in action. (p. 47)

postconventional morality In Kohlberg's theory, the level of morality in which individuals follow abstract, self-defined principles which may or may not accord with the dominant mores or morals of the times. (p. 500)

posttraumatic stress disorder (PTSD) An anxiety disorder characterized by symptoms such as flashbacks and recurrent thoughts of a psychologically distressing event outside the normal range of experience. (p. 546)

pragmatics The way language is used and understood in everyday life. (p. 264)

preconscious mental processes Thoughts that are not conscious but could become conscious at any point, much like information stored in long-term semantic memory. (pp. 308, 405)

preconventional morality In Kohlberg's theory, the level of morality in which children follow moral rules either to avoid punishment or to obtain reward. (p. 500)

prejudice Judging people based on negative stereotypes. (p. 606)

preoperational stage Piaget's second stage of cognitive development, beginning roughly around age 2 and lasting until age 5 to 7, characterized by the emergence of symbolic thought. (p. 458)

prepared learning Responses to which an organism is predisposed because they were selected through natural selection. (p. 168)

presbycusis The inability to hear high-frequency sounds, which usually occurs with aging. (p. 451)

primary appraisal The first stage in the process of stress and coping in which the person decides whether the situation is benign, stressful, or irrelevant. (p. 389)

primary area The area of the cortex involved in sensory functions and in the direct control of motor movements. (p. 88)

primary drive An innate drive such as hunger, thirst, and sex. (p. 341)

primary process thinking Associative thinking described by Freud, in which ideas connected in people's minds through experience come to mind automatically when they think about related ideas; primary process thought is also wishful and unrealistic. (p. 410)

primary reinforcer A stimulus that is innately rewarding to an organism. (p. 182)

priming effects The processing of specific information is facilitated by prior exposure to the same or similar information. (p. 209)

proactive interference A phenomenon in which old memories that have already been stored interfere with the retrieval of new information. (p. 226)

probability value The probability that obtained findings were accidental or just a mater of chance; also called *p*-value. (p. 59)

problem solving The process of transforming one situation into another that meets a goal. (p. 245)

problem-solving strategy A technique used to solve problems. (p. 246)

procedural memory Knowledge of procedures or skills that emerges when people engage in activities that require them. (p. 207)

projection A defense mechanism in which a person attributes his own unacknowledged feelings or impulses to others. (p. 411)

projective test A personality assessment method in which subjects are confronted with an ambiguous stimulus and asked to define it in some way; the assumption underlying these tests is that when people are faced with an unstructured, undefined stimulus, they will project their own thoughts, feelings, and wishes into their responses. (p. 414)

proprioceptive senses Senses that provide information about body position and movement; the two proprioceptive senses are kinesthesia and vestibular sense. (p. 138)

prosocial behavior Behavior that benefits either specific individuals or society as a whole. (p. 501)

prospective memory Memory for things that need to be done in the future. (p. 212)

prototype A particularly good example of a category. (p. 238)

proximity A Gestalt rule of perception which states that, other things being equal, the brain groups objects together that are close to each other. (p. 140)

psychoactive substance Any drug that operates on the nervous system to alter patterns of mental activity. (p. 327)

psychoanalysis An intensive therapeutic process in which the patient meets with the therapist three to five times in week, lies on a couch, and uses free association, interpretation, and transference. (p. 563)

psychodynamic formulation A set of hypotheses about the patient's personality structure and the meaning of a symptom. (p. 520)

psychodynamic perspective The perspective initiated by Sigmund Freud that focuses on the dynamic interplay of mental forces. (p. 11)

psychodynamic psychotherapy A form of psychotherapy based on psychodynamic principles, in which the patient meets the therapist somewhat less frequently than in psychoanalysis and sits face to face with the therapist. (p. 563)

psychodynamics A view analogous to dynamics among physical forces in which psychological forces such as wishes, fears, and intentions have a direction and an intensity. (pp. 11, 404)

psychological anthropologist Person who studies psychological phenomena in other cultures by observing the way the natives behave in their daily lives. (p. 6)

psychology The scientific investigation of mental processes and behavior. (p. 3)

psychometric approach An approach to the study of intelligence, personality, and psychopathology which tries to derive some kind of theoretical meaning empirically from statistical analysis of psychometric test findings. (p. 289)

psychometric instruments Tests that quantify psychological attributes such as personality traits or intellectual abilities (p. 281)

psychomotor slowing An increase in the time required for processing and acting on information that occurs with age (p. 468)

psychopathology Problematic patterns of thought, feeling, or behavior that disrupt an individual's sense of well-being or social or occupational functioning. (p. 516)

psychophysics Branch of psychology that studies the relationship between attributes of the physical world and the psychological experience of them. (p. 104)

psychosexual stages Freud's hypothesized stages in the development of personality, sexuality, and motivation. (p. 407)

psychosis A gross disturbance involving a loss of touch with reality. (p. 520)

psychosocial needs Personal and interpersonal motives that lead people to strive for such ends as mastery, achievement, power, self-esteem, affiliation, and intimacy with other people. (p. 361)

psychosocial stages In Erikson's theory, the stages in the development of the person as a social being. (p. 507)

psychosurgery Brain surgery to reduce psychological symptoms. (p. 583)

psychotherapy integration The use of theory or technique from multiple theoretical perspectives (p. 576)

psychoticism A dimension whose low end is defined by people who display empathy and impulse control and the high end is defined by people who are aggressive, egocentric, impulsive, and antisocial. (p. 423)

psychotropic medications Drugs that act on the brain to affect mental processes. (p. 579)

puberty The stage at which individuals become capable of reproduction. (p. 449)

punishment A conditioning process that decreases the probability that a behavior will occur. (p. 172)

pupil The opening in the center of the iris that constricts or dilates to regulate the amount of light entering the eye. (p. 113)

Q

quasi-experimental design A research design that employs the logic of experimental methods but lacks absolute control over variables. (p. 40)

questionnaire A research tool in which the investigator asks subjects to respond to a written list of questions or items. (p. 43)

R

random sample A sample of subjects selected from the population in a relatively arbitrary manner. (p. 43)

range A measure of variability that represents the difference between the highest and the lowest value on a variable obtained in a sample. (p. 56)

rapid eye movement (REM) sleep The period of sleep during which darting eye movements occur, autonomic activity increases, and patterns of brain activity resemble those observed in waking states. (p. 318)

ratio schedules of reinforcement Operant conditioning procedures in which an organism is reinforced for some proportion of responses. (p. 177)

rational-emotive behavior therapy A psychological treatment in which the therapist helps uncover and alter the illogical thoughts that provoke psychological distress. (p. 570)

rationalist philosophy A school of philosophical thought that emphasizes the role of reason in creating knowledge. (p. 17)

rationalization A defense mechanism that involves explaining away actions in a seemingly logical way to avoid uncomfortable feelings. (p. 412)

reaction formation A defense mechanism in which the person turns unacceptable feelings or impulses into their opposites. (p. 411)

reasoning The process by which people generate and evaluate arguments and beliefs. (p. 242)

recall The explicit (conscious) recollection of material from long-term memory. (p. 208)

receptive field A region within which a neuron responds to appropriate stimulation. (p. 115)

receptors In neurons, protein molecules in the postsynaptic membrane that pick up neurotransmitters; in sensation, specialized cells of the sensory systems that respond to the environmental stimuli and typically activate sensory neurons. (p. 70)

reciprocal altruism The theory that natural selection favors animals that behave altruistically if the likely benefit to each individual over time exceeds the likely cost to each individual's reproductive success. (p. 636)

recognition Explicit (conscious) knowledge of whether something currently perceived has been previously encountered. (p. 208)

recognition-by-components The theory that asserts that we perceive and categorize objects in our environment by breaking them down into component parts and then matching the components and the way they are arranged against similar "sketches" stored in memory. (p. 141)

reference group The group to which a person refers when taking a particular action. (p. 651)

reflex A behavior that is elicited automatically by an environmental stimulus. (pp. 79, 160)

regression Reverting to conflicts or modes of managing emotion characteristic of an earlier particular stage. (p. 408)

rehearsal Repeating or studying information to retain it in memory. (p. 198)

reinforcement A conditioning process that increase the probability that a response will occur. (p. 172)

reinforcer An environmental consequence that occurs after an organism has produced a response and makes the response more likely to recur. (p. 172)

rejected children Children who are disliked by their peers. (p. 489)

relatedness motives Interpersonal motives for connectedness with other people; also called communion motives. (p. 361)

relational theories Theories that propose that the need for relatedness is a central motive in humans and that people will distort their personalities to maintain ties to important people in their lives. (p. 413)

reliability A measure's ability to produce consistent results. (p. 33)

religious experiences Subjective experiences of being in contact with the divine, which can range from relatively ordinary experiences, such as listening passively to a sermon, to altered states of consciousness in which a person feels at one with nature or the supernatural. (p. 330)

representative A sample that reflects characteristics of the population as a whole. (p. 31)

representativeness heuristic A cognitive shortcut used to assess whether an object or incident belongs in a particular class. (p. 250)

repression A defense mechanism in which thoughts that are too anxiety-provoking to acknowledge are kept from conscious awareness. (p. 411)

reproductive success The capacity to survive and reproduce offspring. (p. 20)

resistance Barriers to psychotherapy created by the patient in an effort to reduce anxiety. (p. 562)

response bias In signal detection theory, the subject's readiness to report detecting a signal when uncertain; also called decision criterion. (p. 107)

response prevention Preventing the patient from producing responses that allow avoidance of the feared stimulus. (p. 568)

resting potential Condition in which the neuron is not firing. (p. 68)

retest reliability The tendency of a test to yield relatively similar scores for the same individual over time. (p. 33)

reticular formation A diffuse network of neurons that extends from the lowest parts of the medulla in the hindbrain to the upper end of the midbrain, serving to maintain consciousness, regulate arousal levels, and modulate the activity of neurons throughout the central nervous system. (p. 83)

retina The light-sensitive layer of tissue at the back of the eye that transduces light into neural impulses. (p. 113)

retrieval Bringing information from long-term memory into short-term, or working, memory. (p. 199)

retrieval cues Stimuli or thoughts that can be used to stimulate retrieval. (p. 215)

retroactive interference Interference of new information with the retrieval of old information. (p. 226)

retrospective memory Memory for events that have already occurred. (p. 212)

rods One of two types of photoreceptors; allow vision in dim light. (p. 114)

role A position within a group that defines appropriate behavior for the person occupying it. (p. 651)

Rorschach inkblot test A projective personality test in which a subject views a set of inkblots and tells the tester what each inkblot resembles. (p. 414)

S

sample A subgroup of a population likely to be representative of the population as a whole. (p. 31)

satiety mechanisms Processes that turn off ingestive behavior. (p. 349)

Schacter-Singer theory The theory that asserts that emotion involves cognitive interpretation of general physiological arousal. (p. 383)

schema Integrated pattern of knowledge stored in memory that organizes information and guides the acquisition of new information. (p. 154, 456)

schizophrenia Psychotic disorders characterized by disturbances in thought, perception, behavior, language, communication, and emotion. (p. 533)

secondary appraisal The second stage in the process of stress and coping during which the person evaluates the options and decides how to respond. (p. 389)

secondary drive A motive learned through classical conditioning and other leaning mechanisms such as modeling; also called acquired drive. (p. 342)

secondary process thinking Rational, logical, goal-directed thinking. (p. 410)

secondary reinforcer A stimulus that acquires reinforcement value after an organism learns to associate it with stimuli that are innately reinforcing. (p. 182)

secure attachment style Response to separation in which infants welcome the mother's return and seek closeness to her. (p. 477)

selective inattention The process by which important information is ignored. (p. 305)

selective serotonin reuptake inhibitor (SSRI) A class of antidepressant medications, including Prozac, that blocks the presynaptic membrane from taking back serotonin, and hence leaves it acting longer in the synapse. (p. 582)

self The person, including mental processes, body, and attributes. (p. 617)

self-actualization needs In Maslow's theory, the needs to express oneself, grow, and actualize or attain one's potential. (p. 345)

self-concept A person's view of him/herself. (pp. 430, 491, 617)

self-consistency The motivation to interpret information to fit the self-concept and to prefer people who verify rather than challenge it. (p. 620)

self-determination theory A theory of motivation that proposes that people have three innate needs-competence, autonomy, and relatedness to others-and that intrinsic motivation flourishes when these needs are fulfilled rather than compromised. (p. 343)

self-efficacy expectancy A person's conviction that he can perform the actions necessary to produce an intended behavior. (p. 419)

self-esteem The degree to which a person likes, respects, or esteems the self. (p. 617)

self-fulfilling prophecies False impressions of a situation that evoke behavior that, in turn, makes impressions become true. (p. 647)

self-help groups Groups that are leaderless or guided by a nonprofessional, in which members assist each other in coping with a specific problem, as in Alcoholics Anonymous. (p. 573)

self-perception theory Alternative explanation of cognitive dissonance phenomena which holds that individuals become aware of their attitudes, emotions, and other internal states by observing their own behavior. (p. 602)

self-regulation Setting goals, evaluating one's own performance, and adjusting one's behaviors flexibly to achieve these goals in the context of ongoing feedback. (p. 419)

self-representations Mental models of the self. (p. 618)

self-schema A schema or pattern of thought about the self. (p. 618)

self-serving bias A phenomenon in which people tend to see themselves in a more positive light than they deserve. (p. 615)

semantic memory General world knowledge or facts; also called generic memory. (p. 207)

semantics The rules that govern the meanings, rather than the order, of morphemes, words, phrases, and sentences. (p. 263)

sensation The process by which the sense organs gather information about the environment. (p. 102)

sensitive period Developmental period during which environmental input is especially important, but not absolutely required, for future development in a domain. (p. 443)

sensorimotor stage Piaget's first stage of cognitive development, from birth to about 18 months of age, with thinking primarily characterized by action. (p. 458)

sensory adaptation The tendency of sensory systems to respond less to stimuli that continue without change. (p. 111)

sensory neuron Neuron that transmits information from sensory cells in the body called receptors to the brain. (p. 66)

sensory receptors Specialized cells in the nervous system that transform energy in the environment into neural impulses that can be interpreted by the brain. (p. 105)

sensory registers Memory systems that hold information for a very brief period of time. (p. 197)

sensory representation Information that is represented in one of the sense modalities. (p. 196)

sentence A unit of language that combines a subject and predicate and expresses a thought or meaning. (p. 262)

separation anxiety Distress at separation from attachment figures. (p. 477)

sequential study Type of research in which multiple cohorts are studied over time. (p. 445)

serial position effect The phenomenon that people are more likely to remember information that appears first and last in a list than information in the middle of the list. (p. 199)

serotonin A neurotransmitter involved in the regulation of mood, sleep, eating, arousal, and pain. (p. 73)

set point The value of some variable that the body is trying to maintain, such as temperature. (p. 349)

set-point theory The theory that suggests each person has a natural weight to which his or her body gravitates. (p. 354)

sex-role ideology Beliefs about appropriate behaviors of the sexes. (p. 495)

sex typing The process by which children come to acquire personality traits, emotional responses, skills, behaviors, and preferences that are culturally considered to be appropriate to their sex. (p. 487)

sexual orientation The direction of a person's enduring sexual attraction-to members of the same sex, the opposite sex, or both. (p. 359)

sexual response cycle The pattern of physiological changes during sexual stimulation, consisting of four phases: excitement, plateau, orgasm, and resolution. (p. 356)

sexual strategies Tactics used in selecting mates. (p. 630)

s-factors Specific cognitive abilities. (p. 289)

shape constancy The perception that an object's shape remains constant despite the changing shape of the retinal image as the object is viewed from varying perspectives. (p. 147)

shaping The process of teaching a new behavior by reinforcing closer and closer approximations of the desired response. (p. 180)

short-term memory (STM) Memory for information that is available to consciousness for roughly 20 to 30 seconds; also called working memory. (p. 198)

similarity A Gestalt rule of perception which states that the brain tends to group similar elements within a perceptual field. (p. 140)

simplicity A Gestalt rule of perception which states that people tend to perceive the simplest pattern possible. (p. 140)

single-blind study A study in which subjects are kept blind to crucial information, notably about the experimental condition in which they have been placed. (p. 38)

situational variables Aspects of the situation that interact with aspects of the person to produce behavior. (pp. 426, 626)

size constancy The perception that an object's size of the retinal image as the subject is seen from different distances. (p. 147)

skills training A technique that involves teaching behaviors or procedures for accomplishing specific goals. (p. 569)

social cognition The processes by which people make sense of others, themselves, social interactions, and relationships. (pp. 490, 604)

social development Predictable changes in interpersonal thought, feeling, and behavior. (p. 474)

social-emotional leader A role that may emerge in a group in which that member seeks to maximize group cohesion and minimize hostility. (p. 652)

social exchange theories Theories based on behaviorist principles that suggest the foundation of relationships is reciprocal reward. (p. 628)

social facilitation The phenomenon in which the presence of other people facilitates performance. (p. 646)

social influence The ways in which the presence of other people influences a person's thought, feeling, or behavior. (p. 646)

socialization The process by which children and adults learn the rules, beliefs, values, skills, attitudes, and patterns of behavior of their society. (p. 482)

social learning Learning in which individuals learn many things from the people around them, with or without reinforcement. (p. 189)

social phobia A marked fear that occurs when a person is in a specific social or performance situation. (p. 545)

social psychology A subdiscipline that examines the influence of social processes on the way people think, feel, and behave. (p. 593)

social skills training A cognitive-behavioral technique that involves instruction and modeling, and was designed to help people develop interpersonal competence. (p. 569)

social support Relationships with others that provide resources for coping with stress. (p. 398)

sociobiology A field that explores possible evolutionary and biological bases of human social behavior. (p. 20)

somatic nervous system The division of the peripheral nervous system that consists of sensory and motor neurons that transmit sensory information and control intentional actions. (p. 75)

somatosensory cortex The primary area of the parietal lobes, located behind the central tissue, which receives sensory information from different sections of the body. (p. 89)

sound localization Identifying the location of a sound in space. (p. 130)

sound wave A pulsation of acoustic energy. (p. 124)

spacing effect The superior long-term retention of information rehearsed in sessions spread out over longer intervals of time. (p. 215)

spinal cord The part of the central nervous system that transmits information from sensory neurons to the brain, and from the brain to motor neurons that initiate movement; it is also capable of reflex actions. (p. 81)

split brain The condition that results when the corpus callosum has been surgically cut, blocking communication between the two cerebral hemispheres. (p. 92)

spontaneous recovery The spontaneous re-emergence of a response or an operant that has been extinguished. (p. 166)

spreading activation theory The theory that the presentation of a stimulus triggers activation of closely related nodes. (p. 218)

SQ3R method A mnemonic device designed for helping students remember material from textbooks, which includes five steps: survey, question, read, recite, and review. (p. 216)

stages Relatively discrete steps through which everyone progresses in the same sequence. (p. 443)

stagnation A feeling that the promise of youth has gone unfulfilled. (p. 509)

standard deviation (SD) The amount that the average subject deviates from the mean of the sample on a measure. (p. 56)

standardized procedures Procedures applied uniformly to subjects to minimize unintended variation. (p. 31)

states of consciousness Different ways of orienting to internal and external events, such as awake states and sleep states. (p. 303)

statistical significance The degree to which the results of a study are likely to have occurred simply by chance. (p. 58)

status The amount of power a member of a group holds in that group. (p. 651)

stereotypes Schemas about characteristics ascribed to a group of people based on qualities such as race, ethnicity, or gender rather than achievements or actions. (p. 606)

Stevens's power law A law of sensation proposed by S. S. Stevens, which states that the subjective intensity of a stimulus grows as a proportion of the actual intensity raised to some power. (p. 111)

stimulant A drug that increases alertness, energy, and autonomic reactivity. (p. 328)

stimulus An object or event in the environment that elicits a response in an organism. (p. 160)

stimulus discrimination The tendency for an organism to respond to a very restricted range of stimuli. (p. 166)

stimulus generalization The tendency for learned behavior to occur in response to stimuli that were not present during conditioning but that are similar to the conditioned stimulus. (p. 165)

stratified random sample A sample selected to represent subpopulations proportionately, randomizing only within groups (such as age or race). (p. 43)

stress A challenge to a person's capacity to adapt to inner and outer demands, which may be physiologically arousing, emotionally taxing, and cognitively and behaviorally activating. (p. 388)

stressors Situations that often lead to stress, including life events, catastrophes, and daily hassles. (p. 389)

structural model Freud's model of conflict between desires and the dictates of conscience or the constraints of reality, which posits three sets of mental forces or structures: id, ego, and superego. (p. 410)

structuralism An early school of thought in psychology developed by Edward Titchener, which attempted to use introspection as a method for uncovering the basic elements of consciousness and the way they combine with each other into ideas. (p. 9)

structure of personality The way enduring patterns of thought, feeling, and behavior are organized within an individual. (p. 403)

structure of thought In Piaget's theory, a distinct underlying logic used by a child at a given stage. (p. 457)

subcortical structures Structures within the cerebrum, such as the basal ganglia and limbic system, which lie below the cortex. (p. 84)

subgoals Mini-goals on the way to achieving a broader goal. (p. 246)

subjects The individuals whom a researcher observes in a study; also called participants. (p. 31)

sublimation A defense mechanism that involves converting sexual or aggressive impulses into socially acceptable activities. (p. 411)

subliminal perception The perception of stimuli below the threshold of consciousness. (p. 308)

subordinate level A level of categorization below the basic level in which more specific attributes are shared by members of a category. (p. 239)

substance-related disorders Disorders involving continued use of a substance (such as alcohol or cocaine) that negatively affects psychological and social functioning. (p. 530)

superego In Freudian theory, the structure that acts as conscience and source of ideals, or the parental voice within the person, established through identification. (p. 410)

superordinate goals Goals requiring groups to cooperate for the benefit of all. (p. 612)

superordinate level The most abstract level of categorization in which members of a category share few common features. (p. 239)

superstitious behavior A phenomenon that occurs when the learner erroneously associates an operant and an environmental event. (p. 173)

survey research Research asking a large sample of subjects questions, often about attitudes or behaviors, using questionnaires or interviews. (p. 43)

syllogism A formal statement of deductive reasoning, which consists of two premises that lead to a logical conclusion. (p. 243)

sympathetic nervous system A branch of the autonomic nervous system, typically activated in response to threats to the organism, which readies the body for "fight-or-flight" reactions. (p. 76)

synapse The place at which transmission of information between neurons occurs. (p. 68)

syntax Rules that govern the placement of specific words or phrases within a sentence. (p. 262)

system A group with interdependent parts. (p. 523)

systematic desensitization A cognitive-behavioral procedure in which the patient is induced to approach feared stimuli gradually, in a state that inhibits anxiety. (p. 566)

systems approach An approach that explains an individual's behavior in the context of a social group, such as a couple, family, or larger group. (p. 523)

T

tardive dyskinesia A serious, unpredictable, irreversible side effect of prolonged use of antipsychotic medications, in which a patient develops involuntary or semivoluntary twitching, usually of the tongue, face, and neck. (p. 581)

task leader The group member who takes responsibility for seeing that the group completes its tasks. (p. 652)

taste buds Structures that line the walls of the papillae of the tongue (and elsewhere in the mouth) that contain taste receptors. (p. 132)

tectum A midbrain structure involved in vision and hearing. (p. 84)

tegmentum A midbrain structure that includes a variety of neural structures, related mostly to movement and conscious arousal and activation. (p. 84)

telegraphic speech Speech used by young children that leaves out all but the essential words in a sentence. (p. 271)

temperament Basic personality dispositions heavily influenced by genes. (p. 426)

temporal lobes Brain structures located in the lower side portion of the cortex that are important in audition (hearing) and language. (p. 90)

teratogen A harmful environmental agent, such as drugs, irradiation, and viruses that cause maternal illness, which can produce fetal abnormalities or death. (p. 446)

terminal buttons Structures at the end of the neuron that receive nerve impulses from the axon and transmit signals to adjacent cells. (p. 67)

testosterone The hormone produced by the male gonads (testes). (p. 75)

thalamus A structure located deep in the center of the brain that acts as a relay station for sensory information, processing it and transmitting it to higher brain centers. (p. 85)

Thematic Apperception Test (TAT) A projective test consisting of a series of ambiguous pictures about which subjects are asked to make up a story. (p. 340)

theory A systematic way of organizing and explaining observations. (p. 30)

theory of mind An implicit set of ideas about the existence of mental states, such as beliefs and feelings, in oneself and others that children begin to develop in the toddler years. (p. 493)

theory of multiple intelligences Howard Gardner's theory of seven intelligences used to solve problems or produce culturally significant products. (p. 293)

therapeutic alliance The patient's degree of comfort with the therapist, which allows him or her to speak about emotionally significant experiences. (p. 560)

thinking Manipulating mental representations for a purpose. (p. 235)

thyroid gland Endocrine structure located next to the trachea and larynx in the neck, which releases hormones that control growth and metabolism. (p. 75)

tip-of-the tongue phenomenon The experience in which people attempting but failing to recall information from memory know the information is "in there" but are not quite able to retrieve it (p. 208)

timbre The psychological property corresponding to a sound wave's complexity; the texture of a sound. (p. 125)

top-down processing Perceptual processing that starts with the observer's expectations and knowledge. (p. 151)

topographic model Freud's model of conscious, preconscious, and unconscious processes. (p. 405)

traits Emotional, cognitive, and behavioral tendencies that constitute underlying dimensions of personality on which individuals vary. (p. 421)

transduction The process of converting physical energy into neural impulses. (p. 105)

transference The phenomenon in which the patient displaces thoughts, feelings, fears, wishes, and conflicts from past relationships, especially childhood relationships, onto the therapist. (p. 562)

trichromatic theory of color A theory of color vision initially proposed by Thomas Young and modified by Herman Von Helmholtz that proposes that the eye contains three types of receptors, each sensitive to wavelengths of light that produce sensations of blue, green, and red; by this theory, the colors that humans see reflect blends of the three colors to which the retina is sensitive; also called the Young-Helmholtz theory. (p. 122)

tricyclic antidepressant A class of medications for depression that compensates for depleted neurotransmitters. (p. 581)

true self A core aspect of being, untainted by the demands of others. (p. 430)

t-test An inferential statistic that compares the mean scores of two groups. (p. 61)

tutelage The teaching of concepts or procedures primarily through verbal explanation or instruction. (p. 189)

two-factor theory of intelligence A theory derived by Charles Spearman that holds that two types of factors or abilities underlie intelligence. (p. 289)

tympanic membrane Eardrum. (p. 126)

Type A behavior pattern A pattern of behavior and emotions that includes ambition, competitiveness, impatience, and hostility. (p. 395)

U

unconditional positive regard An attitude of total acceptance expressed by the therapist toward the client in client-centered therapy (p. 572)

unconditioned reflex A reflex that occurs naturally, without any prior learning. (p. 162)

unconditioned response (UCR) An organism's unlearned, automatic response to a stimulus. (p. 162)

unconditioned stimulus (UCS) A stimulus that produces a reflexive response without any prior learning. (p. 162)

unconscious mental processes In Freud's theory, mental processes that are inaccessible to consciousness, many of which are repressed. (pp. 308, 405)

unipolar depression A mood disorder involving only depression; see also bipolar disorder. (p. 540)

universal grammar An innate, shared set of linguistic principles. (p. 267)

V

valid Said of a study whose procedures are sound. (p. 31)

validation Demonstrating the validity of a measure by showing that it consistently relates to other phenomena in theoretically expected ways. (p. 33)

validity The extent to which a test measures the construct it attempts to assess, or a study adequately addresses the hypothesis it attempts to assess. (p. 33)

variability The extent to which subjects tend to vary from each other in their scores on a measure. (p. 56)

variable A phenomenon that changes across circumstances or varies among individuals. (p. 30)

variable-interval (VI) schedule of reinforcement An operant conditioning procedure in which an organism receives a reward for its responses after an amount of time that is not constant. (p. 177)

variable-ratio (VR) schedule of reinforcement An organism receives a reward for a certain percentage of behaviors that are emitted, but this percentage is not fixed. (p. 177)

ventricles Fluid-filled cavities of the brain that are enlarged in schizophrenics suggesting neuronal atrophy. (p. 536)

ventromedial prefrontal cortex An area in the brain that serves many functions, including helping people use their emotional reactions to guide decision making and behavior. (p. 259)

verbal representations Information represented in words. (p. 196)

vestibular sense The sense that provides information about the position of the body in space by sensing gravity and movement. (p. 138)

vicarious conditioning The process by which an individual learns the consequences of an action by observing its consequences for someone else. (p. 189)

visual cliff A clear table with a checkerboard directly beneath it on one side and another checkerboard that appears to drop off like a cliff on the other, used especially with human infants in direct perception studies. (p. 150)

W

wavelength The distance over which a wave of energy completes a full oscillation. (p. 112)

Weber's law The perceptual law described by Ernst Weber that states that for two stimuli to be perceived as differing in intensity, the second must differ from the first by a constant proportion. (p. 109)

Wechsler Adult Intelligence Scale, Third Edition (WAIS-III) An intelligence test for adults that yields scores for both verbal and nonverbal (performance) IQ scores. (p. 283)

Wechsler Intelligence Scale for Children (WISC-III) An intelligence test for children up to age 16 that yields verbal and nonverbal (performance) IQ scores. (p. 283)

weighted utility value In expectancy value theory, a combined measure of the importance of an attribute and how well a given option satisfies it. (p. 249)

well-defined concept A concept that has properties clearly setting it apart from other concepts. (p. 237)

well-defined problem Problems in which there is adequate information to solve the problem and clear criteria by which to determine whether the problem has been solved. (p. 245)

Wernicke's area A brain structure located in the left temporal lobe involved in language comprehension. (p. 90)

what pathway The pathway running from the striate cortex in the occipital lobes through the lower part of the temporal lobes, involved in determining what an object is. (p. 120)

where pathway The pathway running from the striate cortex through the middle and upper regions of the temporal lobes and up into the parietal lobes, involved in locating an object in space, following its movement, and guiding movement toward it. (p. 121)

Whorfian hypothesis of linguistic relativity
The notion that language shapes thought. (p. 260)

working memory Conscious "work-space" used for retrieving and manipulating information, maintained through maintenance rehearsal; also called short-term memory. (p. 201)

Y

Young-Helmholtz theory A theory of color vision initially proposed by Young and modified by Helmholtz which proposes that the eye contains three types of receptors, each sensitive to wavelengths of light that produce sensations of blue, green, and red; by this theory, the colors that humans see reflect blends of the three colors to which the retina is sensitive; also called trichromatic theory. (p. 122)

References

AARP News Bulletin. (January 1989). New study finds older drivers "capable, safe." *30*, 14.

Abelson, R. B. (1995). *Statistics as principled argument.* Hillsdale, NJ: Lawrence Erlbaum Associates

Abelson, R. P. (1983). Whatever became of consistency theory? *Personality and Social Psychology Bulletin, 9*, 37–54.

Abelson, R. P. (1997). On the surprising longevity of flogged horses: Why there is a case for the significance test. *Psychological Science, 8*, 12–15.

Aber, J. L., Belsky, J., Slade, A., & Crnic, K. (1999). Stability and change in mothers' representations of their relationship with their toddlers. *Developmental Psychology, 35*(4), 1038–1047.

Ablon, J. S., & Jones, E. E. (1999). Psychotherapy process in the National Institute of Mental Health Treatment of Depression Collaborative Research Program. *Journal of Consulting and Clinical Psychology, 67*, 64–75.

Abraham, H. D., & Duffy, F. H. (1996). Stable quantitative EEG difference in post-LSD visual disorder by split-half analysis: Evidence for disinhibition. *Psychiatry Research: Neuroimaging, 67*, 173–187.

Abramov, I., & Gordon, J. (1994). Color appearance: On seeing red—or yellow, or green, or blue. *Annual Review of Psychology, 45*, 451–485.

Abrams, D. B., & Wilson, G. T. (1983). Alcohol, sexual arousal, and self control. *Journal of Personality and Social Psychology, 45*, 188–198.

Abrams, R., Swartz, C. M., & Vedak, C. (1989). Antidepressant effects of right versus left unilateral ECT and the lateralization theory of ECT action. *American Journal of Psychiatry, 146*, 1190–1192.

Abramson, L. Y., Metalsky, G. I, & Alloy, L. B. (1989) Hopelessness depression: A theory-based subtype of depression. *Psychological Review, 96*, 358–372.

Abramson, L. Y., Seligman, M. E. P., & Teasdale, J. D. (1978). Learned helplessness in humans: Critique and reformulation. *Journal of Abnormal Psychology, 87*, 49–74.

Abrous, D. N., Rodriquez, J., le Moal, M., Moser, P. C., & Barneoud, P. (1999). Effects of mild traumatic brain injury on immunoreactivity for the inducible transcription factors c-Fos, c-Jun, JunB, and Krox-24 in cerebral regions associated with conditioned fear responding. *Brain Research, 826*, 181–192.

Ackerman, S. J., Clemence, A., J., Weatherill, R., & Hilsenroth, M. J. (1999). Use of the TAT in the assessment of DSM-IV Cluster B personality disorders. *Journal of Personality Assessment, 73*(3), 422–442.

Adams, B. D. (1985). Age, structure, and sexuality. *Journal of Homosexuality, 11*, 19–33.

Adams, C. (1991). Qualitative age differences in memory for text: A life-span development perspective. *Psychology and Aging, 6*, 323–336.

Adams, H. E., Wright, L. W., & Lohr, B. A. (1996). Is homophobia associated with homosexual arousal? *Journal of Abnormal Psychology 105*, 440–445.

Adams, P. R., & Adam, G. R. (1984). Mount Saint Helens' Ashfall: Evidence for a disaster stress reaction. *American Psychologist, 39*, 252–260.

Adcock, R. A., Constable, R. T., Gore, J. C., & Goldman-Rakic, P. S. (2000). Functional neuroanatomy of executive processes involved in dual-task performance. *Proceedings of the National Academy of Science, USA, 97*, 3567–3572.

Adelson, E., & Fraiberg, S. (1974). Gross motor development in infants blind from birth. *Child Development, 45*, 114–126.

Ader, R., & Cohen, N. (1985). CNS immune system interactions: Conditioning phenomena. *Behavioral and Brain Sciences, 8*, 379–426.

Adolphs, R. (1999). Social cognition and the brain. *Trends in Cognitive Sciences, 3*, 469–479).

Adorno, T. W., Frenkel–Brunswik, E., Levinson, D., & Sanford, R. N. (1950). *The authoritarian personality.* New York: W. W. Norton.

Aggleton, J. P. (Ed). (1992). *The amygdala: Neurobiological aspects of emotion, memory, and mental dysfunction.* New York: Wiley-Liss.

Agras, W. S., Walsh, T., Fairburn, C. G., Wilson, G. T., & Kraemer, H. C. (2000). A multicenter comparison of cognitive-behavioral therapy and interpersonal psychotherapy for bulimia nervosa. *Archives of General Psychiatry, 57*, 459–466.

Ainsworth, M. D. (1991). Attachments and other affectional bonds across the life cycle. In C. M. Parkes, J. Stevenson-Hinde, et al. (Eds.), *Attachment across the life cycle* (pp. 33–51). London: Tavistock/Routledge.

Ainsworth, M. D. S. (1967). *Infancy in Uganda.* Baltimore, MD: Johns Hopkins University.

Ainsworth, M. D. S. (1973). The development of infant–mother attachment. In B. Caldwell & H. Ricciuti (Eds.), *Review of Child Development Research* (Vol. 3).Chicago: University of Chicago Press.

Ainsworth, M. D. S. (1979). Infant–mother attachment. *American Psychologist, 34*, 932–937.

Ainsworth, M. D. S., & Bell, S. M. (1970). Attachment, exploration, and separation: Illustrated by the behavior of one-year-olds in a strange situation. *Child Development, 41*, 49–67.

Ajzen, I. (1996). The directive influence of attitudes on behavior. In P. M. Gollwitzer & J. A. Bargh (Eds.), *The psychology of action: Linking cognition and motivation to behavior.* (pp. 385-403). New York: Guilford Press.

Ajzen, I., & Fishbein, M. (1977). Attitude-behavior relations: A theoretical analysis and review of empirical research. *Psychological Bulletin, 84*, 888 918.

al-Absi, M., & Rokke, P. D. (1991). Can anxiety help us tolerate pain? *Pain, 46*, 43–51.

Albert, D. J., Jonik, R. H., & Walsh, M. (1991). Hormone-dependent aggression in the female rat: Testosterone plus estradiol implants prevent the decline in aggression following ovariectomy. *Physiology & Behavior, 49*, 673–677.

Albert, M. K. (1993). Parallelism and the perception of illusory contours. *Perception, 22*, 589–595.

Alberts, A. C. (1989). Ultraviolet visual sensitivity in desert iguanas: Implications for pheromone detection. *Animal Behaviour, 38*, 129–137.

Alderfer, C. (1972). Existence, relatedness, and growth: *Human needs in organizational settings.* New York: Free Press.

Alderfer, C. P. (1989). Theories reflecting my personal experience and life development. *Journal of Applied Behavioral Science, 25*, 351–365.

Alexander, G. M., Swerdloff, R. S., Wang, C. W., & Davidson, T. (1997). Androgen-behavior correlations in hypogonadal men and eugonadal men: I. Mood and response to auditory sexual stimuli. *Hormones & Behavior, 31*, 110–119.

Alexander, I. (1990). *Personology: Method and content in personality assessment and psychobiography.* Durham, NC: Duke University Press.

Alexander, J. M., & Schwanenflugel, P. J. (1994). Strategy regulation: The role of intelligence, metacognitive attributions, and knowledge base. *Developmental Psychology, 30*, 709–723.

Allen, S. W., & Brooks, L. R. (1991). Specializing the operation of an explicit rule. *Journal of Experimental Psychology: General, 120*, 3–19.

Allison, D. B., Heshka S., Neale, M. C., & Lykken, D. T. (1994). A genetic analysis of relative weight among 4,020 twin pairs, with an emphasis on sex effects. *Health Psychology, 13*, 362–365.

Alloy, L. B., Abramson, L. Y., Hogan, M. E., Whitehouse, W. G., Rose, D. T., Robinson, M. S., Kim, R. S., & Lapkin, J. B. (2000). The Templen-Wisconsin Cognitive Vulnerability to Depression Project: Lifetime history of Axis I psychopathology in individuals at high and low cognitive risk for depression. *Journal of Abnormal Psychology, 109*, 403–418.

Allport, G. (1935). Attitudes. In C. Murchison (Ed.), *Handbook of social psychology* (pp. 798–844). Worcester, MA: Clark University Press.

Allport, G. (1937). *Personality: A psychological interpretation.* New York: Henry Holt

Allport, G. (1954). *The nature of prejudice.* Cambridge, MA: Addison-Wesley.

Allport, G. (1968). The historical background of modern social psychology. In G. Lindzey & E. Aronson (Eds.), *Handbook of social psychology* (Vol. I.) Reading, MA: Addison-Wesley.

Allport, G., & Odbert, H. (1936). *Trait-names: A Psycho-lexical study.* Psychological Monographs, Vol. 47, No. 1. Princeton, NJ: Psychological Review

Altamura, A. C., Pioli, R., Vitto, M., & Mannu, P. (1999). Venlafaxine in social phobia: A study in selective serotonin reuptake inhibitor nonresponders. *International Clinical Psychopharmacology, 14,* 239–245.

Alvarez–Borda, B., Ramirez–Amaya, V., Perez–Montfort, R., & Bermudez–Rattoni, F. (1995). Enhancement of antibody production by a learning paradigm. *Neurobiology of Learning & Memory, 64,* 103–105.

Amabile, T. M. (1996). Creativity in context. *Update to "The Social Psychology of Creativity."* Boulder, CO: Westview.

Ambady, N., & Rosenthal, R. (1993). Half a minute: Predicting teacher evaluations from thin slices of nonverbal behavior and physical attractiveness. *Journal of Personality and Social Psychology, 64,* 431–441.

American Association on Mental Retardation. (1992). *Mental retardation: Definition, classification, and systems of supports* (9th ed.). Washington, DC: American Association on Mental Retardation.

American Psychiatric Association. (1994). *Diagnostic and statistical manual of mental disorders* (4th ed.). Washington, DC: Author.

American Psychological Association, Committee for the Protection of Human Participants in Research. (1973). *Ethical principles in the conduct of research with human subjects.* Washington, DC.

American Psychological Association. (1997). Report of the ethics committee, 1996. *American Psychologist, 52,* 897–905.

Amminger, G. P., Pape, S., Rock, D., Roberts, S. A., Ott, S. L., Squires-Wheeler, E., Kestenbaum, C., & Erlenmeyer-Kimling, L. (1999). Relationship between childhood behavioral disturbance and later schizophrenia in the New York High-Risk Project. *American Journal of Psychiatry, 156,* 525–530.

Amsterdam, B. (1972). Mirror self–image reactions before age two. *Developmental Psychology, 5,* 297–305.

Anand, B., & Brobeck, J. (1951). Hypothalamic control of food intake in rats and cats. *Yale Journal of Biological Medicine, 24,* 123–140.

Anastasi, A. (1958). Heredity, environment, and the question "How?" *Psychological Review, 65,* 197–208.

Anastasi, A., & Urbina, S. (1997). *Psychological testing* (7th ed.). Upper Saddle River, NJ: Prentice-Hall.

Andersen, S., & Cole, S. (1991). Do I know you? The role of significant others in general social

perception. *Journal of Personality and Social Psychology, 59,* 384–399.

Andersen, S. M., Reznik, L., & Manzella, L. M. (1996). Eliciting facial affect, motivation, and expectancies in transference: Significant-other representations in social relations. *Journal of Personality and Social Psychology, 71,* 1108–1129.

Anderson, C. (1989). Temperature and aggression: Ubiquitous effects of heat on occurrence of human violence. *Psychological Bulletin, 106,* 74–96.

Anderson, C. A., & Dill, K. E. (2000). Video games and aggressive thoughts, feelings, and behavior in the laboratory and in life. *Journal of Personality and Social Psychology, 78*(4), 772–790.

Anderson, D. J., & Ricklefs, R. E. (1995). Evidence of kin-selected tolerance by nestlings in a siblicida bird. *Behavioral Ecology & Sociobiology, 37,* 163–168.

Anderson, J. (1983). *The architecture of cognition.* Cambridge, MA: Harvard University Press.

Anderson, J. R. (1985). *Cognitive psychology and its implications* (2nd ed.). New York: Freeman.

Anderson, J. R. (1993). Problem solving and learning. *American Psychologist, 48,* 35–44.

Anderson, J. R. (1995). *Learning and memory: An integrated approach.* New York: John Wiley.

Anderson, J. R. (1996). ACT: A simple theory of complex cognition. *American Psychologist, 51,* 355–365.

Andreasen, N. C. (1999). A unitary model of schizophrenia: Bleuler's "fragmented phrene" as schizencephaly. *Archives of General Psychiatry, 56,* 781-787.

Andreasen, N. C., Arndt, S., Miller, D., Flaum, M., et al. (1995). Correlational studies of the Scale for the Assessment of Negative Symptoms and the Scale for the Assessment of Positive Symptoms: An overview and update. *Psychopathology, 28,* 7–17.

Andreasen, N. C., Rice, J., Endicott, J., Coryell, W., Grove, W. M., & Reich, T. (1987). Familial rates of affective disorder: A report from the National Institute of Mental Health collaborative study. *Archives of General Psychiatry, 44,* 461–469.

Andreason, N., Swayze, V., Flaum, M., Alliger, R., & Cohen, G. (1990). Ventricular abnormalities in affective disorder: Clinical and demographic correlates. *American Journal of Psychiatry, 147,* 893–900.

Andreasson, S., & Brandt, L. (1997). Mortality and morbidity related to alcohol. *Alcohol & Alcoholism, 32,* 173–178.

Andrzejewski, S. J., Moore, C. M., Corvette, M., & Hermann, D. (1991). Prospective memory skill. *Bulletin of the Psychonomic Society, 29,* 304–306.

Angel, I., Hauger, R., Giblin, B., & Paul, S. (1992). Regulation of the anorectic drug recognition site during glucoprovic feeding. *Brain Research Bulletin, 28,* 201–207.

Angrist, B., Sathananthan, G., Wilk, S., & Gershon, S. (1974). Amphetamine psychosis: Behavioral and biochemical aspects. *Journal of Psychiatric Research, 11,* 13–23.

Anthony, E., & Cohler, B. (Eds.). (1987). *The invulnerable child.* New York: Guilford Press.

Antoch, M. P., Song, E. J., Chang, A. M., Vitaterna, M. H., Zhao, Y. L., Wilsbacher, L. D., et al. (1997). Functional identification of the mouse circadian clock gene by transgenic bac rescue. *Cell, 89,* 655–667.

Antrobus, J. (1991). Dreaming: Cognitive processes during cortical activation and high afferent thresholds. *Psychological Review, 98,* 96–121.

Aponte, H. J., & VanDeusen, J. M. (1981). Structural family therapy. In A. S. Gurman and D. P. Kniskern (Eds.), *Handbook of family therapy.* New York: Brunner/Mazel.

Applebaum, P. S., Uyehara, L. A., & Elin, M. R. (Eds.). (1997). *Trauma and memory: Clinical and legal controversies.* New York: Oxford University Press.

Archer D. (1994). American violence: How high and why? *Law Studies, 19,* 12–20.

Archer, J. (1991). The influence of testosterone on human aggression. *British Journal of Psychology, 82,* 1–28.

Archer, J., & Lloyd, B. (1985). *Sex and gender* (2nd ed.). New York: Cambridge University Press.

Arena, J. G., & Blanchard, E. B. (1996). Biofeedback and relaxation therapy for chronic disorders. In R. J. Gatchel, D. C. Turk, et al. (Eds.), *Psychological approaches to pain management: A practitioner's handbook.* (pp. 179–230). New York: Guilford Press.

Arendt, J., Skene, D. J., Middleton, B., Lockley, S. W., & Deacon, S. (1997). Efficacy of melatonin treatment in jet lag, shift work, and blindness. *Journal of Biological Rhythms, 12*(6), 604–617.

Arendt, R. E., Minnes, S., & Singer, L. T. (1996). Fetal cocaine exposure: Neurologic effects and sensory-motor delays. In L. S. Chandler & S. J. Lane (Eds.), *Children with prenatal drug exposure* (pp. 129–144). New York: Haworth Press.

Arkes, H., Boehm, L., & Xu, G. (1991). Determinants of judged validity. *Journal of Experimental Social Psychology, 27,* 576–605.

Arkowitz, H. (1997). Integrative theories of therapy. In P. L. Wachtel, S. B. Messer et al. (Eds.), *Theories of psychotherapy: Origins and evolution* (pp. 227–288). Washington, DC: American Psychological Association.

Arkowitz, H., & Messer, S. B. (Eds.). (1984). *Psychodynamic therapy and behavior therapy: Is integration possible?* New York: Plenum Press.

Armony, J. L., & LeDoux, J. E. (2000). How danger is encoded: Toward a systems, cellular, and computational understanding of cognitive-emotional interactions in fear. In M. S. Gazzaniga (Ed.), *The new cognitive neurosciences* (2nd ed. pp. 1067–1080). Cambridge, MA: MIT Press.

Arndt, J., Greenberg, J., Solomon, S., Pyszczynski, T., & Simon, L. (1997). Suppression, accessibility of death-related thoughts, and cultural worldview defense: Exploring the psychodynamics of terror management. *Journal of Personality and Social Psychology, 73,* 5–18.

Arnett, J. J. (1999). Adolescent storm and stress, reconsidered. *American Psychologist, 54,* 317–326.

Arnkoff, D., Victor, B., & Glass, C. (1993). Empirical research on factors in psychotherapeutic change. In G. Stricker & J. Gold (Eds.), *Comprehensive handbook of psychotherapy integration* (pp. 27–42). New York: Plenum Press.

Arnsten, A. F. T. (1998). Catecholamine modulation of prefrontal cortical cognitive function. *Trends in Cognitive Sciences, 2,* 436–447.

Aron, L. (1996). *A meeting of minds: Mutuality in psychoanalysis.* Hillside, NJ: Analytic Press.

Arrigo, J. A., & Pezdek, K. (1997). Lessons from the study of psychogenic amnesia. *Current Directions in Psychological Science, 5,* 148–152.

Arvey, R. D., McCall, B., & Bouchard, T. J. (1994). Genetic influence on job satisfaction and work values. *Personality and Individual Differences, 17,* 21–33.

Asch, S. E. (1955). Opinions and social pressure. *Scientific American, 193,* 31–35.

Asch, S. E. (1956). Studies of independence and conformity: A minority of one against unanimous majority. *Psychological Monographs: General and Applied, 70,* 1–69.

Asendorpf, J., & Baudonniere, P. (1993). Self-awareness and other-awareness: Mirror self-recognition and synchronic imitation among unfamiliar peers. *Developmental Psychology, 29,* 88–95.

Asendorpf, J., & Scherer, K. (1983). The discrepant repressor: Differentiation between low anxiety, high anxiety, and repression of anxiety by autonomic-facial-verbal patterns of behavior. *Journal of Personality and Social Psychology, 45,* 1334–1346.

Ashby, F. G., & Waldron, E. M. (2000). The neuropsychological bases of category learning. *Current Directions in Psychological Science, 9,* 10–14.

Ashford, J. W., Schmitt, F. A., & Kumar, V. (1996). Diagnosis of Alzheimer's disease. *Psychiatric Annals, 26,* 262–268.

Atkinson, J. W. (1977). Motivation for achievement. In T. Blass (Ed.), *Personality Variables in Social Behavior.* Hillsdale, NJ: Erlbaum.

Atkinson, J. W., & Litwin, G. H. (1960). Achievement motive and test anxiety conceived as motive to approach success and motive to avoid failure. *Journal of Abnormal and Social Psychology, 60,* 52–63.

Atkinson, R. C., & Shiffrin, R. N. (1968). Human memory: A proposed system and its control processes. In K. W. Spence & J. T. Spense (Eds.), *The psychology of learning and motivation,* (Vol. 2.) New York: Academic Press.

Baars, B. (1995). Tutorial commentary: Surprisingly small subcortical structures are needed for the stage of waking consciousness, while cortical projection areas seem to provide perceptual contents of consciousness. *Consciousness and Cognition, 4,* 159–162.

Baars, B. J. (1988). Momentary forgetting as a "resetting" of a conscious global workspace due to competition between incompatible contexts. In M. J. Horowitz (Ed.), *Psychodynamics and cognition* (pp. 269–293). University of California.

Baars, B. J. (1997). *In the theater of consciousness: The workspace of the mind.* New York: Oxford University Press.

Baars B. J., & McGovern, K. (1996). Cognitive views of consciousness: What are the facts? How can we explain them? In M. Velmans (Ed.), *The science of consciousness: Psychological, neuropsychological and clinical reviews* (pp. 63–95). London.

Babor, T., Hoffman, M., DelBoca, F., Hesselbrock, V., Meyer, R. E., Dolinsky, Z., & Rounsaville, B. (1992). Types of alcoholics, I: Evidence for an empirically derived typology based on indicators of vulnerability and severity. *Archives of General Psychiatry, 49,* 599–608.

Babor, T. F., Miller, W. R., DiClemente, C., & Longabaugh, R. (1999). A study to remember: Response of the project MATCH research group. *Addiction, 94,* 66–69.

Baddeley, A., Gathercole, S., & Papagno, C. (1998). The phonological loop as a language learning device. *Psychological Review, 105,* 158–173.

Baddeley, A. D. (1992). Working memory. *Science, 255,* 556–559.

Baddeley, A. D. (1995). Working memory. In M. Gazzaniga (Ed.), *The cognitive neurosciences* (pp. 754–764). Cambridge, MA: Bradford/MIT Press.

Baddeley, A. D., & Patterson, K. (1971). The relation between long-term and short-term memory. *British Medical Bulletin, 27,* 237–242.

Baer, L., Rauch, S. L., Ballantine, H. T., Martuza, R., Cosgrove, R., Cassem, E., et al. (1995). Cingulotomy for intractable obsessive-compulsive disorder: Prospective long term follow up of 18 patients. *Archives of General Psychiatry, 52,* 384–392.

Bahrick, H. P. (1985). Associationism and the Ebbinghaus legacy. *Journal of Experimental Psychology: Learning, Memory, & Cognition, 11,* 439–443.

Bahrick, H. P., Bahrick, L. E., Bahrick, A. S., & Bahrick, P. E. (1993). Maintenance of foreign language vocabulary and the spacing effect. *Psychological Science, 4,* 316–321.

Bahrick, H. P., & Hall, L. K. (1991). Lifetime maintenance of high school mathematics content. *Journal of Experimental Psychology: General, 120,* 20–33.

Bahrick, H. P., Hall, L. K., & Berger, S. A. (1996). Accuracy and distortion in memory for high school grades. *Psychological Science, 7,* 265–271.

Bahrick, L. E., & Lickliter, R. (2000). Intersensory redundancy guides attentional selectivity and perceptual learning in infancy. *Developmental Psychology, 36,* 190–201.

Bailey, C. H., & Kandel, E. R. (1995). Molecular and structural mechanisms underlying long-term memory. In M. S. Gazzaniga et al. (Eds.), *The cognitive neurosciences* (pp. 19–36). Cambridge, MA: MIT Press.

Bailey, J. M., & Pillard, R. (1991). A genetic study of male sexual orientation. *Archives of General Psychiatry, 48,* 1089–1096.

Bailey, J. M., Pillard, R. C., Dawood, K., Miller, M. B., Farrer, L. A., Trivedi, S., & Murphy, R. L. (1999). A family history study of male sexual orientation using three independent samples. *Behavior Genetics, 29*(2), 79–86.

Bailey, J. M., Pillard, R. C., Neale, M. C., & Agyei, Y. (1993). Heritable factors influence sexual orientation in women. *Archives of General Psychiatry, 50,* 217–223.

Baillargeon, R., & DeVos, J. (1991). Object permanence in young infants: Further evidence. *Child Development, 62,* 1227–1246.

Bakan, D. (1966). The duality of human existence: An essay on psychology and religion. New York: Rand McNally.

Baker, L., Silk, K. R., Westen, D., Nigg, J. T., & Lohr, N. E. (1992). Malevolence, splitting, and parental ratings by borderlines. *Journal of Nervous and Mental Disease, 180,* 258–264.

Baker, R. W., & Trzepacz, P. T. (1998). Mental status examination. In G. P. Koocher, J. C. Norcross, & S. S. Hill (Eds.), *Psychologists' desk reference* (pp. 6–11). New York: Oxford University Press.

Baldessarini, R. J., & Tohen, M., & Tondo, L. (2000). Maintenance treatment in bipolar disorder. *Archives of General Psychiatry, 57,* 490–492.

Baldwin, M. (1992). Relational schemas and the processing of social information. *Psychological Bulletin, 112,* 461–484.

Bales, R. F. (1953). The equilibrium problem in small groups. In T. Parsons, R. F. Bales, & E. A. Shils (Eds.), *Working papers in the theory of action.* Glencoe, IL: Free Press.

Baltes, P. (1987). Theoretical propositions of life-span developmental psychology: On the dynamics between growth and decline. *Developmental Psychology, 23,* 611–626.

Baltes, P. B. (1997). On the incomplete architecture of human ontogeny: Selection, optimization, and compensation as foundation of developmental theory. *American Psychologist, 52,* 366–380.

Baltes, P. B. (1998). Theoretical propositions of life-span developmental psychology: On the dynamics between growth and decline. In M. P. Lawton & T. A. Salthouse (Eds.), *Essential papers on the psychology of aging. Essential papers in psychoanalysis.* (pp. 86–123). New York,: New York University Press.

Baltes, P. B., & Staudinger, U. M. (2000). Wisdom: A metaheuristic (pragmatic) to orchestrate mind and virtue toward excellence. *American Psychologist, 55,* 122–136.

Bandler, R. (1982). Identification of neuronal cell bodies mediating components of biting attack behavior in the cat: Induction of jaw opening following microinjections of glutamate into hypothalamus. *Brain Research, 245,* 192–197.

Bandura, A. (1967). The role of modeling personality development. In C. Lavatelli & F. Stendler (Eds.), *Readings in childhood and development* (pp. 334–343). New York: Harcourt Brace Jovanovich.

Bandura, A. (1977a). Self-efficacy: Toward a unifying theory of behavioral change. *Psychological Review, 84,* 191–215.

Bandura, A. (1977b). *Social learning theory.* Englewood Cliffs, NJ: Prentice-Hall.

Bandura, A. (1982). Self-efficacy mechanisms in human agency. *American Psychologist, 37,* 122–147.

Bandura, A. (1986). *Social foundations of thought and action: A social cognitive theory,* Englewood Cliffs, NJ: Prentice-Hall.

Bandura, A. (1989). Human agency in social cognitive theory. *American Psychologist, 44,* 1175–1184.

Bandura, A. (1991). Social cognitive theory of self-regulation. *Organizational Behavior and Human Decision Processes 50,* 248–287.

Bandura, A. (1995). *Self-efficacy in changing societies.* New York: Cambridge University Press.

Bandura, A. (1999a). Social cognitive theory of personality. In L. Pervin & O. John (Eds.), *Handbook of personality: Theory and research*, 2nd ed., pp. 154–196). New York: Guilford Press.

Bandura, A. (1999b). Social cognitive theory of personality. In L. A. Pervin, and O. P. John (Eds.), Handbook of personality: Theory and research (2nd ed.). (pp. 154-196). New York, NY, US: The Guilford Press.

Bandura, A., Blanchard, E. B., & Ritter, B. (1969). Relative efficacy of desensitization and modeling approaches for inducing behavioral, affective, and attitudinal changes. *Journal of Personality and Social Psychology, 13,* 173–199.

Bandura, A., Ross, D., & Ross, S. (1961). Transmission of aggression through imitation of aggressive models. *Journal of Abnormal and Social Psychology, 66,* 3–11.

Bandura, A., Ross, D., & Ross, S. (1963). Vicarious reinforcement and imitative learning. *Journal of Abnormal and Social Psychology, 67,* 601–607.

Banerjee, M. (1997). Hidden emotions: Preschoolers' knowledge of appearance-reality and emotion display rules. *Social Cognition 15(2),* 107–132.

Banks, M. S., & Salapatek, P. (1983). Infant visual perception. In M. M. Haith & J. J. Campos (Eds.), *Handbook of child psychology: Vol. 2. Infancy and developmental psychobiology.* New York: John Wiley.

Bar, M., & Biederman, I. (1998). Subliminal visual priming. *Psychological Science, 9,* 464–469.

Bard, P. (1934). On emotional expression after desortication with some remarks on certain theoretical views. *Psychological Review, 41,* 309–328.

Bardwick, J. (1971). *Psychology of women.* New York: Harper & Row.

Bargh, J. (1997). The automaticity of everyday life. In J. S. Wyer, Jr. (Ed.), *Advances in social cognition* (Vol. 10). Hillsdale, NJ: Lawrence Erlbaum.

Bargh, J., & Barndollar, K. (1996). Automaticity in action: The unconscious as repository of chronic goals and motives. In P. M. Gollwitzer & J. Bargh (Eds.), *The psychology of action: Linking cognition and motivation to behavior* (pp. 457–481). New York: Guilford.

Bargh, J. A., & Chartrand, T. L. (1999). The unbearable automaticity of being. *American Psychologist, 54(7),* 462–479.

Bargh, J. A., & Tota, M. E. (1988). Context-dependent automatic depression: Accessibility of negative constructs with regard to self but not others. *Journal of Personality and Social Psychology, 54,* 925–939.

Barinag, M. (1997). New imaging methods provide a better view into the brain. *Science, 276,* 1974–1976.

Barlow, D. (in press). *Anxiety and its disorders.* New York: Guilford Press.

Barlow, D. H., Esler, J. L., & Vitali, A. E. (1998). Psychosocial treatments for panic disorders, phobias, and generalized anxiety disorder. In P. E. Nathan, J. M. Gorman, et al. (Eds.), *A guide to treatments that work* (pp. 288–318). New York: Oxford University Press.

Barnes, D. M. (1990). Silver Spring monkeys yield unexpected data on brain reorganization. *Journal of NIH, 2,* 19–20.

Baroff, G. S., & Gregory, O. J. (1999). *Mental retardation: Nature, cause, and management.* Bristol, PA: Brunner/Mazel.

Baroff, G. S., & Olley, J. G. (1999). *Mental retardation: Nature, cause, and management* (3rd ed.). Bristol, PA: Brunner/Mazel.

Baron, A., & Mattila, W. (1989). Response slowing of older adults: Effects of time-limit contingencies on single- and dual-task performances. *Psychology and Aging, 4.*

Baron, R. S., Cutrona, C. E., Hicklin, D., Russel, D. W., & Lubaroff, D. M. (1990). Social support and immune function among spouses of cancer patients. *Journal of Personality and Social Psychology, 59,* 344–352.

Baron-Cohen, S., Baldwin, D. A., & Crowson, M. (1997). Do children with autism use the speaker's direction of gaze strategy to crack the code of language? *Child Development, 68,* 48–57.

Barr, H., Pytkowicz, Streissguth, Darby, B., & Sampson, P. (1990). Prenatal exposure to alcohol, caffeine, tobacco, and aspirin: Effects on fine and gross motor performance in 4-year-old children. *Developmental Psychology, 26,* 339–348.

Barrett, D. H., Resnick, H. S., Foy, D. W., Dansky, B. S., Flanders, W. D., & Stroup, N. E. (1996a). Combat exposure and adult psychosocial adjustment among U.S. Army veterans serving in Vietnam, 1965–1971. *Journal of Abnormal Psychology, 105,* 575–581.

Barrett, G. V., & Depinet, R. L. (1991). A reconsideration of testing for competence rather than for intelligence. *American Psychologist, 46,* 1012–1024.

Barrett, G. V., & Franke, R. H. (1969). Communication preference and performance: A cross-cultural comparison. *Proceedings of the 77th Annual American Psychological Association Convention,* 597–598.

Barrett, P. M., Dadds, M. R., & Rapee, R. M. (1996b). Family treatment of childhood anxiety: A controlled trial. *Journal of Consulting and Clinical Psychology, 64,* 333–339.

Barron, F., & Harrington, D. M. (1981). Creativity, intelligence, and personality. *Annual Review of Psychology, 32,* 439–476.

Barron, J. W. (1998). *Making diagnosis meaningful: Enhancing evaluation and treatment of psychological disorders.* Washington, DC, USA: American Psychological Association.

Barry, H. M., et al. (1957). A cross-cultural survey of some sex differences in socialization. *Journal of Abnormal Social Psychology, 55,* 327–332.

Barta, P., Pearlson, G., Powers, R. E., Richards, S. S., & Tune, L. (1990). Auditory hallucinations and smaller superior temporal gyral volume in schizophrenia. *American Journal of Psychiatry, 147,* 1457–1462.

Bartlett, F. C. (1932). *Remembering: A study in experimental and social psychology.* Cambridge: Cambridge University Press.

Bartoshuk, L. M., & Beauchamp, G. K. (1994). Chemical senses. *Annual Review of Psychology, 45,* 419–449.

Basoglu, M. (1997). Torture as a stressful life event: A review of the current status of knowledge. In T. W. Miller (Ed.), *Clinical disorders and stressful life events* (pp. 45–70). Madison, CT: International Universities Press.

Basoglu, M., Paker, M., Paker, O., Ozmen, E., Marks, I., Sahin, D., & Sarimurat, N. (1994). Psychological effects of torture: A comparison of tortured with nontortured political activists in Turkey. *American Journal of Psychiatry, 151,* 6–81.

Bassili, J. N., & Krosnick, J. A. (2000). Do strength-related attitude properties determine susceptibility to response effects? New evidence from response latency, attitude extremity, and aggregate indices. *Political Psychology, 21 ,* 107-132.

Bateman, A., & Fonagy, P. (1999). Effectiveness of partial hospitalization in the treatment of borderline personality disorder: A randomized controlled trial. *American Journal of Psychiatry, 156,* 1563–1569.

Bates, J., Pettit, G., Dodge, K., & Ridge, B. (1998). Interaction of temperamental resistance to control and restrictive parenting in the development of externalizing behavior. *Developmental Psychology, 34,* 982–995.

Bates, M. S. (1987). Ethnicity and pain: A biocultural model. *Social Science and Medicine, 24,* 47–50.

Batson, C. D. (1991). Evidence for altruism: Toward a pluralism of prosocial motives. *Psychological Inquiry, 2,* 107–122.

Batson, C. D. (1995). Altruism. In A. Tesser (Ed.), *Advanced social psychology.* New York: McGraw-Hill.

Batson, C. D. (1998). Altruism and prosocial behavior. In D. T. Gilbert, S. T. Fiske, & G. Lindzey (Eds.), *The handbook of social psychology* (Vol. 2, 4th ed., pp. 282–316). Boston, MA: McGraw-Hill.

Batson, C. D., & Moran, T. (1999). Empathy-induced altruism in a prisoner's dilemma. *European Journal of Social Psychology, 29(7),* 909–924.

Battacchi, M. W., Pelamatti, G., Umilta, C., & Michelotti, E. (1981). On the acoustic information stored in echoic memory. *International Journal of Psycholonguistics, 8,* 17–29.

Batteau, D. W. (1967). The role of the pinna in human localization. *Proceedings of the Royal Society of London, Series, B, 168,* 158–180.

Batuev, A. S., & Gafurov, B. G. (1993). The chemical nature of the hypothalamocortical activation underlying drinking behavior. *Neuroscience of Behavioral Psychology, 23,* 35–41.

Baumeister, R. (1991). *Meanings of life.* New York: Guilford Press.

Baumeister, R., & Leary, M. R. (1995). The need to belong: Desire for interpersonal attachments as a fundamental human motive. *Psychological Bulletin, 117,* 497–529.

Baumeister, R. F., & Bratlavsky, E. (1999). Passion, intimacy, and time: Passionate love as a function of change in intimacy. *Personality and Social Psychology Review, 3,* 49–67.

Baumeister, R. F., Bushman, B. J., & Campbell, W. K. (2000). Self-esteem, narcissism, and aggression. Does violence result from low self-esteem or from threatened egotism? *Current Directions in Psychological Science, 9*(1), 26–29.

Baumeister, R. F., Smart, L., & Boden, J. M. (1996). Relation of threatened egotism to violence and aggression: The dark side of high self-esteem. *Psychological Review, 103,* 5–33.

Baumeister, R. F., Stillwell, A. M., & Heatherton, T. F. (1994). Guilt: An interpersonal approach. *Psychological Bulletin, 115,* 243–267.

Baumeister, R. J. (1998). The self. In D. T. Gilbert, S. T. Fiske, & G. Lindzey (Eds.), *The handbook of social psychology* (Vol. 2, 4th ed., pp. 680–740). Boston, MA: McGraw-Hill.

Baumrind, D. (1967). Child care practices anteceding three patterns of preschool behavior. *Genetic Psychology Monographs, 75,* 43–88.

Baumrind, D. (1971). Current patterns of parental authority. *Developmental Psychology Monograph, 4,* 1–103.

Baumrind, D. (1987). A developmental perspective on adolescent risk taking in contemporary America. *New Directions for Child Development, 37,* 93–125.

Baumrind, D. (1991). The influence of parenting style on adolescent competence and substance use. *Journal of Early Adolescence, 11,* 56–95.

Beach, S. R., Tesser, A., Fincham, F. D., Jones, D. J., Johnson, D., & Whitaker, D. J. (1998). Pleasure and pain in doing well, together: An investigation of performance-related affect in close relationships. *Journal of Personality and Social Psychology, 74,* 923–938.

Beaman, A. L., Cole, C. M., Preston, M., Klentz, B., & Steblay, N. M. (1983). Fifteen years of foot-in-the-door research: A meta-analysis. *Personality and Social Psychology Bulletin, 9,* 181–196.

Bechara, A., Tranel, D., Damasio, H., Adolphs, R., Rockland, C., & Damasio, A. (1995). Double dissociation of conditioning and declarative knowledge relative to the amygdala and hippocampus in humans. *Science, 29,* 1115–1118.

Beck, A. (1985). *Anxiety disorders and phobias: A cognitive perspective.* New York: Basic Books.

Beck, A. (1989). *Cognitive therapy in clinical practice: An illustrative casebook.* New York: Routledge.

Beck, A. (1991). Cognitive therapy: A 30-year retrospective. *American Psychologist, 46,* 368–375.

Beck, A. (1992). Cognitive therapy: A 30 year ret-

rospective. In J. Cottraux, P. Legeron, et al. (Eds.), *Which psychotherapies in year 2000? Annual series of European research in behavior therapy.* (Vol. 6, pp. 13–28). Amsterdam, The Netherlands: Swets & Zeitlinger.

Beck, A. T. (1976). *Cognitive therapy and the emotional disorders.* New York: International Universities Press.

Beck, A. T. (1993). Cognitive therapy: Past, present, and future. *Journal of Consulting and Clinical Psychology, 61,* 194–198.

Becker, E. (1973). *The denial of death.* New York: Free Press.

Beckwith, J., Geller, L., & Sarkar, S. (1991). Sources of human psychological differences: The Minnesota Study of Twins Reared Apart: Comment. *Science, 252,* 191.

Bee, H. (1982). Prediction of IQ and language skill from perinatal status, child performance, family characteristics, and mother-infant interaction. *Child Development, 53,* 1134–1156.

Bekesy, G. von. (1959). Synchronism of neural discharges and their demultiplication in pitch perception on the skin and in learning. *Journal of the Acoustical Society of America, 31,* 338–349.

Bekesy, G. von. (1960). *Experiments in hearing.* New York: McGraw-Hill.

Bekesy, G. von, & Rosenblith, W. A. (1951). The mechanical properties of the ear. In S. S. Stevens (Ed.), *Handbook of experimental psychology.* New York: John Wiley.

Bell, A. J., & Cook, H. (1998). Empirical evidence for a compensatory relationship between dream content and repression. *Psychoanalytic Psychology, 15,* 154–163.

Bell, A. P., Weinberg, M. S., & Hammersmith, S. (1981). *Sexual preference: Its development in men and women.* Bloomington: University of Indiana Press.

Bell, M., Billington, R., Cicchetti, D., & Gibbons, J. (1998). Do object relations deficits distinguish BPD from other diagnostic groups? *Journal of Clinical Psychology, 44,* 511–516.

Bell, R. M. (1985). *Holy anorexia.* Chicago: University of Chicago Press.

Bell, R. Q. (1968). A reinterpretation of the direction of effects in studies of socialization. *Psychological Review, 75,* 71–85.

Bellack, L., Hurvich, M., & Geldman, H. (1973). *Ego functions in schizophrenics, neurotics, and normals.* New York: Wiley.

Bellivier, F., Leboyer, M., Courtet, P., Buresi, C., Beufils, B., Samolyk, D., et al. (1998). Association between the tryptophan hydroxylase gene and manic-depressive illness. *Archives of General Psychiatry, 55,* 33–37.

Belsky, J., & Hsieh, K. (1998). Patterns of marital change during the early childhood years: Parent personality, coparenting, and division-of-labor correlates. *Journal of Family Psychology, 12,* 511-528.

Belsky, J., & Isabella, R. (1988). Maternal, infant, and social-contextual determinants of attachment security. In J. Belsky & T. Nezworsky (Eds.), *Clinical implications of attachment* (pp. 41–94). Hillsdale, NJ: Erlbaum.

Belsky, J., & Pensky, E. (1988). Marital change across the transition to parenthood. *Marriage and Family Review, 12,* 133–156.

Belsky, J., & Rovine, M. (1990). Patterns of marital change across the transition to parenthood. Pregnancy to three years postpartum. *Journal of Marriage and the Family, 52,* 5–20.

Bem, D. J. (1967). Self perception: An alternative interpretation of cognitive dissonance phenomena. *Psychological Review, 74,* 183–200.

Bem, D. J. (1972). Self-perception theory. In L. Berkowitz (Ed.), *Advances in experimental social psychology* (Vol. 6). New York: Academic Press.

Bem, D. J., & Allen, A. (1974). On predicting some of the people some of the time: The search for cross-situational consistencies in behavior. *Psychological Review, 81,* 506–520.

Bem, S. L. (1983). Gender schema theory and its implications for child development: Raising gender-aschematic children in a gender-schematic society. *Signs, Journal of Women in Culture and Society, 8,* 354–364.

Bem, S. L. (1985). Androgyny and gender schema theory: A conceptual and empirical integration. In T. B. Sonderegger (Ed.), *Nebraska symposium on motivation: Psychology and gender* (Vol. 32). Lincoln: University of Nebraska Press.

Bemporad, J. R. (1996). Self-starvation through the ages: Reflections on the pre-history of anorexia nervosa. *International Journal of Eating Disorders, 19,* 217–237.

Benasich, A. A., & Brooks-Gunn, J. (1996). Maternal attitudes and knowledge of child-rearing: Associations with family and child outcomes. *Child Development, 67,* 1186–1205.

Benbow, C., & Stanley, J. (1983). Sex differences in mathematical reasoning ability: More facts. *Science, 222,* 1029–1030.

Bendersky, M., & Lewis, M. (1998). Arousal modulation in cocaine-exposed infants. *Developmental Psychology, 34,* 555–564.

Benedict, R. (1934). *Patterns of culture.* New York: Mentor/New American Library.

Benes, F. (1989). Myelination of cortical-hippocampal relays during late adolescence. *Schizophrenia Bulletin, 15,* 585–593.

Benes, F., Turtle, M., Khan, Y., & Farol, P. (1994). Myelination of a key relay zone in the hippocampal formation occurs in the human brain during childhood, adolescence, and adulthood. *Archives of General Psychiatry, 51,* 477–484.

Benes, F. M. (1998). Brain development, VII: Human brain growth spans decades. *American Journal of Psychiatry, 155,* 1489.

Benet-Martinez, V., & John, O. P. (1998). Los Cinco Grandes across cultures and ethnic groups: Multitrait-multimethod analyses of the Big Five in Spanish and English. *Journal of Personality & Social Psychology, 75,* 729-750.

Benet-Martinez, V., & Waller, J. G. (1997). Further evidence for the cross-cultural generality of the Big Seven factor model: Indigenous and imported Spanish personality constructs. *Journal of Personality, 65,* 567–598.

Benotsch, E. G., Brailey, K., Vasterling, J. J., Uddo, M., Constans, J. I., & Sutker, P. B.

(2000). War zone stress, personal and environmental resources, and PTSD symptoms in Gulf War veterans: A longitudinal perspective. *Journal of Abnormal Psychology, 109,* 205–213.

Berg, C. (1992). Perspectives for viewing intellectual development throughout the life course. In R. J. Sternberg & C. A. Berg (Eds.), *Intellectual development* (pp. 1–15). New York: Cambridge University Press.

Berg, F. M. (1999). Health risks associated with weight loss and obesity treatment programs. *Journal of Social Issues, 55*(2), 277–297.

Berger, R. J., & Phillips, N. H. (1995). Energy conservation and sleep. *Behavioural Brain Research, 69,* 65–73.

Bergin, A. E., & Garfield, S. L. (1994). *Handbook of psychotherapy and behavior change* (4th ed.) New York: John Wiley & Sons.

Berkowitz, L. (1989). Frustration-aggression hypothesis: Examination and reformulation. *Psychological Bulletin, 106,* 59–73.

Berkowitz, L. B. (1994). *Aggression: Its causes, consequences, and control.* New York: McGraw-Hill.

Berman, P. W., & Pedersen, F. A. (1987). Research on men's transitions to parenthood: An integrative discussion. In P. W. Berman & F. A. Pederson (Eds.), *Men's transitions to parenthood: Longitudinal studies of early family experience.* Hillsdale, NJ: Erlbaum.

Bermond, B., Nieuwenhuyse, B., Fasotti, L., Schuerman, J. (1991). Spinal cord lesions, peripheral feedback, and intensities of emotional feelings. *Cognition & Emotion, 5,* 201-220.

Bernhardt, P. C. (1997). Influences of serotonin and testosterone in aggression and dominance: Convergence with social psychology. *Current Directions in Psychological Science, 6,* 44–48.

Bernstein, I. L. (1991). Aversion conditioning in response to cancer and cancer treatment. *Clinical Psychology Review, 11,* 185–191.

Berridge, K., & Zajonc, R. (1991). Hypothalamic cooling effects elicit eating: Differential effects on motivation and pleasure. *Psychological Science, 2,* 184–189.

Berridge, K. C. (1996). Food reward: Brain substrates of wanting and liking. Special Issue: Society for the Study of Ingestive Behavior, Second Independent Meeting. *Neuroscience & Biobehavioral Reviews, 20,* 1–25.

Berry, J. W. (1979). A cultural ecology of social behavior. In L. Berkowitz (Ed.), *Advances in experimental social psychology* (Vol. 12). New York: Academic Press.

Berry, J. W. (1989). Psychology of acculturation. In J. Berman (Ed.), *Nebraska Symposium on Motivation,* (Vol. 37, pp. 201–234). Lincoln: University of Nebraska Press.

Berry, J. W., & Bennet, J. A. (1992). Cree conceptions of cognitive competence. *International Journal of Psychology, 27,* 73–88.

Berry, J. W., Dasen, P. R., Saraswathi, T. S. (Eds.). (1997). *Handbook of cross-cultural psychology: Vol. 2. Basic processes and human development* (2nd ed.). Boston: Allyn & Bacon.

Berry, J. W., & Irvine, S. H. (1986). Bricolage: Savages do it daily. In R. J. Sternberg, & R. K. Wagner (Eds.), *Practical intelligence: Nature and origins of competence in the everyday world* (pp. 271–303). New York: Cambridge University Press.

Berry, J. W., Poortinga, Y. H., Segall, M. H., & Dasen, P. R. (1992). *Cross-cultural psychology: Research and applications.* New York: Cambridge University Press.

Berscheid, E., Dion, K., Walster, E., & Walster, G. (1971). Physical attractiveness and dating choice: A test of the matching hypothesis. *Journal of Experimental Social Psychology, 7,* 173–189.

Berscheid, E., & Reis, H. T. (1998). Attraction and close relationships. In D. T. Gilbert, S. T. Fiske, et al. (Eds.), *The handbook of social psychology* (Vol. 2, 4th ed., pp. 193–281). Boston, MA: McGraw-Hill.

Bersoff, D. N. (Ed.). (1999). *Ethical conflicts in psychology* (2nd ed.). Washington, DC: American Psychological Association.

Bertenthal, B. I. (1996). Origins and early development of perception, action, and representation. *Annual Review of Psychology, 47,* 431–459.

Bertenthal, B. I., & Clifton, R. K. (1998) Perception and action. In W. Damon (Ed. in Chief) and N. Eisenberg (Vol. Ed.), *Handbook of Child Psychology, Vol. 2.* (pp. 51-102). New York: John Wiley.

Bertolino, A., Esposito, G., Callicott, J. H., Mattay, V. S., Van Horn, J. D., Frank, J. A., Berman, K. F., & Weinberger, D. R. (2000). Specific relationship between prefrontal neuronal *N*-acetylaspartate and activation of the working memory cortical network in schizophrenia. *American Journal of Psychiatry, 157,* 26–33.

Best, D. L. (1993). Inducing children to generate mnemonic organizational strategies: An examination of long-term retention and materials. *Developmental Psychology, 29,* 324–336.

Best, D. L., & Williams, J. E. (1998). Masculinity and femininity in the self and ideal self descriptions of university students in 14 countries. In G. Hofstede (Ed.), *Masculinity and femininity: The taboo dimension of national cultures. Cross-cultural psychology series,* Vol. 3. (pp. 106-116). Thousand Oaks, CA: Sage Publications, Inc.

Best, D. L., Williams, J. E., Cloud, J. M., Davis, S. W. Robertson, L. S., Edwards, J. R., Giles, H., & Fowles, J. (1977). Development of sex-trait stereotypes among young children in the United States, England, and Ireland. *Child Development, 48,* 1375–1384.

Beutler, L. E. (1991). Have all won and must all have prizes? Revisiting Luborsky et al's verdict. *Journal of Consulting and Clinical Psychology, 59,* 226–232.

Beutler, L. E., Williams, R. E., Wakefield, P. J., & Entwistle, S. R. (1995). Bridging scientist and practitioner perspectives in clinical psychology. *American Psychologist, 50,* 984-994.

Beyene, Y. (1986). Cultural significance and physiological manifestations of menopause. A biocultural analysis. *Culture, Medicine, & Psychiatry, 10,* 47–71.

Beyer, C., Caba, M., Banas, C., & Komisaruk, B. R. (1991). Vasoactive intestinal polypeptide (VIP) potentiates the behavior effect of substance P intrathecal administration. *Pharmacology, Biochemistry, and Behavior, 39,* 695–698.

Bickel, W. K., Green, L., & Vuchinich, R. E. (1995). Behavioral economics. Special Issue: Behavioral economics. *Journal of the Experimental Analysis of Behavior, 64,* 257–262.

Bidell, T. R., & Fischer, K. W. (1992). Beyond the stage debate: Action, structure, and variability in Piagetian theory and research. In R. Sternberg & C. Berg (Eds.), *Intellectual development* (pp. 100–140). Cambridge: Cambridge University Press.

Bidell, T. R., & Fischer, K. W. (2000). The role of cognitive structure in the development of behavioral control: A dynamic skills approach. In W. J. Perrig, & A. Grob (Eds.). *Control of human behavior, mental processes, and consciousness: Essays in honor of the 60th birthday of August Flammer* (pp. 183–201). Mahwah, NJ: Lawrence Erlbaum Associates, Inc., Publishers.

Biederman, I. (1987). Recognition by components: A theory of human image understanding. *Psychological Review, 94,* 115–147.

Biederman, I. (1990). Higher-level vision. In D. N. Osherson, S. M. Kosslyn, et al. (Eds.), *Visual cognition and action: An invitation to cognitive science* (Vol. 2, pp. 41–72). Cambridge, MA, USA: MIT Press.

Biederman, I., Glass, A. L., & Stacy, E. W., Jr. (1973). Searching for objects in real-world scenes. *Journal of Exerimental Psychology, 97,* 22–27.

Biederman, I., Mezzanotte, R. J., & Rabinowitz, J. C. (1982). Scene perception: Detecting and judging objects undergoing relational violations. *Cognitive Psychology, 14,* 143–177.

Biederman, I., Mezzanotte, R. J., Rabinowitz, J. C., Francolini, C. M., & Plude, D. (1981). Detecting the unexpected in photointerpretation. *Human Factors, 23,* 153–164.

Biederman, J., Faraone, S., Milberger, S., Guite, J., Mick, E., Chen, L., et al. (1996). A prospective 4-year follow-up study of attention-deficit hyperactivity and related disorders. *Archives of General Psychiatry, 53,* 437–446.

Biederman, J., Mick, E., & Faraone, S. V. (2000). Age-dependent decline of symptoms of attention deficit hyperactivity disorder: Impact of remission definition and symptom type. *American Journal of Psychiatry, 157,* 816-818.

Biederman, J., Milberger, S., Faraone, S. V., Kiely, K., Guite, J., Mick, E., et al. (1995). Family-environment risk factors for attention-deficit hyperactivity disorder: A test of Rutter's indicators of adversity. *Archives of General Psychiatry, 52,* 464–470.

Bieling, P. J., Beck, A. T., & Brown, G. K. (2000). The Sociotropy-Autonomy Scale: Structure and implications. *Cognitive Therapy and Research, 24,* 763–780.

Bierer, L. M., Hof, P. R., Purohit, D. P., Carlin, L., et al. (1995). Neocortical neurofibrillary tangles correlate with dementia severity in Alzheimer's disease. *Archives of Neurology, 52,* 81–88.

Bieri, J. (1966). Cognitive complexity and personality development. In O. J. Jarvey (Ed.), *Experience, structure and adaptability.*

Bierut, L. J., Dinwiddie, S. H, Begleiter, H., Crowe, R. R, Hesselbrock, V., Nurnberger, J. I. Jr., Porjesz, B., Schuckit, M. A, & Reich, T. (1998). Familial transmission of substance dependence: Alcohol, marijuana, cocaine, and habitual smoking: A report from the collaborative study on the genetics of alcoholism. *Archives of General Psychiatry, 55,* 982-988.

Bierut, L. J., Heath, A. C., Bucholz, K., K., Dinwiddie, S. H., Madden, P. A. F., Statham, D. J., Dunne, M. P., & Martin, N. G. (1999). Major depressive disorder in a community-based twin sample: Are there different genetic and environmental contributions for men and women? *Archives of General Psychiatry, 57,* 557–563.

Biesanz, J., West, S. G., & Graziano, W. (1998). Moderators of self-other agreement: Reconsidering temporal stability in personality. *Journal of Personality and Social Psychology, 75,* 467–477.

Biesanz, J. C., West, S. G., & Graziano, W. G. (1998). Moderators of self-other agreement: Reconsidering temporal stability in personality. *Journal of Personality & Social Psychology, 75,* 467-477.

Binder, J. L., Strupp, H. H., & Henry, W. P. (1995). Psychodynamic therapies in practice: Time-limited dynamic psychotherapy. In M. B. Bongar, and L. E. Beutler (Eds.), *Comprehensive textbook of psychotherapy: Theory and practice. Oxford textbooks in clinical psychology, Vol. 1.* (pp. 48-63). New York: Oxford University Press.

Binet, A., & Simon, T. (1908). Le developpement de l'intelligence chez les enfants. *L'Annee Psychologique, 14,* 1–94.

Birnbaum, D. W. (1983). Preschooler's stereotypes about sex differences in emotionality: A reaffirmation. *Journal of Genetic Psychology, 143,* 139–140.

Bishop, J. A., & Cook, L. M. (1975). Moths, melanism and clean air. *Scientific American, 232,* 90–99.

Bjork, E. L., & Bjork, R. A. (1996). Continuing influences of to-be-forgotten information. *Consequences & Cognition: An International Journal, 5,* 176–196.

Bjorklund, A., & Gage, F. (1985). Neural grafting of neutrodegenerative diseases in animal models. *Annals of the New York Academy of Sciences, 457,* 53–81.

Bjorklund, D., & Harnishfeger, K. (1990). The resources construct in cognitive development: Diverse sources of evidence and a theory of efficient inhibition. *Developmental Review, 10,* 48–71.

Black, D. W., Goldstein, R. B., & Mason, E. E. (1992). Prevalence of mental disorder in 88 morbidly obese bariatric clinic patients. *American Journal of Psychiatry, 149,* 227–234.

Black, M. M., Dubowitz, H., & Starr, R. H. (1999). African American fathers in low income, urban families: Development, behavior, and home environment of their three-year-old children. *Child Development, 70,* 967–978.

Blair, I. V., & Banaji, M. R. (1996). Automatic and controlled processes in stereotype priming. *Journal of Personality & Social Psychology, 70,* 1142-1163.

Blake, R., & Hirsch, H. V. B. (1975). Deficits in binocular depth perception in cats after alternating monocular deprivation. *Science, 190,* 1114–1116.

Blake, R., & Mouton, J. (1964). *The managerial grid.* Houston, TX: Gulf.

Blakemore, C., & Cooper, G. F. (1970). Development of the brain depends on the visual environment. *Nature, 228,* 477–478.

Blampied, N. M. (1999). A legacy neglected: Restating the case for single-case research in cognitive-behaviour therapy. *Behaviour Change, 16,* 89–104.

Blanchard-Fields, F., & Chen, Y. (1996). Adaptive cognition and aging. *American Behavioral Scientist, 39,* 231–248.

Blascovich, J., & Mendes, W. B. (2000). Feeling and thinking: The role of affect in social cognition. In J. P. Forges et al. (Eds.), *Challenge and threat appraisals: The role of affective cues.* New York: Cambridge University Press.

Blasko, D. G. (1999). Only the tip of the iceberg: Who understands what about metaphors. *Journal of Pragmatics, 31,* 1675–1683.

Blass, T. (1991). Understanding behavior in the Milgram obedience experiment: The role of personality, situations, and their interactions. *Journal of Personality and Social Psychology, 60,* 398–413.

Blass, T. (1999). The Milgram Paradigm after 35 years: Some things we now know about obedience to authority. *Journal of Applied Social Psychology, 29*(5), 955–978.

Blass, T. (2000). *Obedience to authority: Current perspectives on the Milgram paradigm.* Mahwah, NJ: Lawrence Erlbaum Associates.

Blatt, S., Ford, R., Berman, W., Cook, B., Cramer, P., & Robins, C. E. (1994). *Therapeutic change: An object relations perspective.* New York: Plenum Press.

Blatt, S., & Zuroff, D. (1992). Interpersonal relatedness and self-definition: Two prototypes for depression. *Clinical Psychology Review, 12,* 527–562.

Blatt, S. J., Auerbach, J. S., & Levy, K. N. (1997). Mental representations in personality development, psychopathology, and the therapeutic process. *Review of General Psychology, 1,* 351-374.

Blatt, S. J., & Homann, E. (1992). Parent child interaction in the etiology of dependent and self-critical depression. *Clinical Psychology Review, 12,* 47–91.

Blaustein, A. R., & Waldman, B. (1992). Kin recognition in anuran amphibians. *Animal Behavior, 44,* 207–221.

Bliss, T. V., & Lomo, T. (1973). Long-lasting potentiation of synaptic transmission in the dentate area of the anaesthetized rabbit following stimulation of the perforant path. *Journal of Physiology, 232,* 331–356.

Block, J. (1995). A contrarian view of the five-factor approach to personality description. *Psychological Bulletin, 117,* 187–215.

Block, J., Block, J. H., & Keyes, S. (1988). Longitudinally foretelling drug usage in adolescence: Early childhood personality and environmental precursors. *Child Development, 59,* 336–355.

Block, J., & Kremen, A. (1996). IQ and ego-resiliency: Conceptual and empirical connections and separateness. *Journal of Personality and Social Psychology, 70,* 349–361.

Block, J. H. (1976). Issues, problems, and pitfalls in assessing sex differences: A critical review of "The Psychology of Sex Differences." *Merrill Palmer Quarterly, 22,* 283-308.

Block, J. H. (1978). Another look at sex differentiation in the socialization behaviors of mothers and fathers. In J. Sherman & F. L. Denmark (Eds.), *The psychology of women: Future directions of research.* New York: Psychological Dimensions.

Block, J. H., Gjerde, P., & Block, J. H. (1991). Personality antecedents of depressive tendencies in 18-year-olds: A prospective study. *Journal of Personality and Social Psychology, 60,* 726–738.

Block, R., Farinpour, R., & Schlechte, J. (1991a). Effects of chronic marijuana use of testosterone. *Drug and Alcohol Dependence, 28,* 121–128.

Block, R. I., Farinpour, R., & Schlechte, J. A. (1991b). Effects of chronic marijuana use on testosterone, luteinizing hormone, follicle stimulating hormone, prolactin and cortisol in men and women. *Drug & Alcohol Dependence, 28,* 121–128.

Blokland, A. (1997). Acetylcholine: A neurotransmitter for learning and memory? *Brain Research Reviews, 21,* 285–300.

Bloom, L. (1993). *The transition from infancy to language: Acquiring the power of expression.* New York: Cambridge University Press.

Blos, P. (1962). *On adolescence: A psychoanalytic interpretation.* New York: Free Press.

Blos, P. (1967). The second individuation process of adolescence. *Psychoanalytic study of the Child, 22,* 162–186.

Blouin, A., Blouin, J., Aubin, P., Carter, J., Goldstein, C., Boyer, H., & Perez, E. (1992). Seasonal patterns of bulimia nervosa. *American Journal of Psychiatry, 149,* 73–81.

Blowers, G. H., & O'Connor, K. P. (1996). *Personal construct psychology in the clinical context.* Ottawa, Canada: University of Ottawa Press.

Blum, G. S. (1954). An experimental reunion of psychoanalytic theory with perceptual vigilance and defense. *Journal of Abnormal and Social Psychology, 49,* 94–98.

Blumer, D., & Benson, D. (1984). Personality changes with frontal and temporal lesions. In D. F. Benson & F. Blumer (Eds.), *Psychiatric aspects of neurologic disease.* New York: Grune & Stratton.

Blurton-Jones, N., & Konner, M. (1976). !Kung knowledge of animal behavior. In R. B. Lee & I. DeVore (Eds.), *Kalahari hunter-gatherers* (pp. 326–348). Cambridge, MA: Harvard University Press.

Boden, J. M., & Baumeister, R. F. (1997). Repressive coping: Distraction using pleasant thoughts and memories. *Journal of Personality and Social Psychology, 73*, 45–62.

Bodenhausen, G. (1993). Emotions, arousal, and stereotypic judgments: A heuristic model of affect and stereotyping. In D. Mackie & D. Hamilton (Eds.), *Affect, cognition, and stereotyping: Interactive processes in group perception.* New York: Academic.

Boersch, E. E. (1982). Ritual und Psychotherapie. *Zeitschrift fur Klinische Psychologie und Psychotherapie, 30*, 214–234.

Bogdan, R. J. (2000). Minding minds: Evolving a reflexive mind by interpreting others. Cambridge, MA: The MIT Press.

Bogen, J. E. (1995). On the neurophysiology of consciousness: I. An overview. *Consciousness & Cognition: An International Journal, 4*, 52–62.

Bohannon, J. N., & Bonvillian, J. D. (1997). Theoretical approaches to language acquisition. In J. B. Gleason (Ed.), *The development of language,* (4th ed., pp. 259–316). Boston: Allyn and Bacon.

Bolger, K. E., Patterson, C. J., & Kupersmidt, J. B. (1998). Peer relationships and self-esteem among children who have been maltreated. *Child Development, l 69*, 1171-1197.

Bolger, N., Foster, M., Vinokur, A. D., & Ng, R. (1996). Close relationships and adjustment to a life crisis: The case of breast cancer. *Journal of Personality and Social Psychology, 70*, 283–294.

Bond, R., & Smith, P. B. (1996). Culture and conformity: A meta-analysis of studies using Asch's (1952b, 1956) line judgment task. *Psychological Bulletin, 119*(1), 111–137.

Bondareff, W. (1985). The neural basis of aging. In J. Birren & K. W. Schaie (Eds.). *Handbook of the psychology of aging* (2nd ed.). New York: Van Nostrand.

Bonebakker, A. E., Bonke, B., Klein, J., & Wolters, G. (1996). Information processing during general anesthesia: Evidence for unconscious memory. *Memory & Cognition, 24*, 766-776.

Bonvillian, J. D. (in press). Sign language development. In M. Barrett (Ed.), *The development of language.* London: UCL Press.

Borbély, A. (1986). *Secrets of sleep.* New York: Basic.

Borden, V. M. H., & Levinger, G. (1991). Interpersonal transformations in intimate relationships. In W. H. Jones, D. Perlman, et al. (Eds.), *Advances in personal relationships: A research annual: Vol. 2. Advances in personal relationships* (pp. 35–56). London: Jessica Kingsley Publishers.

Boring, E. G. (1930). A new ambiguous figure. *American Journal of Psychology, 42*, 444–445.

Borjeson, M. (1976). The aetiology of obesity in children. *Acta Paediatrica Scandinavica, 65*, 279–287.

Borkovec, T. D., & Costello, E. (1993). Efficacy of applied relaxation and cognitive-behavioral therapy in the treatment of generalized anxiety disorder. *Journal of Consulting and Clinical Psychology, 61*, 611–619.

Borkovec, T. D., & Costonguay, L. G. (1998). What is the scientific meaning of empirically supported therapy? *Journal of Consulting & Clinical Psychology, 66*, 136-142.

Bornstein, M. H. (1989). Sensitive periods in development: Structural characteristics and causal interpretations. *Psychological Bulletin, 105*, 179–197.

Borod, J. (1992). Interhemispheric and intrahemispheric control of emotion: A focus on unilateral brain damage. *Journal of Consulting and Clinical Psychology, 60*, 339–348.

Bors, D. A., & Forrin, B. (1998). The effects of post-weaning environment, biological dam, and nursing dam on feeding neophobia, open field activity, and learning. *Canadian Journal of Experimental Psychology, 50*, 197–204.

Bosson, J. K., & Swann, W. B., Jr. (1999). Self-liking, self-competence, and the quest for self-verification. *Personality and Social Psychology Bulletin, 25*(10), 1230–1241.

Bosworth, H. B., & Schaie, K. W. (1999). Survival effects in cognitive function, cognitive style and sociodemographic variables in the Seattle longitudinal study. *Experimental Aging Research, 25*, 121–139.

Bosworth, H. B., Schaie, K., Willis, S. L., & Siegler, I. C. (1999). Age and distance to death in the Seattle Longitudinal Study. *Research on Aging, 21*, 723–738.

Boszormenyi, N. J, & Spark, G. M. (1973). *Invisible loyalties: Reciprocity in intergenerational family therapy.* New York: Harper and Row.

Bouchard, C. (1989). Genetic factors in obesity. *Medical Clinics of North America, 73*, 67–81.

Bouchard, T. J., Lykken, D. T., McGue, M., & Segal, N. L. (1990). Sources of human psychological differences: The Minnesota study of twins reared apart. *Science, 250*, 223–228.

Bourguignon, E. (1979). *Psychological anthropology: An introduction to human nature and cultural differences.* New York: Holt, Rinehart & Winston.

Bovasso, G. B., Eaton, W. W., & Armenian, H. K. (1999). The long-term outcomes of mental health treatment in a population-based study. *Journal of Consulting and Clinical Psychology, 67*, 529–538.

Bovbjerg, D., Redd, W. H., Maier, L. A., Holland, J. C., Leske, L. M., Niedzwiecki, D., Rubin, S. C., & Herkes, T. B. (1990). Anticipatory immune suppression and nausea in women receiving cyclic chemotherapy for ovarian cancer. *Journal of Consulting and Clinical Psychology, 58*, 153–157.

Bowd, A. D. (1990). A decade of animal research in psychology: Room for consensus? *Canadian Psychology, 31*, 74–82.

Bowden, S. C. (1990). Separating cognitive impairment in neurologically asymptomatic alcoholism from Wernicke-Korsakoff syndrome: Is the neuropsychological distinction justified? *Psychological Bulletin, 107*, 355–366.

Bowen, M. (1978). *Family therapy in clinical practice.* New York: Jason Aronson.

Bowen, M. (1991). Alcoholism as viewed through family systems theory and family psychotherapy. *Family Dynamics of Addiction Quarterly, 1*, 94–102.

Bower, G. (1975). Cognitive psychology: an introduction. In W. K. Estes, (Ed.), *Handbook of Learning and Cognitive Processes: Vol. 1. Introduction to concepts and Issues* (pp. 25–80). Hillsdale, NJ: Erlbaum.

Bower, G. H. (1970). Analysis of a mnemonic device. *American Scientist, 58*, 496–510.

Bower, G. H. (1981). Mood and memory. *American Psychologist, 36*, 129–148.

Bower, G. H. (1989). In search of mood-dependent retrieval. *Journal of Social Behavior & Personality, 4*, 121–156.

Bower, T. G. R. (1971). The object in the world of the infant. *Scientific American, 225*, 30–38.

Bower, T. G. R. (1982). *Development in infancy* (2nd ed.). San Francisco: W. H. Freeman.

Bowers, J. S., & Schacter, D. L. (1990). Implicit memory and test awareness. *Journal of Experimental Psychology: Learning, Memory, and Cognition, 16*, 404–416.

Bowers, K. (1976). *Hypnosis for the seriously curious.* Monterey, CA: Brooks/Cole Publishing Co.

Bowers, K., Regenr, G., Balthazard, C., & Parker, K. (1990). Intuition in the context of discovery. *Cognitive Psychology, 22*, 72–110.

Bowlby, J. (1969). *Attachment and loss: Vol. I. Attachment.* New York: Basic Books.

Bowlby, J. (1973). *Separation, attachment, and loss (Vol. 2).* New York: Basic Books.

Bowlby, J. (1982). Attachment and loss: Retrospect and prospect. *American Journal of Orthopsychiatry, 52*, 664-678.

Boysen, S. T., & Himes, G. T. (1999). Current issues and emerging theories in animal cognition. *Annual Review of Psychology, 50*, 683–705.

Bradley, C. L., & Marcia, J. E. (1998). Generativity-stagnation: A five-category model. *Journal of Personality, 66*, 39–64.

Brainerd, C. J. (1996). Piaget: A centennial celebration. *Psychological Science, 7*, 191–195.

Brandao, M., Cardoso, S. H., Melo, L. L., Motta, V., & Coimbra, N. C. (1994). Neural substrate of defensive behavior in the midbrain tectum. *Neuroscience and Biobehavioral Reviews, 18*, 339–346.

Brandimonte, M., Einstein, G. O., & McDaniel, M. A. (Eds.). (1996). *Prospective memory: Theory and applications.* Mahwah: Lawrence Erlbaum.

Braun, A. R., Balkin, T. J., Wesensten, N. J., Gwadry, F., Carson, R. E., Varga, M., et al. (1998). Dissociated pattern of activity in visual cortices and their projections during human rapid movement sleep. *Science, 279*, 91–95.

Braun, S. (1996). New experiments underscore warnings on maternal drinking. *Science, 273*, 738–739.

Braungart, J., Plomin, R., DeFries, J., & Fulker, D. (1992). Genetic influence on tester-rated infant temperament as assessed by Bayley's infant behavior record: Nonadoptive and adoptive siblings and twins. *Developmental Psychology, 28*, 40–47.

Brazelton, T. B. (1972). Implications of infant development among the Mayan Indians of Mexico. *Human Development, 15*, 90–111.

Breer, H., Wanner, I., & Strogmann, J. (1996). Molecular genetics of mammalian olfaction. *Behavior Genetics, 26,* 209–219.

Breland, K., & Breland, M. (1961). The misbehavior of organisms. *American Psychologist, 16,* 681–684.

Bremner, J. D. (1998). Neuroimaging of posttraumatic stress disorder. *Psychiatric Annals, 28,* 445–450.

Bremner, J. D. (1999). Does stress damage the brain? *Biological Psychiatry, 45,* 797–805.

Brennan, K. A., Clark, C. L., & Shaver, P. R. (19998). Self-report measurement of adult attachment: An integrative overview. In J. A. Simpson & W. S. Rholes (Eds.), *Attachment theory and close relationships.* (pp. 46-76). New York: The Guilford Press.

Brennan, P.A., Grekin, E.R., & Mednick, S.A. (1999). Maternal smoking during pregnancy and adult male criminal outcomes. *Archives of General Psychiatry, 56,* 215-219.

Brennen, T., Baguley, T., Bright, J., & Bruce, V. (1990). Resolving semantically induced tip-of-the-tongue states for proper nouns. *Memory & Cognition, 18,* 339–347.

Brenner, C. (1982). *The mind in conflict.* New York: International Universities Press.

Breslau, N., Chilcoat, H. D., Kessler, R. C., & Davis, G. C. (1999). Previous exposure to trauma and PTSD effects of subsequent trauma: Results from the Detroit Area Survey of Trauma. *American Journal of Psychiatry, 156,* 902–907.

Breslau, N., Davis, G. C., Andreski, P., Peterson, E. L., & Schultz, L. R. (1997). Sex differences in posttraumatic stress disorder. *Archives of General Psychiatry, 54,* 1044–1048.

Bretherton, I. (1985). Attachment theory: Retrospect and prospect. In I. Bretherton & E. Waters (Eds.), Growing points of attachment theory and research. *Monographs of the Society for Research in Children Development, 50* (1–2, serial No. 209), 3–35.

Bretherton, I. (1990). Communication patterns, internal working models, and the intergenerational transmission of attachment relationships. *Infant Mental Health Journal, 11,* 237–257.

Breuer, K. (1985). Intentionality and perception in early infancy. *Human Development, 28,* 71–83.

Brewer, J. B., Zhao, Z., Desmond, J. E., Glover, G. H., & Gabrieli, J. D. E. (1998). Making memories: Brain activity predicts how well visual experience will be remembered. *Science, 281,* 1185–1187.

Brewer, M. B., & Brown, R. J. (1998). Intergroup relations. In D. T. Gilbert, S. T. Fiske, et al. (Eds.), *The handbook of social psychology* (Vol. 2, 4th ed., pp. 554–594). Boston: McGraw-Hill.

Brewer, W. F., & Treyens, J. C. (1981). Role of schemata in memory for places. *Cognitive Psychology, 13,* 207–230.

Brewerton, T. D. (1995). Toward a unified theory of serotonin dysregulation in eating and related disorders. *Psychoneuroendocrinology, 20,* 561–590.

Brewin, C. R., Andrews, B., & Valentine, John D. (2000). Meta-analysis of risk factors for posttraumatic stress disorder in trauma-exposed adults. *Journal of Consulting and Clinical Psychology, 68,* 748–766.

Briere, J., & Conte, J. R. (1993). Self-reported amnesia for abuse in adults molested as children. *Journal of Traumatic Stress, 6,* 21–31.

Brislin, R. M. (1986). The culture general assimilator: Preparation for various types of sojourns. Special issue: Theories and methods in cross-cultural orientation. *International Journal of Intercultural Relations, 10,* 215–234.

Brislin, R. W., & Keating, C. F. (1976). Cultural differences in the perception of a three-dimensional Ponzo illusion. *Journal of Cross-Cultural Psychology, 7,* 397–412.

Broadbent, D. E. (1958). The hidden preattentive processes. *American Psychologist, 32,* 109–118.

Brody, L. & Hall, J. (2000). Gender, emotion, and expression. In M. Lewis & J. Haviland-Jones (Eds.), *Handbook of Emotions,* 2nd edition. (pp. 338-349). New York: Guilford Press.

Brody, L. R. (1999). *Gender, emotion, and the family.* Cambridge, MA: Harvard University Press.

Brody, L. R., Lovas, G. S., & Hay, D. H. (1995). Gender differences in anger and fear as a function of situational context. *Sex Roles, 32*(1–2), 47–78.

Brody, N. (1992). *Intelligence* (2nd ed.). San Diego, CA: Academic Press.

Broocks, A., Bandelow, A., Pekrun, G., George, A., Meyer, T., Bartmann, U., et al. (1998). Comparison of aerobic exercise, clomipramine, and placebo in the treatment of panic disorder. *American Journal of Psychiatry, 155,* 603–609.

Brookoff, D., O'Brien, K., Cook, C. S., & Thompson, T. D. (1997). Characteristics of participants in domestic violence. *Journal of the American Medical Association, 277,* 1369–1373.

Brooks-Gunn, J., Duncan, G., & Aber, L., Eds. (1997). *Neighborhood poverty: Context and consequences for children.* NY: Russell Sage Foundation.

Brosschot, J. F., & Janssen, E. (1998). Continuous monitoring of affective-autonomic response dissociation in repressors during negative emotional stimulation. *Personality and Individual Differences, 25,* 69–84.

Broughton, J. (1978). Development of concepts of self, mind, reality, and knowledge. *New Directions for Child Development, 1,* 75–100.

Brown, A., Bransford, J., Ferrara, R., & Campione, J. (1983). Learning, remembering, and understanding. In E. M. Markman & J. H. Flavell (Eds.), *Carmichael's manual of child psychology* (Vol. III). New York: John Wiley.

Brown, A. S., Cohen, P., Greenwald, S., & Susser, E. (2000a). Nonaffective psychosis after prenatal exposure to rubella. *American Journal of Psychiatry, 157,* 438–443.

Brown, A. S., van Os, J., Driessens, C., Hoek, H. W., & Susser, E. S. (2000b). Further evidence of relation between prenatal famine and major affective disorder. *American Journal of Psychiatry, 157,* 190–195.

Brown, G., Bhrolchain, M., & Harris, T. (1975). Social class and psychiatric disturbance among women in an urban poulation. *Sociology, 9,* 225–254.

Brown, G. L., Goodwin, F. K., Ballenger, J. C., Goyer, P. F., & Major, L. F. (1979). Aggression in humans correlates with cerebrospinal fluid amine metabolites. *Psychiatry Research, 1,* 131–139.

Brown, G. W., & Harris, T. O. (1978). *Social origins of depression: A study of psychiatric disorder in women.* New York: Free Press.

Brown, G. W., & Harris, T. O. (1989). Depression. In G. W. Brown & T. O. Harris (Eds.), *Life events and illnesses.* New York: Guilford Press.

Brown, G. W., Harris, T. O., & Hepworth, C. (1994). Life events and endogenous depression: A puzzle reexamined. *Archives of General Psychiatry, 51,* 525–534.

Brown, J., & Smart, S. A. (1991). The self and social conduct: Linking self-representations to prosocial behavior. *Journal of Personality and Social Psychology, 60,* 368–375.

Brown, J. B. (1991). Staying fit and staying well: Physical fitness as a moderator of life stress. *Journal of Personality and Social Psychology, 61,* 555–561.

Brown, L. L., Tomarken, A. J., Orth, D. N., Loosen, P. T., Kalin, N. H., & Davidson, R. J. (1996). Individual differences in repressive-defensiveness predict basal salivary cortisol levels. *Journal of Personality and Social Psychology, 70,* 362–371.

Brown, N. O. (1959). *Life against death: The psychoanalytic meaning of history.* Middleton, CT: Wesleyan University Press.

Brown, P. K., & Wald, G. (1964). Visual pigments in single rods and cones in the human retina. *Science, 144,* 45–52.

Brown, R. (1973). *A first language: The early stages.* Cambridge, MA: Harvard University Press.

Brown, R., & Chiesa, M. (1990). An introduction to repertory grid theory and technique. *British Journal of Psychotherapy, 6,* 411–419.

Brown, R., & Fraser, C. (1963). The acquisition of syntax. In C. N. Cofer & B. Musgrave (Eds.), *Verbal behavior and learning: Problems and processes* (pp. 158–201). New York: McGraw-Hill.

Brown, R., & Hanlon, C. (1970). Derivational complexity and order of acquisition in child speech. In J. R. Hayes (Ed.), *Cognition and the development of language.* New York: John Wiley.

Brown, R. P., & Josephs, R. A. (1999). A burden of proof: Stereotype relevance and gender differences in math performance. *Journal of Personality and Social Psychology, 76,* 246–257.

Brown, R. W., Galanter, E., Hess, D., & Mandler, G. (1962). *New directions in psychology.* New York: Holt.

Brown, R. W., & McNeill, D. (1966). The tip-of-the-tongue phenomenon. *Journal of Verbal Learning and Verbal Behavior, 5,* 325–337.

Brown, S. L. (1985). Two adolescents at risk for schizophrenia: A family case study: Discussion. *International Journal of Family Therapy, 7,* 149–154.

Brown, T. A., Chorpita, B. F., & Barlow, D. H. (1998) Structural relationships among dimensions of the DSM-IV anxiety and mood disorders and dimensions of negative affect, positive affect, and autonomic arousal. *Journal of Abnormal Psychology, 107,* 179-192.

Brownell, K. D., & Rodin, J. (1994). The dieting maelstrom: Is it possible and advisable to lose weight? *American Psychologist, 49,* 781–791.

Bruce, D., & Bahrick, H. P. (1992). Perceptions of past research. *American Psychologist, 47,* 319–328.

Bruch, H. (1970). Eating disorders in adolescence. *Proceedings of the American Psychopathology Association, 59,* 181–202.

Bruch, H. (1973). *Eating disorders: Obesity, anorexia nervosa, and the person within.* New York: Basic Books.

Bruder, G., Kayser, J., Tenke, C., Amador, X., Friedman, M., Sharif, Z., & Gorman, J. (1999). Left temporal lobe dysfunction in schizophrenia: Event-related potential and behavioral evidence from phonetic and tonal dichotic listening tasks. *Archives of General Psychiatry. 56,* 267-276.

Bruner, J. S. (1992). Another look at New Look 1. *American Psychologist, 47,* 780–783.

Bruyer, R. (1991). Covert face recognition in prosopagnosia: A review. *Brain and Cognition, 15,* 223–235.

Bryant, P. E., & Trabasso, T. (1971).Transitive inferences and memory in young children. *Nature, 232,* 456-458

Bucci, W. (1997). *Psychoanalysis and cognitive science: A multiple code theory.* New York: Guilford Press.

Buchan, H., Johnstone, E., McPherson, K., & Palmer, R. L. (1992). Who benefits from electroconvulsive therapy? Combined results of the Leicester and Northwick Park trials. *British Journal of Psychiatry, 160,* 355–359.

Buck, L., & Axel, R. (1991). A novel multigene family may encode odorant receptors: A molecular basis for odor recognition. *Cell, 65,* 175–187.

Buck, R. (1986). The psychology of emotion. In J. E. LeDoux and W. Hirst (Eds.), *Mind and brain: Dialogues in cognitive neuroscience.* New York: Cambridge University Press.

Buck, R., Losow, J., & Murphy, M. (1992). Social facilitation and inhibition of emotional expression and communication. *Journal of Personality and Social Psychology, 63,* 962–968.

Bugental, D. B., & Goodnow, J. J. (1998) Socialization processes. In W. Damon (Ed. in Chief) and N. Eisenberg (Vol. Ed.), *Handbook of Child Psychology, Vol. 3.* (pp. 389-462). New York: John Wiley.

Buhrich, N., Bailey, J. M., Martin, N. G. (1991). Sexual orientation, sexual identity, and sex-dimorphic behaviors in male twins. *Behavior Genetics, 21,* 75–96.

Buhrmester, D. (1990). Intimany of friendship, interpersonal competence, and adjustment during preadolescence and adolescence. *Child Development, 61,* 1101–1111.

Bukowski, W., Gauze, C., Hoza, B., & Newcomb, A. (1994). Differences and consistency beween same-sex and other-sex peer relation-ships during early adolescence. *Developmental Psychology, 29,* 255–263.

Bunge, S. A., Klingberg, T., Jacobsen, R. B., & Gabrieli, J. D. E. (2000). A resource model of the neural basis of executive working memory. *Proceedings of the National Academy of Science, USA, 97,* 3573–3578.

Burchinal, M. R., Roberts, J. E., Riggins, R., Zeisel, S. A., Neebe, E., & Bryant D. (2000). Relating quality of center-based child care to early cognitive and language development longitudinally. *Child Development, 71,* 339–357.

Burgess, N., & Hitch, G. J. (1999). Memory for serial order: A network model of the phonological loop and its timing. *Psychological Review 106(3),* 551–581.

Buri, J., Louiselle, P., Misukanis, T., & Mueller, R. (1988). Effects of parental authoritarianism on self-esteem. *Personality and Social Psychology Bulletin, 14,* 271–282.

Burke, W., & Cole, A. M. (1978). Extra-retinal influences on the lateral geniculate nucleus. *Review of Physiology, Biochemistry, and Pharmacology, 80,* 105–166.

Burks, B. (1938). On the relative contributions of nature and nurture to average group differences in intelligence. *Proceedings of the National Academy of Sciences, 24,* 276–282.

Burks, B. S. (1928). The relative influence of nature and nurture upon mental development: A comparative study of foster parent-foster child resemblance and true parent-true child resemblance. *27th Yearbook of the National Society for the Study of Education, 27,* 219–316.

Burnstein, E., Crandall, C., & Kitayama, S. (1994). Some neo-Darwinian decision rules for altruism: Weighing cues for inclusive fitness as a function of the biological importance of the decision. *Journal of Personality & Social Psychology, 67,* 773–789.

Bushman, B. J. (1995). Moderating role of trait aggressiveness in the effects of violent media on aggression. *Journal of Personality & Social Psychology, 69,* 950-960.

Bushman, B. J. (1997). Effects of alcohol on human aggression: Validity of proposed explanations. In M. Galanter (Ed.). *Recent developments in alcoholism, Vol. 13. Alcohol and violence: Epidemiology, neurobiology, psychology, family issues* (pp. 227–243). New York: Plenum Press.

Bushman, B. J., & Baumeister, R. F. (1998). Threatened egotism, narcissism, self-esteem, and direct and displaced aggression: Does self-love or self-hate lead to violence? *Journal of Personality and Social Psychology, 75(1),* 219–229.

Bushman, B. J., Baumeister, R. F., & Stack, A. D. (1999). Catharsis, aggression, and persuasive influence: Self-fulfilling or self-defeating prophecies? *Journal of Personality and Social Psychology, 76(3),* 367–376.

Bushman, B. J., & Cooper, H. M. (1990). Effects of alcohol on human aggression: An integrative research review. *Psychological Bulletin, 107,* 341–354.

Buss, D. (1999). Human nature and individual differences: The evolution of human personality. In L. Pervin & O. John (Eds.), *Handbook of personality: Theory and research,* (2nd ed., pp. 31–56). New York: Guilford Press.

Buss, D. M. (1991). Evolutionary personality psychology. *Annual Review of Psychology, 42,* 459–492.

Buss, D. M. (1999). Human nature and individual differences: The evolution of human personality. In L. A. Pervin & O. P. John (Eds.), *Handbook of personality: Theory and research* (2nd ed.). New York: The Guilford Press (pp. 31-56).

Buss, D. M. (2000). The evolution of happiness. *American Psychologist, 55,* 15-23.

Buss, D. M., & Angleitner, A. (1989). Mate selection preferences in Germany and the United States. *Personality & Individual Differences, 10,* 1269-1280.

Buss, D. M., & Kenrick, D. T. (1998). Evolutionary social psychology. In D. T. Gilbert, S. T. Fiske, et al. (Eds.), *The handbook of social psychology,* (Vol. 2, 4th ed., pp. 982–1026). Boston: McGraw-Hill.

Buss, D. M., & Schmitt, D. P. (1993). Sexual strategies theory: An evolutionary perspective on human mating. *Psychological Review, 100,* 1–29.

Buss, D. M., Larsen, R. J., Westen, D., & Semmelroth, J. (1992). Sex differences in jealousy: Evolution, physiology, and psychology. *Psychological Science, 3,* 251–255.

Bussey, K. (1999). Children's categorization and evaluation of different types of lies and truths. *Child Development, 70,* 1338-1347.

Butler, A. B., & Hodos, W. (1996). *Comparative vertebrate neuroanatomy: Evolution and adaptation.* New York: Wiley-Liss.

Butler, C. A. (1976). New data about female sexual response. *Journal of Sex and Marital Therapy, 2,* 40–46.

Butler, R. N. (1969). Ageism: Another form of bigotry. *Gerontologist, 9,* 243–246.

Butler, R. N. (1975). *Why survive? Being old in America.* New York: Harper & Row.

Butler, R. N. (1984). Senile dementia: Reversible and irreversible. *Counseling Psychology, 12,* 75–79.

Butt, A., Testylier, G., & Dykes, R. (1997). Acetylcholine release in rat frontal and somatosensory cortex is enhanced during lactile discrimination learning. *Psychobiology, 25,* 18–33.

Butters, N., Heindel, W. C., & Salmon, D. (1990). Dissociation of implicit memory in dementia: Neurological implications. *Bulletin of the Psychonomic Society, 28,* 359–366.

Butterworth, A. (1978). A review of a primer of infant development. *Perception, 17,* 363–364.

Butzlaff, R. L., & Hooley, J. M. (1998). Expression emotion and psychiatric relapse: A meta-analysis. *Archives of General Psychiatry, 55,* 547–552.

Buunk, B. P., Angleitner, A., Oubaid, V., & Buss, D. M. (1996). Sex differences in jealousy in evolutionary and cultural perspective: Tests from the Netherlands, Germany, and the United States. *Psychological Science, 7,* 359–363.

Bynum, C. W. (1987). *Holy feast and holy fast.* Berkeley: University of California Press.

Byrne, D., et al. (1968). The effects of physical attractiveness, sex, and attitude similarity on interpersonal attraction. *Journal of Personality, 36,* 259–271.

Byrne, D., & Murnen, S. (1988). Maintaining loving relationships. In R. Sternberg & M. L. Barnes (Eds.), *The psychology of love* (pp. 293–310). New Haven, CT: Yale University Press.

Cacioppo, J. T., Crites, S. L., & Gardner, W. L. (1996). Attitudes to the right: Evaluative processing is associated with lateralized late positive event-related brain potentials. *Personality and Social Psychology Bulletin, 22,* 1205–1219.

Cacioppo, J. T., Ernst, J. M., Burleson, M. H., McClintock, M. K., Malarkey, W. B., Hawkley, L. C., Kowalewski, R. B., Paulsen, A., Hobson, J. A., Hugdahl, K., Spiegel, D., & Berntson, G. G. (2000). Lonely traits and concomitant physiological processes: The MacArthur social neuroscience studies. *International Journal of Psychophysiology, 35,* 143–154.

Cacioppo, J. T., Gardner, W. L., & Berntson, G. G. (1997). Beyond bipolar conceptualizations and measures: The case of attitudes and evaluative space. *Personality and Social Psychology Review, 1,* 3–25.

Cadenhead, K. S., Light, G. A., Geyer, M. A., & Braff, D. L. (2000). Sensory gating deficits assessed by the P50 event-related potential in subjects with schizotypal personality disorder. *American Journal of Psychiatry, 157,* 55–59.

Cadoret, R. J., O'Gorman, T. W., Troughton, E., & Heywood, E. (1985). Alcoholism and antisocial personality. *Archives of General Psychiatry, 42,* 161–167.

Cadoret, R. J., Yates, W. R., Troughton, E., Woodworth, G., & Stewart, M. A. (1995). Genetic-environmental interaction in the genesis of aggressivity and conduct disorders. *Archives of General Psychiatry, 52,* 916–924.

Caggiula, A. R., Epstein, L. H., Antelman, S., Seymour, M., & Taylor, S. S. (1991). Conditioned tolerance to the anorectic and corticosterone-elevating effects of nicotine. *Pharmacology, Biochemistry, and Behavior, 40,* 53–59.

Calhoun, K. S., Moras, K., Pilkonis, P. A., & Rehm, L. P. (1998). Empirically supported treatments: Implications for training. *Journal of Consulting & Clinical Pshcology, 66,* 151–162.

Cameron, L. D., Leventhal, H., & Love, R. R. (1998). Trait anxiety, symptom perceptions, and illness-related responses among women with breast cancer in remission during a tamoxifen clinical trial. *Health Psychology, 17*(5): p. 459–469.

Camp. B. W. & Bash, M. A. S. (1981) *Think aloud: Increasing social and cognitive skills—a problem solving program for children (primary level).* Champaign, IL: Research Press.

Campbell, D. T., & Stanley, J. C. (1963). *Experimental and quasiexperimental designs for research.* Chicago: Rand McNally.

Campbell, J. D. (1986). Similarity and uniqueness: The effects of attribute type, relevance, and individual differences in self-esteem and depression. *Journal of Personality and Social Psychology, 50,* 281–294.

Campbell, S. B. (1985). Hyperactivity in preschoolers: Correlates and prognostic implications. *Clinical Psychology Review, 5,* 405–428.

Campbell, W. K., & Sedikides, C. (1999). Self-threat magnifies the self-serving bias. A meta-analytic integration. *Reviews of General Psychology, 3,* 23–43.

Campfield, L., Arthur, S., Francoise, J., Rosenbaum, M., & Hirsch, J. (1996). Human eating: Evidence for a physiological basis using a modified paradigm. Special Issue: Society for the Study of Ingestive Behavior, Second Independent Meeting. *Neuroscience & Biobehavioral Reviews, 20,* 133–1137.

Campfield, L., Brandon, P., & Smith, F. J. (1985). On-line continuous measurement of blood glucose and meal pattern in free-feeding rats: The role of glucose in meal initiation. *Brain Research Bulletin, 14,* 605–617.

Campione, J. C., Brown, A. L., & Ferrara, R. A. (1982). Mental retardation and intelligence. In R. J. Sternberg (Ed.), *Handbook of human intelligence* (pp. 393–490). New York: Cambridge University Press.

Campos, J. J., Barrett, K. C., Lamb, M. E., Goldsmith, H. H., & Stenberg, C. (1983). Socioemotional development. In P. H. Mussen (Ed.), *Handbook of Child Psychology: Vol. II. Infancy and developmental psychobiology.* New York: John Wiley.

Canfield, R. L., & Ceci, S. J. (1992). Integrating learning into a theory of intellectual development. In R. J. Sternberg & C. A. Berg (Eds.), *Intellectual development.* New York. Cambridge University Press.

Canivez, G. L., & Watkins, M. W. (1998). Long-term stability of the *Wechsler Intelligence Scale for Children, third edition. Psychological Assessment, 10,* 285–291.

Cannon, T. D., Kaprio, J., Lönnqvist, J., Huttunen, M., & Koskenvuo, M. (1998). The genetic epidemiology of schizophrenia in a Finnish twin cohort: A population-based modeling study characterization of psychotic conditions. *Archives of General Psychiatry, 55,* 67–74.

Cannon, W. B. (1927). The James-Lange theory of emotions: A critical examination and an alternative theory. *American Journal of Psychiatry, 39,* 106–124.

Cannon, W. B. (1932). *The wisdom of the body.* New York: W. W. Norton.

Cantor, N. (1990). From thought to behavior: Having and doing in the study of personality and cognition. *American Psychologists, 45,* 735–750.

Cantor, N., & Blanton, H. (1996). Effortful pursuit of personal goals in daily life. In P. M. Gollwitzer, J. A. Bargh, et al. (Eds.), *The psychology of action: Linking cognition and motivation to behavior* (pp. 338–359). New York: Guilford Press.

Cantor, N., & Harlow, R. (1994). Personality, strategic behavior, and daily-life problem solving. *Current Directions in Psychologial Science 3,* 169–172.

Cantor, N., & Kihlstrom, J. F. (1987). Personality and social intelligence. Englewood Cliffs, NJ: Prentice-Hall.

Capaldi, E., & VandenBos, G. (1991). Taste, food exposure, and eating behavior. *Hospital and Community Psychiatry, 42,* 787–789.

Caplan, D., & Waters, G. S. (1990). Short-term memory and language comprehension: A critical review of the neuropsychological literature. In G. Vallar and T. Shallice (Eds.), *Neuropsychological impairments of short-term memory* (pp. 337–389). Cambridge: Cambridge University Press.

Caporael, L. R., & Baron, R. M. (1997). Groups as the mind's natural environment. In J. A. Simpson & D. T. Kenrick (Eds.), *Evolutionary social psychology.* (pp. 317-344). Mahwah, NJ: Lawrence Erlbaum Associates.

Cardno, A. G., Bowen, T., Guy, C. A., Jones, L. A., McCarthy, G., Williams, N. M, Murphy, K. C, Spurlock, G., Gray, M., Sanders, R. D., Craddock, N., McGuffin, P., Owen, M. J., & O'Donovan, M. C. (1999). CAG repeat length in the hKCa3 gene and symptom dimensions in schizophrenia. *Biological Psychiatry, 45,* 1592-1596.

Cardno, A. G., Marshall, E. J., Coid, B., Macdonald, A. M., Ribchester, T. R., Davies, N. J. Venturi, P., Jones, L. A., Lewis, S. W., Sham, P. C., Gottesman, I. I., Farmer, A. E., McGuffin, P., Reveley, A. M., & Murray, R. M. (1999). Heritability estimates for psychotic disorders: The Maudsley Twin Psychosis Series *Archives of General Psychiatry, 56,* 162–168.

Cardozo, B. L., Vergara, A., Agani, F., & Gotway, C. A. (2000). 162–168. Mental health, social functioning, and attitudes of Kosovar Albanians following the War in Kosovo. *Journal of the American Medical Association, 284,* 569–577.

Carlsmith, J. M., & Anderson, C. A. (1979). Ambient temperature and the occurrence of collective violence: A new analysis. *Journal of Personality and Social Psychology, 37,* 337–344.

Carlson, E. A. (1998). A prospective longitudinal study of attachment disorganization/disorientation. *Child Development, 69,* 1107-1128.

Carlson, E. B., & Rosser-Hogan, R. (1991). Trauma experiences, posttraumatic stress, dissociation, and depression in Cambodian refugees. *American Journal of Psychiatry, 148,* 1548–1551.

Carlson, N. R. (1999). *Foundations of physiological psychology* (4th ed.). New York: Allyn & Bacon.

Carmagnani, A., & Carmagnani, E.-F. (1999). Biofeedback: Present state and future possibilities. *International Journal of Mental Health, 28*(3), 83–86.

Carolsfeld, J., Tester, M., Kreiberg, H., & Sherwood, N. M. (1997). Pheromone-induced spawning of Pacific herring: I. Behavioral characterization. *Hormones & Behavior, 31,* 256–268.

Carone, B. J., Harrow, M., & Westermeyer, J. F. (1991). Posthospital course and outcome in schizophrenia. *Archives of General Psychiatry, 48,* 247–253.

Carpenter, P. A., Miyaka, A., & Just, M. A.

(1995). Language comprehension: Sentence and discourse processing. *Annual Review, 46,* 91–120.

Carroll, J. B. (1993). *Human cognitive abilities: A survey of factor-analytic studies.* New York: Cambridge University Press.

Carroll, J. M., & Russell, J. A. (1996). Do facial expressions signal specific emotions? Judging emotion from the face in context. *Journal of Personality & Social Psychology, 70,* 205-218.

Carskadon, M. A., & Dement, W. (1982). Nocturnal determinants of daytime sleepiness, *Sleep,* 5, 73-81.

Carstensen, L. L. (1992). Social and emotional patterns in adulthood: Support for socioemotional selectivity theory. *Psychology & Aging, 7,* 331-338.

Cartwright, R. D. (1996). Dreams and adaptation to divorce. In D. Barrett (Ed.), *Trauma and dreams* (pp. 179–185). Cambridge, MA: Harvard University Press.

Carver, C. S. (1998). Resilience and thriving: Issues, models, and linkages. *Journal of Social Issues, 54*(2), 245–266.

Carver, C. S., Scheier, M. F., & Weintraub, J. K. (1989). Assessing coping strategies: A theoretically based approach. *Journal of Personality and Social Psychology, 56,* 267–283.

Case, R. (1984). The process of stage transitions: A neo-Piagetian view. In R. J. Sternberg (Ed.), *Mechanisms of cognitive development.* New York: Freeman.

Case, R. (1992). Neo-Piagetian theories of child development. In R. J. Sternberg & C. A. Berg, *Intellectual development* (pp. 161–196). New York: Cambridge University Press.

Case, R. (1998) The development of conceptual structures. In W. Damon (Ed. in Chief) and N. Eisenberg (Vol. Ed.), *Handbook of Child Psychology, Vol. 2.* (pp. 745-800). New York: John Wiley.

Casey, M. B., Nuttall, R. L., & Pezaris, E. (1997). Mediators of gender differences in mathematics college entrance test scores: A comparison of spatial skills with internalized beliefs and anxieties. *Development Psychology, 33,* 669–680.

Cash, T. F., Gillen, B., & Burns, D. S. (1977). Sexism and "beautyism" in personnel consultant decision making. *Journal of Applied Psychology, 62,* 301–310.

Cashmore, J. A., & Goodnow, J. J. (1986). Influences on Australian parents' values: Ethnicity versus socioeconomic status. *Journal of Cross-Cultural Psychology, 17,* 441–454.

Casper, R. C., Hedeker, D., & McClough, J. F. (1992). Personality dimensions in eating disorders and their relevance for subtyping. *Journal of the American Academy of Child and Adolescent Psychiatry, 31,* 830–840.

Caspi, A. (1998). Personality development across the lifespan. In W. Damon (Ed.), *Handbook of child psychology: Vol. 3. Social, emotional, and personality development* (N. Eisenberg, Vol. Ed.) (pp. 311–388). New York: Wiley.

Caspi, A. (2000). The child is father of the man: Personality continuities from childhood to adulthood. *Journal of Personality and Social Psychology, 78*(1), p. 158–172.

Caspi, A., Elder, G. E., & Herbener, E. (1990). Childhood personality and the prediction of life-course patterns. In L. N. Robins & M. Rutter (Eds.), *Straight and devious pathways from childhood to adulthood* (pp. 13–35). New York: Cambridge University Press.

Caspi, A., Lynam, D., Moffitt, T., & Silva, P. (1993). Unraveling girls' delinquency: Biological, dispositional, and contextual contributions to adolescent misbehavior. *Developmental Psychology, 29,* 19–30.

Cassidy, J., & Shaver, P. R. (Eds.). (1999). *Handbook of attachment: Theory, research, and clinical applications.* New York: Guilford Press.

Cassidy, J., Kirsh, S. J., Scolton, K., & Parke, R. D. (1996). Attachment and representations of peer relationships. *Developmental Psychology, 32,* 892–904.

Castle, D. J., & Ames, F. R. (1996). Cannabis and the brain. *Australian & New Zealand Journal of Psychiatry, 30,* 179–183.

Cattell, R. B. (1941). Some theoretical issues in adult intelligence testing. *Psychological Bulletin, 38,* 592.

Cattell, R. B. (1957). *Personality and motivation: Structure and measurement.* Yonkers-on-Hudson, NY: World Book Co.

Cattell, R. B. (1990). Advances in Cattellian personality theory. In L. Pervin (Ed.), *Handbook of personality: Theory and research* (pp. 101–110). New York: Guilford Press.

Cavallero, C., & Foulkes, D. (1993). *Dreaming as cognition.* London: Harvester Wheatsheaf.

Cave, C. B. (1997). Very long-lasting priming in picture naming. *Psychological Science, 8,* 322–325.

Ceci, S. J. (1990). Framing intellectual assessment in terms of a person-process-context model. *Educational Psychologist, 25,* 269–291.

Ceci, S. J., & Bronfenbrenner, U. (1991). On the demise of everyday memory: "The rumors of my death are much exaggerated" (Mark Twain). *American Psychologist, 46,* 27–31.

Cerella, J. (1990). Aging and information-processing rate. In J. E. Birren & K. W. Schaie (Eds.), *Handbook of the psychology of aging* (3rd ed.). New York: Van Nostrand Reinhold.

Cervantes, C. A., & Callahan, M. (1998). Labels and explanations in mother-child emotion talk: Age and gender differentiation. *Developmental Psychology, 34,* 88–98.

Chaiken, M. L., Gentner, T. Q., & Hulse, S. H. (1997). Effects of social interaction on the development of startling song and the perception of these effects by conspecifics. *Journal of Comparative Psychology, 111,* 379-392.

Chaiken, S. (1980). Heuristic versus systematic information processing and the use of source versus message cues in persuasion. *Journal of Personality and Social Psychology, 39,* 752–766.

Chaiken, S. R., Kyllonen, P. C., & Tirre, W. C. (2000). Organization and components of psychomotor ability. *Cognitive Psychology, 40,* 198–226.

Chambless, D. C., & Gillis, M. M. (1993). Cognitive therapy of anxiety disorders. *Journal of Consulting and Clinical Psychology, 61,* 248–260.

Chambless, D. L., & Hollon, S. D. (1998). Defining empirically supported therapies. *Journal of Consulting & Clinical Psychology, 66,* 7–18.

Chambless, D. L., & Steketee, G. (2000). Expressed emotion and behavior therapy outcome: A prospective study with obsessive-compulsive and agoraphobic outpatients. *Journal of Consulting and Clinical Psychology, 67,* 658–665.

Chamove, A. S. (1978). Therapy of isolate rhesus: Different partners and social behavior. *Child Development, 49,* 43-50

Champoux, M., & Suomi, S. J. (1994). Behavioral and adrenocortical responses of rhesus macaque mothers to infant separation in an unfamiliar environment. *Primates, 35,* 191–202.

Chance, P. (1988). *Learning and behavior.* (2nd ed.). Belmont, CA: Wadsworth.

Chandler, L. S., Richardson, G. A., Gallagher, J. D., & Day, N. L. (1996). Prenatal exposure to alcohol and marijuana: Effects on motor development of preschool Children. *Alcoholism: Clinical & Experimental Research, 20,* 455–461.

Chen, J., & Gardner, H. (1997). Alternative assessment from a multiple intelligences theoretical perspective. In D. P. Flanagen, J. L. Genshaft, and P. L. Harrison (Eds.) *Contemporary intellectual assessment: Theories, tests, and issues* (pp. 105–121). New York: Guilford Press.

Chen, S., & Chaiken, S. (1999). The heuristic-systematic model in its broader context. In S. Chaiken & Y. Trope (Eds.), *Dual-process theories in social psychology.* (pp. 73-96). New York: The Guilford Press.

Cherry, E. C. (1953). Some experiments on the recognition of speech, with one and with two ears. *Journal of the Acoustical Society of America, 25,* 975-979.

Chess, S., & Thomas, A. (1986). *Temperament in clinical practice.* New York: Guilford Press.

Chess, S., & Thomas, A. (1987). *Origins and evolution of behavior disorders: From infancy to early adult life.* Cambridge, MA: Harvard University Press.

Cheyette, S. R., & Cummings, J. L. (1995). Encephalitis lethargica: Lessons for contemporary neuropsychiatry. *Journal of Neuropsychiatry & Clinical Neurosciences, 7,* 125–134.

Chi, M. T. H. (1978). Knowledge structures and memory development. In R. Siegler (Ed.), *Children's thinking: What deficits?* Hillsdale, NJ: Erlbaum.

Chi, M. T. H., Glaser, R., & Rees, E. (1982). Expertise in problem solving. In R. J. Sternberg (Ed.), *Advances in the psychology of human intelligence,* (Vol. 1, pp. 7–76). Hillsdale, NJ: Erlbaum.

Chiu, L-H. (1990). A comparison of moral reasoning in American and Chinese school children. *International Journal of Adolescence and Youth, 2,* 185–198.

Chomsky, N. (1957). *Syntactic structures.* The Hague: Mouton.

Chomsky, N. (1959). Review of Skinner's Verbal Behavior. *Language, 35,* 26–58.

Chomsky, N. (1986). *Knowledge of language: Its nature, origins, and use.* New York: Praeger.

Christenfeld, N. (1997). Memory for pain and the

delayed effects of distraction. *Health Psychology, 16,* 327–330.

Christensen, A., & Heavey, C. L. (1999). Interventions for couples. *Annual Review of Psychology, 50,* 165-190.

Christianson, S. A. (1992). Emotional stress and eyewitness memory: A critical review. *Psychological Bulletin, 112(2)Z,* 284–309.

Christie, R., & Geis, F. I. (1970). *Studies in Machiavellianism.* New York: Academic Press.

Chrobak, J. J., & Buzsaki, G. (1994). Selective activation of deep layer (V-VI) retrohippocampal cortical neurons during hippocampal sharp waves in the behaving rat. *Journal of Neuroscience, 14,* 1660–1670.

Chu, J. A., Frey, L. M., Ganzel, B. L., & Matthews, J. A. (1999). Memories of childhood abuse: Dissociation, amnesia, and corroboration. *American Journal of Psychiatry, 156,* 749–755.

Chung, K. K. K., Martinez, M., & Herbert, J. (2000). c-fos expression, behavioural, endocrine and autonomic responses to acute social stress in male rats after chronic restraint: Modulation by serotonin. *Neuroscience, 95,* 453–463.

Church, A. T., & Lonner, W. J. (1998). The cross-cultural perspective in the study of personality: Rationale and current research. *Journal of Cross-Cultural Psychology, 29,* 32 62.

Civic, D. (2000). College students' reasons for nonuse of condoms within dating relationships. *Journal of Sex & Marital Therapy, 26,* 95-105.

Clancy, S. A., Schacter, D. L., McNally, R. J., & Pitman, R. K. (2000). False recognition in women reporting recovered memories of sexual abuse. *Psychological Science, 11,* 26–31.

Clark, A. S., & Goldman-Rakic, P. (1989). Go nadal hormones influence the emergence of cortical function in nonhuman primates. *Behavioral Neuroscience, 103,* 1287–1295.

Clark, D. A., Beck, A. T., & Alford, B. A. (1999). *Scientific foundations of cognitive theory and therapy of depression.* New York: Wiley.

Clark, D. M. (1994). Cognitive therapy for panic disorder. In B. E. Wolfe, J. D. Maser, et al. (Eds.), *Treatment of panic disorder: A consensus development conference* (pp. 121–132). Washington: American Psychiatric Press.

Clark, K. E., & Ladd, G. W. (2000). Connectedness and autonomy support in parent-child relationships: Links to children's socioemotional orientation and peer relationships. *Developmental Psychology, 36,* 485-498.

Clark, M. S., & Pataki, S. (1995). Interpersonal processes influencing attraction and relationships. In A. Tesser (Ed.), *Advanced social psychology.* New York: McGraw-Hill.

Claustrat, B., Brun, J., David, M., et al. (1992). Melatonin and jet lag: Confirmatory result using a simplified protocol. *Biological Psychiatry, 32(8),* 705 711.

Cleare, A., & Bond, A. (1997). Does central oserotonergic function correlate inversely with aggression? A study using *d*-fenfluramine in healthy subjects. *Psychiatry Research, 69,* 89–95.

Cleghorn, J. M., Peterfy, G., Pinter, E. J., & Pat-

tee, C. J. (1970). Verbal anxiety and the beta adrenergic receptors: A facilitating mechanism? *Journal of Nervous and Mental Disease, 151,* 266–272.

Clifford, M. M., & Walster, E. (1973). The effect of physical attractiveness on teacher expectations. *Sociological Education, 46,* 248–258.

Cloninger, C. R., Bohman, M., & Sigvardsson, S. (1981). Inheritance of alcohol abuse. *Archives of General Psychiatry, 38,* 861–868.

Cody, H., & Kamphaus, R. W. (1999). Down syndrome. In S. Goldstein, C. R. Reynolds, et al. (Eds.), Handbook of neurodevelopmental and genetic disorders in children (pp. 385–405). New York: Guilford Press.

Cohen, D. (1983). *Piaget: Critique and reassessment.* New York: St. Martin's Press.

Cohen, D., & Nisbett, R. E. (1997). Field experiments examining the culture of honor: The role of institutions in perpetuating norms about violence. *Personality and Social Psychology Bulletin, 23(11),* 1188–1199.

Cohen, D., Nisbett, R. E., Bowdle, B. F., & Schwarz, N. (1996). Insult, aggression, and the southern culture of honor: An "experimental ethnography." *Journal of Personality & Social Psychology, 70,* 945-960.

Cohen, J. D., Schooler, J. W. (1997). *Scientific approaches to consciousness.* Mahwah, NJ: Lawrence Erlbaum Associates, Inc.

Cohen, L. B., Diehl, R. L., Oakes, L. M., & Loehlin, J. L. (1992a). Infant perception of /aba/ versus /apa/: Building a quantitative model of infant categorical discrimination. *Developmental Psychology, 28,* 261–272.

Cohen, R. M., Gross, M., Nordahl, T., Semple, W., Oren, D., & Rosenthal, N. (1992b). Preliminary data on the metabolic brain pattern of patients with Winter seasonal affective disorder. *Archives of General Psychiatry, 49,* 545–552.

Cohen, S., & Herbert, T. B. (1996). Health psychology: Psychological factors and physical disease from the perspective of human psychoneuroimmunology. *Annual Review of Psychology, 47,* 113–142.

Cohen, S., Tyrrell, D. A. J., & Smith, A. P. (1991). Psychological stress and susceptibility to the common cold. *New England Journal of Medicine, 325,* 606–612.

Cohen, S., & Williamson, G. M. (1991). Stress and infectious disease in humans. *Psychological Bulletin, 109,* 5–24.

Cohen, S., & Wills, T. A. (1985). Stress, social support, and the buffering hypothesis. *Psychological Bulletin, 98,* 310–357.

Colby, A., & Kohlberg, L. (1984). Invariant sequence and internal consistency in moral judgment stages. In W. M. Kurtines & J. L. Gewirtz (Eds.), *Morality, moral behavior and moral development.* New York: John Wiley.

Cole, D. A., Martin, J. M., Peeke, L. A., Seroczynski, A. D., & Fier, J. (1999). Children's over- and underestimation of academic competence: A longitudinal study of gender differences, depression, and anxiety. *Child Development, 70,* 459–473.

Cole, M. (1975). An ethnographic psychology of cognition. In R. Brislin et al. (Eds.), *Cross-cultural perspectives on learning.* New York: Sage Publications.

Cole, M. (1997). Cultural mechanisms of cognitive development. In E. Amsel, K. A. Renninger, et al. (Eds.), *Change and development: Issues of theory, method, and application. The Jean Piaget symposium series* (pp. 245–263). Mahwah, NJ: Lawrence Erlbaum Associates.

Cole, M., Gay, J., Glick, J. A., & Sharp, D. W. (1971). *The cultural context of learning and thinking.* New York: Basic Books.

Cole, P. M., Zahn-Waxler, C., Fox, N. A., & Usher, B. A. (1996). Individual differences in emotion regulation and behavior problems in preschool children. *Journal of Abnormal Psychology, 105,* 518–529.

Cole, S. W., Kemeny, M. E., & Taylor, S. E. (1997). Social identity and physical health: Accelerated HIV progression in rejection-sensitive gay men. *Journal of Personality and Social Psychology, 72,* 320–335.

Collett, T. S., & Baron, J. (1994). Biological compasses and the coordinate frame of landmark memories in honeybees. *Nature, 368,* 137–140.

Collier, G., Johnson, D. F., & Berman, J. (1998). Patch choice as a function of procurement cost and encounter rate. *Journal of the Experimental Analysis of Behavior, 69,* 5–16.

Collings, S., & King, M. (1994). Ten-year follow-up of 50 patients with bulimia nervosa. *British Journal of Psychiatry, 164,* 80–87.

Collins, A., & Loftus, E. F. (1975). A spreading-activation theory of semantic processing. *Psychological Review, 82,* 407–428.

Collins, R. L., Lapp, W. M., Emmons, K. M., & Isaac, L. M. (1990). Endorsement and strength of alcohol expectancies. *Journal of Studies on Alcohol, 51,* 336–342.

Collins, W. A., & Gunnar, M. R. (1990). Social and personality development. *Annual Review of Psychology, 41,* 387–416.

Collins, W. A., Maccoby, E. E., Steinberg, L., Hetherington, E. M. & Bornstein, M. H. (2000). Contemporary research on parenting: The case for nature and nurture. *American Psychologist, 55,* 218–232.

Cologer-Clifford, A., Simon, N., & Jubilan, B. (1992). Genotype, uterine position, and testosterone sensitivity in older female mice. *Physiology and Behavior, 51,* 1047–1050.

Colvin, C. R. (1993). Judgable people: Personality, behavior, and competing explanations. *Journal of Personality and Social Psychology, 64,* 861–873.

Colvin, C. R., Block, J., & Funder, D. C. (1995). Overly positive self-evaluations and personality: Negative implications for mental health. *Journal of Personality & Social Psychology, 68,* 1152–1162.

Comaroff, J. (1980). Healing and the cultural order: The case of the Barolong boo Ratshidi of Southern Africa. *American Ethnologist, 7,* 637–657.

Compas, B., Hinden, B. R., & Gerhardt, C. (1995). Adolescent development: Pathways and processes of risk and resilience. *Annual Review of Psychology, 46,* 265–293.

Compton, W. M., Helzer, J., Hai-Gwo, H., Eng-Kung, Y., McEvoy, L., Tipp, J., & Spitznagel, E. (1991). New methods in cross-cultural psychiatry: Psychiatric illness in Taiwan and the United States. *American Journal of Psychiatry, 148,* 1697–1704.

Conger, R., Conger, K., Elder, G., Lorenz, F., Simons, R., & Whitbeck, L. (1993). Family economic stress and adjustment of early adolescent girls. *Developmental Psychology, 29,* 206–219.

Conklin, H. M., Curtis, C. E., Katsanis, J., & Iacono, W. G. (2000). Verbal working memory impairment in schizophrenia patients and their first-degree relatives: Evidence from the Digit Span Task. *American Journal of Psychiatry, 157,* 275–277.

Conway, M. A. (1995). *Flashbulb memories.* Mahwah, NJ: Lawrence Erlbaum.

Conway, M. A., Collins, A. F., Gathercole, S. E., & Anderson, S. J. (1996). Recollections of true and false autobiographical memories. *Journal of Experimental Psychology: General, 125,* 69–95.

Coombs, C., & Lehner, P. E. (1984). Conjoint design and analysis of the bilinear model: An application to judgments of risk. *Journal of Mathematical Psychology, 28,* 1–42.

Cooper, L. A. (1976). Demonstration of a mental analog of an external rotation. *Perception and Psychophysics, 19,* 296–302.

Cooper, L. A., & Shepard, R. N. (1973a). Chronometric studies of the rotation of mental images. In W. G. Chase (Ed.), *Visual information processing.* New York: Academic.

Coopersmith, S. (1967). *The antecedents of self-esteem.* San Francisco: Freeman.

Cork, R. C. (1996). Implicit memory during anesthesia. In S. R. Hameroff, A. W. Kaszniak, & A. C. Scott (Eds.), *Toward a science of consciousness: The first Tucson discussions and debates. Complex adaptive systems* (pp. 295–302). Cambridge: MIT Press.

Cornblatt, B. A., & Kelip, J. G. (1994). Impaired attention, genetics, and the pathophysiology of schizophrenia. *Schizophrenia Bulletin, 20,* 31–46.

Corr, P. J., Pickering, A. D., & Gray, J. A. (1995). Personality and reinforcement in associative and instrumental learning. *Personality & Individual Differences, 19,* 47–71.

Coryell, W., Endicott, J., & Winokur, G. (1992). Anxiety syndromes as epiphenomena of primary major depression: Outcome and familial psychopathology. *American Journal of Psychiatry, 149,* 100–107.

Cosmides, L. (1989). The logic of social exchange: Has natural selection shaped how humans reason? Studies with the Wason selection task. *Cognition, 31,* 187–276.

Cosmides, L., & Tooby, J. (1995). From evolution to adaptations to behavior. Toward an integrated evolutionary psychology. In R. Wong et al. (Eds.), *Biological perspectives on motivated activities* (pp. 11–74). Norwood: Ablex Publishing.

Cosmides, L., & Tooby, J. (1999). Toward an evo-

lutionary taxonomy of treatable conditions. *Journal of Abnormal Psychology, 108,* 453–464.

Costa, P. T., & McCrae, R. (1977). Age differences in personality structure revisited: Studies in validity, stability, and change. *International Journal of Aging and Human Development, 8,* 261-275.

Costa, P. T. Jr., & McCrae, R. R. (1988). Personality in adulthood: A six-year longitudinal study of self-reports and spouse ratings on the NEO Personality Inventory. *Journal of Personality and Social Psychology, 54,* 853–863.

Costa, P. T. Jr., & McCrae, R. R. (1990). Personality: Another "hidden factor" in stress research. *Psychological Inquiry, 1,* 22–24.

Costa, P. T. Jr., & McCrae, R. R. (1997). Stability and change in personality assessment: The Revised NEO Personality Inventory in the Year 2000. *Journal of Personality Assessment, 68,* 86–94.

Cotman, C. W. (1990). Synaptic plasticity, neurotropic factors, and transplantation in the aged brain. In E. L. Schneider & J. W. Rowe (Eds.), *Handbook of the biology of aging* (3rd ed.). San Diego: Academic Press.

Coull, J. T., & Sahakian, B. J. (2000). Psychopharmacology of memory. In G. E. Berrios & J. R. Hodges (Eds.). *Memory disorders in psychiatric practice.* (pp. 75–98). New York: Cambridge University Press.

Courtney, S. M., et al. (1998). An area specialized for spatial working memory in human frontal cortex. *Science, 279,* 1347–1351.

Courtney, S. M., Ungerleider, L. G., Keil, K., & Haxby, J. V. (1997). Transient and sustained activity in a distributed neural system for human working memory. *Nature, 386,* 608–611.

Cousins, S. (1989). Culture and self-perception in Japan and the United States. *Journal of Personality and Social Psychology, 56,* 124–131.

Cowan, C. P., & Cowan, P. A. (1992). *When partners become parents.* New York: Basic Books.

Cowan, N. (1994). Mechanisms of verbal short-term memory. *Current Directions in Psychological Science, 3,* 185–189.

Cowan, W. M. (1979). The development of the brain. *Science American, 241,* 112–133.

Cowdry, R. W., & Gardner, D. L. (1988). Pharmacotherapy of borderline personality disorder: Alprazolam, carbamazepine, trifluoperazine, and tranylcypromine. *Archives of General Psychiatry, 45,* 111–119.

Cowey, A. (1991). Grasping the essentials. *Nature, 349,* 102–103.

Cowgill, D. O., & Holms, L. D. (1972). *Aging and modernization.* New York: Appleton-Century Crofs.

Coyle, J. (1991). Molecular biological and neurobiological contributions to our understanding of Alzheimer's disease. In A. Tasman & S. Goldfinger, (Eds.), *American Psychiatric Press Review of Psychiatry* (Vol. 10, pp. 515–527). Washington, DC: American Psychiatric Press.

Craig, A. D., Reiman, E. M., Evans, A., & Bushnell, M. C. (1996). Functional imaging of an illusion of pain. *Nature, 384,* 258–260.

Craig, J. C., & Rollman, G. B. (1999). Somesthesis. *Annual Review of Psychology, 50,* 305–331.

Craik, F., & Lockhart, R. (1972). Levels of processing: A framework for memory research. *Journal of Verbal Learning and Verbal Behavior, 11,* 671–684.

Craik, F. I. M., & Salthouse, T. A. (2000). *The handbook of aging and cognition* (2nd ed.). Mahwah, NJ: Lawrence Erlbaum Associates.

Craik, F. I. M., Govoni, R., Naveh-Benjamin, M., & Anderson, N. D. (1996). The effects of divided attention on encoding and retrieval processes in human memory. *Journal of Experimental Psychology: General, 125,* 159–180.

Crair, M. C., Gillespie, D. C., & Stryker, M. P. (1998). The role of visual experience in the development of columns in cat visual cortex. *Science, 279,* 566–570.

Cramer, P. (1996). *Storytelling, narrative, and the Thematic Apperception Test.* New York: Guilford Press.

Cramer, P. (in press). Identity, narcissism, and defense mechanisms in late adolescence. *Journal of Research in Personality.*

Cramer, P., & Block, J. (1998). Preschool antecedents of defense mechanism use in young adults: A longitudinal study. *Journal of Personality and Social Psychology, 74,* 159–169.

Crandall, C. (1994). Prejudice against fat people: Ideology and self-interest. *Journal of Personality and Social Psychology, 66,* 882–894.

Crews, F. C. (1998). *Unauthorized Freud: Doubters confront a legend.* New York: Viking Penguin, Inc.

Crick, F. (1993) The astonishing hypothesis: The scientific search for the soul. New York: Charles Scribner's Sons.

Crick, F., & Koch, C. (1998). Consciousness an neuroscience. *Cerebral Cortex, 8,* 97–107.

Crick, F., & Mitchison, G. (1983). The function of dream sleep. *Nature, 304,* 111–114.

Crick, N. R., & Dodge, K. A. (1994). A review and reformulation of social information-processing mechanisms in children's social adjustment. *Psychological Bulletin, 115,* 74-101.

Critchley, H., Daly, E., Phillips, M., Brammer, M., Bullmore, E., Williams, S., Amelsvoort, T. V., Robertson, D., David, A., & Murphy, D. (2000). Explicit and implicit neural mechanisms for processing of social information from facial expressions: A functional magnetic resonance imaging study. *Human Brain Mapping, 9,* 93–105.

Crits-Christoph, P. (1992). The efficacy of brief dynamic psychotherapy: A meta-analysis. *American Journal of Psychiatry, 149,* 151–158.

Crook, T. H., Youngjohn, J., Larrabee, G., & Salama, M. (1992). Aging and everyday memory. *Neuropsychology, 6,* 123–136.

Cross, S. E., & Markus, H. (1999). The cultural constitution of personality. In L. Pervin & O. John (Eds.), *Handbook of personality: Theory and research,* (2nd ed., pp. 378–396). New York: Guilford Press.

Crow, T. J. (1980). Molecular pathology of schizophrenia: More than one disease process? *British Medical Journal, 280,* 66–68.

Crowder, R. (1993). Systems and principles in memory theory: Another critique of pure memory. In A. F. Collins, S. Gathercole, M. A. Conway, & P. E. Morris (Eds.), *Theories of memory* (pp. 139–161). Hillsdale: Lawrence Erlbaum Associates.

Crowell, J. A., & Feldman, S. S. (1991). Mothers' working models of attachment relationships and mother and child behavior during separation and reunion. *Developmental Psychology, 27,* 597–605.

Crowne, D. P., & Marlow, D. (1964). *The approval motive: Studies in evaluative dependence.* New York: John Wiley.

Csikszentmihalyi, M., & Larson, R. (1984). *Being adolescent: Conflict and growth in the teenage years.* New York: Basic Books.

Cummins, R. A., Livesey, P. J., & Evans, J. G. M. (1977). A developmental theory of environmental enrichment. *Science, 197,* 692–694.

Cunningham, M. R., Roberts, A. R., Barbee, A. P., Druen, P. B., et al. (1995)."Their ideas of beauty are, on the whole, the same as ours": Consistency and variability in the cross-cultural perception of female physical attractiveness. *Journal of Personality & Social Psychology, 68,* 261–279.

Curran, J. P., & Lippold, S. (1975). The effects of physical attraction and attitude similarity on attraction in dating dyads. *Journal of Personality and Social Psychology, 43,* 528–539.

Curtiss, S. (1977). *Genie: A psycholinguistic study of a modern-day wild child.* New York: Academic Press.

Curtiss, S. (1989). The independence and task-specificity of language. In A. Bornstein & J. Bruner (Eds.), *Interaction in human development.* Mahwah, NJ: Erlbaum.

D'Amico, E. J., & Fromme, K. (1997). Health risk behaviors of adolescent and young adult siblings. *Health Psychology, 16,* 426–432.

D'Andrade, R. G. (1992). Cognitive anthropology. In T. Schwartz, G. M. White, et al. (Eds.), *New directions in psychological anthropology.* Publications of the Society for Psychological Anthropology (Vol. 3, pp. 47–58). Cambridge, UK: Cambridge University Press.

D'Esposito, M., Detre, J., Aquirre, G., Stallcup, M., Alsop, D., Tippet, L., & Farah, M. (1997). A functional MRI study of mental image generation. *Neuropsychologia, 35,* 725–730.

D'Zurilla, T., & Sheedy, C. (1991). Relation between social problem-solving and subsequent level of psychological stress in college students. *Journal of Personality and Social Psychology, 61,* 841–846.

Daley, S. E., Hammen, C., Burge, D., Davila, J., Paley, B., Lindberg, N., & Herzberg, D. S. (1999). Depression and Axis II symptomatology in an adolescent community sample: Concurrent and longitudinal associations. *Journal of Personality Disorders, 13,* 47–59.

Dalgleish, T., & Power, M. J. (1999). *Handbook of cognition and emotion.* Chichester, England: John Wiley & Sons Ltd.

Daly, M., & Wilson, M. (1988). Evolutionary social psychology and family homicide. *Science, 242,* 519–524.

Damasio, A. R. (1994). *Descartes' error: Emotion, reason, and the human brain.* New York: Grosset/Putnam.

Damon, W. (1977). *The social world of the child.* San Francisco: Jossey-Bass.

Damon, W., & Hart, D. (1988). Self-understanding in childhood and adolescence. New York: Cambridge University Press.

Daneman, M., & Merikle, P. (1996). Working memory and language comprehension: A meta-analysis. *Psychonomic Bulletin and Review, 3,* 422–433.

Darley, J. M., & Latane, B. (1968). When will people help in a crisis ? *Psychology Today, 2,* 54-57, 70-71.

Darley, J. M., & Shultz, T. R. (1990). Moral rules: Their content and acquisition. *Annual Review of Psychology, 41,* 525-556.

Dartnall, H. J., Bowmaker, J. K., & Mollon, J. D. (1983). Human visual pigments: Microspectrophotometric results from the eyes of seven persons. *Proceedings of the Royal Society of London, Series B: Biological Sciences, 220,* 115–130.

Darwin, C. (1872). *The expression of the emotions in man and animals.* London: John Murray/Julian Friedmann, 1979.

Dasen, P. (1975). Concrete operational development in three cultures. *Journal of Cross-Cultural Psychology, 6,* 156–172.

Dasen, P., & Heron, A. (1981). Cross-cultural tests of Piaget's theory. In H. C. Triandis & A. Heron (Eds.), *Handbook of cross-cultural psychology: Vol. 4. Developmental psychology.* Boston: Allyn & Bacon.

Davanloo, H. (1985). Short-term dynamic psychotherapy. In H. I. Kaplan & B. J. Sadock (Eds.), *Comprehensive Textbook of Psychiatry* (4th ed.). Baltimore, MD: Williams & Wilkins.

Davidson, R. (1992). Emotion and affective style: Hemispheric substrates. *Psychological Science, 3,* 39-43.

Davidson, R. (1995). Cerebral asymmetry, emotion and affective style. In R. J. Davidson & K. Hugdahl (Eds.), *Brain asymmetry* (pp. 361–387). Cambridge, MA: MIT Press.

Davis, D. L., & Whitten, R. G. (1987). The cross-cultural study of human sexuality. *Annual Review of Anthropology, 16,* 69–98.

Davis, H. (1996). Underestimating the rat's intelligence. *Cognitive Brain Research, 3,* 291–298.

Davis, H., & Perusse, R. (1988). Numerical competence in animals: Definitional issues, current evidence, and a new research agenda. *Behavioral and Brain Sciences, 11,* 561–615.

Davis, J. M. (1985). Minor tranquilizers, sedatives, and hypnotics. In H. I. Kaplan & B. J. Sadock (Eds.), *Comprehensive textbook of psychiatry* (4th ed.). Baltimore, MD: Williams & Wilkins.

Davis, S. (1990). Men as success objects and women as sex objects: A study of personals advertisements. *Sex Roles, 23,* 43–50.

Davison, K. P., Pennebaker, J. W., & Dickerson, S. S. (2000). Who talks? The social psychology of illness support groups. *American Psychologist, 55,* 205-217.

Dawes, R. (1997). Judgment, decision making, and interference. In D. Gilbert, S. Fiske, & G.

Lindzey (Eds.), *Handbook of social psychology* (pp. 497–549). Boston: McGraw-Hill.

Day, N.L., Richardson, G.A., Goldschmidt, L., & Cornelius, M.D. (2000). Effects of prenatal tobacco exposure on preschoolers' behavior. *Journal of Developmentsl and Behavioral Pediatrics, 21,* 180-188.

Deacon, T. W. (1996). *The making of language.* Edinburgh: Edinburgh University Press.

Deak, G. O., Flom, R. A., & Pick, A. D. (2000). Effects of gesture and target on 12- and 18-month-olds' joint visual attention to objects in front of or behind them. *Developmental Psychology, 36,* 511–523.

Deater-Deckard, K., Dodge, K. A., Bates, J. E., & Pettit, G. S. (1996). Physical discipline among African American and European American mothers: Links to children's externalizing behaviors. *Developmental Psychology, 32,* 1065–1072.

de Castro, J., & Brewer, M. (1992). The amount eaten in meals by humans is a power function of the number of people present. *Physiology and Behavior, 51,* 121–125.

de Castro, J. M. (1993). Genetic influences on daily intake and meal patterns of humans. *Physiology & Behavior, 53,* 777–782.

Deci, E. L., Koestner, R., & Ryan, R. M. (1999). A meta-analytic review of experiments examining the effects of extrinsic rewards on intrinsic motivation. *Psychological Bulletin, 125,* 627-668.

Deglin, V. L., & Kinsbourne, M. (1996). Divergent thinking styles of the hemispheres: How syllogisms are solved during transitory hemisphere suppression. *Brain & Cognition, 31,* 285–307.

DeKay, T. (1998). *An evolutionary-computational approach to social cognition: Grandparental investment as a test case.* Unpublished doctoral dissertation, University of Michigan.

De La Ronde, C. & Swann, W.B., Jr. (1988). Partner verification: Restoring shattered images of our intimates. *Journal of Personality and Social Psychology, 75,* 374 382.

DeLoache, J. S., Miller, K. F., & Rosengren, K. S. (1997). The credible shrinking room: Very young children's performance with symbolic and nonsymbolic relations. *Psychological Science, 8,* 308–313.

DeLongis, A., Folkman, S., & Lazarus, R. S. (1988). The impact of daily stress on health and mood: Psychological and social resouces as mediators. *Journal of Personality and Social Psychology, 54*(3), 486–495.

Dembroski, T. M., & Costa, P. T. (1987). Coronary prone behavior: Components of the Type A pattern and hostility. *Journal of Personality, 55,* 211–235.

Dement, W. C., & Kleitman, N. (1957). The relation of eye movements during sleep to dream activity: An objective method for the study of dreaming. *Journal of Experimental Psychology, 55,* 543–553.

Demorest, A. P., & Siegel, P. F. (1996). Personal influences on professional work: An empirical case study of B. F. Skinner. *Journal of Personality, 64,* 243–261.

Demorest, M. E. (1986). Problem solving: Stages, strategies, and stumbling blocks. *Journal of Academic Rehabilitation Audiology, 19,* 13–26.

Dempster, F. N. (1996). Distributing and managing the conditions of encoding and practice. In E. L. Bjork, & R. A. Bjork, (Eds.), *Memory. Handbook of perception and cognition* (2nd ed., pp. 317–344). San Diego: Academic Press.

DeMulder, E. K., Denham, S., Schmidt, M., & Mitchell, J. (2000). Q-sort assessment of attachment security during the preschool years: Links from home to school. *Developmental Psychology, 36,* 274–282.

Denham, S., & Holt, R. W. (1993). Preschoolers' likability as cause or consequence of their social behavior. *Developmental Psychology, 29,* 271–275.

Denney, N. R., & Denney, N. W. (1973). The use of classification for problem solving: A comparison of middle and old age. *Developmental Psychology, 9,* 275–278.

De Pascalis, V., & Perrone, M. (1996). EEG asymmetry and heart rate during experience of hypnotic analgesia in high and low hypnotizables. International *Journal of Psychophysiology, 21,* 163–175.

DePaulo, B. M., & Friedman, H. S. (1998). Nonverbal communication. In D. T. Gilbert, S. T. Fiske, & G. Lindzey (Eds.), The handbook of social psychology (4th ed.). New York: McGraw-Hill.

Deregowski, J. B. (1970). Effect of cultural value of time upon recall. *British Journal of Social and Clinical Psychology, 9*(11), 37–41.

DeRosier, M., & Kupersmidt, J. (1991). Costa Rican children's perceptions of their social networks. *Developmental Psychology, 27,* 656–662.

DeSteno, D. A., & Salovey, P. (1996). Genes, jealousy, and the replication of misspecified models. *Psychological Science, 7,* 376–377.

Deutsch, H. (1945). *Psychology of women: A psychoanalytic interpretation.* New York: Grune & Stratton.

Deutsch, J. A., & Gonzalez, M. E. (1980). Gastric nutrient content signals satiety. *Behavioral and Neural Biology, 30,* 113–116.

DeValois, R. L., & DeValois, K. (1975). Neural coding of color. In E. C. Carterette & M. P. Friedman (Eds.), *Handbook of perception.* New York: Academic Press.

Devine, P. (1989). Stereotypes and prejudice: Their automatic and controlled components. *Journal of Personality and Social Psychology, 56,* 5–18.

Devine, P., Monteith, M., Zuwerink, J., & Elliot, A. (1991). Prejudice with and without compunction. *Journal of Personality and Social Psychology, 60,* 817–830.

Devine, P. G., & Monteith, M. J. (1993). The role of discrepancy-associated affect in prejudice reduction. In D. M. Mackie, D. L. Hamilton, et al. (Eds.), *Affect, cognition and stereotyping: Interactive processes in group perception* (pp. 317–344). San Diego: Academic Press.

Devlin, M. J., Yanovski, S. Z., & Wilson, G. T. (2000). Obesity: What mental health professionals need to know. *American Journal of Psychiatry, 157,* 854–866.

de Waal, F. (1989). *Peacemaking among primates.* Cambridge: Harvard University Press.

de Wijk, R. A., Schab, F. R., & Cain, W. S. (1995). Odor identification. In F. R. Schab, R. G. Crowder, et al. (Eds.), *Memory for odors* (pp. 21–37). Mahwah, NJ: Lawrence Erlbaum Associates.

De Witte, P. (1996). The role of neurotransmitters in alcohol dependence: Animal research. *Alcohol and Alcoholism, 31,* 13–16.

Dews, P. B. (1959). Some observations on an operant in the octopus. *Journal of the Experimental Analysis of Behavior, 2,* 57–63.

Diamond, M. C. (1978). The aging brain: Some enlightening and optimistic results. *American Psychologist, 66,* 66–71.

Diaz-Guerrero, R. (1979). The development of coping style. *Human Development, 2,* 320–331.

Di Blas, L., & Forzi, M. (1999). Refining a descriptive structure of personality attributes in the Italian language: The abridged big three circumplex structure. *Journal of Personality and Social Psychology, 76,* 451–481.

Di Chiara, G., Acquas, E., & Tanda, G. (1996). Ethanol as a neurochemical surrogate of conventional reinforcers: The dopamine-opioid link. *Alcohol, 13,* 13–17.

Dick, D. M., Rose, R. J., Viken, R. J., & Kaprio, J. (2000). Pubertal timing and substance use: Associations between and within families across late adolescence. *Developmental Psychology, 36,* 180–189.

Diener, E. (1998). Subjective well-being: Three decades of progress. *Psychological Bulletin, 125,* 276–302.

Diener, E. (2000). Subjective well-being: The science of happiness and a proposal for a national index. *American Psychologist, 55,* 34–43.

Diener, E., Lucas, R. E., Brody, L. R., Hall, J. A., Forgas, J. P., Vargas, P. T., Hess, U., Kirouac, G., Bates, J. E., Shweder, R. A., & Haidt, J. A. (2000). Part IV: Social/personality issues. In M. Lewis, and J. M. Haviland-Jones (Eds.), *Handbook of emotions* (2nd ed.). (pp. 325-414). New York: The Guilford Press.

Dies, R. (1992). The future of group therapy. *Psychotherapy, 29,* 58–64.

Dil, N. (1984). Noverbal communication in young children. *Topics in Early Childhood Special Education, 4,* 82–99.

Dion, K. K., & Berscheid, E. (1974). Physical attractiveness and peer perception among children. *Sociometry, 37,* 1–12.

Dion, K. K., & Dion, K. L. (1996). Cultural perspectives on romantic love. *Personal Relationships, 3,* 5–17.

Dion, K. L., & Dion, K. K. (1988). Romantic love: Individual and cultural perspectives. In R. Sternberg, and M. Barnes (Eds.), *The psychology of love.* New Haven CT: Yale University Press.

Dipboye, R. L. (1997). Organizational barriers to implementing a rational model of training. In M. A. Quinones, and A. Ehrenstein (Eds.), *Training for a rapidly changing workplace: Applications of psychological research.* (pp. 31-60). Washington: American Psychological Association.

DiPietro, J. A., Hodgson, D. M., Costigan, K. A., & Johnson, T. R. B. (1996a). Fetal antecedents of infant temperament. *Child Development, 67,* 2568–2583.

DiPietro, J. A., Hodgson, D. M., Costigan, K. A., Hilton, S. C., & Johnson, T. R. B. (1996b). Fetal neurobehavioral development. *Child Development, 67,* 2553–2567.

Dittes, J. E. (1959). Effect of changes in self-esteem upon impulsiveness and deliberation in making judgments. *Journal of Abnormal Social Psychology, 53,* 100–107.

Dixit, A. R., & Crum, R. M. (2000). Prospective study of depression and the risk of heavy alcohol use in women. *American Journal of Psychiatry, 157,* 751–758.

Dixon, N. F. (1971). *Subliminal perception: The nature of a controversy.* New York: McGraw-Hill.

Dixon, N. F. (1981). *Preconscious processing.* New York: John Wiley.

Doane, J. A., et al. (1981). Parental communication deviance and affective style: Predictors of subsequent schizophrenia spectrum disorders in vulnerable adolescents. *Archives of General Psychiatry, 38,* 679–685.

Dobson & Teller (1978). Visual acuity in human infants: A review and comparison of behavioral and electrophysiological studies. *Visual Research, 18,* 1469–1483.

Dodd, B. (1979). Lip reading in infants: Attention to speech presented in- and out-of-synchrony. *Cognitive Psychology, 11,* 478–484.

Dodge, K., Lochman, J., Harnish, J., Bates, J. E., & Pettit, G. (1997). Reactive and proactive aggression in school chidlren and psychiatrically impaired chronically assaultive youth. *Journal of Abnormal Psychology, 106,* 37–51.

Dodge, K., Pettit, G., Bates, J. E., & Valente, E. (1995). Social information-processing patterns partially mediate the effect of early physical abuse on later conduct problems. *Journal of Abnormal Psychology, 104,* 632–643.

Doi, T. (1992). On the concept of amae. *Infant Mental Health Journal, 13,* 7–11.

Dollard, J., Doob, L., Miller, N. E., Mowrer, O., & Sears, R. (1939). *Frustration and aggression.* New Haven CT: Yale University Press.

Dollard, J., & Miller, N. (1950). *Personality and psychotherapy: An analysis in terms of learning, thinking, and culture.* New York: McGraw-Hill.

Domhoff, G. W. (1996). *Finding meaning in dreams: A quantitative approach.* New York: Plenum Press.

Donovan, S. J., Stewart, J. W., Nunes, E. V., Quitkin, F. M., Parides, M., Daniel, W., Susser, E., & Klein, D. F. (2000). Divalproex treatment for youth with explosive temper and mood lability: A double-blind, placebo-controlled crossover design. *American Journal of Psychiatry, 157,* 818–820.

Doty, R. L., Green, P. A., Ram, C., & Tandeil, S. L. (1982). Communication of gender from human breath odors: Relationship to perceived intensity and pleasantness. *Hormones and Behavior, 16,* 13–22.

Dougall, A. L., Herberman, H. B., Delahanty, D.

L., Inslicht, S. S., & Baum, A. (2000). Similarity of prior trauma exposure as a determinant of chronic stress responding to an airline disaster. *Journal of Consulting and Clinical Psychology, 68,* 290–295.

Douvan, E., & Adelson, J. (1966). *The adolescent experience.* New York: John Wiley.

Dovidio, J., & Gaertner, S. (1993). Stereotypes and evaluative intergroup bias. In D. Mackie & D. Hamilton (Eds.), *Affect, cognition, and stereotyping: Interactive processes in group perception.* San Diego: Academic Press.

Dovidio, J. F., Kawakami, K., & Gaertner, S. L. (2000). Reducing contemporary prejudice: Combating explicit and implicit bias at the individual and intergroup level. In S. Oskamp (Ed.), *Reducing prejudice and discrimination.* 'The Claremont Symposium on Applied Social Psychology (pp. 137-163). Mahwah, NJ: Lawrence Erlbaum Associates.

Downey, G., Freitas, A. L., Michaelis, B., & Khouri, H. (1998). The self-fulfilling prophecy in close relationships: Rejection sensitivity and rejection by romantic partners. *Journal of Personality and Social Psychology, 75,* 545–560.

Downey, G., Lebolt, A., Rincon, C., & Freitas, A. L. (1998). Rejection sensitivity and children's interpersonal difficulties. *Child Development, 69,* 1074 1091.

Dozier, M., & Kobak, R. (1992). Psychophysiology in attachment interviews: Converging evidence for deactivating strategies. *Child Development, 63,* 1473–1480.

Draguns, J. G. (1990). Normal and abnormal behavior in cross-cultural perspective: Specifying the nature of their relationship. In J. J. Beeman (Ed.), *Cross-Cultural perspectives. Current theory and research in motivation.*

Drasdo, N. (1977). The neural representation of visual space. *Nature, 266,* 554–556.

Drepper, J., Timmann, D., Kolb, F. P., & Diener, H. C. (1999). Non-motor associative learning in patients with isolated degenerative cerebellar disease. *Brain, 122,* 87–97.

Dreyfus, H., & Dreyfus, S. (1986). Why computers may never think like people. *Technology Review, 89,* 42–61.

Drigotas, S. M., Rusbult, C. E., Wieselquist, J., & Whitton, S. W. (1999). Close partner as sculptor of the ideal self: Behavioral affirmation and the Michelangelo phenomenon. *Journal of Personality and Social Psychology, 77,* 293–323.

Dryer, D. C., & Horowitz, L. M. (1997). When do opposites attract? Interpersonal complementarity versus similarity. *Journal of Personality & Social Psychology, 72,* 592-603.

DuBois, C. (1944). *The people of Alor: A social psychological study of an East Indian.* Minneapolis: University of Minnesota Press.

Duckitt, J. (1992). Psychology and prejudice: A historical analysis and integrative framework. *American Psychologist, 47,* 1182–1197.

Dudley, R. (1991). IQ and heritability. *Science, 252,* 191–192.

Duman, R. S., Heninger, G. R., & Nestler, E. J. (1997). A molecular and cellular theory of depression. *Archives of General Psychiatry, 54,* 597–606.

Dumaret, A. (1985). I.Q., scholastic performance and behavior of sibs raised in contrasting environments. *Journal of Child Psychology and Psychiatry and Allied Disciplines, 26,* 553–580.

Duncan, G., & Brooks, G. J. (2000). Family poverty, welfare reform, and child development. *Child Development, 71,* 188–196.

Duncan, J., Seitz, R., Kolodny, J., et al. (2000). A neural basis for general intelligence. *Science, 289,* 457–460.

Duncker, K. (1946). On problem solving. *Psychological Monographs, 158, 5,* #270.

Dunfon, R., & Duncan, G. J. (1998). Long-run effects of motivation on labor-market success. *Social Psychology Quarterly, 61,* 33–48.

Dunn, J., Bretherton, I., & Munn, P. (1987). Conversations about feeling states between mothers and their young children. *Developmental Psychology, 23,* 132–139.

Dunn, J., & McGuire, S. (1992). Sibling and peer relationships in childhood. *Journal of Child Psychology and Psychiatry, 33,* 67–105.

Durbin, C. E., Klein, D. N., & Schwartz, J. E. (2000). Predicting the 2-sup-1/-sub-2-year outcome of dysthymic disorder: The roles of childhood adversity and family history of psychopathology. *Journal of Consulting and Clinical Psychology, 68,* 57–63.

Durkheim, E. (1915). *The elementary forms of the religious life.* New York: Free Press.

Dutton, D. G. (1996). *The domestic assault of women.* Vancouver: University of British Columbia Press.

Dweck, C. (1975). The role of expectations and attributions in the alleviation of learned helplessness. *Journal of Personality and Social Psychology, 31,* 674–685.

Dweck, C. (1986). Motivational processes affecting learning. *American Psychologist, 41,* 1040–1048.

Dworkin, R. H., Hartsetin, G., Rosner, H., Walther, R., Sweeney, E. W., & Brand, L. (1992). A high-risk method for studying psychosocial antecedents of chronic pain: The prospective investigation of herpes zoster. *Journal of Abnormal Psychology, 101,* 200–205.

Eagle, M. (1959). The effects of subliminal stimuli of aggressive content upon conscious cognition. *Journal of Personality, 27,* 678–688.

Eagly, A., Ashmore, R., Makhijani, M., & Longo, L. (1991). What is beautiful is good, but: A meta-analytic review of research on the physical attractiveness stereotype. *Psychological Bulletin, 110,* 109–128.

Eagly, A., & Chaiken, S. (1992). *The psychology of attitudes.* San Diego: Harcourt, Brace.

Eagly, A. H. (1983). Gender and Social Influence: A social psychological analysis. *American Psychologist, 38,* 971–981.

Eagly, A. H. (1995). The science and politics of comparing men and women. *American Psychologist, 50,* 145–158.

Eagly, A. H., & Chaiken, S. (1998). Attitude structure and function. In D. T. Gilbert, S. T. Fiske, et al. (Eds.), *The handbook of social psychology,* (Vol. 2, 4th ed., pp. 269–322). Boston: McGraw-Hill.

Eagly, A. H., & Wood, W. (1999). The origins of sex differences in human behavior: Evolved dispositions versus social roles. *American Psychologist, 54,* 408–423.

Ebbinghaus, H. (1885). *Memory.* New York: Columbia University/Dover, 1964.

Eder, R. (1990). Uncovering young children's psychological selves: Individual and developmental differences. *Child Development, 61,* 849–863.

Edelman, G. M. (1989). *The remembered present: A biological theory of consciousness.* New York: Basicbooks, Inc.

Edwards, C. P., & Whiting, B. B. (1983). Differential socialization of girls and boys in light of cross-cultural research. In W. Damon (Ed.), *Social and personality development: Essays on the growth of the child.* New York: W. W. Norton.

Edwards, D. A., & Einhorn, L. C. (1986). Preoptic and midbrain control of sexual motivation. *Physiology and Behavior, 37,* 329–335.

Edwards, W. (1977). How to use multiattribute utility measurement for social decision making. *IEEE Transactions in Systems Man and Cybernetics, 17,* 326–340.

Edwards, W., & Newman, J. R. (1986). Multiattribute choice. In H. R. Arkes & K. R. Hammond (Eds.), *Judgment and decision making: An interdisciplinary reader.* Cambridge, England: Cambridge University Press.

Egger, M. D., & Flynn, J. P. (1963). Effect of electrical stimulation of the amygdala on hypothalamically elicited attack behavior in cats. *Journal of Neurophysiology, 26,* 705–720.

Ehlers, A., & Breuer, P. (1992). Increased cardiac awareness in panic disorder. *Journal of Abnormal Psychology, 101,* 371–382.

Ehrman, R., Ternes, J., O'Brien, C. P., & McLellan, A. T. (1992). Conditioned tolerance in human opiate addicts. *Psychopharmacology, 108,* 218–224.

Eichenbaum, H. (1997). Declarative memory: Insights from cognitive neurobiology. *Annual Review, 48,* 547–572.

Eimas, P. D., Siqueland, E. R., Jusczyk, P., & Vigorito, J. (1971). Speech perception in infants. *Science, 171,* 303–306.

Einstein, G. O., & McDaniel, M. A. (1990). Normal aging and prospective memory. *Journal of Experimental Psychology: Learning, Memory, & Cognition, 16,* 717–726.

Einstein, G. O., Smith, R. E., McDaniel, M. A., & Shaw, P. (1997). Aging and prospective memory: The influence of increased task demands at encoding and retrieval. *Psychology & Aging, 12,* 479–488.

Eisenberg, N., Fabes, R. A., & Murphy, B. C. (1996). Parent's reactions to children's negative emotions: Relations to children's social competence and comforting behavior. *Child Development, 67,* 2227–2247.

Eisenberg, N., Miller, P. A., Shell, R., McNalley, S., & Shea, C. (1991). Prosocial development in adolescence: A longitudinal study. *Developmental Psychology 27,* 849–857.

Eisenberg, N., & Zhou, Q. (2000). Regulation from a developmental perspective. *Psychological Inquiry, 11,* 166-171.

Ekelund, J., Lichtermann, D., Jaervelin, M., & Peltonen, L. (1999). Association between novelty seeking and type 4 dopamine receptor gene in a large Finnish cohort sample. *American Journal of Psychiatry, 156,* 1453–1455.

Ekman, P. (1971). Universals and cultural differences in facial expression. In J. K. Cole (Ed.), *Nebraska Symposium on Motivation.* Lincoln: University of Nebraska Press.

Ekman, P. (1977). Biological and cultural contributions to body and facial movement. In J. Blacking (Ed.), *The anthropology of the body.* A.S.A. Monograph 15. London: Academic Press.

Ekman, P. (1992). Facial expressions of emotion: New findings, new questions. *Psychological Science, 3,* 34–38.

Ekman, P. (1999). Facial expressions. In T. Dalgleish & M. Power (Eds.), *The handbook of cognition and emotion* (pp. 301–320). New York: John Wiley & Sons.

Ekman, P., & Davidson, R. J. (1993). Voluntary smiling changes regional brain activity. *Psychological Science, 4,* 342–345.

Ekman, P., & Friesen, W. V. (1975). *Unmasking the face: A guide to recognizing emotions from facial cues.* Englewood Cliffs, NJ: Prentice-Hall.

Elder, G. (1998). The life course as developmental theory. *Current Directions in Psychological Science, 69,* 1–12.

Elder, G. H., Jr. (1998). The life course as developmental theory. *Child Development, 69,* 1–12.

Eldridge, L., Knowlton, B., & Engel, S. (2000). *Hippocampus selectively encodes episodic memories.* Unpublished manuscript, UCLA.

Elias, M., Elias, J., & Elias, P. (1990). Biological and health influences on behavior. In J. Birren & K. W. Schaie (Eds.), *Handbook of the psychology of aging* (3rd ed., pp. 80–102). New York: Academic Press.

Elkin, I., Shea, M. T., Watkins, J., & Imber, S. (1989). National Institute of Mental Health Treatment of Depression Collaborative Research Program: General effectiveness of treatments. *American Journal of Psychiatry, 46,* 971–982.

Elkind, D. (1981). Children's discovery of the conservation of mass, weight, and volume: Piaget replications studies II. *Journal of Genetic Psychology, 98,* 37–46.

Elkins, I. J., Mcgue, M., & Iacono, W. G. (1997). Genetic and environmental influences on parent-son relationships: Evidence for increasing genetic influence during adolescence. *Developmental Psychology, 33,* 351–363.

Elkis, H., Friedman, L., Wise, A., Meltzer, H. Y. (1995). Meta-analyses of studies of ventricular enlargement and cortical sulcall prominence in mood disorders: Comparisons with controls or patients with schizophrenia. *Archives of General Psychiatry. 52,* 735-746.

Ellicott, A., Hammen, C., Gitlin, M., Brown, G., & Jamison, K. (1990). Life events and the course of bipolar disorder. *American Journal of Psychiatry, 147,* 1194–1198.

Elliot, A. J., & Church, M. A. (1997). A hierarchical model of approach and avoidance achievement motivation. *Journal of Personality & Social Psychology, 72,* 218–232.

Elliot, A. J., & Harackiewicz, J. M. (1996). Approach and avoidance achievement goals and intrinsic motivation: A mediational analysis. *Journal of Personality and Social Psychology, 70,* 461–475.

Elliott, J. (1977). The power and pathology of prejudice. In P. G. Zimbardo & F. L. Ruch (Eds.), *Psychology and Life* (9th ed.). Glenview, IL: Scott, Foresman.

Ellis, A. (1962). *Reason and emotion in psychotherapy.* New York: Lyle Stuart.

Ellis, A. (1977). The basic clinical theory of rational-emotive therapy. In A. Ellis & R. Grieger (Eds.), *Handbook of rational-emotive therapy.* New York: Springer.

Ellis, A. (1984). Rational-emotive therapy. In R. J. Corsini (Ed.), *Current psychotherapies.* (2nd ed.). Itasca, IL: Peacock Publishers.

Ellis, A. (1987). Cognitive therapy and rational-emotive therapy: A dialogue. *Journal of Cognitive Psychotherapy, 1,* 205–255.

Ellis, A. (1989). *Inside rational-emotive therapy: A critical appraisal of the theory and therapy of Albert Ellis.* New York: Academic.

Ellis, A. (1999). Why rational-emotive therapy to rational emotive behavior therapy? *Psychotherapy, 36,* 154–159.

Ellis, L., & Ames, M. A. (1987). Neurohormonal functioning and sexual orientation: A theory of homosexuality-heterosexuality. *Psychological Bulletin, 101,* 233–258.

Emery, R. E., Waldron, M., Kitzmann, K. M., & Aaron, J. (1999). Delinquent behavior, future divorce or nonmarital childbearing, and externalizing behavior among offspring: A 14-year prospective study. *Journal of Family Psychology, 13,* 568–579.

Emmons, R., & King, L. A. (1988). Conflict among personal strivings: Immediate and long-term implications for psychological and physical well-being. *Journal of Personality and Social Psychology, 54,* 1040–1048.

Engel, S., Zhang, X., & Wandell, B. (1997). Colour tuning in human visual cortex measured with functional magnetic resonance imaging. *Nature, 388,* 68–71.

Engen, T. (1982). *The perception of odors.* New York: Academic.

Epley, N., & Dunning, D. (2000). Feeling "holier than thou": Are self-serving assessments produced by errors in self or social prediction? *Journal of Personality and Social Psychology, 79,* 861–875.

Epley, N., & Gilovich, T. (1999). Just going along: Nonconscious priming and conformity to social pressure. *Journal of Experimental Social Psychology, 35(6),* 578–589.

Epstein, S. (1973). The self-concept revisited, or a theory of a theory. *American Psychologist, 28,* 404–416.

Epstein, S. (1979). The stability of behavior: On predicting most of the people much of the time.

Journal of Personality and Social Psychology, 37, 1097–1126.

Epstein, S. (1986). Does aggregation produce spuriously high estimates of behavior stability? *Journal of Personality and Social Psychology, 50,* 1199–1210.

Epstein, S. (1992). Coping ability, negative self-evaluation, and overgeneralization: Experiment and theory. *Journal of Personality and Social Psychology, 62,* 826–836.

Epstein, S. (1994). Integration of the cognitive and the psychodynamic unconscious. *American Psychologist, 49,* 709–724.

Epstein, S. (1997). This I have learned from over 40 years of personality research. *Journal of Personality, 65,* 3–32.

Epstein, S. (1998). Cognitive-experiential self-theory. In D. F. Barone, M. Hersen, et al. (Eds.), *Advanced personality. The Plenum series in social/clinical psychology* (pp. 211–238). New York: Plenum Press.

Epstein, S., & Katz, L. (1992). Coping ability, stress, productive load, and symptoms. *Journal of Personality and Social Psychology, 62,* 813–825.

Era, P., Jokela, J., & Heikkinen, E. (1986). Reaction and movement times in men of different ages: A population study. *Perceptual and Motor Skills, 63,* 111–130.

Erdelyi, M. H. (1985). *Psychoanalysis: Freud's cognitive psychology.* New York: W. H. Freeman.

Erdmann, G., & Van-Lindern, B. (1980). The effects of beta-adrenergic stimulation and beta-adrenergic blockade on emotional reactions. *Psychophysiology, 17,* 332-338.

Erhardt, A. A., & Baker, S. W. (1974). Fetal androgens, human central nervous system differentiation, and behavior sex differences. In R. C. Friedman, R. M. Richart, & R. L. Vande Wiele (Eds.), *Sex differences in behavior.* New York: John Wiley.

Erickson, M. A., & Kruschke, J. K. (1998). Rules and exemplars in category learning. *Journal of Experimental Psychology: General, 127,* 107–140.

Erikson, E. (1963). *Childhood and society.* New York: W. W. Norton.

Erikson, E. (1968). *Identity: Youth and crisis.* New York: W. W. Norton.

Erikson, E. (1969). *Gandhi's truth: On the origin of militant nonviolence.* New York: W. W. Norton.

Erlenmeyer-Kimling, L., Adamo, U. H., Rock, D., Roberts, S. A., Bassett, A. S., Squires-Wheeler, E., et al. (1997). The New York High-Risk Project Prevalence and Comorbidity of Axis I Disorders in Offspring of Schizophrenic Parents at 25-Year Follow-up. *Archives of General Psychiatry, 54,* 1096–1102.

Estes, W. K. (1994). *Classification and cognition.* New York: Oxford University Press.

Euler, H. A., & Weitzel, B. (1996). Discriminative grandparental solicitude as reproductive strategy. *Human Nature, 7,* 39–59.

Evans, G. W., Palsane, M. N., & Carrere, S. (1987). Type A behavior and occupational stress: A cross-cultural study of blue-collar workers. *Journal of Personality and Social Psychology, 52,* 1002–1007.

Evans, K. K., & Singer, J. A. (1994). Studying intimacy through dream narratives: The relationship of dreams to self-report and projective measures of personality. *Imagination, Cognition & Personality, 14*, 211–226.

Evans-Pritchard, E. E. (1956). *Nuer religion.* Oxford: Clarendon Press.

Everson, C. A. (1997). Sleep deprivation and the immune system. In M. R. Pressman, & W. C. Orr (Eds.), *Understanding sleep: The evaluation and treatment of sleep disorders. Application and practice in health psychology* (pp. 401–424). Washington, DC: American Psychological Association.

Eysenck, H. (1987a). The growth of a unified scientific psychology: Ordeal by quakery. In A. Staats & L. Mos (Eds.), *Annals of theoretical psychology,* (Vol. 5, pp. 91–113). New York: Plenum Press.

Eysenck, H. (1987b). *Theoretical foundations of behavior therapy.* New York: Plenum Press.

Eysenck, H. J. (1952). The effects of psychotherapy: an evaluation. *Journal of Consulting Psychology, 16*, 319-324.

Eysenck, H. J. (1953). *The structure of human personality.* New York: John Wiley.

Eysenck, H. J. (1982). Development of a theory. In H. J. Eysenck (Ed.), *Personality, Genetics and Behavior: Selected papers.* (p. 593-595). New York: Praeger.

Eysenck, H. J. (1983a). Human learning and individual differences: The genetic dimension. *Educational Psychology, 3*, 169–188.

Eysenck, H. J. (1983b). The roots of creativity: Cognitive ability or personality trait? *Roeper Review, 5*, 10–12.

Eysenck, H. J. (1990). Biological dimensions of personality. In L. A. Pervin (Ed.), *Handbook of personality: Theory and research* (pp. 244–276). New York: Guilford Press.

Eysenck, H. J. (1993). Creativity and personality: Suggestions for a theory. *Psychological Inquiry, 4*, 147–178.

Fabrega, H. (1994). International systems of diagnosis in psychiatry. *Journal of Nervous & Mental Disease, 182*, 256-263.

Fagot, B. I. (1985). Changes in thinking about early sex role development. *Developmental Review, 5*, 83–98.

Fagot, B. I., & Patterson, G. R. (1969). An in vivo analysis of reinforcing contingencies for sex-role behaviors in the preschool child. *Developmental Psychology.*

Fairbairn, W. (1954). *An object-relations theory of personality.* New York: Basic Books.

Fairburn, C. G., Cooper, Z., Doll, H. A., & Welch, S. L. (1999). Risk factors for anorexia nervosa: Three integrated case-control comparisons. *Archives of General Psychiatry, 56*, 468–476.

Faith, M. S., Rha, S. S., Neale, M. C., & Allison, D. B. (1999). Evidence for genetic influences on human energy intake: Results from a twin study using measured observations. *Behavior Genetics, 29*(3), 145–154.

Fanselow, M. S. (1998). Pavlovian conditioning, negative feedback, and blocking: Mechanisms that regulate association formation. *Neuron, 20*, 625–627.

Fanselow, M. S., & LeDoux, J. E. (1999). Why we think plasiticity underlying Pavlovian fear conditioning occurs in the basolateral amygdala. *Neuron, 23*, 229–232.

Fantz, R. L. (1966). Pattern discrimination and selective attention as determinants of perceptual developmental from birth. In A. H. Kidd & L. J. Rivoire (Eds.), *Perceptual development in children.* New York: International Universities Press.

Fantz, R. L., Fagan, J. F., III, & Miranda, S. B. (1975). Early visual selectivity. In L. B. Cohen & P. Salapatek (Eds.), *Infant perception: From sensation to cognition: Vol. I. Basic visual processes.* New York: Academic Press.

Faraone, S. V., Biederman, J., & Milberger, S. (1995). How reliable are maternal reports of their children's psychopathology? One-year recall of psychiatric diagnoses of ADHD children. *Journal of the American Academy of Child & Adolescent Psychiatry, 34*, 1001-1008.

Faraone, S. V., Biederman, J., Feighner, J. A., & Monuteaux, M. C. (2000). Assessing symptoms of attention deficit hyperactivity disorder in children and adults: Which is more valid? *Journal of Consulting and Clinical Psychology, 68*, 830–842.

Faravelli, C., & Pallanti, S. (1989). Recent life events and panic disorder. *American Journal of Psychiatry, 146*, 622–626.

Farber, N. B., Newcomer, J. W., & Olney, J. W. (1999). Glycine agonists: What can they teach us about schizophrenia? *Archives of General Psychiatry, 56*, 13–17.

Farmer, C. M., O'Donnell, B. F., Niznikiewicz, M. A., Voglmaier, M. M., McCarley, R. W., & Shenton, M. E. (2000). Visual perception and working memory in schizotypal personality disorder. *American Journal of Psychiatry, 157*, 781–786.

Farmer, I. P., Meyer, P. S., Ramsey, D. J., & Goff, D. C. (1996). Higher levels of social support predict greater survival following acute myocardial infarction: Corpus Christi Heart Project. *Behavioral Medicine, 22*, 59–66.

Fass, P. S. (1980). The I.Q.: A cultural and historical framework. *American Journal of Education*, 431–458.

Fazio, R. (1990). Multiple processes by which attitudes guide behavior: The MODE model as an integrative framework. In L. Berkowitz (Ed.), *Advances in Experimental Social Psychology, 23*, 75–109.

Fazio, R., Jackson, J. R., Dunton, B., & Williams, C. J. (1995). Variability in automatic activation as an unobtrusive measure of racial attitudes: A bona fide pipeline? *Journal of Personality and Social Psychology, 69*, 1013–1027.

Fazio, R., & Zanna, M. (1981). Direct experience and attitude-behavior consistency. In L. Berkowitz (Ed.), *Advances in experimental social psychology* (Vol. 14). New York: Academic.

Fazio, R. H. (1986). How do attitudes guide behavior? In R. M. Sorrentino & E. T. Higgins (Eds.), *The handbook of motivation and cognition: Foundations of social behavior.* New York: Guilford Press.

Fazio, R. H. (1995). Attitudes as object-evaluation associations: Determinants, consequences, and correlates of attitude accessibility. In R. E. Petty, J. A. Krosnick, et al. (Eds.), *Attitude strength: Antecedents and consequences.* Ohio State University series on attitudes and persuasion, (Vol. 4, pp. 247–282). Mahwah, NJ: Lawrence Erlbaum Associates.

Fazio, R. H., Ledbetter, J. E., & Towles-Schwen, T. (2000). On the costs of accessible attitudes: Detecting that the attitude object has changed. *Journal of Personality and Social Psychology, 78* (2), 197–210.

Fehm-Wolfsdorf, G., Soherr, U., Arndt, R., Kern, W., et al. (1993). Auditory reflex thresholds elevated by stress-induced cortisol secretion. *Psychoneuroendocrinology, 18*, 579–589.

Fein, S., & Spencer, S. J. (1997). Prejudice as self-image maintenance: Affirming the self through derogating others. *Journal of Personality & Social Psychology, 73*, 31-44.

Feingold, A. (1992). Good-looking people are not what we think. *Psychological Bulletin, 111*, 304–341.

Feingold, A. (1994). Gender differences in personality: A meta-analysis. *Psychological Bulletin, 116*, 429–456.

Feldman, D. E., Brainard, M. S., & Knudsen, E. I. (1996). Newly learned auditory responses mediated by NMDA receptors in the owl inferior colliculus. *Science, 271*, 525–528.

Feng, A. S., & Ratnam, R. (2000). Neural basis of hearing in real-world situations. *Annual Review of Psychology, 51*, 699–725.

Ferguson, E. D. (2000). *Motivation: A biosocial and cognitive integration of motivation and emotion.* New York: Oxford University Press.

Fernald, A., & Kuhl, P. (1987). Acoustic determinants of infant preference for motherese speech. *Infant Behavior and Development, 10*, 279–293.

Fernald, R. D. (1996). Recognition of visual signals; Eyes specialize. In C. F. Moss, S. J. Shettleworth, et al. (Eds.), *Neuroethological studies of cognitive and perceptual processes* (pp. 229–249). Boulder: Westview Press.

Ferro, T., Verdeli, H., Pierre, F., & Weissman, M. M. (2000). Screening for depression in mothers bringing their offspring for evaluation or treatment of depression. *American Journal of Psychiatry, 157*, 375–379.

Ferster, D., & Miller, K. D. (2000). Neural mechanisms of orientation selectivity in the visual cortex. *Annual Review of Neuroscience, 23*, 441–471.

Festinger, L. (1957). *A theory of cognitive dissonance.* New York: Harper & Row.

Festinger, L. (1962). Cognitive dissonance. *Scientific American, 107*, 409–415.

Festinger, L., & Carlsmith, J. M. (1959). Cognitive consequences of forced compliance. *Journal of Abnormal and Social Psychology, 58*, 203–210.

Festinger, L., Schachter, S., & Back, K. (1950). *Social pressures in informal groups: A study of human factors in housing.* New York: Harper Bros.

Field, A. E., Camargo, C. A., Jr., Taylor, C. B., Berkey, C. S., Frazier, L., Gillman, M. W., & Colditz, G. A. (1999). *Journal of the American Academy of Child and Adolescent Psychiatry, 38*(6), 754–760.

Fincham, F. D. (1998). Child development and marital relations. *Child Development, 69,* 543-574.

Fincham, F. D., & Beach, S. R. H. (1999). Conflict in marriage: Implications for working with couples. *Annual Review of Psychology, 50,* 47-77.

Finkelhor, D. (1994). The international epidemiology of child sexual abuse. *Child Abuse & Neglect, 18,* 409–417.

Finkelhor, D., Hotaling, G., Lewis, I. A., & Smith, C. (1990). Sexual abuse in a national survey of adult men and women: Prevalence, characteristics, and risk factors. *Child Abuse & Neglect, 14,* 19–28.

Finlay, B. L., & Darlington, R. (1995). Linked regularities in the development and evolution of mammalian brains. *Science, 268,* 1578–1583.

Finlay-Jones, R., & Brown, G. W. (1981). Types of stressful life event and the onset of anxiety and depressive disorders. *Psychological Medicine, 11,* 803-815.

Finn, P. R., Sharkansky, E. J., Brandt, K. M., & Turcotte, N. (2000). The effects of familial risk, personality, and expectancies on alcohol use and abuse. *Journal of Abnormal Psychology, 109,* 122–133.

Fischer, A. H. (Ed.) (2000). *Gender and emotion: Social psychological perspectives.* New York: Cambridge University Press

Fischer, K. W. (1980). A theory of cognitive development: The control and construction of hierarchies of skills. *Psychological Review, 87,* 477–531.

Fischer, K. W., Shaver, P. R., & Carnochan, P. (1990). How emotions develop and how they organize development. *Cognition and Emotion, 4,* 81–127.

Fiset, P., Paus, T., Daloze, T., Plourde, G., Meuret, P., Bonhomme, V., Hajj-Ali, N., Backman, S. B., & Evans, A. C. (1999). Brain mechanisms of propofol-induced loss of consciousness in humans: A positron emission tomographic study. *Journal of Neuroscience, 19,* 5506–5513.

Fishbein, M., & Ajzen, I. (1974). Attitudes towards objects as predictors of single and multiple behavioral criteria. *Psychologial Review, 81,* 59–74.

Fisher, S., & Greenberg, R. (1985). *The scientific credibility of Freud's theories and therapy.* New York: Columbia University Press.

Fisher, S., & Greenberg, R. P. (1996). *Freud scientifically reappraised: Testing the theories and therapy.* New York: John Wiley & Sons.

Fiske, A. P., Kitayama, S., Markus, H. R., & Nisbett, R. E. (1998). The cultural matrix of social psychology. In D. T. Gilbert & S. T. Fiske (Eds.). *The handbook of social psychology, Vol. 2* (4th ed.). (pp. 915-981). Boston: McGraw-Hill.

Fiske, S. (1992). Thinking is for doing: Portraits of social cognition from daguerreotype to laserphoto. *Journal of Personality and Social Psychology, 63,* 877–889.

Fiske, S. (1995). Social cognition. In A. Tesser (Ed.), *Constructing social psychology.* New York: McGraw-Hill.

Fiske, S. T. (1993). Social cognition and social perception. *Annual Review of Psychology, 44,* 155–194.

Fiske, S. T. (1998). Stereotyping, prejudice, and discrimination. In D. T. Gilbert, S. T. Fiske, et al. (Eds.), *The handbook of social psychology,* (Vol. 2, 4th ed., pp. 357–411). Boston: McGraw-Hill.

Fiske, S. T., & Taylor, S. E. (1991). *Social cognition* (2nd ed.) New York: McGraw-Hill.

Flavell, J., Green, F. L., Flavell, E., & Grossman, J. B. (1997). The development of children's knowledge about inner speech. *Child Development, 68,* 39–47.

Flavell, J. H. (1982). Structures, stages, and sequences in cognitive development. In W. A. Collins (Ed.), *The concept of development:* (Vol. 15). Hillsdale, NJ: Erlbaum.

Flavell, J. H. (1992). Perspectives on perspective taking. In H. Beilin & P. B. Pufall (Eds.), *Piaget's theory: Prospects and possibilities. The Jean Piaget symposium series.* (pp. 107-139). Hillsdale, NJ: Lawrence Erlbaum Associates, Inc.

Flavell, J. H. (1999). Cognitive development: Children's knowledge about the mind. *Annual Review of Psychology, 50,* 21-45.

Flavell, J. H., Botkin, P. T., Fry, C. L. Jr., Wright, J. W., & Jarvis, P. E. (1968). *The development of role-taking and communications skills in children.* New York: John Wiley.

Flavell, J. H., Friedrichs, A. G., & Hoyt, J. D. (1970). Developmental changes in memorization processes. *Cognitive Psychology, 1,* 324–340.

Flavell, J. H., Green, F. L., Flavell, E. R., & Grossman, J. B. (1997). The development of children's knowledge about inner speech. *Child Development, 68,* 39-47.

Flavell, J. H., Green, F. L., Flavell, E. R., & Lin, N. T. (1999). Development of children's knowledge about unconsciousness. *Child Development, 70,* 396–412.

Flavell, J. H., & Miller, P. H. (1998) Social cognition. In W. Damon (Ed. in Chief) and N. Eisenberg (Vol. Ed.), *Handbook of Child Psychology, Vol. 2.* (pp. 851-898). New York: John Wiley.

Flavell, J. H., & Wellman, H. M. (1977). Metamemory. In R. V. Kail Jr. & J. W. Hagen (Eds.). *Perspectives on the development of memory and cognition.* Hillsdale, NJ: Erlbaum.

Fletcher, G. O., Simpson, J. A., Thomas, G., & Giles, L. (1999). Ideals in intimate relationships. *Journal of Personality and Social Psychology, 76,* 72–89.

Flor, H., Haag, G., & Turl, D. C. (1986). Long term efficacy of EMG biofeedback for chronic rheumatic back pain. *Pain, 27,* 195–202.

Flynn, J. R. (1987). Massive IQ gains in 14 nations: What IQ tests really measure? *Psychological Bulletin, 101,* 171–191.

Flynn, J. R. (1999). Searching for justice: The discovery of IQ gains over time. *American Psychologist, 54,* 5–20.

Foa, E. B., Dancu, C. V., Hembree, E. A., Jaycox, L. H., Meadows, E. A., & Street, G. P. (1999). A comparison of exposure therapy, stress inoculation training, and their combination for reducing posttraumatic stress disorder in female assault victims. *Journal of Consulting and Clinical Psychology, 67,* 194–200.

Fodor, J. (1983). *The modularity of mind.* Cambridge, MA: MIT.

Fogel, A., Melson, G. F., & Mistry, J. (1986). Conceptualizing the determinants of nurturance: A reassessment of sex differences. In A. Fogal & G. F. Melson (Eds.), *Origins of nurturance.* Hillsdale, NJ: Erlbaum.

Folkman, S., and Moskowitz, J. T. (2000). Positive affect and the other side of coping. *American Psychologist, 55,* 647–654.

Fonagy, P., Steele, H., & Steele, M. (1991). Maternal representations of attachment during pregnancy predict the organization of infant-mother attachment at one year of age. *Child Development, 62,* 891–905.

Ford, M. (1979). The construct validity of egocentrism. *Psychological Bulletin, 86,* 1169–1188.

Foreyt, J. P. (1987). Issues in the assessment and treatment of obesity. *Journal of Consulting and Clinical Psychology, 55,* 677–684.

Forgas, J. P. (1995). Mood and judgment: The affect infusion model (AIM). *Psychological Bulletin, 117,* 39–66.

Foster, G. (1965). Peasant society and the image of limited good. *American Anthropologist, 67,* 293–315.

Foulkes, D. (1982). REM-dream perspectives on the development of affect and cognition. *Psychiatric Journal of the University of Ottawa, 7,* 48-55.

Fouts, R. S., Hirsch, A. D., & Fouts, D. H. (1982). Cultural transmission of a human language in a chimpanzee mother-infant relationship. In H. E. Fitzgerald, J. A. Mullins, & P. Gage (Eds.), *Child Nurturance,* (Vol. 3). New York: Plenum Press.

Fowles, D. C. (1992). Schizophrenia: Diathesis-stress revisited. *Annual Review of Psychology, 43,* 303–336.

Fox, N. (1991a). Hemispheric specialization and attachment behaviors: Developmental processes and individual differences in separation protest. In J. Gewirtz & W. Kurtines (Eds.), *Intersections with attachment* (pp. 147–164). Hillsdale, NJ: Erlbaum.

Fox, N. (1991b). If it's not left, it's right: Electroencephalograph asymmetry and the development of emotion. *American Psychologist, 46,* 863–872.

Fox, N. A., Rubin, K. H., Calkins, S. D., Marshall, T. R., Coplan, R. J., Porges, S. W., et al. (1995). Frontal activation asymmetry and social competence at four years of age. *Child Development, 66,* 1770–1784.

Fozard, J. (1990). Vision and hearing in aging. In J. Birren & K. W. Schaie (Eds.), *Handbook of the psychology of aging* (3rd ed.). New York: Academic Press.

Fraiberg, S. (1975). The development of human attachments in infants blind from birth. *Merrill-Palmer Quarterly, 21,* 315–334.

Fraley, R. C., & Shaver, P. R. (1998). Airport separations: A naturalistic study of adult attachment dynamics in separating couples. *Journal of Personality & Social Psychology, 75,* 1198–1212.

Frank, E., Anderson, B., Reynolds, C. F., Ritenour, A., & Kupfer, D. J. (1994). Life events and the research diagnostic criteria endogenous subtype: A confirmation of the distinction using the Bedford College methods. *Archives of General Psychiatry, 51,* 519–524.

Frank, E., Swartz, H. A., Mallinger, A. G., Thase, M. E., Weaver, E. V., & Kupfer, D. J. (1999). Adjunctive psychotherapy for bipolar disorder. Effects of changing treatment modality. *Journal of Abnormal Psychology, 108,* 579–587.

Frank, J. D. (1978). *Psychotherapy and the human predicament: A psychosocial approach.* New York: Schocken.

Frankl, V. (1959). *Man's search for meaning: An introduction to logotherapy.* New York: Pocket Books.

Franklin, J., Donohew, L., Dhoundiyal, V., & Cook, P. L. (1988). Attention and our recent past: The scaly thumb of the reptile. *American Behavioral Scientist, 31,* 312–326.

Franklin, M. E., Abramowitz, J. S., Kozak, M. J., Levitt, J. T., & Foa, E. B. (2000). Effectiveness of exposure and ritual prevention for obsessive-compulsive disorder: Randomized compared with nonrandomized samples. *Journal of Consulting and Clinical Psychology, 68,* 594–602.

Franz, C., McClelland, D., & Weinberger, J. (1991). Childhood antecedents of conventional social accomplishment in midlife adults: A 36-year prospective study. *Journal of Personality and Social Psychology, 60,* 586–595.

Free, M., & Beekhuis, M. (1985). A successful adaptation of systematic desensitization in the treatment of a phobia of babies. *Behaviour Change, 2,* 1985, 59–64.

Freedman, J. L., & Fraser, S. C. (1966). Compliance without pressure: The foot-in-the-door technique. *Journal of Personality and Social Psychology, 4,* 195–202.

Freedman, N., Hoffenberg, J. D., Vorus, N., & Frosch, A. (1999). The effectiveness of psychoanalytic psychotherapy: The role of treatment duration, frequency of sessions, and the therapeutic relationship. *Journal of the American Psychoanalytic Association, 47,* 741–772.

Freeman, W. (1959). Psychosurgery. In S. Aneti (Ed.), *American handbook of psychiatry II.* New York: Basic Books.

Freud, A. (1936). *The ego and the mechanisms of defense.* New York: International Universities Press.

Freud, A. (1958). Adolescence. *Psychoanalytic Study of the Child, 13,* 255–278.

Freud, S. (1895). Project for a scientific psychology. In J. Strachey (Ed.), *The standard edition of the complete psychological works of Sigmund Freud* (Vol. 1). London: Hogarth Press, 1966.

Freud, S. (1900). *The interpretation of dreams.* New York: Avon, 1965.

Freud, S. (1905). *Three contributions to the theory of sexuality.* New York: E. P. Dutton, 1962.

Freud, S. (1912). The dynamics of transference. In J. Strachey (Ed., Trans.), *The standard edition of the complete psychological works of Sigmund Freud,* (Vol. 12, pp. 97–108). London: Hogarth, 1958.

Freud, S. (1915). The unconscious. In P. Rieff (Ed.), *Freud: General psychological theory.* New York: Collier, 1963.

Freud, S. (1917). Mourning and melancholia. In P. Reiff (Ed.), *Freud: General psychological theory.* New York: Collier, 1963.

Freud, S. (1922). Certain neurotic mechanisms in jealousy, paranoia, and homosexuality. In J. Strachey (Ed., Trans.), *The standard edition of the complete psychological works of Sigmund Freud* (Vol. 1). London: Hogarth Press, 1966.

Freud, S. (1923). *The ego and the id.* New York: W. W. Norton.

Freud, S. (1925). An autobiographical study. In J. Strachey (Ed., Trans.), *The standard edition of the complete psychological works of Sigmund Freud,* (Vol. 20). London: Hogarth Press, 1952.

Freud, S. (1928). *The Future of an Illusion. International psychoanalytical library, no. 15.* New York: Liveright.

Freud, S. (1933). *New introductory lectures on psychoanalysis.* New York: W. W. Norton, 1965.

Frick, R. W. (1985). Communicating emotion: The role of prosodic features. *Psychological Bulletin, 97,* 412–429.

Fried, C. B., & Aronson, E. (1995). Hypocrisy, misattribution, and dissonance reduction. *Personality and Social Psychology Bulletin, 21,* 925–933.

Fried, P. A. (1995). The Ottawa Prenatal Prospective Study (OPPS): Methodological issues and findings: It's easy to throw the baby out with the bath water. Special Issue: 1994 International Symposium on Cannabis and the Cannabinoids: Developmental effects. *Life Sciences, 56,* 2159–2168.

Friedman, H. R., & Goldman-Rakic, P. (1994). Coactivation of prefrontal cortex and inferior parietal cortex in working memory tasks revealed by 2DG functional mapping in the rhesus monkey. *Journal of Neuroscience, 14,* 2775–2788.

Friedman, M., & Rosenman, R. H. (1959). Association of specific overt behavior pattern with blood and cardiovascular findings—blood cholesterol level, blood clotting time, incidence of arcus senilis, and clinical coronary heart disease. *Journal of the American Medical Association, 162,* 1286–1296.

Friedman, M. A., & Brownell, K. D. (1995). Psychological correlates of obesity: Moving to the next research generation. *Psychological Bulletin, 117,* 3–20.

Frieze, I. H., & Browne, A. (1989). Violence in marriage. In L. Ohlin & M. Tonry (Eds.), *Family violence.* Chicago: University of Chicago Press.

Frisch, R. E., Wyshak, G., & Vincent, L. (1980). Delayed menarch and amenorrhea of ballet dancers. *New England Journal of Medicine, 303,* 17–19.

Frith, C., & Dolan, R. (1996). The role of the prefrontal cortex in higher cognitive functions. *Cognitive Brain Research, 5,* 175–181.

Frock, J., & Money, J. (1992). Sexuality and the menopause. *Psychotherapy and Psychosomatics, 57,* 29–33.

Fromkin, V., Krashen, S., Curtiss, S., Rigler, D., & Rigler, M. (1974). The development of language in Genie: A case of language acquisition beyond the critical period. *Brain and Language, 1,* 81–107.

Fromm, E. (1955). *The sane society.* Greenwich, CT: Fawcett Books.

Fry, A. F., & Hale, S. (1996). Processing speed, working memory, and fluid intelligence: Evidence for a developmental cascade. *Psychological Science, 7,* 237–241.

Fukunishi, I., Maeda, K., Kubota, M., & Tomino, Y. (1997). Association of alexithymia with low utilization and perception on a measure of social support in patients on peritoneal dialysis. *Psychological Reports, 80,* 127–130.

Fuller, J. L., & Thompson, W. R. (1978). *Foundations of behavior genetics.* New York: John Wiley.

Funder, D., & Colvin, C. R. (1991). Explorations in behavioral consistency: Properties of persons, situations, and behaviors. *Journal of Personality and Social Psychology, 60,* 773–794.

Furman, W., & Buhrmester, D. (1992). Age and sex differences in perceptions of networks of personal relationships. *Child Development, 63,* 103–115.

Fussell, S. R., & Krauss, R. M. (1992). Coordination of knowledge in communication: Effects of speakers' assumptions about what others know. *Journal of Personality and Social Psychology, 62,* 378–391.

Fuster, J. (1989). *The prefrontal cortex* (2nd ed.). New York: Raven.

Fyer, A. J., Mannuzza, S., Chapman, T. F., Martin, L. Y., & Klein, D. F. (1995). Specificity in familial aggregation of phobic disorders. *Archives of General Psychiatry, 52,* 564–573.

Gabbard, G. (1992). Psychodynamic psychiatry in the "decade of the brain." *American Journal of Psychiatry, 149,* 991–998.

Gabbay, F. (1992). Behavior-genetic strategies in the study of emotion. *Psychological Science, 3,* 50–55.

Gable, S. L., & Reis, H. T. (1999). Now and then, them and us, this and that: Studying relationships across time, partner, context, and person. *Personal Relationships, 6,* 415–432.

Gable, S. L., & Reis, H. T. (in press). Appetitive and aversive social interaction. In J. H. Harvey & A. E. Wenzel (Eds.), *Close romantic relationship maintenance and enhancement.* New York: Guilford.

Gabrieli, J. D., Desmond, J. E., Demb, J. B., Wagner, A. D., Stone, M. V., Vaidya, C. J., & Glover, G. H. (1996). Functional magnetic resonance imaging of semantic memory processes in the frontal lobes. *Psychological Science, 7,* 278–283.

Gabrieli, J. D. E. (1998). Cognitive neuroscience

of human memory. *Annual Review of Psychology, 49,* 87–115.

Gadow, K., & Sprafkin, J. (1993). Television violence and children with emotional and behavioral disorders. *Journal of Emotional and Behavioral Disorders, 1,* 54–63.

Gaensbauer, T., Chatoor, I., Drell, M., Siegel, D., et al. (1995). Traumatic loss in a one-year old girl. *Journal of the American Academy of Child and Adolescent Psychiatry, 34,* 520–528.

Galinsky, A. D., & Moskowitz, G. B. (2000). Perspective-taking: Decreasing stereotype expression, stereotype accessibility, and in-group favoritism. *Journal of Personality and Social Psychology, 78*(4), 708–724.

Gallup, G. G., McClure, M. K., Hill, S. D., & Bundy, R. A. (1971). Capacity for self-recognition in differentially reared chimpanzees. *Psychological-Record, 21,* 69-74

Gamsa, A. (1990). Is emotional disturbance a precipitator or a consequence of chronic pain? *Pain, 42,* 183–195.

Ganley, R. (1989). Emotion and eating in obesity: A view of the literature. *International Journal of Eating Disorders, 8,* 343–361.

Gannon, P. J., Holloway, R. L., Broadfield, D. C., & Braun, A. R. (1998). Asymmetry of chimpanzee planum temporale: Humanlike pattern of Wernicke's brain language, area homolog. *Science, 279,* 220–222.

Garb, H. N. (1984). The incremental validity of information used in personality assessment. *Clinical Psychological Review, 40,* 641–655.

Garcia, J. (1979). I.Q.: The conspiracy. In J. B. Maas (Ed.), *Readings in psychology today* (4th ed., pp. 198–202). New York: Random House.

Garcia, J., & Garcia y Robertson, R. (1985). Evolution of learning mechanisms. In B. L. Hammonds (Ed.), *The Master Lecture Series* (Vol. 4). Washington, DC: American Psychological Association.

Garcia, J., & Koelling, R. (1966). Relation of cue to consequence in avoidance learning. *Psychonomic Science, 4,* 123–124.

Garcia, J., Lasiter, P., Bermudez-Rattoni, & Deems, D. (1985). A general theory of aversion learning. *Annals of the New York Academy of Sciences, 443,* 8–21.

Gardner, B. T., & Gardner, R. A. (1975). Evidence for sentence constituents in the early utterances of child and chimpanzee. *Journal of Experimental Psychology: General, 104,* 244–267.

Gardner, H. (1975). *The shattered mind.* New York: Alfred A. Knopf.

Gardner, H. (1983). *Frames of mind: The theory of multiple intelligences.* New York: Basic Books.

Gardner, H. (1985). *The mind's new science: A history of the cognitive revolution.* New York: Basic Books.

Gardner, H. (1999). *Intelligence reframed: Multiple intelligences for the 21st century.* New York: Basic Books.

Gardner, H. (2000). The giftedness matrix: A developmental perspective. In R. C. Friedman, B. M. Shore, et al. (Eds.), *Talents unfolding: Cognition and development* (pp. 77–88). Washington, DC: American Psychological Association.

Garner, D. M., & Garfinkel, P. E. (1979). The Eating Attitudes Test: An index of the symptoms of anorexia nervosa. *Psychological Medicine, 9,* 273-279.

Garner, D. M., & Wooley, S. (1991). Confronting the failure of behavioral and dietary treatments for obesity. *Clinical Psychology Review, 11,* 729–780.

Garver, D. L. (1997). The etiologic heterogeneity of schizophrenia. *Harvard Review of Psychiatry, 4,* 317–327.

Gaudreau, D., & Peretz, I. (1999). Implicit and explicit memory for music in old and young adults. *Brain & Cognition, 40,* 126–129.

Gauthier, J. G., Ivers, H., & Carrier, S. (1996). Nonpharmacological approaches in the management of recurrent headache disorders and their comparison and combination with pharmacotherapy. *Clinical Psychology Review, 16,* 543–571.

Gazzaniga, M. (1967). The split brain in man. *Scientific American, 217,* 24–29.

Ge, X., Conger, R. D., & Elder, G. (1996). Coming of age too early: Pubertal influences on girls' vulnerability to psychological distress. *Child Development, 67,* 3386–3400.

Geary, D. C., Rumsey, M., Bow-Thomas, C. C., & Hoard, M. K. (1995). Sexual jealousy as a facultative trait: Evidence from the pattern of sex differences in adults from China and the United States. *Ethology & Sociobiology, 16,* 355–383.

Gebhard, P. H. (1971). Human sexual behavior: A summary statement. In D. S. Marshall & R. C. Suggs (Eds.), *Human sexual behavior: Variations in the ethnographic spectrum.* New York: Basic Books.

Geen, R. (1990). *Human aggression.* Pacific Grove, CA: Brooks-Cole.

Geen, R. G. (1995). Human aggression. In A. Tesser (Ed.), *Advanced social psychology.* New York: McGraw-Hill.

Geen, R. G. (1998). Aggression and antisocial behavior. In D. T. Gilbert, S. T. Fiske, et al. (Eds.), *The handbook of social psychology,* (Vol. 2, 4th ed., pp. 317–356). Boston: McGraw-Hill.

Geertz, C. (1963). The integrative revolution: Primordial sentiments and civil politics in the new states. In C. Geertz (Ed.), *Old societies and new states.* New York: Free Press.

Geertz, C. (1974). From the natives' point of view. *American Academy of Arts and Sciences Bulletin, 28,* 26–43.

Geis, F. (1978). Machiavellianism. In H. London and J. E. Exner (Eds.), *Dimensions of personality.* New York: Wiley.

Geldard, G. A. (1972). *The human senses* (2nd ed.). New York: Wiley.

Gelinas, D. J. (1983). The persisting negative effects of incest. *Psychiatry, 46,* 312–332.

Gelman, R., & Baillargeon, R. (1983). A review of Piagetian concepts. In J. H. Flavell & E. M. Markman (Eds.), *Handbook of child psychology: Cognitive development* (Vol. 3). New York: John Wiley.

Gentner, D., & Holyoak, K. J. (1997). Reasoning and learning by analogy: Introduction. *American Psychologist, 52,* 32–34.

Gentner, D., & Markman, A. B. (1997). Structure mapping in analogy and similarity. *American Psychologist, 52,* 45–46.

George, M. S., Lisanby, S. H., & Sackeim, H. A. (1999). Transcranial magnetic stimulation: Applications in neuropsychiatry. *Archives of General Psychiatry, 56,* 300–311.

Gerken, L., & McIntosh, B. J. (1993). Interplay of function morphemes and prosody in early language. *Developmental Psychology, 29,* 448–457.

Gershon, S., & Soares, J. C. (1997). Current therapeutic profile of lithium. *Archives of General Psychiatry, 54,* 16–20.

Gerstner, C., & Day, D. V. (1994). Cross-cultural comparison of leadership prototypes. *Leadership Quarterly, 5,* 121–134.

Gest, S. D. (1997). Behavioral inhibition: Stability and associations with adaptation from childhood to early adulthood. *Journal of Personality and Social Psychology, 72,* 467–475.

Gibbs, R. W., Jr. (1981). Your wish is my command: Convention and context in interpreting indirect requests. *Journal of Verbal Learning and Verbal Behavior, 20,* 431–444.

Gibson, E. J. (1969). *Principals of perceptual learning and its development.* Englewood-Cliffs, NJ: Prentice Hall.

Gibson, E. J. (1984). Perceptual development from the ecological approach. In M. E. Lamb, A. L. Brown, & B. Rogoff (Eds.), *Advances in developmental psychology* (Vol. 3).

Gibson, E. J., & Walk, R. D. (1960). The "visual cliff." *Scientific American, 202,* 64–71.

Gibson, H. B. (1996). Sexual functioning in later life. In R. T. Woods et al. (Eds.), *Handbook of the clinical psychology of ageing* (pp. 183–193). Chichester, UK: John Wiley & Sons.

Gibson, J. J. (1966). *The senses considered as perceptual systems.* Boston: Houghton Mifflin.

Gibson, J. J. (1979). *The ecological approach to visual perception.* Boston: Houghton Mifflin.

Giesler, R. B., Josephs, R. A, & Swann, W. B. Jr. (1996). Self-verification in clinical depression: The desire for negative evaluation. *Journal of Abnormal Psychology, 105,* 358-368.

Gigerenzer, G., & Goldstein, D. G. (1996). Reasoning the fast and frugal way: Models of bounded rationality. *Psychological Review, 103,* 650–669.

Gilbert, D. (1989). Thinking lightly about others: Automatic components of the social inference process. In J. S. Uleman & J. A. Bargh (Eds.), *Unintended thought* (pp. 189–211). New York: Guilford Press.

Gilbert, D. T., Fiske, S. T., & Lindzey, G. (1998). *The handbook of social psychology, Vol. 1* (4th ed.). Boston: McGraw-Hill.

Gilbert, D. T., Pinel, E. C., Wilson, T. C., Blumberg, S. J., & Wheatley, T. P. (1998). Immune neglect: A source of durability bias in affective forecasting. *Journal of Personality and Social Psychology, 75,* 617–638.

Gilbert, P. L., Harris, M. J., McAdams, L. A., & Jeste, D. V. (1995). Neuroleptic withdrawal in schizophrenic patients: A review of the literature. *Archives of General Psychiatry, 52,* 173–188.

Gilboa, E., & Gotlib, I. H. (1997). Cognitive biases and affect persistence in previously dysphoric and never-dysphoric individuals. *Cognition & Emotion, 11*, 517-538.

Gilert, D. T., & Malone, P. S. (1995). The correspondence bias. *Psychological Bulletin, 117*, 21–38.

Gilhooly, K. J. (1989). Human and machine problem solving: Toward a comparative cognitive science. In K. J. Gilhooly (Ed.), *Human and machine problem solving.* New York: Plenum Press.

Gill, M. (1982). *The analysis of transference: Vol. 1. Theory and technique. Psychological Issues, Monograph,* No. 53.

Gilleard, C. J. (2000). Is Alzheimer's disease preventable? A review of two decades of epidemiological research. *Aging & Mental Health, 4*, 101–118.

Gilligan, C. (1982). *In a different voice.* Cambridge, MA: Harvard University Press.

Gilligan, J. (1996). Exploring shame in special settings: A psychotherapeutic study. In C. Cordess, M. Cox, et al. (Eds.), *Forensic psychotherapy: Crime, psychodynamics and the offender patient, Vol. 2: Mainly practice. Forensic focus series, No. 1* (pp. 475–489). London: Jessica Kingsley Publishers.

Gilmore, R. O., & Johnson, M. H. (1995). Working memory in infancy: Six month-olds' performance on two versions of the oculomotor delayed response task. *Journal of Experimental Child Psychology, 59*, 397-418.

Gilovich, T., Medvec, V. H., & Savitsky, K. (2000). The spotlight effect in social judgment: An egocentric bias in estimates of the salience of one's own actions and appearance. *Journal of Personality and Social Psychology, 78*(2), 211–222.

Gladis, M. M., Gosch, E. A., Dishuk, N. M., & Crits-Christoph, P. (1999). Quality of life: Expanding the scope of clinical significance. *Journal of Consulting and Clinical Psychology, 67*, 320–331.

Gladue, B. A., Green, R., & Hellman, R. E. (1984). Neuroendocrine response to estrogen and sexual orientation. *Science, 225*, 1496–1499.

Gladwin, T. (1970). *East is a big bird.* Cambridge, MA: Belknap Press.

Glass, G. V., & Smith, M. L. (1980). Ask not for whom the bell tolls. *American Psychologist, 35*, 223.

Glassman, N., & Andersen, S. (1997). *Activating transference without consciousness: Using significant-other representations to go beyond the subliminally given information.* Unpublished manuscript, Department of Psychology, New York University.

Gleason, T. R., Sebanc, A. M., & Hartup, W. W. (2000). Imaginary companions of preschool children. *Developmental Psychology, 36*, 419–428.

Gleitman, L. R., Gleitman, H., Landau, B., & Warner, E. (1988). Where learning begins: Initial representations for language learning. In F. Newmeyer (Ed.), *Linguistics: The Cambridge survey. Vol. III. Language: Psychological and biological aspects.* Cambridge: Cambridge University Press.

Gluck, M. A., & Myers, C. E. (1997). Psychobiological models of hippocampal function in learning and memory. *Annual Review, 48*, 481–514.

Godden, D. R., & Baddeley, A. D. (1975). Context-dependent memory in two natural environments: On land and underwater. *British Journal of Psychology, 66*, 325–331.

Goff, D. C., Bagnell, A. L., & Perlis, R. H. (1999). Glutamatergic augmentation strategies for cognitive impairment in schizophrenia. *Psychiatric Annals, 29*, 649-654.

Gold, J. M., Carpenter, C., Randolph, C., Goldberg, T. E., Weinberger, D. E. (1997). Auditory working memory and Wisconsin card sorting test performance in schizophrenia. *Archives of General Psychiatry, 54*, 159–165.

Gold, M. S., & Pearsall, H. R. (1983). Hypothyroidism—or is it depression? *Psychosomatics, 24*, 646–656.

Goldberg, L. R. (1981). Language and individual differences: The search for universals in personality lexicons. In L. Wheeler (Ed.), *Review of personality and social psychology.* Beverly Hills, CA: Sage Publications.

Goldberg, L. R. (1993). The structure of phenotypic personality traits. *American Psychologist, 48*, 26–34.

Golden, R. M., & Rumelhart, D. E. (1993). A parallel distributed processing model of story comprehension and recall. *Discourse Processes, 16*, 203–237.

Goldfield, B. A., & Snow, C. E. (1989). Individual differences in language acquisition. In J. Berko Gleason (Ed.), *The development of language* (2nd ed.). Columbus, OH: Merrill.

Goldfried, M. R., & Davison, G. C. (1994). *Clinical behavior therapy* (2nd ed.). New York: Wiley.

Goldin-Meadow, S., & Mylander, C. (1984). Gestural communication in deaf children: The effects and noneffects of parental input on early language development. *Monographs of the Society for Research in Child Development, 49*, 1–121.

Goldin-Meadow, S., & Mylander, C. (1998). Spontaneous sign systems created by deaf children in two cultures. *Nature, 391*, 279–281.

Goldman-Rakic, P. (1995). Cellular basis of working memory. *Neuron, 14*, 477–485.

Goldman-Rakic, P. (1996). Regional and cellular fractionation of working memory. *Proceedings of the National Academy of Sciences, 93*, 13473–13476.

Goldner, E. M., Srikameswaran, S., Schroeder, M. L., Livesley, W. J., & Birmingham, C. L. (1999). Dimensional assessment of personality pathology in patients with eating disorders. *Psychiatry Research, 85*, 151–159.

Goldsmith, H. H., & Alansky, J. A. (1987). Maternal and infant temperamental predictors of attachment: A meta-analytic review. *Journal of Consulting and Clinical Psychology, 55*, 805–816.

Goldsmith, S. K., Shapiro, R. M., & Joyce, J. N. (1997). Disrupted pattern of D2 dopamine receptors in the temporal lobe in schizophrenia: A postmortem study. *Archives of General Psychiatry, 54*, 649–658.

Goldsmith, T. H. (1994). Ultraviolet receptors and color visions: Evolutionary implications and a dissonance of paradigms. *Vision Research, 34*, 1479–1487.

Goldstein, A. J., & Chambless, D. J. (1978). A reanalysis of agoraphobia. *Behavior Therapy, 9*, 47–59.

Goldstein, J. M. Goodman, J. M., Seidman, L. J., Kennedy, D. N., Makris, N., Lee, H., Tourville, J., Caviness, V. S., Faraone, S. V., & Tsuang, M. T. (1999). Cortical abnormalities in schizophrenia identified by structural magnetic resonance imaging. *Archives of General Psychiatry, 57*, 537–547.

Goldstein, M. J. (1988). The family and psychopathology. *Annual Review of Psychology, 39*, 283–299.

Goldstein, R. B., Wickramaratne, P. J., Horwath, E., & Weissman, M. M. (1997). Familial aggregation and phenomenology of "early"-onset (at or before age 20 years) panic disorder. *Archives of General Psychiatry, 54*, 271–278.

Goleman, D. (1995). *Emotional intelligence.* New York: Bantam Books.

Golomb, A., Ludolph, P., Westen, D., Block, M. J., et al. (1994). Maternal empathy, family chaos, and the etiology of borderline personality disorder. *Journal of the American Psychoanalytic Association, 42*, 525–548.

Goodenough, B., & Gillam, B. (1997). Gradients as visual primitives. *Journal of Experimental Psychology: Human Perception and Performance, 23*, 370–387.

Goodman, L., Koss, M., Fitzgerald, L., Russo, N., & Keita, G. (1993). Male violence against women: Current research and future directions. *American Psychologist, 48*, 1054–1058.

Goodnow, J. J. (1976). The nature of intelligent behavior: Questions raised by cross-cultural studies. In L. B. Resnick (Ed.), *The nature of intelligence* (pp. 169–188). Hillsdale, NJ: Erlbaum.

Goodwin, F. K., & Ghaemi, S. N. (1997). Future directions in mood disorder research. In A. Honig & H. M. van Praag (Eds.), *Depression: Neurobiological, psychopathological and therapeutic advances. Wiley series on clinical and neurobiological advances in psychiatry, Vol. 3.* (pp. 627-643). New York: John Wiley & Sons, Inc.

Goodwin, F. K., & Ghaemi, S. N. (1998). Understanding manic-depressive illness. *Archives of General Psychiatry, 55*, 23–25.

Goodwin, F. K., & Roy-Byrne, P. (1987). Treatment of bipolar disrorders. In A. J. Frances and R. E. Hales (Eds.), *Psychiatric Update Annual Review* (Vol. 6).

Goody, J. (1977). *The domestication of the savage mind.* Cambridge University Press.

Gopnik, A. (1993). How we know our minds: The illusion of first-person intentionality. *Behavioral and Brain Sciences, 16*, 1–14.

Gordis, E. (1996). Alcohol research: At the cutting edge. *Archives of General Psychiatry, 53*, 199–201.

Gordon, M., & Shankweiler, P. J. (1971). Different equals less: Female sexuality in recent marriage manuals. *Journal of Marriage and the Family, 33*, 459–466.

Gordon, P. (1990). Learnability and feedback. *Developmental Psychology, 26,* 217–220.

Gorman, J. M., Kent, J. M., Sullivan, G. M., & Coplan, J. D. (2000). Neuroanatomical hypothesis of panic disorder, revised. *American Journal of Psychiatry, 157,* 493–505.

Gorski, R. A., & Barraclough, C. A. (1963). Effects of low dosages of androgen on the differentiation of hypothalamic regulatory control of ovulation in the rat. *Endocrinology, 73,* 210–216.

Goschke, T., & Kuhl, J. (1993). Representations of intentions: Persisting activation in memory. *Journal of Experimental Psychology: Learning, Memory, and Cognition, 19,* 1211–1226.

Goto, H. (1971). Auditory perception by normal Japanese adults of the sounds "l" and "r." *Neuropsychologia, 9,* 317–323.

Gottesman, I. I. (1991). *Schizophrenia genesis: The origins of madness.* New York: W. H. Freeman & Co.

Gottesman, I. I., & Bertelsen, A. (1989). Confirming unexpressed genotypes for schizophrenia: Risks in the offspring of Fischer's Danish identical and fraternal discordant twins. *Archives of General Psychiatry, 50,* 527–540.

Gottlieb, G. (1991). Experiential canalization of behavioral development: Theory. *Developmental Psychology, 27,* 4–13.

Gottlieb, J. P., Kusunoki, M., & Goldberg, M. E. (1998). The representation of visual salience in monkey parietal cortex. *Nature, 391,* 481-484.

Gottman, J. (1998). Psychology and the study of marital processes. *Annual Review of Psychology, 49,* 169–197.

Gould, E., Tanapat, P., McEwen, B. S., Flugge, G., & Fuchs, E. (1998). Proliferation of granule cell precursors in the dentate gyrus of adult monkeys is diminished by stress. *Proceedings of the National Academy of Sciences, 95,* 3168–3171.

Gould, S. J. (1981). *The mismeasure of man.* New York: W. W. Norton.

Gould, S. J. (1984). Human equality is a contingent fact of history. *Natural History, 92,* 26–33.

Gracely, R., Lynch, S., & Bennett, G. J. (1992). Painful neuropathy: Altered central processing maintained dynamically by peripheral input. *Pain, 51,* 175–194.

Graesser, A. C., Millis, K. K., & Zwaan, R. (1997). Discourse comprehension. *Annual Review of Psychology, 48,* 163–189.

Graf, P., & Schacter, D. L. (1987). Selective effects of interference on implicit and explicit memory for new associations. *Journal of Experimental Psychology: Learning, Memory, & Cognition, 13,* 45–53.

Graham, K. S., Patterson, K., & Hodges, J. R. (1999). Episodic memory: New insights from the study of semantic dementia. *Current Opinion in Neurobiology, 9,* 245–250.

Gray, J. A. (1987). *The psychology of fear and stress* (2nd ed.). New York: Cambridge University Press.

Gray, J. A. (1990). Brain systems that mediate both emotion and cognition. *Cognition and Emotion, 4,* 269–288.

Gray, J. A. (1994). Framework for a taxonomy of psychiatric disorder. In S. H. M. van Goozen & N. E. Van de Poll, (Eds.), *Emotions: Essays on emotion theory.* (pp. 29-59). Hillsdale, NJ: Lawrence Erlbaum Associates, Inc.

Graziadei, P. P. C. (1969). The ultra-structure of vertebrate taste buds. In C. Pfaffman (Ed.), *Olfaction and taste,* (Vol. 3). New York: Rockefeller University Press.

Green, L., & Freed, D. E. (1993). The substitutability of reinforcers. *Journal of the Experimental Analysis of Behavior, 60,* 141–158.

Green, R. (1987). *The "sissy boy" syndrome and the development of homosexuality.* New Haven, CT: Yale University Press.

Greenberg, J. (1977). The brain and emotions: Crossing a new frontier. *Science News, 112,* 74–75.

Greenberg, J., Pyszczynski, T., Solomon, S., Rosenblatt, A., Veeder, M., Kirkland, S., & Lyon, D. (1990). Evidence for terror management theory II: The effects of mortality salience on reactions to those who threaten or bolster the cultural worldview. *Journal of Personality and Social Psychology, 58,* 308–318.

Greenberg, J., Pyszczynski, T., Solomon, S., Simon, L., et al. (1994). Role of consciousness and accessibility of death-related thoughts in mortality salience effects. *Journal of Personality & Social Psychology, 67,* 627–637.

Greenberg, L. S., & Safran, J. D. (1990). Emotional-change processes in psychotherapy. In R. Plutchik & H. Kellerman, Henry (Eds.), *Emotion, psychopathology, and psychotherapy. Emotion: Theory, research, and experience, Vol. 5.* (pp. 59-85). San Diego: Academic Press, Inc.

Greenberger, E., Chen, C., Tally, S. R., & Dong, Q. (2000). Family, peer, and individual correlates of depressive symptomatology among U.S. and Chinese adolescents. *Journal of Consulting and Clinical Psychology, 68,* 209–219.

Greene, D. M., & Swets, J. A. (1966). *Signal detection theory and psychophysics.* New York: Wiley.

Greeno, C. G., & Wing, R. R. (1994). Stress-induced eating. *Psychological Bulletin, 115,* 444–464.

Greeno, J. G. (1978). Natures of problem-solving abilities. In W. K. Estes (Ed.), *Handbook of Learning and Cognitive Processes,* (Vol. 5). Hillsdale, NJ: Erlbaum.

Greenough, W., Black, J., & Wallace, C. (1987). Experience and brain development. *Child Development, 58,* 539–559.

Greenough, W. T. (1991). Experience as a component of normal development: Evolutionary considerations. *Developmental Psychology, 27,* 14–17.

Greenwald, A. G. (1980). The totalitarian ego: Fabrication and revision of personal history. *American Psychologist, 35,* 603–618.

Greenwald, A. G., & Banaji, M. (1995). Implicit social cognition: Attitudes, self-esteem, and stereotypes. *Psychological Review, 102,* 4–27.

Greenwald, A. G., McGhee, D. E., & Schwartz, J. L. K. (1998). Measuring individual differences in implicit cognition: The implicit association test. *Journal of Personality and Social Psychology, 74*(6), 1464–1480.

Gregory, R. (1978). *Eye and brain: The psychology of seeing* (3rd ed.). New York: McGraw-Hill.

Gregory, R. I. (1970). *The intelligent eye.* New York: McGraw-Hill.

Grencavage, L. M., & Norcross, J. C. (1990). Where are the commonalities among the therapeutic common factors? *Professional Psychology: Research and Practice, 21,* 372–378.

Grice, H. P. (1975). Logic and conversation. In P. Cole & J. L. Morgan (Eds.), *Syntax and semantics: Speech acts* (pp. 41–58). San Diego: Academic Press.

Griffin, D. W., & Ross, L. (1991). Subjective construal, social inference, and human misunderstanding. In M. Zanna (Ed.), *Advances in experimental social psychology* (Vol. 24, pp. 319–356). New York: Academic Press.

Griffith, D. R., Azuma, S. D., & Chasnoff, I. J. (1994). Three-year outcome of children exposed prenatally to drugs. Special Section: Cocaine babies. *Journal of the American Academy of Child and Adolescent Psychiatry, 33,* 20–27.

Griffith, E. E., Young, J. L., & Smith. (1984). An analysis of the therapeutic elements in a Black church service. *Hospital and Community Psychiatry, 35,* 464–469.

Griffitt, W. (1987). Females, males, and sexual responses. In K. Kelley (Ed.), *Females, males, and sexuality: Theories and research.* Albany: State University of New York Press.

Griggs, R. A., & Cox, J. R. (1982). The elusive thematic-materials effect in Wason's selection task. *British Journal of Psychology, 73,* 407–420.

Grimshaw, G. M., Bryden, M. P., & Finegan, J. K. (1995). Relations between prenatal testosterone and cerebral lateralization in children. *Neuropsychology, 9,* 68–79.

Grob, C., & Dobkin de Rios, M. (1992). Adolescent drug use in cross-cultural perspective. *Journal of Drug Issues, 22,* 121–138.

Gross, J. J. (1998). Antecedent- and response-focused emotion regulation: Divergent consequences for experience, expression, and physiology. *Journal of Personality & Social Psychology, 74,* 224–237.

Gross, R. T., & Duke, P. M. (1980). The effect of early versus late physical maturation on adolescent behavior. *Pediatric Clinic of North America, 27.*

Group for the Advancement of Psychiatry (GAP) Committee on Alcoholism and the Addictions (1991). Substance abuse disorders: A psychiatric priority. *American Journal of Psychiatry, 148,* 1291–1300.

Grunbaum, A. (1984). *The foundations of psychoanalysis: A philosophical critique.* Berkeley: University of California Press.

Grusec, J. E., & Goodnow, J. J. (1994). Summing up and looking to the future. *Developmental Psychology, 30,* 29–31.

Guarnaccia, P. J., & Rogler, L. H. (1999). Research on culture-bound syndromes: New directions. *American Journal of Psychiatry, 156,* 1322–1327.

Gumperz, J. J., & Levinson, S. C. (Eds.). (1996). *Rethinking linguistic relativity.* Cambridge: Cambridge University Press.

Gunderson, J. G. (1986). Pharmacotherapy for patients with borderline personality disorder. *Archives of General Psychiatry, 43,* 698–700.

Gunnar, M. R., & Nelson, C. A. (1992). *Developmental behavioral neuroscience.* Hillsdale, NJ: Lawrence Erlbaum Associates, Inc.

Gunter, B., & McAleer, J. (1990). *Children and television: The one eyed monster?* London: Routledge.

Gur, R. E., Cowell, P. E., Latshaw, A., Turetsky, B. I., Grossman, R. I., Arnold, S. E., Bilker, W. B., & Gur, R. C. (2000). Reduced dorsal and orbital prefrontal gray matter volumes in schizophrenia. *Archives of General Psychiatry, 57,* 761–768.

Gur, R. E, Turetsky, B. I., Bilker, W. B., Gur, R. C. (1999). Reduced gray matter volume in schizophrenia. *Archives of General Psychiatry, 56,* 905-911.

Gurevich, E. V., Bordelon, Y., Shapiro, R. M., Arnold, S. E., Gur, R. E., & Joyce, J. N. (1997). Mesolimbic dopamine D3 receptors and use of antipsychotics in patients with schizophrenia: A postmortem study. *Archives of General Psychiatry, 54,* 225–232.

Gust, D., Gordon, T., Brodie, A., & McClure, H. (1994). Effect of a preferred companion in modulating stress in adult female rhesus monkeys. *Physiology and Behavior, 4,* 681 684.

Gustavson, C. R., Kelly, D. J., Sweeny, M., & Garcia, J. (1976). Prey-lithium aversions: I: Coyotes and wolves. *Behavioral Biology, 17,* 61–72.

Guzowski, J. F., Lyford, G. L., Stevenson, G. D., Houston, F. P., McGaugh, J. L., Worley, P. F., & Barnes, C. A. (2000). Inhibition of activity-dependent arc protein expression in the rat hippocampus impairs the maintenance of long-term potentiation and the consolidationof long-term memory. *Journal of Neuroscience, 20,* 3993–4001.

Hagan, M. M., Castaneda, E., Sumaya, I. C., Fleming, S. M., Galloway, J., & Moss, D. E. (1998). The effect of hypothalamic peptide YY on hippocampal acetylcholine release in vivo: Implications for limbic function in binge-eating behavior. *Brain Research, 805,* 20–28.

Hahn, C., Pawlyk, A. C., Whybrow, P. C., Gyulai, L., & Tejani-Butt, S. M. (1999). Lithium administration affects gene expression of thyroid hormone receptors in rat brain. *Life Sciences, 64,* 1793–1802.

Hahn, S. E., & Smith, C. S. (1999). Daily hassles and chronic stressors: Conceptual and measurement issues. *Stress Medicine, 15*(2), 89–101.

Halasz, P. (1993). Arousals without awakening: Dynamic aspect of sleep. *Physiology & Behavior, 54,* 795–802.

Halbertstadt, J., & Rhodes, G. (2000). The attractiveness of nonface averages: Implication for an evolutionary explanation of the attractiveness of average faces. *Psychological Science, 11,* 285–289.

Hale, S., Bronik, M., & Fry, A. (1997). Verbal and spatial working memory in school-age children:

Differences in susceptibility to interference. *Developmental Psychology, 33,* 364–371.

Haley, J. (1971). Family therapy: A radical change. In J. Haley (Ed.), *Changing families: A family therapy reader.* New York: Grune & Stratton.

Haley, J. (1976). *Problem-solving therapy.* San Francisco: Jossey-Bass.

Halford, G. (1989). Reflections on 25 years of Piagetian cognitive developmental psychology, 1963–1988. *Human Development, 32,* 325–357.

Hall, G. C. N., & Hirschman, R. (1991). Toward a theory of sexual aggression: A quadripartite model, *Journal of Consulting & Clinical Psychology, 662–669.*

Hall, G. S. (1904). *Adolescence: Its psychology and its relations to physiology, anthropology, sociology, sex, crime, religion, and education.* (Vols. 1–2.). New York: Appleton-Century-Crofts.

Hall, J. A. (1984). Nonverbal sex differences: *Communication accuracy and expressive style.* Baltimore: Johns Hopkins University Press.

Hallowell, A. I. (1955). *Culture and experience.* Philadelphia: University of Pennsylvania Press.

Halmi, K. A., Goldberg, S., & Cunningham, S. (1977). Perceptual distribution of body image in adolescent girls: Distortion of body image in adolescence. *Psychological Medicine, 7,* 253–257.

Halms, K. A. (1999). Eating disorders: Defining the phenotype and reinventing the treatment. *American Journal of Psychiatry, 156,* 1673–1675.

Hamermesh, D. S., & Biddle, J. E. (1994). Beauty and the labor market. *American Economic Review, 94,* 1174–1195.

Hamilton, D., & Sherman, J. (1994). Stereotypes. In R. S. Wyer, Jr., & T. K. Srull (Eds.), *Handbook of social cognition: Vol. 1. Basic processes* (2nd ed., pp. 1–68). Hillsdale, NJ: Erlbaum.

Hamilton, R. H., & Pascual-Leone, A. (1998). Cortical plasticity associated with Braille learning. *Trends in Cognitive Neuroscience, 2,* 168–174.

Hamilton, W. D. (1964). The genetical theory of social behavior. *Journal of Theoretical Biology, 6,* 1–52.

Hanin, B., Sprour, N., Margolin, J., & Braun, P. (1993). Electroconvulsive therapy in mania: Successful outcome despite short duration of convulsions. *Convulsive Therapy, 9,* 50–53.

Hansen, W. B., & O'Malley, P. M. (1996). Drug use. In R. J. DiClemente, W. B. Hansen, et al. (Eds.), *Handbook of adolescent health risk behavior. Issues in clinical child psychology* (pp. 161–192). New York: Plenum Press.

Harari, H., Harari, O., & White, R. V. (1985). The reaction to rape by American male bystanders. *Journal of Social Psychology, 125,* 653–658.

Harlow, H. F., & Zimmerman, R. R. (1959). Affectional responses in the infant monkey. *Science, 130,* 421–432.

Harlow, R., & Cantor, N. (1994). Personality as problem solving: A framework for the analysis of change in daily-life behavior. *Journal of Personality Integration, 4,* 355–386.

Harmon-Jones, E., & Allen, J. J. B. (1998). Anger and frontal brain activity: EEG asymmetry consistent with approach motivation despite negative affective valence. *Journal of Personality & Social Psychology, 74,* 1310–1316.

Harper, J. M., Schaalje, B. G., & Sandberg, J. G. (2000). Daily hassles, intimacy, and marital quality in later life marriages. *American Journal of Family Therapy, 28*(1), 1–18.

Harris, B. (1979). Whatever happened to little Albert? *American Psychologist, 34,* 151–160.

Harris, C. R., & Christenfeld, N. (1996). Gender, jealousy, and reason. *Psychological Science, 7,* 364–366.

Harris, J. E. (1980). Memory aids people use: Two interview studies. *Memory and Cognition, 8,* 31–38.

Harris, J. R. (1998). *The nurture assumption: Why children turn out the way they do.* New York: Free Press.

Harris, J. R. (2000). The outcome of parenting: What do we really know? *Journal of Personality, 68,* 625-637.

Harris, M. B., Walters, L. C., & Waschull, S. (1991). Gender and ethnic differences in obesity-related behaviors and attitudes in a college sample. *Journal of Applied Social Psychology, 21,* 1545–1566.

Harris, Y. H. (1995). *The opportunity for romantic love among hunter-gatherers.* Paper presented at the annual convention of the Human Behavior and Evolution Society, June, Santa Barbara, CA.

Hart, B., & Risley, T. (1992). American parenting of language-learning children: Persisting differences in family-child interactions observed in natural home environments. *Developmental Psychology, 28,* 1096–1105.

Harter, S. (1998) The development of self-representations. In W. Damon (Ed. in Chief) and N. Eisenberg (Vol. Ed.), *Handbook of Child Psychology, Vol. 3.* (pp. 553 618). New York: John Wiley.

Harter, S., & Monsour, A. (1992). Development analysis of conflict caused by opposing attributes in the adolescent self-portrait. *Developmental Psychology, 28,* 251–260.

Harter, S., Waters, P., & Whitesell, N. R. (1998). Relational self-worth: Differences in perceived worth as a person across interpersonal contexts among adolescents. *Child Development, 69,* 756-766.

Hartline, H. K. (1938). The response of single optic nerve fibers of the vertebrate eye to illuminate of the retina. *American Journal of Physiology, 121,* 400–415.

Hartmann, H. (1939). *Ego psychology and the problem of adaptation.* New York: International Universities Press.

Hartup, W. (1989). Social relationships and their developmental significance. *American Psychologist, 44,* 120–126.

Hartup, W. W. (1977). Aggression in childhood: Developmental perspectives. In M. Hertherington and D. Ross (Eds.), *Contemporary readings in child psychology.* New York: McGraw-Hill.

Hartup, W. W. (1996). The company they keep: Friendships and their developmental significance. *Child Development, 67,* 1–13.

Hartup, W. W. (1998). Cooperation, close relationships, and cognitive development. In W. M. Bukowski, A. F. Newcomb, et al. (Eds.), *The company they keep: Friendship in childhood and* adolescence. *Cambridge studies in social and emotional development* (pp. 213–237). New York: Cambridge University Press.

Hartup, W. W., & Stevens, N. (1997). Friendships and adaptation in the life course. *Psychological Bulletin, 121,* 355–370.

Harway, M. (2000). Families experiencing violence. In W. C. Nichols & M. A. Pace-Nichols (Eds.), *Handbook of family development and intervention. Wiley series in couples and family dynamics and treatment.* (pp. 391-414). New York: John Wiley & Sons, Inc

Harwood, R. L., Schoelmerich, A., Schulze, P. A., & Gonzalez, Z. (1999). Cultural differences in maternal beliefs and behaviors: A study of middle-class Anglo and Puerto Rican mother-infant pairs in four everyday situations. *Child Development, 70,* 1005–1016.

Harwood, R. L., Schoelmerich, A., Ventura-Cook, E., Schulze, P. A., & Wilson, S. P. (1996). Culture and class influence on Anglo and Puerto Rican mothers' beliefs regarding long-term socialization goals and child behavior. *Child Development, 67,* 2446–2461.

Haselton, M. G., & Buss, D. M. (2000). Error management theory: A new perspective on biases in cross-sex mind reading. *Journal of Personality and Social Psychology, 78,* 81–91.

Hasselhorn, M. (1990). The emergence of strategic knowledge activation in categorical clustering during retrieval. *Journal of Experimental Child Psychology, 50,* 59–80.

Hasselquist, D., & Bensch, S. (1991). Trade-off between mate guarding and mate attraction in the polygynous great reed warbler. *Behavioral Ecology and Sociobiology, 28,* 187–193.

Haugtvedt, C., & Petty, R. (1992). Personality and persuasion: Need for cognition moderates the persistence and resistance of attitude changes. *Journal of Personality and Social Psychology, 63,* 308–319.

Hauser, S. T., & Safyer, A. W. (1994). Ego development and adolescent emotions. *Journal of Research on Adolescence, 4,* 487-502.

Hay, D. F., Caplan, M., Castle, J., & Stimson, C. A. (1991). Does sharing become increasinngly "rational" in the second year of life? *Developmental Psychology, 27,* 987–993.

Hayes, S. C., & Wilson, K. (1994). Acceptance and commitment therapy: Altering the verbal support for experiential avoidance. Special section: Clinical behavior analysis. *Behavior Analysis, 17,* 289–303.

Hazan, C., & Diamond, L. M. (2000). The place of attachment in human mating. *Review of General Psychology, l 4,* 186-204.

Hazan, C., & Shaver, P. (1987). Romantic love conceptualized as an attachment process. *Journal of Personality and Social Psychology, 57,* 731–739.

Healy, A. F., & McNamara, D. S. (1996). Verbal learning and memory: Does the modal model still work? *Annual Review, 47,* 143–172.

Healy, S. D. (1996). Ecological specialization in the avian brain. In C. F. Moss, S. J. Shettleworth, et al. (Eds.), *Neuroethological studies of cognitive and*

perceptual processes (pp. 84–110). Boulder, CO: Westview Press.

Heath, A. C., Madden, P. A., Cloninger, C. R., & Martin, N. G. (1999). Genetic and environmental structure of personality. In C. R. Cloninger (Ed.), *Personality and psychopathology.* (pp. 343-367). Washington: American Psychiatric Press, Inc.

Heatherton, T. F., & Baumeister, R. F. (1991). Binge eating as escape from self-awareness. *Psychological Bulletin, 110*(1), 86–108.

Hebb, D. O. (1949). *The organization of behavior: A neuropsychological theory.* New York: Wiley.

Hebl, M. R., & Heatherton, T. F. (1998). The stigma of obesity in women: The difference is black and white. *Personality & Social Psychology Bulletin, 24,* 417–426.

Heckers, S., Goff, D., Schacter, D. L., Savage, C. R., Fischman, A. J., Alpert, N. M., & Rauch, S. L., (1999). Functional imaging of memory retrieval in deficit vs nondeficit schizophrenia. *Archives of General Psychiatry, 56,* 1117–1123.

Hedricks, C. A. (1994). Female sexual activity across the human menstrual cycle. *Annual Review of Sex Research, V,* 122–172.

Hegarty, J., Baldessarini, R., Tohen, M., Waternaux, C., & Oepen, G. (1994). One hundred years of schizophrenia: A meta-analysis of the outcome literature. *American Journal of Psychiatry, 151,* 1409–1416.

Heider, F. (1958). *The psychology of interpersonal relations.* New York: John Wiley.

Heine, S. J., & Lehman, D. R. (1997). Culture, dissonance, and self-affirmation. *Personality & Social Psychology Bulletin, 23,* 389–400.

Heller, D. (1986). *The children's God.* Chicago: University of Chicago Press.

Helmholtz, H. von. (1863). *Die Lehre von den tonempfindungen als physiolgisdne grundlage fur die theorie der musik.* Brunswick: Vierweg-Verlag.

Helson, R., & Klohnen, E. C. (1998). Affective coloring of personality from young adulthood to midlife. *Personality & Social Psychology Bulletin, 24,* 241–252.

Henderson, N. D. (1982). Human behavior genetics. *Annual Review of Psychology, 33,* 403–440.

Henss, R. (2000). Waste-to-hip ratio and female attractiveness. Evidence from photographic stimuli and methodological considerations. *Personality and Individual Differences, 28,* 501–513.

Herdt, G. (1997). *Same sex, different cultures: Gays and lesbians across cultures.* Boulder, CO: Westview Press.

Herdt, G. H. (Ed.). (1984). *Ritualized homosexuality in Melanesia.* Berkeley, CA: University of California Press.

Hering, E. (1878). *Zur lehre vom lichtsinne.* Vienna: Gerold.

Hering, E. (1920). *Grundzuge, der Lehr vs. Lichtsinn.* Berlin: Springer-Verlag.

Heritch, A., Henderson, K., & Westfall, T. (1990). Effects of social isolation on brain catecholamines and forced swimming in rats. *Journal of Psychiatric Research, 24,* 251–258.

Herman, J., Perry, J. C., & Van der Kolk, B. A.

(1989). Childhood trauma in borderline personality disorder. *American Journal of Psychiatry, 146,* 490–495.

Herman, J. L. (1992). *Trauma and recovery: The aftermath of violence—from domestic violence to political terror.* New York: Basic Books.

Herrigel, E. (1953). *Zen in the art of archery.* New York: Vintage Books.

Herrmann, D., McEvoy, C., Hertzod, C., Hertel, P., & Johnson, M. K. (Eds.). (1996). *Basic and applied memory research* (Vols. 1–2). Mahwah, NJ: Lawrence Erlbaum Associates.

Herrmann, D. J., Crawford, M., & Holdsworthy, M. (1992). Gender-linked differences in everyday memory performance. *British Journal of Psychology, 83,* 221–231.

Herrnstein, R. J. (1970). On the law of effect. *Journal of the Experimental Analysis of Behavior, 13,* 243–266.

Hersen, M., & Bellack, A. S. (Eds.). (1999). *Handbook of comparative interventions for adult disorders* (2nd ed.). New York: Wiley.

Hersey, P., & Blanchard, K. (1982). *Management of organizational behavior: Utilizing human resources* (2nd ed.). Englewood Cliffs, NJ: Prentice-Hall.

Herzog, D. B, Dorer, D. J, Keel, P. K, Selwyn, S. E., Ekeblad, E. R, Flores, A. T., Greenwood, D. N., Burwell, R. A., & Keller, M. B. (1999). Recovery and relapse in anorexia and bulimia nervosa: A 7.5-year follow-up study. *Journal of the American Academy of Child & Adolescent Psychiatry, 38,* 829-837.

Hess, E. H. (1959). Two conditions limiting critical age for imprinting. *Journal of Comparative and Physiological Psychology, 52,* 515-518

Hick, K. M., & Katzman, D. K. (1999). Self-assessment of sexual maturation in adolescent females with anorexia nervosa. *Journal of Adolescent Health, 24,* 206–211.

Hicks, R. A., & Pelligrini, R. (1991). The changing sleep habits of college students. *Perceptual & Motor Skills, 72,* 631–636.

Higgins, E. T. (1987). Self-discrepancy: A theory relating self and affect. *Psychological Review, 94,* 319–340.

Higgins, E. T. (1999). Self-discrepancy: A theory relating self and affect. In R. F. Baumeister (Ed.). *The self in social psychology. Key readings in social psychology.* (pp. 150-181). Philadelphia: Psychology Press/Taylor & Francis.

Higgins, E. T., & Bargh, J. A. (1987). Social cognition and social perception. *Annual Review of Psychology, 38,* 369–425.

Higley, J., Mehlman, P., Taub, D., Higley, S., Suomi, S., Linnoila, M., & Vickers, J. H. (1992). Cerebrospinal fluid momoamine and adrenal correlates of aggression in free-ranging rhesus monkeys. *Archives of General Psychiatry, 49,* 436–441.

Higley, J. D., Mehlman, P. T., Poland, R. E., Taub, D. M., Vickers, J., Suomi, S. J., & Linnoila, M. (1996). CSF testosterone and 5-HIAA correlate with different types of aggressive behaviors. *Biological Psychiatry, 40,* 1067–1082.

Hill, A. (1999). Phantom limb pain: A review of the literature on attributes and potential mechanisms. *Journal of Pain and Symptom Management, 17,* 125–412.

Hill, J. O., & Peters, J. C. (1998). Environmental contributions to the obesity epidemic. *Science, 280*(5368), 1371–1374.

Hilliard, R. B., Henry, W. P., & Strupp, H. H. (2000). An interpersonal model of psychotherapy: Linking patient and therapist developmental history, therapeutic process, and types of outcome. *Journal of Consulting and Clinical Psychology, 68,* 125–133.

Hillman, D. C., Siffre, M., Milano, G., & Halberg, F. (1994). Free-running psychophysiologic circadians and three-month pattern in a woman isolated in a cave. *New Trends in Experimental and Clinical Psychiatry, 10,* 127–133.

Hilgard, E. R. (1965). *Hypnotic susceptibility.* New York: Harcourt Brace Jovanovich.

Hilgard, E. R. (1986). *Divided consciousness: Multiple controls in human thought and action.* New York: John Wiley.

Hilgard, E. R., & Hilgard, J. R. (1975). *Hypnosis in the relief of pain.* Los Altos, CA: William Kaufman.

Hinde, R. (1982). *Ethology: Its nature and relations with other sciences.* New York: Oxford University Press.

Hirsch, J. (1997). Some history of heredity-vs-environment, genetic inferiority at Harvard (?), and the (incredible) Bell curve. *Genetica, 99,* 207–224.

Hirsch, J., & Knittle, J. L. (1970). Cellularity of obese and nonobese human adipose tissue. *Federation Proceedings, 29,* 1516–1521.

Hirshberg, L. M. (1990). When infants look to their parents: II Twelve-month-olds' response to conflicting parental emotional signals. *Child Development, 61,* 1187-1191.

Hirshman, E., & Henzler, A. (1998). The role of decision processes in conscious recollection. *Psychological Science, 9,* 61–65.

Hirst, W. (1994). The remembered self in amnesics. In U. Neisser & R. Fivush (Eds.), *The remembering self: Construction and accuracy in self-narrative* (pp. 252–277). New York: Cambridge University Press.

Hirt, E. R., Zillmann, D., Erickson, G. A., Kennedy, C. (1992). Costs and benefits of allegiance: Changes in fans' self-ascribed competencies after team victory versus defeat. *Journal of Personality & Social Psychology, 63,* 724–738.

Hittner, J. B. (1997). Alcohol-related outcome expectancies: Construct overview and implications for primary and secondary prevention. *Journal of Primary Prevention, 17,* 297–314.

Hobson, J. A. (1988). *The dreaming brain.* New York: Basic Books.

Hobson, J. A., & McCarley, R. W. (1977). The brain as a dream state generator: An activation-synthesis hypothesis of the dream process. *American Journal of Psychiatry, 134,* 1335-1348.

Hodges, E. V. E., & Perry, D. G. (1999). Personal and interpersonal antecedents and consequences of victimization by peers. *Journal of Personality & Social Psychology, 76,* 677–685.

Hoek, H. W. (1993). Review of the epidemiological studies of eating disorders. *International Review of Psychiatry, 5,* 61–74.

Hoff-Ginsberg, E. (1990). Maternal speech and the child's development of syntax: A further look. *Journal of Child Language, 17,* 85–99.

Hoff-Ginsberg, E., & Shatz, M. (1982). Linguistic input and the child's acquisition of language. *Psychological Review, 92,* 3–26.

Hoffman, L. (1981). *Foundations of family therapy.* New York: Basic Books.

Hoffman, L. (1991). A reflexive stance for family therapy. *Journal of Strategic and Systemic Therapies, 10,* 4–17.

Hoffman, M. A., & Levy-Shiff, R. (1994). Coping and locus of control: Cross-generational transmission between mothers and adolescents. *Journal of Early Adolescence, 14,* 391-405.

Hoffman, M. L. (1978). Psychological and biological perspectives on altruism. *International Journal of Behavioral Development, 1,* 323–339.

Hoffman, M. L. (1982). Development of prosocial motivation: Empathy and guilt. In N. Eisenberg (Ed.), *The development of prosocial behavior.* New York: Academic Press.

Hoffman, M.L. (2000) *Empathy and moral development: Implications for caring and justice.* New York: Cambridge University Press.

Hoffman, M. L., & Saltzstein, H. D. (1967). Parent discipline and the child's moral development. *Journal of Personality and Social Psychology, 5,* 45–47.

Hoffman, P. (1997). The endorphin hypothesis. In W. P. Morgan et al. (Eds.), *Physical activity and mental health. Series in health psychology and behavioral medicine* (pp. 163–177). Washington: Taylor & Francis.

Hofmann, S., & DiBartolo, P.M., Eds. (2001). *From social anxiety to social phobia: Multiple perspectives.* Boston: Allyn & Bacon.

Hogan, R. (1983). What every student should know about personality psychology. In A. M. Rogers & J. Scheirer (Eds.), *G. Stanley Hall lecture series,* (Vol. 6). Washington, DC: American Psychological Association.

Hogan, R. (1987). Personality psychology: Back to basics. In J. Aronoff et al. (Eds.), *The emergence of personality.* New York: Springer.

Hogan, R., Curphy, G., & Hogan, J. (1994). What we know about leadership: Effectiveness and personality. *American Psychologist, 49,* 493–304.

Hohmann, G. W. (1966). Some effects of spinal cord lesions on experienced emotional feelings. *Psychophysiology, 3,* 143–156.

Holahan, C. K., & Holahan, C. J. (1999). Being labeled as gifted, self-appraisal, and psychological well-being: A life span developmental perspective. *International Journal of Aging and Human Development, 48,* 161–173.

Holden, C. (1980). Identical twins reared apart. *Science, 207,* 1323–1325.

Holland, A. J., & Oliver, C. (1995). Down's syndrome and the links with Alzheimer's disease. *Journal of Neurology, Neurosurgery & Psychiatry, 59,* 111–114.

Holland, J., Holyoak, K., Nisbett, R., & Thagard, P. (1986). *Induction: Processes of inference, learning, and discovery.* Cambridge, MA: MIT Press.

Hollander, E., Stein, D. J., DeCaria, C. M., Cohen, L., Saoud, J. B., Skodol, A. E., Kellman, D., Rosnick, L., & Oldham, J. M. (1994). Serotonergic sensitivity in borderline personality disorder: Preliminary findings. *American Journal of Psychiatry, 151,* 277–280.

Hollis, K. L. (1997). Contemporary research on Pavlovian conditioning: A "new" functional analysis. *American Psychologist, 52,* 956–965.

Hollon, S. (1988). Cognitive therapy. In Lyn Y. Abramson (Ed.), *Social cognition and clinical psychology: A synthesis* (pp. 204–253). New York: Guilford Press.

Hollon, S. D., Shelton, R. C., & Davis, D. D. (1993). Cognitive therapy for depression: Conceptual issues and clinical efficacy. *Journal of Consulting & Clinical Psychology, 61,* 270-275.

Holmes, D. (1990). The evidence for repression: An examination of sixty years of research. In J. L. Singer, (Ed.), *Repression and dissociation: Implications for personality theory, psychopathology, and health* (pp. 85–102). Chicago, IL: University of Chicago Press.

Holmes, T. H., & Rahe, R. H. (1967). The social readjustment rating scale. *Journal of Psychosomatic Research, 11,* 213–218.

Holmgren, R. A., Eisenberg, N., & Fabes, R. A. (1998). The relations of children's situational empathy-related emotions to dispositional prosocial behaviour. *International Journal of Behavioral Development, 22,* 169-193.

Holscher, C., Anwyl, R., & Rowan, M. J., (1997). Stimulation on the positive phase of hippocampal theta rhythm induces long-term potentiation that can be depotentiated by stimulation on the negative phase in area C1 in vivo. *Journal of Neuroscience, 17,* 6470–6477.

Holt, R. (1976). Drive or wish? A reconsideration of the psychoanalytic theory of motivation. In M. Gill & P. Holzman (Eds.), *Psychology vs. metapsychology: Psychoanalytic essays in memory of George Klein. Psychological Issues,* Monograph 36, Vol. 9, No. 4.

Holt, R. R. (1985). The current status of psychoanalytic theory. *Psychoanalytic Psychology, 2,* 289–315.

Holyoak, K. J., & Simon, D. (1999). Bidirectional reasoning in decision making by constraint satisfaction. *Journal of Experimental Psychology: General, 128,* 3–31.

Holyoak, K. J., & Spellman, B. A. (1993). Thinking. *Annual Review of Psychology, 44,* 265–315.

Holyoak, K. J., & Thagard, P. (1995). *Mental leaps: Analogy in creative thought.* Cambridge: MIT Press.

Homans, G. (1961). *Social behavior: Its elementary forms.* London: Routledge & Kegan Paul.

Honeybourne, C., Matchett, G., & Davey, G. (1993). Expectancy models of laboratory preparedness effects: A UCS-expectancy bias in phylogenetic and ontogenetic fear-relevant stimuli. *Behavior Therapy, 24,* 253–264.

Hooks, M. S., Jones, G. H., Juncos, J. L., Neill, D. B., et al. (1994). Individual differences in schedule-induced and conditioned behaviors. *Behavioural Brain Research, 60,* 199–209.

Hooley, J., & Teasdale, J. D. (1989). Predictors of relapse in unipolar depressives: Expressed emotion, marital distress and perceived criticism. *Journal of Abnormal Psychology, 98,* 229–235.

Hooley, J. M. (1998). Expressed emotion and locus of control. *Journal of Nervous & Mental Disease, 186,* 374-378.

Hooley, J. M., & Hiller, J. B. (1998). Expressed emotion and the pathogenesis of relapse in schizophrenia. In M. F. Lenzenweger & R. H. Dworkin (Eds.), *Origins and development of schizophrenia: Advances in experimental psychopathology.* (pp. 447-468). Washington: American Psychological Association.

Horn, J. (1998). A basis for research on age differences in cognitive capabilities. In J. J. McArdle & R. W. Woodcock (Eds.). *Human cognitive abilities in theory and practice.* (pp. 57–91). Mahwah, NJ: Lawrence Erlbaum Associates.

Horn, J. C., & Meer, J. (1987). The vintage years. *Psychology Today, 21,* 76–90.

Horn, J. L. (1968). Organization of abilities and the development of intelligence. *Psychological Review, 75,* 242–259.

Horn, J. L., & Cattell, R. B. (1967). Age differences in fluid and crystallized intelligence. *Acta Psychologica, 26,* 107–129.

Horn, J. L., & Hofer, S. M. (1992). Major abilities and development in the adult period. In R. J. Sternberg & C. A. Berg (Eds.), *Intellectual development* (pp. 44–99). New York: Cambridge University Press.

Horn, J. L., & Noll, J. (1997). Human cognitive capabilities: gf-gc theory. In D. P. Flanagen, J. L. Genshaft, & P. L. Harrison (Eds.), *Contemporary intellectual assessment: Theories, tests and issues* (pp. 53–91). New York: Guilford Press.

Horn, J. M., Loehlin, J. C., & Willerman, L. (1979). Intellectual resemblance among adoptive and biological relatives: The Texas Adoption Project. *Behavior Genetics, 9,* 177–207.

Horner, T. M., & Chethik, L. (1986). Conversation attentiveness and following in 12- and 18-week-old infants. *Infant Behavior and Development, 9,* 203–213.

Horowitz, M. (1988). *Introduction to psychodynamics: A synthesis.* New York: Basic Books.

House, J. S., Landis, K. R., & Umberson, D. (1988a). Social relationships and health. *Science, 241,* 540–545.

House, J. S., Umberson, D., & Landis, K. R. (1988b). Structures and processes of social support. *American Review of Sociology, 14,* 293–318.

House, R. J. (1977). A 1976 theory of charismatic leadership. In J. G. Hunt & L. L. Larson (Eds.), *Leadership: The cutting edge* (pp. 189–207). Carbondale, IL: Southern Illinois University Press.

House, R. J., & Singh, J. V. (1987). Organizational behavior: Some new directions for I/O psychology. *Annual Review of Psychology, 38,* 669–718.

Hovland, C. (1937). The generalization of conditioned responses: IV. The effects of varying amounts of reinforcement upon the degree of generalization of conditioned responses. *Journal of General Psychology, 21,* 261–276.

Hovland, C. I., & Janis, I. (1959). *Personality and persuasibility.* New Haven, CT: Yale University Press.

Howard, K. I., Kopta, S. M., Krause, M. S., & Orlinsky, D. E. (1986). The dose-effect relationship in psychotherapy. *American Psychologist, 41,* 159–164.

Howard, K. I., Orlinsky, D. E., & Lueger, R. J. (1994). Clinically relevant outcome research in individual psychotherapy: New models guide the researcher and clinician. *British Journal of Psychiatry, 165,* 4-8.

Howard, W. T., Evans, K. K., Quintero-Howard, C. V., Bowers, W. A., & Andersen, A. E. (1999). Predictors of success or failure of transition to day hospital treatment for inpatients with anorexia nervosa. *American Journal of Psychiatry, 156,* 1697–1702.

Howes, C., & Hamilton, C. E. (1992). Children's relationships with child care teachers: Stability and concordance with parental attachments. *Child Development, 63,* 867–878.

Howes, C., Hamilton, C. E., & Philiopsen, L. C. (1998). Stability and comorbidity of child-caregiver and child-peer relationships. *Child Development, 69,* 418–426.

Hsu, F. L. K. (1981). *Americans and Chinese: Passage to difference* (3rd ed.). Honolulu: University Press of Hawaii.

Hsu, L. K. G. (1989). The gender gap in eating disorders: Why are the eating disorders more common among women. *Clinical Psychology Review, 9,* 393–407.

Hubel, D. H., & Wiesel, T. N. (1959). Receptive fields of single neurons in the cat's striate cortex. *Journal of Physiology, 148,* 574–591.

Hubel, D. H., & Wiesel, T. N. (1963). Single-cell responses in striate cortex of kittens deprived of vision in one eye. *Journal of Neuropsychology, 26,* 1003–1009.

Hubel, D. H., & Wiesel, T. N. (1979). Brain mechanisms of vision. *Scientific American, 241,* 150–162.

Hulka, B. S., & Meirik, O. (1996). Research on the menopause. *Maturitas, 23,* 109–112.

Hull, C. L. (1943). *Principles of behavior: An introduction to behavior theory.* New York: Oxford University Press.

Hull, C. L. (1952). *A behavior system: An introduction to behavior theory concerning the individual organism.* New Haven, CT: Yale University Press.

Hull, J. G., & Bond, C. F. (1986). Social and behavioral consequences of alcohol consumption and expectancy: A meta-analysis. *Psychological Bulletin, 99,* 347–360.

Hulme, C., Maughan, S., & Brown, G. D. A. (1991). Memory for familiar and unfamiliar words: Evidence for a long-term memory contribution to short-term memory span. *Journal of Memory and Language, 30,* 685–701.

Hultsch, D., & Dixon, R. (1990). Learning and memory in aging. In J. Birren & K. W. Schaie (Eds.), *Handbook of the psychology of aging* (3rd ed.). New York: Academic Press.

Hunter, J. E. (1997). Needed: A ban on the significance test. *Psychological Science, 8,* 3–7.

Hupka, R. B., Zaleski, Z., Otto, J., Reidl, L., et al. (1997). The colors of anger, envy, fear, and jealousy: A cross-cultural study. *Journal of Cross-Cultural Psychology, 28,* 156–171.

Hurvich, L. M., & Jameson, D. (1957). An opponent-process of color vision. *Psychological Review, 64,* 384–404.

Huston, A. C. (1983). Sex-typing. In M. Hetherington (Ed.), *Handbook of child psychology: Vol. 4. Social and personality development.* New York: John Wiley.

Huston, T. L. (1973). Ambiguity of acceptance, social desirability, and dating choice. *Journal of Experimental Social Psychology, 9,* 32–42.

Huston, T. L. (1994). Courtship antecedents of marital satisfaction and love. In R. Erber, R. Gilmour, et al. (Eds.), *Theoretical frameworks for personal relationships* (pp. 43–65). Hillsdale, NJ: Lawrence Erlbaum Associates.

Huttenlocher, J., & Hedges, L. V. (1994). Combining graded categories: Membership and typicality. *Psychological Review, 101,* 157–165.

Hyde, J. S. (1990). Meta-analysis and the psychology of gender differences. *Signs, 16,* 55–73.

Hyman, I. E., & Billings, F. J. (1998). Individual differences and the creation of false childhood memories. *Memory, 6,* 1–20.

Ikonomov, O. C., & Manji, H. K. (1999). Molecular mechanisms underlying mood stabilization in manic-depressive illness: The phenotype challenge. *American Journal of Psychiatry, 156,* 1506–1514.

Ilardi, S. S., & Craighead, W. E. (1999). The relationship between personality pathology and dysfunctional cognitions in previously depressed adults. *Journal of Abnormal Psychology, 108,* 51–57.

Impey, S., Smith, D. M., Obrietan, K., Donahue, R., Wade, C., & Storm, D. R. (1998). Stimulation of cAMP response element (CRE)-mediated transcription during contextual learning. *Nature Neuroscience, 1,* 595–601.

Inciardi, J. A., Surratt, H. L., & Saum, C. A. (1997). *Cocaine-exposed infants: Social, legal, and public health issues.* Thousand Oaks, CA: Sage Publications.

Inglehart, M. R. (1991). *Reactions to critical life events: A social psychological analysis.* New York: Praeger Publishers.

Inhelder, B., & Piaget, J. (1958). *The growth of logical thinking from childhood to adolescence.* New York: Basic Books.

Inkeles, A., & Smith, D. H. (1974). *Becoming modern: Individual change in six developing countries.* Cambridge, MA: Harvard University Press.

Innis, N. K. (1992). Early research on the inheritance of the ability to learn. *American Psycologist, 47,* 190–197.

Insko, C. A. (1964). Primacy versus recency in persuasion as a function of the timing of arguments and measures. *Journal of Abnormal and Social Psychology, 69,* 381–391.

Insko, C. A., Arkoff, A., & Insko, V. M. (1965).

Effects of high and low fear-arousing communications upon opinions toward smoking. *Journal of Experimental Social Psychology, 1,* 156–266.

Intons-Peterson, M. J., & Fournier, J. (1986). External and internal memory aids: When and how often do we use them? *Journal of Experimental Psychology, General, 115,* 267–280.

Irwin, M., Schafer, G., & Fieden, C. (1974). Emic and unfamiliar category sorting of Mano farmers and U.S. undergradutes. *Journal of Cross-Cultural Psychology, 5,* 407–423.

Irwin, M. H., & McLaughlin, D. H. (1970). Ability and preference in category sorting by Mano school children and adults. *Journal of Social Psychology, 82,* 15–24.

Isen, A. (1984). Toward understanding the role of affect in cognition. In R. S. Wyer, Jr. & T. K. Srull (Eds.), *Handbook of social cognition* (Vol. 3). Hillsdale, NJ: Erlbaum.

Isen, A. (1993). Positive affect and decision making. In M. Lewis, & J. M. Haviland (Eds.), *Handbook of emotions* (pp. 261–277). New York: Guilford.

Ishai, A., Ungerleier, L. G., Martin, A., Schouten, J. L., & Haxby, J. V. (1999). Distributed representation of objects in the human ventral visual pathway. *Proceedings of the National Academy of Science, USA, 96,* 9379–9384.

Islam, M. R., & Hewstone, M. (1993). Intergroup attributions and affective consequences in majority and minority groups. *Journal of Personality and Social Psychology, 64,* 936–950.

Ismail, B., Cantor-Graae, E., & McNeil, T. F. (1998). Minor physical anomalies in schizophrenic patients and their siblings. *American Journal of Psychiatry, 155,* 1695–1702.

Ito, T. A., Miller, N., & Pollock, V. E. (1996). Alcohol and aggression: A meta-analysis on the moderating effects of inhibitory cues, triggering events, and self-focused attention. *Psychological Bulletin, 120,* 60–82.

Iyengar, S. S., & Lepper, M. R. (1999). Rethinking the value of choice: A cultural perspective on intrinsic motivation. *Journal of Personality & Social Psychology, 76,* 349-366.

Izard, C. (1990). Facial expressions and the regulation of emotions. *Journal of Personality and Social Psychology, 58,* 487–498.

Izard, C. E. (1971). *The face of emotion.* New York: Appleton.

Izard, C. E. (1977). *Human emotions.* New York: Plenum Press.

Izard, C. E. (1997). *Emotions and facial expressions: A perspective from Differential Emotions Theory.* New York: Cambridge University Press.

Izard, C. E., & Buechler, S. (1980). Aspects of consciousness and personality in terms of differential emotions theory. In R. Plutchik & H. Kellerman (Eds.), *Emotion: Theory, research, and experience: Vol. I. Theories of emotion.* New York: Academic Press.

Izquierdo, I., & Medina, J. H. (1997). The biochemistry of memory formation and its regulation by hormones and neuromodulators. *Psychobiology, 25,* 1–9.

Jablenski, A. (1989). Epidemiology and cross-cul-

tural aspects of schizophrenia. *Psychiatric Annals, 19,* 516–524.

Jackendoff, R. (1996). The architecture of the linguistic-spatial interface. In P. Bloom, M. A. Peterson, et al. (Eds.), *Language and space. Language, speech, and communication* (pp. 1–30). Cambridge: MIT Press.

Jacklin, C. (1989). Female and male: Issues of gender. *American Psychologist, 44,* 127–133.

Jacobs, T. J., & Charles, E. (1980). Life events and the occurrence of cancer in children. *Psychosomatic Medicine, 42,* 11–24.

Jacobsen, L. K., Staley, J. K., Malison, R. T., Zoghbi, S. S., Seibyl, J. P., Kosten, T. R., & Innis, R. B. (2000). Elevated central serotonin transporter binding availability in acutely abstinent cocaine-dependent patients. *American Journal of Psychiatry, 157,* 1134–1140.

Jacobsen, T., & Hofmann, V. (1997). Children's attachment representations: Longitudinal relations to school behavior and academic competency in middle childhood and adolescence. *Developmental Psychology, 33,* 703–710.

Jacobson, E. (1964). The self and the object world. *Psychoanalytic Study of the Child, 9,* 75–127.

Jacobson, J. L., Jacobsen, S. W., Sokol, R. J., & Martier, S. S. (1993). Teratogenic effects of alcohol on infant development. *Alcoholism: Clinical and Experimental Research, 17,* 174–183.

Jacobson, N. S., Christensen, A., Prince, S. E., Cordova, J., & Eldridge, K. (2000). Integrative behavioral couple therapy: An acceptance-based, promising new treatment for couple discord. *Journal of Consulting and Clinical Psychology, 68,* 351–355.

Jacobson, N. S., Roberts, L. J., Berns, S. B., & McGlinchey, J. B. (1999). Methods for defining and determining the clinical significance of treatment effects: Description, application, and alternatives. *Journal of Consulting and Clinical Psychology, 67,* 300–307.

Jacoby, L. L., & Kelley, C. M. (1987). Unconscious influences of memory for a prior event. *Personality and Social Psychology Bulletin, 13,* 314–336.

Jacques, E. (1965). Death and the mid-life crisis. *International Journal of Psychoanalysis, 46,* 502–514.

Jaeger, T., & van der Kooy, D. (1996). Separate neural substrates mediate the motivating and discriminative properties of morphine. *Behavioral Neuroscience, 110,* 181–201.

Jaffee, S., & Hyde, J. S. (2000). Gender differences in moral orientation: A meta-analysis. *Psychological Bulletin, 126,* 703-726.

Jahoda, M. (1988). Opening address: The range of convenience of personal construct psychology—an outsider's view. In F. Fransella & L. F. Thomas (Eds.), *Experimenting with personal construct psychology.* (pp. 1-14). London: Routledge & Kegan Paul, Inc.

James, W. (1884). What is emotion? *Mind, 19,* 188–205.

James, W. (1890). *Principles of psychology* (Vol. 1). New York: Henry Holt.

James, W. (1902). *Varieties of religious experience.* New York: American Library, 1958.

James, W. (1910). The self. *In Psychology: The briefer course.* New York: Henry Holt and Co. Reprinted in C. Gordon & K. J. Gergen, *The self in social interaction,* 1968. New York: John Wiley.

Jang, K. L., McCrae, R., Angleitner, A., Reimann, R., & Livesley, W. J. (1998). Heritability of facet-level traits in a cross-cultural twin sample: Support for a hierarchical model of personality. *Journal of Personality and Social Psychology, 74,* 1556–1575.

Jangid, R. K., Vyas, J. N., & Shukla, T. R. (1988). The effects of the transcendental meditation programme on the normal individuals. *Journal of Personality and Clinical Studies, 4,* 145–149.

Janoff-Bulman, R. (1992). *Shattered assumptions: Towards a new psychology of trauma.* New York: Free Press.

Janowitz, H. D., & Grossman, M. I. (1949). Some factors affecting the food intake of normal dogs and dogs esophagostomy and gastric fistula. *American Journal of Physiology, 159,* 143–148.

Jarvis, W. B. G., & Petty, R. E. (1996). The need to evaluate. *Journal of Personality and Social Psychology, 70,* 172–194.

Jasmos, T. M., & Hakmiller, K. I. (1975). Some effects of lesion level, and emotional cues of affective expression in spinal cord patients. *Psychological Reports, 37,* 859–870.

Jeffery, K. J. (1997). LTP and spatial learning—where to next? *Hippocampus, 7,* 95–110.

Jemmott, J. B., III, Boryseko, J. Z., Borysenko, M., McClelland, D. C., Chapman, R., Meyer, D., & Benson, H. (1983). Academic stress, power motivation, and decrease in salivary secretory immunoglobulin A secretion rate. *Lancet, 1,* 1400–1402.

Jencks, C. (1998). Racial bias in testing. In C. Jencks & M. Phillips (Eds.), *The Black-White test score gap* (pp. 55–85). Washington, DC: Brookings Institution.

Jencks, C., & Phillips, M. (1998). *The Black-White test score gap.* Washington, DC: Brookings Institution.

Jenike, M., Baer, L., Ballantine, T., & Martuza, R. (1991). Cingulotomy for refractory obsessive-compulsive disorder: A long-term follow-up of 33 patients. *Archives of General Psychiatry, 48,* 548–555.

Jenike, M. A. (1983). Obsessive compulsive disorder. *Comprehensive Psychiatry, 24,* 99–111.

Jenkins, J. H., & Karno, M. (1992). The meaning of expressed emotion: Theoretical issues raised by cross-cultural research. *American Journal of Psychiatry, 149,* 9–21.

Jensen, A. R. (1969). How much can we boost IQ and scholastic achievement? *Harvard Educational Review, 39,* 1–123.

Jensen, A. R. (1973). *Educability and group differences.* New York: Harper & Row.

Jensen, A. R. (1998). Jensen on "Jensenism." *Intelligence, 26,* 181–208.

Jewesbury, E. C. O. (1951). Insensitivity to pain. *Brain, 74,* 336–353.

Jockin, V., McGue, M., & Lykken, D. (1996). Personality and divorce: A genetic analysis. *Journal of Personality and Social Psychology, 71,* 288–299.

John, O., & Robins, R. (1994). Accuracy and bias in self-perception: Individual differences in self-enhancement and the role of narcissism. *Journal of Personality and Social Psychology, 66,* 206–219.

John, O. P. (1990). The big five factor taxonomy: Dimensions of personality in the natural language and in questionnaires. In L. Pervin (Ed.), *Handbook of personality: Theory and research* (pp. 66–100). New York: Guilford Press.

John, O. P., & Srivastava, S. (1999). The Big Five Trait taxonomy: History, measurement, and theoretical perspectives. In L. A. Pervin & O. P. John (Eds.), *Handbook of personality: Theory and research* (2nd ed.). (pp. 102-138). New York: The Guilford Press.

Johnson, J. V., Stewart, W., Hall, E. M., Fredlund, P., et al. (1996a). Long-term psychosocial work environment and cardiovascular mortality among Swedish men. *American Journal of Public Health, 86,* 324–331.

Johnson, K., Churchill, L., Klitenick, M. A., & Hooks, M. S. (1996b). Involvement of the ventral tegmental area in locomotion elicited from the nucleus accumbens or ventral pallidum. *Journal of Pharmacology & Experimental Therapeutics, 277,* 1122–1131.

Johnson, K. O., & Lamb, G. H. (1981). Neural mechanisms of spatial tactile discrimination: Neural patterns evoked by Braille-like dot patterns in the monkey. *Journal of Physiology, 310,* 117–144.

Johnson, M. K., Kim, J. K., & Risse, G. (1985). Do alcoholic Korsakoff's syndrome patients acquire affective reactions? *Journal of Experimental Psychology: Learning, Memory, & Cognition, 11,* 22–36.

Johnson, R., & Murray, F. (1992). Reduced sensitivity of penile mechanoreceptors in aging rats with sexual dysfunction. *Brain Research Bulletin, 28,* 61–64.

Johnson, S. L., & Jacob, T. (2000). Sequential interactions in the marital communication of depressed men and women. *Journal of Consulting & Clinical Psychology, 68,* 4-12.

Johnson, S. L., & Miller, I. (1997). Negative life events and time to recovery from episodes of bipolar disorder. *Journal of Abnormal Psychology, 106,* 449-457.

Johnson-Laird, P. N. (1995). Mental models, deductive reasoning, and the brain. In M. S. Gazzaniga et al. (Eds.), *The cognitive neurosciences* (pp. 999–1008). Cambridge: MIT Press.

Johnson-Laird, P. N. (1996). The process of deduction. In D. Steier & T. M. Mitchell (Eds.), *Mind matters: A tribute to Allen Newell. Carnegie Mellon Symposia on cognition* (pp. 363–399). Hollsdale, NJ: Lawrence Erlbaum Associates.

Johnson-Laird, P. N. (1999). Deductive reasoning. *Annual Review of Psychology, 50,* 109–135.

Johnson-Laird, P. N., Legrenzi, P., Girotto, V., & Legrenzi, M. S. (2000). Illusions in reasoning about consistency. *Science, 288,* 531–532.

Johnson-Laird, P. N., Legrenzi, P., & Legrenzi, M. S. (1972). Reasoning and a sense of reality. *British Journal of Psychology, 63,* 395–400.

Joiner, T. E. (2000). Depression's vicious scree: Self-propagating and erosive processes in depression chronicity. *Clinical Psychology—Science and Practice, 7,* 203–218.

Jones, E. G. (2000). Cortical and subcortical contributions to activity-dependent plasticity in primate somatosensory cortex. *Annual Review of Neuroscience, 23,* 1–37.

Jones, K. L., Smith, D. W., Ulleland, C. N., & Streissguth, A. (1973). Pattern of malformation in offspring of chronic alcoholic mothers. *Lancet, 1,* 1267–1271.

Jones, M. C., & Mussen, P. H. (1958). Self-conceptions, motivations, and interpersonal attitudes of early- and late-maturing girls. *Child Development, 29,* 491-501.

Josephson, B. R., Singer, J. A., & Salovey, P. (1996). Mood regulation and memory: Repairing sad moods with happy memories. *Cognition & Emotion, 10,* 437-444.

Judd, C. M., & Park, B. (1988). Out-group homogeneity: Judgments of variability at the individual and group levels. *Journal of Personality and Social Psychology, 54,* 778–788.

Jung, C. G. (1923). *Psychological types.* New York: Pantheon Books.

Jung, C. G. (1961). *Memories, dreams, reflections.* New York: Random House.

Jung, C. G. (1968). *Analytical psychology: Its theory and practice.* New York: Vintage Books.

Jusczyk, P. W., Houston, D. M., & Newsome, M. (1999). The beginnings of word segmentation in English-learning infants. *Cognitive Psychology, 39,* 159–207.

Just, M. A., & Carpenter, P. A. (1992). A capacity theory of comprehension: Individual differences in working memory. *Psychological Review, 99,* 122–149.

Kaas, J. H. (1987). Somatosensory cortex. In G. Adelman (Ed.), *Encyclopedia of neuroscience* (Vol. 2). Boston: Birkhauser.

Kagan, J. (1976). Emergent themes in human development. *American Scientist, 64,* 186–196.

Kagan, J. (1983). Stress and coping in early development. In N. Garmezy & M. Rutter (Eds.), *Stress, coping, and development in children.* New York: McGraw-Hill.

Kagan, J. (1984). *The nature of the child.* New York: Basic Books.

Kagan, J. (1989). Temperamental contributions to social behavior. *American Psychologist, 44,* 668–674.

Kagan, J., Kearsley, R. B., & Zelazo, P. R. (1978). *Infancy: Its place in human development.* Cambridge, MA: Harvard University Press.

Kagan, J., & Snidman, N. (1991). Temperamental factors in human development. *American Psychologist, 46,* 856–862.

Kagan, J., & Zentner, M. (1996). Early childhood predictors of adult psychopathology. *Harvard Review of Psychiatry, 3,* 341-350.

Kahn, R. S., Davidson, M., & Davis, K. L. (1996). Dopamine and schizophrenia revisted. In S. J. Watson et al. (Eds.), *Biology of schizophrenia and affective disease.* (pp. 369–391). Washington: American Psychiatric Press.

Kahn, S., Zimmerman, G., Csikszentmihalyi, M., & Getzels, J. (1985). Relations between identity in young adulthood and intimacy at midlife. *Journal of Personality and Social Psychology, 49,* 1316–1322.

Kahneman, D., & Tversky, A. (1979). Prospect theory: An analysis of decision under risk. *Econometrica, 47,* 263–291.

Kail, R. (1991a). Developmental change in speed of processing during childhood and adolescence. *Psychological Bulletin, 109,* 490–501.

Kail, R. (1991b). Processing time declines exponentially during childhood and adolescence. *Developmental Psychology, 27,* 259–266.

Kail, R. (2000). Speed of information processing: Developmental change and links to intelligence. *Journal of School Psychology, 38,* 51–61.

Kail, R., & Pelligrino, J. W. (1985). *Human intelligence: Perspectives and prospects.* New York: Freeman.

Kalamas, A. D., & Gruber, M. L. (1998). Electrodermal responses to implied versus actual violence on television. *Journal of General Psychology, 125*(1), 31–37.

Kalick, S. M., Zebrowitz, L. A., Langlois, J. H., & Johnson, R. M. (1998). Does human facial attractiveness honestly advertise health? Longitudinal data on an evolutionary question. *Psychological Science, 9,* 8–13.

Kalter, N. (1990). *Growing up with divorce: Helping your child avoid immediate and later emotional problems.* New York: Free Press; London: Collier Macmillan.

Kamen, L. P., & Seligman, M. E. P. (1987). Explanatory style and health. *Current Psychological Research & Reviews, 6,* 207–218.

Kamil, A. C., & Jones, J. E. (1997). The seed-storing corvid Clark's nutcracker learns geometric relationships among landmarks. *Nature, 390,* 276–279.

Kamin, L. J. (1969). Predictability, surprise, attention, and conditioning. In B. A. Campbell & R. M. Church (Eds.), *Punishment and aversive behavior.* New York: Appleton-Century-Crofts.

Kamin, L. J. (1974). *The science and politics of I.Q.* Hillsdale, NJ: Erlbaum.

Kaminer, Y., & Hrecznyj, B. (1991). Lysergic acid diethylamide-induced chronic visual disturbances in an adolescent. *Journal of Nervous and Mental Disease, 179,* 173–174.

Kandel, E. R. (1998). A new intellectual framework for psychiatry. *American Journal of Psychiatry, 155,* 457–469.

Kandel, E. R. (1999). Biology and the future of psychoanalysis: A new intellectual framework for psychiatry revisited. *American Journal of Psychiatry, 156,* 505–524.

Kanizsa, G. (1976). Subjective contours. *Scientific American, 234,* 48–52.

Kanner, A. D., Coyne, J. C., Schaefer, C., & Lazarus, R. S. (1981). Comparison of two modes of stress measurement: Daily hassles and uplifts versus major life events. *Journal of Behavioral Medicine, 491,* 1–39.

Kanwisher, N., McDermott, J., & Chun, M. M. (1997). The fusiform face area: A module in human extrastriate cortex specialized for face perception. *Journal of Neuroscience, 17,* 4302–4311.

Kaplan, J. P. (1996). Psychologists' attitudes towards corporal punishment. *Dissertation Abstracts International: Section B: the Sciences & Engineering, 56,* 5151.

Kaplan, J. S., & Sue, S. (1997). Ethnic psychology in the United States. In D. F. Halpern & A. E. Voiskounsky (Eds.), *States of mind: American and post-Soviet perspectives on contemporary issues in psychology.* (pp. 342-369). New York: Oxford University Press.

Kapur, S., Tulving, E., Cabeza, R., & McIntosh, A. R. (1996). The neural correlates of intentional learning of verbal materials: A PET study in humans. *Cognitive Brain Research, 4,* 243–249.

Kapur, S., Zipursky, R., Jones, C., Remington, G., & Houle, S. (2000). Relationship between dopamine D-sub-2 occupancy, clinical response, and side effects: A double-blind PET study of first-episode schizophrenia. *American Journal of Psychiatry, 157,* 514–520.

Kardiner, A. (1945). *The psychological frontiers of society.* New York: Columbia University Press.

Karney, B. R., & Bradbury, T. N. (2000). Attributions in marriage: State or trait? A growth curve analysis. *Journal of Personality & Social Psychology, 78,* 295-309.

Karni, A., Tanne, D., Rubenstien, B. S., & Askenasy, J. J. M. (1994). Dependence on REM sleep of overnight improvement of a perceptual skill. *Science, 265,* 679–682.

Kassin, S., & Kiechel, K. (1996). The social psychology of false confessions: Compliance, internationalization, and confabulation. *Psychologial Science, 7,* 125–128.

Katahn, M., & McMinn, M. (1990). Obesity: A biobehavioral point of view. *Annals of the New York Academy of Arts and Sciences, 602,* 189–204.

Katigbak, M., Church, A. T., & Akamine, T. (1996). Cross-cultural generalizability of personality dimensions: Relating indigenous and imported dimensions in two cultures. *Journal of Personality and Social Psychology, 70,* 99–114.

Katz, H., & Beilin, H. (1976). A test of Bryant's claims concerning the young children's understanding of quantitative invariance. *Child Development, 47,* 877–880.

Katz, I., & Hass, R. (1988). Racial ambivalence and American value conflict: Correlational and priming studies of dual cognitive structures. *Journal of Personality and Social Psychology, 55,* 893–905.

Katz, J., & Melzack, R. (1990). Pain "memories" in phantom limbs: Review and clinical observations. *Pain, 43,* 319–336.

Kaufman, L., & Rock, I. (1989). The moon illusion thirty years later. In M. Hershenson (Ed.), *The moon illusion* (pp. 193–234). Hillsdale, NJ: Erlbaum.

Kawakami, K., Dovidio, J. F., Moll, J., Hermsen, S., & Russin, A. (2000). Just say no (to stereotyping): Effects of training in the negation of stereotypic associations on stereotype activation. *Journal of Personality and Social Psychology, 78*(5), 871–888.

Kaye, W. H, Gendall, K., Strober, M. (1998) Serotonin neuronal function and selective serotonin reuptake inhibitor treatment in anorexia and bulimia nervosa. *Biological Psychiatry, 44,* 825-838.

Kazdin, A. E. (1999). The meanings and measurement of clinical significance. *Journal of Consulting and Clinical Psychology, 67,* 332–339.

Kazdin, A. E., & Tuma, A. H. (1982). *Single-case research designs.* San Francisco: Jossey-Bass.

Keel, P. K, & Mitchell, J. E. (1997). Outcome in bulimia nervosa. *American Journal of Psychiatry, 154,* 313-321.

Keesey, R. E., & Corbett, S. W. (1984). Metabolic defense of the body weight set-point. In A. J. Stunkard & E. Stellar (Eds.), *Eating and its disorders.* New York: Raven Press.

Keesey, R. E., & Powley, T. L. (1986). The regulation of body weight. *Annual Review of Psychology, 37,* 109–134.

Keller, L. S., & Butcher, J. N. (1991). Assessment of chronic pain patients with the MMPI-2. Minneapolis: University of Minnesota Press.

Kelley, H. H. (1973). The process of causal attribution. *American Psychologist, 28,* 107–128.

Kelley, H. H. (1979). *Personality relationships.* Hillsdale, NJ: Erlbaum.

Kelley, H. H. (1992). Common-sense psychology and scientific psychology. *Annual Review of Psychology, 43,* 1–23.

Kelley, H. H., & Thibaut, J. W. (1978). *Interpersonal relations: A theory of interdependence.* New York: Wiley.

Kelley, J. E., Lumley, M. A., & Leisen, J. C. C. (1997). Health effects of emotional disclosure in rheumatoid arthritis patients. *Health Psychology, 16,* 331–340.

Kelley, S. A., Brownell, C. A., & Campbell, S. B. (2000). Mastery motivation and self-evaluative affect in toddlers: Longitudinal relations with maternal behavior. *Child Development, 71,* 1061–1071.

Kelly, G. A., (1955) *Psychology of personal constructs.* New York: W. W. Norton.

Keltner, D., & Bonanno, G. A. (1997). A study of laughter and dissociation: Distinct correlates of laughter and smiling during bereavement. *Journal of Personality and Social Psychology, 73,* 687–702.

Keltner, D., Kring, A. M., & Bonanno, G. A. (1999). Fleeting signs of the course of life: Facial expression and personal adjustment. *Current Directions in Psychological Science, 8,* 18–22.

Kemeny, M. E., & Laudenslager, M. L. (1999). Beyond stress: The role of individual difference factors in psychoneuroimmunology. *Brain, Behavior and Immunity, 13*(2), 73–75.

Kenardy, J., Evans, L., & Tian, P. (1992). The latent structure of anxiety symptoms in anxiety disorders. *American Journal of Psychiatry, 149,* 1058–1061.

Kendall, P. C. (1993). Treating anxiety disorders in children: Results of a randomized clinical trial. *Journal of Consulting and Clinical Psychology, 62,* 100–110.

Kendall, P. C. (1998). Empirically supported psy-

chological therapies. *Journal of Consulting & Clinical Psychology, 66,* 3–6.

Kendall, P. C. (1999). Clinical significance. *Journal of Consulting and Clinical Psychology, 67,* 283–284.

Kendall, P. C., Marrs-Garcia, A., Nath, S. R., & Sheldrick, R. C. (1999). Normative comparisons for the evaluation of clinical significance. *Journal of Consulting and Clinical Psychology, 67,* 285–299.

Kendler, K., MacLean, C., Neale, M., Kessler, R., Heath, A., & Eaves, L. (1991). The genetic epidemiology of bulimia nervosa. *American Jounal of Psychiatry, 148,* 1627–1637.

Kendler, K., Neale, M., Kessler, R., Heath, A., & Eaves, L. (1992b). The genetic epidemiology of phobias in women: The interrelationship of agoraphobia, social phobia, situational phobia, and simple phobia. *Archives of General Psychiatry, 49,* 273–281.

Kendler, K. S. (1995). Adversity, stress and psychopathology: A psychiatric genetic perspective. *International Journal of Methods in Psychiatric Research, 5,* 163-170.

Kendler, K. S., & Gardner, C. O., Jr. (1998). Boundaries of major depression: An evaluation of DSM-IV criteria. *American Journal of Psychiatry, 155,* 172–177.

Kendler, K. S., Gardner, C. O., & Prescott, C. A. (1999a). Clinical characteristics of major depression that predict risk of depression in relatives. *Archives of General Psychiatry, 56,* 322–327.

Kendler, K. S., Karkowski, L. M., Neale, M. C., & Prescott, C. A. (2000). Illicit psychoactive substance use, heavy use, abuse and dependence in a U.S. population-based sample of male twins. Archives of General Psychiatry, 57, 261–269.

Kendler, K. S., Karkowski, L. M., & Prescott, C. A. (1999b). Causal relationship between stressful life events and the onset of major depression. *American Journal of Psychiatry, 156,* 837–848.

Kendler, K. S., Myers, J. M., O'Neill, F. A., Martin, R., Murphy, B., MacLean, C. J., Walsh, D., & Straub, R. E. (2000). Clinical features of schizophrenia and linkage to chromosomes 5q, 6p, 8p, and 10p in the Irish Study of High Density Schizophrenia Families. *American Journal of Psychiatry, 157,* 402–408.

Kendler, K. S., Neale, M. C., Heath, A. C., Kessler, R. C., & Eaves, L. J. (1994). A twinfamily study of alcoholism in women. *American Journal of Psychiatry, 151,* 707–715.

Kendler, K. S., Neale, M. C., Kessler, R.C., & Heath, A. C. (1993). A test of the equal-environment assumption in twin studies of psychiatric illness. *Behavior Genetics, 23,* 21–27.

Kendler, K. S., Walters, E. E., Neale, M. C., Kessler, R. C., Heath, A. C., & Eaves, L. J. (1995). The structure of the genetic and environmental risk factors for six major psychiatric disorders in women: Phobia, generalized anxiety disorder, panic disorder, bulimia, major depression, and alcoholism. *Archives of General Psychiatry, 52,* 374–383.

Kenealy, P. M. (1997). Mood-state-dependent retrieval: The effects of induced mood on memory reconsidered. *Quarterly Journal of Experimental Psychology: Human Experimental Psychology, 50,* 290–317.

Kenrick, D., & Keefe, R. (1992). Age preferences in mates reflect sex differences in human reproductive strategies. *Behavioral and Brain Sciences, 15,* 75–113.

Kenrick, D., Groth, G., Trost, M., & Sadalla, E. (1993). Integrating evolutionary and social exchange perspectives on relationships: Effects of gender, self-appraisal, and involvement level on mate selection criteria. *Journal of Personality and Social Psychology, 64,* 951–969.

Kenrick, D. T., & Stringfield, D. O. (1980). Personality traits and the eye of the beholder: Crossing some traditional philosophical boundaries in the search for consistency in all of the people. *Psychological Review, 87,* 88–104.

Kernberg, O. (1975). *Borderline conditions and pathological narcissism.* New York: Aronson.

Kernberg, O. (1984). *Severe personality disorders: Psychotherapeutic strategies.* New Haven, CT: Yale University Press.

Kernberg, O. F., Selzer, M. A., Koenigsberg, H. W., Carr, A. C., & Appelbaum, A. H. (1989). *Psychodynamic psychotherapy of borderline patients.* New York: Basic Books.

Kerr, N. H., Foulkes, D., & Jurkovic, G. J. (1978). Reported absence of visual dream imagery in a normally sighted subject with Turner's syndrome. *Journal of Mental Imagery, 2,* 247-264.

Kessler, R. C., House, J. S., & Turner, J. B. (1987a). Unemployment and health in a community sample. *Journal of Health and Social Behavior, 28,* 51–59.

Kessler, R. C., McGonagle, K. A., Zhao, S., Nelson, C. B., Hughes, M., Eshleman, S., Wittchen, H., & Kendler, K. S. (1994). Lifetime and 12-month prevalence of DSM-III-R psychiatric disorders in the United States. *Archives of General Psychiatry, 51,* 8–19.

Kessler, R. C., Price, R. H., & Wortman, C. B. (1985). Social factors in psychopathology: Stress, social support, and coping processes. *Annual Review of Psychology, 36,* 531–572.

Kessler, R. C., Stein, M. B., & Berglund, P. (1998). Social phobia subtypes in the National Comorbidity Survey. *American Journal of Psychiatry, 155,* 613–619.

Kessler, R. C., Turner, J. B., & House, J. S. (1987b). Intervening processes in the relationship between unemployment and health. *Psychological Medicine, 17,* 949–961.

Kessler, R. C., Turner, J. B., & House, J. S. (1989). Unemployment, reemployment, and emotional functioning in a community sample. *American Sociological Review, 54,* 648–657.

Kessler, R. C., Zhao, S., Katz, S. J., Kouzis, A. C., Frank, R. G., Edlund, M., & Leaf, P. (1999). Past-year use of outpatient services for psychiatric problems in the National Comorbidity Survey. *American Journal of Psychiatry, 156,* 115–123.

Ketelaar, T., & Ellis, B. J. (2000). Are evolutionary explanations unfalsifiable? Evolutionary psychology and the Lakotosian philosophy of science. *Psychological Inquiry, 11,* 1–21.

Kety, S. S., Rosenthal, D., Wender, P. H., Schulsinger, F., & Jacobsen, B. (1975). Mental illness in the biological and adoptive families of adopted individuals who have become schizophrenic: A preliminary report based on psychiatric interviews. In Fieve, Rosenthal, & Brill (Eds.), *Genetic research in psychiatry.* Baltimore, MD: Johns Hopkins University Press.

Kihlstrom, J. F. (1987). The cognitive unconscious. *Science, 237,* 1445–1452.

Kihlstrom, J. F. (1996). Unconscious processes in social interaction. In S. R. Hameroff, A. W. Kasniak, & A. C. Scott (Eds.), *Toward a science of consciousness: The first Tucson discussions and debates. Complex adaptive systems* (pp. 93–104). Cambridge: MIT Press.

Kihlstrom, J. F., & Cantor, N. (1983). Mental representations of the self. In L. Berkowitz (Ed.), *Advances in experimental social psychology* (Vol. 15). New York: Academic Press.

Killackey, H. P. (1995). Evolution of the human brain: A neuroanatomical perspective. In M. S. Gazzaniga (Ed.), *The cognitive neurosciences* (pp. 1243–1253). Cambridge, MA: MIT Press.

Kim, H., & Markus, H. R. (1999). Deviance or uniqueness, harmony or conformity? A cultural analysis. *Journal of Personality and Social Psychology, 77*(4), 785–800.

Kim, J. J., & Fanselow, M. S. (1992). Modality-specific retrograde amnesia of fear. *Science, 256,* 675–677.

Kim, J. M. S., Andreasen, N. C., O'Leary, D. S., Watkins, G. L., Ponto, L. L. B., & Hichwa, R. D. (2000). Regional neural dysfunctions in chronic schizophrenia studied with positron emission tomography. *American Journal of Psychiatry, 157,* 542–548.

Kimble, D. P. (1992). *Biological psychology* (2nd ed.). Ft. Worth: Harcourt Brace Jovanovich.

Kimura, D. (1987). Are men's and women's brains really different? *Canadian Psychology, 28,* 133–148.

King, A. J., & Carlile, S. (1995). Neural coding for auditory space. In M. S. Gazzaniga et al. (Eds.), *The cognitive neurosciences* (pp. 279–293). Cambridge: MIT Press.

King, H. E. (1961). Psychological effects of excitation in the limbic system. In D. E. Sheer (Ed.), *Electrical stimulation of the brain.* Austin: University of Texas Press.

King, W., & Ellison, G. (1989). Long-lasting alterations in behavior and brain neurochemistry following continuous low-level LSD administration. *Pharmacology, Biochemistry & Behavior, 33,* 69–73.

Kinney, D. K., Holzman, P. S., Jacobsen, B., Jansson, L., Faber, B., Hildebrand, W., et al. (1997). Thought disorder in schizophrenic and control adoptees and their relatives. *Archives of General Psychiatry, 54,* 475–479.

Kinomura, S., Larsson, J., Gulyas, B., & Roland, P. E. (1996). Activation of attention by the human reticular formation and thalamic intralaminar nuclei. *Science, 271,* 512–515.

Kinsbourne, M., & Smith, W. L. (1974). *Hemispheric disconnection and cerebral function.* Springfield, IL: Charles C. Thomas.

Kinsey, A. C., Pomeroy, W. B., & Martin, C. E. (1948). *Sexual behavior in the human male.* Philadelphia: W. B. Saunders.

Kinsey, A. C., Pomeroy, W. B., Martin, C. E., & Gebhard, P. (1953). *Sexual behavior in the human female.* Philadelphia: W. B. Saunders.

Kintsch, W., & Greeno, J. G. (1985). Understanding and solving word arithmetic problems. *Psychological Review, 92,* 109–129.

Kirasic, K. C., Allen, G. A., Dodson, S. H., & Binder, K. S. (1996). Aging, cognitive resources, and declarative learning. *Psychology & Aging, 11,* 658–670.

Kirkpatrick-Steger, K., Wasserman, E. A., & Biederman, I. (1998). Effects of geon deletion, scrambling, and movement on picture recognition in pigeons. *Journal of Experimental Psychology: Animal Behavior Processes, 24,* 34–46.

Kirsch, I., & Lynn, S. J. (1998). Social-cognitive alternatives to dissociation theories of hypnotic involuntariness. *Review of General Psychology, 2,* 66–80.

Kirsch, I., Montgomery, G., & Sapirstein, G. (1995). Hypnosis as an adjunct to cognitive behavioral psychotherapy: A meta-analysis. *Journal of Consulting & Clinical Psychology, 63,* 214–220.

Kitayama, S., & Markus, H. R. (Eds.). (1994). *Emotion and culture: Empirical studies of mutual influence.* Washington, DC: American Psychological Association.

Klaczynski, P. (1997). Bias in adolescents' everyday reasoning and its relationship with intellectual ability, personal theories, and self-serving motivation. *Developmental Psychology, 33,* 273–283.

Klaczynski, P. (2000). Motivated scientific reasoning biases, epistemological beliefs, and theory polarization: A two-process approach to adolescent cognition. *Child Development, 71,* 1347–1366.

Klayman, J., & Ha, Y. (1989). Hypothesis testing in rule discovery: Strategy, structure, and content. *Journal of Experimental Psychology: Learning, Memory, and Cognition, 15,* 596–604.

Klein, D. N., Schwartz, J. E., Rose, S., & Leader, J. B. (2000). Five-year course and outcome of dysthymic disorder: A prospective, naturalistic follow-up study. *American Journal of Psychiatry, 157,* 931–939.

Kleinke, C. L., Peterson, T. R., & Rutledge, T. R. (1998). Effects of self-generated facial expressions on mood. *Journal of Personality & Social Psychology, 74,* 272-279.

Kleinman, A. (1988). *Rethinking psychiatry: From cultural category to personal experience.* New York: Macmillan.

Kleven, M., & Seiden, L. (1991). Repeated injection of cocaine potentiates methamphetamine-induced toxicity to dopamine-containing neurons in rat striatum. *Brain Research, 557,* 340–343.

Klinger, E. (1992). What will they think of next?

Understanding daydreaming. In G. Brannigan & M. Merrens (Eds.), *The undaunted psychologist: Adventures in research.* New York: McGraw-Hill.

Klinger, M. R., & Greenwald, A. G. (1994). Preferences need no inferences? The cognitive basis of unconscious mere exposure effects. In P. M. Niedenthal, S. Kitayama, et al. (Eds.), *The heart's eye: Emotional influences in perception and attention* (pp. 67–85). San Diego, CA: Academic Press.

Klinnert, M. D., Campos, J. J., Sorce, J. F., Emde, R. R., & Svejda, M. (1983). Emotions as behavior regulators: Social reference in infancy. In R. Plutchik & H. Kellerman (Eds.), *Emotion: Theory, research, and experience: Vol. 2. Emotions in early development.* San Diego: Academic Press.

Kluckhohn, F., & Strodtbeck, F. (1961). *Variations in value orientations.* Evanston, IL: Row, Peterson.

Kluger, A., & DeNisi, A. (1996). The effects of feedback interventions on performance: A historical review, a meta-analysis, and a preliminary feedback intervention theory. *Psychological Bulletin, 119,* 254–284.

Kluver, H., & Bucy, P. (1939). Preliminary analysis of functions of the temporal lobe in monkeys. *Archives of Neurology and Psychiatry, 42,* 979–1000.

Knapp, M. L., & Hall, J. A. (1992). *Nonverbal communication in human interaction.* New York: Harcourt Brace Jovanovich College Publishers.

Knowlton, B. J., Mangels, J. A., & Squire, L. R. (1996). A neostriatal habit learning system in humans. *Science, 273,* 1399–1402.

Knupfer, G. (1991). Abstaining for foetal health: The fiction that even light drinking is dangerous. *British Journal of Addiction, 86,* 1063–1073.

Kochanska, G., Murray, K. T., & Harlan, E. T. (2000). Effortful control in early childhood: Continuity and change, antecedents, and implications for social development. *Developmental Psychology, 36,* 220–232.

Koerner, K., & Linehan, M. M. (2000). Research on dialectical behavior therapy for patients with borderline personality disorder. *Psychiatric Clinics of North America, 23,* 151–167.

Koestner, R., Weinberger, J., & McClelland, D. C. (1991a). Task-intrinsic and social-extrinsic sources of arousal for motives assessed in fantasy and self-report. *Journal of Personality, 59,* 57–82.

Koestner, R., Zuroff, D., & Powers, T. (1991b). Family origins of adolescent self-criticism and its continuity into adulthood. *Journal of Abnormal Psychology, 100,* 191–197.

Kohlberg, L. (1963). The development of children's orientations toward a moral order. I. Sequence in the development of moral thought. *Vita Humana, 6,* 11–33.

Kohlberg, L. (1976). Moral stages and moralization: The cognitive-developmental perspective. In T. Lickona (Ed.), *Moral development and behavior: Theory, research, and social issues.* New York: Holt, Rinehart, & Winston.

Kohlberg, L., & Kramer, R. (1969). Continuities and discontinuities in childhood and adult moral development. *Human Development, 12,* 93–120.

Kohlberg, L. A. (1966). A cognitive-developmental analysis of children's sex-role concepts and attitudes. In E. E. Maccoby (Ed.), *The development of sex differences.* Stanford, CA: Stanford University Press.

Kohlenberg, R. J., & Tsai, M. (1994). Improving cognitive therapy for depression with functional analytic psychotherapy: Theory and case study. *Behavior Analyst, 17,* 305–319.

Kohler, W. (1925). *The mentality of apes.* New York: Harcourt Brace.

Kohut, H. (1971). *The analysis of the self: A systematic approach to the treatment of narcissistic personality disorders.* New York: International Universities Press.

Kohut, H. (1977). *The restoration of the self.* New York: International Universities Press.

Kolb, B. (1989). Brain development, plasticity, and behavior. *American Psychologist, 44,* 1203-1212.

Kolb, B., & Gibb, R. (1991). Environmental enrichment and cortical injury: Behavioral and anatomical consequences of frontal cortex lesions. *Cerebral Cortex, 1,* 189–198.

Kolb, B., & Wishaw, I. Q. (1996). *Fundamentals of neuropsychology.* New York: W. H. Freeman.

Konishi, M. (1995). Neural mechanisms of auditory image formation. In M. S. Gazzaniga et al. (Eds.), *The cognitive neurosciences* (pp. 269–277). Cambridge, MA: MIT Press.

Konner, M. (1991). Universals of behavioral development in relation to brain myelination. In K. R. Gibson & A. C. Petersen (Eds.), *Brain maturation and cognitive development: Comparative and cross-cultural perspectives.* New York: Aldine de Gruyter.

Konrad, A. M., Ritchie, J. Edgar Jr; Lieb, Pamela; Corrigall, Elizabeth. (2000). Sex differences and similarities in job attribute preferences: A meta-analysis. *Psychological Bulletin, 126,* 593–641.

Kopp, C. B. (1989). Regulation of distress and negative emotions: A developmental view. *Developmental Psychology, 25,* 343–354.

Korfine, L., & Hooley, J. M. (2000). Directed forgetting of emotional stimuli in borderline personality disorder. *Journal of Abnormal Psychology, 109,* 214–221.

Koriat, A., Goldsmith, M., & Pansky, A. (2000). Toward a psychology of memory accuracy. *Annual Review of Psychology, 51,* 481–537.

Korn, J. H., Davis, R., & Davis, S. F. (1991). Historians' and chairpersons' judgments of eminence among psychologists. *American Psychologist, 46,* 789–792.

Korten, A. E., Henderson, A. S., Christensen, H., Jorm, A. F., et al. (1997). A prospective study of cognitive function in the elderly. *Psychological Medicine, 27,* 919–930.

Kosmitzki, C., & John, O. (1993). The implicit use of explicit conceptions of social intelligence. *Personality and Individual Differences, 15,* 11–23.

Koss, M. (1993). Rape: Scope, impact, interventions, and public policy responses. *American Psychologist, 48,* 1062–1069.

Kosslyn, S. M. (1983). *Ghosts in the mind's machine.* New York: Norton.

Kosslyn, S. M., Alpert, N. M., Thompson, W. L., Maljokovic, V., et al. (1993). Visual imagery activates topographically organized visual cortex: PET investigations. *Journal of Cognitive Neuroscience, 5*(3), 263–287.

Kosslyn, S. M., Thompson, W. L., Costantini-Ferrando, M. F., Alpert, N. M., & Spiegel, D. (2000). Hypnotic visual illusion alters brain color processing. *American Journal of Psychiatry, 157.*

Kosslyn, S. M., Thompson, W. L., Kim, I. J., & Alpert, N. M. (1995). Topographical representations of mental images in primary visual cortex. *Nature, 378,* 496–498.

Kouri, E., Pope, H. G., Yurgelun-Todd, D., Gruber, S. (1995). Attributes of heavy vs. occasional marijuana smokers in a college population. *Biological Psychiatry, 38,* 475–481.

Kourtzi, Z., & Kanwisher, N. (2000b). Activation in human MT/MST by static images with implied motion. *Journal of Cognitive Neuroscience, 12,* 48–55.

Kovacs, D. M., Parker, J. G., & Hoffman, L. W. (1996). Behavioral, affective, and social correlates of involvement in cross-sex friendship in elementary school. *Child Development, 67,* 2269–2286.

Kraemer, G. (1992). A psychobiological theory of attachment. *Behavioral and Brain Sciences, 15,* 493–541.

Kramer, L., & Gottman, J. (1992). Becoming a sibling: "With a little help from my friends." *Developmental Psychology, 28,* 685–699.

Kramer, L., Perozynski, L. A., & Chung, T. (1999). Parental responses to sibling conflict: The effects of development and parent gender. *Child Development, 70,* 1401–1414.

Kramer, P. (1993). *Listening to Prozac.* New York: Viking Press.

Kraus, N., Malmfors, T., & Slovic, P. (1992). Intuitive toxicology: Expert and lay judgments of chemical risks. *Risk Analysis, 12,* 215–232.

Kraus, S. J. (1995). Attitudes and the prediction of behavior: A meta-analysis of the empirical literature. *Personality & Social Psychology Bulletin, 21,* 58–75.

Kremen, A. M., & Block, J. (1998). The roots of ego-control in young adulthood: Links with parenting in early childhood. *Journal of Personality & Social Psychology, 75,* 1062-1075.

Kring, A. M., & Gordon, A. H. (1998). Sex differences in emotion: Expression, experience, and physiology. *Journal of Personality & Social Psychology, 74,* 686–703.

Kripke, D., Simons, R. N., Garfinkel, L., & Hammond, E. C. (1979). Short and long sleep and sleeping pills. *Archives of General Psychiatry, 36,* 103–116.

Kruesi, M., Hibbs, E., Zahn, T., & Keysor, C. (1992). A 2-year prospective follow-up study of children and adolescents with disruptive behavior disorders: Prediction by cerebrospinal fluid 5-hydroxyindoleacetic acid, homovanillic acid, and autonomic measures? *Archives of General Psychiatry, 49,* 429–435.

Krystal, A. D., Dean, M. D., Weiner, R. D., Tramontozzi, L. A., Connor, K. M., Lindahl, V. H., & Massie, R. W. (2000). ECT stimulus intensity: Are present ECT devices too limited? *American Journal of Psychiatry, 157,* 963–967.

Kuebli, J., Butler, S., & Fivush, R. (1995). Mother-child talk about past emotions: Relations of maternal language and child gender over time. *Cognition and Emotion, 9,* 265–283.

Kuffler, S. W. (1953). Discharge patterns and functional organization of mammalian retina. *Journal of Neurophysiology, 16,* 37–68.

Kuhlmeier, V. A., Boysen, S. T., & Mukobi, K. L. (1999). Scale-model comprehension by chimpanzees *(Pan troglodytes). Journal of Comparative Psychology, 113,* 396–402.

Kuhl, P. K., & Meltzoff, A. N. (1988). Speech and an intermodal object of perception. In A. Tonas (Ed.), *Minnesota symposium on child psychology: Vol. 20. Perceptual development in infancy.* Hillsdale, NJ: Erlbaum.

Kuhn, D. (1976). Short-term longitudinal evidence for the sequentiality of Kohlberg's early stages of moral judgment. *Developmental Psychology, 12,* 162–166.

Kuhn, T. S. (1970). *The structure of scientific revolutions* (2nd ed.). Chicago: University of Chicago Press.

Kuiper, N. A., & Derry, P. A. (1982). Depressed and nondepressed content self-reference in mild depression. *Journal of Personality, 50,* 67–79.

Kuiper, N. A., Olinger, L. J., MacDonald, M. R., & Shaw, B. F. (1985). Self-schema processing of depressed and nondepressed content: The effects of vulnerability on depression. *Social Cognition, 3,* 77–93.

Kunda, Z. (1990). The case for motivated reasoning. *Psychological Bulletin, 108,* 480–498.

Kunda, Z., & Thagard, P. (1996). Forming impressions from stereotypes, traits, and behaviors: A parallel-constraint-satisfaction theory. *Psychological Review, 103,* 284–308.

Kunzendorf, R. G., Spanos, N. P., & Wallace, B. (Eds.). (1996). *Hypnosis and imagination. Imagery and human development series.* New York: Baywood Publishing Co.

Kuo-shu, Y., & Bond, M. H. (1990). Exploring implicit personality theories with indigenous or imported constructs: The Chinese case. *Journal of Personality and Social Psychology, 58,* 1087–1095.

Kushner, M. G., Abrams, K., & Borchardt, C. (2000). The relationship between anxiety disorders and alcohol use disorders: A review of major perspectives and findings. *Clinical Psychology Review, 20*(2), 149–171.

Kvavilashvili, L. (1987). Remembering intention as a distinct form of memory. *British Journal of Psychology, 78,* 507–518.

LaBar, K. S., & LeDoux, J. E. (1996). Partial disruption of fear conditioning in rats with unilateral amygdala damage: Correspondence with unilateral temporal lobectomy in humans. *Behavioral Neuroscience, 110,* 991–997.

Labarre, W. (1966). The Aymaya: History and world view. *Journal of American Folklore, 79,* 130-144.

Labouvie-Vief, G., & Schell, D. A. (1982). Learning and memory in late life. In B. B. Wolman (Ed.), *Handbook of developmental psychology.* Englewood Cliffs, NJ: Prentice-Hall.

Ladd, G. W. (1999). Peer relationships and social competence during early and middle childhood. *Annual Review of Psychology, 50,* 333–359.

Ladd, G. W., & Burgess, K. B. (1999). Charting the relationship trajectories of aggressive, withdrawn, and aggressive/withdrawn children during early grade school. *Child Development, 70,* 910–929.

Ladd, G. W., & Mize, J. (1983). A cognitive-social learning model of social skill training. *Psychologial Review, 90,* 127–157.

LaFreniere, P. J., & Sroufe, L. A. (1985). Profiles of peer competence in the preschool: Interrelations between measures, influences of social ecology, and relation to attachment history. *Developmental Psychology, 21,* 56–69.

Laing, D. G., Prescott, J., Bell, G. A., & Gilmore, R. (1993). A cross-cultural study of taste discrimination with Australians and Japanese. *Chemical Senses, 18,* 161–168.

Lakoff, G. (1985). *Women, fire, and dangerous things.* Chicago: University of Chicago Press.

Lakoff, G. (1989). A suggestion for a linguistics with connectionist foundations. In D. Touretzky, G. E. Hinton, et al. (Eds.), *Proceedings of the 1988 Connectionist Models Summer School.* (pp. 301–314). San Mateo, CA: Morgan Kaufmann.

Lakoff, G. (1997). How unconscious metaphorical thought shapes dreams. In D. J. Stein (Ed.), *Cognitive science and the unconscious. Progress in psychiatry* (No. 52, pp. 89–120). Washington, DC: American Psychiatric Press.

Lalumiere, M. L., Blanchard, R., & Zucker, K. J. (2000). Sexual orientation and handedness in men and women: A meta-analysis. *Psychological Bulletin, 126,* 575-592.

Lamb, M. E. (1987). Introduction: The emergent American father. In M. E. Lamb (Ed.), *The father's role: Cross-cultural perspective.* Hillsdale, NJ: Erlbaum.

Lamb, M. E., & Roopnarine, J. L. (1979). Peer influences on sex-role development in preschoolers. *Child Development, 50,* 1219–1222.

Lambert, M. J., Shapiro, D. A., & Bergin, A. E. (1986). The effectiveness of psychotherapy. In S. L. Garfield and A. E. Bergin (Eds.), *Handbook of psychotherapy and behavior change.* New York: John Wiley.

Lame Deer, J., & Erdoes, R. (1972). *Lame Deer, seeker of visions.* New York: Simon & Schuster.

Landau, E., & Weissler, K. (1993). Parental environment in families with gifted and nongifted children. *Journal of Psychology, 127,* 129–142.

Landman, J. T., & Dawes, R. M. (1982). Psychotherapy outcome: Smith and Glass' conclusions stand up under scrutiny. *American Psy-*
chologist, 37, 504–516.

Landy, D., & Aronson, E. (1969). The influence of the character of the criminal and his victim on the decisions of simulated jurors. *Journal of Experimental Social Psychology, 5,* 141-152.

Lane, C., & Hobfoll, S. E. (1992). How loss affects anger and alienates potential supporters. *Journal of Consulting and Clinical Psychology, 6,* 935–942.

Lang, P. (1995). The emotion probe: Studies of motivation and attention. *American Psychologist, 50,* 372–385.

Lang, P. J. (1994). The varieties of emotional experience: A meditation on James-Lange theory. *Psychological Review, 101,* 212–221.

Lange, C. G. (1885). The emotions: A psychophysiological study, trans. I. A. Haupt. In C. G. Lange & W. James (Eds.), *Psychology classics,* (Vol. I). Baltimore, MD: Williams & Wilkins, 1922.

Langer, E. J. (1978). Rethinking the role of thought in social interaction. In J. H. Harvey, W. I. Ickes, & R. F. Kidd (Eds.), *New directions in attribution research* (Vol. 2, pp. 35–58). Hillsdale, NJ: Earlbaum.

Langlois, J., Ritter, J. M., Roggman, L., & Vaughn, L. S. (1991). Facial diversity and infant preferences for attractive faces. *Developmental Psychology, 27,* 79–84.

Langlois, J. H., & Downs, A. C. (1980). Mothers, fathers, and peers as socialization agents of sex-typed play behaviors in young children. *Child Development, 51,* 1217–1247.

Langlois, J. H., & Roggman, L. A. (1990). Attractive faces are only average. *Psychological Science, 1,* 115–121.

Lanzetta, J. T., Cartwright-Smith, J., & Kleck, R. E. (1976). Effects of nonverbal dissimulation on emotional experience and autonomic arousal. *Journal of Personality and Social Psychology, 33,* 354–370.

Larose, H., & Standing, L. (1998). Does the halo effect occur in the elderly? *Social Behavior & Personality, 26,* 147-150.

Larson, R. W. (1997). The emergence of solitude as a constructive domain of experience in early adolescence. *Child Development, 68,* 80–93.

Larson, R. W., Richards, M. H., Moneta, G., Holmbeck, G., & Duckett, E. (1996). Changes in adolescents' daily interactions with their families from ages 10 to 18: Disengagement and transformation. *Developmental Psychology, 32,* 744–754.

Larzelere, R. E., Schneider, W. N., Larson, D. B., & Pike, P. L. (1996). The effects of discipline responses in delaying toddler misbehavior recurrences. *Child & Family Behavior Therapy, 18,* 35–57.

Lasswell, H. D. (1948). The structure and function of communication in society. In L. Bryson (Ed.), *Communication of ideas.* New York: HarperCollins.

Latimer, P. R. (1979). The behavior treatment of self-excoriation in a twelve-year-old girl. *Journal of Behavioral Therapy and Experimental Psychiatry, 10,* 349–352.

Laub, J. B., & Sampson, R. J. (1995). The long-term effect of punitive discipline. In J. McCord (Ed.), *Coercion and punishment in long-term perspectives* (pp. 247–258). New York: Cambridge University Press.

Lavie, P. (1996). *The enchanted world of sleep* (A. Berris, Trans.). New Haven: Yale University Press.

Lawrence, C. B., Turnbull, A. V., & Rothwell, N. J. (1999). Hypothalamic control of feeding. *Current Opinion in Neurobiology, 9*(6), 778–783.

Lazarus, R. (1981). The stress and coping paradigm. In C. Eisdorfer, D., Cohen, A. Kleinman & P. Maxim (Eds.), *Models for clinical psychopathology.* New York: Spectrum.

Lazarus, R. S. (1991). *Emotion and adaptation.* New York: Oxford University Press.

Lazarus, R. S. (1993). From psychological stress to the emotions: A history of changing outlooks. *Annual Review of Psychology, 44*, 1–21.

Lazarus, R. S. (1999a). *Stress and emotion: A new synthesis.* New York: Springer.

Lazarus, R. S. (1999b). The cognition-emotion debate: A bit of history. In T. Dalgleish & M. Power (Eds.), *The handbook of cognition and emotion* (pp. 3–20). New York: John Wiley & Sons.

Lazarus, R. S., & McCleary, R. A. (1951). Autonomic discrimination without awareness: A study of subception. *Psychological Review, 58*, 113–122.

Leaper, C., Anderson, K. J., & Sanders, P. (1998). Moderators of gender effects on parents' talk to their children: A meta-analysis. *Developmental Psychology, 34*, 3–27.

Lecky, P. (1945). *Self-consistency: A theory of personality.* New York: Island Press.

LeDoux, J. (1995). Emotion: Clues from the brain. *Annual Review of Psychology, 46*, 209–235.

LeDoux, J. (1998). Fear and the brain: Where have we been, and where are we going? *Biological Psychiatry, 44*, 1229–1238.

LeDoux, J. E. (1989). Cognitive-emotional interactions in the brain. *Cognition and Emotion, 3*, 267–289.

LeDoux, J. E. (2000). Emotion circuits in the brain. *Annual Review of Neuroscience, 23*, 155–184.

LeDoux, J. E., Wilson, D. H., & Gazzinaga, M. S. (1977). Manipulo-spatial aspects of central lateralization. *Neuropsychologia, 15*, 743–750.

Lee, D. (1950). The conception of the self among the Wintu Indians. In D. Lee (Ed.), *Freedom and culture.* Englewood Cliffs, NJ: Prentice-Hall, 1959.

Lee, E. (1951). Negro intelligence and selective migration: A Philadelphia test of Klineberg's hypothesis. *American Sociological Review, 61*, 227–233.

Lee, J. (1995). *Facing the fire: Experiencing and expressing anger appropriately.* New York: Bantam.

Lee, Y., & Seligman, M. E. P. (1997). Are Americans more optimistic than the Chinese? *Personality & Social Psychology Bulletin, 23*, 32–40.

Lehman, D. R., Wortman, C. B., & Williams, A. F. (1987). Long-term effects of losing a spouse or child in a motor vehicle crash. *Journal of Personality and Social Psychology, 52*, 218–231.

Lehmann, H. E. (1985). Affective disorders: Clinical features. In H. I. Kaplan & B. J. Sadock (Eds.), *Comprehensive textbook of psychiatry* (4th ed.), Baltimore, MD: Williams & Wilkins.

Lehrman, D. S. (1956). On the organization of maternal behavior and the problem of instinct. In *L'instinct dans le Comportement des Animaux et de l'homme.* Paris: Masson et Cie.

Lempers, J. D., Flavell, E. R., & Flavell, J. H. (1977). The development in very young children of tacit knowledge concerning visual perception. *Genetic Psychology Monographs, 95*, 3–53.

Lenneberg, E. (1967). *The biological foundations of language.* New York: John Wiley.

Lenzenweger, M. F, Loranger, A. W., Korfine, L., & Neff, C. (1997) Detecting personality disorders in a nonclinical population: Application of a 2-stage for case identification. *Archives of General Psychiatry, 54*, 345-351.

Lepper, M. R., Greene, D., & Nisbett, R. E. (1996). Undermining children's intrinsic interest with extrinsic reward: A test of the "overjustification" hypothesis. In F. Fein, Steven, and S. Spencer (Eds.), *Readings in social psychology: The art and science of research.* (pp. 10-18). Boston: Houghton Mifflin Co.

Lerner, R. (1991). Changing organism-context relations as the basic process of development: A developmental contextual perspective. *Developmental Psychology, 27*, 27–32.

LeVay, S. (1991). A difference in hypothalamic structure between heterosexual and homosexual men. *Science, 253*, 1034–1037.

Levenson, J. L., & Bemis, C. (1991). The role of psychological factors in cancer onset and progression. *Psychosomatics, 32*, 124–132.

Levenson, R., & Ruef, A. (1992). Empathy: A physiological substrate. *Journal of Personality and Social Psychology, 63*, 234–246.

Levenson, R. W. (1992). Autonomic nervous system differences among emotions. *Psychological Science, 3*, 23–27.

Levenson, R. W., Ekman, P., & Friesen, W. (1990). Voluntary facial action generates emotion-specific autonomic nervous system activity. *Psychophysiology, 27*, 363–385.

Levenson, R. W., Ekman, P., Heider, K., & Friesen, W. V. (1992). Emotion and autonomic nervous system activity in the Minangkabau of West Sumatra. *Journal of Personality and Social Psychology, 62*, 972–988.

Leventhal, E. A., Leventhal, H., Shacham, S., & Easterling, D. V. (1989). Active coping reduces reports of pain from childbirth. *Journal of Consulting and Clinical Psychology, 57*, 365–371.

Leventhal, H., & Leventhal, E. A. (1993). Affect, cognition, and symptom perception. In C. R. Chapman & K. M Foley, (Eds.), *Current and emerging issues in cancer pain: Research and practice. Bristol-Myers Squibb Symposium on Pain Research series.* (pp. 153-173). New York: Raven Press.

Leventhal, H., & Tomarken, A. J. (1986). Emotion: Today's problems. *Annual Review of Psychology, 37*, 565–610.

Levine, L. J., & Burgess, S. L. (1997). Beyond general arousal: Effects of specific emotions on memory. *Social Cognition, 15*, 157–181.

LeVine, R. (1982). *Culture, behavior, and personality* (2nd ed.). Chicago: Aldine.

LeVine, R. A., & LeVine, B. B. (1963). Nyasongo: A Gusii community in Kenya. In B. Whiting (Ed.), *Six cultures: Studies in child rearing* (pp. 19–202). New York: John Wiley.

Levine, R. V., Martinez, T., Brase, G., & Sorenson, K. (1994). Helping in 36 U.S. cities. *Journal of Personality and Social Psychology, 67*, 69–82.

Levinger, G. (1976). Social psychological perspectives on marital dissolution. *Journal of Social Issues, 32*, 21–47.

Levinson, D. (1978). *The seasons of a man's life.* New York: Ballantine Books.

Levinson, D. J., Darrow, C. N., Klein, E. B., Levinson, M. H., & McKee, B. (1978). *The seasons of a man's life.* New York: Alfred A. Knopf.

Levy-Shiff, R. (1994). Individual and contextual correlates of marital change across the transition to parenthood. *Developmental Psychology, 30*, 591–601.

Lewicki, P. (1986) *Nonconscious social information processing.* New York: Academic Press.

Lewin, K. (1939). Field theory and experiment in social psychology: Concepts and methods. *American Journal of Sociology, 44*, 868–897.

Lewinsohn, P. M., Allen, N. B., Seeley, J. R., & Gotlib, I. H. (1999). First onset versus recurrence of depression: Differential processes of psychosocial risk. *Journal of Abnormal Psychology, 108*, 483–489.

Lewinsohn, P. M., Gotlibm, I. H., Lewinsohn, M., Seeley, J. R., & Allen, N. B. (1998). Gender differences in anxiety disorders and anxiety symptoms in adolescents. *Journal of Abnormal Psychology, 107*,109–117.

Lewinsohn, P. M., Solomon, A., Seeley, J. R., & Zeiss, A. (2000). Clinical implications of "subthreshold" depressive symptoms. *Journal of Abnormal Psychology, 109*, 345–351.

Lewis, D. A. (2000). Distributed disturbances in brain structure and function in schizophrenia. *American Journal of Psychiatry, 157*, 1–2.

Lewis, D. O., Yeager, C. A., Swica, Y., Pincus, J. H., & Lewis, M. (1997a). Objective documentation of child abuse and dissociation in 12 murderers with dissociative identity disorder. *American Journal of Psychiatry, 154*, 1703–1710.

Lewis, J. E., Malow, R. M., & Ireland, S. J. (1997b). HIV/AIDS in heterosexual college students: A review of a decade of literature. *Journal of American College Health, 45*, 147–158.

Lewis, M., & Bendersky, M. (1995). *Mothers, babies, and cocaine: The role of toxins in development.* Hillsdale, NJ: Lawrence Erlbaum Associates.

Lewis, M., Feiring, C., & Rosenthal, S. (2000). Attachment over time. *Child Development, 71*, 707–720.

Lewis, M. B. G. J. (1979). *Social cognition and the acquisition of self.* New York: Plenum Press.

Lewis, N., & Brooks-Gunn, J. (1979). *Social cognition and the acquisition of self.* New York: Plenum Press.

Lewkowicz, D. J. (2000). The development of intersensory temporal perception: An epigenetic systems/limitations view. *Psychological Bulletin, 126*, 281–308.

Liberman, A., & Chaiken, S. (1992). Defensive processing of personally relevant health messages. *Journal of Experimental Social Psychology.*

Lichtenberg, J. (1983). *Psychoanalysis and motivation.* Hillsdale, NJ: Analytic Press.

Lickliter, R., & Bahrick, L. E. (2000). The development of infant intersensory perception: Advantages of a comparative convergent-operations approach. *Psychological Bulletin, 126,* 260–280.

Lieberman, M., Doyle, A., & Markiewicz, D. (1999). Developmental patterns in security of attachment to mother and father in late childhood and early adolescence: Associations with peer relations. *Child Development, 70,* 202–213.

Lieberman, M. D. (2000). Intuition: A social cognitive neuroscience approach. *Psychological Bulletin, 126,* 109–136.

Lieberman, M. D., Ochsner, K. N., Gilbert, D. T., & Schacter, D. L. (in press). Do amnesics exhibit cognitive dissonance reduction? The role of explicit memory and attention in attitude change. *Psychological Science.*

Lieberman, S. (1956). The effects of changes in roles on the attitudes of role occupants. *Human Relations, 9,* 385–402.

Lifton, R. J. (1963). *Thought reform and the psychology of totalism: A study of brainwashing in China.* New York: W. W. Norton.

Light, L. (1990). Interactions between memory and language in old age. In J. E. Birren & K. W. Schaie (Eds.), *Handbook of the psychology of aging.* (3rd ed.). New York: Van Nostrand Reinhold.

Limongelli, L., Boysen, S. T., & Visalberghi, E. (1995). Comprehension of cause-effect relations in a tool-using task by chimpanzees *(Pan troglodytes). Journal of Comparative Psychology, 109,* 18–26.

Lindberg, M. (1980). Is knowledge base development a necessary and sufficient condition for memory development? *Journal of Experimental Child Psychology, 30,* 401–410.

Lindemann, C. G. (Ed). (1996). *Handbook of the treatment of the anxiety disorders* (2nd ed.). Northvale, NJ: Jason Aronson.

Lindley, R. H., & Smith, W. R. (1992). Coding tests as measures of IQ: Cognitive or motivation? *Personality and Individual Differences, 13,* 25–29.

Linehan, M. (1987a). Dialectical behavior therapy for borderline personality disorder: Theory and method. *Bulletin of the Menninger Clinic, 51,* 261–276.

Linehan, M. M. (1987b). Dialectical behavioral therapy: A cognitive behavioral approach to parasuicide. *Journal of Personality Disorders, 1,* 328–333.

Linehan, M. M. (1993). *Cognitive-behavioral treatment of borderline personality disorder.* New York: Guilford Press.

Linehan, M. M. (2000) Behavioral treatments of suicidal behaviors: Definitional obfuscation and treatment outcomes. In R. W. Maris & S. S. Canetto (Eds.), *Review of suicidology, 2000.* (pp. 84-111). New York: The Guilford Press.

Lisspers, J., & Ost, L. (1990). Long-term follow-up of migraine treatment: Do the effects remain up to six years? *Behaviour Therapy and Research, 28,* 313–322.

Litt, M., Babor, T., DelBoca, F., Kadden, R., & Cooney, N. (1992). Types of alcoholics, II: Application of an empirically derived typology to treatment matching. *Archives of General Psychiatry, 49,* 609–614.

Livesley, W. J., & Bromley, D. B. (1973). *Person perception in childhood and adolescence.* London: John Wiley.

Livingstone, M., & Hubel, D. H. (1988). Segregation of form, color, movement, and depth: Anatomy, physiology, and perception. *Science, 240,* 740–749.

Locke, E., & Latham, G. (1990). *A theory of goal-setting and task performance.* Englewood Cliffs, NJ: Prentice-Hall.

Locke, E. A. (1991). Goal theory vs. control theory: Contrasting approaches to understanding work motivation. *Motivation and Emotion, 15,* 9–27.

Locke, E. A. (1996). Motivation through conscious goal setting. *Applied and Preventive Psychology, 5,* 117–124.

Lockhart, R. S., & Craik, F. (1990). Levels of processing: A retrospective commentary on a framework for memory research. *Canadian Journal of Psychology, 44,* 87–112.

Loeb, R. C., Horst, L., & Horton, P. J. (1980). Family interaction patterns associated with self-esteem in preadolescent girls and boys. *Merill-Palmer Quarterly, 26,* 203–217.

Loehlin, J. (1992). *Genes and environment in personality development.* New York: Guilford Press.

Loehlin, J. C., Horn, J. M., & Willerman, L. (1989). Modeling IQ change: Evidence from the Texas Adoption Project. *Child Development, 60,* 993–1004.

Loehlin, J. C., Horn, J. M., & Willerman, L. (1997). Heredity, environment and IQ in the Texas Adoption Project. In R. J. Sternberg, E. L. Grigorenko, et al. (Eds.), *Intelligence, heredity, and environment* (pp. 105–125). New York: Cambridge University Press.

Loehlin, J. C., Willerman, L., & Horn, J. M. (1988). Human behavior genetics. *Annual Review of Psychology, 39,* 101–133.

Loevinger, J. (1976). *Ego development.* San Francisco: Jossey-Bass.

Loevinger, J. (1985). Revision of the sentence completion test for ego development. *Journal of Personality and Social Psychology, 48,* 420–427.

Loewenstein, W. R. (1960). Biological transducers. *Scientific American, 98*–108.

Loftus, E. (1997a). Creating false memories. *Scientific American, 277,* 70–75.

Loftus, E. (1997b). Memory for a past that never was. *Current Directions in Psychological Science, 6,* 60–65.

Loftus, E. F. (1993). The reality of repressed memories. *American Psychologist, 48*(5), 518–537.

Loftus, E. F., Levidow, B., & Duensing, S. (1992). Who remembers best? Individual differences in memory for events that occurred in a science museum. *Applied Cognitive Psychology, 6,* 93–107.

Loftus, E. F., & Palmer, J. C. (1974). Reconstruction and automobile destruction. An example of the interaction between language and memory. *Journal of Verbal Learning and Verbal Behavior, 13,* 585–589.

Loftus, E. F., Polonsky, S., & Fullilove, M. T. (1994). Memories of childhood sexual abuse: Remembering and repressing. *Psychology of Women Quarterly, 18,* 67–84.

Loftus, E. F., & Zanni, G. (1975). Eyewitness testimony: The influence of the wording of a question. *Bulletin of the Psychonomic Society, 5,* 86–88.

Logie, R. (1996). The seven ages of working memory. In J. T. E. Richardson, R. W. Engle, L. Hasher, R. Logie, E. Stoltzfus, & R. Zacks (Eds.), *Working memory and human cognition* (pp. 31–65). New York: Oxford University Press.

Lonner, W., & Malpass R. (Eds.) (1994a). *Readings in psychology and culture.* Boston: Allyn & Bacon.

Lonner, W. J., & Malpass, R. (1994b). *Psychology and Culture.* Needham Heights, MA: Allyn and Bacon.

Lopez, A., Atran, S., Coley, J. D., Medin, D. L., & Smith, E. E. (1997). The tree of life: Universal and cultural features of folkbiological taxonomies and inductions. *Cognitive Psychology, 32,* 251–295.

Lore, R., & Schultz, L. A. (1993). Control of human aggression: A comparative perspective. *American Psychologist, 48,* 16–25.

Lorenz, K. (1935). The companion in the bird's world. The fellow-member of the species as releasing factor of social behavior. *Journal fuer Ornithologie, 83,* 137-213.

Lorenz, K. (1937). Ueber den Begriff der Instinkthandlung. / The concept of instinctive action. *Folia Biotheoretica, 2,* 17-50.

Lorenz, K. (1966). *On aggression.* New York: Harcourt, Brace & World.

Lorenz, K. (1979). *King Solomon's ring.* New York: HarperCollins.

Lott, A., & Lott, B. (1974). The role of reward in the formation of positive interpersonal attitudes. In T. Huston (Ed.), *Foundations of interpersonal attraction.* New York: Academic.

Lovaas, O. I. (1977). *The autistic child.* New York: Wiley.

Lovaas, O. I. (1987). Behavioral treatment and normal educational and intellectual functioning in young autistic children. *Journal of Consulting and Clinical Psychology, 55,* 3–9.

Low, B. S. (1989). Cross-cultural patterns in the training of children: An evolutionary perspective. *Journal of Comparative Psychology, 103,* 311–319.

Lu, C., Shaikh, M. B., & Siegel, A. (1992). Role of NMDA receptors in hypothalamic facilitation of feline defensive rage elicited from the midbrain pariaqueductal gray. *Brain Research, 581,* 123–132.

Luborsky, L. (1985). Therapist success and its determinants. *Archives of General Psychiatry, 42,* 602-611.

Luborsky, L., Barber, J. P., & Crits-Christoph, P.

(1990). Theory-based research for understanding the process of dynamic psychotherapy. *Journal of Consulting and Clinical Psychology, 58,* 281–287.

Luborsky, L., & Crits-Christoph, P. (1990). *Understanding transference: The core conflictual relationship theme method.* New York: Basic Books.

Luborsky, L., Docherty, J. P., Miller, N. E., & Barber, J. P. (1993). What's here and what's ahead in dynamic therapy research and practice? In N. E. Miller, L. Luborsky, et al. (Ed.), *Psychodynamic treatment research: A handbook for clinical practice* (pp. 536–553). New York: Basic Books.

Luborsky, L., McLellan, A. T., Diguer, L., Woody, G., & Seligman, D. A. (1997). The psychotherapist matters. Comparison of outcomes across twenty-two therapists and seven patient samples. *Clinical Psychology-Science & Practice, 4,* 53-65.

Lubow, R. E., & Gewirtz, J. C. (1995). Latent inhibition in humans: Data, theory, and implications for schizophrenia. *Psychological Bulletin, 117,* 87–103.

Luchins, A. (1957). Primacy-recency in impression formation. In C. Hovland (Ed.), *The order of presentation in persuasion* (pp. 33–61). New Haven, CT: Yale University Press.

Ludolph, P. S., Westen, D., Misle, B., Jackson, A., et al. (1990). The borderline diagnosis in adolescents: Symptoms and developmental history. *American Journal of Psychiatry, 147,* 470–476.

Lumer, E. D., & Rees, G. (1999). Covariation of activity in visual and prefrontal cortex associated with subjective visual perception. *Proceedings of the National Academy of Science, USA, 96,* 1669–1673.

Lundh, L., Wikstrom, J., Westerlund, J., & Ost, L. (1999). Preattentive bias for emotional information in panic disorder with agoraphobia. *Journal of Abnormal Psychology, 108,* 222–232.

Luria, A. R. (1973). *The working brain.* Harmondsworth, UK: Penguin.

Luthar, S. S., Cicchetti, D., & Becker, B. (2000). Research on resilience: Response to commentaries. *Child Development, 71,* 573–575.

Lutz, C. (1988). Ethnographic perspectives on the emotion lexicon. In V. Hamilton, G. H. Bower, & N. Frijda (Eds.), *Cognitive perspectives on emotion and motivation* (pp. 399–419). Kluwer: Dordrecht.

Lyketsos, C. G., Chen, L., & Anthony, J. C. (1999). Cognitive decline in adulthood: An 11.5-year follow-up of the Baltimore Epidemiologic Catchment Area Study. *American Journal of Psychiatry, 156,* 58–65.

Lykken, D. T., Bouchard, T. J., McGue, M., & Tellegen, A. (1993). Heritability of interests: A twin study. *Journal of Applied Psychology, 78,* 649–661.

Lykken, D. T., McGue, M., Tellegen, A., & Bouchard, T. J. (1992). Emergenesis: Genetic traits that may not run in families. *American Psychologist, 47,* 1565–1577.

Lynch, O. M. (1990). The social construction of emotion in India. In O. M. Lynch (Ed.), *Divine passions: The social construction of emotion in India* (pp. 3–34). Berkeley: University of California Press.

Lynd-Stevenson, R. M. (1999). Expectancy-value theory and predicting future employment status in the young unemployed. *Journal of Occupational and Organizational Psychology, 72*(1), 101–106.

Lynn, S. J., Lock, T., Myers, B., & Payne, D. G. (1997). Recalling the unrecallable: Should hypnosis be used to recover memories in psychotherapy? *Current Directions in Psychological Science, 6,* 79–83.

Lyons, M. J., Eisen, S. A., Goldberg, J., True, W., Lin, N., Meyer, J. M., et al. (1998). A registry-based twin study of depression in men. *Archives of General Psychiatry, 55,* 468–472.

Lyons, M. J., True, W. R., Eisen, S. A., & Goldberg, J. (1995). Differential heritability of adult and juvenile antisocial traits. *Archives of General Psychiatry, 52,* 906-915.

Lyons-Ruth, K., Connell, D., Grunebaum, H., & Botein, S. (1990). Infants at social risk: Maternal depression and familiy support services as mediators of infant development and security of attachment. *Child Development, 61,* 85–98.

Lyons-Ruth, K., Easterbrooks, M. A., & Cibelli, C. D. (1997). Infant attachment strategies, infant mental lag, and maternal depressive symptoms. Predictors of internalizing and externalizing problems at age 7. *Developmental Psychology, 33,* 681–692.

Lytton, H. (1990). Child and parent effects in boys' conduct disorder: A reinterpretation. *Developmental Psychology, 26,* 683–697.

Maccoby, E. (1992). The role of parents in the socialization of children: An historical overview. *Developmental Psychology, 28,* 1006–1017.

Maccoby, E. E., & Jacklin, C. N. (1974). *The psychology of sex differences.* Stanford, CA: Stanford University Press.

Maccoby, E. E., & Jacklin, C. N. (1980). Sex differences in aggression: A rejoinder and reprise. *Child Development, 51,* 964–980.

MacCorquodale, K. (1970). On Chomsky's review of Skinner's verbal behavior. *Journal of the Experimental Analysis of Behavior, 13,* 83–89.

MacCoun, R. J. (1998). Biases in the interpretation and the use of research results. *Annual Review of Psychology, 49,* 259–287.

MacDonald, A. W., Cohen, J. D., Stenger, V. A., & Carter, C. S. (2000). Dissociating the role of the dorsolateral prefrontal and anterior cingulate cortex in cognitive control. *Science, 288,* 1835–1838.

Mace, R. (1996). Biased parental investment and reproductive success in Gabbra pastoralists. *Behavioral Ecology & Sociobiology, 38,* 75–81.

Macfie, J., Toth, S. L., Rogosch, F. A., Robinson, J., Emde, R. N., & Cicchetti, D. (1999). Effect of maltreatment on preschoolers' narrative representations of responses to relieve distress and of role reversal. *Developmental Psychology, 35,* 460–465.

MacKinnon-Lewis, C., Starnes, R., Volling, B., & Johnson, S. (1997). Perceptions of parenting as predictors of boys' sibling and peer relations. *Developmental Psychology, 33,* 1024–1031.

Mackintosh, N. J. (1998). *IQ and human intelligence.* New York: Oxford University Press.

Macklin, M. L., Metzger, L. J., Litz, B. T., McNally, R. J., Lasko, N. B., Orr, S. P., & Pitman, R. K. (1998). Lower precombat intelligence is a risk factor for posttraumatic stress disorder. *Journal of Consulting & Clinical Psychology, 66,* 323–326.

MacLean, P. D. (1982). On the origin and progressive evolution of the triune brain. In E. Armstrong & D. Falk, (Eds.), *Primate brain evolution.* New York: Plenum Press.

MacLean, P. D. (1990). A reinterpretation of memorative functions of the limbic system. In E. Goldberg et al. (Eds.), *Contemporary neuropsychology and the legacy of Luria. Institute for research in behavioral neuroscience.* (pp. 127–154). Hillsdale, NJ: Lawrence Erlbaum Associates, Inc.

Macrae, C. N., Bodenhausen, G. V., & Milne, A. B. (1998). Saying no to unwanted thoughts: Self-focus and the regulation of mental life. *Journal of Personality & Social Psychology, 74,* 578–589.

Macrae, C. N., Milne, A. B., & Bodenhausen, G. (1994). Stereotypes as energy-saving devices: A peek inside the cognitive toolbox. *Journal of Personality and Social Psychology, 66,* 37–47.

MacWhinney, B. (1998). Models of the emergence of language. *Annual Review of Psychology, 49,* 199–227.

Madden, P. A. F., Heath, A. C., Rosenthal, N. E., & Martin, N. G. (1996). Seasonal changes in mood and behavior: The role of genetic factors. *Archives of General Psychiatry, 53,* 47–55.

Madrid, A., & Schwartz, M. (1991). Maternal-infant bonding and pediatric asthma: An initial investigation. *Pre- and Peri-natal Psychology Journal, 5,* 347–358.

Magee, W. J., Eaton, W. W., Wittchen, H., McGonagle, K. A., & Kessler, R. C. (1996). Agoraphobia, simple phobia, and social phobia in the National Comorbidity Survey. *Archives of General Psychiatry, 53,* 159–168.

Mahler, M., Pine, F., & Bergman, A. (1975). *The psychological birth of the human infant: Symbiosis and individualization.* New York: Basic Books.

Main, M. (1990). Cross-cultural studies of attachment organization: Recent studies, changing methodologies, and the concept of conditional strategies. *Human Development, 33,* 48–61.

Main, M. (1995). Recent studies in attachment: Overview, with selected implications for clinical work. In S. Goldberg, R. Muir, et al. (Eds.). *Attachment Theory: Social, Developmental, and Clinical Perspectives.* (pp. 407–474). Hillsdale, NJ: Analytic Press, Inc.

Main, M., Kaplan, N., & Cassidy, J. (1985). Security in infancy, childhood, and adulthood: A move to the level of representation. In I. Bretherton & E. Waters (Eds.), Growing points of attachment theory and research. *Monographs of the Society for Research in Child Development,*

50 (No. 1–2), 67–104.

Main, M., & Solomon, J. (1986). Discovery of a new, insecure-disorganized/disoriented attachment pattern. In T. Brazelton & M. Yogman, (Eds.), *Affective development in infancy* (pp. 95–124). Norwood, NJ: Ablex.

Maj, M., Veltro, F., Pirozzi, R., Lobrace, S., & Magliano, L. (1992). Pattern of recurrence of illness after recovery from an episode of major depression: A prospective study. *American Journal of Psychiatry, 149*, 795–800.

Major, B., Zubek, J. M., Cooper, M. L., Cozzarelli, C., et al. (1997). Mixed messages: Implications of social conflict and social support within close relationships for adjustment to a stressful life event. *Journal of Personality & Social Psychology, 72*, 1349–1363.

Malamuth, N. M., & Donnerstein, E. (1982). The effects of aggressive-pornographic mass media stimuli. In L. Berkowitz (Ed.) *Advances in Experimental Social Psychology*, Vol. 15. New York: Academic Press.

Malpass, R. S., & Devine, P. G. (1980). Realism and eyewitness identification research. *Law and Human Behavior, 4*, 347-358.

Malt, B., & Smith, E. E. (1984). Correlated properties in natural categories. *Journal of Verbal Learning and Verbal Behavior, 23*, 250–269.

Mandler, G. (1980). Recognizing: The judgment of previous occurrence. *Psychological Review, 87*, 252–271.

Mandler, G. (1997). *Human nature explored*. New York: Oxford University Press.

Mandler, G., & Nakamura, Y. (1987). Aspects of consciousness. *Personality and Social Psychology Bulletin, 13*, 299–313.

Mandler, J. M. (1997). Development of categorisation: Perceptual and conceptual categories. In G. Bremner & A. Slater (Eds.), *Infant development: Recent advances.* (pp. 163-189). Hove, England: Psychology Press/Erlbaum (UK) Taylor & Francis.

Mangelsdorf, S., Gunnar, M., Kestenbaum, R., Lang, S., & Andreas, D. (1990). Infant proneness-to-distress temperament, maternal personality, and mother-infant attachment: Associations and goodness of fit. *Child Development, 61*, 820–831.

Manji, H. K., Chen, G., Shimon, H., Hsiao, J. K., Potter, W. Z., & Belmaker, R. H. (1995) Guanine nucleotide-binding proteins in bipolar affective disorder: Effects of long-term lithium treatment. *Archives of General Psychiatry, 52*, 135–144.

Mann, J. (1982). *A casebook in time-limited psychotherapy.* New York: McGraw-Hill.

Mann, J. J., Huang, Y., Underwood, M. D., Kassir, S. A., Oppenheim, S., Kelly, T. M., Dwork, A. J., & Arango, V. (2000). A serotonin transporter gene promoter polymorphism (5-HTTLPR) and prefrontal cortical binding in major depression and suicide. *Archives of General Psychiatry, 57*, 729–738.

Mannuzza, S., Klein, R. G., Bessler, A., Malloy, P., & Lpadula, M. (1998). Adult psychiatric status of hyperative boys grown up. *American Journal of Psychiatry, 155*, 493–498.

Manson, J. E., Colditz, G. A., Stampfer, M. J., Willett, W. C., Rosner, B., Monson, R. R., Speizer, F., & Hennekens, C. (1990). A prospective study of obesity and risk of coronary heart disease in women. *New England Journal of Medicine, 322*, 882–889.

Manuck, S. B., Flory, J. D., Ferrell, R. E., Dent, K. M., Mann, J. J., & Muldoon, M. F. (1999). Aggression and anger-related traits associated with a polymorphism of the tryptophan hydroxylase gene. *Biological Psychiatry, 45*, 603–614.

Maquet, P., Peters, J., Aerts, J., & Delfiore, G. (1996). Functional neuroanatomy of human rapid-eye-movement sleep and dreaming. *Nature, 383*, 163-166.

Maquire, E. A., Frackowiak, R. S. J., & Frith, C. D. (1997). Recalling routes around London: Activation of the right hippocampus in taxi drivers. *Journal of Neuroscience, 17*, 7103–7110.

Maquire, E. A., Gadian, D. G., Johnsrude, I. S., Good, C. D., Ashburner, J., Frackowiak, R. S. J., & Frith, C. D. (2000). Navigation-related structural change in the hippocampi of taxi drivers. *Proceedings of the National Academy of Science, USA, 97*, 4398–4403.

Marcel, A. J. (1983). Conscious and unconscious perception: Experiments on visual masking and word recognition. *Cognitive Psychology, 15*, 197–237.

Marcia, J. (1987). The identity status approach to the study of ego identity development. In T. Honess & K. Yardley (Eds.), *Self and identity: Perspectives across the lifespan* (pp. 161–171). Boston: Routledge & Kegan Paul.

Marcia, J. E. (1999). Representational thought in ego identity, psychotherapy, and psychosocial developmental theory. In I. E. Sigel (Ed.), *Development of mental representation: Theories and applications.* (pp. 391-414). Mahwah, NJ: Lawrence Erlbaum Associates.

Marcotte, A., & Morere, D. (1990). Speech lateralization in deaf populations: Evidence for a developmental critical period. *Brain & Language, 39*, 134–152.

Marcus, D. E., & Overton, W. E. (1978). The development of cognitive gender constancy and sex role preferences. *Child Development, 49*, 434–444.

Marcus, G. F. (1993). Negative evidence in language acquisition. *Cognition, 46*, 53–85.

Marengo, J., Harrow, M., Sands, J., & Galloway, C.. (1991). European versus U.S. data on the course of schizophrenia. *American Journal of Psychiatry, 148*, 606-611.

Margolskee, R. (1995). Receptor mechanisms in gustation. In R. L. Doty (Ed.), *Handbook of olfaction and gustation.* New York: Marcel Dekker.

Marks, I. M. (1969). *Fears and phobias.* New York: Academic Press.

Markus, H. (1977). Self-schemata and processing information about the self. *Journal of Personality and Social Psychology, 35*, 63–78.

Markus, H., & Cross, S. (1990). The interpersonal self. In L. Pervin (Ed.), *Handbook of personality: Theory and research* (pp. 576–608). New York:

Guilford Press.

Markus, H., & Kitayama, S. (1991). Culture and the self: Implications for cognition, emotion, and motivation. *Psychological Review, 98*, 224–253.

Markus, H., & Nurius, P. (1986). Possible selves. *American Psychologist, 41*, 954–969.

Markus, H., & Wurf, E. (1987). The dynamic self-concept: A social psychological perspective. *Annual Review of Psychology, 38*, 299–337.

Marlatt, G. A., & Baer, J. S. (1988). Addictive behaviors: Etiology and treatment. *Annual Review of Pychology, 39*, 223–252.

Marsh, R. L., Hiscks, J. L., & Bink, M. L. (1998). Activation of completed, uncompleted, and partially completed intentions. *Journal of Experimental Psychology: Learning, Memory and Cognition, 24*, 350–361.

Marshall, D. A., & Moulton, D. G. (1981). Olfactory sensitivity to a-ionone in humans and dogs. *Chemical Senses, 6*, 53–61.

Marshall, G., & Zimbardo, P. G. (1979). Affective consequences of inadequately explained physiological arousal. *Journal of Personality and Social Psychology, 37*, 970–988.

Martikainen, P., & Valkonen, T. (1996). Mortality after the death of a spouse: Rates and causes of death in a large Finnish cohort. *American Journal of Public Health, 86*, 1087–1093.

Martin, C. L., & Ruble, D. N. (1997). A developmental perspective of self-construals and sex differences: Comment on Cross and Madson (1997). *Psychological Bulletin, 122*, 45-50.

Martin, D. J., Garske, J. P., & Davis, M. K. (2000). Relation of the therapeutic alliance with outcome and other variables: A meta-analytic review. *Journal of Consulting and Clinical Psychology, 68*, 438–450.

Martin, J., & Sugarman, J. (1999). *The psychology of human possibility and constraint.* Albany, NY: State University of New York Press.

Martin, M. (1986). Ageing patterns of change in everyday memory and cognition. *Human Learning Journal of Practical Research and Application, 5*, 63–74.

Martin, M. A. (1985). Students' applications of self-questioning study techniques: An investigation of their efficacy. *Reading Psychology, 6*, 69–83.

Martinez, J. L., & Derrick, B. E. (1996). Long-term potentiation and learning. *Annual Review, 47*, 173–203.

Marx, K. (1972). *The Marx-Engels reader,* (R. Tucker, Ed.) New York: Norton.

Maslach, C. (1979). Negative emotional biasing of unexplained arousal. *Journal of Personality and Social Psychology, 37*, 953–969.

Masling, J. M., & Bornstein, R. F. (Eds.). (1994). *Empirical perspectives on object relations theory.* Washington, DC: American Psychological Association.

Maslow, A. H. (1962). *Toward a psychology of being.* Princeton, NJ: Van Nostrand.

Maslow, A. H. (1970). *Motivaiton and personality* (2nd ed.). New York: Harper & Row.

Masserman, J. H., Wechkin, S. & Terris, W.

(1964). "Altruistic" behavior in rhesus monkeys. *American Journal of Psychiatry, 121,* 584-585.

Masters, W., & Johnson, V. (1966). *Human sexual response.* Boston: Little, Brown.

Mathews, A., & Macleod, C. (1994). Cognitive approaches to emotion. *Annual Review of Psychology, 45,* 25–50.

Matlin, M. M. (1983). *Perception.* Boston: Allyn & Bacon.

Matsumoto, D., Kasri, F., & Kooken, K. (1999). American-Japanese cultural differences in judgements of expression intensity and subjective experience. *Cognition and Emotion, 13,* 201–218.

Matsuoka, S. (1990). Theta rhythms: State of consciousness. *Brain Topography, 3,* 203–208.

Matthews, K.A. (1992). Myths and realities of the menopause. *Psychosomatic Medicine, 54,* 1-9.

Maurer, D., Stager, C. L., & Mondloch, C. J. (1999). Cross-modal transfer of shape is difficult to demonstrate in one-month-olds. *Child Development, 70,* 1047–1057.

Mauro, R., Sato, K., & Tucker, J. (1992). The role of appraisal in human emotions: A cross-cultural study. *Journal of Personality and Social Psychology, 62,* 301–317.

Mavissakalian, M., & Perel, J. (1992). Protective effects of imipramine maintenance treatment in panic disorder with agoraphobia. *American Journal of Psychiatry, 149,* 1053–1057.

May, R. (1953). *Man's search for himself.* New York: Signet Books.

May, R., Angel, E., & Ellenberger, H. F. (1958). *Existence: A new dimension in psychiatry and psychology.* New York: Basic Books.

Mayberry, R., & Eichen, E. B. (1991). The long lasting advantage of learning sign language in childhood: Another look at the critical period for language acquisition. *Journal of Memory and Language, 30,* 486–512.

Mayer, J., Gasche, Y., Braverman, D., & Evans, T. (1992). Mood-congruent judgment is a general effect. *Journal of Personality and Social Psychology, 63,* 119–132.

Mayer, J. D., & Salovey, P. (1997). What is emotional intelligence? In P. Salovey & D. Sluyter (Eds.), *Emotional development and emotional intelligence: Implications for educators.* New York: Basic Books.

Mayer, J. D., Salovey, P., & Caruso, D. (2000). Models of emotional intelligence. In R. J. Sternberg (Ed.), *Handbook of intelligence* (pp. 396–420). New York: Cambridge University Press.

McAdams, D. (1992a). The five-factor model in personality: A critical appraisal. *Journal of Personality, 60,* 329–361.

McAdams, D. (1992b). The intimacy motive. In C. P. Smith, J. W. Atkinson, D. McClelland, & J. Veroff (Eds.), *Motivation and personality: Handbook of thematic content analysis* (pp. 224–228). Cambridge: Cambridge University Press.

McAdams, D., & Vaillant, G. (1982). Intimacy motivation and psychosocial adjustment: A longitudinal study. *Journal of Personality Assessment, 46,* 586–593.

McAdams, D., & West, S. G. (1997). Introduction: Personality psychology and the case study. *Journal of Personality, 65,* 757–783.

McAdams, D. P. (1999). Motives. In V. J. Derlega, B. A. Winstead, et al. (Eds.), *Personality: Contemporary theory and research. Nelson-Hall series in psychology* (2nd ed., pp. 162–194). Chicago, IL: Nelson-Hall Publishers.

McAdams, D. P., & de St. Aubin, E. (1998). *Generativity and adult development: How and why we care for the next generation.* Washington, DC: American Psychological Association.

McAdams, D. P., Hart, H. M., & Maruna, S. (1998). The anatomy of generativity. In D. P. McAdams & E. de St. Aubin (Eds.), *Generativity and adult development: How and why we care for the next generation.* (pp. 7-43). Washington, DC: American Psychological Association.

McAdams, D. P., Hoffman, B. J., Mansfield, E. D., & Day, R. (1996). Themes of agency and communion in significant autobiographical scenes. *Journal of Personality, 64,* 339–377.

McAdams, J. (1986). Status polarization of social welfare attitudes. *Political Behavior, 8,* 313–334.

McCaul, K. D., & Malott, J. M. (1984). Distraction and coping with pain. *Psychological Bulletin, 95,* 516–533.

McClelland, D. C. (1978). Managing motivation to expand human freedom. *American Psychologist, 33,* 201–210.

McClelland, D. C. (1985). *Human motivation.* Glenview, IL: Scott, Foresman.

McClelland, D. C., Atkinson, J. W., Clark, R. A., & Lowell, E. L. (1953). *The achievement motive.* New York: Appleton-Century-Crofts.

McClelland, D. C., Koestner, R., & Weinberger, J. (1989). How do self-attributed and implicit motives differ? *Psychological Review, 96,* 690–792.

McClelland, D. C., & Pilon, D. A. (1983). Sources of adult motives in patterns of parent behavior in early childhood. *Journal of Personality and Social Psychology, 44,* 564–554.

McClelland, D. C., & Winter, D. G. (1969). *Motivating economic achievement.* New York: Free Press.

McClelland, J. L. (1995). Constructive memory and memory distortions: A parallel-distributed processing approach. In D. L. Schacter (Ed.), *Memory distortions: How minds, brains, and societies reconstruct the past* (pp. 69–90). Cambridge: Harvard University Press.

McClintock, M. K. (1971). Menstrual synchrony and suppression. *Nature, 229,* 244–245.

McCloskey, M., & Macaruso, P. (1995). Representing and using numerical information. *American Psychologist, 50,* 351–363.

McComb, K., Packer, C., & Pusey, A. (1994). Roaring and numerical assessment in contests between groups of female lions, Panthera leo. *Animal Behaviour, 47,* 379–387.

McConaghy, N. (1979). Maternal deprivation: Can its ghost be laid? *Australian and New Zealand Journal of Psychiatry, 13,* 209–217.

McConahay, J., & Hough, J. (1976). Symbolic racism. *Journal of Social Issues, 32,* 23–45.

McConkey, K. M. (1995). *Hypnosis, memory, and behavior in criminal investigation.* New York: Guilford Press.

McCrae, C. N., Bodenhausen, G., & Milne, A. B. (1998b). Saying no to unwanted thoughts: Self-focus and the regulation of mental life. *Journal of Personality and Social Psychology, 74,* 578–589.

McCrae, R. R. (1996). Social consequences of experiential openness. *Psychological Bulletin, 120,* 323–337.

McCrae, R. R., & Costa, P. (1997). Personality trait structure as a human universal. *American Psychologist, 52,* 509–516.

McCrae, R. R., & Costa, P. T. (1990). *Personality in adulthood.* New York: Guilford Press.

McCrae, R. R., Costa, P., del Pilar, G., Rolland, J-P., & Parker, W. D. (1998a). Cross-cultural assessment of the five-factor model: The revised NEO Personality Inventory. *Journal of Cross-Cultural Psychology, 29,* 171–188.

McDaniel, M. A., Robinson-Riegler, B., & Einstein, G. O. (1998). Prospective remembering: Perceptually driven or conceptually driven processes? *Memory and Cognition, 26,* 121–134.

McDonald, J. L. (1997). Language acquisition: The acquisition of linguistic structure in normal and special populations. *Annual Review, 48,* 215–241.

McDonough, L., & Mandler, J. M. (1994). Very long-term recall in infants: Infantile amnesia reconsidered. *Memory, 2,* 339-352.

McEvoy, G. M., & Cascio, W. F. (1989). Cumulative evidence of the relationship between employee age and job performance. *Journal of Applied Psychology, 74,* 11–17.

McEwan, B. S. (1999). Stress and hippocampal plasticity. *Annual Review of Neuroscience, 22,* 105-122.

McGaugh, J., Weinberger, N., & Lynch, G. (Eds.). (1995). *Brain and memory: Modulation and mediation of neuroplasticity.* New York: Oxford University Press.

McGaugh, J. L. (2000). Memory: A century of consolidation. *Science, 287,* 248–251.

McGeorge, P., Crawford, J. R., & Kelley, S. W. (1996). The relationship between WAIS—R abilities and speed of processing in a word identification task. *Intelligence, 23,* 175–190.

McGlynn, F. D., Mealies, W. L. Jr., & Landau, D. L. (1981). The current status of systematic desensitization. *Clinical Psychology Review, 1,* 149–179.

McGrober, S. (2000). Family, school, and community parenting among low-income, African-American single mothers with preschool-age children: Patterns, pPredictors, and developmental correlates. *Child Development, 71,* 752–771.

McGue, M., & Bouchard, T. J. (1998). Genetic and environmental influences on human behavioral differences. *Annual Review of Neuroscience, 21,* 1–24.

McGue, M., Bacon, S., & Lykken, D. (1993). Personality stability and change in early adulthood: A behavior genetic analysis. *Developmen-*

tal Psychology, 29, 96–109.

McGue, M., Pickens, R. W., & Svikis, D. (1992). Sex and age effects on the inheritance of alcohol problems: A twin study. Journal of Abnormal Psychology, 101, 3–17.

McGuire, S., Manke, B., Saudino, K. J., Reiss, D., Hetherington, E. M., & Plomin, R. (1999). Perceived competence and self-worth during adolescence: A longitudinal behavioral genetic study. Child Development, 70, 1283–1296.

McGuire, W. (1986). The myth of massive media impact: Savagings and salvagings. In G. Comstock (Ed.), Public communication and behavior (Vol. 1). New York: Academic Press.

McGuire, W. J. (1961). The effectiveness of supportive and refutational defenses in immunizing and restoring beliefs against persuasion. Sociometry, 24, 184–197.

McGuire, W. J. (1985). Attitudes and attitude change. In G. Lindzey & E. Aronson (Eds.), Handbook of Social Psychology. Reading, MA: Addison-Wesley.

McGuire, W. J., & Papageorgis, D. (1962). Effectiveness of forewarning in developing resistance to persuasion. Public Opinion Quarterly, 26, 24–34.

McHale, S. M., Crouter, A. C., & Tucker, C. J. (1999). Family context and gender role socialization in middle childhood: Comparing girls to boys and sisters to brothers. Child Development, 70, 990–1004.

McIntosh, A. R., & Gonzalez-Lima, F. (1998) Large-scale functional connectivity in associative learning: Interrelations of the rat auditory, visual, and limbic systems. Journal of Neurophysiology, 80, 3148–3162.

McKoon, G., & Ratcliff, R. (1998). Memory-based language processing: Psycholinguistic research in the 1990s. Annual Review of Psychology, 49, 25–42.

McLoyd, V. (1989). Socialization and development in a changing economy: The effects of paternal job and income loss on children. American Psychologist, 44, 293–302.

McNally, R. (1987). Preparedness and phobias: A review. Psychologial Bulletin, 101, 283–303.

McNally, R. J., Clancy, S. A., Schacter, D. L., & Pitman, R. K. (1999). Cognitive processing of trauma cues in adults reporting repressed, recovered, or continuous memories of childhood sexual abuse. Journal of Abnormal Psychology, 109, 355–359.

McNeil, T. F, Cantor-Graae, E., & Weinberger, D. R. (2000). Relationship of obstetric complications and differences in size of brain structures in monozygotic twin pairs discordant for schizophrenia. American Journal of Psychiatry, 157, 203-212.

Mead, M. (1928). Coming of age in Samoa: A psychological study of primitive youth for Western civilization. New York: Morrow & Co.

Meaney, M., & McEwen, B. (1986). Testosterone implants into the amygdala during the neonatal period masculinize the social play of juvenile female rats. Brain Research, 398, 324–328.

Medin, D., L., & Heit, E. (1999). Categorization. In B. M. Bly & D. E. Rumelhart (Eds.), Cognitive science: Handbook of perception and cognition (2nd ed., pp. 99–143). San Diego, CA: Academic Press.

Medin, D. L., Lynch, E. B., Coley, J. D., & Atran, S. (1997). Categorization and reasoning among tree experts: Do all roads lead to Rome? Cognitive Psychology, 32, 49–96.

Medin, D. L., Lynch, E. B., & Solormon, K. O. (2000). Are there kinds of concepts? Annual Review of Psychology, 51, 121–147.

Medin, D. L., & Smith, E. E. (1981). Strategies and classification learning. Journal of Experimental Psychology: Human Learning and Memory, 7, 241–253.

Medin, D. L., & Smith, E. E. (1985). Concepts and concept formation. Annual Review of Psychology, 35, 113–138.

Meece, J. L., Wigfield, A., & Eccles, J. S. (1990). Predictors of math anxiety and its influence on young adolescents' course enrollment intentions and performance in mathematics. Journal of Educational Psychology, 82, 60–70.

Meichenbaum, D. (1977). Cognitive-behavior modification: An integrative approach. New York: Plenum Press.

Meichenbaum, D. (1990). Cognitive perspective on teaching self-regulation. American Journal of Mental Retardation, 94, 367–369.

Melcher, J. M., & Schooler, J. W. (1996). The misremembrance of wines past: Verbal and perceptual expertise differentially mediate verbal overshadowing of taste memory. Journal of Memory and Language, 35, 231–245.

Mellers, B., Schwartz, A., & Cooke, A. D. J. (1998). Judgment and decision making. Annual Review of Psychology, 49, 447–477.

Mellers, B., Schwartz, A., Ho, K., & Ritov, I. (1997). Decision affect theory: Emotional reactions to the outcomes of risky options. Psychological Science, 8, 423–429.

Mellers, B., Schwartz, A., & Ritov, I. (1999). Emotion-based choice. Journal of Experimental Psychology: General, 128, 332–345.

Meltzoff, A. (1990). Towards a developmental cognitive science: The implications of cross-modal matching and imitation for the development of representation and memory in infancy. Annals of the New York Academy of Sciences, 608, 1–7.

Meltzoff, A. N. (1995). What infant memory tells us about infantile amnesia: Long-term recall and deferred imitation. Special Issue: Early memory. Journal of Experimental Child Psychology, 59, 497–515.

Meltzoff, A. N., & Borton, R. W. (1979). Inter-modal matching by human neonates. Nature, 282, 403–404.

Meltzoff, A. N., & Moore, M. K. (1977). Imitation of facial and manual gestures by human neonates. Science, 198, 75–78.

Melzack, R. (1970). Phantom limbs. Psychology Today, 63–68.

Melzack, R. (1993). Pain: Past, present and future. Canadian Journal of Experimental Psychology, 47, 615–629.

Melzack, R., & Wall, P. D. (1965). Pain mecha-nisms: A new theory. Science, 150, 971–979.

Melzack, R., & Wall, P. D. (1983). The challenge of pain. New York: Basic Books.

Menard, M. T., Kosslyn, S., Thompson, W. L., Alpert, N. M., et al. (1996). Encoding words and pictures: A positron emission tomography study. Neuropsychologia, 34, 185–194.

Mendlowicz, M. V., & Stein, M. B. (2000). Quality of life in individuals with anxiety disorders. American Journal of Psychiatry, 157, 669–682.

Mendola, J. D., Dale, A. M., Fischl, B., Liu, A. K., & Tootell, R. B. H. (1999). The representation of illusory and real contours in human cortical visual areas revealed by functional magnetic resonance imaging. Journal of Neuroscience, 19, 8560–8572.

Mendoza, S. P., & Mason, W. A. (1997). Attachment relationships in New World primates. In C. S. Carter, I. I. Lederhendler, & B. Kirkpatrick (Eds.), The integrative neurobiology of affiliation (Vol. 807, pp. 203–209). New York: New York Academy of Sciences.

Menon, T., Morris, M. W., Chiu, C., & Hong, Y. (1999). Culture and the construal of agency: Attribution to individual versus group disposi-tions. Journal of Personaity and Social Psychology, 76, 701–717.

Merckelbach, H., Arntz, A., & de Jong, P. (1991). Conditioning experiences in spider phobics. Behaviour Research & Therapy, 29, 333–335.

Merikangas, K. R., Dierker, L. C., & Szamari, P. (1998). Psychopathology among offspring of parents with substance abuse and/or anxiety disorders: A high risk study. Journal of Child Psychology & Psychiatry & Allied Disciplines, 39, 711-720.

Merriam, A. P. (1971). Aspects of sexual behavior among the Bala (Basongye). In D. S. Marshall, & R. C. Suggs (Eds.), Human sexual behavior: Variations in the ethnographic spectrum. New York: Basic Books.

Merton, R. K. (1957). Social theory and social structure. Glencoe, IL: Free Press.

Mervis, C. B., & Rosch, E. (1981). Categorization of natural objects. Annual Review of Psychology, 32, 89–115.

Messer, S., & Winokur, M. (1980). Some limits to the integration of psychodynamic and behavior therapy. American Psychologist, 35, 818–827.

Messer, S., Sass, L. H., & Woolfolk, R. L., (Eds.). (1988). Hermeneutics and psychological theory. New Brunswick, NJ: Rutgers University Press.

Metcalfe, J. (2000). Metamemory: Theory and data. In E. Tulving & F. I. Craik (Eds.). The Oxford handbook of memory. (pp. 197–211). New York: Oxford University Press.

Mezzacappa, E. S., Katkin, E. S., & Palmer, S. N. (1999). Epinephrine, arousal, and emotion: A new look at two-factor theory. Cognition and Emotion, 13, 181–199.

Mezzich, J. E., Kirmayer, L. J., Kleinman, A., Fabrega, H., Parron, D. L., Good, B. J., Lin, K., & Manson, S M. (1999). The place of culture in DSM-IV. Journal of Nervous & Mental Disease, 187, 457-464.

Mezzich, J. E., Kleinman, A., Fabrega, H., &

Parron, D. L. (1996). Culture and psychiatric diagnosis: A DSM-IV perspective. Washington, DC: American Psychiatric Press, Inc.

Michelson, D., Bancroft, J., Targum, S., Kim, Y., & Tepner, R. (2000). Female sexual dysfunction associated with antidepressant administration: A randomized, placebo-controlled study of pharmacologic intervention. *American Journal of Psychiatry, 157,* 239–243.

Mickelson, K. D., Kessler, R. C., & Shaver, P. R. (1997). Adult attachment in a nationally representative sample. *Journal of Personality & Social Psychology, 73,* 1092–1106.

Mikulincer, M., & Florian, V. (1997). Are emotional and instrumental supportive interactions beneficial in times of stress? The impact of attachment style. *Anxiety, Stress & Coping: an International Journal, 10,* 109-127.

Mikulincer, M., Florian, V., & Weller, A. (1993). Attachment styles, coping strategies, and post-traumatic psychological distress: The impact of the Gulf War in Israel. *Journal of Personality and Social Psychology, 64,* 817–826.

Milgram, S. (1963). Behavioral study of obedience. *Journal of Abnormal and Social Psychology, 67,* 371–378.

Milgram, S. (1965). Some conditions of obedience and disobedience to authority. *Human Relations, 18,* 57–76.

Milgram, S. (1974). *Obedience to authority: An experimental view.* New York: Harper & Row.

Miller, C. T., & Downey, K. T. (1999). A meta-analysis of heavyweight and self-esteem. *Personality and Social Psychology Review, 3*(1), 68–84.

Miller, C. T., Rothblum, E. D., Barbour, L., & Brand, P. A. (1990). Social interactions of obese and nonobese women. *Journal of Personality, 58,* 365-380.

Miller, D. T. (1999). The norm of self-interest. *American Psychologist, 54*(12), 1053–1060.

Miller, G. A. (1956). The magical number seven, plus or minus two: Some limits in our capacity for processing information. *Psychological Review, 63,* 81–97.

Miller, G. A., Galanter, E., & Pribram, K. H. (1960). *Plans and the structure of behavior.* New York: Holt, Rinehart & Winston.

Miller, I. J., Jr. (1995). Anatomy of the peripheral taste system. In R. L. Doty (Ed.), *Handbook of olfaction and gustation.* New York: Marcel Dekker.

Miller, J. G. (1994). Cultural diversity in the morality of caring: Individually oriented versus duty-based interpersonal moral codes. *Cross-Cultural Research, 28,* 3–39.

Miller, J. G. (1997). A cultural-psychology perspective on intelligence. In R. J. Sternberg & E. L. Grigorenko (Eds.), *Intelligence, heredity, and environment* (pp. 269–302). New York: Cambridge University Press.

Miller, J. L., & Eimas, P. (1995). Speech perception: From signal to word. *Annual Review of Psychology, 46,* 467–492.

Miller, L. C., Bettencourt, B. A., DeBro, S., & Hoffman, V. (1993). Negotiating safer sex: Interpersonal dynamics. In J. Pryor and G. Reeder (Eds.), *The social psychology of HIV infection.*

Hillsdale, NJ: Erlbaum.

Miller, L. T., & Vernon, P. A. (1997). Developmental changes in speed of information processing in young children. *Developmental Psychology, 33,* 549–554.

Miller, N., & Campbell, D. T. (1959). Recency and primacy in persuasion as a function of the timing of speeches and measurement. *Journal of Abnormal and Social Psychology, 59,* 1–9.

Miller, P. A., Eisenberg, N., Fabes, R., & Shell, R. (1996). Relations of moral reasoning and vicarious emotion to young children's prosocial behavior toward peers and adults. *Developmental Psychology, 32,* 210–219.

Miller, T. W., & Kraus, R. F. (1990). An overview of chronic pain. *Hospital and Community Psychiatry, 41,* 433–440.

Miller, W. A., Ratliff, F., & Hartline, H. K. (1961). How cells receive stimuli. *Scientific American, 222*–238.

Miller, W. C. (1999). Fitness and fatness in relation to health: Implications for a paradigm shift. *Journal of Social Issues, 55*(2), 207–219.

Mills, J., & Clark, M. S. (1994). Communal and exchange relationships: Controversies and research. In R. Erber, R. Gilmour, et al. (Eds.), *Theoretical frameworks for personal relationships* (pp. 29–42). Hillsdale, NJ: Lawrence Erlbaum Associates.

Mills, M. (1995). *Characteristics of personals ads differ as a function of publication readership SES.* Paper presented at the annual convention of the Human Behavior and Evolution Society, June, Santa Barbara, CA.

Milner, B., Corkin, S., & Teuber, H. L. (1968). Further analysis of the hippocampal amnesic syndrome: Fourteen year follow-up study of H.M. *Neuropsychologia, 6,* 215–234.

Milner, P. (1991). Brain-stimulation reward: A review. *Canadian Journal of Psychology, 45,* 1–36.

Mineka, S., & Sutton, S. K. (1992). Cognitive biases and the emotional disorders. *Psychological Science, 3,* 65–69.

Mineka, S., Watson, D., & Clark, L. A. (1998). Comorbidity of anxiety and unipolar mood disorders. *Annual Review of Psychology, 49,* 377–412.

Minsky, M. (1975). A framework for representing knowledge. In P. H. Winston (Ed.), *The psychology of computer vision.* New York: McGraw-Hill.

Minuchin, S. (1974). *Families and family therapy.* Cambridge, MA: Harvard University Press.

Mirsky, A. F., & Duncan, C. C. (1986). Etiology and expression of schizophrenia: Neurobiological and psychosocial factors. *Annual Review of Psychology, 37,* 291–319.

Mischel, W. (1968). *Personality and assessment.* New York: John Wiley.

Mischel, W. (1973). Toward a cognitive social learning reconceptualization of personality. *Psychological Review, 39,* 351–364.

Mischel, W. (1979). On the interface of cognitive and personality: Beyond the person-situation debate. *American Psychologist, 34,* 740–754.

Mischel, W., & Mischel, H. N. (1976). A cognitive social-learning approach to morality and

self-regulation. In T. Lickona (Ed.), *Moral development and behavior: Theory, research, and social issues.* New York: Holt, Rinehart, & Winston.

Mischel, W., & Shoda, Y. (1995). A cognitive-affective system theory of personality: Reconceptualizing situations, dispositions, dynamics, and invariance in personality structure. *Psychological Review, 102,* 246–268.

Mischel, W., & Shoda, Y. (1998). Reconciling processing dynamics and personality dispositions. *Annual Review of Psychology,* 229–258.

Mishra, R. C. (1997). Cognition and cognitive development. In J. W. Berry, P. R. Dasen, & T. S. Swanaswathi (Eds.), *Handbook of cross-cultural psychology: Vol. 2. Basic processes and human development* (2nd ed., pp. 143–175). Boston: Allyn & Bacon.

Mistry, J., & Rogoff, B. (1985). A cultural perspective on the development of talent. In F. D. Horowitz & M. O'Brien (Eds.), *The gifted and talented: Developmental perspectives* (pp. 125–144). Washington, DC: American Psychological Association.

Misumi, J., & Peterson, M. F. (1985). The performance-maintenance (PM) theory of leadership: Review of a Japanese research program. *Administrative Science Quarterly, 30,* 198-223.

Mitchell, S. A. (1988). *Relational concepts in psychoanalysis: An integration.* Cambridge, MA: Harvard University Press.

Mitchell, S. A., & Aron, L. (Eds.). (1999). *Relational perspectives book series: Vol. 14. Relational psychoanalysis: The emergence of a tradition.* Hillsdale, NJ: Analytic Press.

Moatti, J., Hausser, D., & Agrafiotis, D. (1997). Understanding HIV risk-related behaviour: A critical overview of current models. In L.V. Campenhoudt, M. Cohen, G. Guizzardi, & D. Hausser (Eds.), *Sexual interactions and HIV risk: New conceptual perspective in European research. Social aspects of AIDS* (pp. 100–126). Washington, DC: Taylor & Francis.

Moeller, G., & Applezweig, M. M. (1957). A motivational factor in conformity. *Journal of Abnormal Social Psychology, 55,* 114–120.

Moerk, E. L. (1992). *A first language taught and learned.* Baltimore, MD: Brookes.

Moffit, T.E., Caspi, A., Dickson, N., Silva, P., & Stanton, W. (1996). Childhood-onset versus adolescent-onset antisocial conduct problems in males: Natural history from ages 3 to 18 years. *Development & Psychopathology, 8,* 399-424.

Mogil, J. S., Yu, L., & Basbaum, A. I. (2000). Pain genes? Natural variation and transgenic mutants. *Annual Review of Neuroscience, 23,* 777–811.

Moloney, D. P., Bouchard, T., & Segal, N. (1991). A genetic and environmental analysis of the vocational interests of monozygotic and dizygotic twins reared apart. *Journal of Vocational Behavior, 39,* 76–109.

Money, J. (1987). Sin, sickness, or status? Homosexual gender identity and psychoneuroendocrinology. *American Psychologist, 42,* 384–399.

Money, J., & Ehrhardt, A. A. (1972). *Man and woman. Boy and girl.* Baltimore, MD: Johns

Hopkins University Press.

Money, J., Schwartz, M., & Lewis, V. G. (1984). Adult heterosexual status and fetal hormonal masculinization and demasculinization. *Psychoneuroendocrinology, 9*, 405–414.

Monk, T. H. (1997). Shift work. In M. R. Pressman & W. C. Orr (Eds.), *Understanding sleep: The evaluation and treatment of sleep disorders. Application and practice in health psychology* (pp. 249–266). Washington, DC: American Psychological Association.

Monroe, S. M., & Simons, A. D. (1991). Diathesis-stress theories in the context of life stress research: Implications for the depressive disorders. *Psychological Bulletin, 110*, 406–425.

Montemayor, R., & Eisen, M. (1977). A developmental sequence of self-conceptions from childhood to adolescence. *Developmental Psychology, 13*, 314–319.

Montgomery, S. (1994a). Long-term treatment of depression. *British Journal of Psychiatry, 165*, 31–36.

Montgomery, S. A. (1994b). Antidepressants in long-term treatment. *Annual Review of Medicine, 45*, 447–457.

Moos, R. H., & Billings, A. G. (1982). Conceptualizing and measuring coping resources and processes. In L. Goldberger & S. Breznitz (Eds.), *Handbook of stress.* New York: Macmillan.

Moos, R. H., & Schaefer, J. A. (1986). Life transitions and crises. In R. H. Moos & J. A. Schaefer (Eds.), *Coping with life crises: An integrated approach.* New York: Plenum Press.

Moray, N. (1969). *Attention: Selective processes in vision and hearing.* London: Hutchinson.

Moreland, R. L. (1985). Social categorization and the assimilation of new group members. *Journal of Personality and Social Psychology, 48*, 1173–1190.

Morelli, G., Rogoff, B., Oppenheim, D., & Goldsmith, D. (1992). Cultural variation in infants' sleeping arrangements: Questions of independence. *Developmental Psychology, 28*, 604–613.

Moretti, M. M., & Higgins, E. T. (1999). Own versus other standpoints in self-regulation. Developmental antecedents and functional consequences. *Review of General Psychology, 3*(3), 188–223.

Morgan, J. (1986). *From simple input to complex grammar.* Cambridge, MA: MIT Press.

Morling, B., & Epstein, S. (1997). Compromises produced by the dialectic between self-verification and self-enhancement. *Journal of Personality & Social Psychology, 73*, 1268–1283.

Morris, J. S., Frith, C. D., Perrett, D. I., Rowland, D., Young, A. W., Calder, A. J., & Dolan, R. J. (1996). A differential neural response in the human amygdala to fearful and happy facial expressions. *Nature, 383*, 812–815.

Morris, J. S., Oehman, A., & Dolan, R. J. (1998). Conscious and unconscious emotional learning in the human amygdala. *Nature, 393*, 467–470.

Morris, R. G., & Baddeley, A. D. (1988). Primary and working memory functioning in Alzheimer-type dementia. *Journal of Clinical and Experimental Neuropsychology, 10*, 279–296.

Morse, J. M., & Park, C. (1988). Differences in cultural expectations of the perceived painfulness of childbirth. In K. Michaelson (Ed.), *Childbirth in America: Anthropological perspectives.* South Hadley, MA: Bergin & Garvey.

Mowrer, O. H. (1960). *Learning theory and behavior.* New York: John Wiley.

Moyer, K. E. (1983). The physiology of motivation: Aggression as a model. In C. James Scheirer & Anne M. Rogers (Eds.), *G. Stanley Hall Lecture Series* (Vol. 3). Washington, DC: American Psychological Association.

Mroczek, D. K., & Kolarz, C. M. (1998). The effect of age on positive and negative affect: A developmental perspective on happiness. *Journal of Personality and Social Psychology, 75*, 1333–1349.

Mueller, T. I., Leon, A. C., Keller, M. B., Solomon, D. A., Endicott, J., Coryell, W., Warshaw, M., & Maser, J. D. (1999). Recurrence after recovery from major depressive disorder during 15 years of observational follow-up. *American Journal of Psychiatry, 156*, 1000–1006.

Mulligan, R. (1966). Dental pain. In J. Barber (Ed.), *Hypnosis and suggestion in the treatment of pain: A clinical guide* (pp. 185–208). New York: W. W. Norton & Co.

Mumaw, R., & Pellegrino, J. (1984). Individual differences in complex spatial processing. *Journal of Educational Psychology, 76*, 920–939.

Mumford, D. B. (1993). Eating disorders in different cultures. *International Review of Psychiatry, 5*, 109–113.

Munk, M., Roelfsema, P., Konig, P., Engel, A. K., & Singer, W. (1996). Role of reticular activation in the modulation of intracortical synchronization. *Science, 272*, 271–274.

Muraven, M., & Baumeister R. F. (2000). Self-regulation and depletion of limited resources: Does self-control resemble a muscle? *Psychological Bulletin, 126*(2), 247–259.

Murphy, G. L., & Medin, D. L. (1985). The role of theories in conceptual coherence. *Psychological Review, 92*, 289–316.

Murphy, J. M. (1976). Psychiatric labeling in cross-cultural perspective. *Science, 191*, 1019–1028.

Murphy, J. M., Laird, N. M., Monson, R. R., Sobol, A. M., & Leighton, A. H. (2000). A 40-year perspective on the prevalence of depression: The Stirling County Study. *Archives of General Psychiatry, 57*, 209–215.

Murphy, S. T., & Zajonc, R. (1993). Affect, cognition, and awareness: Affective priming with optimal and suboptimal stimulus exposures. *Journal of Personality and Social Psychology, 64*, 723–739.

Murray, H. A. (1938). *Explorations in personality.* New York: Oxford University Press.

Murray, S. L., & Holmes, J. G. (1997). A leap of faith? Positive illusions in romantic relationships. *Personality and Social Psychology Bulletin, 23*, 586–604.

Murray, S. L., & Holmes, J. G. (1999). The (mental) ties that bind: Cognitive structures that predict relationship resilience. *Journal of Personality and Social Psychology, 77*, 1228–1244.

Murray, S. L., Holmes, J. G., & Griffin, D. W. (2000). Self-esteem and the quest for felt security: How perceived regard regulates attachment processes. *Journal of Personality and Social Psychology, 78*, 478–498.

Murray, S. L., Holmes, J. G., MacDonald, G., & Ellsworth, P. C. (1998). Through the looking glass darkly? When self-doubts turn into relationship insecurities. *Journal of Personality and Social Psychology, 75*, 1459–1480.

Murrey, G. J., Cross, H. J., & Whipple, J. (1992). Hypnotically created pseudomemories: Further investigation into the "memory distortion or response bias" question. *Journal of Abnormal Psychology, 101*, 75–77.

Myers, D. G. (2000). The funds, friends, and faith of happy people. *American Psychologist, 55*, 56–67.

Myers, D. G., & Diener, E. (1995). Who is happy? *Psychological Science, 6*, 10–19.

Nader, K., & van der Kooy, D. (1997). Deprivation state switches the neurobiological substrates mediating opiate reward in the ventral tegmental area. *Journal of Neuroscience, 17*, 383–390.

Nakao, M., Nomura, S., Shimosawa, T., Fujita, T., & Kuboki, T. (1999). Blood pressure biofeedback treatment, organ damage and sympathetic activity in mild hypertension. *Psychotherapy and Psychosomatics, 68*(6), 341–347.

Nakao, M., Nomura, S., Shimosawa, T., Yoshiuchi, K., Kumano, H., Kuboki, T., et al. (1997). Clinical effects of blood pressure biofeedback treatment on hypertension by auto-shaping. *Psychosomatic Medicine, 59*, 331–338.

Narita, K., Sasaki, T., Akaho, R., Okazaki, Y., Kusumi, I., Kato, T., Hashimoto, O., Fukuda, R., Koyama, T., Matsuo, K., Okabe, Y., Nanko, S., Hohjoh, H., Tokunaga, K. (2000) Human leukocyte antigen and season of birth in Japanese patients with schizophrenia. *American Journal of Psychiatry, 157*, 1173-1175.

Nash, M. R. (1988). Hypnosis as a window on regression. *Bulletin of the Menninger Clinic, 52*, 383–403.

Nathan, P. E. (1998). *The DSM-IV and its antecedents: Enhancing syndromal diagnosis. Making diagnosis meaningful: Enhancing evaluation and treatment of psychological disorders.* Barron, J. W. (Ed). (pp. 3-27). Washington: American Psychological Association.

Nathans, J. (1987). Molecular biology of visual pigments. *Annual Review of Physiology, 10*, 163–194.

National Institute of Child Health and Human Development Early Child Care Research Network. (2000). The relation of child care to cognitive and language development. *Child Development, 71*, 960–980.

National Research Council. (1989). Obesity and eating disorders. In *Diet and health: Implications for reducing chronic disease risk* (pp. 563–592.).

Washington, DC: National Academy Press.

Negandhi, A. R. (1973). *Management and economic development: The case of Taiwan.* The Hague: Martinus Nijhoff.

Neher, A. (1991). Maslow's theory of motivation: A critique. *Journal of Humanistic Psychology, 31,* 89–112.

Neisser, U. (1967). *Cognitive psychology.* New York: Appleton-Century-Crofts.

Neisser, U. (1976a). *Cognition and reality.* San Francisco: Freeman.

Neisser, U. (1976b). General, academic, and artificial intelligence. In L. Resnick (Ed.), *Human intelligence: Perspectives on its theory and measurement* (pp. 179–189). Norwood, NJ: Ablex.

Neisser, U. (1978). Anticipations, images, and introspection. *Cognition, 6,* 169–174.

Neisser, U. (1991). A case of misplaced nostalgia. *American Psychologist, 46,* 34–36.

Neisser, U., Boodoo, G., Bouchard, T. J., Boykin, A. W., Brody, N., Ceci, S. J., Halpern, D. F., Loehlin, J. C., Perloff, R., Sternberg, R. J., & Urbina, S. (1998). Intelligence: Knowns and unknowns. In M. E. Hertzig & E. A. Farber (Eds.), *Annual progress in child psychiatry and child development: 1997* (pp. 95–133). Bristol, PA: Brunner/Mazel.

Neisser, U., et al. (Eds.) (1998). *The rising curve: Long-term gains in IQ and related measures.* Washington, DC: American Psychological Association.

Nelson, C. A. (1995). The ontogeny of human memory: A cognitive neuroscience perspective. *Developmental Psychology, 31,* 723–738.

Nelson, D. A., & Crick, N. R. (1999). Rose-colored glasses: Examining the social information-processing of prosocial young adolescents. *Journal of Early Adolescence, 19,* 17-38.

Nelson, K. (1987). What's in a name? Reply to Seidenberg and Petitto. *Journal of Experimental Psychology: General, 116,* 293–296.

Nelson, K. (1997). Cognitive change as collaborative construction. In E. Amsel, K. A. Renninger, et al. (1997), *Change and development: Issues of theory, method, and application. The Jean Piaget symposium series.* (pp. 99–115). Mahwah, NJ: Lawrence Erlbaum Associates.

Nelson, M. D., Saykin, A. J., Flashman, L. A., & Riordan, H. J. (1998). Hippocampal volume reduction in schizophrenia as assessed by magnetic resonance imaging: A meta-analytic study. *Archives of General Psychiatry, 55,* 433–440.

Nesbitt, E. B. (1973). An escalator phobia overcome in one session of flooding in vivo. *Journal of Behavior Therapy and Experimental Psychiatry, 4,* 405–406.

Nestadt, G., Samuels, J., Riddle, M., Bienvenu, J., Liang, K., LaBuda, M., Walkup, J., Grados, M., & Hoehn-Saric, R. (2000). A family study of obsessive-compulsive disorder. *Archives of General Psychiatry, 57,* 358–363.

Nettelbeck, T., & Wilson, C. (1997). Speed of information processing and cognition. In W. E. MacLean Jr. (Ed.), *Ellis' handbook of mental deficiency, psychological theory and research* (3rd ed., pp. 245–274). Hillsdale, NJ: Lawrence Erlbaum

Associates.

Neugarten, B. L. (1977). Personality and aging. In J. E. Birren & K. W. Schaie (Eds.), *Handbook of the psychology of aging.* New York: Academic.

Neugarten, B. L. (1979). Time, age and the life cycle. *American Journal of Psychiatry, 136,* 887-894.

Neutra, M., & Leblond, C. P. (1969). The Golgi apparatus. *Scientific American,* 100–107.

Newcomb, T. M. (1956). The predictions of interpersonal attraction. *American Psychologist, II,* 575–586.

Newcomb, T. M. (1961). *The acquaintance process.* New York: Holt, Rinehart, & Winston.

Newcombe, N., Drummey, A. B., & Lie, E. (1995). Children's memory for early experience. Special issue: Early memory. *Journal of Experimental Child Psychology, 59,* 337–342.

Newcombe, N., & Dubas, J. S. (1992). A longitudinal study of predictors of spatial ability in adolescent females. *Child Development, 63,* 37–46.

Newell, A. (1969). Heuristic programming: Ill-structured problems. In J. Aronofsky (Ed.), *Progress in operations research,* (Vol. 3). New York: John Wiley.

Newell, A., & Simon, H. A. (1972). *Human problem solving.* Englewood Cliffs, NJ; Prentice-Hall.

Newman, E. A., & Hartline, P. H. (1982). The infrared "vision" of snakes. *Scientific American,* 116–127.

Newman, H. G., Freeman, F. N., & Holzinger, K. J. (1937). *Twins: A study of heredity and environment.* Chicago: University of Chicago Press.

Newman, J. (1995). Thalamic contributions to attention and consciousness. *Consciousness and Cognition, 4,* 172–193.

Newman, L. S., Duff, K., & Baumeister, R. (1997). A new look at defensive projection: Thought suppression, accessibility, and biased person perception. *Journal of Personality and Social Psychology, 72,* 980–1001.

Newport, E. L. (1990). Maturational constraints on language learning. *Cognitive Science, 14,* 11–28.

Newport, E. L., Gleitman, H., & Gleitman, L. R. (1977). Mother, I'd rather do it myself: Some effects and noneffects of maternal speech style. In C. Snow & C. A. Ferguson (Eds.), *Talking to children: Language input and acquisition.* Cambridge, England: Cambridge University Press.

Newsom, C., Flavall, J., & Rincover, A. (1983). Side effects of punishment. In S. Axelrod & J. Apsche (Eds.), *The effects of punishment on human behavior.* New York: Academic.

Newsome, W. T., Britten, K. H., & Moushon, J. A. (1989). Neuronal correlates of a perceptual decision. *Nature, 341,* 52–54.

Nickerson, R. S. (1998). Confirmation bias: A ubiquitous phenomenon in many guises. *Review of General Psychology, 2,* 175–220.

Niedenthal, P., Setterlund, M., & Wherry, M. B. (1992). Possible self-complexity and affective reactions to goal-relevant evaluation. *Journal of Personality and Social Psychology, 63,* 5–16.

Nielsen, D. A., Jenkins, G. L., Stefanisko, K. M., Jefferson, K. K., & Goldman, G. (1997).

Sequence, splice site, and population frequency distribution analyses of polymorphic human tryptophan hydroxylase intron 7. *Molecular Brain Research, 45,* 145–148.

Nigg, J. T., & Goldsmith, H. H. (1994). Genetics of personality disorders: Perspectives from personality and psychopathology research. *Psychological Bulletin, 115,* 346–380.

Nigg, J. T., Lohr, N. E., Westen, D. Gold, L. J., & Silk, K. (1992). Malevolent object representations in borderline personality disorder and major depression. *Journal of Abnormal Psychology, 101,* 61–67.

Nisbett, R. E., & Ross, L. (1980). *Human inference: Strategies and shortcomings of social judgment.* Englewood Cliffs, NJ: Prentice-Hall.

Nisbett, R. E., & Wilson, T. D. (1977). Telling more than we can know: verbal reports on mental processes. *Psychological Review, 84,* 231–259.

Nishith, P., Mechanic, M. B., & Resick, P. A. (2000). Prior interpersonal trauma: The contribution to current PTSD symptoms in female rape victims. *Journal of Abnormal Psychology, 109,* 20–25.

Nix, R. L., Pinderhughes, E. E., Dodge, K. A., Bates, J. E., Pettit, G. S., & McFadyen-Ketchum, S. A. (1999). The relation between mothers' hostile attribution tendencies and children's externalizing behavior problems: The mediating role of mothers' harsh discipline practices. *Child Development, 70,* 896–909.

Nolde, S. F., Johnson, M. K., & Raye, C. L. (1998). The role of prefrontal cortex during tests of episodic memory. *Trends in Cognitive Sciences, 2,* 399-406.

Nolen-Hoeksema, S., Girgus, J. S., & Seligman, M. E. (1992). Predictors and consequences of childhood depressive symptoms: A 5-year longitudinal study. *Journal of Abnormal Psychology. 101,* 405-422.

Noll, R. (1994). Hypnotherapy for warts in children and adolescents. *Journal of Developmental and Behavioral Pediatrics, 15,* 170–173.

Norcross, J., Karg, R., & Prochaska, J. (1997). Clinical psychologists in the 1990s: Part 1. *Clinical Psychologist, 50,* 4–8.

Norenzayan, A., & Nisbett, R. E. (2000). Culture and causal cognition. *Current Directions in Psychological Science, 9*(4), 132–135.

Norman, W. T. (1963). Toward an adequate taxonomy of personality attributes: Replicated factor structure in peer nomination personality ratings. *Journal of Abnormal and Social Psychology, 66,* 574–583.

Novak, M. A., & Harlow, H. F. (1975). Social recovery of monkeys isolated for the first year of life: Rehabilitation and therapy. *Developmental Psychology, 11,* 453–465.

Nwadiora, E., & McAdoo, H. (1996). Acculturative stress among Amerasian refugees: Gender and racial differences. *Adolescence, 31,* 477–487.

Nyber, L. (1998). Mapping episodic memory. *Behavioral Brain Research, 90,* 107–114.

Nyborg, H., & Jensen, A. R. (2000). Black-white differences on various psychometric tests:

Spearman's hypothesis tested on American armed services veterans. *Personality and Individual Differences, 28*, 593–599.

Oakhill, J., Johnson-Laird, P. N., & Garnham, A. (1989). Believability and syllogistic reasoning. *Cognition, 31*, 117–140.

Oatley, K., & Jenkins, J. M. (1992). Human emotion: Function and dysfunction. *Annual Review of Psychology, 43*, 55–85.

O'Brien, T. B., & DeLongis, A. (1996). The interactional context of problem-, emotion-, and relationship-focused coping: The role of the Big Five personality factors. *Journal of Personality, 64*, 775–813.

Ochsner, K. N. (2000). Are affective events richly recollected or simply familiar? The experience and process of recognizing feelings past. *Journal of Experimental Psychology: General, 129*(2), 242–261.

Ochsner, K. N., & Schacter, D. L. (2000). A social cognitive neuroscience approach to emotion and memory. In J. C. Borod, et al. (Eds.), *The neuropsychology of emotion* (pp. 163–193). New York: Oxford University Press.

O'Connor, T. G., McGuire, S., Reiss, D., Hetherington, E. M., & Plomin, R. (1998). Co-occurrence of depressive symptoms and antisocial behavior in adolescence: A common genetic liability. *Journal of Abnormal Psychology, 107*, 27–37.

O'Connor, T. G., Rutter, M., Beckett, C., Keaveney, L., Kreppner, J., & the English and Romanian Adoptees Study Team. (2000). The effects of global severe privation on cognitive competence: Extension and longitudinal follow-up. *Child Development, 71*, 376–390.

Oettingen, G., & Seligman, M. (1990). Pessimism and behavioral signs of depression in East versus West Berlin. *European Journal of Social Psychology, 20*, 207–220.

Oettingen, G., Little, T. D., Lindenberger, U., & Baltes, P. B. (1994). Causality, agency, and control beliefs in East versus West Berlin children: A natural experiment on the role of context. *Journal of Personality and Social Psychology, 66*, 579–595.

Offer, D., & Offer, J. (1975). *From teenage to young manhood: A psychological study.* New York: Basic Books.

Offer, D., Ostrov, E., Howard, K., & Atkinson, R. (1990). Normality and adolescence. *Psychiatric Clinics of North America, 13*, 377–388.

Ogata, N., Voshii, M., & Narahashi, T. (1989). Psychotropic drugs block voltage-gated ion channels in neuroblastoma cells. *Brain Research, 476*, 140–144.

Ogbu, J. (1991). Minority coping responses and school experience. *Journal of Psychohistory, 18*, 434–456.

Ohman , A. (1994)."Unconscious anxiety": Phobic responses to masked stimuli. *Journal of Abnormal Psychology, 103*, 231–240.

Ohman, A., Esteves, F., & Soares, J. F. (1995). Preparedness and preattentive associative learning: Electrodermal conditioning to masked stimuli. *Journal of Psychophysiology, 9*, 99–108.

Ohman, A., Fredrikson, M., Hugdahl, K., & Rimmon, P. (1976). The premise of equipotentiality in human classical conditioning. *Journal of Experimental Psychological General, 105*, 313–337.

Okasha, A., El Akabaw, A. S., Snyder, K. S., Wilson, A. K., Youssef, I. & El Dawla, A. S. (1994). Expressed emotion, perceived criticism, and relapse in depression: A replication. *American Journal of Psychiatry, 151*, 1001–1005.

Olds, J., & Milner, P. (1954). Positive reinforcement produced by electrical stimulation of septal areas and other regions of rat brains. *Journal of Comparative and Physiological Psychology, 47*, 419–427.

O'Leary, A. (1992). Self-efficacy and health: Behavioral and stress-physiological mediation. *Cognitive Therapy & Research, 16*, 229-245.

O'Leary, A., Brown, S., & Suarez-Al-Adam, M. (1997). Stress and immune function. In T. W. Miller (Ed.), *Clinical disorders and stressful life events* (pp. 181–215). Madison, CT: International Universities Press.

Oliner, S., & Oliner, P. (1988). *The altruistic personality: Rescuers of Jews in Nazi Europe.* New York: Free Press.

Olson, D. (1985). Circumplex model VII: Validation and FACES III. *Family Process, 25*, 337–351.

Olson, D. H. (2000). Circumplex model of marital and family systems. *Journal of Family Therapy, 22*, 144–167.

Olson, G. B. (1981). Perception of melodic contour through intrasensory matching and intersensory transfer by elementary school students. *Journal of Educational Research, 74*, 358–362.

Olson, J. M., & Zanna, M. (1993). Attitudes and attitude change. *Annual Review of Psychology, 44*, 117–154.

Olster, D. H., & Blaustein, J. D. (1989). Development of progesterone-facilitated lordosis in female guinea pigs: Relationship to neural estrogen and progestin receptors. *Brain Research, 484*, 168-176.

Olweus, D. (1980). Familial and temperamental determinants of aggressive behavior in adolescent boys: A causal analysis. *Developmental Psychology, 16*, 644–666.

Olweus, D., Mattsson, A., Schalling, D., & Loew, H. (1980). Testosterone, aggression, physical, and personality dimensions in normal adolescent males. *Psychosomatic Medicine, 42*, 253-269

O'Neill, R. M., Greenberg, R. P., & Fisher, S. (1992). Humor and anality. *Humor: International Journal of Humor Research, 5*, 283–291.

Oppenheim, D., Nir, A., Warren, S., & Emde, R. N. (1997). Emotion regulation in mother-child narrative co-construction: Associations with children's narratives and adaptation. *Developmental Psychology, 33*, 284-294.

Orne, M. T., Sheehan, P. W., & Evans, F. J. (1968). *Journal of Personality and Social Psychology, 9*, 189–196.

Ornstein, R. E. (1986). *The psychology of consciousness.* (2nd ed.). New York: Penguin Books.

Ortony, A., Clore, G. L., & Collins, A. (1988). *The cognitive structure of emotions.* New York: Cambridge University Press.

Ortony, A., & Turner, T. J. (1990). What's basic about basic emotions? *Psychological Review, 97*, 315–331.

Oskamp, S. (1991). Factors influencing household recycling behavior. *Environment & Behavior, 23*, 494–519.

Ost, L. (1991). Acquisition of blood and injection phobia and anxiety response patterns in clinical patients. *Behavior Research and Therapy, 29*, 323–332.

Ouellette, J. A., & Wood, W. (1997). Habit: Predicting frequently-occurring behaviors in constant contexts. Manuscript submitted.

Packwood, J., & Gordon, B. (1975). Steropsis in normal domestic cat, Siamese cat, and cat raised with alternating monocular occlusion. *Journal of Neurophysiology, 38*, 1485–1499.

Paivio, A. (1991). Dual coding theory: Retrospect and current status. *Canadian Journal of Psychology, 45*, 255–287.

Paivio, S. C., & Greenbery, L. S. (1995). Resolving "unfinished business"; efficacy of experimental therapy using empty-chair dialogue. *Journal of Consulting and Clinical Psychology, 63*, 419–425.

Palme, G., & Palme, J. (1999). Personality characteristics of female seeking treatment for obesity, bulimia nervosa and alcoholic disorders. *Personality and Individual Differences, 26*(2), 255–263.

Palumbo, R., & Gillman, I. (1984). Effects of subliminal activation of Oedipal fantasies on competitive performance. *Journal of Nervous and Mental Disease, 172*, 737–741.

Pantel, J., Schroeder, J., Schad, L. R., & Friedlinger, M. (1997). Quantitative magnetic resonance imaging and neuropsychological functions in dementia of the Alzheimer type. *Psychological Medicine, 27*, 221-229.

Papez, J. W. (1937). A proposed mechanism of emotion. *Archives of Neurology and Psychiatry, 38*, 725–743.

Pargament, K. I., & Park, C. L. (1995). Merely a defense? The variety of religious means and ends. *Journal of Social Issues, 51*, 13–32.

Park, D. C., Smith, A. D., Lautenschlager, G., & Earles, J. L. (1996). Mediators of long-term memory performance across the life span. *Psychology & Aging, 11*, 621–637.

Park, D. C., & Schwarz, N. (2000). *Cognitive aging: A primer.* Philadelphia, PA: Psychology Press/Taylor & Francis.

Park, S., & Holzman, P. S. (1993). Association of working memory deficit and eye tracking dysfunction in schizophrenia. *Schizophrenia Research, 11*, 55–61.

Parke, R. D., & Buriel, R. (1998) Socialization in the family: Ethnic and ecological perspectives. In W. Damon (Ed. in Chief) and N. Eisenberg (Vol. Ed.), *Handbook of Child Psychology, Vol. 3.* (pp. 463-552). New York: John Wiley.

Parker, J. G., & Asher, S. R. (1987). Peer relations and later personal adjustment: Are low-accepted children at risk? *Psychological Bulletin,*

102, 357-389.

Parkin, A. J., & Java, R. I. (1999). Deterioration of frontal lobe function in normal aging: Influences of fluid intelligence versus perceptual speed. *Neuropsychology, 13*, 539–545.

Parkin, A. J., Walter, B. M., & Hunkin, N. M. (1995). Relationships between normal aging, frontal lobe function, and memory for temporal and spatial information. *Neuropsychology, 9*, 304–312.

Parloff, M. B., London, P., & Wolfe, B. (1986). Individual psychotherapy and behavior change. *Annual Review of Psychology, 37*, 321–349.

Parsons, T. (1951). *The social system.* Glencoe, IL: Free Press.

Pascual-Leone, A., & Torres, F. (1993). Plasticity of the sensorimotor cortex representations of the reading finger in Braille. *Brain.*

Pascual-Leone, A., Walsh, V., & Rothwell, J. (2000). Transcranial magnetic stimulation in cognitive neuroscience—virtual lesion, chronometry, and functional connectivity. *Current Opinion in Neurobiology, 10*, 232–237.

Passaro, K. T., & Little, R. E. (1997). Childbearing and alcohol use. In R. W. Wilsnack & S. C. Wilsnack (Eds.), *Gender and alcohol: Individual and social perspectives* (pp. 90–113). Rutgers, NJ: Rutgers Center of Alcohol Studies.

Pattatucci, A., & Hamer, D. (1995). Development and familiarity of sexual orientation in females. *Behavior Genetics, 25*, 407–420.

Patterson, D. R., & Ptacek, J. T. (1997). Baseline pain as a moderator of hypnotic analgesia for burn injury treatment. *Journal of Consulting & Clinical Psychology, 65*, 60–67.

Patterson, D. R., Everett, J. J., Burns, G. L., & Marvin, J. A. (1992). Hypnosis for the treatment of burn pain. *Journal of Consulting & Clinical Psychology, 60*, 713–717.

Patterson, G. R., & Bank, L. (1986). Bootstrap ping your way in the nomological thicket. *Behavioral Assessment, 8*, 49–73.

Paulesu, E., Frith, U., Snowling, M., Gallagher, A., Morton, J., Frackowiak, R. S. J., & Frith, C. D. (1996). Is developmental dyslexia a disconnection syndrome? Evidence from PET scanning. *Brain, 119*, 143–157.

Paulhus, D., Fridhandler, B., & Hayes, S. (1997). Psychological defense: Contemporary theory and research. In R. Hogan, J. Johnson, & S. R. Briggs (Eds.), *Handbook of personality psychology* (pp. 543–579). San Diego: Academic Press.

Paunonen, S. V., Jackson, D. N., Trzebinski, J., & Forsterling, F. (1992). Personality structure across cultures: A multimethod evaluation. *Journal of Personality and Social Psychology, 62*, 447–456.

Pause, B. M., Bernfried, S., Krauel, K., Fehm-Wolfsdorf, Gabriele, & Ferstl, R. (1996). Olfactory information processing during the course of the menstrual cycle. *Biological Psychology, 44*, 31–54.

Pavlov, I. P. (1927). *Conditioned reflexes.* New York: Oxford University Press.

Pavone, L., Meli, C., Nigro, F., Lisi, R., et al.

(1993). Late diagnosed phenylketonuria patients: Clinical presentation and results of treatment. *Developmental Brain Dysfunction, 6*, 184–187.

Payne, D. G., Neuschatz, Lampien, J., & Lynn, S. J. (1997). Compelling memory illusions: The qualitative characteristics of false memories. *Current Directions in Psychological Science, 6*, 56–60.

Pedersen, D. M., & Wheeler, J. (1983). The Muller-Lyer illusion among Navajos. *Journal of Social Psychology, 121*, 3–6.

Pederson, D. R., Moran, G., Sitko, C., Campbell, K., Ghesquire, K., & Acton, H. (1990). Maternal sensitivity and the security of infant-mother attachment: A q-sort study. *Child Devleopment, 61*, 1974–1983.

Peele, S. (1986). Implications and limitations of genetic models of alcoholism and other addictions. *Journal of Studies on Alcohol, 47*, 63–73.

Peng, D., & Nisbett, R. E. (1999). Culture, dialectics, and reasoning about contradiction. *American Psychologist, 54*(9), 741–754.

Pennebaker, J. (1997a). *Opening up: The healing power of expressing emotions* (rev. ed.). New York: Guilford Press.

Pennebaker, J. (1997b). Writing about emotional experiences as a therapeutic process. *Psychological Science, 8*, 162–166.

Pennebaker, J., Colder, M., & Sharp, L. K. (1990). Accelerating the coping process. *Journal of Personality and Social Psychology, 58*, 528–537.

Pennebaker, J. W., Barger, S. D., & Tiebout, J. (1989). Disclosure of traumas and health among Holocaust survivors. *Psychosomatic Medicine, 51*, 577–589.

Pennebaker, J. W., Mayne, T. J., & Francis, M. E. (1997). Linguistic predictors of adaptive bereavement. *Journal of Personality & Social Psychology, 72*, 863–871.

Pennebaker, J. W., & Seagal, J. D. (1999). Forming a story: The health benefits of narrative. *Journal of Clinical Psychology, 55*(10), 1243–1254.

Perdue, C., & Gurtman, M. (1990). Evidence for the automaticity of ageism. *Journal of Experimental Social Psychology, 26*, 199–216.

Perlmutter, M. (1983). Learning and memory through adulthood. In M. W. Riley, B. B. Hess, & K. Bond (Eds.), *Aging in society: Selected reviews of recent research.* Hillsdale, NJ: Erlbaum.

Perlmutter, M., Dams, C., Berry, J., Kaplan, M., Pearson, D., & Verdonik, J. (1990). Aging and memory. *Annual Review of Gerontology and Geriatrics, 7*, 57–92.

Perls, F. S. (1969). *Ego, hunger and aggression: The beginning of Gestalt therapy.* New York: Random House.

Perls, F. S. (1989). Theory and technique of personality integration. *TACD Journal, 17*, 35-52.

Perris, E. E., Myers, N. A., & Clifton, R. K. (1990). Long-term memory for a single infancy experience. *Child Development, 61*, 1796–1807.

Perruchet, P. (1989). The effect of spaced practice on explicit and implicit memory. *British Journal of Psychology, 80*, 113–130.

Perry, E., Walker, M., Grace, J., & Perry, R.

(1999). Acetylcholine in mind: A neurotransmitter correlate of consciousness? *Trends in Neurosciences, 22*, 273–280.

Perry, G. D., & Bussey, K. (1979). The social learning theory of sex differences: Imitation is alive and well. *Journal of Personality and Social Psychology, 37*, 1699–1712.

Perry, J. C., & Cooper, S. H. (1987). Empirical studies of psychological defense mechanisms. In R. Michels & J. O. Cavenar, Jr. (Eds.), *Psychiatry.* Philadelphia: J. B. Lippincott.

Pervin, L. (1996). Personality: A view of the future based on a look at the past. *Journal of Research in Personality, 30*, 309–318.

Peskin, J. (1992). Ruse and representations: On children's ability to conceal information. *Developmental Psychology, 28*, 84–89.

Petersen, M. R., et al. (1984). Neural lateralization of vocalizations by Japanese macaques: Communicative significance is more important than acoustic structure. *Behavioral Neuroscience, 98*, 779–790.

Peterson, B. S., Leckman, J. F., Tucker, D., Scahill, L., Staib, L., Zhang, H., King, R., Cohen, D. J., Gore, J. C., & Lombroso, P. (2000). Preliminary findings of antistreptococcal antibody titers and basal ganglia volumes in tic, obsessive-compulsive, and attention-deficit/hyperactivity disorders. *Archives of General Psychiatry, 57*, 364–372.

Peterson, C. (1988). Explanatory style as a risk factor for illness. *Cognitive Therapy and Research, 12*, 119–132.

Peterson, C. (1995). Explanatory style and health. In G. M. Buchanan, M. E. P. Seligman, et al. (Eds.), *Explanatory style* (pp. 233–246). Hillsdale, NJ: Lawrence Erlbaum Associates.

Peterson, C. (2000). The future of optimism. *American Psychologist, 55*, 44–55.

Peterson, C., & Seligman, M. E. P. (1984). Causal explanations as a risk factor for depression: Theory and evidence. *Psychological Review, 91*, 347–374.

Peterson, C., Seligman, M., & Vaillant, G. (1988). Pessimistic explanatory style is a risk factor for physical illness: A thirty-five-year longitudinal study. *Journal of Personality & Social Psychology, 55*, 23–27.

Peterson, C. B., & Mitchell, J. E. (1999). Psychosocial and pharmacological treatment of eating disorders: A review of research findings. *Journal of Clinical Psychology, 55*, 685–697.

Peterson, J. (1925). *Early conceptions and tests of intelligence.* Yonkers-on-Hudson, NY: World Book Co.

Petrinovich, L. F. (1999). *Darwinian dominion: Animal welfare and human interests.* Cambridge, MA: MIT Press.

Petry, N. M., Martin, B., Cooney, J. L., & Kranzler, H. R. (2000). Give them prizes and they will come: Contingency management for treatment of alcohol dependence. *Journal of Consulting and Clinical Psychology, 68*, 250–257.

Pettigrew, T. (1958). Personality and socio-cultural factors in intergroup attitudes: A cross-national comparison. *Journal of Conflict Resolution, 2*,

29–42.

Pettigrew, T. F., & Meertens, R. W. (1995). Subtle and blatant prejudice in western Europe. *European Journal of Social Psychology, 25,* 57-75.

Pettit, G. S. (1997). The developmental course of violence and aggression: Mechanisms of family and peer influence. *Psychiatric Clinics of North America, 20,* 283-299.

Petty, F. (1995). GABA and mood disorders: A brief review and hypotheses. *Journal of Affective Disorders, 34,* 275–281.

Petty, R., & Cacioppo, J. (1981). *Attitudes and persuasion: Classic and contemporary approaches.* Dubuque, IA: W. C. Brown.

Petty, R., & Cacioppo, J. (1986a). *Communication and persuasion: Central and peripheral routes to attitude change.* New York: Springer-Verlag.

Petty, R., & Cacioppo, J. T. (1986b). The elaboration likelihood model of persuasion. *Advances in Experimental Social Psychology, 19,* 123–205.

Petty, R., & Krosnick, J. (1994). *Attitude strength: Antecedents and consequences.* Hillsdale, NJ: Erlbaum.

Petty, R. E., & Wegener, D. T. (1998). Matching versus mismatching attitude functions: Implications for scrutiny of persuasive messages. *Personality & Social Psychology Bulletin, 24,* 227–240.

Phelps, E. A., O'Connor, K. J., Cunningham, W. A., Funayama, E. S., Gatenby, J. C., Gore, J. C., & Banaji, M. (2000). Performance on indirect measures of race evaluation predicts amygdala activation. *Journal of Cognitive Neuroscience, 12,* 729–738.

Phillips, M. L., Young, A. W., Senior, C., Brammer, M., Andrews, C., Calder, A. J., et al. (1997). A specific neural substrate for perceiving facial expressions of disgust. *Nature, 389,* 495–498.

Piaget, J. (1926). *The language and thought of the child.* New York: Humanities Press, 1951.

Piaget, J. (1932). *The moral judgment of the child* (M. Gabrain, Trans.). New York: Free Press.

Piaget, J. (1965). The moral judgment of the child. New York, NY, US: The Free Press.

Piaget, J. (1970). Piaget's theory. In P. Mussen, (Ed.), *Carmichael's manual of child psychology.* New York: John Wiley.

Piaget, J. (1972). Development and learning. In C. S. Lavatelli & F. Stendler (Eds.), *Readings in child behavior and development* (3rd ed.). New York: Harcourt Brace Jovanovich.

Piaget, J., & Inhelder, B. (1956). *The child's conception of space* (F. J. Langdon & J. L. Lunzer, Trans.). London: Routledge & T. K. Paul.

Piaget, J., & Inhelder, B. (1969). *The psychology of the child.* New York: Basic Books.

Pickens, R., Svikis, D., McGue, M., Lykken, D., Heston, L., & Clayton, P. (1991). Heterogeneity in the inheritance of alcoholism: A study of male and female twins. *Archives of General Psychiatry, 48,* 19–28.

Piers, G., & Singer, M. (1953). *Shame and guilt: A psychoanalytic and a cultural study.* Springfield, IL: C. Thomas.

Pihl, R., Peterson, J., & Finn, P. (1990). Inherited predisposition to alcoholism: Characteristics of sons of male alcoholics. *Journal of Abnormal Psychology, 99,* 291–301.

Pilkington, C. J., Tesser, A., & Stephens, D. (1991). Complementarity in romantic relationships: A self-evaluation maintenance perspective. *Journal of Social & Personal Relationships, 8,* 481-504.

Pillard, R. C., Poumadere, J., & Carretta, R. A. (1981). Is homosexuality familial? A review, some data, and a suggestion. *Archives of Sexual Behavior, 10,* 465–73.

Pillard, R. C., Poumadere, J., & Carretta, R. A. (1982). A family study of sexual orientation. *Archives of Sexual Behavior, 11,* 511–520.

Pillemer, D. B. (1984). Flashbulb memories of the assassination attempt on President Reagan. *Cognition, 16,* 63–80.

Pinel, E. C., & Swann, W. B. Jr. (2000). Finding the self through others: Self-verification and social movement participation. In S. Stryker & T. J. Owens (Ed.), *Self, identity, and social movements. Social movements, protest, and contention, Vol. 13.* (pp. 132-152). Minneapolis: University of Minnesota Press.

Pinker, S. (1994). *The language instinct: How the mind creates language.* New York: HarperCollins.

Piper, W. E., McCallum, M., Joyce, A. S., Azim, H. F., & Ogrodniczuk, J. S. (1999). Follow-up findings for interpretive and supportive forms of psychotherapy and patient personality variables. *Journal of Consulting and Clinical Psychology, 67,* 267–273.

Piper, W. E., Ogrodniczuk, J. S., Joyce, A. S., McCallum, M., Rosie, J. S., O'Kelly, J. G., & Steinberg, P. I. (1999). Prediction of dropping out in time-limited, interpretive individual psychotherapy. *Psychotherapy, 36,* 114-122.

Plomin, R. (1990). *Nature and nurture.* Pacific Grove, CA: Brooks-Cole.

Plomin, R., & Caspi, A. (1999). Behavioral genetics and personality. In L. Pervin & O. John (Eds.), *Handbook of personality: Theory and research* (2nd ed., pp. 251–276). New York: Guilford Press.

Plomin, R., Chipuer, H., & Loehlin, J. C. (1990). Behavioral genetics and personality. In L. Pervin (Ed.), *Handbook of personality: Theory and research* (pp. 225–243). New York: Guilford Press.

Plomin, R., & DeFries, J. (1980). Genetics and intelligence: Recent data. Intelligence, 4, 15–24.

Plomin, R., DeFries, J. C., McClearn, G. E., & Rutter, R. (1997). *Behavioral genetics* (3rd ed.). New York: W. H. Freeman.

Plomin, R., Reiss, D., Hetherington, E. M., & Howe, G. W. (1994). Nature and nurture: Genetic contributions to measures of the family environment. *Developmental Psychology, 30,* 32–43.

Plomin, R., Willerman, L., & Loehlin, J. C. (1976). Resemblance in appearance and the equal environments assumption in twin studies of personality. *Behavior Genetics, 6,* 43–52.

Plutchik, R. (1980). *Emotions: A psychoevolutionary synthesis.* New York: Harper & Row.

Plutchik, R. (1997). The circumplex as a general model of the structure of emotions and personality. In R. Plutchik, H. R. Conte, et al. (Eds.). *Circumplex models of personality and emotions* (pp. 17–45). Washington: American Psychological Association.

Poldrack, R. A., Desmond, J. E., Glover, G. H., & Gabrieli, J. D. E. (1998). The neural basis of visual skill learning: An fMRI study of mirror reading. *Cerebral Cortex, 8,* 1–10.

Pollen, D. A. (1999). On the neural correlates of visual perception. *Cerebral Cortex, 9,* 4–19.

Pollock, V. E., Briere, J., Schneider, L., Knop, J., Mednick, S., & Goodwin, D. W. (1990). Childhood antecedents of antisocial behavior: Parental alcoholism and physical abusiveness. *American Journal of Psychiatry, 147,* 1290–1293.

Ponds, R., Brouwer, W., & Van Wolffelaar, P. (1988). Age differences in divided attention in a simulated driving task. *Journal of Gerontology, 43,* 151–156.

Poon, L., Clayton, P. M., Martin, P., Johnson, M. A., Courtenay, B., Sweaney, A., Merriam, S., Pless, B. S., & Thielman, S. (1992). The Georgia Centenarian study. *International Journal of Aging and Human Development, 34,* 1–17.

Pope, H. G., Gruber, A. J., & Yurgelun-Todd, D. (1995). The residual neuropsychological effects of cannabis: The current status of research. *Drug & Alcohol Dependence, 38,* 25–34.

Popper, K. (1963). *Conjectures and refutations: The growth of scientific knowledge.* New York: Basic Books.

Porath, M. (2000). Social giftedness in childhood: A developmental perspective. In R. C. Friedman, B. M. Shore, et al. (Eds.), *Talents unfolding: Cognition and development.* (pp. 195–215). Washington, DC: American Psychological Association.

Porcerelli, J., Hill, K., & Dauphin, V. B. (1995). Need-gratifying object relations and psychopathology. *Bulletin of the Menninger Clinic, 59,* 99–106.

Porkka-Heiskanen, T., Strecker, R. E., Thakkar, M., & Bjorkum, A. A. (1997). Adenosine: A mediator of the sleep-induced effects of prolonged wakefulness. *Science, 276,* 1265–1268.

Posner, M. I. (1995). Attention in cognitive neuroscience: An overview. In M. S. Gazzaniga et al. (Eds.), *The cognitive neurosciences* (pp. 615–624). Cambridge: MIT Press.

Posner, M. I., & DiGirolamo, G. J. (2000). Attention in cognitive neuroscience: An overview. In M. S. Gazzaniga (Ed.), *The new cognitive neurosciences (2nd Ed.),* pp.623–631). Cambridge, MA: MIT Press.

Posner, N. I., & Raichle, M. E. (1996). Precis of image and mind. *Behavioral and Brain Sciences, 18,* 327–383.

Posner, R. M., Boies, S., Eichelman, W. H., & Taylor, R. L. (1969). Retention of visual and name codes of single letters. *Journal of Experimental Psychology, 79.*

Pospisil, L. (1963). *Kapauka Papuan political economy.* New Haven, CT: Yale University Publications in Anthropology, No. 67.

Postle, B. R., D'Esposito, M. (1999)

"What"–then–"where" in visual working memory: An event-related fMRI study. *Journal of Cognitive Neuroscience, 11,* 585–597.

Povinelli, D., & Simon, B. B. (1998). Young children's understanding of briefly versus extremely delayed images of the self: Emergence of the autobiographical stance. *Developmental Psychology, 34,* 188–194.

Pratkanis, A. R., Eskenazi, J., & Greenwald, A. G. (1994). What you expect is what you believe (but not necessarily what you get): A test of the effectiveness of subliminal self-help audiotapes. *Basic & Applied Social Psychology, 15,* 251-276.

Preisig, M., Bellivier, F., Fenton, B. T., Baud, P., Berney, A., Courtet, P., Hardy, P., Golaz, J., Leboyer, M., Mallet, J., Matthey, M., Mouthon, D., Neidhart, E., Nosten-Bertrand, M., Stadlemann-Dubuis, E., Guimon, J., Ferrero, F., Buresi, C., & Malafosse, A. (2000). Association between bipolar disorder and monoamine oxidase a gene polymorphisms: Results of a multicenter study. *American Journal of Psychiatry, 157,* 948–955.

Premack, A. J., & Premack, D. (1972). Teaching language to an ape. *Scientific American, 227,* 92–99.

Premack, D. (1962). Reversibility of the reinforcement relation. *Science, 136,* 235 237.

Premack, D. (1965). *Reinforcement theory.* In D. Levine (Ed.), *Nebraska symposium on motivation* (Vol. 3, pp. 123–180). Lincoln: University of Nebraska Press.

Prescott, C. A., & Kendler, K. S. (1999). Genetic and environmental contributions to alcohol abuse and dependence in a population-based sample of male twins. *American Journal of Psychiatry, 156,* 34–40.

Preti, G., Cutler, W. B., Garcia, G. R., Huggins, M., & Lawley, J. J. (1986). Human axillary secretions influence women's menstrual cycles: The role of donor extract from females. *Hormones and Behavior, 20,* 474 482.

Pribram, K. H. (1980). The biology of emotions and other feelings. In R. Plutchik & H. Kellerman (Eds.), *Emotion: Theory, research, and experience: Vol. I. Theories of emotion.* New York: Academic Press.

Price-Williams, D. (1981). Concrete and formal operations. In R. H. Munroe, R. L. Munroe, & B. D. Whiting (Eds.), *Handbook of cross-cultural human development.* New York: Garland Press.

Price-Williams, D., Gordon, W., & Ramirez, M. (1969). Skill and conservation: A study of pottery-making children. *Developmental Psychology, 1,* 769.

Price-Williams, D. R. (1985). In G. Lindzey and E. Aronson (Eds.), *Handbook of social psychology.* Reading, MA: Addison-Wesley.

Priester, J. R., & Petty, R. E. (1996). The gradual threshold model of ambivalence: Relating the positive and negative bases of attitudes to subjective ambivalence. *Journal of Personality & Social Psychology, 71,* 431-449.

Prince, A., & Smolensky, P. (1997). Optimality: From neural networks to universal grammar. *Science, 275,* 1604–1610.

Prochaska, J. D. (1984). *The transtheoretical approach: Crossing traditional boundaries of therapy.* Homewood, IL: Dow Jones-Irwin.

Puce, A., Allison, T., Asgari, M., Gore, J. C., & McCarthy, G. (1996). Differential sensitivity of human visual cortex to faces, letterstrings, and textures: A functional magnetic resonance imaging study. *Journal of Neuroscience, 16,* 5205–5215.

Puce, A., Alison, T., Bentin, S., Gore, J. C., & McCarthy, G. (1998). Temporal cortex activation in humans viewing eye and mouth movements. *Journal of Neuroscience, 18,* 2188–2199.

Putnam, F. W. (1991). Dissociative disorders in children and adolescents: A developmental perspective. *Psychiatric Clinics of North America, 14,* 519–531.

Putnam, H. (1973). Reductionism and the nature of psychology. *Cognition, 2,* 131–146.

Quitkin, F. M., Rabkin, J. G., Gerald, J., Davis, J. M., & Klein, D. F. (2000). Validity of clinical trials of antidepressants. *American Journal of Psychiatry, 157,* 327–337.

Rachlin, H., Green, L., Kagel, J. H., & Battalio, R. C. (1976). Economic demand theory and psychological studies of choice. In G. H. Bower (Ed.), *The psychology of learning and motivation* (Vol. 10, pp. 129–154). New York: Academic.

Rain, A., & Venables, P. H. (1984). Electrodermal nonresponding, antisocial behavior, and schizoid tendencies in adolescents. *Psychophysiology, 21,* 424–433.

Rallison, M. (1986). *Growth disorders in infants, children, and adolescents.* New York: John Wiley.

Ralston, D., Gustafson, D., Elsass, P., & Cheung, F. (1992). Eastern values: A comparison of managers in the United States, Hong Kong, and the People's Republic of China. *Journal of Applied Psychology, 77,* 664–671.

Ramachandran, V. S., & Hirstein, W. (1998). The perception of phantom limbs: The D. O. Hebb lecture. *Brain, 121,* 1603–1630.

Ramirez-Amaya, V., & Bermudez-Rattoni, F. (1999). Conditioned enhancement of antibody production is disrupted by insular cortex and amygdala but not hippocampal lesions. *Brain, Behavior and Immunity, 13,* 46–60.

Ramos, A., Berton, O., Mormede, P., & Chaouloff, F. (1997). A multiple-test study of anxiety-related behaviours in six inbred rat strains. *Behavioural Brain Research, 85,* 57–69.

Ramus, F., Hauser, M., Miller, C., Morris, D., & Mehler, J. (2000). Language discrimination by human newborns and by cotton-top tamarin monkeys. *Science, 288,* 349–351.

Rand, C. S., & Kuldau, J. M. (1990). The epidemiology of obesity and self-defined weight problem in the general population: Gender, race, age, and social class. *International Journal of Eating Disorders, 9,* 329-343.

Randhawa, B. (1991). Gender differences in academic achievement: A closer look at mathematics. *Alberta Journal of Educational Research, 37,* 241–257.

Rao, S. C., Rainier, G., & Miller, E. K. (1997). Integration of what and where in the primate prefrontal cortex. *Science, 276,* 821–824.

Rao, S. M., Huber, S. J., & Bornstein, R. A. (1992). Emotional changes with multiple sclerosis and Parkinson's disease. *Journal of Consulting and Clinical Psychology, 60,* 369–378.

Rapee, R. (1991). Generalized anxiety disorder: A review of clinical features and theoretical concepts. *Clinical Psychology Review, 11,* 419–440.

Rapee, R. M., Brown, T. A., Antony, M., & Barlow, D. (1992). Response to hyperventilation and inhalation of 5.5% carbon dioxide-enriched air across the DSM-III-R anxiety disorders. *Journal of Abnormal Psychology, 101,* 538–552.

Rashidy-Pour, A., Motaghed-Larijani, Z., & Bures, J. (1995). Reversible inactivation of the medial septal area impairs consolidation but not retrieval of passive avoidance learning in rats. *Behavioural Brain Research, 72,* 185–188.

Rawsthorne, L. J., & Elliott, A. J. (1999). Achievement goals and intrinsic motivation: A meta-analytic review. *Personality and Social Psychology Review, 3*(4), 326–344.

Rea, C. P., & Modigliani, V. (1988). Educational implications of the spacing effect. In M. M. Gruneberg, P. E. Morris, et al. (Eds.), *Practical aspects of memory: Current research and issues: Vol. 1. Memory in everyday life* (pp. 402–406). New York: John Wiley & Sons.

Read, S. J., Vanman, E. J., & Miller, L. C. (1997). Connectionism, parallel constraint satisfaction processes, and Gestalt principles: (Re)introducing cognitive dynamics to social psychology. *Personality and Social Psychology Review, 1,* 26–53.

Reber, A. S. (1989). Implicit learning and tacit knowledge. *Journal of Experimental Psychology: General, 118,* 219–235.

Reber, A. S. (1992). The cognitive unconscious: An evolutionary perspective. *Consciousness and Cognition, 1,* 93 133.

Reber, A. S. (1993). *Implicit learning and tacit knowledge: An essay on the cognitive unconscious.* New York: Oxford University Press.

Recanzone, G. H., Schreiner, C. E., & Merzenich, M. M. (1993). Plasticity in the frequency representation in the primary auditory cortex following discontinuous training in adult owl monkeys. *Journal of Neuroscience.*

Reder, L. M., & Schunn, C. D. (1996). Metacognition does not imply awareness: Strategy choice is governed by implicit learning and memory. In L. M. Reder (Ed.), *Implicit memory and metacognition* (pp. 45–77). Mahwah, NJ: Erlbaum.

Rees, G., Frackowiak, R., & Firth, C. (1997). Two modulatory effects of attention that mediate object categorization in human cortex. *Science, 275,* 835–838.

Regan, D., & Fazio, R. (1977). On the consistency between attitudes and behavior: Look to the method of attitude formation. *Journal of Experimental Social Psychology, 13,* 28–45.

Regan, P. C. (1996). Rhythms of desire: The association between menstrual cycle phases and female sexual desire. *Canadian Journal of Human Sexuality, 5,* 145–215.

Regan, T. (1997). The rights of humans and other animals. *Ethics and Behavior, 7,* 103–111.

Reifman, A., Larrick, R., & Fein, S. (1991). Temper and temperature on the diamond: The heat-aggression relationship in major league baseball. *Personality & Social Psychology Bulletin, 17,* 580–585.

Reiman, E. M. (1997). The application of positron emission tomography to the study of normal and pathologic emotions. *Journal of Clinical Psychiatry, 58,* 4-12.

Reiman, P., & Chi, M. T. H. (1989). Human expertise. In K. J. Gilhooly (Ed.), *Human and machine problem solving.* New York: Plenum Press.

Reinisch, J. M. (1981). Prenatal exposure to synthetic progestins increases potential for aggression in humans. *Science, 211,* 1171–1173.

Reis, H. J., & Shaver, P. (1988). Intimacy as an interpersonal process. In S. Duck (Ed.), *Handbook of personal relationships: Theory, relationships and interventions.* New York: John Wiley.

Reisberg, D. (1997). *Cognition: Exploring the science of the mind.* New York: Norton.

Reisenzein, R. (1983). The Schachter theory of emotion: Two decades later. *Psychological Bulletin, 94,* 239–264.

Repacholi, B., & Gopnik, A. (1997). Early reasoning about desires: Evidence from 14- and 18-month-olds. *Developmental Psychology, 33,* 12–21.

Rescorla, R. A. (1966). Predictability and number of pairings in Pavlovian fear conditioning. *Psychonomic Science, 4,* 383–384.

Rescorla, R. A. (1973). Second order conditioning: Implications for theories of learning. In F. J. McGuigan and D. B. Lumsden (Eds.), *Contemporary approaches to conditioning and learning.* New York: Wiley.

Rescorla, R. A. (1988). Pavlovian conditioning: It's not what you think it is. *American Psychologist, 43,* 151–160.

Rescorla, R. A. (1999). Partial reinforcement reduces the associative change produced by nonreinforcement. *Journal of Experimental Psychology: Animal Behavior, 25,* 403–414.

Rescorla, R. A., & Holland, P. C. (1982). Behavioral studies of associative learning in animals. *Annual Review of Psychology, 33,* 265–308.

Rescorla, R. A., & Wagner, A. R. (1972). A theory of Pavlovian conditioning: Variations in the effectiveness of reinforcement and non-reinforcement. In A. H. Black & W. F. Prokasy (Eds.), *Classical conditioning: II. Current research and theory.* New York: Appleton.

Rest, J. R. (1983). Morality. In J. H. Flavell & E. M. Markman (Eds.), *Handbook of child psychology: Vol. 3. Cognitive development.* New York: John Wiley.

Reuter-Lorenz, P. A., & Stanczak, L. (2000). Differential effects of aging on the functions of the corpus callosum. *Developmental Neuropsychology, 18,* 113-137.

Reynolds, A. J., Mehana, M., & Temple, J. A. (1995). Does preschool intervention affect children's perceived competence? *Journal of Applied Development Psychology, 16,* 211–230.

Rhee, S. H., Waldman, I. D., Hay, D. A., & Levy, F. (1999). Sex differences in genetic and environmental influences on DSM-III-R attention-deficit/hyperactivity disorder. *Journal of Abnormal Psychology, 108,* 24–41.

Rholes, W. S., Simpson, J. A., Blakely, B. S., Lanigan, L., & Allen, E. A. (1997). Adult attachment styles, the desire to have children, and working models of parenthood. *Journal of Personality, 65,* 357–385.

Richard, T. C., Romero, S. G., Basso, G., Wharton, C., Flitman, S., & Grafman, J. (2000). The calculating brain: An fMRI study. *Neuropsychologia, 38,* 325–335.

Richards, B. J. (1990). Language development and individual differences: A study of auxiliary verb learning. Cambridge: Cambridge University Press.

Richards, J. B., Sabol, K. E., & Freed, C. R. (1990). Conditioned rotation: A behavioral analysis. *Physiology and Behavior, 47,* 1083–1087.

Richards, J. M., & Gross, J. J. (in press). Emotion regulation and memory: The cognitive costs of keeping one's cool. *Journal of Personality and Social Psychology.*

Richards, R., Kinney, D., Lunde, I., Benet, M., & Merzel, A. (1988). Creativity in manic-depressives, cyclothymes, and their normal relatives, and control subjects. *Journal of Abnormal Psychology, 97,* 281–288.

Richardson, D. (1991). Structural and strategic family therapy techniques: Application to chemically dependent families. *Journal of Chemical Dependency Treatment, 4,* 29–39.

Richardson, J. T. E. (1996a). Evolving concepts of working memory. In J. T. E. Richardson, R. W. Engle, L. Hasher, R. Logie, E. Stoltzfus, & R. Zacks (Eds.), *Working memory and human cognition* (pp. 3–29). New York: Oxford University Press.

Richardson, J. T. E. (1996b). Evolving issues in working memory. In J. T. E. Richardson, R. W. Engle, L. Hasher, R. Logie, E. S. Stoltzfus, & R. Zacks (Eds.), *Working memory and human cognition* (pp. 121–152). New York: Oxford University Press.

Richardson, S. A., & Koller, H. (1996). *Twenty-two years: Causes and consequences of mental retardation.* Cambridge: Harvard University Press.

Ricks, M. H. (1985). The social transmission of parental behavior: Attachment across generations. In I. Bretherton & E. Waters (Eds.), *Growing points of attachment theory and research. Monographs of the Society for Research in Child Development, 50,* (1–2, Serial No. 209), 211–227.

Riesen, A. H. (1960). The effects of stimulus deprivation on the development and atrophy of the visual sensory system. *American Journal of Orthopsychiatry, 30,* 23–36.

Riley, A. J. (1991). Sexuality and the menopause. *Sexual and Marital Therapy, 6,* 135–145.

Rinn, W. E. (1984). The neuropsychology of facial expression: A review of the neurological and psychological mechanisms for producing facial expressions. *Psychological Bulletin, 95,* 52–77.

Ripple, C. H., Gilliam, W. S., Chanana, N., & Zigler, E. (1999). Will fifty cooks spoil the broth? The debate over entrusting Head Start to the states. *American Psychologist, 54,* 327–343.

Rips, L. (1990). Reasoning. *Annual Review of Psychology, 41,* 321–353.

Rips, L. J. (1995). Deduction and cognition. In E. E. Smith, D. N. Osherson, et al. (Eds.), *Thinking: An invitation to cognitive science: Vol. 3. An invitation to cognitive science* (2nd ed., pp. 297–343). Cambridge: MIT Press.

Rizzolatti, G., & Arbib, M. A. (1998). Language within our grasp. *Trends in Neuroscience, 21,* 188–194.

Rizzolatti, G., Fadiga, L., Matelli, M., Bettinardi, V., Paulesu, E., Perani, D., & Fazio, F. (1996). Localization of grasp representations in humans by PET: 1. Observation versus execution. *Experimental Brain Research, 111,* 246–252.

Robben, H. S., Webley, P., Weigel, R., & Warneryd, K-E. (1990). Decision frame and opportunity as determinants of tax cheating: An international experimental study. *Journal of Economic Psychology, 11,* 341–364.

Robbins, T. W. (1997). Arousal systems and attentional processes. *Biological Psychology, 45,* 57–71.

Robbins, T. W., & Everitt, B. J. (1999). Interaction of the dopaminergic system with mechanisms of associative learning and cognition: Implications for drug abuse. *Psychological Science, 10,* 199–202.

Roberts, L. C., & Rafal, R. (2000). Disorders of visual attention. In M. S. Gazzaniga (Ed.), *The new cognitive neurosciences* (2nd ed., pp. 633–649). Cambridge, MA: MIT Press.

Roberts, W. A. (1995). Simultaneous numerical and temporal processing in the pigeon. *Current Directions in Psychological Science, 4,* 47–51.

Robertson, D., Davidoff, J., & Braisby, N. (1999). Similarity and categorization: Neuropsychological evidence for a dissociation in explicit categorization tasks. *Cognition, 71,* 1–42.

Robertson, J., & Robertson, J. (1971). Young children in brief separation: A fresh look. *Psychoanalytic study of the child, 26,* 264–315.

Robin, A. A. (1958). A controlled study of the effects of leucotomy. *Journal of Neurology, Neurosurgery and Psychiatry, 21,* 262–269.

Robin, N., & Holyoak, K. (1995). Relational complexity and the functions of the prefrontal cortex. In M. Gazzaniga (Ed.), *The cognitive neurosciences* (pp. 987–997). Cambridge: MIT Press.

Robins, R. W., & Beer, J. S. (2001). Positive illusions about the self: Short-term benefits and long-term costs. *Journal of Personality & Social Psychology, 80,* 340-352.

Robinson, B. W., et al. (1969). Dominance reversal resulting from aggressive responses evoked by brain telestimulation. *Physiology and Behavior, 4,* 749–752.

Robinson, D., Woerner, M. G., Alvir, J. M. J., Bilder, R., Goldman, R., Geisler, S., Koreen, A., Sheitman, B., Chakos, M., Mayerhoff, D., & Lieberman, J. A. (1999). Predictors of relapse following response from a first episode of schizophrenia or schizoaffective disorder.

Archives of General Psychiatry, 56, 241-247.

Robinson, F. P. (1961). *Effective study.* New York: Harper & Row.

Robinson, G. (1996). Cross cultural perspectives on menopause. *The Journal of Nervous and Mental Disease, 184,* 453–458.

Robinson, K. J., & Roediger, H. L., III. (1997). Associative processes in false recall and false recognition. *Psychological Science, 8,* 231–237.

Robinson, T. N. (1999). Reducing children's television viewing to prevent obesity a randomized controlled trial. *Journal of the American Medical Association, 282,* 1561-1567.

Rodin, J. Schank, D., & Striegel-Moore, R. (1989). Psychological features of obesity. *Medical Clinics of North America, 73,* 47–66.

Rodkin, P., Farmer, T. W., Pearl, R., & Van Acker, R. (2000). Heterogeneity of popular boys: Antisocial and prosocial configurations. *Developmental Psychology, 36,* 14–24.

Rodman, H. R. (1997). Temporal cortex. In G. Adelman & B. Smith (Eds.), *Encyclopedia of Neuroscience.* Amsterdam: Elsevier.

Rodman, H. R., & Albright, T. D. (1989). Single-unit analysis of pattern-motion selective properties in the middle temporal visual area (MT). *Experimental Brain Research, 75,* 53–64.

Roediger, H. L. (1990). Implicit memory: Retention without remembering. *American Psychologist, 45*(9), 1043–1056.

Roediger, H. L., & McDermott, K. B. (1995). Creating false memories: Remembering words not presented in lists. *Journal of Experimental Psychology: Learning, Memory, and Cognition, 21,* 803–814.

Rogan, M. T., Staeubli, U. V., & LeDoux, J. E. (1997). AMPA receptor facilitation accelerates fear learning without altering the level of conditioned fear acquired. *Journal of Neuroscience, 17,* 5928-5935.

Roger, T. B., Kuiper, N. A., & Kirker, W. S. (1977). Self-reference and the encoding of personal information. *Journal of Personality and Social Psychology, 35,* 677-688.

Rogers, C. (1959). A theory of therapy, personality, and interpersonal relationships, as developed in the client-centered framework. In S. Koch (Ed.), *Psychology: A study of a science,* (Vol. 3). New York: McGraw-Hill.

Rogers, C. R. (1951). *Client-centered therapy: Its current practice, implications, and theory.* Boston: Houghton Mifflin.

Rogers, C. R. (1961). *On becoming a person: A therapist's view of psychotherapy.* Boston: Houghton Mifflin.

Rogers, C. R. (1980). *A way of being.* Boston: Houghton Mifflin.

Rogers, C. R., & Sanford, M. A. (1985). Client-centered psychotherapy. In H. I. Kaplan, H., & B. J. Sadock (Eds.), *Comprehensive textbook of psychiatry* (4th ed.). Baltimore, MD: Williams & Wilkins.

Rogler, L. H., Cortes, D. E., & Malgady, R. G. (1991). Acculturation and mental health status among hispanics: Convergence and new directions for research. *American Psychologist, 46,*

585–592.

Rogoff, B., & Lave, J. (Eds.), (1984). *Everyday cognition: Its development in social context.* Cambridge, MA: Harvard University Press.

Rohner, R. (1975a). Parental acceptance-rejection and personality development: A universalist approach to behavioral science. In R. W. Brislin et al. (Eds.), *Cross-cultural perspectives on learning* (pp. 251–269). New York: Sage.

Rohner, R. (1975b). *They love me, they love me not.* New Haven, CT: HRAF Press.

Rohner, R. P. (1986). *The warmth dimension: Foundations of parental acceptance-rejection theory.* Beverly Hills, CA: Sage Publications.

Rollin, B. E. (1985). The moral status of research animals in psychology. *American Psychologist, 40,* 920–926.

Ron, M. (1989). Psychiatric manifestations of frontal lobe tumours. *British Journal of Psychiatry, 155,* 735–738.

Ron, M. A., & David, A. S. (1998). *Disorders of brain and mind.* New York: Cambridge University Press.

Rosch, E. (1973). On the internal structure of perceptual and semantic categories. In T. E. Moore (Ed.), *Cognitive development and the acquisition of language.* New York: Academic Press.

Rosch, E. (1978). Principles of categorization. In E. Rosch & B. Lloyd (Eds.), *Cognition and categorization.* New York: John Wiley.

Roseman, I. J., Dhawan, N., Rettek, S. I., Naidu, R. K., et al. (1995). Cultural differences and cross-cultural similarities in appraisals and emotional responses. *Journal of Cross-Cultural Psychology, 26,* 23–48.

Rosen, A. B., & Rozin, P. (1993). Now you see it, now you don't: The preschool child's conception of invisible particles in the context of dissolving. *Developmental Psychology, 29,* 300–311.

Rosen, J. C., & Gross, J. (1987). The prevalence of weight reducing and weight gaining in adolescent girls and boys. *Health Psychology, 6,* 131–147.

Rosen, K. S., & Rothbaum, F. (1993). Quality of parental caregiving and security of attachment. *Developmental Psychology, 29,* 358–367.

Rosenberg, M. (1979). *Conceiving the self.* New York: Basic Books.

Rosenberg, S. D., Rosenberg, H. J., & Farrell, M. P. (1999). The midlife crisis revisited. In S. L. Willis & J. D. Reid (Eds.), *Life in the middle: Psychological and social development in middle age.* (pp. 25–45, 47-73). San Diego: Academic Press, Inc.

Rosenblatt, A., Greenberg, J., Solomon, S., Pyszczynski, T., & Lyon, D. (1989). Evidence for terror management theory: I. The effects of mortality salience on reactions to those who violate or uphold cultural values. *Journal of Personality and Social Psychology, 57,* 681–690.

Rosenblum, G. D., & Lewis, M. (1999). The relations among body image, physical attractiveness, and body mass in adolescence. *Child Development, 70,* 50–64.

Rosenhan, D. L. (1973). On being sane in insane places. *Science, 179,* 252–258.

Rosenheck, R., Dunn, L., Peszke, M., Cramer, J.,

Xu, W., Thomas, J., & Charney, D. (1999). Impact of clozapine on negative symptoms and on the deficit syndrome in refractory schizophrenia. *American Journal of Psychiatry, 156,* 88–93.

Rosenthal, D. (1970). *Genetic theory and abnormal behavior.* New York, NY, US: McGraw-Hill.

Rosenthal, R. & Jacobson, L. (1966). Teachers' expectancies: Determinants of pupils' IQ gains. *Psychological Reports, 19,* 115-118.

Rosenthal, R., & Rubin, D. G. (1978). Interpersonal expectancy effects: The first 345 studies. *Behavioral and Brain Sciences, 1*(3), 377–415.

Rosenwald, G. (1988). The multiple case study method. *Journal of Personality, 56,* 239–264.

Rosenzweig, M. R. (1966). Environmental complexity, cerebral change, and behavior. *American Psychologist, 21,* 321-332

Rosenzweig, M. R. (1984). Experience, memory, and the brain. *American Psychologist, 39,* 365–376.

Rosenzweig, M. R., Bennett, E. L., & Diamond, M. C. (1972). Brain changes in response to experience. *Scientific American, 226,* 22–29.

Ross, C. A., Anderson, G., Fleisher, W., & Norton, G. R. (1991). The frequency of multiple personality disorder among psychiatric inpatients. *American Journal of Psychiatry, 148,* 1717–1720.

Ross, L. (1977). The intuitive psychologist and his shortcomings: Distortions in the attribution process. *Advances in Experimental Social Psychology, 10,* 173–220.

Ross, L., Greene, D., & House, P. (1977). The false consensus effect: An egocentric bias in social perception and attribution processes. *Journal of Experimental Social Psychology, 13*(3), 279–301.

Ross, M., & Sicoly, F. (1979). Egocentric biases in availability and attribution. *Journal of Personality and Social Psychology, 37,* 322–336.

Ross, S. M., & Ross, L. E. (1971). Comparison of trace and delay classical eyelid conditioning as a function of interstimulus interval. *Journal of Experimental Psychology, 91,* 165–167.

Rosso, I. M., Cannon, T. D., Huttunen, T., Huttunen, M. O., Loennqvist, J., & Gasperoni, T. L. (2000). Obstetric risk factors for early-onset schizophrenia in a Finnish birth cohort. *American Journal of Psychiatry, 157,* 801–807.

Roth, A., Fonagy, P., Parry, G., & Target, M. (1996). *What works for whom? A critical review of psychotherapy research.* New York: Guilford Press.

Roth, M. (1978). Epidemiological studies. In R. Katzman, R. D. Terry, & K. L. Bick (Eds.), *Alzheimer's disease: Senile dementia and related disorders.* New York: Raven.

Rothbaum, B. O., Hodges, L., Smith, S., Lee, J. H., & Price, L. (2000). A controlled study of virtual reality exposure therapy for the fear of flying. *Journal of Consulting and Clinical Psychology, 68,* 1020–1026.

Rothbaum, F., Pott, M., Azuma, H., Miyake, K., & Weisz, J. (2000). The development of close relationships in Japan and the United States:

Paths of symbiotic harmony and generative tension. *Child Development, 71*, 1121–1142.

Rothgerber, H. (1997). External intergroup threat as an antecedent to perceptions in in-group and out-group homogeneity. *Journal of Personality & Social Psychology, 73*, 1206-1212.

Rotter, J. (1971). External control and internal control. *Psychology Today*, June, 40–45.

Rotter, J. B. (1954). *Social learning and clinical psychology.* New York: Englewood Cliffs, NJ: Prentice-Hall.

Rotter, J. B. (1966). Generalized expectancies for internal versus external control of reinforcement. *Psychological Monographs* (Whole No. 609).

Rotter, J. B. (1990). Internal versus external control of reinforcement: A case history of a variable. *American Psychologist, 45*, 489–493.

Rotton, J., & Cohn, E. G. (2000). Violence is a curvilinear function of temperature in Dallas: A replication. *Journal of Personality and Social Psychology, 78*(6), 1074–1081.

Rotton, J., et al. (1979). The air pollution experience and physical aggression. *Journal of Applied Social Psychology, 9*, 397–442.

Rovee-Collier, C. (1990). The"memory system"of prelinguistic infants. In A. Diamond (Ed.), *Development and neural bases of higher cognitive functions* (pp. 517–542). New York: New York Academy of Sciences Press.

Rowe, D. C., Jacobson, K. C., & Van den Oord, E. J. C. G. (1999). Genetic and environmental influences on vocabulary IQ: Parental education level as moderator. *Child Development, 70*, 1151–1162.

Rowe, J. W., & Kahn, R. L. (1997). Successful aging. *Gerontologist, 37*, 433-440.

Rowe, J. W., & Kahn, R. L. (1998). *Successful aging.* New York: Pantheon Books.

Rubin, D. C. (1995). *Memory in oral traditions: The cognitive psychology of epic, ballads, and counting-out rhymes.* New York: Oxford University Press.

Rubin, D. C., & Kozin, M. (1984).Vivid memories. *Cognition, 16*, 81–95.

Rubin, D. C., Rahhal, T. A., & Poon, L. W. (1998). Things learned in early childhood are remembered best. *Memory and Cognition, 26*, 3–19.

Ruble, D. N., & Martin, C. L. (1998) Gender development. In W. Damon (Ed. in Chief) and N. Eisenberg (Vol. Ed.), *Handbook of Child Psychology, Vol. 3.* (pp. 933-1016). New York: John Wiley.

Rudman, L. A., Greenwald, A. G., Mellott, D. S., & Schwartz, J. L. K. (1999). Measuring the automatic components of prejudice: Flexibility and generality of the Implicit Association Test. *Social Cognition, 17*(4), 437–465.

Ruffman, T. (1999). Children's understanding of logical inconsistency. *Child Development, 70*, 872–886.

Rumbaugh, D. M. (1992). Learning about primates' learning, language, and cognition. In G. G. Brannigan & M. R. Merrens (Eds.), *The undaunted psychologist: Adventures in research.* New York: McGraw-Hill.

Rumbaugh, D. M., & Gill, T. V. (1977). Lana's acquisition of language skills. In D. M. Rumbaugh (Ed.), *Language learning by a chimpanzee: The Lana project* (pp. 165–192). New York: Academic Press.

Rumelhart, D. (1984). Schemata and the cognitive system. In R. S. Wyer & T. K. Srull (Eds.), *Handbook of social cognition* (Vol. 1). Hillsdale, NJ: Erlbaum.

Rumelhart, D. E., McClelland, J. L., & the PDP Research Group. (1986). *Parallel distributed processing: Explorations in the microstructure of cognition.* Cambridge, MA: MIT Press.

Rundus, D. (1971). Analysis of rehearsal process in free recall. *Journal of Experimental Psychology, 89*, 63–77.

Runyan, W. M. (1984). *Life histories and psychobiography: Explanations in theory and method.* New York: Oxford University Press.

Rusbult, C. E., & Van Lange, P. A. M. (1996). Interdependence processes. In E. T. Higgins, A. W. Kruglanski, et al. (Eds.), *Social psychology: Handbook of basic principles* (pp. 564–596). New York: Guilford Press.

Ruscio, J., & Ruscio, A. M. (2000). Informing the continuity controversy: A taxometric analysis of depression. *Journal of Abnormal Psychology, 109*, 473–487.

Rushton, J. P. (1986). Altruism and aggression: The heritability of individual differences. *Journal of Personality and Social Psychology, 50*, 1192–1198.

Rushton, W. A. H. (1962).Visual pigments in man. *Scientific American*, 120–132.

Russell, J. A. (1994). Is there universal recognition of emotion from facial expression? A review of the cross-cultural studies. *Psychological Bulletin, 115*, 102–141.

Russell, J. D., & Roxanas, M. (1990). Psychiatry and the frontal lobes. *Australian and New Zealand Journal of Psychiatry, 24*, 113–132.

Russell, M. J. (1976). Human olfactory communication. *Nature, 260*, 520–522.

Russo, R., & Parkin, A. J. (1993). Age differences in implicit memory: More apparent than real. *Memory and Cognition, 21*, 73–80.

Rutter, M., Quinton, D., & Liddle, C. (1983). Parenting in two generations: Looking backwards and looking forwards. In N. Madge (Ed.), *Families at risk* (pp. 60–98). London: Heineman.

Ryan, J. J., Sattler, J. M., & Lopez, S. J. (2000). Age effects on Wechsler Adult Intelligence Scale-III subtests. *Archives of Clinical Neuropsychology, 15*, 311–317.

Ryan, R. M., & Deci, E. L. (2000). Intrinsic and extrinsic motivations: Classic definitions and new directions. *Contemporary Educational Psychology, 25*, 54-67.

Rypma, B., & D'Esposito, M. (2000). Isolating the neural mechanisms of age-related changes in human working memory. *Nature Neuroscience, 3*, 509–515.

Saarni, C. (1998). Issues of cultural meaningfulness in emotional development. *Developmental Psychology, 34*, 647-652.

Sacks, O. (1973). *Awakenings.* London: Duckworth.

Sacks, O. (1993). A neurologist's notebook: To see and not see. *New Yorker*, May 10, 59–73.

Saegert, S., & Winkel, G. H. (1990). Environmental psychology. *Annual Review of Psychology, 41*, 441–477.

Saffran, J., Aslin, R., & Newport, E. (1996). Statistical learning by 8-month-old infants. *Science, 274*, 1926–1928.

Sagi, A. (1990). Attachment theory and research from a cross-cultural perspective. *Human Development, 33*, 10–22.

Sagi, A., van IJzendoorn, M. H., Aviezer, O., Donnell, F., & Mayseless, O. (1994). Sleeping out of the home in a kibbutz communal arrangement: It makes a difference for infant-mother attachment. *Child Development, 65*, 971–991.

Sahraie, A., Weiskrantz, L., Barbur, J. L., Simmons, A., Williams, S. C., & Brammer, M. J. (1997). Pattern of neuronal activity associated with conscious and unconscious processing of visual signals. *Proceedings of the National Academy of Sciences of the United States of America, 94*, 9406–9411.

Sakurai, T., et al. (1998). Orexins and orexin receptors: A family of hypothalamic neuropeptides and g protein-coupled receptors that regulate feeding behavior. *Cell, 92*, 573–585.

Salkovskis, P. M., Jones, D. R., & Clark, D. M. (1986). Respiratory control in the treatment of panic attacks: Replication and extension with concurrent measurement of behavior and PCPs. *British Journal of Psychiatry, 148*, 526–532.

Salovey, P., Rothman, A. J., & Rodin, J. (1998). Health behavior. In D. T. Gilbert, S. T. Fiske, et al. (Eds.), *The handbook of social psychology*, (Vol. 2, 4th ed., pp. 633–683). Boston: McGraw-Hill.

Salthouse, T. (1992). The information-processing perspective on cognitive aging. In R. Sternberg & C. Berg (Eds.), *Intellectual development.* Cambridge: Cambridge University Press.

Salthouse, T. A. (1996). General and specific speed mediation of adult age differences in memory. *Journals of Gerontology Series B- Psychological Sciences and Social Sciences, 51B*, P30–P42.

Salthouse, T. A. (2000). Item analyses of age relations on reasoning tests. *Psychology & Aging, 15*, 3–8.

Salthouse, T. A. (2000). Pressing issues in cognitive aging. In D. C. Park & N. Schwarz (Eds.). *Cognitive aging: A primer.* (pp. 43–54). Philadelphia: Psychology Press/Taylor & Francis.

Sameroff, A., Seifer, R., Baldwin, A., & Baldwin, C. (1993). Stability of intelligence from preschool to adolescence: The influence of social and family risk factors. *Child Development, 64*, 80–97.

Sandler, J., & Rosenblatt, B. (1962). The concept of the representational world. *Psychoanalytic Study of the Child, 17*, 128–145.

Sanfilipo, M., Lafargue, T., Rusinek, H., Arena, L., Loneragan, C., Lautin, A., Feiner, D., Rotrosen, J., & Wolkin, A. (2000).Volumetric measure of the frontal and temporal lobe regions in schizophrenia: Relationship to negative symptoms. *Archives of General Psychiatry,*

57, 471–480.

Sanger, T. M., Lieberman, J. A., Tohen, M., Grundy, S., Beasley, C., & Tollefson, G. D. (1999). Olanzapine versus haloperidol treatment in first-episode psychosis. *American Journal of Psychiatry, 156,* 79–87.

Sapir, E. (1949). *Culture, language and personality.* Berkeley: University of California Press.

Sarason, B. R., Sarason, I. G., & Gurung, R. A. R. (1997). Close personal relationships and health outcomes: A key to the role of social support. In S. Duck et al. (Eds.), *Handbook of personal relationships: Theory, research and interventions* (2nd ed., pp. 547–573). Chichester, UK: John Wiley & Sons.

Saraswathi, T., & Dutta, R. (1988). Current trends in developmental psychology: A life span perspective. In J. Pandey (Ed.), *Psychology in India: The state-of-the-art: Vol. 1. Personality and mental processes* (pp. 93–152). London: Sage.

Sarnat, H. B., & Netsky, M. G. (1974). *Evolution of the nervous system.* New York: Oxford University Press.

Sarter, M., & Markowitsch, H. J. (1985). Involvement of the amygdala in learning and memory: A critical review, with emphasis on anatomical relation. *Behavioral Neuroscience, 99,* 342–380.

Sartre, J. P. (1971). Being and nothingness: An essay in phenomenological ontology (H. E. Barnes, Trans.). New York: Citadel Press.

Satel, S. L., Southwick, S. M., & Gawin, F. H. (1991). Clinical features of cocaine-induced paranoia. *American Journal of Psychiatry, 148,* 495–498.

Saundino, K. (1997). Moving beyond the heritability question: New directions in behavioral genetic studies of personality. *Current Directions in Psychological Science, 6,* 86–89.

Savage-Rumbaugh, E. S. (1990). Language acquisition in a nonhuman species: Implications for the innateness debate. *Developmental Psychobiology, 23,* 599–620.

Savage-Rumbaugh, E. S., Pate, J. L., Lawson, J., Smith, S. T., & Rosenbaum, S. (1983). Can a chimpanzee make a statement? *Journal of Experimental Psychology: General, 112,* 457–492.

Savage-Rumbaugh, E. S., Rumbaugh, D. M., & Boysen, S. (1978). Symbolic communication between two chimpanzees. *Science, 201,* 641–644.

Savage-Rumbaugh, S., McDonald, K., Sevcik, R., Hopkins, W., & Rupert, E. (1986). Spontaneous symbol acquisition and communicative use by pygmy chimpanzees (pan paniscus). *Journal of Experimental Psychology: General, 115,* 211–235.

Savin-Williams, R. C., & Small, S. A. (1986). The timing of puberty and its relationship to adolescent and parent perceptions of family interactions. *Developmental Psychology, 22,* 342–47.

Scarr, S., & Carter-Saltzman, L. (1982). Genetics and intelligence. In R. J. Sternberg (Ed.), *Handbook of human intelligence* (pp. 792–896). New York: Cambridge University Press.

Scarr, S., Pakstis, A. J., Katz, S. H., & Barker, W. B. (1977). The absence of a relationship between degree of white ancestry and intellectual skills within a black population. *Human Genetics, 39,* 69–86.

Scarr, S., & Weinberg, R. A. (1976). IQ test performance of black children adopted by white families. *American Psychologist, 31,* 726–739.

Scarr, S., & Weinberg, R. A. (1983). The Minnesota adoption studies: Genetic differences and malleability. *Child Development, 54,* 260–267.

Schab, F. R., & Crowder, R. G. (1995). Odor recognition memory. In F. R. Schab, F. R. G. Crowder, et al. (Eds.), *Memory for odors* (pp. 9–20). Mahwah, NJ: Lawrence Erlbaum Associates.

Schachter, F. F., Shore, E., Hodapp, R., Chalfin, S., & Bundy, C. (1978). Do girls talk earlier? Mean length of utterance in toddlers. *Developmental Psychology, 14,* 388–392.

Schachter, S., & Singer, J. (1962). Cognitive, social, and physiological determinants of emotional state. *Psychological Review, 69,* 379–399.

Schacter, D. (1995a). Implicit memory: A new frontier for cognitive neuroscience. In M. Gazzaniga (Ed.), *The cognitive neurosciences* (pp. 815–824). Cambridge: MIT Press.

Schacter, D. (1995b). *Memory and distortion: How minds, brains, and societies recollect the past.* Cambridge: Harvard University Press.

Schacter, D. (1997). False recognition and the brain. *Current Directions in Psychological Science, 6,* 65–70.

Schacter, D., Cooper, L. A., & Valdiserri, M. (1992). Implicit and explicit memory for novel visual objects in older and younger adults. *Psychology and Aging, 7,* 299–308.

Schacter, D. L. (1966). *Searching for memory: The brain, the mind, and the past.* New York: Basic Books.

Schacter, D. L. (1992). Understanding implicit memory: A cognitive neuroscience approach. *American Psychologist, 47,* 559–569.

Schacter, D. L. (1999). The seven sins of memory: Insights from psychology and cognitive neuroscience. *American Psychologist, 54*(3), 182–203.

Schacter, D. L., & Buckner, R. L. (1998). Priming and the brain. *Neuron, 20,* 185–195.

Schacter, D. L., Verfaellie, M., Anes, M., & Racine, C. (in press). When true recognition suppresses false recognition: Evidence from amnesic patients. *Journal of Cognitive Neuroscience.*

Schafe, G. E., & Bernstein, I. L. (1996). Taste aversion learning. In E. D. Capaldi (Ed.), *Why we eat what we eat: The psychology of eating* (pp. 31–51). Washington, DC: American Psychological Association.

Schaie, K. W. (1988). Ageism in psychological research. *American Psychologist, 43,* 179–183.

Schaie, K. W. (1990). Intellectual development in adulthood. In J. E. Birren & K. W. Schaie (Eds.), *Handbook of the psychology of aging* (3rd ed.). New York: Van Nostrand Reinhold.

Schaie, K. W. (1994). The course of adult intellectual development. *American Psychologist, 49,* 304–313.

Schatzberg, A. F. (2000). New indications for antidepressants. *Journal of Clinical Psychiatry, 61,* 9–17.

Scheel, K. R. (2000). The empirical basis of dialectical behavior therapy: Summary, critique, and implications. *Clinical Psychology–Science and Practice, 7,* 68–86.

Scheff, T. J. (1970). Schizophrenia as ideology. *Schizophrenia Bulletin, 1,* 15–20.

Scheier, M., & Carver, C. (1993). On the power of positive thinking: The benefits of being optimistic. *Current Directions in Psychological Science, 2,* 26–30.

Scheier, M. F., Matthews, K. A., Owens, J., Magovern, G. J., Lefebvre, R. C., Abbott, R., & Carver, C. S. (1989). Dispositional optimism and recovery from coronary artery bypass surgery: The beneficial effects on physical and psychological well-being. *Journal of Personality and Social Psychology, 57,* 1024–1040.

Scheper-Hughes, N. (1979). *Saints, scholars, and schizophrenics: Mental illness in rural Ireland.* Berkeley: University of California Press.

Scher, S., & Cooper, J. (1989). Motivational basis of the dissonance: The singular role of behavioral consequences. *Journal of Personality and Social Psychology, 56,* 899–906.

Scherer, K., & Wallbott, H. (1994). Evidence for universality and cultural variation of differential emotion response patterning. *Journal of Personality & Social Psychology, 66,* 310–328.

Scherer, K. R. (1997). Profiles of emotion-antecedent appraisal: Testing theoretical predictions across cultures. *Cognition & Emotion, 11,* 113–150.

Scherer, K. R. (1999). Appraisal theory. In T. Dalgleish & M. Power (Eds.), *The handbook of cognition and emotion* (pp. 637–664). New York: John Wiley & Sons.

Schiavi, R. C., Schreiner-Engel, P., White, D., & Mandeli, J. (1991). The relationship between pituitary-gonadal function and sexual behavior in healthy aging men. *Psychosomatic Medicine, 53,* 363–374.

Schiavi, R. C., Schreiner-Engle, P., Mandeli, J., Schanzer, H., et al. (1990). Healthy aging and male sexual function. *American Journal of Psychiatry, 147,* 766–771.

Schiff, M., Duyme, M., Dumaret, A., & Tomkiewicz, S. (1982). How much could we boost scholastic achievement and IQ scores? A direct answer from a French adoption study. *Cognition, 12,* 165–196.

Schiffman, H. R. (1996). *Sensation and perception* (4th ed.). New York: John Wiley.

Schlegel, A., & Barry, H, III. (1991). *Adolescence: An anthropological inquiry.* New York: Free Press.

Schlesser, M. A., & Altshuler, K. Z. (1983). The genetics of affective disorder: Date, theory, and clinical applications. *Hospital and Community Psychiatry, 34,* 415–422.

Schmidt, F. L., & Hunter, J. E. (1998). The validity and utility of selection methods in personnel psychology: Practical and theoretical implications of 85 years of research findings. *Psychological Bulletin, 124,* 262–274.

Schmidt, N. B., Lerew, D. R., & Trakowski, J. H.

(1997a). Body vigilance in panic disorder: Evaluating attention to bodily perturbations. *Journal of Consulting and Clinical Psychology, 65,* 214–220.

Schmidt, N. B., Trakowski, J. H., & Staab, J. P. (1997b). Extinction of a panicogenic effects of a 3% CO_2 challenge in patients with panic disorder. *Journal of Abnormal Psychology, 106,* 630–640.

Schmolck, H., Buffalo, E. A., & Squire, L. R. (2000). Memory distortions develop over time: Recollections of the O. J. Simpson trial verdict after 15 and 32 months. *Psychological Science, 11,* 39–45.

Schnapf, J., Kraft, T., Nunn, B., & Baylor, D. (1989). Transduction in primate cones. *Neuroscience Research,* Suppl. 10, 9–14.

Schneider, M. L., Roughton, E. C., Koehler, A. J., & Lubach, G. R. (1999). Growth and development following prenatal stress exposure in primates: An examination of ontogenetic vulnerability. *Child Development, 70,* 263–274.

Schneider, M. L., Roughton, E. C., & Lubach, G. R. (1997). Moderate alcohol consumption and psychological stress during pregnancy induce attention and neuromotor impairments in primate infants. *Child Development, 68,* 747–759.

Schnurr, P. P., Ford, J. D., Friedman, M. J., Green, B. L., Dain, B. J., & Sengupta, A. (2000). Predictors and outcomes of posttraumatic stress disorder in World War II veterans exposed to mustard gas. *Journal of Consulting and Clinical Psychology, 68,* 258–268.

Schraw, G. Dunkle, M. E., & Bendixen, L. D. (1995). Cognitive processes in well-defined and ill-defined problem solving. *Applied Cognitive Psychology, 9,* 523–538.

Schreiber, F. R. (1973). *Sybil.* Chicago: Regnery.

Schreiner, C. E., Read, H. L., & Sutter, M. L. (2000). Modular organization of frequency integration in primary auditory cortex. *Annual Review of Neuroscience, 23,* 501–529.

Schuckit, M. (1984). Relationship between the course of primary alcoholism in men and family history. *Journal of Studies on Alcohol, 45,* 334–338.

Schuckit, M. A. (1994). Low level of response to alcohol as a predictor of future alcoholism. *American Journal of Psychiatry, 151,* 184–189.

Schultz, T., & Schliefer, M. (1983). Towards a refinement of attribution concepts. In J. Jaspars, F. Fincham, & M. Hewstone (Eds.), *Attribution theory and research: Conceptual, developmental, and social dimensions* (pp. 37–62). New York: Academic Press.

Schultz, W. (1998). Predictive reward signal of dopamine neurons. *Journal of Neurophysiology, 80,* 1–27.

Schultz, W., Dayan, P., & Montague, P. R. (1997). A neural substrate of prediction and reward. *Science, 275,* 1593–1599.

Schuster, D. T. (1990). Fulfillment of potential, life satisfaction, and competence: Comparing four cohorts of gifted women at midlife. *Journal of Educational Psychology, 82,* 471–478.

Schwartz, D., Dodge, K. A., Pettit, G. S., &

Bates, J. E. (2000). Friendship as a moderating factor in the pathway between early harsh home environment and later victimization in the peer group. *Developmental Psychology, 36,* 646–662.

Schwartz, G. E. (1987). Personality and health: An integrative health science approach. In V. P. Makosky (Ed.), *The G. Stanley Hall Lecture Series* (Vol. 7). Washington, DC: American Psychological Association.

Scott, S. K., Young, A. W., Calder, A. J., & Hellawell, D. J. (1997). Impaired auditory recognition of fear and anger following bilateral amygdala lesions. *Nature, 385,* 254–257.

Scoville, W. B., & Milner, B. (1957). Loss of recent memory after bilateral hippocampal lesions. *Journal of Nerology, Neurosurgery, and Psychiatry, 20,* 11–21.

Scribner, S. (1986). Thinking in action: Some characteristics of practical thought. In R. J. Sternberg & R. K. Wagner (Eds.), *Practical intelligence: Nature and origins of competence in the everyday world* (pp. 13–40). New York: Cambridge University Press.

Scroppo, J. C., Drob, S. L., Weinberger, J. L., & Eagle, P. (1998). Identifying dissociative identity disorder: A self-report and projective study. *Journal of Psychology, 107,* 272–284.

Scully, D., & Bart, P. (1973). A funny thing happened on the way to the orifice: Women in gynecology textbooks. In J. Huber (Ed.), *Changing women in a changing society.* Chicago: University of Chicago Press.

Searle, J. (1987). Minds, brains and programs. In Rainer Born (Ed.), *Artificial intelligence: The case against.* London: Croom Helm.

Searle, J. R. (2000) Consciousness. *Annual Review of Neuroscience, 23,* 557–578.

Sears, D. O. (1986). College sophomores in the laboratory: Influences of a narrow data base on social psychological view of human nature. *Journal of Personality and Social Psychology, 51,* 515–530.

Sears, R. R. (1977). Sources of life satisfactions of the Terman gifted men. *American-Psychologist, 32,* 119-128.

Seelinger, G., & Schuderer, B. (1985). Release of male courtship display in Periplaneta americana: Evidence for female contact sex pheromone. *Animal Behaviour, 33,* 599–607.

Segal, M. W. (1974). Alphabet and attraction: An unobtrusive measure of the effect of propinquity in a field setting. *Journal of Personality and Social Psychology, 30,* 654–657.

Segal, N. L. (1997). Same-age unrelated siblings: A unique test of within-family environmental influences on IQ similarity. *Journal of Educational Psychology, 89,* 381–390.

Segall, M. H. (1988). Cultural roots of aggressive behavior. In M. H. Bond (Ed.), *The cross-cultural challenge to social psychology.* Newbury Park, CA: Sage.

Segall, M. H., Campbell, D. T., & Herskovitz, M. J. (1966). *Influence of culture on visual perception.* New York: Bobbs-Merrill.

Segall, M. H., Dasen, P. R., Berry, J. W., & Poortinga, Y. H. (1990). *Human behavior in global perspective: An introduction to cross-cultural psychology.* New York: Pergamon Press.

Seger, C. A. (1994). Implicit learning. *Psychological Bulletin, 115,* 163–196.

Seidenberg, M. S. (1997). Language acquisition and use: Learning and applying probabilistic constraints. *Science, 275,* 1599–1603.

Seidenberg, M. S., & Petitto, L. A. (1987). Communication, symbolic communication, and language: Comment on Savage-Rumbaugh, McDonald, Sevcik, Hopkins, & Rupert (1986). *Journal of Experimental Psychology: General, 116,* 279–287.

Sekular, R., & Blake, R. (1994). *Perception* (3rd ed.). New York: McGraw-Hill.

Seligman, L. (1975). Skin potential as an indicator of emotion. *Journal of Counseling Psychology, 22,* 489–493.

Seligman, M. E. P. (1971). Phobias and preparedness. *Behavior Therapy, 193,* 323–325.

Seligman, M. E. P. (1995). The effectiveness of psychotherapy: The Consumer Reports study. *American Psychologist, 50,* 965–974.

Selman, R. L. (1980). *The growth of interpersonal understanding.* New York: Academic Press.

Selye, H. (1936). A syndrome produced by diverse nocuous agents. *Nature, 138,* 32.

Selye, H. (1976). *The stress of life.* New York: McGraw-Hill.

Serpell, L., Treasure, J., Teasdale, J., & Sullivan, V. (1999). Anorexia nervosa: Friend or foe? *International Journal of Eating Disorders, 25,* 177–186.

Serpell, R. (1989). Dimensions endogenes de l'intelligence chez les A-chewa et autres peuples africans. In J. Retschitzky, M. Bossel-Lagos, & P. Dasen (Eds.), *La recherche interculturelle.* Paris: L'Harmattan.

Sethi, S., & Seligman, M. (1993). Optimism and fundamentalism. *Psychological Science, 4,* 256–259.

Sewall, L., & Wooten, B. R. (1991). Stimulus determinants of achromatic constancy. *Journal of the Optical Society of America, 8,* 1794–1809.

Sewell, K. W., Adams-Webber, J., Mitterer, J., & Cromwell, R. L. (1992). Computerized repertory grids: Review of the literture. *International Journal of Personal Construct Psychology, 5,* 1–23.

Shantz, C. U. (1983). Social cognition. In J. H. Flavell & E. M. Markman (Eds.), *Handbook of child psychology: Vol. 3. Cognitive Development.* New York: John Wiley.

Shapira, Z. (1995). *Risk taking: A managerial perspective.* New York: Russell Sage Foundation.

Shapiro, S., & Vukovich, K. R. (1970). Early experience effects upon cortical dendrites: A proposed model for development. *Science, 167,* 292–294.

Shapley, R. (1995). Parallel neural pathways and visual function. In M. S. Gazzaniga et al. (1995), *The cognitive neurosciences* (pp. 315–324). Cambridge: MIT Press.

Shaver, P., Hazan, C., & Bradshaw, D. (1988). Love as attachment. In R. J. Sterberg & M. L. Barnes, *The psychology of love.* New Haven, CT: Yale University Press.

Shaver, P., Schwartz, J., Kirson, D., & O'Connor, G. (1987). Emotion knowledge: Further exploration of a prototype approach. *Journal of Personality and Social Psychology, 52,* 1061–1086.

Shaver, P. R., Collins, N., & Clark, C. L. (1996). Attachment styles and internal working models of self and relationship partners. In G. O. Fletcher, J. Fitness, et al. (Eds.), *Knowledge structures in close relationships: A social psychological approach* (pp. 25–61). Mahwah, NJ: Lawrence Erlbaum Associates.

Shaywitz, B. A., Shaywitz, S. E., Pugh, K. R., Constable, R. T., et al. (1995). Sex differences in the functional organization of the brain for language. *Nature, 373,* 607–609.

Shaywitz, S., Shaywitz, B., Pugh, K. R., Fulbright, R. K., Constable, R. T., Mencl, W. E., et al. (1998). Functional disruption in the organization of the brain for reading in dyslexia. *Proceedings of the National Academy of Science, 95,* 2636–2641.

Shea, M., Glass, D., Pilkonis, P., Watkins, J., & Docherty, J. (1987). Frequency and implications of personality disorders in a sample of depressed outpatients. *Journal of Personality Disorders, 1,* 27–42.

Shea, M. T., Elkin, I., Imber, S., & Sotsky, S. (1992). Course of depressive symptoms over follow-up: Findings from the National Institute of Mental Health Treatment of Depression Collaborative Research Program. *Archives of General Psychiatry, 49,* 782–787.

Shedler, J., & Block, J. (1990). Adolescent drug use and psychological health: A longitudinal inquiry. *American Psychologist, 45,* 612–630.

Shedler, J., Mayman, M., & Manis, M. (1993). The illusion of mental health. *American Psychologist, 48,* 1117–1131.

Sheehy, G. (1976). *Passages.* New York: E. P. Dutton.

Shefler, G., Dasberg, H., & Ben-Shakhar, G. (1995). A randomized controlled outcome and follow-up study of Mann's time-limited psychotherapy. *Journal of Consulting and Clinical Psychology, 63,* 585–593.

Shepher, J. (1978). Reflections on the origins of human pair-bonds. *International Journal of Social and Biological Structures, 1,* 253–264.

Sherif, M., et al. (1961). *Intergroup conflict and cooperation: The Robber's Cave experiment.* Norman: University of Oklahoma Press.

Sherif, M., & Sherif, C. W. (1979). Research on intergroup relations. In W. G. Austin & S. Worchel (Eds.), *The social psychology of intergroup relations.* Monterey, CA: Brooks/Cole.

Sherman, R. L. (1994). The rock ceiling: A study of African-American women managers' experiences and perceptions of barriers restricting advancement in the corporation. Dissertation Abstracts International Section A. *Humanities & Social Sciences, 54,* 3226.

Sherwin, B. (1993). *Menopause myths and realities.* Washington, DC: American Psychiatric Press.

Shettleworth, S. J. (1988). Foraging as operant behavior and operant behavior as foraging: What have we learned? In G. H. Bower et al. (Eds.), *The psychology of learning and motivation: Advances in research and theory* (Vol. 22, pp. 1–49). San Diego: Academic Press.

Shevrin, H., Bond, J. Brakel, L., Hertel, R., & Williams, W. J. (1996). *Conscious and unconscious processes: Psychodynamic, cognitive, and neurophysiological convergences.* New York: Guilford.

Shields, J. (1962). *Monozygotic twins brought up apart and brought together.* London: Oxford University Press.

Shimamura, A. P. (1995). Memory and frontal lobe function. In M. S. Gazzaniga et al. (Eds.), *The cognitive neurosciences.* (pp. 803–813). Cambridge: MIT Press.

Shoda, Y., & Mischel, W. (1996). Toward a unified, intra-individual dynamic conception of personality. *Journal of Research in Personality, 30,* 414–428.

Shultz, T. R., & Lepper, M. R. (1995). Cognitive dissonance reduction as constraint satisfaction. *Psychological Review, 103,* 219–240.

Shweder, R. A. (1980). Scientific thought and social cognition. In W. A. Collins (Ed.), *Development of cognition, affect, and social relations: Minnesota Symposium on Child Development* (Vol. 13). Hillsdale, NJ: Erlbaum.

Shweder, R. A. & Bourne, E. J. (1982). Does the concept of the person vary cross-culturally? In A. J. Marsella & G. M. White (Eds.), *Cultural conceptions of mental health and therapy.* Boston: D. Reidel.

Siegel, A., Roeling, T. A. P., Gregg, T. R., & Kruk, M. R. (1999). Neuropharmacology of brain-stimulation-evoked aggression. *Neuroscience and Biobehavioral Reviews, 23,* 359–389.

Siegel, R. K. (1990). *Intoxication.* New York: Pocket Books.

Siegel, S. (1984). Pavlonian conditioning and heroin overdose: Reports by overdose victims. *Bulletin of the Psychonomic Society, 22,* 428–430.

Siegler, R. S. (1991). *Children's thinking* (2nd ed.). Englewood Cliffs, NJ: Prentice-Hall.

Siegler, R. S. (1996) *Emerging minds: The process of change in children's thinking.* New York,: Oxford University Press.

Siegler, R. S., & Ellis, S. (1996). Piaget on childhood. *Psychological Science, 7,* 211–215.

Siegman, A. W. (1994). From Type A to hostility to anger: Reflections on the history of coronary-prone behavior. In A. W. Siegman, T. W. Smith, et al. (Eds.). *Anger, hostility, and the heart* (pp. 1–21). Hillsdale, NJ: Lawrence Erlbaum Associates.

Sifneos, P. (1973). The prevalence of alexithymic characteristics in psychosomatic patients. *Psychotherapy and Psychosomatics, 22,* 255–262.

Sifneos, P. (1987). *Short-term dynamic psychotherapy: Evaluation and technique* (2nd ed.). New York: Plenum.

Sigall, H., Page, R., & Brown, A. C. (1971). Effort expenditure as a function of evaluation and evaluator attractiveness. *Representative Research in Social Psychology, 2,* 19–25.

Sigel, I. E., Sander, A., Cunningham, H., & Harkness, S. (1996). Disciplinary approaches to images of childhood: Religion, history, anthropology, and psychology. In C. P. Hwang, and M. E. (Eds.), *Images of childhood.* (pp. 13-73). Mahwah, NJ: Lawrence Erlbaum Associates.

Sillars, A. L., & Zietlow, P. (1993). Investigations of marital communication and lifespan development. In N. Coupland & J. Nussbaum (Eds.), *Discourse and lifespan identity: Language and language behaviors* (Vol. 4, pp. 237–261). Newbury Park, CA: Sage Publications.

Silverstein, L. B., & Auerbach, C. F. (1999). Deconstructing the essential father. *American Psychologist, 54,* 397–407.

Simmons, L. W. (1990). Pheromonal cues for the recognition of kin by female field crickets, Gryllus bimaculatus. *Animal Behaviour, 40,* 192–195.

Simon, H. (1990). Invariants of human behavior. *Annual Review of Psychology, 41,* 1–19.

Simon, H. A. (1978). Information-processing theory of human problem solving. In W. K. Estes (Ed.), *Handbook of learning and cognitive processes.* Hillsdale, NJ: Erlbaum.

Simon, R. (1985). Family therapy. In H. I. Kaplan & B. J. Sadock (Eds.), *Comprehensive textbook of psychiatry* (4th ed.). Baltimore, MD: Williams & Wilkins.

Simonoff, E., Bolton, P., & Rutter, M. (1998). Genetic perspectives on mental retardation. In J. A. Burack, R. M. Hodapp, et al. (Eds.), *Handbook of mental retardation and development* (pp. 41–79). New York: Cambridge University Press.

Simons, H. W., Berkowitz, N. N., & Moyer, R. J. (1970). Similarity, credibility, and attitude change: A review and a theory. *Psychological Bulletin, 73,* 1–16.

Simonton, D. K. (1994). *Greatness: Who makes history and why?* New York: Guilford.

Simonton, D. K. (1997). Creative productivity: A predictive and explanatory model of career trajectories and landmarks. *Psychological Review, 104,* 66–89.

Simpson, J., Gangestad, S., & Lerma, M. (1990). Perception of physical attractiveness: Mechanisms involved in the maintenance of romantic relationships. *Journal of Personality and Social Psychology, 59,* 1192–1201.

Singer, J. L. (1975). *The inner world of day-dreaming.* New York: Harper & Row.

Singer, J. L. (1990). *Repression and dissociation: Implications for personality theory, psychopathology, and health.* Chicago: University of Chicago Press.

Singer, J. L., & Kolligian, J., Jr. (1987). Personality: Developments in the study of private experience. *Annual Review of Psychology, 38,* 533–574.

Singer, J. L., & Singer, D. G. (1981). Television, imagination, and aggression: A study of preschoolers, Hillsdale, NJ: Erlbaum.

Singh, D. (1993). Adaptive significance of female physical attractiveness: Role of waist-to-hip ratio. *Journal of Personality and Social Psychology, 65,* 293–307.

Skeels, H. M. (1966). Adult states of children with contrasting early life experiences: A follow-up study. *Monographs of the Society for Research in Child Development, 31* (serial No. 105), 70.

Skinner, B. F. (1938). *The behavior of organisms.* New York: Appleton-Century-Crofts.

Skinner, B. F. (1948). *Walden Two.* New York: Macmillan.

Skinner, B. F. (1951). How to teach animals. *Scientific American, 185,* 26–29.

Skinner, B. F. (1953). *Science and human behavior.* New York: Macmillan.

Skinner, B. F. (1957). *Verbal behavior.* New York: Appleton-Century-Crofts.

Skinner, B. F. (1974). *About behaviorism.* New York: Vintage Books.

Skinner, B. F. (1977). Hernstein and the evolution of behaviorism. *American Psychologist, 32,* 1006–1012.

Skinner, B. F. (1990). Can psychology be a science of mind? *American Psychologist, 45,* 1206–1210.

Skodak, M., & Skeel, H. M. (1949). A final follow-up study of one hundred adopted children. *Journal of Genetic Psychology, 75,* 85–125.

Skoog, G. & Skoog, I. (1999). A 40-year follow-up of patients with obsessive-compulsive disorder. *Archives of General Psychiatry, 56,* 121-127.

Slaby, R. G., & Frey, K. S. (1976). Development of gender constancy and selective attention to same-sex models. *Child Development, 46,* 849-856.

Slade, L. A., & Rush, M. C. (1991). Achievement motivation and the dynamics of task difficulty choices. *Journal of Personality and Social Psychology, 60,* 165–172.

Sloboda, J. A., Hermelin, B., & O'Connor, N. (1985). An exceptional music memory. *Music Perception, 3,* 155–169.

Slochower, J. (1987). The psychodynamics of obesity: A review. *Psychoanalytic Psychology, 4,* 145–159.

Slutske, W. S., Heath, A. C., Kinwiddie, S. H., Madden, P. A. F., Buholz, K. K., Dunne, M. P., et al. (1997). Modeling genetic and environmental influences in the etiology of conduct disorder: A study of 2682 adult twin pairs. *Journal of Abnormal Psychology, 106,* 266–279.

Smith, C. (1985). Sleep states and learning: A review of the animal literature. *Neuroscience and Biobehavioral Review, 9,* 157–168.

Smith, C., & Lloyd, B. (1978). Maternal behavior and perceived sex of infant: Revisited. *Child Development, 49,* 1263–1265.

Smith, C. A., & Ellsworth, P. (1985). Patterns of cognitive appraisal in emotion. *Journal of Personality and Social Psychology, 48,* 813–838.

Smith, D. E., & Seumour, R. B. (1994). LSD: History and toxicity. *Psychiatric Annals, 24,* 145–147.

Smith, E. E. (1995). Concepts and categorization. In E. E. Smith, D. N. Osherson, et al. (Eds.), *Thinking: An invitation to cognitive science: Vol. 3. An invitation to cognitive science* (2nd ed., pp. 3–33). Cambridge: MIT Press.

Smith, E. E. (2000). Neural bases of human working memory. *Current Directions in Psychological Science, 6,* 45–49.

Smith, E. E., Patalano, A. L., & Jonides, J. (1998). Alternative strategies of categorization. *Cognition, 65,* 167–196.

Smith, E. R. (1996). What do connectionism and social psychology offer each other? *Journal of Personality and Social Psychology, 70,* 893–912.

Smith, E. R. (1998). Mental representation and memory. In D. T. Gilbert, S. T. Fiske, et al. (Eds.), *The handbook of social psychology,* (Vol. 2, 4th ed., pp. 391–445). Boston: McGraw-Hill.

Smith, J., & Baltes, P. B. (1999). Trends and profiles of psychological functioning in very old age. In P. B. Baltes & K. U. Mayer (Eds.). *The Berlin Aging Study: Aging from 70 to 100.* (pp. 197–226). New York: Cambridge University Press.

Smith, J. A., Hauenstein, N. M. A., & Buchanan, L. B. (1996). Goal setting and exercise performance. *Human Performance, 9,* 141–154.

Smith, K. (1984). Drive: In defence of a concept. *Behaviorism, 12,* 71–114.

Smith, M. B. (1978). Perspectives on self-hood. *American Psychologist, 33,* 1053–1063.

Smith, M. B. (1988). Can there be a human science? *Symposium of the American Psychological Association,* Atlanta, GA.

Smith, M. B. (1994). Selfhood at risk: Postmodern perils and the perils of postmodernism. *American Psychologist, 49,* 405–411.

Smith, M. L., & Glass, G. V. (1977). Meta-analysis of psychotherapy outcome studies. *American Psychologist, 32,* 752–760.

Smith, M. W., Sharit, J., & Czaja, S. J. (1999). Aging, motor control, and the performance of computer mouse tasks. *Human Factors, 41,* 389–396.

Smith, P. K., & Daglish, L. (1977). Sex differences in parent and infant behavior. *Child Development, 48,* 1250–1254.

Smith, R. E., & Swinyard, W. R. (1983). Attitude-behavior consistency: The impact of product trial versus advertising. *Journal of Marketing Research, 20,* 257–267.

Smith, S. M., & Petty, R. E. (1995). Personality moderators of mood congruency effects on cognition: The role of self-esteem and negative mood regulation. *Journal of Personality and Social Psychology, 68*(6), 1092–1107.

Smotherman, W. P., & Robinson, S. R. (1996). The development of behavior before birth. *Developmental Psychology, 32,* 425–434.

Snyder, D. K., Wills, R. M., & Grady-Fletcher, A. (1991). Long-term effectiveness of behavioral versus insight-oriented marital therapy: A 4-year follow-up study. *Journal of Consulting and Clinical Psychology, 59,* 138–141.

Snyder, M., & Cantor, N. (1979). Testing hypotheses about other people: The use of historical knowledge. *Journal of Experimental Social Psychology, 15*(4), 330–342.

Snyder, M., & Ickes, W. (1985). In G. Lindzey and E. Aronson (Eds.), *Handbook of social psychology,* Reading, MA: Addison-Wesley.

Snyder, M., Tanke, E. D., & Berscheid, E. (1977). Social perception and interpersonal behavior: On the self-fulfilling nature of social stereotypes. *Journal of Personality and Social Psychology, 35* 656–666.

Sobal, J., & Stunkard, A. (1989). Socioeconomic status and obesity: A review of the literature. *Psychological Bulletin, 105,* 260–275.

Sohlberg, S., & Strober, M. (1994). Personality in anorexia nervosa: An update and a theoretical integration. *Acta Psychiatrica Scandinavica, 89* (Suppl 37), 16.

Solomon, D. A., Keller, M. B., Leon, A. C., Mueller, T. I, Lavori, P. W., Shea, M. T., Coryell, W., Warshaw, M., Turvey, C., Maser, J. D, & Endicott, J. (2000). Multiple recurrences of major depressive disorder. *American Journal of Psychiatry, 157,* 229-233.

Solomon, D. A., Keller, M. B., Leon, A. C., Mueller, T. I., Shea, M. T., Warshaw, M., et al. (1997). Recovery from major depression: A 10-year prospective follow-up across multiple episodes. *Archives of General Psychiatry, 54,* 1001–1006.

Solomon, L. Z., Solomon, H., & Maiorca, J. (1982). The effects of bystander's anonymity, situational ambiguity, and victim's status on helping. *Journal of Social Psychology, 117,* 285-294.

Solomon, S., Greenberg, J., & Pyszczynski, T. (1991). A terror management theory of social behavior: The psychological functions of self-esteem and cultural worldviews. In L. Berkowitz (Ed.), *Advances in Experimental Social Psychology, 24,* 93–159.

Somer, O., & Goldberg, L. (1999). The structure of Turkish traits—descriptive adjectives. *Journal of Personaity and Social Psychology, 76,* 431–450.

Sommer, R., & Sommer, B. A. (1983). Mystery in Milwaukee: Early intervention, I.Q., and psychology textbooks. *American Psychologist, 38,* 982–985.

Sorensen, P. W. (1996). Biological responsiveness to pheromones provides fundamental and unique insight into olfactory function. *Chemical Senses, 21,* 245–256.

Sorrentino, R. M., & Higgins, E. T. (Eds.). (1996). *Handbook of motivation and cognition: Vol. 3. The interpersonal context.* New York: Guilford Press.

Souchay, C., Isingrini, M., & Espagnet, L. (2000). Aging, episodic memory feeling-of-knowing, and frontal functioning. *Neuropsychology, 14,* 299–309.

Spain, D. (Ed.). (1992). *Psychoanalytic anthropology after Freud.* New York: Psyche Press.

Spanos, N. P., Burgess, C. A., Wallace-Capretta, S., & Ouaida, N. (1996). Simulation, surreptitious observation and the modification of hypnotizability: Two tests of the compliance hypothesis. *Contemporary Hypnosis, 13,* 161–176.

Spanos, N. P., Stenstrom, R. J., & Johnston, J. C. (1988). Hypnosis, placebo, and suggestion in the treatment of warts. *Psychosomatic Medicine, 50,* 245–260.

Spearman, C. (1904). General intelligence, objectively determined and measured. *American Journal of Psychology, 15,* 201–293.

Spearman, C. (1927). *The abilities of man: Their nature and measurement.* New York: Macmillan.

Speicher, B. (1994). Family patterns of moral judgement during adolescence and early adulthood. *Developmental Psychology, 30,* 624–632.

Spelke, E., Hirst, W., & Neisser, U. (1976). Skills of divided attention. *Cognition, 4*, 215-230

Spellman, B. A., & Holyoak, K. (1992). If Saddam is Hitler then who is George Bush? Analogical mapping between systems of social roles. *Journal of Personality and Social Psychology, 62*, 913–933.

Spence, A. P. (1989). *Biology of human aging*. Englewood Cliffs, NJ: Prentice-Hall.

Spence, S. A., Liddle, P. F., Stefan, M. D., Hellewell, J. S. E., Sharma, T., Friston, K. J., Hirsch, S. R., Frith, C. D., Murray, R. M., Deakin, J. F. W., & Grasby, P. M. (2000). Functional anatomy of verbal fluency in people with schizophrenia and those at genetic risk: Focal dysfunction and distributed disconnectivity reappraised. *British Journal of Psychiatry, 176*, 52–60.

Spencer, M. B., & Markstrom-Adams, C. (1990). Identity processes among racial and ethnic minority children in America. *Child Development, 61*, 290–310.

Sperling, G. (1960). The information available in brief visual presentations. *Psychological Monographs, 74*, 1–29.

Sperry, R. (1984). Consciousness, personal identity and the divided brain. *Neuropsychologia, 22*, 661–673.

Spiegel, D. (1999). Healing words - Emotional expression and disease outcome. *Journal of the American Medical Association, 281*, 1328-1329.

Spiegel, D., & Kato, P. M. (1996). Psychological influences on cancer incidence and progression. *Harvard Review of Psychiatry, 4*, 10–26.

Spillman, L. (1994). The Mermann grid illusion: A tool for studying human perceptive field organization. *Perception, 23*, 691–708

Spirduso, W., & MacRae, P. (1990). Motor performance and aging. In J. E. Birren & K. W. Schaie (Eds.), *Handbook of the psychology of aging* (3rd ed.). New York: Van Nostrand Reinhold.

Spiro, M. (1965). *Context and meaning in cultural anthropology*. New York: Free Press.

Spitz, R. A. (1945). Hospitalism: An inquiry into the genesis of psychiatry conditions in early childhood. *Psychoanalytic Study of the Child, 1*, 53–74.

Spitzer, R., Williams, J. B. W., Gibbon, M., & First, M. (1992). The structured clinical interview for DSM-III-R (SCID) I: History, rationale, and description. *Archives of General Psychiatry, 49*, 624–629.

Spitzer, R. L. (1985). DSM-III and the politics-science dichotomy syndrome: A response to Thomas E. Schacht's"DSM-III and the politics of truth."*American Psychologist, 40*, 522–526.

Sporer, S., Malpass, R., & Koehnken, G., (Eds.). (1996). *Psychological issues in eyewitness identification*. Mahwah, NJ: Lawrence Erlbaum.

Spreen, O., Tupper, D., Risser, A., Tuokko, H., & Edgell, D. (1984). *Human developmental neuropsychology*. New York: Oxford University Press.

Squier, L. H., & Domhoff, G. W. (1998). The presentation of dreaming and dreams in introductory psychology textbooks: A critical examination with suggestions for textbook authors and course instructors. *Dreaming: Journal of the Association for the Study of Dreams, 8*, 149-168.

Squire, L. R. (1986). Mechanisms of memory. *Science, 232*, 1612–1619.

Squire, L. R. (1989). On the course of forgetting in very long-term memory. *Journal of Experimental Psychology: Learning, Memory, and Cognition, 15*, 241–245.

Squire, L. R. (1992). Declarative and nondeclarative memory: Multiple brain systems supporting learning and memory. *Journal of Cognitive Neuroscience, 4*, 232–243.

Squire, L. R. (1995). Memory and brain systems. In R. D. Broadwell et al. (Eds.), *Neuroscience, memory, and language. Decade of the brain*, (Vol. 1, pp. 59–75). Washington: U.S. Government Printing Office.

Squire, L. R., & Zola-Morgan, S. (1991). The medial temporal lobe memory system. *Science, 253*, 1380–1386.

Srinivas, K., Breedin, S. D., Coslett, H. B., & Saffran, E. M. (1997). Intact perceptual priming in a patient with damage to the anterior inferior temporal lobes. *Journal of Cognitive Neuroscience, 9*, 490–511.

Srivastava, A., Borries, C., & Sommer, V. (1991). Homosexual mounting in free-ranging female langurs (*Presbytis entellus-R*). *Archives of Sexual Behavior, 20*, 487-512.

Staal, W. G., Hulshoff Pol, H. E., Schnack, H. G., Hoogendoorn, M. L. C., Jellema, K., & Kahn, R. S. (2000). Structural brain abnormalities in patients with schizophrenia and their healthy siblings. *American Journal of Psychiatry, 157*, 416–421.

Stacy, A. W. (1997). Memory activation and expectancy as prospective predictors of alcohol and marijuana use. *Journal of Abnormal Psychology, 106*, 61–73.

Stadler, M. A., & Frensch, P. A. (1998). *Handbook of implicit learning*. London: Sage.

Stallings, M., Hewitt, J., Cloninger, C. R., Heath, A. C., & Eaves, L. J. (1996). Genetic and environmental structure of the Tridimensional Personality Questionnaire: Three or four temperament dimensions? *Journal of Personality and Social Psychology, 70*, 127–140.

Stanley, B., Molcho, A., Stanley, M., Winchel, R., Gameroff, M. J., Parsons, B., & Mann, J. J. (2000). Association of aggressive behavior with altered serotonergic function in patients who are not suicidal. *American Journal of Psychiatry, 157*, 609–614.

Stanton, A. L., Danoff-Burg, S., Cameron, C. L., Bishop, M., Collins, C. A., Kirk, S. B., Sworowski, L. A., & Twillman, R. (2000). Emotionally expressive coping predicts psychological and physical adjustment to breast cancer. *Journal of Consulting and Clinical Psychology, 68*, 875–882.

Stattin, H., & Magnusson, D. (1989). The role of early aggressive behavior in the frequency, seriousness, and types of later crime. *Journal of Consulting and Clinical Psychology, 57*, 710–718.

Steele, C., & Aronson, J. (1995). Stereotype threat and the intellectual test performance of African Americans. *Journal of Personality and Social Psychology, 69*, 797–811.

Steele, C. M. (1997). A threat in the air: How stereotypes shape intellectual identity and performance. *American Psychologist, 52*, 613-629.

Steele, C. M. (1988). The psychology of self-affirmation: Sustaining the integrity of the self. In L. Berkowitz (Ed.), *Advances in experimental social psychology, Vol. 21: Social psychological studies of the self: Perspectives and programs*. (pp. 261-302). San Diego: Academic Press, Inc.

Steele, H., Steele, M., & Fonagy, P. (1996). Associations among attachment classifications of mothers, fathers, and their infants. *Child Development, 67*, 541–555.

Stein, B. E., & Meredith, M. A. (1990). Multisensory integration: Neural and behavioral solutions for dealing with stimuli from different sensory modalities. *Annals of the New York Academy of Sciences, 608*, 51–70.

Stein, J., Newcomb, M., & Bendler, P. (1994). Psychosocial correlates and predictors of AIDS risk behaviors, abortion, and drug use among a community sample of young adult women. *Health Psychology, 13*, 308–318.

Steinberg, L., Lamborn, S. D., Darling, N., & Mounts, N. S. (1994). Over-time changes in adjustment and competence among adolescents from authoritative, authoritarian, indulgent, and neglectful families. *Child Development, 65*, 754–770.

Steinhausen, H. C., Willms J., & Spohr, H. L. (1993). Long-term psychopathological and cognitive outcome of children with fetal alcohol syndrome. *Journal of the American Academy of Child and Adolescent Psychiatry, 32*, 990–994.

Stephan, W. G. (1987). The contact hypothesis in intergroup relations. In C. Hendrick (Ed.), *Group processes and intergroup relations. Review of personality and social psychology, Vol. 9*. (pp. 13-40). Beverly Hills: Sage Publications, Inc.

Stephens, D. W., & Krebs, J. R. (1986). *Foraging theory*. Princeton: Princeton University Press.

Stephens, R. S., Roffman, R. A., & Curtin, L. (2000). Comparison of extended versus brief treatments for marijuana use. *Journal of Consulting and Clinical Psychology, 68*, 898–908.

Stepper, S., & Strack, F. (1993). Proprioceptive determinants of emotional and nonemotional feelings. *Journal of Personality & Social Psychology, 64*, 211-220.

Stern, D. (1985). *The interpersonal world of the infant*. New York: Basic Books.

Stern, K., & McClintock, M. K. (1998). Regulation of ovulation by human pheromones. *Nature, 392*, 177–179.

Sternbeger, R. J., Forsythe, G. B., Hedlund et al. (2000). *Practical intelligence in everyday life*. New York: Cambridge University Press.

Sternberg, R. J. (Ed.). (1984). *Mechanisms of cognitive development*. New York: Freeman.

Sternberg, R. J. (1985). *Beyond IQ: A triarchic theory of human intelligence*. New York: Cambridge University Press.

Sternberg, R. J. (1988). Triangulating love. In R.

Sternberg & M. L. Barnes (Eds.), *The psychology of love.* New Haven, Conn.: Yale University Press.

Sternberg, R. J. (1996). Costs of expertise. In K. A. Ericsson (Ed.), *The road to excellence: The acquisition of expert performance in the arts and sciences, sports, and games* (pp. 347–354). Hinsdale,NJ: Lawrence Erlbaum Associates, Inc.

Sternberg, R. J. (1997a). *Satisfaction in close relationships.* New York: Guilford Press.

Sternberg, R. J. (1997b). The triarchic theory of intelligence. In D. P. Flanagan, J. L. Genshaft, & P. L. Harrison (Eds.), *Contemporary intellectual assessment: Theories, tests, and issues* (pp. 92–104). New York: Guilford Press.

Sternberg, R. J. (1997c). Construct validation of a triangular love scale. *European Journal of Social Psychology, 27(3),* 313–335.

Sternberg, R. J. (1998). *Handbook of creativity.* New York: Cambridge University Press.

Sternberg, R. J. (1999). Looking back and looking forward on intelligence: Toward a theory of successful intelligence. In M. Bennett et al. (Eds.), *Developmental psychology: Achievements and prospects.* (pp. 289–308). Philadelphia, PA: Psychology Press/Taylor & Francis.

Sternberg, R. J. (2000a). *Handbook of intelligence.* New York: Cambridge University Press.

Sternberg, R. J. (2000b). The concept of intelligence. In R. J. Sternberg (Ed.), *Handbook of intelligence* (pp. 3–15). New York: Cambridge University Press.

Sternberg, R. J., Conway, B. E., Ketron, J. L., & Bernstein, M. (1981). People's conceptions of intelligence. *Journal of Personality and Social Psychology: Attitudes and Social Cognitions, 41,* 37–55.

Sternberg, R. J., & Lubart, T. I. (1996). Investing in creativity. *American Psychologist, 51,* 677–688.

Sternberg, R. J., & O'Hara, L. A. (2000). Intelligence and creativity. In R. J. Sternberg (Ed.), *Handbook of intelligence* (pp. 611–630). New York: Cambridge University Press.

Sternberg, R. J., & Salter, W. (1982). Conceptions of intelligence. In R. J. Sternberg (Ed.), *Handbook of human intelligence* (pp. 3–28). New York: Cambridge University Press.

Sternberg, R. J., & Wagner, R. K. (1993). The geocentric view of intelligence and job performance is wrong. *Current Directions in Psychological Science, 2,* 1–5.

Stevens, A., & Coupe, P. (1978). Distortions in judged spacial relations. *Cognitive Psychology, 10,* 422–437.

Stevens, C. F. (1979). The neuron. *Scientific American, 241,* 54–65.

Stevens, S. S. (1961). Psychophysics of sensory function. In W. Rosenblith (Ed.), *Sensory communication* (pp. 1–33). Cambridge, MA: MIT Press.

Stevens, S. S. (1975). *Psychophysics: Introduction to its perceptual, neural, and social prospects.* New York: John Wiley.

Stevens, S. S., & Newman, E. B. (1934). The localization of pure tone. *Proceedings of the National Academy of Sciences, 20,* 593–596.

Stewart, D. E., & Robinson, G. E. (1997). *A clinician's guide to menopause.* Washington, DC: Health Press International.

Stewart, W. A. (1969). On the use of Negro dialect in the teaching of reading. In J. C. Baratz & R. W. Schuy (Eds.), *Teaching black children to read* (pp. 156–219). Washington, DC: Center for Applied Linguistics.

Stice, E., & Barrera, M. (1995). A longitudinal examination of the reciprocal relations between perceived parenting and adolescents' substance use and externalizing behaviors. *Developmental Psychology, 31,* 322–334.

Stickgold, R. (1998). Sleep: Off-line memory reprocessing. *Trends in Cognitive Sciences, 2,* 484–492.

Stoff, D. M., Breiling, J., & Maser, J. D. (Eds.), (1997). *Handbook of antisocial behavior.* New York: Wiley.

Stogdill, R., & Coons, A. (1957). *Leader behavior: Its description and measurement.* Columbus, OH: Ohio State University Bureau of Business Research.

Stokes, J. P. (1985). The relation of social network and individual differences variables to loneliness. *Journal of Personality and Social Psychology, 48,* 981–990.

Stoolmiller, M. (1999). Implications of the restricted range of family environments for estimates of heritability and nonshared environment in behavior-genetic adoption studies. *Psychological Bulletin, 125,* 392–409.

Strang, D. J. (1972). Conformity, ability, and self-esteem. *Representative Research in Social Psychology, 3,* 97–103.

Strauman, T. (1992). Self-guides, autobiographical memory, and anxiety and dysphoria: Toward a cognitive model of vulnerability to emotional distress. *Journal of Abnormal Psychology, 101,* 87–95.

Strauman, T., Lemieux, A., & Coe, C. (1993). Self-discrepancy and natural killer cell activity: Immunological consequences of negative self-evaluation. *Journal of Personality and Social Psychology, 64,* 1042–1052.

Straus, A. S. (1977). Northern Cheyenne ethnopsychology. *Ethos, 5,* 326–357.

Straus, A. S. (1982). The structure of the self in Northern Cheyenne culture. In B. Lee (Ed.), *Psychosocial theories of the self.* New York: Plenum Press.

Straus, M. A., & Mouradian, V. E. (1998). Impulsive corporal punishment by mothers and antisocial behavior and impulsiveness of children. *Behavioral Sciences and the Law, 16,* 353–374.

Strauss, C., & Quinn, N. (1997). *A cognitive theory of cultural meaning.* New York: Cambridge University Press.

Strauss, D. H., Spitzer, R. L., & Muskin, P. R. (1990). Maladaptive denial of physical illness: A proposal for DSM-IV. *American Journal of Psychiatry, 147,* 1168–1172.

Strauss, J., Carpenter, W. T., & Bartko, J. (1974). The diagnosis and understanding of schizophrenia, III: Speculations on the processes that underlie schizophrenic symptoms and signs. *Schizophrenia Bulletin, 1,* 61–69.

Strauss, J., & Ryan, R. M. (1987). Autonomy disturbances in subtypes of anorexia nervosa. *Journal of Abnormal Psychology, 96,* 254–258.

Strayer, J. (1993). Children's concordant emotions and cognitions in response to observed emotions. *Child Development, 64,* 188–201.

Strayer, J., & Roberts, W. (1997). Facial and verbal measures of children's emotions and empathy. *International Journal of Behavioral Development, 20,* 627–649.

Streissguth, A., Barr, H., Johnson, M. D., & Kirchner, G. (1985). Attention and distraction at age 7 years related to maternal drinking during pregnancy. *Alcoholism: Clinical and experimental research, 9,* 195.

Streissguth, A., Sampson, P., & Barr, H. (1989). Neurobehavioral dose-response effects of prenatal alcohol exposure in humans from infancy to adulthood. *Annals of the New York Academy of Sciences, 562,* 145–158.

Stricker, G. (1996). Empirically validated treatment, psychotherapy manuals, and psychotherapy integration. *Journal of Psychotherapy Integration, 6,* 217-226.

Stricker, G., & Healey, B. J. (1990). Projective assessment of object relations: A review of the empirical literature. *Psychological Assessment, 2,* 219–230.

Striegel-Moore, R. H., Silberstein, L. R., & Rodin, J. (1986). Toward an understanding of risk factors for bulimia. *American Psychologist, 41,* 246–263.

Strober, M., Freeman, R., Lampert, C., Diamond, J., & Kaye, W. (2000). Controlled family study of anorexia nervosa and bulimia nervosa: Evidence of shared liability and transmission of partial syndromes. *American Journal of Psychiatry, 157,* 393–401.

Stroebe, M., Gergen, M., Gergen, K., & Stroebe, W. (1996). Broken hearts or broken bonds? In D. Klass, P. R. Silverman, et al. (Eds.), *Continuing bonds: New understandings of grief. Series in death education, aging, and health care.* (pp. 31–44). Washington, DC: Taylor & Francis.

Stroebel, C. F. (1985). Biofeedback and behavioral medicine. In H. I. Kaplan & B. J. Sadock (Eds.), *Comprehensive textbook of psychiatry.* Baltimore, MD: Williams & Wilkins.

Stromme, P., & Magnus, P. (2000). Correlations between socioeconomic status, IQ and aetiology in mental retardation: A population-based study of Norwegian children. *Social Psychiatry and Psychiatric Epidemiology, 35,* 12–18.

Stromswold, K. (1995). The cognitive and neural bases of language acquisition. In M. S. Gazzaniga (Ed.), *The cognitive neurosciences.* (pp. 855–870). Cambridge: MIT Press.

Stroufe, L. A., & Fleeson, J. (1986). Attachment and the construction of relationships. In W. W. Hartup & Z. Rubin (Eds.), *Relationships and development* (pp. 51–72). Hillsdale, NJ: Erlbaum.

Stroufe, L. A., & Waters, E. (1977). Attachment as an organizational construct. *Child Development, 48,* 1184–1199.

Strupp, H., & Binder, J. L. (1984). *Psychotherapy in a new key: A guide to time-limited dynamic psy-*

chotherapy. New York: Basic Books.

Stuart, G. L., Treat, T. A., & Wade, W. A. (2000). Effectiveness of an empirically based treatment for panic disorder delivered in a service clinic setting: 1-year follow-up. *Journal of Consulting and Clinical Psychology, 68,* 506–512.

Stumpf, H. (1993). The factor structure of the Personality Research Form: A cross-national evaluation. *Journal of Personality, 61,* 1–26.

Stunkard, A., Sorensen, T. I. A., Harris, C., Teasdale, T. W., Chakraborty, R., Schull, W., & Schulsinger, F. (1986). An adoption study of human obesity. *New England Journal of Medicine, 314,* 193–198.

Stuss, D. T., & Benson, D. F. (1984). Neuropsychological studies of the frontal lobes. *Psychological Bulletin, 95,* 3–28.

Stuss, D. T., Gw, C. A., & Hetherington, C. R. (1992). "No longer Gage": Frontal lobe dysfunction and emotional changes. *Journal of Consulting and Clinical Psychology, 60,* 349–359.

Suarez-Orozco, M., Spindler, G., & Spindler, L. (1994). *The making of psychological anthropology II.* Fort Worth, TX: Harcourt Brace Jovanovich.

Suedfeld, P., & Granatstein, J. L. (1995). Leader complexity in personal and professional crises: Concurrent and retrospective information processing. *Political Psychology, 16,* 509–544.

Suedfeld, P., & Pennebaker, J. W. (1997). Health outcomes and cognitive aspects of recalled negative life events. *Psychosomatic Medicine, 59,* 172–177.

Suh, E., Diener, E., Oishi, S., & Triandis, H. C. (1998). The shifting basis of life satisfaction judgments across cultures: Emotions versus norms. *Journal of Personality & Social Psychology, 74,,* 482-493.

Sullivan, H. S. (1953). *The interpersonal theory of psychiatry.* New York: W. W. Norton.

Suls, J., David, J. P., & Harvey, J. H. (1996). Personality and coping: Three generations of research. *Journal of Personality, 64,* 711–735.

Suls, J., Green, P., & Hillis, S. (1998). Emotional reactivity to everyday problems, affective inertia, and neuroticism. *Personality & Social Psychology Bulletin, 24,* 127–136.

Sundstrom, L., Chapuisat, M., & Keller, L. (1996). Conditional manipulation of sex ratios by ant workers: A test of kin selection theory. *Science, 274,* 993–995.

Suomi, S. J. (1999). Behavioral inhibition and impulsive aggressiveness: Insights from studies with rhesus monkeys. In L. Balter & C. S. Tamis-LeMonda (Eds.), *Child psychology: A handbook of contemporary issues.* (pp. 510-525). Philadelphia: Psychology Press/Taylor & Francis.

Suomi, S. J. (2000). A biobehavioral perspective on developmental psychopathology: Excessive aggression and serotonergic dysfunction in monkeys. In A. J. Sameroff, & M. Lewis (Eds.), *Handbook of developmental psychopathology* (2nd Ed.) (pp. 237–256) New York: Kluwer Academic/Plenum Publishers.

Super, C. M. (1981). Cross-cultural research on infancy. In H. C. Triandis & A. Heron (Ed.), *Hand-book of cross-cultural psychology: Vol. 4. Developmental psychology.* Boston: Allyn & Bacon.

Super, C. M., & Harkness, S. (1980). *Anthropological perspectives on child development.* San Francisco: Jossey-Bass.

Surman, O. S., Gottlieb, S. K., Hackett, T. P., & Silverberg, E. L. (1983). Hypnosis in the treatment of warts. *Advances, 1,* 19–24.

Susser, E., Neugebauer, R., Hoek, H. W., Brown, A. S., Lin, S., Labovitz, D., & Gorman, J. M. (1996). Schizophrenia after prenatal famine further evidence. *Archives of General Psychiatry, 53,* 25–31.

Sutker, P., Winstead, D., Galina, Z., & Allai, A. (1991). Cognitive deficits and psychopathology among former prisoners of war and combat veterans of the Korean conflict. *American Journal of Psychiatry, 148,* 67–72.

Sutton, S. K., & Davidson, R. J. (1997). Prefrontal brain asymmetry: A biological substrate of the behavioral approach and inhibition systems. *Psychological Science, 8,* 204–210.

Swain, I., Zelano, P., & Clifton, R. K. (1993). Newborn infants' memory for speech sounds retained over 24 hours. *Developmental Psychology, 29,* 312–323.

Swain, S. A., Polkey, C. E., Bullock, P., & Morris, R. G. (1998). Recognition memory and memory for order in script-based stories following frontal lobe excisions. *Cortex, 34,* 25–45.

Swann, W. (1990). To be adored or to be known: The interplay of self-enhancement and self-verification. In R. M. Sorrentino & E. T. Higgins (Eds.), *Handbook of motivation and cognition.* (Vol. 2, pp. 408–448). New York: Guilford Press.

Swann, W., Stein-Seroussi, A., & Giesler, R. B. (1992a). Why people self-verify. *Journal of Personality and Social Psychology, 62,* 392–401.

Swann, W., Wenzlaff, R., Krull, D. S., & Pelham, B. (1992b). Allure of negative feedback: Self-verification strivings among depressed persons. *Journal of Abnormal Psychology, 101,* 293–306.

Swann, W. B. (1997). The trouble with change: Self-verification and allegiance to the self. *Psychological Science, 8,* 177-180.

Swann, W. D. (1984). Quest for accuracy in person perception: A matter of pragmatics. *Psychological Review, 91,* 457–477.

Sweet, R. A., Mulsant, B. H., Gupta, B., Rifai, A. H., Pasternak, R. E., McEachran, A., & Zubenko (1995). Duration of neuroleptic treatment and prevelence of tardive dyskinesia in late life. *Archives of General Psychiatry, 52,* 478–486.

Swendsen, J. D., Tennen, H., Carney, M. A., Affleck, G., Willard, A., & Hromi, A. (2000). Mood and alcohol consumption: An experience sampling test of the self-medication hypothesis. *Journal of Abnormal Psychology, 109,* 198–204.

Swets, J. A. (1992). The science of choosing the right decision threshold in high-stakes diagnostics. *American Psychologist, 47,* 522–532.

Szasz, T. (1974). *The myth of mental illness: Foundations of a theory of personal conduct,* (rev. ed.). New York: Harper & Row.

Szeszko, P. R., Robinson, D., Alvir, J. M. J., Bilder, R. M., Lencz, T., Ashtari, M., Wu, H., & Bogerts, B. (1999). Orbital frontal and amygdala volume reductions in obsessive-compulsive disorder. *Archives of General Psychiatry, 56,* 913-919.

Szymusiak, R., Iriye, T., & McGinty, D. (1989). Sleep-walking discharge of neurons in the posterior lateral hypothalamic area of cats. *Brain Research Bulletin, 23,* 111–120.

Tajfel, H. (1981). *Human groups and social categories: Studies in social psychology.* Cambridge: Cambridge University Press.

Tamminga, C., Thaker, G., Buchanon, R., Kirkpatrick, B., Alpha, L., Chase, T., & Carpenter, W. T. (1992). Limbic system abnormalities identified in schizophrenia using positron emission tomography with fluorodeoxyglucose and neocortical alterations with deficit syndrome. *Archives of General Psychiatry, 49,* 522–530.

Tan, C. C. (1991). Occupational health problems among nurses. *Scandinavian Journal of Work, Environment, and Health. 17,* 221–230.

Tanaka, J. W., & Taylor, M. (1991). Object categories and expertise: Is the basic level in the eye of the beholder? *Cognitive Psychology, 23,* 457–482.

Tandberg, E., Larsen, J. P., Aarsland, D., & Cummings, J. L. (1996). The occurrence of depression in Parkinson's disease: A community-based study. *Archives of Neurology, 53,* 175–179.

Tanner, J. E., & Byrne, R. W. (1996). Representation of action through iconic gesture in a captive lowland gorilla. *Current Anthropology, 37,* 162–173.

Tarr, M. J., Buelthoff, H. H., Zabinski, M., & Blanz, V. (1997). To what extent do unique parts influence recognition across changes in viewpoint? *Psychological Science, 8,* 282–289.

Tassinary, L. G., & Cacioppo, J. (1992). Unobservable facial actions and emotion. *Psychological Science, 3,* 28–33.

Taylor, G. J., & Taylor, H. L. (1997). Alexithymia. In M. McCallum, and W. E. Piper (Eds.), *Psychological mindedness: A contemporary understanding. The LEA series in personality and clinical psychology.* (pp. 77-104). Mahwah, NJ: Lawrence Erlbaum Associates, Inc., Publishers.

Taylor, S. (1991). *Health psychology* (2nd ed.). New York: McGraw-Hill.

Taylor, S., & Crocker, J. (1980). Schematic bases of social information processing. In E. T. Higgins, P. Herman, & M. Zanna (Eds.), *Social cognition: The Ontario Symposium.* Hillsdale, NJ: Erlbaum.

Taylor, S. E., & Armor, D. A. (1996). Positive illusions and coping with adversity. *Journal of Personality, 64,* 873–898.

Taylor, S. E., & Brown, J. D. (1988). Illusion and well-being: A social psychological perspective on mental health. *Psychological Bulletin, 103,* 193–210.

Taylor, S. E., Kemeny, M. E., Reed, G. M., Bower, J. E., & Gruenewald, T. L. (2000). Psychological resources, positive illusions, and health. *American Psychologist, 55,* 99–109.

Taylor, S. E., Klein, L. C., Lewis, B. P., Gruenewald, T. L., Gurung, R. A. R., & Updegraff, J. A. (in press). Biobehavioral responses to stress in females: Tend-and-befriend, no fight-or-flight. *Psychological Review.*

Taylor, S. E., Pham, L., Rivkin, I., & Armor, D. (1998). Harnessing the imagination: Mental stimulation, self-regulation, and coping. *American Psychologist, 53,* 429–439.

Teitelbaum, P. (1961). Disturbances in feeding and drinking behavior after hypothalamic lesions. *Nebraska Symposium on Motivation,* 39–68.

Tellegen, A., Lykken, D. T., Bouchard, T. J. Jr., Wilcox, K. J., & Rich, S. (1988). Personality similarity in twins reared apart and together. *Journal of Personality and Social Psychology, 54,* 1031–1039.

Terman, L. M. (1916). *The measurement of intelligence.* Boston: Houghton-Mifflin.

Terman, L. M. (1925). *Genetic studies of genius: Vol. 1. Mental and physical traits of a thousand gifted children.* Stanford, CA: Stanford University Press.

Terman, L. M., & Oden, M. H. (1947). *Genetic studies of genius: Vol. 4. The gifted child grows up: Twenty-five years' follow-up of a superior group.* Stanford, CA: Stanford University Press.

Terman, L. M., & Oden, M. H. (1959). *Genetic studies of genius: Vol. 5. The gifted group at midlife.* Stanford, CA: Stanford University Press.

Terman, M., Terman, J. S., & Ross, D. C. (1998) A controlled trial of timed bright light and negative air ionization for treatment of winter depression. *Archives of General Psychiatry, 55,* 875–882.

Terrace, H. S. (1979). How Nim Chimsky changed my mind. *Psychology Today, 3,* 65–76.

Tetlock, P., & Levi, A. (1982). Attributional bias: On the inconclusiveness of the cognitive-motivation debate. *Journal of Experimental Social Psychology, 18,* 68–88.

Tetlock, P. E. (1989). Structure and function in political belief systems. In A. R. Pratkanis, S. J. Breckler, et al. (Eds.), *Attitude structure and function. The third Ohio State University volume on attitudes and persuasion* (pp. 129–151). Hillsdale, NJ: Lawrence Erlbaum Associates.

Thase, M., Simons, A. D., Cahalane, J., McGeary, J., & Harden, T. (1991). Severity of depression and response to cognitive behavior therapy. *American Journal of Psychiatry, 148,* 784–789.

Thase, M. E. (2000). Relapse and recurrence of depression: An updated practical approach for prevention. In K. J. Palmer (Ed.), *Drug treatment issues in depression.* (pp. 35-52). Kwai Chung, Hong Kong: Adis International Publications.

Thase, M. E., & Kupfer, D. J. (1996). Recent developments in the pharmacotherapy of mood disorders. *Journal of Consulting & Clinical Psychology, 64,* 646-659.

Thelen, E. (1995). Motor development: A new synthesis. *American Psychologist, 50,* 79–95.

Thigpen, C. H., & Cleckley, H. (1954). *The thress faces of Eve.* Kingsport, TN: Kingsport Press.

Thomas, D. G., & Lykins, M. S. (1995). Event-related potential measures of 24-hour retention in 5-month-old infants. *Developmental Psychology, 31,* 946–957.

Thompson, D. A., & Campbell, R. G. (1977). Hunger in humans induced by 2-deoxy-D-glucose: Clucoprivic control of taste preference and food intake. *Science, 198,* 1065–1068.

Thompson, V. A., & Paivio, A. (1994). Memory for pictures and sounds: Independence of auditory and visual codes. *Canadian Journal of Experimental Psychology, 48,* 380–398.

Thorndike, E. L. (1911). *Animal intelligence: Experimental studies.* New York: Macmillan.

Thurstone, L. L. (1938). Primary mental abilities. *Psychometric Monographs* (Vol. 1). Chicago: Chicago University Press.

Thyer, B. A. (1980). Prolonged in vivo exposure therapy with a 70-year-old woman. *Journal of Behavior Therapy and Experimental Psychiatry, 11.*

Tienari, P. (1991). Interaction between genetic vulnerability and family environment: The Finnish adoptive family study of schizophrenia. *Act Psychiatrica Scandinavica, 84,* 460–465.

Tinbergen, N. (1951). *The study of instinct.* Oxford: Clarendon Press.

Tizard, B., & Hodges, J. (1978). The effects of early institutional rearing on the development of eight-year old children. *Journal of Child Psychology and Psychiatry, 19,* 99–108.

Tohen, M., Hennen, J., Zarate, C. M., Baldessarini, R. J., Strakowski, S. M., Stoll, A. L., Faedda, G. L., Suppes, T., Gebre-Medhin, P., & Cohen, B. M. (2000). Two-year syndromal and functional recovery in 219 cases of first-episode major affective disorder with psychotic features. *American Journal of Psychiatry, 157,* 220–228.

Tolliver, L. M. (1983). Social and mental health needs of the aged. *American Psychologist, 38,* 316–318.

Tolman, E. C. (1948). Cognitive maps in rats and men. *Psychological Review, 55,* 189–208.

Tolman, E. C., & Honzik, C. H. (1930). Insight in rats. *University of California Publications in Psychology, 4,* 215–232.

Tomarken, A. J., Davidson, R. J., Wheeler, R. E., & Doss, R. C. (1992). Individual differences in anterior brain asymmetry and fundamental dimensions of emotion. *Journal of Personality & Social Psychology, 62,* 676–687.

Tomkins, S. S. (1962). *Affect, imagery, consciousness: Vol. 1. The positive affects.* New York: Springer-Verlag.

Tomkins, S. S. (1980). Affect as amplification: Some modifications in theory. In R. Plutchik & H. Kellerman (Eds.), *Emotion: Theory, research, and experience: Vol. I. Theories of emotion.* New York: Academic Press.

Tomkins, S. S. (1986). Script theory. In J. Aronoff, A. I. Radin, & R. Zucker (Eds.), *The emergence of personality* (pp. 147–216). New York: Springer.

Tomlinson-Keasey, C., & Little, T. D. (1990). Predicting educational attainment, occupational achievement, intellectual skill, and personal adjustment among gifted men and women. *Journal of Educational Psychology, 82,* 442–455.

Tonigan, J. S., Miller, W. R., & Connors, G. J. (2000). Project MATCH client impressions about Alcoholics Anonymous: Measurement issues and relationship to treatment outcome. *Alcoholism Treatment Quarterly, 18,* 25–41.

Tooby, J., & Cosmides, L. (1992). The psychological foundations of culture. In J. H. Barkow, L. Cosmides, & J. Tooby (Eds.), *The adapted mind: Evolutionary psychology and the generation of culture* (pp. 19–136). New York: Oxford University Press.

Toorey, E. F. (1986). *Witchdoctors and psychiatrists: The common roots of psychotherapy and its future.* New York: Aronson.

Tootell, R. B. H., Reppas, J. B., Dale, A. M., & Look, R. B. (1995a). Visual motion aftereffect in human cortical area MT revealed by functional magnetic resonance imaging. *Nature, 375,* 139–141.

Tootell, R. B. H., Reppas, J. B., Kwong, K. K., & Malach, R. (1995b). Functional analysis of human MT and related visual cortical area using magnetic resonance imaging. *Journal of Neuroscience, 15,* 3215–3230.

Tootell, R. B. H., Silverman, M. S., Switkes, E., & De Valois, R. L. (1982). Deoxyglucose analysis of retinotopic organization in primate striate cortex. *Science, 218,* 902–904.

Toppino, T. C., & Schneider, M. A. (1999). The mix-up regarding mixed and unmixed lists in spacing-effect research. *Journal of Experimental Psychology: Learning, Memory, & Cognition, 25,* 1071–1076.

Traiwick, M. (1990). The ideology of love in a Tamil family. In O. M. Lynch (Ed.), *Divine passions: The social construction of emotion in India.* Berkeley: University of California Press.

Trappey, C. (1996). A meta-analysis of consumer choice and subliminal advertising. *Psychology & Marketing, 13,* 517–530.

Triandis, H. (Ed.). (1980). *Handbook of cross-cultural psychology* (6 vols.). Boston: Allyn & Bacon.

Triandis, H. (1989). The self and social behavior in differing cultural contexts. *Psychological Bulletin, 96,* 506–520.

Triandis, H. (1994). *Culture and social behavior.* New York: McGraw-Hill.

Triandis, H. C., Valsiner, J., Berry, J. W., Hui, C. H., & Keats, D. M. (1989). Culture and socialisation. In J. P. Forgas, J. M. Innes, et al. (Eds.), *Recent advances in social psychology: An international perspective* (pp. 491–534). Amsterdam, The Netherlands: North-Holland.

Triesman, A. (1986). Properties, parts and objects. In K. Boff, L. Kaufman, & J. Thomas (Eds.), *Handbook of perception and human performance* (Vol. 2, pp. 3501–3570). New York: Wiley.

Triplett, N. (1897). The dynamogenic factors in pacemaking and competition. *American Journal of Psychology, 9,* 507–533.

Trivers, R. (1972). Parental investment and sexual selection. In B. Campbell (Ed.), *Sexual selection and the descent of man: 1871–1971* (pp. 136–179). Chicago: Aldine.

Trivers, R. L. (1971). The evolution of reciprocal altruism. *Quarterly Review of Biology, 46,* 35–57.

Tronick, E., Morelli, G., & Ivey, P. (1992). The Efe forager infant and toddler's pattern of social relationships: Multiple and simultaneous. *Developmental Psychologist, 28,* 568–577.

Trope, Y., & Liberman, A. (1996). Social hypothesis testing: Cognitive and motivational mechanisms. In E. T. Higgins, W. Kruglanski, et al. (Eds.), *Social psychology: Handbook of basic principles* (pp. 239–270). New York: Guilford Press.

Tsuang, M. T., Lyons, M. J., Meyer, J. M., Doyle, T., Eisen, S. A., Goldberg, J., True, W., Lin, N., Toomey, R., & Eaves, L. (1998). Co-occurrence of abuse of different drugs in men: The role of drug-specific and shared vulnerabilities. *Archives of General Psychiatry, 55,* 967–972.

Tsuang, M. T., Stone, W. S., & Faraone, S. V. (2000). Toward reformulating the diagnosis of schizophrenia. *American Journal of Psychiatry, 157,* 1041–1050.

Tucker, D. M., Novelly, R. A., & Walker, P. J. (1987). Hyperreligiosity in temporal lobe epilepsy: Redifining the relationship. *Journal of Nervous and Mental Disease, 175,* 181–184.

Tuddenham, R. D. (1962). The nature & measurement of intelligence. In L. Postman (Ed.), *Psychology in the making: Histories of selected research problems* (pp. 469–525). New York: Alfred A. Knopf.

Tulving, E. (1972). Episodic and semantic memory. In E. Tulving and W. Donaldson (Eds.), *Organization of memory* (pp. 381–403). New York: Academic Press.

Tulving, E. (1987). Multiple memory systems and consciousness. *Human Neurobiology, 6*(2), 67–80.

Tulving, E., & Thomson, D. M. (1973). Encoding specificity and retrieval processes in episodic memory. *Psychological Review, 80,* 359–380.

Turiel, E. (1998). The development of morality. In W. Damon (Ed.), *Handbook of child psychology: Vol. 3. Social, emotional, and personality development* (N. Eisenberg, Vol. Ed.) (pp. 863–932). New York: Wiley.

Turkheimer, E. (1991). Individual and group differences in adoption studies of IQ. *Psychological Bulletin, 110,* 392–405.

Turner, J. R., Sherwood, A., & Light, K. (Eds.). (1992a). *Individual differences in cardiovascular response to stress.* New York: Guilford Press.

Turner, S. M., Beidel, D. C., Long, P. J., & Greenhouse, J. (1992b). Reduction of fear in social phobics: An examination of extinction patterns. *Behavior Therapy, 23,* 389–403.

Turner, V. (1969). *The ritual process.* Chicago: Aldine.

Turner, V. W. (1967). *A forest of symbols: Aspects of Ndembu ritual.* Ithaca, NY: Cornell University Press.

Tversky, A. (1977). Features of similarity. *Psychological Review, 84,* 327–352.

Tversky, A., & Kahneman, D. (1973). Availability: A heuristic for judging frequency and probability. *Cognitive Psychology, 5,* 207–232.

Tversky, A., & Kahneman, D. (1974). Judgment under uncertainty: Heuristics and biases. *Science, 185,* 1124–1131.

Tversky, A., & Kahneman, D. (1981). Extensional vs. intuitive reasoning: The conjunction fallacy in probability judgment. *Psychological Review, 90,* 293–315.

Udry, J. R., Billy, J. O. G., Morris, N. M., Groff, T. R., & Raj, J. H. (1985). Serum androgenic hormones motivate sexual behavior in adolescent boys. *Fertility and Sterility, 43,* 90–94.

Uleman, J. S., & Bargh, J. A. (Eds.). (1989). *Unintended thought.* New York: Guilford Press.

Ullman, S. (1989). Aligning pictorial descriptions: An approach to object recognition. *Cognition, 32,* 193–254.

Ullman, S. (1995). The visual analysis of shape and form. In M. S. Gazzaniga et al. (Eds.), *The cognitive neurosciences.* (pp. 339–350). Cambridge: MIT Press.

Ulrich, R. E. (1991). Animal rights, animal wrongs, and the question of balance. *Psychological Science, 2,* 197–201.

Ulrich, R. S. (1984). View through a window may influence recovery from surgery. *Science, 224,* 420–421.

Ungerleider, L. G., & Haxby, J. V. (1994). "What" and "where" in the human brain. *Current Opinion in Neurobiology, 4,* 157–165.

U.S. Bureau of the Census (1998). *Current Population Reports, P23-194, Population Profile of the United States: 1997.* Washington: US: Government Printing Office.

US Bureau of the Census (1998). Statistical Abstract of the United States. Washington, DC: US Census Bureau.

Vaillant, C., & Vaillant, L. M. (1998). The role of ego mechanisms of defense in the diagnosis of personality disorders. In J. Barron (Ed.), *Making diagnosis meaningful* (pp. 139–158). Washington, D.C.: American Psychological Association.

Vaillant, G. (1977). *Adaptation to life.* Boston: Little, Brown.

Vaillant, G. (Ed.). (1992). *Ego mechanisms of defense: A guide for clinicians and researchers.* Washington: American Psychiatric Association Press.

Vaillant, G., & Perry, J. C. (1985). Personality disorders. In H. I. Kaplan & B. J. Sadock (Eds.), *Comprehensive textbook of psychiatry* (4th ed.). Baltimore, MD: Williams & Wilkins.

Vaillant, G., & Vaillant, C. (1990). Natural history of male psychology health: XII. A 45-year study of predictors of successful aging at age 65. *American Journal of Psychiatry, 147,* 31–37.

Vaillant, G. E. (1992). The historical origins and future potential of Sigmund Freud's concept of the mechanisms of defence. *International Review of Psycho-Analysis, 19,* 35–50.

Vaillant, G. E. (1996). A long-term follow-up of male alcohol abuse. *Archives of General Psychiatry, 53,* 243–249.

Valenstein, E. S. (1986). *Great and desperate cures.* New York: Basic Books.

Valenstein, E. S. (1988). The history of lobotomy: A cautionary tale. *Michigan Quarterly, 27,* 417–437.

Vallacher, R. R., & Wegner, D. M. (1987). What do people thing they're doing? Action identification and human behavior. *Psychological Review, 94,* 3–15.

Vance, E. B., & Wagner, N. N. (1976). Written descriptions of orgasm: A study of sex differences. *Archives of Sexual Behavior, 5,* 87–98.

van der Staay, F. J., & Blockland, A. (1996). Behavioral differences between outbred Wistar, inbred Fischer 344, Brown Norway, and hybrid Fischer 344 Brown Norway rats. *Physiology & Behavior, 60,* 97–109.

van Duijn, C. M. (1996). Epidemiology of the dementias: Recent developments and new approaches. *Journal of Neurology, Neurosurgery & Psychiatry, 60,* 478–488.

Van Essen, D. C., Anderson, C. H., & Felleman, D. J. (1992). Information processing in the primate visual system: An integrated systems perspective. *Science, 255,* 419–423.

van IJzendoorn, M. (1995). Adult attachment representations, parental responsiveness, and infant attachment: A met-analysis on the predictive validity of the Adult Attachment Interview. *Psychological Bulletin, 117,* 387–403.

van IJzendoorn, M., & Kroonenberg, P. (1988). Cross-cultural patterns of attachment: A meta-analysis of the strange situation. *Child Development, 59,* 147–156.

van IJzendoorn, M. H., & Bakermans-Kranenburg, M. J. (1996). Attachment representations in mothers, fathers, adolescents, and clinical groups: A meta-analytic search for normative data. *Journal of Consulting & Clinical Psychology, 64,* 8–21.

van IJzendoorn, M.H., & De Wolf, M. S. (1997). In search of the absent father—Meta-analyses of infant-father attachment: A rejoinder to our discussants. *Child Development, 68,* 604–609.

Varley, C. K. (1984). Attention deficit disorder (the hyperactivity syndrome): A review of selected issues. *Developmental and Behavioral Pediatrics, 5,* 254–258.

Vaughn, B. E., Stevenson-Hinde, J., Waters, E., & Kotsaftis, A. (1992). Attachment security and temperament in infancy and early childhood: Some conceptual clarifications. *Developmental Psychology, 28,* 463–473.

Vedhara, K., Fox, J. D., & Wang, E. C. Y. (1999). The measurement of stress-related immune dysfunction in psychoneuroimmunology. *Neuroscience and Biobehavioral Reviews, 23*(5), 699–715.

Velez-Blasini, C. J. (1997). A cross-cultural comparison of alcohol expectancies in Puerto Rico and the United States. *Psychology of Addictive Behaviors, 11,* 124–141.

Venables, P. H. (1996). Schizotypy and maternal exposure to influenza and to cold temperature: The Mauritius Study. *Journal of Abnormal Psychology, 105,* 53–60.

Veneziano, R. A., & Rohner, R. P. (1998). Perceived paternal acceptance, paternal involvement, and youths' psychological adjustment in a rural, biracial southern community. *Journal of*

Marriage & the Family, 60, 335-343.

Vernon, P. A., & Weese, S. E. (1993). Predicting intelligence with multiple speed of information-processing tests. *Personality and Individual Differences, 14*, 413–419.

Verschueren, K., & Marcoen, A. (1999). Representation of self and socioemotional competence in kindergartners: Differential and combined effects of attachment to mother and father. *Child Development, 70*, 183-201.

Viinamaeki, H., Koskela, K., & Niskanen, L. (1996). Rapidly declining mental well being during unemployment. *European Journal of Psychiatry, 10*, 215–221.

Viken, R. J., Rose, R. J., Kaprio, J., & Koskenvuo, M. (1994). A developmental genetic analysis of adult personality: Extraversion and neuroticism from 18 to 59 years of age. *Journal of Personality and Social Psychology, 66*, 722–730.

Vinogravdov, S., & Yalom, I. (1989). *Concise guide to group psychotherapy.* Washington, DC: American Psychiatric Press.

Vinter, A., & Perruchet, P. (2000). Implicit learning in children is not related to age evidence from drawing behavior. *Child Development, 71*, 1223–1240.

Vitaro, F., Tremblay, R. E., Kerr, M., Pagani, L., & Bukowski, W. M. (1997). Disruptiveness, friends' characteristics, and delinquency in early adolescence: A test of two competing models of development. *Child Development, 68*, 676–689.

Voglmaier, M. M., Seidman, L. J., Niznikiewicz, M. A., Dickey, C. C., Shenton, M. E., & McCarley, R. W. (2000). Verbal and nonverbal neuropsychological test performance in subjects with schizotypal personality disorder. *American Journal of Psychiatry, 157*, 787–793.

Vollrath, D., Nathans, J., & Davis, R. W. (1988). Tandem array of human visual pigment genes at Xq28. *Science, 40*, 1669–1672.

Von Senden, M. (1960). *Space and sight.* Public Health transcript. New York: Free Press.

Vormbrock, J. (1993). Attachment theory as applied to wartime and job-related marital separation. *Psychological Bulletin, 114*, 122–144.

Vygotsky, L. (1978). *Mind in society: The development of higher psychological processes* (M. Cole, V. John-Steiner, S. Scribner, & E. Souberman, Eds.). Cambridge, Cambridge University Press.

Wachtel, P. (1977). *Psychoanalysis and behavior therapy: Toward an integration.* New York: Basic Books.

Wachtel, P. (1993). *Therapeutic communication.* New York: Guilford.

Wachtel, P. (1997). *Psychoanalysis, behavior therapy, and the relational world.* Washington, DC: American Psychological Association Press.

Wachtel, P. L. (1984). On theory, practice, and the nature of integration. In H. Arkowitz & S. B. Messer (Eds.), *Psychoanalytic therapy and behavior therapy: Is integration possible?* (pp. 31-52). New York: Plenum Press.

Wachtel, P. L. (1987). *Action and insight.* New York: Guilford Press.

Wagner, A. D., Schacter, D. L., Rotte, M., Kout-

staal, Maril, A., Dale, A. M., Rosen, B. R., & Buckner, R. L. (1998). Building memories: Remembering and forgetting of verbal experiences as predicted by brain activity. *Science, 281*, 1188–1191.

Wagner, A. W., & Linehan, M. (1999). Facial expression recognition ability among women with borderline personality disorder: Implications for emotion regulation. *Journal of Personality Disorders, 13*, 329–344.

Wagstaff, G. F. (1984). The enhancement of witness memory by "hypnosis": A review and methodological critique of the experimental literature. *British Journal of Experimental and Clinical Hypnosis, 2*, 3–12.

Wahlbeck, K., Cheine, M., Essali, A., & Adams, C. (1999). Evidence of clozapine's effectiveness in schizophrenia: A systematic review and meta-analysis of randomized trials. *American Journal of Psychiatry, 156*, 990–999.

Wakeling, A. (1996). Epidemiology of anorexia nervosa. *Psychiatry Research, 62*, 3–9.

Wald, G. (1968). Molecular basis of visual excitation. *Science, 162*, 230–239.

Waldinger, R. J., & Gunderson, J. G. (1984). Completed psychotherapies with borderline patients. *American Journal of Psychotherapy, 38*, 190-202.

Walker, E. F., & Diforio, D. (1997). Schizophrenia: A neural diathesis-stress model. *Psychological Review, 104*, 667–685.

Walker, E. F., Savoie, T., & Davis, D. (1994). Neuromotor precursors of schizophrenia. *Schizophrenia Bulletin, 20*, 441–451.

Wallace, A. F. C. (1956). Revitalization movements. *American Anthropologist, 58*, 264–281.

Wallace, A. F. C. (1959). Cultural determinants of response to hallucinatory experiences. *Archives of General Psychiatry, 1*, 58–69.

Wallace, B. (1993). Day persons, night persons, and variability in hypnotic susceptibility. *Journal of Personality and Social Psychology, 64*, 827–833.

Wallace, P. (1977). Individual discrimination of humans by odor. *Physiology and Behavior, 19*, 577–579.

Waller, N., Kojetin, B., Bouchard, T., & Lykken, D. (1990). Generic and environmental influences on religious interests, attitudes, and values: A study of twins reared apart and together. *Psychological Science, 1*, 138–142.

Waller, N. G., & Ross, C. A. (1997). The prevalence and biometric structure of pathological dissociation in the general population: Taxometric and behavior genetic findings. *Journal of Abnormal Psychology, 106*, 499–510.

Wallerstein, J. S. (1988a). Children after divorce: Wounds that don't heal. *Perspectives in Psychiatric Care, 24*, 107–113.

Wallerstein, J. S., & Corbin, S. B. (1999). The child and the vicissitudes of divorce. In R. M. Galatzer-Levy, Kraus, L., et al. (Eds.), *The scientific basis of child custody decisions* (pp. 73–95). New York: Wiley.

Wallerstein, R. S. (1988b). One psychoanalysis or many? *International Journal of Psycho-Analysis, 69*, 5–22.

Wallerstein, R. S. (1989). The psychotherapy re-

search project of the Menninger Foundations: An overview. *Journal of Consulting and Clinical Psychology, 57*, 195–205.

Walsh, J. K., & Lindblom, S. S. (1997). Psychophysiology of sleep deprivation and disruption. In M. R. Pressman, W. C. Orr, et al. (Eds.), *Understanding sleep: The evaluation and treatment of sleep disorders. Application and practice in health psychology* (pp. 73–110). Washington: American Psychological Association.

Walster, E., Aronson, V., Abrahams, D., & Rottman, L. (1966). The importance of physical attractiveness in dating behavior. *Journal of Personality and Social Psychology, 4*, 508–516.

Walters, J. M., & Gardner, H. (1986). The theory of multiple intelligences: Some issues and answers. In R. J. Sternberg & R. K. Walters (Eds.), *Practical intelligence: Nature and origins of competence in the everyday world.* New York: Cambridge University Press.

Wang, Q., & Leichtman, M. D. (2000). Same beginnings, different stories: A comparison of American and Chinese children's narratives. *Child Development, 71*, 1329-1346.

Warner, L. A., Kessler, R. C., Hughes, M., Anthony, J. C., & Nelson, C. B. (1995). Prevalence and correlates of drug use and dependence in the United States: Results from the national comorbidity survey. *Archives of General Psychiatry, 52*, 219–229.

Warwick, Z. S., Hall, W. G., Pappas, T. N., & Schiffman, S. S. (1993). Taste and smell sensations enhance the satiating effect of both a high-carbohydrate and a high-fat meal in humans. *Physiology and Behavior, 53*, 553–563.

Wason, P., & Johnson-Laird, P. (1972). *The psychology of reasoning: Structure and content.* Cambridge, MA: Harvard University Press.

Wason, P. C. (1960). On the failure to eliminate hypotheses in a conceptual task. *Quarterly Journal of Experimental Psychology, 12*, 129–140.

Wason, P. C. (1968). Reasoning about a rule. *Quarterly Journal of Experimental Psychology, 20*, 273–281.

Wasserman, E. A., & Miller, R. R. (1997). What's elementary about associative learning? *Annual Review, 48*, 573–607.

Watanabe, T., Sasaki, Y., Miyauchi, S., et al., (1998). Attention-regulated activity in human primary visual cortex. *Journal of Neurophysiology, 79*, 2218–2221.

Waters, E., Hamilton, C. E., & Weinfield, N. S. (2000). The stability of attachment security from infancy to adolescence and early adulthood: General introduction. *Child Development, 71*, 678–683.

Waters, E., Merrick, S., Treboux, D., Crowell, J., & Albersheim, L. (2000). Attachment security in infancy and early adulthood: A twenty-year longitudinal study. *Child Development, 71*, 684–689.

Waters, E., Weinfield, N. S., & Hamilton, C. E. (2000). The stability of attachment security from infancy to adolescence and early adulthood: General discussion. *Child Development, 71*, 703–706.

Waters, E. Wippman, J., & Sroufe, J. A. (1979).

Attachment, positive affect, and competence in the peer group: Two studies of construct validation. *Child Development, 50*, 821–829.

Watkin, L. R., & Mayer, D. J. (1982). Organization of endogenous opiate and nonopiate pain control systems. *Science, 216*, 1185–1193.

Watkins, L. R., & Maier, S. F. (2000). The pain of being sick: Implications of immune-to-brain communication for understanding pain. *Annual Review of Psychology*, 29–57.

Watson, D. (2000). *Mood and temperament.* New York: Guilford Press.

Watson, D., & Clark, L. A. (1992). Affects separable and inseparable: On the hierarchical arrangement of the negative affects. *Journal of Personality and Social Psychology, 62*, 489–505.

Watson, D., & Tellegen, A. (1985). Toward a consensual structure of mood. *Psychological Bulletin, 98*, 219–225.

Watson, J. (1925). *Behaviorism.* New York: W. W. Norton, 1970.

Watson, J., & Rayner, R. (1920). Conditioned emotional reactions. *Journal of Experimental Psychology, 3*, 1–14.

Watson, M. W., & Getz, K. (1990). The relationship between Oedipal behaviors and children's family role concepts. *Merrill-Palmer Quarterly, 36*, 487–505.

Weale, R. (1982). *Focus on vision.* Cambridge, MA: Harvard University Press.

Weber, M. (1924). Bureaucracy. In H. Gerth & C. W. Mills (Eds.), *From Max Weber: Essays in sociology.* New York: Oxford University Press, 1946.

Wechsler, D. (1939). *Measurement of adult intelligence.* Baltimore: Williams and Wilkins.

Wechsler, D. (1997). *WAIS-III: Administration and scoring manual.* Psychological Corporation.

Wedekind, C., & Milinski, M. (2000). Cooperation through image scoring in humans. *Science, 288* (5467), 850–852.

Wegesin, D. J. (1998). A neuropsychologic profile of homosexual and heterosexual men and women. *Archives of Sexual Behavior, 27*, 91–108.

Wegner, D. (1992). You can't always think what you want: Problems in the suppression of unwanted thoughts. *Advances in Experimental Social Psychology, 25*, 193–225.

Wegner, D., Shortt, J., Blake, A. W., & Page, M. S. (1990). The suppression of exciting thoughts. *Journal of Personality and Social Psychology, 58*, 409–418.

Wegner, D. M., & Bargh, J. A. (1998). Control and automaticity in social life. In D. Gilbert, S. T. Fiske, & G. Lindzey (Eds.), *Handbook of social psychology* (4th ed., pp. 446–496). New York: McGraw-Hill.

Wegner, D. M., & Wheatley, T. (1999). Apparent mental causation: Sources of the experience of will. *American Psychologist, 54*, 480–492.

Weinberg, R. A. (1989). Intelligence and IQ: Landmark issues and great debates. *American Psychologist, 44*, 98–104.

Weinberg, R. A., Scarr, S., & Waldman, I. D. (1992). The Minnesota Transracial Adoption Study: A follow-up of IQ test performance at adolescence. *Intelligence, 16*, 117–135.

Weinberger, D. A. (1990). The construct validity of the repressive coping style. In J. L. Singer (Ed.), *Repression and dissociation: Implications for personality, psychopathology and health.* Chicago: University of Chicago Press.

Weinberger, J. (1995). Common factors aren't so common: The common factors dilemma. *Clinical Psychology—Science and Practice, 2*, 45–69.

Weinberger, J. (in press). Heart and head: Are they one? In H. Kurtzman (Ed.), *Cognition and psychodynamics.* New York: Oxford University Press.

Weinberger, J., & Hardaway, R. (1990). Subliminal separating science from myth in subliminal psychodynamic activation. *Clinical Psychological Review, 10*, 727–756.

Weinberger, J., & Silverman, L. (1988). *Testability and empirical verification of psychoanalytic dynamic propositions through subliminal psychodynamic activation.* Unpublished manuscript. H. A. Murray Center, Harvard University.

Weiner, B. (1974). *Achievement motivation and attribution theory.* Morristown, NJ: General Learning Press.

Weiner, M. J. (1980). The effect of incentive and control over outcomes upon intrinsic motivation and performance. *Journal of Social Psychology, 112*, 247–254.

Weiner, R. D., & Coffee, C. E. (1988). Indications for use of electroconvulsive therapy. In A. J. Frances & R. E. Hales (Eds.), *Review of Psychiatry* (Vol. 7). Washington, DC: American Psychiatric Press.

Weinfield, N. S., Sroufe, L. A., & Egeland, B. (2000). Attachment from infancy to early adulthood in a high-risk sample: Continuity, discontinuity, and their correlates. *Child Development, 71*, 695–702.

Weinstein, P. (1967). Cybernetics of intra-ocular pressure. *Transactions of the Ophthalmological Society of Australia, 26*, 49–50.

Weisberg, P., & Waldrop, P. R. (1972). Fixed-interval work habits of Congress. *Journal of Applied Behavior Analysis, 5*, 93–97.

Weiskrantz, L. (1997). *Consciousness lost and found: A neuropsychological exploration.* England: Oxford University Press.

Weiskrantz, L., Warrington, E., Sanders, M. D., & Marshall, J. (1974). Visual capacity in the hemianopic field following a restricted occipital ablation. *Brain, 97*, 709–728.

Weiss, B., Dodge, K., Bates, J., & Pettit, G. (1992). Some consequences of early harsh discipline: Child aggression and a maladaptive social information processing style. *Child Development, 63*, 1321–1335.

Weiss, G., Hechtman, L., Milroy, T., & Perlman, T. (1985). Psychiatric status of hyperactives as adults: A controlled prospective 15-year follow-up of 63 hyperactive children. *Journal of the American Academy of Child Psychiatry, 24*, 211–220.

Weiss, L. H., & Schwarz, J. C. (1996). The relationship between parenting types and older adolescents' personality, academic achievements, adjustment, and substance use. *Child Development, 67*, 2101–2114.

Weiss, R. S. (1986). Continuities and transformations in social relationships from childhood to adulthood. In W. W. Hartup & Z. Rubin (Eds.), *Relationships and development* (pp. 95–110). Hillsdale, NJ: Erlbaum.

Weiss, V. (1992). Major genes of general intelligence. *Personality and Individual Differences, 13*, 1115–1134.

Weisse, C. S. (1992). Depression and immunocompetence: A review of the literature. *Psychological Bulletin, 111*, 475–489.

Weissman, M. M., Bland, R. C., Canino, G. J., Faravelli, C., Greenwald, S., Hwu, H., et al. (1997). The cross-national epidemiology of panic disorder. *Archives of General Psychiatry, 54*, 305–309.

Wellman, H. M., Phillips, A. T., & Rodriguez, T. (2000). Young children's understanding of perception, desire, and emotion. *Child Development, 71*, 895–912.

Wells, G. L., & Loftus, E. F. (Eds.). (1984). *Eyewitness testimony: Psychological perspectives.* Cambridge: Cambridge University Press.

Wells, G. L., & Turtle, J. W. (1987). Eyewitness testimony: Current knowledge and emerging controversies. *Canadian Journal of Behavioural Science, 19*(4), 363–388.

Wentzel, K. R., & Asher, S. R. (1995). The academic lives of neglected, rejected, popular, and controversial children. *Child Development, 66*, 754–763.

Werker, J. F., & Tees, R. C. (1984). Cross-language speech perception: Evidence for perceptual reorganization during the first year of life. *Infant Behavior and Development, 7*, 49–63.

Werner, E. (1979). *Cross-cultural child development: A review from the planet earth.* Monterey, CA: Brooks/Cole.

Werner, H. (1948). *Comparative psychology of mental development* (rev. ed.). Chicago: Follett.

Wertenbaker, L. (1981). *The eye: Window to the world.* Washington, DC: U.S. News books.

Wertheimer, M. (1961). Psychomotor coordination of auditory and visual space at birth. *Science., 134*, 1692.

Wertsch, J., & Kanner, B. (1992). A sociocultural approach to intellectual development. In R. Sternberg & C. A. Berg (Eds.), *Intellectual development* (pp. 328–349). New York: Cambridge University Press.

Wesley, F., & Sullivan, E. (1986). *Human growth and development: A psychological approach* (2nd ed.). New York: Human Sciences Press, Inc.

Wessinger, C. M., Fendrich, R., & Gazzaniga, M. S. (1997). Islands of residual vision in hemianopic patients. *Journal of Cognitive Neuroscience, 9*, 203–221.

West, R. L. (1996). An application of prefrontal cortex function theory to cognitive aging. *Psychological Bulletin, 120*, 272–292.

Westen, D. (1985). *Self and society: Narcissism, collectivism, and the development of morals.* New York: Cambridge University Press.

Westen, D. (1991). Social cognition and object relations. *Psychological Bulletin, 109*, 429–455.

Westen, D. (1992). The cognitive self and the psychoanalytic self: Can we put our selves together? *Psychological Inquiry, 3*, 1–13.

Westen, D. (1994). Toward an integrative model of affect regulation: Applications to social-psychological research. *Journal of Personality, 62*, 641–647.

Westen, D. (1995). A clinical-empirical model of personality: Life after the Mischelian ice age and the Neolithic era. *Journal of Personality, 63*, 495–524.

Westen, D. (1997a). Toward an empirically and clinically sound theory of motivation. *International Journal of Psycho-Analysis, 78*, 521–548.

Westen, D. (1997b). Divergences between clinical and research methods for assessing personality disorders: Implications for research and the evolution of Axis II. *American Journal of Psychiatry, 154*, 895–903.

Westen, D. (1998). The scientific legacy of Sigmund Freud: Toward a psychodynamically informed psychological science. *Psychological Bulletin, 124*, 333–371.

Westen, D., & Chang, C. (2000). Personality pathology in adolescence: A review. In A. H. Esman & L. T. Flaherty, Lois T. (Eds,). *Adolescent psychiatry: Developmental and clinical studies, Vol 25. The Annals of the American Society for Adolescent Psychiatry.* (pp. 61-100). Hillsdale, NJ: The Analytic Press, Inc.

Westen, D., & Feit, A. (1999). All the President's women: Cognitive and emotional constraint satisfaction in ambiguous social cognition. Unpublished manuscript, Boston University.

Westen, D., & Gabbard, G. (1999). Psychoanalytic approaches to personality. In L. Pervin & O. John (Eds.), *Handbook of personality: Theory and research* (2nd ed., pp. 57–101). New York: Guilford Press.

Westen, D., & Harnden-Fischer, J. (2001). Classifying eating disorders by personality profiles: Bridging the chasm between Axis I and Axis II. *American Journal of Psychiatry.*

Westen, D., Klepser, J., Ruffins, S., Silverman, M., Lifton, N., & Boekamp, J. (1991). Object relations in childhood and adolescence: The development of working representations. *Journal of Consulting and Clinical Psychology, 59*, 400–409.

Westen, D., Lohr, N., Silk, K., Gold, L., & Kerber, K. (1990). Object relations and social cognition in borderlines, major depressives, and normals: A TAT analysis. *Psychological Assessment: A Journal of Consulting and Clinical Psychology, 2*, 355–364.

Westen, D., & Morrison, K. (2001). A meta-analytic investigation of empirically supported treatments for depression, anxiety, and generalized anxiety disorder. Unpublished manuscript, Boston University.

Westen, D., Muderrisoglu, S., Fowler, C., Shedler, J., & Koren, D. (1997). Affect regulation and affective experience: Individual differences, group differences, and measurement using a Q-sort procedure. *Journal of Consulting and Clinical Psychology, 65*, 429–439.

Wetherick, N. (1975). The role of semantic information in short-term memory. *Journal of Verbal Learning and Verbal Behavior, 14*, 471–480.

Whalen, P. J., Rauch, S. L., Etcoff, N. L.; McInerney, S. C., Lee, M. B., & Jenike, M. A. (1998). Masked presentations of emotional facial expressions modulate amygdala activity without explicit knowledge. *Journal of Neuroscience, 18*(1), 411–418.

Wharton, C. M., & Grafman, J. (1998). Deductive reasoning and the brain. *Trends in Cognitive Sciences, 2*, 54–59.

Wheeler, L., Kim, Y. (1997). What is beautiful is culturally good: The physical attractiveness stereotype has different content in collectivistic cultures. *Personality and Social Psychology Bulletin, 23*(8), 795–800.

Wheeler, M. A., Stuss, D. T., & Tulving, E. (1995). Frontal lobe damage produces episodic memory impairment. *Journal of the International Neuropsychological Society, 1*, 525–533.

Wheeler, M. A., Stuss, D. T., & Tulving, D. (1997). Toward a theory of episodic memory: The frontal lobes and autonoetic consciousness. *Psychological Bulletin, 121*, 331–354.

Whipple, B., Josimovich, J. B., & Komisaruk, B. R. (1990). Sensory thresholds during the antepartum, intrapartum and postpartum periods. *International Journal of Nursing Studies, 27*, 213–221.

Whitam, F., & Mathy, R. (1991). Childhood cross-gender behavior of homosexual females in Brazil, Peru, the Philippines, and the United States. *Archives of Sexual Behavior, 20*, 151–170.

Whitbeck, L. B., Hoyt, D. R., & Bao, W. (2000). Depressive symptoms and co-occurring depressive symptoms, substance abuse, and conduct problems among runaway and homeless adolescents. *Child Development, 71*, 721–732.

Whitbourne, S. K., & Hulicka, I. (1990). Ageism in undergraduate psychology texts. *American Psychologist, 45*, 1127–1136.

Whitbourne, S. K., Zuschlag, M. K., Elliot, L. B., & Waterman, A. S. (1992). Psychosocial development in adulthood: A 22-year sequential study. *Journal of Personality & Social Psychology, 63*, 260–271.

White, R. W. (1959). Motivation reconsidered: The concept of competence. *Psychological Review, 66*, 297–333.

Whiting, B. B., & Whiting, J. W. M. (1975). *Children of six cultures: A psychocultural analysis.* Cambridge, MA: Harvard University Press.

Whiting, J. (1964). The effects of climate on certain cultural practices. In W. Goodenough (Ed.), *Explorations in cultural anthropology: Essays in honor of George Peter Murdock* (pp. 511–544). New York: McGraw-Hill.

Whiting, J. W. M., & Child, I. L. (1953). *Child training and personality: A cross-cultural study.* New Haven, CT: Yale University Press.

Whiting, J. W. M., & Whiting, B. B. (1973). Altruistic and egoistic behavior is six cultures. In L. Nader & T. W. Marekzki (Eds.), *Cultural illness and helath: Essays in human adaptation.* Washington, DC: American Anthropological Association.

Whorf, B. L. (1956). *Language, thought, and reality.* Cambridge, MA: MIT Press.

Wicker, A. W. (1969). Attitudes versus action: The relatonship of verbal and overt behavioral responses to attitude objects. *Journal of Social Issues, 25*, 41–78.

Wicklund, R. A. (1975). Objective self-awareness. In L. Berkowitz (Ed.), *Advances in experimental social psychology* (Vol. 8, pp. 233–275). New York: Academic Press.

Widiger, T. A., & Sankis, L. M. (2000). Adult psychopathology: Issues and controversies. *Annual Review of Psychology, 51*, 377–404.

Wiesel, T. N. (1982). Postnatal development of the visual cortex and the influence of environment. *Nature, 299*, 583–591.

Wiesel, T. N., & Hubel, D. H. (1960). Receptive fields of ganglion cells in the cat's retina. *Journal of Physiology, 153*, 583–594.

Wieselquist, J., Rusbult, C. E., Foster, C. A., & Agnew, C. R. (1999). Commitment, pro-relationship behavior, and trust in close relationships. *Journal of Personality and Social Psychology, 77*(5), 942–966.

Wigfield, A., & Eccles, J. S. (2000). Expectancy-value theory of achievement motivation. *Contemporary Educational Psychology, 25*, 68-81.

Wilkins, M. C. (1982). The effect of changed material on ability to do formal syllogistic reasoning. *Archives of Psychology, 16*, 1–83.

Wilkinson, S. C. (1993). WISC-R profiles of children with superior intellectual ability. *Gifted Child Quarterly, 37*, 84–91.

Williams, C., & Bybee, J. (1994). What do children feel guilty about? Developmental and gender differences. *Developmental Psychology, 30*, 617–623.

Williams, C. D. (1959). The elimination of tantrum behavior by extinction procedures. *Journal of Abnormal and Social Psychology, 59*, 269.

Williams, D. E., & Thompson, J. K. (1993). Biology and behavior: A set-point hypothesis of psychological functioning. *Behavior Modification, 17*, 43–57.

Williams, J. E., & Best, D. L. (1982). *Measuring sex stereotypes: A thirty-nation study.* Beverly Hills, CA: Sage.

Williams, J. H. (1983). The emergence of gender differences. In W. Damon (Ed.), *Social and personality development.* New York: W. W. Norton.

Williams, L. M. (1994). Recall of childhood trauma: A prospective study of women's memories of child sexual abuse. *Journal of Consulting and Clinical Psychology, 62*, 1167–1176.

Williams, R. L. (1974). Scientific racism and IQ: The silent mugging of the black community. *Psychology Today*, 32–41.

Williams, W. M., & Ceci, S. J. (1997). Are Americans becoming more or less alike? Trends in race, class, and ability differences in intelligence. *American Psychologist, 52*, 1226–1235.

Wilson, E. O. (1975). *Sociobiology: A new synthesis.* Cambridge, MA: Harvard University Press.

Wilson, E. O., & Bossert, W. H. (1996). Chemical communication among animals. In L. D. Houck

& L. C. Drickamer (Eds.), *Foundations of animal behavior: Classic papers with commentaries* (pp. 602–645). Chicago: University of Chicago Press.

Wilson, M. A., & McNaughton, B. L. (1994). Reactivation of hippocampal ensemble memories during sleep. *Science, 265,* 676–679.

Wilson, T., Lisle, D., Schooler, J., & Hodges, S. (1993). Introspecting about reasons can reduce post-choice satisfaction. *Personality & Social Psychology Bulletin, 19,* 331–339.

Wilson, T. D., Lindsey, S., & Schooler, T. Y. (2000). A model of dual attitudes. *Psychological Review, 107*(1), 101–126.

Wilson, T. D., Wheatley, T., Meyers, J. M., Gilbert, D. T., & Axsom, D. (2000b). Focalism: A source of durability bias in affective forecasting. *Journal of Personality and Social Psychology, 78*(5), 821–836.

Winn, P. (1995). The lateral hypothalamus and motivated behavior: An old syndrome reassessed and a new perspective gained. *Current Directions in Psychological Science, 4,* 182–187.

Winner, E. (2000). *The origins and ends of giftedness. American Psychologist 55,* 159–169.

Winograd, E., & Neissier, U. (Eds.). (1993). *Affect and accuracy in recall: Studies of "flashbulb" memories.* New York: Cambridge University Press.

Winslow, R. W., Franzini, L., & Hwang, J. (1992). Perceived peer norms, casual sex, and AIDS prevention. *Journal of Applied Psychology, 22,* 1809–1827.

Winson, J. (1985). *Brain and psyche: The biology of the unconscious.* New York: Anchor.

Winter, D. (1993). Power, affiliation, and war: Three tests of a motivational model. *Journal of Personality and Social Psychology, 65,* 532–545.

Winter, D. G. (1987). Enhancement of an enemy's power motivation as a dynamic of conflict escalation. *Journal of Personality and Social Psychology, 42,* 41–46.

Winterbottom, M. R. (1953). *The relation of childhood training in independence to achievement motivation.* Unpublished doctoral dissertation, Univeristy of Michigan, Ann Arbor.

Wise, R. J. S., Howard, D., Mummery, C. J., Fletcher, P., Leff, A., Buchel, C., & Scott, S. K. (2000). Noun imageability and the temporal lobes. *Neuropsychologia, 38,* 985–994.

Wixom, J., Ludolph, P., & Westen, D. (1993). Quality of depression in borderline adolescents. *Journal of the American Academy of Child & Adolescent Psychiatry, 32,* 1172–1177.

Wixted, J., & Ebbesen, E. (1991). On the form of forgetting. *Psychological Science, 2,* 409–415.

Woike, B., & Aronoff, J. (1992). Antecedents of complex social cognitions. *Journal of Personality and Social Psychology, 63,* 97–104.

Woike, B., Gershkovich, I., Piorkowski, R., & Polo, M. (1999). The role of motives in the content and structure of autobiographical memory. *Journal of Personality & Social Psychology, 76,* 600-612.

Wolfe, J., Erickson, D. J., Sharkansky, E. J., King, D. W., & King, L. A. (1999). Course and predictors of posttraumatic stress disorder among Gulf War veterans: A prospective analysis. *Journal of Consulting and Clinical Psychology, 67,* 520–528.

Wolpe, J. (1958). *Psychotherapy by reciprocal inhibition.* Stanford, CA: Stanford University Press.

Wolpe, J. (Ed.). (1964). *The conditioning therapies: The challenge in psychotherapy.* New York: Holt, Rinchart, & Winston.

Wong, M. M., & Csikszentmihalyi, M. (1991). Motivation and academic achievement: The effects of personality traits and the quality of experience. *Journal of Personality, 59,* 539–574.

Wong, P., Shevrin, H., & Williams, W. J. (1994). Conscious and nonconscious processes: An ERP index of an anticipatory response in a conditioning paradigm using visually masked stimuli. *Psychophysiology, 31,* 87–101.

Wong, Q., & Leichtman, M. D. (2000). Same beginnings, different stories: A comparison of American and Chinese children's narratives. *Child Development, 71,* 1329–1346.

Woo, J., Ho, S. C., Yuen, Y. K., Yu, L. M., & Lau, J. (1998). Cardiovascular risk factors and 18-month mortality and morbidity in an elderly Chinese population aged 70 years and over. *Gerontology, 44*(1), 51–55.

Wood, J. M., Lilienfeld, S. O., Garb, H. N., & Nezworski, M. T. (2000). "The Rorschach test in clinical diagnosis": A critical review, with a backward look at Garfield (1947). *Journal of Clinical Psychology, 56,* 395-430.

Wood, R., & Bandura, A. (1989). Social cognitive theory of organizational management. Special issue: Theory development forum. *Academy of Management Review, 14,* 361–384.

Wood, W., Wong, F., & Chachere, J. G. (1991). Effects of media violence on viewers' aggression in unconstrained social interaction. *Psychologial Bulletin, 109,* 371–383.

Woodward, A. L., & Sommerville, J. A. (2000). Twelve-month-old infants interpret action in context. *Psychological Science, 11,* 73–77.

Word, C. O., Zanna, M. P., & Cooper, J. (1974). The nonverbal mediation of self-fulfilling prophecies in interracial interaction. *Journal of Experimental Social Psychology, 10,* 109–120.

Worthington, E. L., Jr., Martin, G. A., Shumate, M., & Carpenter, J. (1983). The effect of brief Lamaze training and social encouragement on pain endurance in a cold pressor tank. *Journal of Applied Social Psychology, 13,* 223–233.

Wright, I. C., Rabe-Hesketh, S., Woodruff, P. W. R., David, A. S., Murray, R. M., & Bullmore, E. T. (2000). Meta-analysis of regional brain volumes in schizophrenia. *American Journal of Psychiatry, 157,* 16–25.

Wright, L. B., Treiber, F. A., Davis, H., & Strong, W. B. (1996). Relationship of John Henryism to cardiovascular functioning at rest and during stress in youth. *Annals of Behavioral Medicine, 18,* 146–150.

Wulff, D. M. (1997). *Psychology of religion: Classic and contemporary* (2nd ed.). New York: John Wiley & Sons.

Wyatt, G. E., Peters, S. D., & Guthrie, D. (1988a). Kinsey revisited: I. Comparisons of the sexual socialization and sexual behavior of White women over 33 years. *Archives of Sexual Behavior, 17,* 201–239.

Wyatt, G. E., Peters, S. D., & Guthrie, D. (1988b). Kinsey revisited: II. Comparisons of the sexual socialization and sexual behavior of Black women over 33 years. *Archives of Sexual Behavior, 17,* 289–332.

Wyatt, R. J. (1996). Neurodevelopmental abnormalities and schizophrenia: A family affair. *Archives of General Psychiatry, 53,* 11–18.

Wynne, L. C. (1961). The study of intrafamilial alignments and splits in exploratory family therapy. In N. Ackerman et al. (Eds.), *Exploring the base for family therapy.* New York: Family Service Association of America.

Wyrwicka, W. (1976). The problem of motivation in feeding behavior. In D. Narwin, W. Wyrwicka, and G. Bray (Eds.), *Hunger: Basic mechanisms and clinical implications.* New York: Raven.

Yadin, E., & Thomas, E. (1996). Stimulation of the lateral septum attenuates immobilization-induced stress ulcers. *Physiology & Behavior, 59,* 883–886.

Yager, J. (2000). Weighty Perspectives: Contemporary challenges in obesity and eating disorders. *American Journal of Psychiatry, 157,* 851–853.

Yahne, C. E., & Miller, W. R. (1999). Enhancing motivation for treatment and change. In B. S. McCrady & E. E. Epstein (Eds.), *Addictions: A comprehensive guidebook* (pp. 235–249). New York: Oxford University Press.

Yalom, I. D. (1995). *The theory and practice of group psychotherapy* (4th ed.). New York: Basicbooks, Inc.

Yalon, I., Brown, S., & Bloch, S. (1975). The written summary as a group psychotherapy technique. *Archives of General Psychiatry, 32,* 605-613.

Yamamoto, D., Ito, H., & Fujitani, K. (1996). Genetic dissection of sexual orientation: Behavioral, cellular, and molecular approaches in *Drosophila melanogaster. Neuroscience Research, 26,* 95–107.

Yaniv, I., Meyer, D. (1987). Activation and metacognition of inaccessible stored information: Potential bases for incubation effects in problem solving. *Journal of Experimental Psychology: Learning, Memory, and Cognition, 13,* 187–205.

Yassa, R., Nair, N., Iskandar, H., & Schwartz, G. (1990). Factors in the development of severe forms of tardive dyskinesia. *American Journal of Psychiatry, 147,* 1156–1163.

Young, A. W. (1994). Face recognition. In G. d'Ydewalle, P. Eelen, et al. (Eds.), *International perspectives on psychological science: Vol. 2. The state of the art.* (pp. 1–27). Hove, UK: Lawrence Erlbaum Associates.

Younger, B. A., & Fearing, D. D. (1999). Parsing items into separate categories: Developmental change in infant categorization. *Child Development, 70,* 291–303.

Youniss, J., & Haynie, D. (1992). Friendship in adolescence. *Developmental and Behavioral Pediatrics, 13,* 59–66.

Yu, B., Zhang, W., Jing, Q., Peng, R., Zhang, G., & Simon, H. A. (1985). STM capacity for Chinese and English language materials. *Memory and Cognition, 13,* 202–207.

Zadra, A., & Donderi, D. C. (2000). Nightmares and bad dreams: Their prevalence and relationship to well-being. *Journal of Abnormal Psychology, 109,* 273–281.

Zahn-Waxler, C., Radke-Yarrow, M., Wagner, E., & Chapman, M. (1992a). Development of concern for others. *Developmental Psychology, 28,* 126–136.

Zahn-Waxler, C., Robinson, J., & Emde, R. (1992b). The development of empathy in twins. *Developmental Psychology, 28,* 1038–1047.

Zajonc, R. (1980). Feeling and thinking: Preferences need no inferences. *American Psychologist, 35,* 151–175.

Zajonc, R. B. (1965). Social facilitation. *Science, 149,* 269–274.

Zajonc, R. B. (1968). The attitudinal effects of mere exposure. *Journal of Personality and Social Psychology, 9,* 1–27.

Zajonc, R. B. (1998). Emotions. In D. T. Gilbert, S. T. Fiske, et al. (Eds.), *The handbook of social psychology* (Vol. 2, 4th ed., pp. 591–632). Boston: McGraw-Hill.

Zanarini, M. C. (Ed.). (1997). *Role of sexual abuse in the etiology of borderline personality disorder.* Washington, DC: American Psychiatric Press.

Zanarini, M., Gunderson, J., Marino, M., Schwartz, E., & Frankenburg, F. (1990). Psychiatric disorders in the families of borderline outpatients. In P. Links (Ed.), *Family environment and borderline personality disorder* (pp. 69–84). Washington, DC: American Psychiatric Press.

Zanarini, M. C., Gunderson, J. G., Marino, M. F., Schwartz, E. D., & Frankenberg, F. R. (1989). Childhood experience of borderline patients. *Comprehensive Psychiatry, 30,* 18–25.

Zanna, M. P., & Cooper, J. (1974). Dissonance and the pill: An attribution approach to studying the arousal properties of dissonance. *Journal of Personality and Social Psychology, 9,* 703–709.

Zaragosta, M., & Mitchell, K. J. (1996). Repeated exposure to suggestion and the creation of false memories. *Psychological Science, 7,* 294–300.

Zatzick, D. F., & Dimsdale, J. E. (1990). Cultural variations in response to painful stimuli. *Psychosomatic Medicine, 52,* 544–557.

Zeanah, C. H., & Zeanah, P. D. (1989). Intergenerational transmission of maltreatment: Insights from attachment theory and research. *Psychiatry, 52,* 177–196.

Zeki, S., Aglioti, S., McKeefry, D., & Berlucchi, G. (1999). The neurological basis of conscious color perception in a blind patient. *Proceedings of the National Academy of Science USA, 96,* 14124–14129.

Zervas, I. M., Augustine, A., & Fricchione, G. L. (1993). Patient delay in cancer: A view from the crisis model. *General Hospital Psychiatry, 15,* 9–13.

Zhang, M., Rost, K. M., & Fortney, J. C. (1999). Earnings changes for depressed individuals treated by mental health specialists. *American Journal of Psychiatry, 156,* 108–114.

Zillman, D., Baron, R. A., & Tamborini, R. (1981). Special costs on smoking: Effects of tobacco smoke on hostile behavior. *Journal of Applied Social Psychology, 11,* 548–561.

Zimbardo, P. G. (1972). Pathology of imprisonment. *Society,* 4–8.

Zimbardo, P. G. (1975). Transforming experimental research into advocacy for social change. In M. Deutsch and H. A. Hornstein (Eds.), *Applying social psychology: Implications for research, practice, and training.* Hillsdale, NJ: Erlbaum.

Zinbarg, R., Barlow, D., Brown, T., & Hertz, R. (1992). Cognitive-behavioral approaches to the nature and treatment of anxiety disorders. *Annual Review of Psychology, 43,* 235–267.

Zinbarg, R. E., & Barlow, D. H. (1996). Structure of anxiety and the anxiety disorders: A hierarchical model. *Journal of Abnormal Psychology, 105,* 181–193.

Zinbarg, R. E., Barlow, D. H., Liebowitz, M., & Street, L. (1994). The DSM-IV field trial for mixed anxiety-depression. *American Journal of Psychiatry, 151,* 1153–1162.

Zipursky, R. B., Lambe, E. K., Kapur, S., & Mikulis, D. J. (1998). Cerebral gray matter volume deficits in first episode psychosis. *Archives of General Psychiatry, 55,* 540–546.

Zoellner, L. A., Foa, E. B., Brigidi, B. D., & Przeworski, A. (2000). Are trauma victims susceptible to "false memories?" *Journal of Abnormal Psychology, 109,* 517–524.

Zornberg, G. L., Buka, S. L., & Tsuang, M. T. (2000). Hypoxic-ischemia-related fetal/neonatal complications and risk of schizophrenia and other nonaffective psychoses: A 19-year longitudinal study. *American Journal of Psychiatry, 157,* 196–202.

Zuckerman, M. (1994). *Behavioral expression and biosocial bases of sensation seeking.* New York: Cambridge University Press.

Zuckerman, M., Koestner, R., DeBoy, T., Garcia, T., Maresca, B., & Sartois, J. (1988). To predict some of the people some of the time. A reexamination of the moderator variable approach in personality theory. *Journal of Personality and Social Psychology, 54,* 1006–1019.

Photo Credits

Chapter 1 Opener: Glenys Barton, *Listen 11*, 1998; ceramic, 50.5x65x50 cm. Photo courtesy Adrian Flowers. From Angela Flowers Gallery. Page 2: Nigel Buchanan/The Image Bank. Page 4: M. Raichle/Peter Arnold, Inc. Page 5 (top): From H. Damasio, T. Grabowski, R. Frank, A.M. Galaburda and A.R. Damasio, *The Return of Phineas Gage: Clues about the Brain from a Famous Patient*, Science 264:1102-1105, 1994. Photo courtesy Hanna Damasio, Department of Neurology and Image Analysis, University of Iowa. Page 5 (bottom): Courtesy of the Institute for Intercultural Studies, Inc., New York. Page 6: Mike Blank/Stone. Page 7: Michael Gallacher/Missoulian/Liaison Agency, Inc. Page 8: Culver Pictures, Inc. Page 11: CORBIS. Page 13 (top): The Far Side ©1993 Farworks, Inc. Used by permission of Universal Press Syndicate. All rights reserved. Page 13 (bottom left): John Marmaras/Woodfin Camp & Associates. Page 13 (bottom right): Terje Rakke/The Image Bank. Page 14: Chris J. Johnson/Stock, Boston. Page 16: The Image Bank. Page 18 (left): Claus C. Meyer/Black Star. Page 18 (right): John Furtunato/Stone. Page 19 (top left): Jim Stamates/Stone. Page 19 (top right): Frank Siteman/Stock, Boston. Page 19 (bottom left): Courtesy J. A. Bishop and L.M. Cook. Page 19 (bottom right): Courtesy Lawrence Cook, University of Manchester. Page 20: CORBIS.

Chapter 2 Opener: Jacob Lawrence, *University*, 1977; tempera and gouache on paper. Private Collection. ©Estate of Jacob and Gwendolyn Lawrence Foundation. Page 28: Moses Soyer, Three Girls, 1955, oil, 9 1/2x 71/2 inches. Image courtesy Hirshorn Museum and Sculpture Garden, Smithsonian Institution/VAGA, New York, NY. Page 33: Brooks Kraft/Black Star. Page 36: Martin Rodgers/Stone. Page 37: Index Stock. Page 42: Jackie Le Fevre/Oxford Scientific Films/Animals Animals. Page 43: The Far Side ©1998 Farworks, INC. Used by permission of Universal Press Syndicate. All rights reserved. Page 44: Christopher Smith/Impact Visuals. Page 46: Michael Newman/PhotoEdit. Page 47: Mehau Kulyk/Photo Researchers. Page 48: Courtesy Mark D'Esposito, University of California, Berkeley. Page 56: ©1990 Jim Unger/Laughing Stock Licensing, Inc. Reprinted with permission by Laughing Stock Licensing Inc., Ottawa, Canada. All rights reserved. Page 57: Marc Romanelli/The Image Bank. Page 60: ©AP/Wide World Photos. Page 61: Ursula Markus/Photo Researchers.

Chapter 3 Opener: Jim Lange/Stockworks. Page 65: The Maas Gallery, London/The Bridgeman Art Library International, Ltd. Page 67 (left): Dennis Kunkel/Phototake. Page 67 (right): M. Abbey Photo/Photo Researchers. Page 71: CNRI/Photo Researchers. Page 72: Will Ryan/Corbis Stock Market. Page 73: Courtesy David Eidelberg, North Shore University Hospital, New York University Medical College. Page 80 (top): Phototake, Inc./PNI. Page 80 (bottom): Brooks Kraft/Corbis Sygma. Page 83 (top): Martin M. Rotker/Photo Researchers. Page 83 (bottom): Jay Silver Man/The Image Bank. Page 86: From Rita Carter, *Mapping the Mind*, University of California Press: Los Angeles, 1998. Reproduced with permission. Page 87: Bonnie Kamin/PhotoEdit. Page 90 (top): M.K. Denny/PhotoEdit. Page 90 (bottom): Al Bello/Allsport. Page 91: From H. Damasio, T. Grabowski, R. Frank, A.M. Galaburda and A.R. Damasio, *The Return of Phineas Gage: Clues about the Brain from a Famous Patient*, Science 264:1102-1105, 1994. Photo courtesy Hanna Damasio, Department of Neurology and Image Analysis, University of Iowa. Page 92: ©Sidney Harris. Page 95: Courtesy Sally Shaywitz, et al., and 1995 NMR Research, Yale Medical School. Page 96: SuperStock. Page 97: Peter Menzel/Stock, Boston. Page 98: T.K. Wanstal/The Image Works.

Chapter 4 Opener: Gail leBoff, *Hand, Ref. No. 20*, From *Smashed Glass* Series, 1986. Page 102: James Reynolds Draper/SuperStock. Page 103: Courtesy R.C. James. Page 104: Joseph van Os/The Image Bank. Page 105: Index Stock Photography, Inc. Page 107: ©1976 Jim Unger/Laughing Stock Licensing, Inc. Page 113 (top): John Clifford/The Kobal Collection. Page 113 (bottom): GJPL/CNRI/Phototake. Page 114: ©Lennart Nilsson, *The Incredible Machine*. Page 119: Courtesy Michael Posner, University of Oregon, and Marcus Raichle, Washington University in St. Louis. Page 121 (top): Robert Brenner/PhotoEdit. Page 121 (bottom): Jeremy Horner/Stone.

Page 123: Courtesy Graham-Field Surgical Company. Page 124: Ed Pritchard/Stone. Page 132: J. & P. Wegner/Animals Animals/Earth Scenes. Page 133: Omikron/Photo Researchers. Page 134: G.W. Willis/B.P.S/Stone. Page 136: ©AP/Wide World Photo. Page 139: Zefa Germany/Corbis Stock Market. Page 140: Adapted from Boring, 1930. Page 142: ©M.C. Escher/Cordon Art-Baarn, Holland. All rights reserved. Page 144: Hilarie Kavanagh/Stone. Page 145 (left): A.K.G., Berlin/SuperStock. Page 145 (right): ©Thomas Warren Enterprises. Page 148: Greg Scott/Masterfile. Page 149 (left): Eric Wheater. Page 149 (right): Marc Romanelli/The Image Bank. Page 150 (top): Topham/The Image Works. Page150 (bottom): Courtesy Cornell University Library, Division of Rare & Manuscript Collections. Page 151: Courtesy Colin Blakemore from Schmitt & Worden, *The Neuroscience's Third Study Program*, MIT Press. Page 152: Courtesy Stephen Kosslyn, Harvard University. Page 153: Tony Craddock/Photo Researchers. Page 155 (left & center): Courtesy San Francisco Convention & Visitors' Bureau. Page 155 (right): Courtesy I. Biederman, R.J. Mezzanotte, and J.C. Rabinotwitz, *Cognitive Psychology*, 14:153, 1982. ©Academic Press. Reproduced with permission.

Chapter 5 Opener: ©Rosa Ibarra/Omni-Photo Communications. Page 160: ©James Balog Photography. Page 162: CORBIS. Page 163: ©John Chase. Page 164: The Far Side ©1998 Farworks, Inc. Used by permission of Universal Press Syndicate. All rights reserved. Page 165 (top): Courtesy Benjamin Harris, University of Wisconsin, Parkside. Page 165 (bottom): Jon Feingersh/Corbis Stock Market. Page 167: Gunter Ziesler/Peter Arnold, Inc. Page 169: Tony Freeman/PhotoEdit. Page 170: Mike Severns/Tom Stack & Associates. Page 172: Tom Cheney ©1993 The New Yorker Collection. All rights reserved. Page 173: Courtesy Julie S. Vargas, B. F. Skinner Foundation. Reproduced with permission. Page 177: Sean Sprague/Impact Visuals. Page 178: Tom Russo/Liaison Agency, Inc. Page 180: J. Widener/Corbis Sygma. Page 181: Photofest. Page 184: David Young-Wolff/PhotoEdit. Page 187: ©Hulton-Deutsch Collection/CORBIS. Page 189: Dan Habib/Impact Visuals. Page 190: Courtesy Albert Bandura.

Chapter 6 Opener: Jan Sawka, *The Memories II*, 1987; acrylic on masonite, 48x74 inches. Page 194: Swanson/The Image Bank. Page 197: A Ruggieri/The Image Bank. Page 198: Pierre August Renoir, *Luncheon of the Boating Party*/SuperStock. Page 200: Courtesy Archives of the History of American Psychology, The University of Akron. Page 201: Wellcome Dept. of Cognitive Neurology/Photo Researchers. Page 204: From Susan Courtney, et al., Nature 386: 610 (1997). Reproduced with permission of Macmillan Magazines, Ltd. Page 208: Courtesy ACLU and DeVito/Verdi. Page 209: Mick Hutson/Retna. Page 221: Courtesy of William Brewer, University of Illinois. Page 222: M&E Bernheim/Woodfin Camp & Associates. Page 225: SuperStock. Page 226: ©Sidney Harris. Page 229: David J. Sams/Stock, Boston. Page 230 (left): Gerald Buthaud/Woodfin Camp & Associates. Page 230 (right): Carol Kohen/The Image Bank.

Chapter 7 Opener: Don Venezia, *The Chess Players*. Page 234: Henry Sims/The Image Bank. Page 237: David Gifford/Photo Researchers. Page 238: Kevin Schafer/Peter Arnold, Inc. Page 240: Robert Brenner/PhotoEdit. Page 242: AFP/CORBIS. Pages 247 & 248: ©Len Speier. Page 249: Frank Herholdt/Stone. Page 251: David Silverman/Liaison Agency, Inc. Page 264: L. D. Gordon/The Image Bank. Page 265: ©1976 Jim Unger/Laughing Stock Licensing, Inc. Page 268: Laguana Photo/Liaison Agency, Inc. Page 270: Jose Polleross/The Image Works. Page 271: D. Greco/The Image Works. Page 273: Courtesy Language Research Center, Georgia State University.

Chapter 8 Opener: Tsing-Fang Chen/SuperStock. Page 278: Rick Raymond/Stone. Page 280: David Hiser/Stone. Page 281: Gabe Palmer/Corbis Stock Market. Page 282: ©Sidney Harris. Page 284: David Young-Wolff/Stone. Page 285: Cindy Karp/Black Star. Page 287: ©Sidney Harris. Page 288: Jed Jacobsohn/Allsport. Page 293 (left): Randi Anglin/The Image Works. Page 293 (right): Markel/Liaison Agency, Inc. Page 294: Vincent van Gogh, *Langlois Bridge*/Private Collection/A.K.G.,

Text and Illustration Credits

Chapter 1 Figure 1.4: From Cave, C. B. (1997). Long-lasting priming in picture naming. *Psychological Science, 8*, 322-325. Copyright © 1997. Reprinted with the permission of Blackwell Science, Inc. Figure 1.6: Based on DeKay, T. (1988). An evolutionary-computational approach to social cognition: Grandparental investment as a test case. Unpublished doctoral dissertation, University of Michigan.

Chapter 2 Figure 2.1: From Pennebaker, J., Colder, M., & Sharp, L. K. (1990). Accelerating the coping process. *Journal of Personality and Social Psychology, 58*, 528-537. Copyright © 1990 by the American Psychological Association. Reprinted and adapted with the permission of the APA and the authors. Figure 2.5: From Bower, G. H. (1981). Mood and memory. *American Psychologist, 36*, 129-148. Copyright © 1981 by the American Psychological Association. Reprinted with the permission of the APA and the author. Table 2.2: Adapted from R. L. Shiner (2000). Linking childhood personality with adaptation: Evidence for continuity and change across time in late adolescence. *Journal of Personality and Social Psychology, 78*, p. 316. Copyright © 2000 by the American Psychological Association. Reprinted and adapted with the permission of the APA and the author.

Chapter 3 Figure 3.8 From *Fundamentals of Human Neuropsychology* by B. Kolb & I. Q. Whishaw. © 1996 by W. H. Freeman and Company. Used with permission of Worth Publisher. Figure 3.13: From Penfield, W., & Rasmussen, T. (1950). *The Cerebral Cortex of Man*. Copyright © 1978 by the Gale Group. Reprinted by permission of The Gale Group. Figure 3.14a: From Gazzaniga, M. S. (August 1967). The split brain in man. Scientific American. Illustration by Eric O. Mose. Copyright 1967. Reprinted and adapted by permission of Eric H. Mose.

Chapter 4 Figure 4.3c: From Stevens, S. S. (1961). Psychophysics of sensory function. In W. Rosenblith (ed.), *Sensory Communication*, 1-33. Cambridge, MA: MIT Press. Used with permission. Figures 4.8 and 4.13: From Sekuler, R., & Blake, R. (1994). Perception, 3rd Edition. New York: McGraw-Hill, Inc. Copyright © 1994, 1990, 1985 by McGraw-Hill, Inc. Reprinted and adapted with the permission of the publisher. Figure 4.16: From Ramachandran, V. S., & Hirstein, W. (1998). The perception of phantom limbs. *The D. O. Heff Lecture. Brain 121*, 1612. Used with permission of the publisher. Figure 4.21: From Sekuler, R., & Blake, R. (1994). *Perception*, 3rd Edition. New York: McGraw-Hill, Inc. Copyright © 1994, 1990, 1985 by McGraw-Hill, Inc. Reprinted and adapted with the permission of the publisher. Figure 4.29e: From Kanisza, G. (April 1976). Subjective contours. *Scientific American, 234*, 48. Copyright © 1976 by Scientific American, Inc. Reprinted with the permission of the publisher. Figure 4.30: From Biederman, I. (1990). Higher level vision. In D. N. Osherson et al. (eds.), *An Invitation to Cognitive Science*, Volume 2. Copyright © 1990 by the Massachusetts Institute of Technology. Reprinted with the permission of The MIT Press. Figure 4.31: From Biederman, I. (1987). Recognition by components. *Computer Visions, Graphics, and Image Processing, 32*, 29-73. Copyright © 1985 by Academic Press, Inc. Reprinted with the permission of the publisher and the author. Table 4.1: From Brown, R., Galanter, E., & Hess, E. H. (1962). *New Directions in Psychology*. New York: Harcourt Brace & Co. Reprinted with the permission of Roger W. Brown, Harvard University.

Chapter 5 Figure 5.2: From Pavlov, I. P. (1927). *Conditioned Reflexes*. New York: Oxford University Press. Copyright 1927. Reprinted with the permission of Oxford University Press, Ltd. Figure 5.4: From Hovland, C. I. (1937). The generalization of conditioned responses: the sensory generalization of conditioned responses with varying frequencies of time. *The Journal of General Psychology, 17*, 125-148, 1937. Reprinted with the permission of the Helen Dwight Reid Educational Foundation. Published by Heldref Publications, 1319 Eighteenth St., NW, Washington, DC 20036-1802. Copyright © 1937. Figure 5.6: From Garcia, J. and Koelling, R. (1966). Relation of cue to consequence in avoidance learning. *Psychonomic Science, 4*, 123-124. Copyright © 1966. Reprinted with the permission of Psychonomic Society, Inc. Figure 5.11: From Gray, J .A. (1988)."Gray's Three Behavioral Systems"from *The Psychology of Fear and Stress, 2nd Edition*. New York: Cambridge University Press. Copyright © 1988. Reprinted with the permission of Cambridge University Press and the author. Figure 5.12: From Tolman, E. C., & Honzik, C. H. (1930). Introduction and removal of reward and maze performance in rats. *University of California Publications in Psychology, 4*, 215-232. Copyright © 1930 The Regents of the University of California. Figure 5.13: From Rotter, J. (1971, June). External control and internal control: Locus of control. *Psychology Today, 42*. Copyright © 1971 by Sussex Publisher, Inc. Reprinted with the permission of Psychology Today Magazine. Figure 5.14: From Bandura, A. (1967). In *The Young Child: Reviews of Research*, W. Hartup and N. Smothergill (eds.). Washington, DC: National Association for the Education of Young Children. Copyright © 1967 by NAEYC. Reprinted with permission from the National Association for the Education of Young Children.

Chapter 6 Figure 6.5: From Rundus, D. (1971). Analysis of rehearsal process in free recall. *Journal of Experimental Psychology, 89*, 63-77. Copyright © 1971 by the American Psychological Association. Reprinted with the permission of the APA and the author. Figure 6.6. From Baddeley A. (1986). *Working memory*. New York: Oxford University Press, Inc. Copyright © 1986 Oxford University Press, Inc. Reprinted with the permission of the publisher. Figure 6.7: From Logie R. (1996). The seven ages of working memory. In J. T. E. Richardson et al., *Working Memory and Human Cognition*. New York: Oxford University Press. Copyright © 1996 Oxford University Press, Inc. Reprinted with the permission of the publisher. Figure 6.8: From Courtney et al. (1997). Transient and sustained activity in a distributed neural system for human working memory. *Nature, 386*, (6625), p. 610. Copyright © 1997 by Macmillan Magazines Ltd. Reprinted with the permission of *Nature* and the authors. Figure 6.11: From Hermann, D. J., Crawford, M., & Holdsworth, M. (1992). Gender-linked differences in everyday memory performance. *British Journal of Psychology, 83*, 221-231. Copyright © 1992. Reprinted with the permission of the British Psychological Society. Figure 6.13: From Gabrieli, et al. (1996). Functional magnetic resonance imaging of semantic memory processes in the frontal lobes. *Psychological Science, 7*, p. 281. Copyright © 1996. Reprinted with the permission of Blackwell Science. Inc. Figure 6.18: Adapted from Bahrick, et al. (1996). Accuracy and distortion in memory for high school grades. Psychological Science, 7, p. 266. Copyright © 1996. Reprinted with the permission of Blackwell Science, Inc.

Chapter 7 Figure 7.1: Adapted from Cooper, L. A., & Shepard, R. N. (1973). The manipulation of visual representations. *Memory and Cognition, 1*, (3), 246-250. Copyright © 1973. Reprinted with the permission of the Psychonomic Society, Inc. Figure 7.4: From Wason, P. C. (1968). Reasoning about a rule. *Quarterly Journal of Experimental Psychology, 20*, 273-281. Copyright © 1968. Reprinted with the permission of Lawrence Erlbaum Associates, Ltd., Hove, UK, and the author. Figure 7.5: Adapted from Griggs, R. A., & Cox, J. R. (1982). The elusive thematic-materials effect in Watson's selection task. *British Journal of Psychology, 73*, 407-420, extract. Reprinted and adapted with the permission of the British Psychological Society and the authors. Figure 7.9: Adapted from Rumelhart, D. (1984). Schemata and the cognitive system. In R. S. Wyler & T. K. Strull (eds.), *Handbook of social cognition*, Vol. 1. Hillsdale, New Jersey: Erlbaum. Copyright © 1984. Reprinted and adapted with the permission of Lawrence Erlbaum Associates and the author. Figure 7.12: From Frith & Dolan (1996). The role of the prefrontal cortex in higher cognitive functions. *Cognitive Brain Research, 5*, 178. Copyright © 1996. Reprinted with the permission of Elsevier Science Limited. Figure 7.13: From Damasio, A. (1994). Descartes' error: Emotion, reason and the human brain, p. 210. Copyright © 1994 by Antonio R. Damasio. Reprinted with the permission of the author. Figure 7.16: From Premack, A. J., & Premack, D. (October 1972). Teaching language to an ape. *Scientific American, 227*, 92-99. Copyright © 1972 by Scientific American, Inc. All rights reserved. Reprinted with permission. Figure 7.18: Adapted from Pinker, S. (1994). *The language instinct: How the mind creates language*. Copyright © 1994 by Stephen Pinker. Reprinted with the permission of HarperCollins Publishers, Inc. Table 7.1: Adapted from Irwin, M., Schafer, G., & Feiden, C. (1974). Emic and unfamiliar category sorting of Mano farmers and U.S. undergraduates. *Journal of Cross-Cultural Psychology, 5*, 407-423. Copyright © 1974 by Sage Publications, Inc. Reprinted and adapted with the permission of the publisher. Tables 7.3 and 7.4: Adapted from Edwards, W. (1977). How to use multiattribute utility measurement for social decision making. *IEEE Transactions in Systems, Man and Cybernetics, 17*, 326-340. Copyright © 1977 by IEEE. Reprinted with the permission of the publisher.

Chapter 8 Figure 8.3: Excerpted and adapted with permission from Duncan, J., Seitz, R., Kolodny, J., Bor, D., Herzog, H., Ahmed, A., Newell, F. N., & Emslie, H. (2000). A neural basis for general intelligence. *Science 289*, 457-460. Figure 8.4: From J. Horn and J. Noll (1997). Human cognitive capacity: Gf - Gc theory. In D. P. Flanagan, J. L. Gershaft, & P. L. Harrison (eds.), *Contemporary Intellectual Assessment.* Copyright" 1997. Reprinted with the permission of The Guilford Press. Figure 8.5: From Mumaw, R., & Pellegrino, J. (1984). Individual differences in complex spatial processing. *Journal of Educational Psychology, 76*, 920-939. Copyright © 1984 by the American Psychological Association. Reprinted with the permission of the APA and the authors. Figure 8.6: From Sameroff, A., Baldwin, A., & Baldwin, C. (1993). Stability of intelligence from preschool to adolescence: The influence of social and family risk factors. *Child Development, 64*, 89. Copyright © 1993 by the Society for Research in Child Development. Reprinted and adapted with permission of the Society for Research in Child Development. Table 8.1: Simulated items similar to those in Wechsler Adult Intelligence Scale, Third Edition. Copyright © 1997 by The Psychological Corporation. Reproduced by permission. All rights reserved. "Wechsler Adult Intelligence Scale" and "WAIS" are trademarks of the Psychological Corporation registered in the United States of America and/or other jurisdictions. Table 8.3: Adapted from Henderson, N. D. (1982). Correlations in IQ for pairs of people with varying degrees of genetic relatedness and shared environment. *Annual Review of Psychology, 33*, 219-243. Copyright © 1982 by Annual Reviews, Inc. Reprinted and adapted with the permission of the author and the publisher.

Chapter 9 Figure 9.5: From Eagle, M. (1959). The effects of subliminal stimuli of aggressive content upon conscious cognition. *Journal of Personality, 27*, 678-688. Copyright © 1959 by Duke University Press. Reprinted with the permission of the publisher. Figure 9.7: Adapted from Squire, L. R. (1986). Priming effects in amnesia. *Science, 232*, 1612-1619. Copyright © 1986 by American Association for the Advancement of Science. Reprinted and adapted with the permission of the publisher and the author. Figure 9.11: Adapted from Kripke, D. F, Simons, R. N., Garfinkel, L., & Hammond, E. C. (1979). Short and long sleep and sleeping pills: Is increased mortality associated? *Archives of General Psychiatry, 36*, 103-116. Copyright © 1979 by the American Medical Association. Reprinted and adapted with permission. Figure 9.13: From Cartwright, R. D. (1978). *A Primer on sleep and dreaming.* Reading: Addison-Wesley, Inc. Copyright © 1978 by R. D. Cartwright. Reprinted with the permission of the author. Figure 9.14: From Hilgard, E. R. (1986). *Divided consciousness* (p. 190). New York: John Wiley & Sons Inc. Copyright © 1986. Reprinted with the permission of the author. Table 9.1: Adapted from Lavie, P. (1996). *In the enchanted world of sleep* (pp. 176-177), translated by A. Berris. New Haven, CT: Yale University Press. Copyright © 1996 by Yale University. Reprinted with the permission of Yale University Press.

Chapter 10 Figure 10.2: Adapted from Simmons, L. W. (1990). Pheromonal cues for the recognition of kin by female field crickets, *Gryllus bimaculutus. Animal Behavior, 40*, 194. Copyright © 1990 by Academic Press Inc. Reprinted and adapted with the permission of the publisher. Figure 10.4: Adapted from Iyengar, S., & Lepper, M. (1999). Rethinking the value of choice: A cultural perspective on intrinsic motivation. *Journal of Personality and Social Psychology, 76*, 349-366. Copyright © 1999 by the American Psychological Association. Reprinted with the permission of the APA and the authors. Figure 10.7: From Thompson, D. A., & Campbell, R. G. (1977). Hunger in humans induced by 2 deoxy-d glucose: Glucoprivic control of taste preference and food intake. *Science, 198*, 1065-1068. Copyright © 1977 by the American Association for the Advancement of Science. Reprinted with the permission of *Science*. Figure 10.8: From Masters, W. H., & Johnson, V. E. (1966). *Human Sexual Response*, p. 5. Boston: Little, Brown and Company. Copyright © 1966 by the Masters and Johnson Institute. Reprinted with permission. Figure 10.9: From Butler, C.A. (1976). New data about female sexual response. *Journal of Sex and Marital Therapy, 10*, 42. Copyright © 1976 by Taylor & Francis, Inc. Reprinted with the permission of Taylor & Francis, Inc., http://www.routledge-ny.com, and the author. Figure 10.10: From Gladue, B. A., Green, R., & Hellman, R. E. (1984). Neuroendocrine response to estrogen and sexual orientation. *Science, 225*, 1496. Copyright © 1984 by American Association for the Advancement of Science. Reprinted with the permission of *Science*. Figure 10.12: Adapted from Elliott, A. J., & Church, M. A. (1997). Journal of Per-

sonality and Social Psychology, 72, 227. Copyright © 1997 by the American Psychological Association. Reprinted with the permission of the publisher. Table 10.1: Adapted from McClelland, D. C., Atkinson, J. W., Clark, R. A., & Lowell, E. L. (1953). *The Achievement Motive*, p. 294. New York: Irvington Publisher. Copyright 1953 by Appleton Century Crofts. Reprinted and adapted with the permission of Ardent Media, Inc.

Chapter 11 Figure 11.2: From Myers, D., & Diener, E. (1995). Who is happy? *Psychological Science, 6*, no. 1, 13. Copyright © 1995. Reprinted with the permission of the publisher. Figure 11.4: From Ekman, P., et al. (1983). Autonomic nervous system activity distinguishes among emotions. *Science, 221*, 1209. Copyright © 1984 by the American Association for the Advancement of Science. Reprinted with the permission of the publisher and the author. Figure 11.6: From Fischer K. W., Shaver, P. R., & Carnochan, P. (1990). How emotions develop and how they organize development. *Cognition and Development, 4*, no. 2: 90. Copyright © 1990. Reprinted with the permission of Lawrence Erlbaum Associates, Ltd., Hove, UK, and Kurt Fischer, Harvard University. Figure 11.7: Adapted from LeDoux, J. E. (1986). The neurobiology of emotion. In J. E. LeDoux & W. Hirst (eds.), *Mind and brain: Dialogues in cognitive neuropsychology*, p. 329. New York: Cambridge University Press. Copyright © 1986. Reprinted and adapted with the permission of Cambridge University Press and the author. Figure 11.8: Adapted from Tomarken, A., Davidson, R.J., Wheeler, R. E., & Doss, R. C. (1992). Individual difference in interior brain asymmetry and fundamental dimensions of emotion. *Journal of Personality and Social Psychology, 62*, 681. Copyright © 1992 by the American Psychological Association. Reprinted and adapted with the permission of the APA and the authors. Figure 11.9: From Shedler, J., Mayman, M., & Maris, M. (1993). The illusion of mental health. *American Psychologist, 11*, 1117-1131. Copyright © 1993 by the American Psychological Association. Reprinted and adapted with the permission of the APA and the authors. Figure 11.11: From Buss, D. M., Larsen, R., Westen, D., & Semmelroth, J. (1992). Sex differences in jealousy: Evolution, Physiology and Psychology. Psychological Science, 3, 251-255. Copyright © 1992. Reprinted with the permission of the publisher and Dr. David M. Buss, Department of Psychology, The University of Michigan. Figure 11.12: From Adams, P. R., & Adams, G. R. (1984). Mount Saint Helens's ashfall: Evidence for a disaster stress reaction. *American Psychologist, 39* (3), 257. Copyright © 1984 by the American Psychological Association. Reprinted with the permission of the APA and the authors. Figure 11.13: Adapted from Cohen, S., & Williamson, G. M. (1991). Stress and infectious diseases in humans. *Psychological Bulletin, 109*, 5. Copyright © 1991 by the American Psychological Association. Reprinted and adapted with the permission of the APA and the authors. Figure 11.14: From Brown, J. B. (1991). Staying fit and staying well: Physical fitness as a moderator of life stress. *Journal of Personality and Social Psychology, 61*, 559. Copyright © 1991 by American Psychological Association. Reprinted and adapted with the permission of the APA and the author. Figure 11.15: From Cohen, S., Ytrrell, P. A. J., & Smith, A. P. (1991). Psychological stress and susceptibility to the common cold. *New England Journal of Medicine, 325*, 609-610. Copyright © 1991 by Massachusetts Medical Society. Reprinted with the permission of The New England Journal of Medicine and the authors. Table 11.1: Adapted from Plutchik, R. (1980). A general psychoevolutionary theory of emotion. In R. Plutchik & H. Kellerman (eds.), *Emotion: Theory, Research and Experience, Volume I: Theory of Emotion*, p. 16. Orlando, FL: Academic Press. Copyright © 1980 by Academic Press, Inc. Reprinted and adapted with the permission of the publisher and the authors. Table 11.2: Excerpt from Holmes, T. H., & Rahe, R. E. (1967). The social readjustment rating scale. *Journal of Psychosomatic Research, 11*, 213-218. Copyright © 1967 by Elsevier Science, Inc. Reprinted with the permission of the publisher. Table 11.3: From Martikainen P., & Valkonen, T. (1996). Mortality after the death of a spouse: Rates and causes of death in a large Finnish cohort. *American Journal of Public Health, 86*, 1090. Copyright © 1996. Reprinted with the permission of American Public Health Association. Text: C. Bukowski (1980). From "the shoelace." Mockingbird Wish Me Luck, p. 114. Santa Rosa: Black Sparrow Press. Copyright © 1972 by Charles Bukowski. Reprinted with the permission of Black Sparrow Press.

Chapter 12 Figure 12.6: From Wood, R., & Bandura, A. (1989). Impact of conceptions of ability on self-regulatory mechanisms and complex decision making. *Journal of Personality and Social Psychology, 56*, 411-413. Copyright © 1988 by the American Psychological Association. Reprinted with the permission of the APA and the authors. Figure 12.7: Adapted from Eysenck, H. J. (1953). *The Structure of Human Personality*, p. 13. London: Methuen & Co. Copyright 1953. Reprinted with the permission of the publisher. Table 12.2: Adapted from McCrae, R. R., & Costa, P. T., Jr. (1997). Personality trait structure as a human universal. *American Psychologist 52*, 513. Copyright © 1997 by the American Psychological Association. Reprinted and adapted with the permission of the APA and the authors. Table 12.3: From Tellegen,

A., Lykken, D. T., Bouchard, T .J., Jr., Wilcox, K. J., & Rich, S. (1988). Personality similarity in twins reared apart and together. *Journal of Personality and Social Psychology, 54,* 1033. Copyright © 1988 by the American Psychological Association. Reprinted with the permission of the APA and the authors. Table 12.4: Adapted from Block, J. M., Gjerde, P., & Block, J. H. (1991). Personality antecedents of depressive tendencies in 18-year-olds: A prospective study. *Journal of Personality and Social Psychology, 60,* 726-738. Copyright © 1991 by the American Psychological Association. Reprinted and adapted with the permission of the APA and the authors.

Chapter 13 Figure 13.4: Adapted from Frankenburg, W. K., & Dodds, J B (1967). The Denver Developmental Screening Test. *Journal of Pediatrics, 91,* 181-191. Copyright © 1991 by Mosby-Year Book, Inc. Reprinted and adapted with permission. Figure 13.5: From Perdue, C., & Gurtman, M. (1990). Evidence for the automaticity of ageism. *Journal of Experimental and Social Psychology, 26,* 12. Copyright © 1990 by Academic Press, Inc. Reprinted with the permission of the publisher and the authors. Figure 13.6: From Meltzoff, A. N., & Borton, R. W. (1979). Intermodal matching by human neonates. *Nature, 282,* 403-404. Copyright © 1979 by Macmillan Magazines Ltd. Reprinted with the permission of *Nature* and the authors. Figure 13.8: Adapted from Bower, T. G. R. (1971). The object in the world of the infant. *Scientific American, 225,* 30-38. Illustration by Eric O. Mose. Copyright 1971. Reprinted and adapted with permission of Eric H. Mose. Figure 13.11: Adapted from Fry, A., & Hale, S. (1996). Processing speed, working memory and fluid intelligence: Evidence for a developmental cascade. *Psychological Science, 7,* 238. Copyright © 1996. Reprinted with the permission of the publisher. Making Connections drawing, p. 466: Adapted from Cerella, J. (1990). Aging and information processing rate. In J. Birren & K. W. Schaie (eds.), *Handbook of the Psychology of Aging (3rd edition),* p. 203. Orlando, FL: Academic Press. Copyright © 1990 by Academic Press, Inc. Reprinted and adapted with the permission of the publisher and the author. Figure 13.13: From Horn, J., & Hofer, S. (1992). Major abilities and development in the adult period. In R. Sternberg & C. Berg (eds.), *Intellectual Development,* p. 79. New York: Cambridge University Press. Copyright © 1992. Reprinted with the permission of the publisher. Figure 13.14: Adapted from Schaie, K. W. (1990). Intellectual development in adulthood. In J. Birren & K. W. Schaie (eds.), *Handbook of the Psychology of Aging (3rd edition),* p. 297. Orlando, FL: Academic Press. Copyright © 1990 by Academic Press, Inc. Reprinted and adapted with the permission of the publisher and the author.

Chapter 14 Figure 14.2: From Kagan, J. (1983). Stress and coping in early development. In N. Garmezy & M. Rutter (eds.), *Stress, Coping and Development in Children,* p. 198. New York: McGraw-Hill, Inc. Copyright © 1983 by Center for Advanced Study in the Behavioral Science. Reprinted with the permission of McGraw-Hill, Inc. Apply & Discuss, p. 493: From Westen, D., Lohr, N., Silk, K., Gold, L., & Kerber, K. (1991). Object relations and social cognition in borderlines, major depressives and normals: A TAT analysis. *Psychological Assessment: A Journal of Consulting and Clinical Psychology, 2,* 355-364. Copyright © 1991 by the American Psychological Association. Reprinted with the permission of the APA and the authors. Figure 14.5: Adapted from Darley, J., & Schultz, T. R. (1990). Moral rules: Their content and acquisition. *Annual Review of Psychology, 41,* 532. Copyright © 1990 by Annual Reviews, Inc. Reprinted and adapted with the permission of the publisher. Figure 14.6: From Rosenblum, G. D., & Lewis, M. (1999). The relations among body image, physical attractiveness, and body mass in adolescence. *Child Development, 70,* 50-64. p. 54. Table 14.1: Adapted from Rohner, R. (1975). Parental acceptance-rejection and personality development: A universalist approach to behavioral science. In R. W. Brislin (ed.), *Cross-cultural perspectives on learning,* p. 260. Thousand Oaks, CA.: Sage Publications, Inc. Copyright © 1975 by Sage Publications, Inc. Reprinted and adapted with the permission of the author and publisher. Table 14.2: From Williams, J. E., & Best, D. L. (1982). *Measuring Sex Stereotypes: A Thirty Nation Study,* p. 77. Thousand Oaks, CA.: Sage Publications, Inc. Copyright © 1982 by Sage Publications, Inc. Reprinted with the permission of the publisher. Table 14.3: Adapted from Kohlberg, L. (1969). Stage and sequence: The cognitive-developmental approach to socialization. In D.A. Goslin (ed.), *Handbook of Socialization and Research,* 347-380. New York: Houghton-Mifflin. Copyright © 1969 by David A. Goslin. Reprinted and adapted with permission.

Chapter 15 Figure 15.3: From Kendler, K. S., Gardner, C. O., & Prescott, C. A. (1999). Clinical characteristics of major depression that predict risk of depression in relatives. *Archives of General Psychiatry, 56,* 322-327. Copyright © 2000 by American Psychiatric Publishing Inc. Reprinted with permission of American Psychiatric Publishing Inc. and the authors. Figure 15.4: From Shedler, J., & Block, J. (1990). Adolescent drug use and emotional health: A longitudinal perspective. *American Psychologist, 45,* 624. Copyright © 1990 by the American Psychological Association.

Reprinted with the permission of the APA and the authors. Figure 15.7: From Mueller, T. I., Leon, A. C., Keller, M. B., Solomon, D. A., Endicott, J., Coryell, W., Warshaw, M., & Maser, J. D. (1999). Recurrence after recovery from major depressive disorder during 15 years of observational follow-up. *American Journal of Psychiatry, 156,* 1000-1006. Copyright © 1999 American Psychiatric Association. Reprinted with the permission of the publisher and the authors. Figure 15.8: From De La Ronde, C, & Swann, W. B., Jr. (1998). Partner verification: Reporting shattered images of our intimates. *Journal of Personality and Social Psychology, 75,* 374-382. Copyright © 1998 by the American Psychological Association. Reprinted with the permission of the APA and the authors. Figure 15.9: From Beck, A. T. (1976). *Cognitive Therapy and the Emotional Disorders,* p. 256. Madison, CT.: International Universities Press, Inc. Copyright © 1976. Reprinted with permission. Figure 15.10: Adapted from Barlow, D. H. (2001). *Anxiety and Its Disorders* (2nd ed.). New York: Guilford. Copyright © 2001 The Guilford Press. Used with permission of the publisher. Figure 15.11: From Rapee, R. M., Brown, J. A., Anthony, M., & Barlow, D. H. (1992). Response to hyperventilation and inhalation of 5.5% carbon dioxide-enriched air across the DSM-III-R anxiety disorders. *Journal of Abnormal Psychology, 101,* 545. Copyright © 1992 by the American Psychological Association. Reprinted with the permission of the APA and the authors. Figure 15.12: Adapted from Cadoret, R. J., Yates, W. R., Troughton, E., Woodworth, G., & Stewart, M. A. (1995). Adoption study demonstrating two genetic pathways to drug abuse. *Archives of General Psychiatry, 52,* 48. Copyright © 1995 by the American Medical Association. Reprinted with the permission of the publisher. Table 15.1: Adapted from Compton, W. M., Helzer, J., Hai-Gwo, H., Eng-Kung, Y., McEvoy, L., Tipp, J., & Spitznagel, E.(1991). New methods in cross-cultural psychiatry: Psychiatric illness in Taiwan and the U.S. *American Journal of Psychiatry, 148,* 1700-1701. Copyright © 1991 by the American Psychiatric Association. Reprinted and adapted with the permission of the publisher and the authors. Table 15.2, 15.3, and 15.6: Adapted from American Psychiatric Association (1994). *Diagnostic and Statistical Manual of Mental Disorders* (4th edition). Washington, DC: American Psychiatric Association. Copyright © 1994 by American Psychiatric Association. Reprinted and adapted with the permission of the publisher. Table 15.5: Adapted from Gottesman, I. (1991). *Schizophrenia Genesis,* p. 96. New York: W. H. Freeman and Company. Copyright © 1991 by Irving I. Gottesman. Reprinted and adapted with the permission of W. H. Freeman and Company.

Chapter 16 Figure 16.1: From Strupp, H., & Binder, J. L. (1984). *Psychotherapy in a new key: A guide to time-limited dynamic psychotherapy.* New York: Basic Books. Copyright © 1984 by Basic Books, Inc. Reprinted with the permission of Basic Books, a member of Perseus Books, L.L.C. Figure 16.3: From Camp, B. W., & Bash, M. A. S. (1981). *Think Aloud: Increasing Social and Cognitive Skills—A Problem-Solving Program for Children* (Primary level), pp. 43-46. Champaign, Illinois: Research Press. Copyright © 1981 by the authors. Reprinted with permission. Figure 16.5: From Herz, M., Lamberti, J. S., Mintz, J., Scott, R., O'Dell, S. P., McCartan, L. & Nix, G (2000). A program for relapse prevention in schizophrenia: A controlled study. *Archives of General Psychiatry, 57,* pp. 277-283. Copyright © 2000 by the American Medical Association. Reprinted with the permission of the publisher and authors. Figure 16.6: Adapted from Davis, J. M. (1985). Minor tranquilizers, sedatives and hypnotics. In H. I. Kaplan & B. J. Sadock (eds.), *Comprehensive textbook of psychiatry* (4th edition). Baltimore, Maryland: Williams & Wilkins. Copyright © 1985 by the Williams & Wilkins Company. Reprinted and adapted with the permission of the publisher. Figure 16.8: From Maj, M., Veltro, R., Lobrace, S., & Magliano, L. (1992). Pattern of recurrence of illness after recovering from an episode of major depression. *American Journal of Psychiatry, 149,* 795-800. Copyright © 1992 by the American Psychiatric Association. Reprinted with the permission of the publisher and the authors. Figure 16.9: Adapted from Smith, M. L., & Glass, G. V. (September 1977). Meta-analysis of psychotherapy outcome studies. *American Psychologist, 32,* 754. Copyright © 1977 by the American Psychological Association. Reprinted with the permission of the APA and the authors. Figure 16.10: From Seligman, M. E P. (1995). The effectiveness of psychotherapy. *American Psychologist, 12,* 968. Copyright © 1995 by American Psychological Association. Reprinted with the permission of the APA and the author.

Chapter 17 Figure 17.1: From Steele, C. M. (1997). A threat in the air: How stereotypes shape intellectual identity and performance. *American Psychologist, 52,* 621. Copyright © 1997 by the American Psychological Association. Reprinted with the permission of the APA and the author. Figure 17.2: From Heine, S. J., & Lehman, D. (1997). Culture, dissonance and self-affirmation. *Personality and Social Psychology Bulletin, 23,* 396. Copyright © 1997. Reprinted with the permission of Sage Publications, Inc. and the authors. Figure 17.3: From Luchins, A .S. (1957). Primacy-recency in impression formation. In C. I. Hovland (ed.), *The Order of Presentation in Persuasion,* pp. 34-35. New Haven, CT: Yale University Press. Copyright © 1957 by Yale University

Press. Reprinted with permission. Figure 17.4: Adapted from Kunda, Z., & Thagard, P. (1996). Forming impressions from stereotypes, traits and behaviors: A parallel-constraint-satisfaction theory. *Psychology Review, 303,* 286. Copyright © 1996 by the American Psychological Association. Reprinted with the permission of the APA and the authors. Figure 17.5: Adapted from Macrae, C. N, Bodenhausen, G.V., & Milne, A. B. (1998). Saying no to unwanted thoughts: Self-focus and the regulation of mental life. *Journal of Personality and Social Psychology, 74,* 585. Copyright © 1998 by the American Psychological Association. Reprinted with the permission of the APA and the authors. Figure 17.6: From Woike, B., & Aronoff, J. (1992). Complexity of social cognition. *Journal of Personality and Social Psychology, 63,* 102. Copyright © 1992 by the American Psychological Association. Reprinted and adapted with the permission of the APA and the authors. Figure 17.7: From Kihlstrom, J. F & Cantor, N. (1983). Mental representations of the self. In L. Berkowitz (ed.), *Advances in Experimental Social Psychology, 15.* Copyright © 1983 by Academic Press, Inc. Reprinted with the permission of the publisher and the authors. Figure 17.18: Adapted from Strauman, T. Lemieux, A., & Coe, C. (1993). Self-discrepancy and natural killer cell activity. *Journal of Personality and Social Psychology, 64,* 1049. Copyright © 1993 by the American Psychological Association. Reprinted and adapted with the permission of the APA and the authors.

Chapter 18 Figure 18.2: From Buss, D. M., & Schmitt, D. P. (1993). Sexual strategies theory: An evolutionary perspective on human mating. *Psychology Review, 100(2),* 204-232. Copyright © 1993 by the American Psychological Association. Reprinted with the permission of the APA and the authors. Figure 18.3: Adapted from Darley, J. M., & Latane, B. (December 1968). When will people help in a crisis? *Psychology Today,* 70-71. Copyright © 1968 by Sussex Publisher, Inc. Reprinted with the permission of *Psychology Today Magazine.* Figure 18.4: From Cohen, D., Nisbett, R., Bowdle, B., & Schwarz, N. (1996). Insult, aggression, and the Southern culture of honor: An experimental ethnography. *Journal of Personality and Social Psychology, 70,* 945-960. Copyright © 1996 by the American Psychological Association. reprinted with the permission of the APA and the authors. Figure 18.6: From Anderson, C. (1989). Temperature and aggression: Ubiquitous effects of heat on occurrence of human violence. *Psychological Bulletin, 106,* 74-96. © 1989 by the American Psychological Association. Reprinted with the permission of the APA and the authors. Figure 18.7: From Milgram, S. (1965). Some conditions of obedience and disobedience to authority. *Human Relations, 18,* 63. Copyright © 1965. Reprinted with the permission of Alexandra Milgram. Figure 18.8 and 18.9: From Asch, S. E. (November 1955). Opinions and social pressure. *Scientific American, 193,* (6), 193. Copyright © 1955 by the Estate of Sara Love.

Name Index

Subject Index